Paris

THE ROUGH GUIDE

Written and researched by
Kate Baillie and Tim Salmon

With additional research by
Emma Salmon

THE ROUGH GUIDES

Help Us Update

We've gone to a lot of effort to ensure that this sixth edition of *The Rough Guide to Paris* is up-to-date and accurate. However, Paris information changes fast: new bars and clubs appear and disappear, museums alter their displays and opening hours, restaurants and hotels change their prices and standards. If you feel there are places we've underpraised or overrated, omitted or ought to omit, please let us know. All suggestions, comments or corrections are much appreciated and we'll send a copy of the next edition (or any other Rough Guide if you prefer) for the best letters.

Please mark letters: Paris 6 update" and send to:
Rough Guides, 1 Mercer St, London, WC2H 9QJ,
or Rough Guides, 375 Hudson St, 9th floor, New York, NY 10014.
Or send email to: paris@roughtravl.co.uk

Online updates about this book can be found on Rough Guides' website at
http://www.roughguides.com

Thanks For Your Help

Many thanks to all the readers who have helped us revise and update this sixth edition by sending information, comments and criticisms:
Richard Bevans, Stanley Blenkinsop, John Broadfoot, Kate Cain, Jamie Carr, C. Earl, Debra Galloway, David Jarman, Jonathan Jarvis, Joanne Latiff, Howard Lewis, Paul Looby, John and Stella Martin, Colin Mclean-Campbell, Denise Nickerson, Geoff Peacock, Niall Petch, Andrew Powner, Cara Slattery, Ashley Spell, Andrew Thomson, Bryony Williams and Gill Williams.

Contents

List of Maps

MAP SYMBOLS

━━━━	Railway	✈	Airport
══════	Main road	ⓘ	Tourist office
══════	Minor road	✉	Post office
──────	Waterway	▮	Building
─ ─ ─	Chapter division boundary	✛	Cemetery
✚	Church	▨	Park
✡	Synagogue	Ⓜ	Metro station
		Ⓡ	RER station

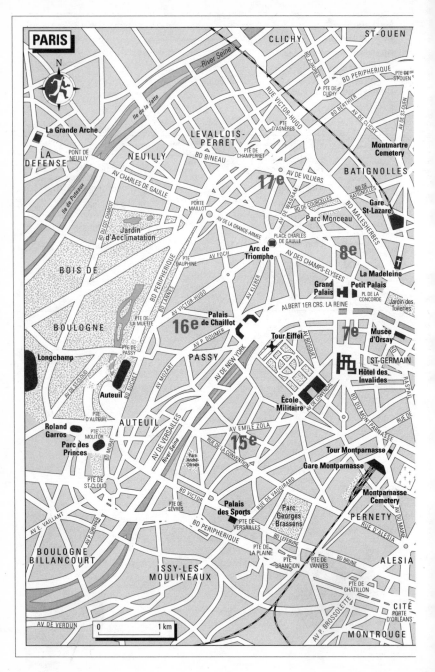

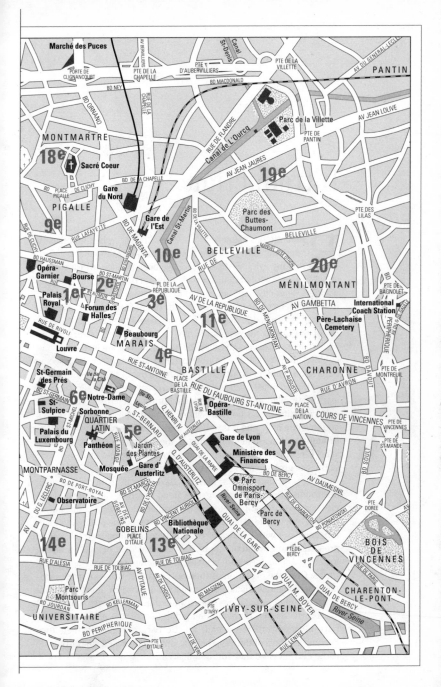

A MAP OF PARIS

Introduction

Romantic . . . glamorous . . . innovative . . . when it comes to summing up Paris, there is no escaping the clichés. More dreamy-eyed, wistful songs have been penned over the years about France's capital than anywhere else on the globe, and it's little wonder. What city experiences could be more seductive than sitting in the gardens of Notre-Dame beneath the drifting cherry blossom, strolling the riverside quais on a summer evening as dusk thickens under the lime trees, sipping coffee and cognac in the early hours while someone plays the blues, or exploring the ancient lanes and cobbled alleyways of the Latin Quarter or Montmartre? Paris seems to have no problem living up to its postcard images and movie myths.

Nor does it falter in its reputation as a great hive of intellectual and artistic stimulation. The new national library, open to all, embodies a cultural attitude that both proclaims Parisian cleverness and invites you to share in it. And it is only the latest in a line of grand and often ground-breaking modern buildings – the Pompidou Centre, the Arab World Institute – that assert modern architecture and design.

But the greatest work of art has to be the city itself. Paris has been fortunate throughout its history. Saved from Hitler's intended destruction, spared the ravages of flood and fire, the centre of the city has been developed purposely to reflect the ever-present power of the French state. And it does so with tremendous pomp and magnificence and with a sense of continuity and homogeneity, however great the changes and the contrasts with what went before. Sweeping avenues, esplanades and bridges link monuments that span centuries. Even the evolution of the Louvre from fortress to glass pyramid has somehow managed to maintain a sense of unity. Time has acted as judge as buildings once swathed in controversy – the Eiffel Tower, the Sacré-Cœur, the Pompidou Centre, the glass pyramid – have blended into the overall artistic backdrop and in their turn become symbols of the city; the new and much-reviled Opéra-Bastille is the current candidate for assimiliation.

Although two thousand years of shaping and reshaping have resulted in monumental buildings and public spaces, the city itself remains on a very human scale, with exquisite, secretive little nooks tucked away from the *grands boulevards* and very definite little communities revolving around games of *boules*, the local *boulangerie*, *charcuterie* and café.

The Parisians are probably the most maligned people in Europe. Their aloofness, indifference and superiority are renowned. But so is their swiftness to enter a quarrel in the street, the habit of falling to their knees on the pavement to coo over a fluffy miniature dog, their ineffable elegance and sexiness, and their attachment to fashion. Outsiders may dismiss it all as posing or attention-seeking, but to a Parisian it's simply a matter of playing a part in the great game of keeping up appearances.

Accustomed to being at the centre of the nation's life, admired, envied and imitated by half the world, Parisians naturally think of themselves as superior beings. But don't be put off by that arrogance and self-absorption; firstly, there is entertainment in it, and, secondly, courtesy and humour lurk not far below the surface. Neither should you be intimidated by the city's reputation for sophistication. Certainly there are expensive pleasures on offer, but you can enjoy Paris without them. The city is so beautiful and its street life so animated and varied that one of the greatest joys of a visit is simply to browse along with eyes and ears at the café-*pâtisserie* level of existence.

One of the most important strands in the kaleidoscopic pattern of the city's life is its **ethnic diversity**. Long a haven and a magnet for foreign refugees and artists, Paris in this century has sheltered aspiring politicians, deposed leaders, dissidents, exiled freedom fighters and members of warring factions from every corner of the globe. It has welcomed black musicians denied civil rights in the United States and others from Africa and Latin America. Writers escaping censorship or just disillusionment in their own countries have flocked to the city.

Some highlights

Paris is a city of great **art** and of dazzling contemporary **architecture**. The general backdrop of the streets is predominantly Neoclassical, the result of nineteenth-century development. But each period since has added, more or less discreetly, novel examples of its own styles – with **Auguste Perret**, **Le Corbusier**, **Mallet-Stevens** and **Gustave Eiffel** among the early twentieth-century innovators. In the last two decades, the architectural additions have been on a dramatic scale, producing new and major landmarks, and recasting down-at-heel districts into important centres of cultural and consumer life. **Beaubourg (the Pompidou Centre)**, **La Villette**, **La Grande Arche**, the **Bastille Opéra**, the **Louvre pyramid**, the **Institut du Monde Arabe** and the new **national library** have all expanded the dimensions of the city, pointing it determinedly towards the future as well as enhancing the monuments of the past.

The **museums and galleries** of Paris are among the finest in western Europe, and, with the tradition of state cultural endowment very much alive, certainly the best displayed. The art of conversion – the **Musée d'Orsay** from a train station, the **Cité des Sciences** from abbatoirs, and spacious well-lit exhibition spaces from mansions and palaces – has given the great collections unparalleled locations. The Impressionists at the **Musée d'Orsay**, the **Orangerie** and **Marmottan**; the moderns at **Beaubourg** and the **Palais de Tokyo**; the ancients in the **Louvre**; **Picasso** and **Rodin** with their own individual museums: all these deservedly entice art-lovers from around the world. In addition, there's the contemporary scene in the **commercial galleries** that fill the Marais, St-Germain, the Bastille and the area round the Champs-Élysées, and an ever-expanding range of museums devoted to other areas of human endeavour – science, history, decoration and performance art.

As for more hedonistic pleasures, few cities can compete with the thousand and one **cafés**, **bars** and **restaurants** – ultra-modern and designer-signed, palatial, traditional and scruffy (and for every pocket) – that line each Parisian street and boulevard. The restaurant choice is not just French, but includes a tempting range of cuisines and social cultures that draws from every ethnic origin represented among the city's millions.

Where **entertainment** is concerned, the city's strong points are movies and music. Paris is the **cinema** capital of Europe, and the **music** on offer encompasses excellent jazz, top-quality classical, avant-garde experimental, international rock, West African *soukous* and French Caribbean *zouk*, Algerian *raï*, and traditional *chansons*. If you want to hear world dance rhythms, Parisian clubs are exciting grounds to discover.

In the final two chapters of this book, we've described an assortment of excursions **beyond the city**. The region surrounding the capital, known as the Île de France, contains cathedrals and châteaux that bear comparison with anything in Paris itself – **Chartres**, **Versailles**, and **Fontainebleau**, for example. It also boasts what can only be seen as a very *un*-French "attraction" – **Disneyland Paris**, which is covered in a separate chapter of this guide.

When to go

When to visit Paris is largely a question of personal taste. The city has a more reliable **climate** than Britain, with uninterrupted stretches of sun (and rain) all year round. However, while it maintains a vaguely southern feel for anyone crossing the English Channel, Mediterranean it is not. Winter temperatures drop well below freezing, with sometimes biting winds. If you're lucky, spring and autumn will be mild and sunny; in summer it can reach the 30s°C (80s°F).

In terms of pure aesthetics, winter sun is the city's most flattering light, when the pale shades of the older buildings become luminescent without any glare, and the lack of trees and greenery is barely relevant. By contrast, Paris in high summer can be choking, with the fumes of congested traffic becoming trapped within the high narrow streets, and the reflected light in the city's open spaces too blinding to enjoy.

If you visit during the **French summer holidays**, from July 15 to the end of August, you will find that large numbers of Parisians have fled the city. It's quieter then, but a lot of shops and restaurants will be closed. There is, too, the **commercial calendar** to consider – fashion shows, trade fairs, etc. Paris hoteliers warn against September and October, and **finding a room** even at the best of times can be problematic. Given the choice, early spring, autumn if you book ahead, or the midwinter months are most rewarding.

The Basics

Getting there from Britain

The quickest way of reaching Paris from Britain is still, usually, by plane, though depending where you live air travel is rivalled closely by the Channel Tunnel rail link that has cut the 340-kilometre London–Paris journey to just three hours. The standard rail- or road-and-sea routes are significantly more affordable, but can be uncomfortable and tiring. Furthermore, if you're going for a short break, the journey time of up to nine hours can drastically eat into the time you have to spend in Paris itself.

By Air

Deals on flights to Paris change all the time. To find the best ones, you should shop around, ideally a month or so before you plan to leave. Students and anyone under 26 can take advantage of a range of special discount fares from London to Paris. Promising sources for checking the possibilities include the classified travel sections in the quality Sunday newspapers and, if you're in London, *Time Out* and *TNT*, the free listings magazine available outside many tube and *British Rail* stations.

General Deals From London

The cheaper choices boil down to either a charter, a Bargain Saver (on *British Midland*) or Apex (on *British Airways* and *Air France* as well as

British Midland) scheduled ticket, or – often cheapest – a flight with an airline that makes a stop in Paris en route to more distant destinations (typically *Malaysia Airlines* or *Pakistan International Airlines*).

Charters are in theory supposed only to be sold in conjunction with accommodation. It is, of course, possible just to buy the air ticket, though doing so is generally a matter of luck, scrounging for whatever seats remain . . . often at the last moment. *Nouvelles Frontières* (see box on p5) sell scheduled flights to Paris for £63 return, with five flights daily. Otherwise they offer daily *British Airways* flights out of Heathrow and Gatwick to Paris; current prices start at £84 return.

British Airways, *Air France* and *British Midland* **Apex** tickets must be reserved two weeks in advance, and you must stay one Saturday night. Your return date has to be fixed when purchasing, and no subsequent changes are allowed. Current cost is £121 return, £136 at weekends. There are fewer restrictions on Apex tickets run by Air France and costing £167, for which you must stay a Saturday night. *British Midland* Bargain Savers can be bought at any time and cost £89 return; once more you have to stay one Saturday night. Their ordinary-availability tickets start from £198 return for an off-peak flight that does not include a Saturday. Apex tickets for departures from airports in the north of England cost £97. *British Airways* ordinary rates start from £215 return, while *Air France* have late availability offers, and discounts if you book within seven days of departure.

Bargains with **long-haul airlines** are harder to predict. Like charters, availability can be chancy, but a good travel agent should usually be able to find you something to Paris. The drawbacks are a much smaller choice of flight times and a considerably higher likelihood of delays. On the other hand, some fares have no maximum stay and do allow you to make changes.

Finally, if you're based in central London and wish to get to Paris with the minimum of hassle, you can fly from **London City Airport** with *Air France* (3 flights daily Mon–Fri; from £220 return). Check-in time has been cut to a minimum and

Air, Rail and Bus Travel Addresses

Air France
177 Piccadilly
London W1V 0LX ☎0181/742 6600

Brit Air
239 Longbridge House
Gatwick Airport,
Crawley
West Sussex, RH6 0NP ☎01293/502044

British Airways
156 Regent St
London W1R 5TA ☎0345/222111

British Midland
Donington Hall
Castle Donington
Derby DE4 2SB ☎0345/554554

British Rail
Victoria Station
European Rail enquiries ☎0171/834 2345

Eurolines, National Express
Victoria Coach Station
164–172 Buckingham Palace Rd
London SW1W 97P ☎0990/808080
23 Crawley Rd, Luton
Beds LU1 1HX ☎01582/404511

Eurostar
EPS House
Waterloo Station
London SE1 1SE ☎01233/617575
or ☎0345/881881

Eurotrain
52 Grosvenor Gardens
London SW1W 0AG ☎0171/730 3402
and regional Campus Travel *offices.*

Le Shuttle
PO Box 300, Crawley
West Sussex RH10 2YW ☎0990/353535

SNCF (French Railways)
179 Piccadilly
London W1V 0VA enquiries ☎0891/515477
reservations ☎0345/300003

Thomas Cook
Head office: 45 Berkeley St
London W1A 1EB ☎0171/499 4000

Wasteels
Platform 2
Victoria Station
London SW1V 1JT ☎0171/834 7066

Note that addresses and telephone numbers may not be in the same location:
some airlines and agents use a single telephone-sales number for several offices.
Note also that 0891 numbers are premium rate and charge around 49p per minute
before 6pm, and 39p thereafter.

tickets can be collected at the check-in desk. Shuttle buses for the airport leave from Liverpool Street station (£4; 30min) and from Canary Wharf (£2; 12min).

General Deals Outside London

As often as not, whether you live in Birmingham or Newcastle, Manchester or Aberdeen, you will find it pays to go to London and then fly on to Paris from there. Scheduled direct flights from British regional airports are very expensive. Charters do exist, though availability is a big problem and prices are unfavourable in relation to London flights, even taking into account the

cost of coach or rail travel to London. What is worth considering, however, is a **package deal**, which often offers exceptional bargain travel – even if you go it alone on the actual holiday. See the box on p.7 for further details.

Student/Youth Flights

STA Travel (see box opposite) offers flights to various cities for which any person under 26, and any student under 32, is eligible. Current return price to Paris (Charles de Gaulle) is £83. *Campus Travel* student/youth charter returns to Paris also start at £83. Both organizations also offer limited special offers. *Air France* do a youth discount for under-26s of £138 for a standard ticket. Special-deal **flight passes** within France with various airlines exist for students, and if you plan to travel elsewhere in France, it's worth enquiring about these from *STA* or *Campus Travel*.

By Train

The Channel Tunnel has slashed travelling time by train from London to Paris and has also led to a multitude of cut-rate deals on regular train and ferry or hovercraft fares via Calais, Boulogne or Dieppe.

Addresses of Specialist Agencies for Independent Travel

Campus Travel
52 Grosvenor Gardens
London SW1W 0AG ☎ 0171/730 8832

541 Bristol Rd, Bournbrook
Selly Oak
Birmingham B29 6AU ☎ 0121/414 1848

39 Queens Rd, Clifton
Bristol BS8 1QE ☎ 0117/929 2494

5 Emmanuel St
Cambridge CB1 1NE ☎ 01223/324283

53 Forrest Rd
Edinburgh EH1 2QP ☎ 0131/6683303

61 Ditchling Rd
Brighton BN1 4SD ☎ 01273/570228

105–106 St Aldates
Oxford OX1 1DD ☎ 01865/242067
Also at YHA shops and university campuses.

Council Travel
28a Poland St
London W1V 3DB ☎ 0171/437 7767
Eight offices in France.

Masterfare
269 Old Brompton Rd
London SW5 9JA ☎ 0171/259 2000
Discount agent with competitive deals.

Nouvelles Frontières
11 Blenheim St
London W1Y 9LE ☎ 0171/629 7772
French agency.

STA Travel
86 Old Brompton Rd
London SW7 3LH,

38 Store St, London WC1

117 Euston Rd tele-sales
London NW1 2SX ☎ 0171/3616161

75 Deansgate tele-sales
Manchester M3 2BW ☎ 0161/834 0668

88 Vicar Lane
Leeds LS1 7JH ☎ 0113/244 8212

25 Queens Rd
Bristol BS8 1QE ☎ 0117/929 4399

38 Sidney St tele-sales
Cambridge CB2 3HX ☎ 01223/366966

36 George St
Oxford OX1 2OJ ☎ 01865/792 800

Other branches in Birmingham, Canterbury,
Cardiff, Coventry, Durham, Glasgow,
Loughborough, Nottingham, Warwick and
Sheffield.

Trailfinders
42–50 Earls Court Rd
London W8 6EJ ☎ 0171/938 3366

194 Kensington High St
London W14 7RG ☎ 0171/938 3839

58 Deansgate
Manchester M3 2FF ☎ 0161/839 6969

22–24 The Priory, Queensway
Birmingham B4 6BS ☎ 0121/236 1234

48 Corn St
Bristol BS1 1HQ ☎ 0117/929 9000

254–284 Sauchiehall St
Glasgow G2 3EH ☎ 0141/353 2224

Travel Bug
597 Cheetham Hill Rd
Manchester M13 5EJ ☎ 0161/721 4000

Union Travel
93 Piccadilly
London W1 ☎ 0171/493 4343

Note that addresses and telephone numbers may not be in the same location: some airlines and agents use a single telephone-sales number for several offices.

Eurostar

Eurostar operate high-speed trains from London Waterloo to Paris Gare du Nord **through the Channel Tunnel** in exactly three hours. There are fifteen trains on weekdays and Saturday, running from around 5am to 7pm, and thirteen on Sunday, running from 8am to 7pm. Fares start at £99 return (lowest fares must be booked 8 days in advance and are subject to restrictions). A three-day excursion ticket, which has to include a Saturday, is £79. Full fare is £77.50 each way in standard class and £110 in first. Various concessions are available if you're under 26, over 60, or hold an international rail pass.

Travelling by *Eurostar* is easy, even bland: you check in at least twenty minutes before departure, passports are checked on the train, and at the other end you emerge onto the station concourse with all the other travellers. There's little sensation of speed, even at 300kph – though the British part of the journey, where new tracks have yet to be laid, does feel incredibly slow by contrast.

Direct services to Paris also run from Edinburgh, Glasgow, Waverley, Newcastle, Darlington, York, Leeds, Doncaster, Newark, Crewe, Peterborough, Manchester, Birmingham, Coventry, Stockport, Stafford, Wolverhampton, Rugby and Milton Keynes.

Rail and sea

Alternatively, catch one of the many trains from London Victoria which connect with cross-Channel ferries or hovercraft and onward services on the other side. On the shortest and most economical Channel crossings the choice is between **train and hovercraft**, on which the total journey time from London to Paris is six hours, or **train and ferry**, taking seven or eight hours. Fare options include special deals on *Eurotrain* (for anyone under 26) and senior citizen reductions for those over 65. If you plan to take in Paris as part of a longer trip you might also consider an *InterRail* or *Euro Domino Pass* (see below).

The **hovercraft** crossing links Dover with Boulogne. Services are frequent (up to 20 a day in peak season) and tie in well with the trains. By **train and ordinary ferry**, the cheapest Channel crossing is currently Newhaven–Dieppe; best deals are on the conveniently scheduled (though slightly slower) night trains. Students and anyone under 26 can buy heavily discounted tickets from *Eurotrain* outlets or *Wasteels* (see box on p.4) and most

student travel agent. The cheapest return ticket costs £35, departing on weekdays and crossing Newhaven–Dieppe, with a coach journey for the last leg. Taking the train for both overland journeys, and crossing at the same point, costs £43. A return ticket on Hoverspeed, 90min faster, is £59 return, or £49 if you book more than a week in advance.

Rail Passes

If you plan to use the rail network to visit other regions of France, you might consider buying a *France Vacances* or *Euro Domino* pass.

The **Euro Domino** pass, available from the International Rail Centre at London Victoria, or from French Railways (*SNCF*), offers unlimited rail travel through France for any three (£108), five (£150) or ten (£222) days within a calendar month; passengers under 26 pay £87, £123 and £183 respectively. The pass also entitles you to reductions of fifty percent on rail/ferry links to France.

The **InterRail** pass, offering one month's unlimited use of all European train services for £275 to anyone under 26 who has been resident in Europe for at least six months, is available from *British Rail* and some travel agents, including branches of *Campus Travel* and *STA Travel*. Cheaper new *InterRail* passes have also been introduced which cover one, two or three "zones". France is within the zone including Belgium, the Netherlands and Luxembourg; a fifteen-day pass to travel this area is £175. A two-zone pass valid for a month is £220, a three-zone £245.

By Bus

Travelling by bus is probably the cheapest way to Paris, but even the buses that take *Le Shuttle* through the Channel Tunnel take almost eight hours from London; barely an hour less than those that use **hovercraft** or **ferry** crossings.

The **Hoverspeed City Sprint** bus service leaves in the morning from London's Victoria Coach Station, catches the hovercraft from Dover to Calais, and arrives in Paris roughly nine hours after setting off. There are four coaches daily and the return fare is £44 with a £2 student discount. Tickets can be purchased through any local agent; for details call *Hoverspeed*.

Eurolines run one bus a day via the Tunnel, plus – on the more traditional routes – three buses overnight and during the day in winter, and four in summer. The regular adult return is £49 if

Packages From Regional Britain

The following is a selection from the wide range of companies selling travel plus accommodation packages to Paris from outside London, either on direct regional charter flights, or including the fare to the capital to catch a flight from London in the overall price, or offering special deals on ferry crossings. More complete lists are available from the *French Government Tourist Office*, 178 Piccadilly, London W1V OAL (☎0171/491 7622).

Allez France (☎01903/742345). *Paris accommodation packages from all major British airports.*

British Airways Holidays (☎01293/723100). *Package deals from around £155 for a Eurostar journey and two nights in Paris.*

Brittany Ferries (☎0990/360360). *Short breaks in Paris for three, six or ten days, including ferry crossing with car in peak season: four nights from £131.*

Gîtes de France (☎0171/493 3480). *Houses, cottages and chalets in the Île-de-France region, mostly about half an hour from Paris by train. One week minimum (Sat to Sat or Tues to Tues) from £102 per person, inclusive of car ferry crossing.*

Kirker European Holidays
(☎0171/231 3333). *Departures from most regional airports. Two nights in a two-star hotel, travelling by coach, from £117.*

Paris Travel Service (☎01920/467467). *Very wide range of packages from £103 for rail and coach trip with basic accommodation. Good for regional flights.*

Sally Holidays (☎0181/395 3030). *Ferry for car and two adults plus two-star hotel accommodation from £122 per person (£28 each subsequent night) in central Paris.*

Time Off Ltd (☎0171/235 8070). *Short breaks to Paris by air, coach and rail (including Orient Express packages). Two nights in a one-star hotel, travelling by coach, from £125; self-drive packages from £105.*

Travelscene Ltd (☎0181/427 4445). *Short breaks in all grades of accommodation, by air, rail or coach. Two nights in a one-star hotel by coach from £99, and £78 self-drive.*

Venice Simplon-Orient-Express
(☎0171/928 6000). *From £590 for two nights, going one way by Eurostar and the other on the Orient Express.*

VFB Holidays; French Weekenders
(☎01242/240300). *Flights from regional destinations including Newcastle, Aberdeen and Belfast. Two nights in two-star hotel accommodation plus flight from Gatwick from £229, or £176 by ferry and car.*

---

you travel by night, £44 by day, with a £5 reduction on off-season tickets. In summer, on certain weekday morning buses, the price drops to £29.

By Car

The most convenient way of taking your car across to France is to drive down to the **Channel Tunnel**, load your car onto the train shuttle, and be whisked under the Channel in 35 minutes, ready for a leisurely drive through northern France to Paris.

The Channel Tunnel entrance is off the M20 at Junction 11A, just outside Folkestone, and *Le Shuttle* services operate round the clock, 365 days a year.

Because of the frequency of the service, you don't have to buy a ticket in advance; although special offers are often available on advance bookings. Even if you do book ahead, you generally won't have a reservation for a particular train: just arrive and wait to board one of the four departures an hour during peak time, with a promised loading time of just ten minutes. You can get out of your car to stretch your legs during the 35-minute crossing.

Tickets are available at the toll booths, or in advance through *Le Shuttle* or from your local travel agent. Fares are per carload: return £109 if you travel between 10pm and 6am, £129 at other times. Comfortable club class is £159. A

1997 FERRY ROUTES AND PRICES

Note: return prices are substantially cheaper but generally need to be booked in advance.

	Operator	Crossing time	Frequency	One-way fares Small car 2 adults	Foot passenger
BRITTANY					
Poole–St-Malo	*Brittany Ferries*	8hr	3–4 wkly	£138–199	£58–74
Portsmouth–St-Malo	*Brittany Ferries*	8hr 45min 1 nightly	Mar–Nov	£151	£40
Plymouth–Roscoff	*Brittany Ferries*	6hr 3–17 wkly	Feb–Dec	£114–158	£23–29
NORMANDY					
Southampton–Cherbourg	*Stena Sealink*	6–10hr	1–2 daily	£67–128	£17–25
Portsmouth–Cherbourg	*P&O European Ferries*	4hr 45min	1–3 daily	£115–164	£23–28
Poole–Cherbourg	*Brittany Ferries*	4hr 15min	Feb–Dec 1–2 daily	£135–317	£34–54
Portsmouth–Caen	*Brittany Ferries*	6hr	3 daily	£135–317	£34–54
Portsmouth–Le Havre	*P&O European Ferries*	5hr 45min	2–3 daily	£135–317	£34–54
Newhaven–Dieppe	*Stena Sealink*	4hr	4 daily	£94–116	£24
PAS-DE-CALAIS					
Folkestone–Boulogne	*Hoverspeed‡*	55 min	3–4 daily	£60–145	£25
Dover–Calais	*Stena Sealink*	1hr 30min	25 daily	£104–128	£24
Dover–Calais	*P&O European Ferries*	1hr 15min	20–25 daily	£104–128	£24
Dover–Calais	*Hoverspeed‡‡*	35min	20–24 daily	£70–160	£25
Ramsgate–Dunkerque	*Sally Line*	2hr 30min	5 daily	£99	£20

SPECIAL OFFERS
Brittany Ferries and *Stena Sealink*: 3-, 5- and 10-day returns; discounts for regular users who own a property abroad.
Sally Line, Hoverspeed and *P&O European Ferries*: 3 and 5-day returns.

ADDRESSES IN BRITAIN

Brittany Ferries
Millbay Docks, Plymouth PL1 3EW
Wharf Rd, Portsmouth PO2 8RU ☎0990/360360

Hoverspeed
Maybrook House, Queens Gardens
Dover CT17 9UQ ☎01304/240101
‡*Seacat high-speed catamaran.*
‡‡*Hovercraft and Seacat.*

P&O European Ferries
Channel House, Channel View Rd
Dover CT17 9TJ ☎0990/980980

Continental Ferry Port, Mile End
Portsmouth PO2 8QW ☎0990/980980

Sally Line
Argyle Centre, York St, Ramsgate
Kent CT11 9DS ☎01843/595522
81 Piccadilly,
London W1V 9HF ☎0181/858 1127

Stena Sealink Line
Charter House, Park St, Ashford
Kent TN24 8EX ☎01233/647047
24-hr information, Dover ☎01304/240028

five-day mini break is £59 if you travel between 10pm and 6am, £69 at other times. One way is half the price of a return ticket.

Cheaper cross-Channel options are the **conventional ferry or hovercraft** links between Dover and Calais or Boulogne, Folkestone and Boulogne, and Ramsgate and Dunkerque. If your starting point is significantly further west than London, it may be worth catching a ferry from one of the south coast ports to Normandy or Brittany – Newhaven to Dieppe; Portsmouth, Southampton, Weymouth or Poole to Le Havre, Caen, Cherbourg and St-Malo; and Plymouth to Roscoff.

Ferry prices vary according to the season and, for motorists, the size of car; details of routes, companies and fares are given on p.8 – look out for special offers. You can either contact the companies direct to reserve space in advance (essential at peak season), or any competent travel agent can do it for you.

Once across the Channel, it's little over three hours' drive **from Calais to Paris** on the fast *autoroutes* A26 amd A1 (tolls payable); Le Havre is even closer and also offers *autoroute* all the way. Worth considering is the *Sally Lines* Ramsgate to Dunkerque crossing, which offers the advantage of access to the toll-free E41 *autoroute* to Lille, almost a third of way to Paris.

Hitching

Hitching from Calais or Boulogne towards Paris is notoriously difficult.; and Dieppe is not a lot easier. Your best policy is to get friendly with drivers on the boat over and ask for a lift before docking. It's a long way to hitch to Paris from the ports in Normandy or Brittany, but actually getting the lifts could well be easier.

Coming back, it may well be worth contacting the ride-share organization *Allostop Provoya*, 8 rue Rochambeau (square Montholon), 8e (Mon–Fri 9am–7.30pm, Sat 9am–1pm & 2–6pm; Mº Cadet/Poissonnière): ☎01.53.20.42.42 for rides out of Paris/Île de France; ☎04.53.20.42.43 for rides to Paris from the rest of France or abroad, so you could check about lifts from the Channel Ports. You pay 30F inscription for a journey of under 200km, then an extra 10F for every 100km up to a maximum of 70F. In addition, there's a charge of 20 centimes for every kilometre. *Allostop-Provoya* can be e-mailed on allostop@ecritel.fr.

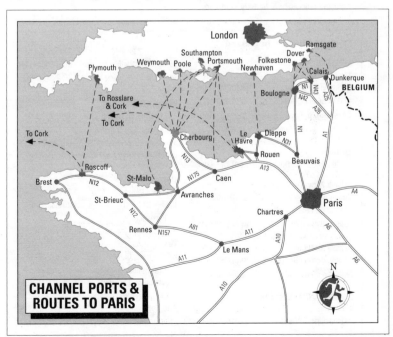

**CHANNEL PORTS &
ROUTES TO PARIS**

Getting there from Ireland

Air Inter and **Aer Lingus** fly direct from Dublin and Cork to Paris, with a midweek fare of £159, £169 on weekends, for which you must stay for one Saturday. Standard fare is £199. There are no direct flights from Belfast to Paris, and a routing through London or Amsterdam is the best option – often airlines like *British Airways* have special deals (from £75 or so); otherwise, the *Paris Travel Service*, based just outside of London (see box on p.7), has package deals including flights from Belfast. Alternatives via Britain are unlikely to be attractive, considering the additional time factor and the cost of a flight from Ireland to Britain. For up-to-date details on the situation, try contacting *USIT*, specialists in student/youth travel (see box below).

By Car and Ferry

The cheapest way of getting to France – although far from the quickest – is by **ferry** from Cork or

---

Packages From Ireland

Irish Ferries
2–4 Merrion Row
Dublin 2   ☎ 01/661 0511
Return to Paris from any Irish Rail station via Le Havre £119. Accommodation in Paris at £29 per head per night is also offered.

Rosslare outside Wexford to various ports in Normandy or Brittany.

Ferry prices vary according to the season and, for motorists, the size of car; details of routes, companies and fares are given in the box opposite. You can either contact the companies direct to reserve space in advance (essential at peak season if you're driving), or any competent travel agent at home or France can do it for you.

Useful Addresses in Ireland

AIRLINES
Aer Lingus
46 Castle St, Belfast   ☎ 01232/314844
40 O'Connell St, Dublin 1   ☎ 01/844 4777
2 Academy St, Cork   ☎ 021/327155
136 O'Connell St, Limerick   ☎ 061/474239

Air Inter
29–30 Dawson St, Dublin   ☎ 01/677 8899

British Airways
Dublin reservations   ☎ 1800/626747
9 Fountain Centre, College St
Belfast, BT1 6ET   ☎ 0345/222111

British Midland
Nutley, Merrion Rd, Dublin 4   ☎ 01/283 8833
Belfast reservations   ☎ 0345/676676

AGENTS AND OPERATORS
Joe Walsh Tours
8–11 Baggot St, Dublin   ☎ 01/876 3053

31 Castle St, Belfast   ☎ 01232/241144
Discount flight agent.

Thomas Cook
118 Grafton St, Dublin   ☎ 01/677 1721
11 Donegal Place, Belfast   ☎ 01232/240833
Mainstream package holiday and flight agent, with occasional discount offers.

USIT
Fountain Centre
Belfast BT1 6ET   ☎ 01232/324073
33 Ferryquay St
Derry   ☎ 01504/371888
Victoria Place
Eyre Square, Galway   ☎ 091/565177
Central Buildings
O'Connell St, Limerick   ☎ 081/415064
36–37 George St
Waterford   ☎ 051/72601
Student and youth specialists.

1997 FERRY ROUTES AND PRICES

Note: return prices are substantially cheaper but generally need to be booked in advance.

	Operator	Crossing time	Frequency	One-way fares Small car 2 adults (£IR)	Foot passenger (£IR)
Cork–Roscoff	*Brittany Ferries*	14hr	mid-March to Oct 1 1–2 wkly	£176–266	£38–106
Cork–St-Malo	*Brittany Ferries*	18hr	mid-May to Sept 1 wkly	£176–226	£38–106
Cork–Le Havre	*Irish Ferries*	21hr 30min	May–Sept 2 wkly	£225–300	£60–87
Cork–Cherbourg	*Irish Ferries*	17hr 30min	July–Sept 1 wkly	£225–300	£60–87
Rosslare–Cherbourg	*Irish Ferries*	18hr	1 wkly	£225–300	£60–87
Rosslare–Le Havre	*Irish Ferries*	22hr	2–3 wkly	£225–300	£60–87
Rosslare–Brest	*Irish Ferries*	15hr	May–Sept 1–2 wkly	£225–300	£60–87
Cork–Brest	*Irish Ferries*	15hr 30 min	June–July 2 wkly	£225–300	£60–87

Special offers
Irish Ferries: 13-night excursion returns (10-night July & Aug).
Brittany Ferries: 3-, 7- and 11-day returns.

Addresses in Ireland

Brittany Ferries		**Irish Ferries**	
42 Grand Parade, Cork		2–4 Merrion Row, Dublin 2	☎ 01/661 0511
reservations	☎ 021/277801	Cork	☎ 021/504333
holidays & information	☎ 021/277705	Rosslare	☎ 053/33158

Getting there from the US and Canada

Getting to Paris from the US or Canada is straightforward. The city is the only French transatlantic gateway and has direct flights from over thirty major North American cities. Nearly a dozen different scheduled airlines operate flights, making Paris one of the cheapest destinations in Europe – especially in these days of cut-throat inter-airline competition. In fact, only London can offer more discounted flights; and while a visit to England may appeal, the price difference is rarely sufficient to make a stopover in London a money-saving idea.

The cheapest way to take any of these scheduled flights is with a non-refundable **Apex** fare, which normally entails booking 21 days in advance of flying, travelling midweek, and staying for at least seven days. Apart from special offers, this is likely to be the best deal you'll get direct from an airline ticket counter.

The best guarantee of a cheap flight, however, is to contact a travel agent specializing in **discounted fares**. The travel sections of the *New York Times, Washington Post* and *Los Angeles Times* advertise them. Restrictions on such tickets

are often not all that stringent; you need not assume that youth or student fares are the best bargain, nor worry if you're not eligible for them. The independent travel specialists **STA Travel** and **Council Travel** are two of the most reliable agents, but not surprisingly the French group **Nouvelles Frontières** has some good offers. These firms, together with several of the other larger agents, act as "consolidators" for particular airlines with which they maintain contracts to sell seats on specific terms, invariably below the airlines' own fares, though sometimes less convenient.

Estimating the cost of **return economy class fares** to Paris is tricky, especially as routes, carriers and the state of the market in general are changing all the time. The return fares shown in the box below are a general guide to what you might expect to pay; startling variations are due to specific airlines engaging in price wars on specific routes. Fares are dependent on **season**, and are highest from around early June to the end of August, when everyone wants to travel; they drop during the "shoulder" seasons,

---

Sample Round-trip Fares to Paris

Typical lowest discounted fares in low season/high season, flying midweek.

Atlanta	$484/715
Boston	$428/659
Charlotte	$484/715
Chicago	$495/726
Dallas	$528/759
Houston	$528/759
Los Angeles	$572/803
Miami	$495/726
Montréal	CDN$449/660
New York	$428/569
San Francisco	$572/803
Toronto	CDN$449/660
Vancouver	CDN$759/1000
Washington DC	$461/692

September–October and April–May, and you'll get the best deals during the low season, November to March (excluding Christmas). Note that Friday, Saturday and Sunday travel tends to carry a premium. One-way fares are generally slightly more than half the return fare. If you have a specific destination in mind in France outside Paris, and you're in a hurry – and if you're prepared to pay extra – it's possible to be ticketed straight through to any of more than a dozen regional airports. Most of these entail connecting flights on *Air Inter*, *Air France*'s domestic arm, and require a change of planes in Paris (check to make sure there's no inconve-

nient transfer between Charles de Gaulle and Orly). Some sample round-trip add-on fares from Paris: Bordeaux, Grenoble, Lyon and Strasbourg around $95; Brest, Marseille, Nice and Toulouse around $125.

Charter flights (a flight chartered by a tour operator from an airline to ferry tourists) can be even cheaper than these prices for scheduled services. But, while discounted scheduled services sometimes carry eligibility restrictions, charter flights hedge you in with restricted dates and major financial penalties if you cancel. They're worth considering if you're very organized and know exactly what you plan to do. Most agents

---

Discount Agents, Consolidators and Travel Clubs in North America

Council Travel
Head office: 205 E 42nd St, New York
NY 10017   ☎1-800/226-8624
Nationwide US student travel organization with branches in 40 US cities including San Francisco, Washington DC, Boston, Austin, Seattle, Chicago, Minneapolis.

Encore Travel Club
4501 Forbes Blvd
Lanham, MD 20706   ☎1-800/444-9800
Discount travel club.

Flight Centre
S Granville Street
Vancouver   ☎1-604/739-9539
Discount air fares from Canadian cities.

High Adventure Travel Inc
253 Sacramento St, Suite 600
San Francisco, CA 94111   ☎1-800/428-8735
Round-the-world tickets. Its new website (http://www.highadv.com) is highly recommended.

Interworld Travel
800 Douglass Rd, Miami
FL 33134   ☎305/443-4929
Consolidator.

New Frontiers/Nouvelles Frontières
12 E 33rd St, New York,
NY 10016   ☎800/366-6387
1001 Sherbrook East, Suite 720
Montréal, H2L 1L3   ☎514/526-8444
French discount travel firm; also markets charters to Paris and Lyon. Other branches in LA, San Francisco and Québec City.

STA Travel
Main office: 10 Downing St, New York
NY 10014   ☎1-800/AIR-ONLY
                                    or 212/573-8980
Worldwide specialist in independent travel with branches in the Los Angeles, San Francisco and Boston areas. Has French branches in Paris and Grenoble.

Travel Cuts
Main office: 187 College St
Toronto, ON M5T 1P7   ☎416/979-2406
Canadian student travel organization with branches all over the country.

Travelers Advantage
3033 S Parker Rd, Suite 900
Aurora, CO 80014   ☎1-800/548-1116
Discount travel club.

Travac TOURS
Main office: 989 6th Ave
New York, NY 10018   ☎1-800/872-8800
Consolidator and charter broker.

Unitravel
1177 N Warson Rd
St Louis, MO 63132   ☎1-800/325-2222
Consolidator.

Worldwide Discount Travel Club
1674 Meridian Ave
Miami Beach, FL 33139   ☎305/534-2082
Discount travel club.

---

sell them. *New Frontiers*, a Canadian discount travel agency, has summer non-stop charters from New York to Paris on *Corsair* from $600 return.

If you're prepared to travel light at short notice and for a short duration it might be worth getting a **courier flight**. Return journeys to Paris are available for around $350, with last-minute specials (booked within three days of departure) as low as $150. Tickets are issued on a first-come, first-served basis, and there's no guarantee that the Paris route will be available at the specific time you want.

Now Voyager (☎212/431-1616) and *Discount Travel International* (☎212/362-3636) arrange such flights to Europe from JFK, Newark and Houston. For more information about what is available, contact the *Air Courier Association*, ☎303/279-3600, the *International Association of Air Couriers* (☎407/582-8320), or get hold of a guide entitled *Courier Bargains: How to Travel Worldwide for Next to Nothing* by Kelly Monaghan ($17.50 postpaid from the *Intrepid Traveler*, PO Box 438, New York, NY 10034).

Flights from the US

The most comprehensive range of flights from the US is offered by **Air France**, the French national carrier, which flies non-stop to Charles de Gaulle airport from Anchorage, Boston, Chicago, Houston, Los Angeles, Miami, New York (JFK and Newark) and Washington DC – in most instances daily. However, *Air France* does tend to be expensive.

Airlines in North America

Only gateway cities are listed for each airline; other routings are always possible using connecting flights.

Air Canada (☎1-800/776-3000; ☎1-800/555-1212 in Canada). *Daily non-stop to Paris from Toronto, Montréal and Los Angeles; three times weekly from Vancouver.*

Air France (☎1-800/237-2747; ☎1-800/667-2747 in Canada). *Daily non-stop to Paris from Toronto, Montréal, Chicago, New York, Los Angeles, San Francisco, Houston, Miami and Washington DC.*

American Airlines (☎1-800/433-7300). *Daily non-stop to Paris from Chicago, Miami, New York and Dallas.*

AOM French Airlines (☎1-310/338-9613). *Non-stop from Los Angeles to Paris three to five times a week depending on the season.*

British Airways (☎1-800/247-9297; ☎1-800/668-1059 in Canada). *Many North American cities to London, with connections to Paris and Nice.*

Canadian Airlines (☎1-800/665-1177 in Canada). *Daily non-stop to Paris from Toronto and other major Canadian cities.*

Continental Airlines (☎1-800/231-0856). *Daily non-stop to Paris from New York and Houston.*

Delta Airlines (☎1-800/241-4141; ☎1-800/555-1212 in Canada). *Daily non-stop to Paris from New York, Cincinnati and Atlanta.*

Iceland Air (☎1-800/223-5500). *New York, Baltimore and Orlando to Reykjavik and on to Paris.*

KLM (☎1-800/374-7747). *Many North American cities to Amsterdam, with connections to Paris, Lyon, Marseille and Nice.*

Northwest Airlines (☎1-800/447-4747). *Boston and Detroit to Paris.*

PIA Pakistan International Airways (☎1-800/221-2552). *Non-stop service from Los Angeles to Paris three to five times a week.*

Tower Air (☎1-800/221-2500). *Daily non-stop from New York to Paris.*

TWA (☎1-800/982-4141). *Daily non-stop from New York and Boston to Paris; three times a week from St Louis.*

United Airlines (☎1-800/538-2929). *Daily non-stop to Paris from Chicago, Los Angeles, San Francisco and Washington DC.*

US Air (☎1-800/622-1015). *Daily non-stop from Philadelphia to Paris.*

Virgin Atlantic Airways (☎1-800/862-8621). *Flights to London from Newark, JFK, Boston, Miami and Orlando.*

The **major American competitors** tend to be cheaper, but offer fewer non-stop routes. *American* and *TWA* have the biggest range of "direct" routes. The former flies to Paris Orly nonstop from Chicago, Dallas, New York (JFK and Raleigh-Durham), or with a stop from LA (via Dallas), San Francisco (via Chicago) and San Diego (via JFK) and has good or guaranteed connections from fourteen cities in the south and west. *TWA* flies nonstop to Paris Charles de Gaulle from Boston, New York, St Louis and Washington DC, and has one-stop flights from Chicago and LA and guaranteed connections (same flight number) from Atlanta, Kansas City, Portland, San Francisco and Seattle. For details of other airlines plying the US to Paris route, see the box below.

Flights from Canada

The strong links between France and Québec's Francophone community ensure regular air services from Canada to Paris. The main route is Vancouver–Toronto–Montréal–Paris (Charles de Gaulle). Most departures originate in Toronto, however, with **Air France** flying daily from Toronto to Charles de Gaulle, either non-stop or

via Montréal. **Air Canada** and **Canadian Airlines** fly direct to Paris from Toronto and Montréal, again pretty well daily, and *Canadian Airlines* flies in from Vancouver twice weekly to guarantee the connection to Paris.. **Travel Cuts** and **Nouvelles Frontières** are the most likely sources of good-value discounted seats; call for details as flights vary from season to season.

There are some excellent **charter deals** in Canada. *Air Transit Holidays*, a Canadian charter operation, is worth trying for its wide selection of non-stop late spring, summer and autumn flights to Paris from Vancouver and Toronto. Toronto–Paris, return, for instance, is CDN$449–660; Vancouver–Paris is CDN$759–1000. *Canada 3000/Fiesta West*, another Canadian charter company, has non-stop flights to Paris from Vancouver and Calgary at CDN$925 for travel between July and September.

Flying via the UK

Although **flying to London** is usually the cheapest way of reaching Europe, price differences these days are minimal enough for there to be little point travelling to France via London unless you've specifically chosen to visit the UK as well.

Tour Operators in North America

Abercrombie & Kent (☎1-800/323-7308). *Rail and canal journeys.*

Air Canada Vacations. *Packages and tours. Contact travel agents or* Air Canada *for brochures.*

American Airlines Fly Away Vacations (☎1-800/433-7300). *Package tours, fly-drive programmes.*

British Airways Holidays (☎1-800/359-8722). *Package tours, fly-drive programmes.*

Canada 3000/Fiesta West *Discount charter flights, cars, hotels, package tours through* BCAA TeleCentre *(☎1-800/663-1956 in Canada) or travel agents.*

CBT Bicycle Tours (☎1-800/736-BIKE). *European bike tours, some starting or ending in Paris.*

Contiki Tours (☎1-800/CONTIKI). *European vacations (most including Paris) for under-35s.*

Cosmos Tourama/Globus (☎1-800/221-0090). *Paris city breaks.*

Delta Dream Vacations (☎1-800/872-7786). *Packages, escorted tours and fly-drive programmes.*

EC Tours (☎1-800/388-0877). *City packages.*

ETT Tours (☎1-800/551-2085). *Independent tours and city packages.*

France Vacations (☎1-800/332-5332). *Flight/hotel packages through* AOM *French Airlines.*

The French Experience (☎1-800/28-FRANCE). *City breaks, self-drive tours, apartment and cottage rentals.*

International Study Tours (☎1-800/833-2111). *Culture/art tours.*

New Frontiers/Nouvelles Frontières (☎1-800/366-6387). *City packages and à la carte accommodation.*

Having said that, you may well be able to pick up a flight to London at an advantageous rate.

In recent years, **Virgin Atlantic** has offered some of the best fares from New York and Newark; and has now added flights from Miami, Orlando and Boston to its schedules (all into London Gatwick). **British Airways** has entered the fray with a series of rival offers. In summer, the savings are bound to be less, but shop around as there may yet be some European bargains. As well as from JFK and Newark, *British Airways* has regular non-stop flights from Philadelphia, Boston, San Francisco, and Los Angeles – and Detroit via Montréal.

Package Tours

Dozens of tour operators offer reasonably priced packages to Paris and the surrounding countryside. Many can put together very **flexible deals**, sometimes amounting to no more than a flight and accommodation; if you're planning to travel in moderate or luxurious style, and especially if your trip is geared around special interests, such packages can work out cheaper than the same arrangements made on arrival. A tour is inevitably more confining than independent travel, but it can help you make the most of time if you're on a tight schedule; and if Paris is your first stop on a longer trip, a tour can ensure a worry-free first few days while you're finding your feet.

Delta Airlines offers a seven-day fly-drive package to Paris starting at $729 for New York departures. *British Airways* has a seven-day Paris tour starting at $949, including transatlantic airfare via London, hotels and sightseeing. Six-day fly-drive tours via London and starting in Paris cost from $709 including airfare from the US and a car. *American Airlines* offer a seven-day England–France fly-drive package, including Channel Tunnel crossing, from $534 per person for hotel, breakfast, rental car and Channel tickets. *American* also has a variety of hotel/sightseeing packages (airfare from the US not included), such as its seven-day Paris package for $673, and the "Paris Stopover", which starts at $52 per person for one night's hotel and breakfast. *AOM French Airlines* offers a six-day Paris package for $689 including return airfare from Los Angeles, hotels and breakfast.

For other possibilities, see the accompanying box or make enquiries at a travel agent (remember, bookings made through a travel agent cost no more than going through the tour operator).

Getting there from Australia and New Zealand

Most people travelling to Paris from Australia and New Zealand will choose to travel via London. There are, however, alternative stopover points in Europe, and these are often available at economical fares. Whichever way you route, most airlines can add on a Paris leg to an Australia/New Zealand–Europe ticket.

From Australia

From Australia, fares to Paris vary according to the season and carrier. Seasons vary slightly depending on the airline, but in general, low season lasts from mid-January to the end of February, and from 1 October to the end of November; high season is the second half of May, from the beginning of June to the end of August, and from the beginning of December to mid-January. Seasonal fare increases are between A$/NZ$200–400.

There is a host of airlines operating a service between major cities in Australia via their home ports to Paris. Those offering several flights a week include Aeroflot, Alitalia, Cathay Pacific, Garuda, Malaysian Airlines and Thai Airways. Daily flights from Sydney, Cairns and Brisbane are run by Air France/Qantas and JAL.

Airlines in Australia and New Zealand

Aeroflot, 388 George St, Sydney (☎ 02/9233 7911). No NZ office.

Air France, 12 Castlereagh St, Sydney (☎ 02/9321 1000); 2nd Floor, Dataset House, 143 Nelson St, Auckland (☎ 09/303 3521).

Alitalia, Orient Overseas Building, 32 Bridge St, Sydney (☎ 02/9247 1308); 6th Floor, Trustbank Building, 229 Queen St, Auckland (☎ 09/379 4457).

British Airways, Level 26, 201 Kent St, Sydney (☎ 02/9258 3300); 154 Queen St, Auckland (☎ 09/356 8690).

Cathay Pacific, Level 12, 8 Spring St, Sydney (☎ 02/9931 5500; local-call rate ☎ 131747); 11f Arthur Andersen Tower, 205–209 Queen St, Auckland (☎ 09/379 0861).

Garuda, 55 Hunter St, Sydney (☎ 02/9334 9944); 120 Albert St, Auckland (☎ 09/366 1855).

JAL, Floor 14, Darling Park, 201 Sussex St, Sydney (☎ 02/9283 1111); Floor 12, Westpac Tower, 120 Albert St, Auckland (☎ 09/379 9906).

KLM, 5 Elizabeth St, Sydney (☎ 02/9231 6333; toll-free 1800/505747). No NZ office.

Lufthansa/Lauda-air, 143 Macquarie St, Sydney (☎ 02/9367 3888); Lufthansa House, 36 Kitchener St, Auckland (☎ 09/303 1529).

Malaysian Airlines, 16 Spring St, Sydney (local-call rate ☎ 132627); Floor 12, Swanson Centre, 12–26 Swanson St, Auckland (☎ 09/373 2741).

Qantas, Chifley Square, cnr Hunter & Phillip streets, Sydney (☎ 02/9957 0111); Qantas House, 154 Queen St, Auckland (☎ 09/357 8900).

Thai Airways, 75–77 Pitt St, Sydney (☎ 02/9844 0999; toll-free ☎ 1800/422 020); Kensington Swan Building, 22 Fanshawe St, Auckland (☎ 09/377 3886).

Discount agents should be able to get you a discount of at least ten percent off the following low-season published fares: *Garuda* (via Bali, Jakarta, Singapore or Bangkok and Abu Dhabi, with two stopovers allowed each way), A$1685 to Paris; *Air France, British Airways* (via London), *KLM* (via Amsterdam), *Lufthansa/Lauda* (via Frankfurt), *Alitalia/Qantas* (via Rome), *JAL* (overnight in Tokyo), A$2199; *Aeroflot* (via Moscow), A$1700; *Thai International* (via Bangkok), A$2055; *Malaysian Airlines* (via Kuala Lumpur), A$2099.

Airpasses, coupons and discounts on further flights within Europe vary with airlines, but the basic rules are that they must be pre-booked with the main ticket, are valid for three months, and are available only with a return fare with the one airline – for example, you have to fly to France with *British Airways* alone to be eligible for their airpass deals. *Air France* offers a **Euroflyer** for use in France and Europe at A$100 each flight; *British Airways* have a zone system: around A$103 for each flight within France, A$135 each for single flights to and around Germany, Italy and Belgium. Both airlines also arrange **fly-drive packages**; check with an agent for current deals as prices are variable. *KLM*'s **Passport to Europe** uses coupons for single flights: three

---

Travel Agents in Australia and New Zealand

Anywhere Travel, 345 Anzac Parade, Kingsford, Sydney (☎02/9663 0411).

Brisbane Discount Travel, 260 Queen St, Brisbane (☎07/3229 9211).

Budget Travel, 16 Fort St, Auckland; other branches around the city (☎09/366 0061; toll-free 0800/808040).

Destinations Unlimited, 3 Milford Rd, Milford, Auckland (☎09/373 4033).

Flight Centres, *Australia*: Level 11, 33 Berry St, North Sydney (☎02/9241 2422); Bourke St, Melbourne (☎03/9650 2899); plus other branches nationwide. *New Zealand*: National Bank Towers, 205–225 Queen St, Auckland (☎09/209 6171); Shop 1M, National Mutual Arcade, 152 Hereford St, Christchurch (☎03/379 7145); 50–52 Willis St, Wellington (☎04/472 8101); other branches countrywide.

Northern Gateway, 22 Cavenagh St, Darwin (☎08/8941 1394).

Passport Travel, 320b Glenferrie Rd, Malvern (☎03/9824 7183).

STA Travel, *Australia*: 702–730 Harris St, Ultimo, Sydney (☎02/9212 1255; toll-free 1800/637 444); 256 Flinders St, Melbourne (☎03/9654 7266); other offices in state capitals and major universities. *New Zealand*: Travellers' Centre, 10 High St, Auckland (☎09/309 0458); 233 Cuba St, Wellington (☎04/385 0561); 90 Cashel St, Christchurch (☎03/379 9098); other offices in Dunedin, Palmerston North, Hamilton and major universities.

Thomas Cook, *Australia*: 321 Kent St, Sydney (☎02/9248 6100); 257 Collins St, Melbourne (☎03/9650 2442); branches in other state capitals. *New Zealand*: Shop 250a St Luke's Square, Auckland (☎09/849 2071).

Topdeck Travel, 65 Glenfell St, Adelaide (☎08/8232 7222).

Tymtro Travel, 428 George St, Sydney (☎02/9223 2211).

Specialist Agents in Australia and New Zealand

European Travel Office, *Australia*: 122 Rosslyn St, West Melbourne (☎03/9329 8844); Level 20, 133 Castlereagh St, Sydney (☎02/9267 7727); *New Zealand*: 407 Great South Rd, Penrose, Auckland (☎09/525 3074).

France Accommodation, 47 North Blackburn Square, Blackburn, Melbourne (☎03/877 6066).

France and Travel, 55 Hardware St, Melbourne (☎03/9670 7253).

France Unlimited, 16 Goldsmith St, Elwood, Melbourne (☎03/9531 8787).

French Bike Tours, 16 Goldsmith St, Elwood, Melbourne (☎03/9531 8787).

French Cottages and Travel, 674 High St, East Kew, Melbourne (☎03/9859 4944).

French Tourist Bureau, 12 Castlereagh Street, Sydney (☎02/231 5244).

French Travel Connection, 90 Mount Street, Sydney (☎02/956 5884).

Renault Eurodrive, cnr Jamieson and York streets, Sydney (☎02/299 3344); branches in other state capitals.

coupons for around US$400, up to six for US$710; Lufthansa start at US$375 for three coupons, with extra flights US$105 each, to a maximum of nine.

From New Zealand

From New Zealand, best deals are (discounted): *Japanese Airlines* (NZ$2200, overnight stop in Tokyo), *Malaysian Airlines* (NZ$2300) and *Garuda* (NZ$2250). For **stopovers** in Europe, *British Airways* charge NZ$2399 via London; *Qantas/Alitalia* are slightly less at NZ$2300 via Rome and London. For **side trips** within Europe, *Qantas/Lufthansa* have a four-coupon deal on a six-month fare for NZ$2600.

Red Tape and Visas

Citizens of EU (European Union) countries, Canada, the United States, New Zealand and Norway do not need any sort of visa to enter. All other passport holders (including British Travel Document holders and Australians) must obtain a visa before arrival in France. Obtaining a visa from your nearest French consulate is fairly automatic, but check their hours before turning up, and leave plenty of time, since there are often queues (particularly in London in summer). Australians can obtain a visa on the spot in London. Note that the British Visitor's Passport is no longer valid.

French Embassies and Consulates Overseas

Australia
492 St Kilda Road, Melbourne, VIC 3001
☎ 03/9820 0921
31 Market St, Sydney, NSW 2000
☎ 02/9261 5779

Canada
Embassy: 42 Promenade Sussex
Ottawa, ON K1M 2C9   ☎ 613/789 1795
Consulates: 1 place Ville Marie
Bureau 22601, Montréal
Québec H3B 4S3   ☎ 514/878 4385
25 rue St-Louis
Québec QC G1R 3Y8
☎ 418/688 0430
130 Bloor Street West, Suite 400
Toronto, ON M5S 1N5   ☎ 416/925 80441
1201-736 Granville St
Vancouver BC V6Z 1H9   ☎ 604/681 4345

Ireland
36 Ailesbury Road, Dublin 4   ☎ 01/260 1666

Netherlands
Vijzelgracht 2, Amsterdam   ☎ 20/624 8346

New Zealand
1 Willeston St, PO Box 1695
Wellington   ☎ 04/720200

Norway
Drammensveien 69, 0244 Oslo   ☎ 02/41820

Sweden
Linnegatan 78, Box 10315
10055 Stockholm   ☎ 08/663 0685

UK
French Consulate General (visas section)
21 Cromwell Road
London SW7   ☎ 0171/838 2051
7–11 Randolph Crescent, Edinburgh
☎ 0131/225 7954; fax 0131/225 8975

USA
Embassy: 4101/Reservoir Rd NW
Washington DC 20007   ☎ 202/944 6000
Consulates: Park Square Building, Suite 750
31 St James Avenue
Boston, MA 02116   ☎ 617/542 7374
737 North Michigan Ave, Olympia Centre
Suite 2020, Chicago, IL 60611   ☎ 312/787 5359
10990 Wilshire Boulevard, Suite 300
Los Angeles, CA 90024   ☎ 310/235 3200
934 Fifth Ave, New York
NY 10021   ☎ 212/606 3689
540 Bush St, San Francisco
CA 94108   ☎ 415/397 4330

Three types of **visa** are currently issued: a transit visa, valid for two months; a short-stay (*court séjour*) visa, valid for ninety days after the date of issue and good for multiple entries; and a long-stay (*long séjour*) visa, which allows for multiple stays of ninety days over three years, but which is issued only after an examination of an individual's circumstances. EU citizens (or other non-visa citizens) who **stay longer than three months** are officially supposed to apply for a **Carte de Séjour**, for which you'll have to show proof of income at least equal to the minimum wage. However, EU passports are rarely stamped, so there is no evidence of how long you've been in the country. If your passport does get stamped, you can cross the border – to Belgium or Germany, for example – and re-enter for another ninety days legitimately.

Health and Insurance

Citizens of all EU and Scandinavian countries are entitled to take advantage of French health services under the same terms as residents, if they have the correct documentaion. British citizens need form E111, available from post offices. North American and other non-EU citizens have to pay for most medical attention and are strongly advised to take out some form of travel insurance.

Under the French Social Security system every hospital visit, doctor's consultation and prescribed medicine incurs a charge. Although all employed French people are entitled to a refund of 70–75 percent of their medical and dental expenses, this can still leave a hefty shortfall, especially after a stay in hospital (accident victims even have to pay for the ambulance that takes them there).

To find a **doctor**, stop at any *pharmacie* and ask for an address, or look under *Médecins Qualifiés* in the Yellow Pages of the Parisian phone directory. To qualify for Social Security refunds, make sure the doctor is a *médecin conventionné*. An average consultation fee would be between 100F and 150F. You will be given a *Feuille de Soins* (Statement of Treatment) for later documentation of insurance claims. Prescriptions should be taken to a *pharmacie* where they must be paid for; the medicines will have little stickers (*vignettes*) attached to them, which you must remove and stick to your *Feuille de Soins*, together with the prescription itself.

Centre Médical Europe (44 rue Amsterdam, 9e; Mº Liège; ☎01.42.81.80.00; Mon–Fri 8am–7pm, Sat 8am–6pm), has a variety of different practitioners charging low consultation fees.

In serious emergencies you will always be admitted to the nearest **hospital** (*hôpital*), either under your own power or by ambulance.

As getting a refund entails a complicated bureaucratic procedure, and in any case does not cover the full cost of treatment, it's always a better idea to take out ordinary travel insurance, which generally allows full reimbursement, less the first few pounds or dollars of every claim, and also covers the cost of repatriation.

If you're travelling in your own car, you may want to have breakdown cover which includes **personal insurance**.

British Cover

When considering any insurance policy, check carefully that it will cover you in case of an accident. Note also that very few insurers will arrange on-the-spot payments in the event of a major expense or loss; you will usually be reimbursed only after going home. In all cases of loss or theft of goods, claims can only be dealt with if a report is made to the local police (the *Commissariat de Police*) within 24 hours and a copy of the report (*constat de vol*) sent with the claim

Most policies are broadly similar, but before signing up you should always read the small print to see what is covered: often money and credit cards are covered only if stolen from your person. If you have any other insurance policies – house and contents insurance, for example – you'll find some of the optional extra cover in travel insurance only duplicates what you already have at home.

Bank and credit cards often have certain levels of medical or other insurance included, especially if you use them to pay for your trip. This can be quite comprehensive, anticipating anything from lost or stolen baggage and missed connections to charter companies going bankrupt. For example, *Barclaycard* automatically insures anything you've purchased with the card for 100 days, gives travel insurance if you pay for your

Medical Help

Emergency numbers

Fire brigade ☎ 18
Ambulance (*Service d'Aide Médicale Urgente*)
☎ 01.45.67.50.50
Emergency medical advice ☎ 15

Doctor call-out (*SOS Médecins*)
☎ 01.47.07.77.77/01.43.37.77.77
Rape crisis (*SOS Viol*) ☎ 08.00.05.95.95

Other medical helplines and services

AIDS see p.25
Burns children: ☎ 01.44.73.74.75
adults: ☎ 01.42.34.17.58
Dentistry ☎ 01.43.37.51.00
SOS Dentaire, 87 bd Port-Royal
13e (Mº Port-Royal)
Poisoning
Centre Anti-Poisons ☎ 01.40.37.04.04
STDs (other than AIDS) ☎ 01.40.78.26.00
Institut A-Fournier, 25 bd St-Jacques,
14e (Mº Glacière/St-Jacques)

SOS Help
In English: ☎ 01.47.23.80.80
(*crisis line/any problem: 3–11pm*)
In French (24hr): ☎ 01.46.08.52.77

International Counselling Service and
American Student & Family Service,
The American Church, 65 quai d'Orsay, 7e (Mº
Invalides/Alma-Marceau; ☎ 01.45.50.26.49)
*Mon–Sat 9.30am–1pm, afternoon and
evening appointments also possible.*

Pharmacies

All **pharmacies**, signalled by an illuminated green cross, are equipped (and obliged) to give first aid
on request – though they will make a charge. **When closed**, they all display the address of the nearest open pharmacy, day or night. **At night and on Sundays** you can call the local police station
(Commissariat de Police) for the address of the nearest open pharmacy or for a doctor on duty.

Pharmacies open at night

Dérhy/Pharmacie des Champs-Elysées, 84
av des Champs-Elysées, 8e (Mº George V;
☎ 01.45.62.02.41). *24 hours.*

Pharmacie Européenne, 6 place Clichy, 9e
(Mº Franklin-D-Roosevelt; ☎ 01.48.74.65.18).
24 hours.

Cariglioli/Pharmacie des Halles, 10 bd
Sébastopol, 4e (Mº Châtelet; ☎ 01.42.72.03.23).
*Mon–Sat 9am–midnight, Sun noon–mid-
night.*

Drugstore Publicis, 149 bd St-Germain, 6e
(Mº St-Germain-des-Près; ☎ 01.42.22.80.00).
Daily 8.30am–2am.

Pharmacie Matignon, 2 rue Jean-Mermoz, 8e
(Mº Franklin-D-Roosevelt; ☎ 01.43.59.86.55).
Daily 8.30am–2am.

Internationale, 17bis bd Rochechouart, 9e (Mº
Anvers/Pigalle; ☎ 01.48.78.03.01). *Daily to 2am.*

La Nation, 13 place de la Nation, 11e (Mº
Nation; ☎ 01.43.73.24.03). *Mon noon–midnight,
Tues–Sat 8am–midnight, Sun 8pm–midnight.*

English-speaking pharmacies

Pharmacie Anglaise, 62 av des Champs-
Elysées, 8e (Mº George-V; ☎ 01.43.59.22.52).
Mon–Sat 9am–7pm.

Pharmacie Swann, 6 rue Castiglione, 1e (Mº
Tuileries; ☎ 01.42.60.72.96). *Mon–Sat
9am–7.30pm. Will translate English prescriptions and make up an equivalent medicine.*

English-speaking hospitals

The American Hospital in Paris, 63 bd
Victor-Hugo, Neuilly-sur-Seine (Mº Porte-
Maillot, then bus #82 to terminus;
☎ 01.46.41.25.25).

The Hertford British Hospital, 3 rue
Barbès, Levallois-Perret (Mº Anatole-France;
☎ 01.46.39.22.22).

To trace someone *who has been hospitalized, call* ☎ 01.40.27.30.81, *8.30am–5.30pm.*

Travel Insurance Companies and Agents

Britain

Campus Travel/STA (see p.5 for addresses).
Endsleigh Insurance (☎0171/436 4451).
Frizzell Insurance (☎01202/292 333).
Columbus Travel Insurance (☎0171/375 0011).

North America

Access America (☎1-800/284-8300).
Carefree Travel Insurance (☎1-800/323-3149).
Desjardins Travel Insurance (Canada only: ☎1-800/463-7830).
International Student Insurance Service (ISIS) – sold by **STA Travel** (☎1-800/777-0112).

Travel Assistance International (☎1-800/821-2828).
Travel Guard (☎1-800/826-1300).
Travel Insurance Services (☎1-800/937-1387).

Australasia

UTAG – United Travel Agents Group (toll-free ☎1800 809 462).
AFTA – Australian Federation of Travel Agents (☎02/956 4800).
Ready Plan (toll-free ☎1-800 337462).
Cover More (☎02/9202 8000; toll-free ☎1800 251 881).

---

holiday with the card and has a free International Rescue Service of legal advice, translation assistance, money transfer, contacting relatives and accompanying children home.

Most travel agents and tour operators will offer you insurance when you book your flight or holiday, and some will insist you take it. These policies are usually reasonable value, though as ever you should check the small print. If you feel the cover is inadequate, or you want to compare prices, any travel agent, insurance broker or bank should be able to help. If you have a good "all risks" home insurance policy it may well cover your possessions against loss or theft even when overseas, and many private medical schemes also cover you when abroad – make sure you know the procedure and the helpline number.

In the UK, travel insurance schemes (from around £45 a month) are sold by almost every travel agent or bank, and by specialist insurance companies. *ISIS* policies, from *STA Travel* or branches of *Endsleigh Insurance*, are usually good value. *Columbus Travel Insurance* also does an annual multi-trip policy which offers twelve months' cover for £125.

The *RAC* and *AA* offer car breakdown cover, including towing costs, labour, dispatch of spare parts and repatriation of the vehicle, plus medical expenses and loss of luggage or money, from around £100 for a family for fifteen days.

North American Cover

Before buying an insurance policy, check that you're not already covered. **Canadian** provincial health plans typically provide some overseas medical coverage, although they are unlikely to pick up the full tab in the event of a mishap. Holders of official **student and youth cards** (see p.39) are entitled to accident coverage and hospital in-patient benefits – the annual membership is far less than the cost of comparable insurance. **Students** may also find that their student health coverage extends during the vacations and for one term beyond the date of last enrolment. Bank and credit cards (particularly *American Express*) often provide certain levels of medical or other insurance, and travel insurance may also be included if you use a major credit or charge card to pay for your trip. **Homeowners'** or **renters' insurance** often covers theft or loss of documents, money and valuables while overseas.

After exhausting the possibilities above, you might want to contact a specialist travel insurance company; your travel agent can usually recommend one (or see the box above). Policies vary: some are comprehensive, while others cover only certain risks (accidents, illnesses, delayed or lost luggage, cancelled flights, etc). In particular, ask whether the policy pays medical costs up front or reimburses you later, and whether it provides for medical evacuation to your home country. For policies that include lost or stolen luggage, check exactly what is and isn't covered, and make sure the per-article limit will cover your most valuable possession.

The best premiums are usually to be had through student/youth travel agencies – *ISIS* policies, for example, cost $48–69 for fifteen days (depending

Alternative Medicine

Acupuncture
Association Française d'Acupuncture,
3 rue Arrivée, 15e (Mo Montparnasse;
☎01.42.29.63.63).

Chiropractice
American Chiropractice Center,
119 rue de l'Université, 7e (Mo Invalides;
☎01.45.51.38.38).

Homeopathy
Académie d'Homéopathie et de Médecines
Douces, 2 rue d'Isly, 8e (Mo St-Lazare;
☎01.43.87.60.33).

*Most pharmacies sell homeopathic
medicines*

on level of coverage), $80–105 for a month,
$149–207 for two months, $510–700 for a year.

Most North American travel policies apply only
to items lost, stolen or damaged while in the cus-
tody of an identifiable, responsible third party –
hotel porter, airline, luggage consignment, etc.
Even in these cases you will have to contact the
local police within a certain time limit to have a
complete report made out so that your insurer
can process the claim.

Australasian Cover

Travel insurance is put together by the airlines
and travel agent groups such as *UTAG, AFTA,
Cover-More* and *Ready Plan* in conjunction with
insurance companies. They are all similar in premium and coverage, however Ready Plan give

the best value for money coverage. A typical pol-
icy will cost A$190/NZ$220 for a month,
A$270/NZ$320 for two months and
A$330/NZ$400 for three months.

AIDS and Safer Sex

If Paris is the city of sex and romance, make sure
it's safer by using condoms (*les préservatifs* or
capotes). Paris has the highest number of people
suffering from **AIDS** of any city in Europe, with
almost equal numbers of heterosexual and
homosexual people who are HIV positive. Among
heterosexuals (excluding drug users), the number
of women who are HIV positive overtook men in
1992.

Anonymous AIDS/HIV **information and support
in English** is available from FACTS-LINE
(☎01.44.93.16.69 Mon, Wed & Fri 6–10pm).
FACTS (*Free AIDS Counselling Treatment Support*)
runs support groups and offers free counselling
at 190, bd de Charonne, 20e (☎01.44.93.16.32;
Mº Alexandre-Dumas). **Information in French** is
available from *Le Kiosque Sida*, 6 rue Dante, 5e
(Mº Maubert-Mutualité), or 36 rue Geoffroy-
l'Asnier, 4e (☎01.44.78.00.00; Mon–Fri
10am–7pm, Sat 2–8pm; Mº St-Paul)

Free HIV tests, with counselling in French, are
available in many hospitals and clinics, including
the *Centre Médico-Social*, 3–5 rue Ridder, 14e
(☎01.45.43.83.78; Mº Plaisance), and *Dispensaire
de la Croix Rouge*, 43 rue de Valois, 1er
(☎01.42.61.30.04; Mº Palais-Royal).

SIDA Info Service (SIS), ☎08.00.36.66.36, is a
free 24-hour nationwide **telephone hotline**.

Disabled Travellers

Paris has no special reputation for providing ease of access or facilities for disabled travellers. The way cars park on pavements makes wheelchair travel a nightmare and the métro system has endless flights of steps. Museums, however, are getting much better; the *Cité des Sciences* has won European awards for its accessibility to those with sight, hearing and mobility disabilities. The *Comédie Française*, the *Théâtre National de l'Odéon*, the planetarium at the *Palais de la Découverte* and the *Studio St-Séverin* cinema have special equipment into which to plug hearing aids.

Travel with a Disability: Useful Contacts

France

APF (*Association des Paralysés de France*)
17 bd Auguste-Blanqui, 13e; ☎01.40.78.69.00.
A national organization providing useful information and lists of new and accessible accommodation. Their guide Où Ferons-Nous Étape *is available at the office or by post to a French address.*

CNRH (*Comité National Français de Liaison pour la Réadaptation des Handicapés*)
236bis rue Tolbiac, 13e; ☎01.53.80.66.66.
Information service whose various useful guides include Paris-Ile de France: Guide Touristique pour les Personnes à Mobilitée Réduite, *available in English for 60F.*

UK

Access Project 33, Blackwall Lane, London SE10; ☎0181/858 2375
Information service giving details of disabled facilities throughout the world.

Holiday Care Service
2nd floor, Imperial Building, Victoria Road Horley, Surrey RH6 9HW; ☎01293/774535.
Information on all aspects of travel.

RADAR (*The Royal Association for Disability and Rehabilitation*)
12 City Forum, 250 City Road
London EC1V 8AF; ☎0171/250 3222.

Minicom ☎0171/250 4119
A good source of advice on holidays and travel.

TRIPSCOPE
The Courtyard, Evelyn Rd
London W4; ☎0181/994 9294.

Phone-in travel information and advice service.

North America
Mobility International USA
PO Box 10767, Eugene
OR 97440; voice and TDD ☎503/343 1248.
Information, access guides, tours and exchange programme. Annual membership $20.

Travel Information Service
Moss Rehabilitation Hospital
1200 West Tabor Rd
Philadelphia, PA 19141; ☎215/456 9600.
Telephone information and referral service.

Twin Peaks Press
Box 129, Vancouver, WA 98666; ☎206/694 2462 or 1-800/637 2256.
Publishes excellent travel guides including the Directory of Travel Agencies for the Disabled *($19.95).*

Australasia
ACROD (*Australian Council for Rehabilitation of the Disabled*)
PO Box 60, Curtin ACT 2605, ☎06/682 4333; 55 Charles St, Ryde; ☎02/9809 4488.
Provides lists of travel agencies and tour operators for people with disabilities.

Disabled Persons Assembly, PO Box 10, 138 The Terrace, Wellington; ☎04/472 2626.
Provides lists of travel agencies and tour operators for people with disabilities.

Up-to-date information is best obtained from organizations at home before you leave or from the French disability organizations. The Paris tourist office touts various unreliable and dated guides.

Access in Paris by Gordon Couch and Ben Roberts, published in Britain by Quiller Press and available from *RADAR* (£6.95), is a thorough **guide** to accommodation, monuments, museums, restaurants and travel to the city. Another guide with the same title is produced by the *Access Project* (£3.50 plus donation towards postage costs). The *Holiday Care Service* has an information sheet on accessible **accommodation** in France.

Most of the cross-Channel ferry companies offer good facilities, though up-to-date information about access is difficult to get hold of. As far as airlines go, *British Airways* has a better-than-average record for treatment of disabled passengers, and from North America, *Virgin* and *Air Canada* come out tops in terms of disability awareness (and seating arrangements) and might be worth contacting first for any information they can provide.

The *French Government Tourist Office* in London has a free booklet on disabled access to hotels, called *Paris, Ile de France: Hôtels et Residences de Tourisme*. For more information, plus first-hand accounts by disabled travellers to France, see the *Rough Guide* special *Able to Travel/Nothing Ventured*, and contact the organizations below.

Getting Around

If you are physically handicapped, **taxis** are obliged by law to carry you and to help you into the vehicle, also to carry your guide dog if you are blind. The suburban agencies **GiHP** (Mon–Fri 8.30am–noon & 2–5/6pm; ☎01.47.71.74.90) and **Le Kangourou** (Mon–Fri 9am–6pm; ☎01.47.08.93.50) have taxicabs and minibuses fully adapted to wheelchairs; 24 hour advance notice is usually needed.

For travel on the **buses**, **métro** or **RER**, the *RATP* offers accompanied journeys for disabled people not in wheelchairs – *Service d'Accompagnement* – which operates Monday to Friday from 8am to 6pm. You have to book your minder on ☎01.42.71.20.53/01.48.93.06.23 a day in advance.

For **wheelchair users**, some stations on *RER* lines A and B are accessible, including Châtelet-les-Halles, Denfert-Rochereau, Gare de Lyon and Grande Arche de la Défense, but only with an official to work the lift for you. A leaflet, *Handicaps et Déplacements en Région Ile-de-France*, giving details, is available free at main métro/*RER* stations. A Braille métro map is obtainable from *L'Association Valentin Haüy*, 5 rue Duroc, 7e (☎01.47.34.07.90). **AIHROP** (Mon–Fri 10am–3pm; ☎01.40.24.34.76) arranges transport to and from the airports and within the city.

Cars with hand controls can be rented from **ITS**, 11 bd Auguste-Blanqui, 13e (☎01.45.88.52.37).

Points of Arrival

There's no great problem, whatever your point of arrival, in getting to any part of Paris. The train stations are all very central with direct access to the fast and efficient métro and RER network; the main bus station, just outside the city proper, is close to a métro station. From the two airports, Charles de Gaulle and Orly, there are trains, buses or taxis to get you to the centre of the city.

By Air

The two main Paris **airports** dealing with international flights are Charles de Gaulle (BA, Air France and most transatlantic flights; 24-hr flight information ☎01.48.62.22.80; two main terminals Aérogare 1 and Aérogare 2, the latter subdivided into 2A, 2B, 2C and 2D) and Orly (flight information ☎01.48.84.52.52; 6am–midnight; two terminals Orly Sud and Orly Ouest). Both airports have information desks providing maps, accommodation listings and money exchanges.

Charles de Gaulle Airport

Charles de Gaulle, 23km to the northeast of the city, is connected with the centre by several means of transport. Ligne B of the **RER** (the suburban express train) runs from the Roissy TGV station (walk from Terminal 2 or take the free airport shuttle from Terminal 1) to Gare du Nord and Châtelet (every 15min from 5.30am until 11.30pm), where you can transfer to the ordinary métro. Taking about 35 minutes, this is the quickest route and costs 45F.

By bus, the cheapest service is run by **Roissy Bus** (30F), from Terminal 2 to the Opéra-Garnier on the corner of rue Auber and rue Scribe, every 15 minutes from 5.45am to 11pm; journey time

For recorded info in French and English on *Air France* buses for both Charles de Gaulle and Orly, phone ☎01.41.56.89.00.

is approximately 45 minutes. The **Air France bus** (every 15 to 20min from 5.40am to 11pm; 48F) terminates at Porte Maillot (métro) on the northwest edge of the city, stopping at av Carnot, between the Arc de Triomphe and rue Tilsitt. Air France buses also link with Montparnasse at 13 bd de Vaugirard every hour 7am to 9pm. Journey times vary from 25 minutes to over an hour in rush hour. **Taxis** into central Paris cost 200–290F, plus a small luggage supplement, and should take between 50 minutes and one hour.

Before leaving the airport, pick up a good free **map** of the city from the information desk.

Orly Airport

Orly, 14km south of Paris, has three links to RER lines and a choice of buses. **Orly-Rail** operates a bus service (every 20min from 5.40am to 11.15pm; 30F) to Pont de Rungis station on RER ligne C for trains to Gare d'Austerlitz, St-Michel, Musée d'Orsay and other stops linked with the métro. The trip takes approximately 35 minutes. At 54F, **Orlyval** (every 4 to 7min from 6.30am to 10.15pm) is a more expensive option of Val train to Anthony on RER ligne B, with connections to Denfert-Rochereau, St-Michel and Châtelet-les-Halles. It takes around 30 minutes to reach the centre. For 30F you can catch the **Orlybus** to Denfert-Rochereau RER station (every 10 to 15min from 6am to 11.30pm); journey time is 30 minutes.

Air France buses connect Orly with the Invalides Air France terminus and Montparnasse (36 av du Maine). The 35-minute services leave every 12 or 15 minutes from 5.40am to 11pm, and cost 48F. Alternatively, **Jetbus** runs to Villejuif-Louis Aragon métro, the terminus of line 7, every 12 minutes from 6am to 10.15pm. It takes 15 minutes and costs 25F (you will then need a métro ticket to get into the centre).

A **taxi** will take around 45 minutes and cost between 140F and 170F.

By Train

Each of Paris' six mainline stations is equipped with cafés, restaurants, *tabacs*, banks, *bureaux de change* (where you can expect lengthy waits in season), and (with the exception of St-Lazare) tourist offices. All are connected with the métro system. They are divided into *Grands Lignes* (main lines) and *Banlieue* (surburban lines), with separate ticket offices (*guichets*).

The central phone number for information is ☎01.45.82.50.50 (or ☎01.45.65.60.00 for suburban lines), for reservations ☎01.45.65.60.60, and on Minitel (see p.43) 3615 SNCF, 8am–8pm. To buy your ticket you have to go to the relevant station; you can use credit cards in automatic vending machines.

The **Gare du Nord**, rue Dunkerque, 10ᵉ (trains from Boulogne, Calais, the UK including Eurostar, Belgium, Holland, northern Germany and Scandinavia) and **Gare de l'Est**, place du 11-Novembre-1918, 10ᵉ (serving eastern France, southern Germany, Switzerland and Austria) are side by side in the northeast of the city. The **Gare St-Lazare** (place du Havre; 8ᵉ; serving the Normandy coast, Dieppe and the UK) is the most central, close to the Madeleine and the Opéra-Garnier.

Still on the Right Bank but towards the southwest corner is the **Gare de Lyon** (place Louis-Armand, 12ᵉ), for trains from the Alps, the south, Italy and Greece. South of the river, **Gare Montparnasse** (bd de Vaugirard, 15ᵉ) is the terminus for Chartres, Brittany, the Atlantic coast and *TGV* lines to southwest France; and **Gare d'Austerlitz**

The central number for **all SNCF information** is ☎01.45.82.50.50.

(bd de l'Hôpital, 13ᵉ), for ordinary trains to south-west France, the Loire Valley, Spain and Portugal.

The motorail station, **Gare de Paris-Bercy**, is down the tracks from the Gare de Lyon, on bd de Bercy, 12ᵉ.

At the time of writing, all the stations' left **luggage lockers are closed** as a security precaution following a spate of bomb attacks in 1995. The only place you can leave luggage is at the manual left luggage office (*consigne*) at the Gare de Lyon.

By Bus

Almost all the **buses** coming into Paris – whether international or domestic – use the **main gare routière** on the eastern edge of the city at 28 av du Général-de-Gaulle, Bagnolet; ☎01.49.72.51.51; the métro station here (Mº Gallieni) is the terminus of line 3.

There are two main exceptions. **Citysprint** buses arrive at and depart from rue St-Quentin, around the corner from the Gare du Nord. Check-in for these services is at 135 rue Lafayette (☎01.42.85.44.55; Mº Gare du Nord). The terminal for **Hoverspeed Voyages** buses is at 164 av de Clichy, 17ᵉ (☎01.40.25.22.00; Mº Porte du Clichy).

By Car

If you're **driving** into Paris, don't try to go straight across the city to your destination. Use the ring road – the **boulevard périphérique** – to get to the *porte* nearest to your destination: it's much quicker, except at rush hour, and easier to find your way.

Once ensconced wherever you're staying, you'd be well advised to garage the car and use public transport. **Parking** is a major problem in the city centre.

Getting around the City

Finding your way around is remarkably easy, as Paris proper, without its suburbs, is compact and relatively small, with a public transport system that is cheap, fast and meticulously signposted.

To help you get your bearings above ground, think of the Louvre as the **centre**. The Seine flows east to west, cutting the city in two. The Eiffel Tower is **west**, the white pimples of the Sacré-Coeur on top of the hill of Montmartre, **north**. These are the landmarks you most often catch glimpses of as you move about. The area north of the river is known as the **Right Bank** or *rive droite*; to the south is the **Left Bank** or *rive gauche*. Roughly speaking, west is smart and east is scruffy.

A more detailed introduction to the topography and demography of Paris is provided in Chapter 1, *The Layout of the City*, on p.62.

Public Transport

The **métro**, combined with the **RER** express lines, is the simplest way of moving around. The métro (abbreviated to M°) runs from 5.30am to 12.45am; the *RER* from 5am to 1am. Stations are far more frequent than on the London Underground though many entrances are a long

Information on the various forms of help offered for **disabled travellers** on Paris' public transport is given on p.26.

way from the platforms and most interchanges involve long walks. Free **maps** are available at most stations. In addition, every station has a big plan of the network outside the entrance and several inside, along with a large-scale map of the immediate neighbourhood.

The métro lines are colour-coded and numbered; the *RER* lines are designated by letters. However, within the system you find your way around by following the signs saying *Direction Porte Dauphine, Direction Gallieni*, etc: the name of the station at the end of the line in the direction in which you are travelling. For instance, if you're travelling from Montparnasse to Châtelet, you follow the sign *Direction Porte de Clignancourt*; from Gare d'Austerlitz to Grenelle you follow *Direction Boulogne Pont-de-St-Cloud*. The numerous interchanges (**correspondances**) make it possible to travel all over the city in a more or less straight line.

For *RER* journeys beyond the city, make sure that the station you want is illuminated on the platform display board.

Don't, however, use the underground system to the exclusion of **buses**. They are easy to use and, of course, allow you to see much more. Free **route maps** are available at métro stations, bus terminals and the tourist office. The best bus map, showing the métro and *RER* as well, is the

The Homeless

There are at least 40,000 **homeless people** in Paris, about a quarter of whom are aged 15–25 and female. Unemployment is over 12 percent. For the long-term unemployed and those who have never worked, benefits are minimal. As a result, large numbers of people end up begging in the streets and, especially, on the métro.

Some of the homeless (*les sans-logement*) make a bit of money by selling magazines along the lines of the *Big Issue*. There are several titles, including *Faim de Siècle* and *Le Lampadaire* which have fun graphics and good articles. Around 7F of the 10F cover price goes to the vendor.

Grand Plan de Paris, available free from the *RATP Bureau de Tourisme*, place de la Madeleine (near rue Royale; M° Madeleine), or from the *RATP* office at 53 quai des Grands-Augustins, 6e (M° St-Michel). Every bus stop displays the numbers of the buses that stop there, a map showing all the stops on the route, and the times of the first and last buses. Each bus has a map of its own route inside and some have a recorded announcement for each approaching stop. Generally speaking, they run from around 6.30am to 8.30pm with some services continuing to 12.30am. Many lines don't operate on Sundays and holidays.

Night buses (Noctambus) run on ten routes every hour from 1am and 5am between place du Châtelet (near the Hôtel de Ville) and *portes* on the edge of the city. There is a reduced service on Sunday.

The **same tickets** are valid for bus, métro and, within the city and immediate suburbs (zones 1

and 2), the *RER* express rail lines, which also extend far out into the Île de France. One ticket only is needed for any métro/*RER* or bus journey, but you cannot switch between buses or between bus and métro/*RER* on the same ticket. Night buses require three tickets, or four if you change buses. Métro journeys beyond zones 1 and 2 require an extra ticket unless you're going to the end of the line. For *RER* journeys beyond zones 1 and 2 you must buy a *RER* ticket. Children under 4 travel free; those from 4 to 10 half price.

For a short stay in the city, tickets can be bought in **carnets** of ten from any station or *tabac* showing a métro ticket sign; the current cost is 46F, as opposed to 8F for a single ticket. There is also a *Formule 1* day pass (30F for the city, 100F to include outer suburbs and airports). Don't buy from the touts who hang round the main stations; you'll pay well over the odds, quite often for a used ticket. Be sure to keep your tick-

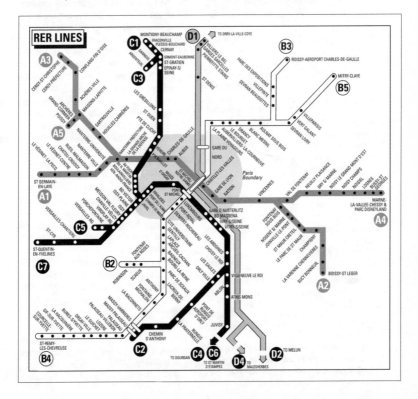

et until the end of the journey: you'll be fined on the spot if you can't produce one. Only the *RER* has a choice of first- or second-class.

If you've arrived early in the week and are staying three days or more, it may be more economical to have a **Carte Orange**, with a weekly coupon (*coupon hebdomadaire*; get zones 1 and 2 to cover the city and close suburbs). It costs 72F, is valid for an unlimited number of journeys from Monday morning to Sunday evening, and is on sale at all métro stations and *tabacs* (you'll need a passport photo – 25F from the booths in the main stations). There is also a monthly coupon (*mensuel*) for 243F. You need to write your *Carte Orange* number on the coupon.

Other possibilities are the 2-, 3- and 5-day visitors' passes (**Paris Visites**) at 70F, 105F and 165F for Paris and close suburbs, or 170F, 230F and 315F to include the airports, Versailles and Disneyland Paris. The main advantage of these is that, unlike the *coupon hebdomadaire* whose validity runs unalterably from Monday to Sunday, they can begin on any day. They also allow you discounts of between 20 and 35 percent on Paris boat trips, the Grande Arche, Parc Astérix, Musée Grevin, the top of Tour Montparnasse and the Cité des Sciences et de l'Industrie.

All these tickets entitle you to **unlimited travel** on bus, métro, *RER*, *SNCF* and the Montmartre funicular. On the métro you put the coupon through the turnstile slot, but make sure to return it to its plastic folder; it is reusable throughout the period of its validity. On a bus you show the whole *carte* to the driver as you board – don't put it into the punching machine.

The Paris transport authority, *RATP* (*Régie Autonome des Transports Parisiens*) also runs numerous **excursions**, some to quite far-flung places, that are far less expensive than those offered by commercial operators. Details are available from the *RATP*'s *Bureau de Tourisme*, place de la Madeleine (nr rue Royale; ☎01.40.06.71.45; M⁰ Madeleine).

Recorded information on all **RATP services** is available on the premium rate number ☎08.36.68.77.14.

Taxis

If it's late at night or you feel like treating yourself, don't hesitate to use **taxis**, as charges are fairly reasonable – between 40F and 60F for a

Touring Paris by Public Transport

The **overground métro** line on the southern route between Charles-de-Gaulle/Étoile and Nation (*ligne* 6) gives you views of the Eiffel Tower, the Île des Cygnes, the Invalides, the new National Library and the Finance Ministry. The northern route (*ligne* 2) is also above ground.

For La Voie Triomphale, take a trip on **bus** #73 between Grande Arche and the Musée d'Orsay. Bus #24 between Porte de Bercy and Gare St-Lazare follows the left bank of the Seine. Bus #20 from Gare de Lyon follows the Grands Boulevards and does a loop through the 1er and 2e *arrondissements*. Many more bus journeys – outside rush hours – are worthwhile trips in themselves.

central daytime journey but considerably more if you call one out. To avoid being ripped off, check that the meter shows the appropriate fare rate. Before you get into the taxi you can see which of the three small indicator lights on its roof is switched on. "A" (passenger side) indicates the daytime rate (around 4F/km) for Paris and the *boulevard périphérique*; "B" is the rate for Paris at night, on Sunday and on public holidays, and for the suburbs during the day (around 6F/km); "C" (driver's side) is the night rate for the suburbs (around 8F/km). In addition there's a pick-up charge of around 12F and a time charge (around 120F/hr) for when the car is stationary.

Taxis will often refuse to take more than three people or charge extra for the fourth. **Tipping** is not mandatory, but fifteen percent will be expected. Finding a taxi rank (*arrêt taxi*) is usually better than trying to hail one down in the street. The large white light means the taxi is free; the orange light below means it's engaged. Taxi ranks will show phone numbers to call for that *arrondissement*.

To call out a taxi, try *Taxis Bleus* (☎01.49.36. 10.10), *Alpha Taxis* (☎01.45.85.85.85), *Artaxi* (☎01.42.41.50.50) or *Taxis Étoile* (☎01.42.70. 41.41).

Boats

There remains one final mode of public transport – **Batobus**, along the Seine. The service operates from May to September and there are five stops: port de la Bourdonnais (Eiffel Tower–Trocadéro), pont de Solférino (Musée d'Orsay), quai Malaquais (Passerelle des Arts/Musée du Louvre), quai de Montebello (Notre-Dame) and quai de l'Hôtel de Ville (Hôtel-de-Ville/Centre Pompidou). Boats run every 30 minutes or so from 10am to 7pm: total journey time is 21 minutes; tickets 12F a stop.

Driving

Travelling around by **car**, in the daytime at least, is hardly worth it because of the difficulty of finding a parking space. Whatever you do, don't park in a bus lane or the *Axe Rouge* express routes (marked with a red square). Should you be **towed away** – and it's extremely expensive – you'll find your car in the pound (*fourrière*) belonging to that particular *arrondissement*: contact the local town hall (*mairie*) to get the address.

In the event of a **breakdown** you can call *SOS Dépannage*, 28bis rue Pascal, 5e (☎01.47.07.99.99), or *Aleveque*, 116 rue de la Convention, 15e (☎01.48.28.12.00), for round-the-clock assistance. Alternatively, ask the police.

For **car rental**, the big international companies have offices at the airports and at several locations in the city: *Avis* (☎01.46.10.60.60); *Europcar* (☎01.30.43.82.82); *Hertz* (☎01.47.88.51.51); and *EuroRent* (freephone ☎08.00.33.22.10 or ☎01.44.38.55.55). Some good local firms are: *Acar*, 99 bd A-Blanqui, 13e (☎01.45.88.28.38) and 85 rue de la Chapelle, 18e (☎01.42.09.42.06); *Dergi*, 60 bd St-Marcel, 5e (Mº Gobelins; Mon–Sat 8am–7pm; ☎01.45.87.27.04); *Locabest*, 3 rue Abel, 12e (Mº Gare-de-Lyon; Mon–Sat 7.30am–7pm; ☎01.43.46.05.05) and at 104 bd Magenta, 10e (Mº Gare du Nord; Mon–Sat 7.30am–7pm; ☎01.44.72.08.05).

If you would like to arrange rental in advance, in London, *Holiday Autos*, 25 Savile Row, W1X 1AA (☎0171/491 1111) have some of the most competitive rates going.

> Remember that you have to be eighteen years of age to drive in France, regardless of whether you hold a licence. Most rental companies will only deal with people over 21.

Cycling

The Mairie de Paris proudly announced in 1996 the existence of 50km of cycle lanes in the city. Unfortunately very few stretches are separate from the roads so, given how Parisians park and drive, the new lanes are very much a token gesture. The best road-free **cycle routes** are the *coulée verte* along the old railway line from Vincennes into the 12e *arrondissement*, rue Vercingétorix from place de Catalogne to Porte de Vanves in the 14e, and the quays of canal St-Martin, the bassin de la Villette and the canal de l'Ourcq. The new bridge across the Seine, Pont Charles-de-Gaulle between the Gare de Lyon and Gare d'Austerlitz, has separate lanes, as do bd d'Auriol, rue Albert-Bayer, av Edison, rues Baudricourt, Château-des-Rentiers and Nationale in the 13e.

Air pollution is very bad in Paris, and the occasional steep and cobbled street does not make for the smoothest of rides. The main hazard, of course, is posed by drivers, though fortunately cycling is becoming increasingly popular amongst Parisians.

You can **rent bikes** from *Paris-Vélo*, 2 rue du Fer-à-Moulin, 5e (Mº Censier-Daubenton; Mon–Sat 10am–7pm, closed public holidays; ☎01.43.37.59.22); *Mountain Bike Trip*, 60 av Jean-Jaurès, 19e (Mº Jaurès/Laumière; ☎01.09.21.14.59); or from the *Maison du Vélo*, which has outlets during the summer at the Gare de l'Est and Gare du Montparnasse (daily 8am–8pm; ☎01.42.81.24.72). A deposit of between 1500F and 2000F (or a credit card) is usually required. Rental rates range from around 80–100F for a day, or 450–600F for a week.

There are also **guided cycling tours** of the city, costing from 130F, organized by *Paris à Velo C'est Sympa*, 9 rue Jacques-Coeur, 4e (Mº Bastille; ☎01.48.87.60.01).

Walking

By far the best way to discover Paris, walking is very pleasant as long as you're away from the main roads. As a general rule it's best to assume that all Parisian cars are out to get you. Be very careful crossing roads, even when there's a green pedestrian light, as cars turning at a junction will ignore your priority. Be aware too of the direction of the traffic (particularly if you're from Britain and are used to it coming from the right). The other, less lethal, but very unpleasant hazard, is dog turds on the pavements.

The best strolling grounds of the city are the quaysides on both banks of the river and around the islands. There's access down to them by each bridge.

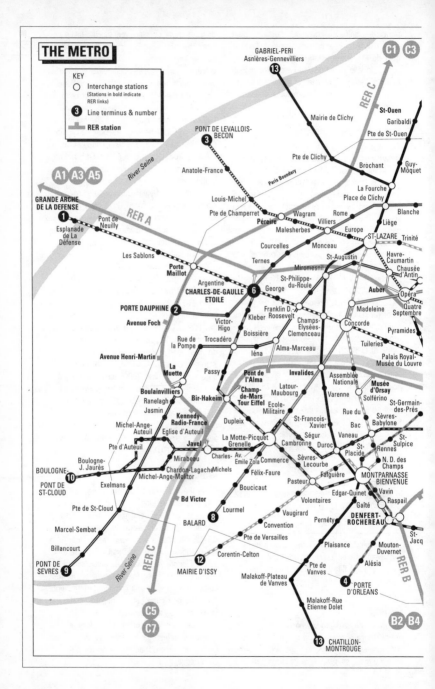

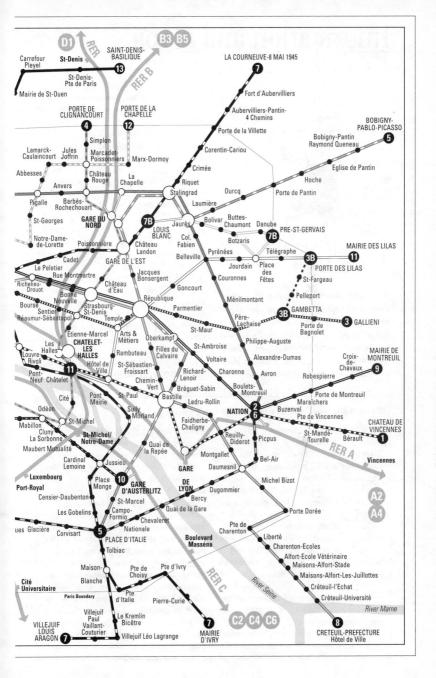

Information and Maps

The French Government Tourist Office gives away large quantities of maps and glossy brochures for every region of France, including lists of hotels and campsites. For Paris, these include some useful fold-out leaflets detailing sights to see, markets, shops, museums, ideas for excursions, useful phone numbers and opening hours, as well as maps and more esoteric information like lists of Paris gardens and squares.

In Paris, the **main tourist office** is at 127 av des Champs-Elysées, 8e (Mº Charles-de-Gaulle–Étoile; daily 9am–8pm all year round, except May 1; ☎01.49.52.53.54, fax 49.52.53.00), where the efficient but overworked staff will answer questions from the predictable to the bizarre. There are **branch offices** at the main train stations: Austerlitz (Mon–Fri 8am–3pm, Sat 8am–1pm; ☎01.45.84.91.70), Est (May–Oct Mon–Sat 8am–9pm, otherwise Mon–Sat 8am–8pm; ☎01.46.07.17.73), Lyon (May–Oct Mon–Sat 8am–9pm, otherwise Mon–Sat 8am–8pm; ☎01.43.43.33.24), Montparnasse (May–Oct Mon–Sat 8am–9pm, otherwise Mon–Sat 8am–8pm; 01.43.22.19.19), Nord (May–Oct Mon–Sat 8am–9pm, otherwise Mon–Sat 8am–8pm; ☎01.45.26.94.82); and at the Eiffel Tower (daily May–Sept 11am–6pm; ☎01.45.51.22.15).

For recorded **tourist information in English**, phone ☎01.49.52.53.56. Alternative sources of

---

Paris Addresses and the Demise of the Concierge

The number after Paris addresses – 3e, 11e, etc – indicates the postal district or **arrondissement**. There are twenty of them altogether. The first, which is written 1er, is centred on the Louvre, with the rest unfurling outwards in a clockwise spiral – see map on p.64. They are an important aid to locating places, and their boundaries are clearly marked on all maps.

The vast majority of Parisians live in flats in apartment buildings, most of which date from the nineteenth century or earlier. They tend to be purpose-built, rather than the conversions typical of London terrace houses. Until very recently they were invariably guarded by a **concierge**, often a woman who lived with her family – if she had one – in dark, pokey rooms beside the main entrance.

Paris *concierges* were a veritable institution. Besides being responsible for looking after the common areas, they took in the mail, relayed messages, ran errands and, above all, kept a very beady eye on all comings and goings within the building and adjacent streets. They ran an effective, if unofficial, neighbourhood watch, and a lightning-fast bush telegraph. They had a reputation for being ferocious, disapproving nosy-parkers. If not always loved individually, they were loved as an institution.

Sadly, they are now an endangered species, partly because stingy landlords won't pay their meagre salaries and partly because there is a general trend towards the dehumanization and depersonalization of life, in Paris as elsewhere.

Instead, most Parisian street doors are protected by **digicode panels**. If you don't know the code, you can't get in. So, when invited to someone's home, remember to ask for the code.

French Government Tourist Offices

Australia
BNP Building, 17th floor
12 Castlereagh St
Sydney NSW 2000   ☎612/9231 5244
    fax 612/9221 8682

Canada
1981 av McGill College, Suite 490
Montréal, QUE H3A 2W9   ☎514/288 4264
    fax 514/845 4868

30 St Patrick St, Suite 700
Toronto ON M5T 3A3   ☎416/593 6423
    fax 416/979 7587

Denmark
NY Ostergade 3.3
DK – 1101 Copenhagen K   ☎33/11 49 12
    fax 33/14 20 48

Ireland
35 Lower Abbey St
Dublin 1   ☎01/703 4046
    fax 01/874 7324

Netherlands
Prinsengracht 670
1017 KX Amsterdam   ☎020/627 3318
    fax 020/620 3339

Norway
Storgaten 10A
0155 Oslo 1   ☎22/42 15 55
    fax 22/42 29 44

Sweden
Norrmalmstorg 1 A, 5 Str
11146 Stockholm   ☎08/679 7975
    ☎08/679 6150
    fax 08/611 3075

UK
178 Piccadilly
London W1V 0AL   ☎0171/629 2869
    ☎0891/244 123*
    fax 0171 493 6594

USA
444, Madison Ave, 16th floor
New York, NY 10022   ☎212/838 7800
    fax 212/838 7855

676 North Michigan Ave
Chicago, IL 60611-2819   ☎312/751 7800
    fax 312/337 6339

9454 Wilshire Blvd, suite 715
Beverly Hills   ☎310/271 6665
CA 90212-2967   ☎310/272 2661
    fax 310/276 2835

* EuropAssistance *premium rated service
(10p/minute) brochures will be sent without
postage charge, and specific queries are
quickly referred to the relevant organization.*

Note that New Zealand does not have a French
Government Tourist Office.

---

information are the Hôtel de Ville information office, the *Bureau d'Accueil* at 29 rue de Rivoli, 4ᵉ (M° Hôtel-de-Ville; Mon–Sat 9am–6pm; ☎01.42.76.43.43), and electronic billboards in the streets. *Paris Le Journal*, published by the *mairie*, is a free **monthly** detailing what's on, available at the *Bureau d'Accueil* or in museums and shops.

For the clearest picture of the layout of the city the best **map** you can get is Michelin no. 10, the 1:10,000 *Plan de Paris*. More convenient is the pocket-sized *Falkplan*, which folds out only as you need it, or, if you're staying any length of time, one of the various A–Z street plans, which have a street index, bus route diagrams, useful addresses, and show car parks and one-way streets – all a great deal more useful than the tourist office free hand-out. The information desk at Roissy airport does, however, provide a helpful, free map.

Some of the A–Zs, like the *Cartes Taride*, include the nearer suburban areas. For a picture of the countryside around Paris – if you plan any of the excursions outlined in Chapter 20 – Michelin no. 106, *Environs de Paris*, is best.

Map Outlets

UK

Daunt Books, 83 Marylebone High St, London W1 (☎0171/224 2295).

John Smith and Sons, 57–61 St Vincent St, Glasgow G2 5TB (☎0141/221 7472).

National Map Centre, 22–24 Caxton St, London SW1 (☎0171/222 4945).

*Stanfords, 12–14 Long Acre, London WC2 (☎0171/836 1321); 52 Grosvenor Gardens, London SW1W 0AG; 156 Regent St, London W1R 5TA.

The Travel Bookshop, 13–15 Blenheim Crescent, London W11 2EE (☎0171/229 5260).

*Maps by **mail or phone order** are available from *Stanfords* (☎0171/836 1321).

Ireland

Easons Bookshop, 40 O'Connell St, Dublin 1 (☎01/873 3811).

Fred Hanna's Bookshop, 27–29 Nassau St, Dublin 2 (☎01/677 1255).

Hodges Figgis Bookshop, 56–58 Dawson St, Dublin 2 (☎01/677 4754).

Waterstone's, Queens Bldg, 8 Royal Ave, Belfast BT1 1DA (☎01232/247355).

USA

Book Passage, 51 Tamal Vista Dr, Corte Madera, CA 94925 (☎415/927 0960).

Complete Traveler Bookstore, 199 Madison Ave, New York, NY 10016 (☎212/685 9007); 3207 Fillmore St, San Francisco, CA 92123 (☎415/923 1511).

Elliot Bay Book Company, 101 S Main St, Seattle, WA 98104 (☎206/624 6600).

Forsyth Travel Library, 9154 W 57th St, Shawnee Mission, KS 66201 (☎1-800/367-7984).

Map Link Inc, 25 E Mason St, Santa Barbara, CA 93101 (☎805/965-4402).

Phileas Fogg's Books & Maps, #87 Stanford Shopping Center, Palo Alto, CA 94304 (☎1-800/233-FOGG in California; ☎%1-800/533-FOGG elsewhere in US).

*Rand McNally, 444 N Michigan Ave, Chicago, IL 60611 (☎312/321-1751); 150 E 52nd St, New York, NY 10022 (☎212/758-7488); 595 Market St, San Francisco, CA 94105 (☎415/777-3131); 1201 Connecticut Ave NW, Washington, DC 20003 (☎202/223-6751).

Sierra Club Bookstore, 730 Polk St, San Francisco, CA 94109 (☎415/923-5500).

Travel Books & Language Center, 4931 Cordell Ave, Bethesda, MD 20814 (☎1-800/220-2665).

Traveler's Bookstore, 22 W 52nd St, New York, NY 10019 (☎212/664-0995).

*Note: For other locations, or for maps by mail order, call ☎1-800/333-0136 (ext 2111).

Canada

Open Air Books and Maps, 25 Toronto St, Toronto, ON M5R 2C1 (☎416/363-0719).

Ulysses Travel Bookshop, 4176 St-Denis, Montréal (☎514/289-0993).

World Wide Books and Maps, 1247 Granville St, Vancouver, BC V6Z 1E4 (☎604/687-3320).

Australia

The Map Shop, 16a Peel St, Adelaide (☎08/8231 2033).

Bowyangs, 372 Little Burke St, Melbourne (☎03/9670 4383).

Perth Map Centre, 891 Hay St, Perth (☎09/9322 5733).

Travel Bookshop, 20 Bridge St, Sydney (☎02/9241 3554).

Specialty Maps, 58 Albert St, Auckland (☎09/307 2217).

Costs, Money and Banks

Because of the relatively low cost of accommodation and eating out, at least by capital city standards, Paris is not an outrageously expensive place to visit, though it's certainly not as cheap as the rest of France. If you are one of two people sharing a hotel room, you can manage a reasonably comfortable existence, including restaurant, museum and café stops, on **500–600F per person per day** (around £66–79/US$102–122). At the bottom line, by watching the pennies, staying at a hostel (91F for bed and breakfast), being strong-willed about cups of coffee and drinks, and admiring monuments and museums from the outside, you could survive on as little as 230F (around £30/US$47) a day, including a cheap restaurant meal – less if you limit eating to street snacks or market food.

For two or more people hotel **accommodation** can be almost as cheap as hostels, though a sensible average estimate for a double room would be around 380F. As for food, you can spend as much or as little as you like. There are large numbers of reasonable, if not very exciting, **restaurants** with three- or four-course menus for between 75F and 150F, and you can get a filling midday plate of hot food for under 60F. **Picnic fare**, obviously, is much less costly, especially when you buy in the markets and cheap supermarket chains; take-away *baguette* sandwiches from cafés are not extortionate. Remember that it's cheaper to be at the bar than at a table in **cafés**; glasses of water are free.

Transport within the city is inexpensive. The *Carte Orange*, for example, with a 72F weekly ticket (see p.32 for more details) gives you a week's unlimited travel on buses and métro/RER.

Reductions and Freebies

Museums and monuments have become a lot more expensive in recent years and are likely to prove one of the biggest wallet-eroders. Although **reduced admission** for young people is a function of age – under 26 – not student status, it is worth carrying the *ISIC* (*International Student Identity Card*), if you are entitled to it, because it's universally accepted as ID, while the British *NUS* card is not. The main tourist office will sell you a *Carte Jeune* (with your passport as proof) for 120F, valid for a year, which will get you all the reductions for under-26s in France and elsewhere in Europe.

For pensioners' (over 60) reductions you will need to carry your passport around with you. If you are going to do a lot of museum duty, it is worth considering buying a museum card (details on p.276). Some museums have free or half-price admission on Sundays, and museums or exhibition spaces with no entry charge at all do still exist.

Cinemas often have half-price admission on Monday or Wednesday; gardens, parks and cemeteries are free, so are the markets. Libraries and the cultural centres of different countries put on films, shows and exhibitions for next to nothing (details in the listings mags). Other **free cultural offerings** appear regularly, from bands in the streets to firework shows, courtesy of the Mairie de Paris (publicized in *Paris Le Journal* – see "Information and Maps", p.37).

Budget-watchers need to be most wary of café-lounging and nightlife; drinks in flash pubs and bars can quickly become a major expense.

Money

The most sensible strategy is to take more than one means of payment and keep them separate. It's always a good idea to have a small amount of French currency on you when you arrive.

Currency and the Exchange Rate

French currency is the **franc** (abbreviated as F or sometimes FF), divided into 100 centimes. Francs come in notes of 500, 100, 50, and 20F, and there are coins of 20, 10, 5, 2, and 1F, and 50, 20, 10 and 5 centimes. At the time of writing the exchange rate, thanks to the insistent *"franc fort"* (strong franc) policy of the French treasury, has been hovering miserably around 7.6F to the pound, 4.9F to the US dollar, 3.6F to the Canadian dollar and 3.8F for the Australian dollar.

Travellers' Cheques

Travellers' cheques are one of the safest ways of carrying your money. Worldwide, they're available from almost any major bank (whether you have an account there or not), usually for a service charge of one percent on the amount purchased. The Bank of Ireland has the lowest rate of 0.2 percent; the highest rate is 2 percent; and some banks have a minimum charge (eg NatWest and the Cooperative Bank of £4). Check with your own bank first as they may offer cheques free of charge provided you meet certain conditions. The most widely recognized brands are *Visa* and *American Express*, which most banks will change. *American Express* travellers' cheques can be cashed at post offices. **French franc travellers' cheques** can be worthwhile: they can often be used as cash, and you should get the face value of the cheques when you change them, so commission is only paid on purchase. Banks being banks, however, this is not always the case.

Eurocheques, available to Europeans with an annual charge of between £4 and £8 and commission of between 1.6 and 2 percent, are no longer such a good idea for France as many banks and post offices now refuse to cash them. You can still use the card, however, in ATMs (cash machines) and as a debit card, and write out cheques in francs in hotels and restaurants, etc.

Credit and Debit Cards

Credit cards are widely accepted; just watch for the window stickers. *Visa* – known as the *Carte Bleue* in France – is almost universally recognized; *Access, Mastercard* – sometimes called *Eurocard* – and *American Express* rank a bit lower. It's always worth checking, however, that restaurants and hotels will accept your card;

> Holders of *Visa, Eurocard* and *American Express* cards can get a free "kit" from the main tourist office of a street plan and museums guide, plus a 10 percent reduction on the *Carte Musées-Monuments*.

some smaller ones don't. Be aware, also, that French cards have a smart chip and machines may reject the magnetic strip of British, American or Australasian cards, even if they are valid. If your card is refused because of this, we suggest you say *"Les cartes britanniques/americaines/ canadiennes/de Nouvelle Zealand ne sont pas cartes à puce, mais à piste magnetique. Ma carte est valable et je vous serais très reconnaissant(e) de demander la confirmation auprès de votre banque ou de votre centre de traitement."*

You can also use credit cards for cash advances at banks and in ATMs. The charge tends to be higher, for example 4.1 percent instead of the 1.5 percent at home for *Visa* cards. The PIN number should be the same as the one you use at home, but check with your credit card company before you leave. Also, because French credit cards are smart cards, some ATMs baulk at foreign plastic and tell you that your request for money has been denied. If that happens, just try another machine. All ATMs give you the choice of instructions in French or English.

Post offices will give cash advances on *Visa* credit cards if you are having a problem using them in ATMs.

Debit cards can also be used in ATMs or to pay for goods and services where there's an "edc" (European acceptance) sign.

Changing Money

Standard **banking hours** are Monday to Friday from 9am to 4 or 5pm. Some close at midday (noon/12.30pm–2/2.30pm); some are open on Saturday 9am to noon. All are closed on Sunday and public holidays. They will have a notice on the door if they do currency exchange, and **rates and commission** vary from bank to bank, so shop around. The usual procedure is a one to two percent commission on travellers' cheques and a flat rate charge on cash. Be wary of banks claiming to charge no commission at all; often they are merely adjusting the exchange rate to their own advantage. Rue de la Paix and other streets around the Opéra-

Bank and Contact Numbers

American Express, 11 rue Scribe, 9e (M⁰ Opéra; ☎01.47.77.77.07). Bureau de Change open Mon–Fri 8.30am–6.30pm, Sat 9am–5.30pm, Sun 10am–6pm, public holidays 9am–5pm.

Barclays, 21 rue Lafitte, 9e (M⁰ Richelieu-Drouot; ☎01.44.79.79.79). Mon–Fri 9am–4.30pm. Branches throughout the city (info on ☎01.42.92.39.08).

Thomas Cook, 52 av des Champs-Elysées, 8e (M⁰ Franklin-D-Roosevelt; ☎01.42.89.80.32). Daily 8.30am–midnight. Branches throughout the city.

Western Union Money Transfer, Banque Rivaud, 4 rue du Cloître-Notre-Dame, 4e (M⁰ Cité; ☎01.43.54.46.12). Daily 9am–5.30pm. Can transfer money from abroad within an hour.

If your credit card is lost or stolen you must ring the number back home to cancel it. Some companies, like *Diners Club* in the UK, allow you to reverse the charges; others will pay for the call if you're absolutely desperate. If you don't have the relevant number to call, contact the French 24-hour lines below; they will speak English.

Access, Mastercard, Eurocard ☎01.45.67.84.84

American Express ☎01.47.77.72.00 (☎08.00.90.86.00 freephone for travellers' cheques)

Diners' Club ☎01.47.62.75.75

Visa ☎01.42.77.11.90

Garnier in the 1er *arrondissement* are full of banks; the *Banque de France* tends to be the most competitive.

There are **money-exchange bureaux** (where rates are inevitably poorer) open every day at Charles-de-Gaulle airport (*CCF;* 6.30am–11.30pm) and Orly airport (*CCF;* 6.30am–11pm); at the train stations: Austerlitz (*Banco Central:* 7am–9pm), Est (*Thomas Cook:* summer 6.45am–10pm, winter 6.45am–7pm), Lyon (*CIC;* 6.30am–11pm), Nord (*Thomas Cook;* 6.15am–10.30pm), St–Lazare (*Thomas Cook;* summer 8am–8pm, winter 8am–6.45pm); at the *Office de Tourisme de Paris* (127, av Champs-Elysées, 8e; 9am–7.30pm; M⁰ Charles-de-Gaulle–Etoile); and at *CCF,* (115 av Champs-Elysées, 8e; 8.30am–8pm; M⁰ George-V).

Visa is currently testing *Visa TravelMoney,* a temporary, disposable debit card that you "load-up" with an amount between £100 and £5,000 and can then use in any *Visa* cashpoint. Like travellers' cheques, they can be replaced if lost or stolen. Called *Visa Cash Cards* in the US, they should be available from 1997.

There are also **automatic exchange machines** at the airports and train stations and outside many money exchange bureaux. They accept £10 and £20 notes as well as dollars and other European currency notes, but offer a very poor rate of exchange.

Communications – Post, Phones and Media

The French term for the post office is **la poste** or **les PTT**; alternatively, **un bureau de poste**. The main Paris post office is at **52 rue du Louvre, 1er (Mº Étienne Marcel)**, and is the best place to have your mail sent, unless you have a particular branch office in mind. It's open 24 hours for letters and telegrams. Poste restante letters should be addressed (preferably with the surname underlined and in capitals, with initials rather than forenames in full) to **Poste Restante, 52 rue du Louvre, 75001 Paris**.

To **collect your mail**, you need a passport or other convincing ID, and there'll be a small charge. You should ask for all your names to be checked, as filing systems are not brilliant.

Other post offices are open 8am–7pm, Monday to Friday, and 9am–noon on Saturday. For sending letters, remember that you can buy **stamps** (*timbres*) with less queuing from *tabacs*. Letters and postcards within France and to European Union countries cost 3F, to North America 4.40F and to the Antipodes 5.20F.

You can send **faxes** from post offices (as well as many newsagents); the official French word is *télécopie*, but *fax* is comonplace. You can also use Minitel (see opposite), cash money and make phone calls.

Phone calls

You can make **international phone calls** from any box (*cabine*) and can receive calls wherever there's a blue logo of a ringing bell. A 50-unit (40.60F) and 120-unit (97.50F) **phone card** (called a *télécarte*) is essential, since coin boxes are being phased out. Phone cards are available from *tabacs* and newsagents as well as post offices. You can also use credit cards in many call boxes.

Phone calls can also be made from **booths at post offices**. You apply at the counter to be assigned a number, and then dial. The disadvantage with these – odd considering the French obsession with technology – is that you can't tell how much you're spending. It's worth counting your units and checking – mistakes are sometimes made.

Cheap rates operate between 9.30pm and 8am Monday to Friday, from midnight to 8am and 2pm to midnight on Saturday, and all day Sunday. Per minute, a cheap rate call to the UK will cost 2.97F; to Ireland 3.09F; to US and Canada 3.96F; to Australia and New Zealand 7.67F.

The major **international calling codes**, are given in the box opposite; remember to omit the initial 0 of the local area code from the subscriber's number. By far the cheapest means of making international calls is to use a **calling card**. Costs are going down all the time, and there's fierce competition. The *AT&T* card is available in France; *Interglobe, Mercury* and *World Telecom* cards need to be purchased in the UK. These cards are either pre-paid or charged to your credit card or on your phone bill if you are a customer. Simply dial the free number (make sure

Telephoning

IDD Codes

From France dial ☎19 + IDD code + area code minus first 0 + subscriber number

Britain ☎44
Ireland ☎353
USA and Canada ☎1
Australia ☎61
New Zealand ☎64

From Britain to Paris: dial ☎00 33 + nine-digit number (leaving out the first 0)

From the USA and Canada to Paris: dial ☎011 33 + nine-digit number (leaving out the first 0)

From Australia to Paris: dial ☎011 33 + nine-digit number (leaving out the first 0)

From New Zealand to Paris: dial ☎044 33 + nine-digit number (leaving out the first 0)

From Paris to elsewhere in France: dial the ten-digit number.

TIME France is one hour ahead of GMT, except for a short period during October, when it's the same. It is six hours ahead of Eastern Standard Time, and nine hours ahead of Pacific Standard Time. This also applies during daylight saving seasons from the end of March to the end of September.

Useful Numbers Within France

Telegrams By phone: internal ☎36.55; external ☎08.00.33.44.11 (all languages)

Time ☎36.99

International operator For Canada & US ☎19.33.11; for all other countries ☎19.33 followed by IDD number

International directory assistance For Canada & US ☎19.33.12.11; for all other countries ☎19.33.12, followed by IDD number

French operator ☎13

French directory assistance ☎12

---

you have with you the relevant number for France), your account number, and then the number you wish to call. The drawback is that the free number is often engaged and you have to dial a great many digits.

To avoid payment altogether, you can, of course, make a reverse charge or **collect call** – known in French as *téléphoner en PCV*. This can also be done through the operator in the UK, by dialling ☎19.00.44 and asking for a "reverse charge call". To get an English-speaking *AT&T* operator for North America, dial ☎19.00.11.

Some British **mobile phones**, as long as they're digital, will work in France.

Minitel

All phone subscribers in Paris (and almost everywhere in France) have **Minitel**, a dinosaurial on-line computer allowing access through the phone lines to directories, databases, chat lines, etc. You will also find them in post offices. Most organizations, from sports federations to government institutions to gay groups, have a code consisting of numbers and letters to call up infor-

mation, leave messages, make reservations, etc. You dial the number on the phone, wait for a fax-type tone, then type the letters on the keyboard. Finally, press *Connexion Fin* (the same key ends the connection). If you're at all computer-literate and can understand basic keyboard terms in French (*retour* – return, *envoi* – enter, etc), you shouldn't find them hard to use. Be warned that most services cost more than phone rates. Directory enquiries (☎12) is free.

The Internet

Having had Minitel since the early 1980s, France has been relatively slow to adopt the **Internet**. Ownership of personal computers is very low (around 15 percent of French homes), and the Minitel is far too slow to link to the Internet. The dominance of English on the Net has been another factor.

In 1996, France Telecom launched its own online service, and there was a rush of media excitement when journalists noticed that cyber-cafés were opening up in Paris (many are listed in the text). Gradually, more people are getting connected, but having an e-mail address as part of your *coordonnées* (contact details) is still considered pretty cool. Most analysts believe France will have to junk the Minitel box altogether if it's going to take part in the Internet revolution. France Telecom is busy selling a Minitel programme for PCs, but the problem is that every home has a comfortably French and familiar Minitel, whose snail speed cannot conceivably be accelerated to even the slowest normal modem.

For information about Paris on the World Wide Web, the biggest site is *The Paris Pages* on http://www.paris.org/city.shtml, but it's not updated very regularly. A better site is the listings magazine *Pariscope* on http://Pariscope.fr/. You can get into a list of all French servers via the *Centre National de Recherche Scientifique* on http://www.urec.fr/ or visit the Ministry of Culture's site on http://web.culture.fr/.

Newspapers and Periodicals

British **newspapers**, the *European*, the *Washington Post*, *New York Times* and the *International Herald Tribune* are widely on sale. The monthly *Paris Free Voice* produced by the American Church at 65 quai d'Orsay, 7e, has good listings, ads for flats and courses, and interesting articles on current events. It's available from the church and from English-language bookshops. *France USA Contacts*, a free American fortnightly available in various cafés, restaurants, shops and colleges, is also useful for flats, jobs, travel, alternative medicine, therapy, etc.

The **listings magazines** *Pariscope* (3F) and *L'Official des Spectacles* (2F) come out on Wednesdays and are indispensable for knowing what's on. *Pariscope*, in particular, has a huge and comprehensive section on films and an English section put together by *Time Out*.

Of the **French daily papers**, *Le Monde* is the most intellectual; it is widely respected, but is somewhat austere, making no concessions to such frivolities as photographs. *Libération* is moderately left-wing, independent, and more colloquial, with good, if choosy, coverage, while rigorous left-wing criticism of the French government

comes from *L'Humanité*, the Communist Party paper. The other nationals, and the local paper *Le Parisien*, are all firmly right-wing in their politics: *Le Figaro* is the most respected. The top-selling national is *L'Équipe*, dedicated to sports coverage.

Weeklies of the *Newsweek/Time* model include the wide-ranging and socialist-inclined *Le Nouvel Observateur*, its right-wing counterpoint *L'Express*, and the boringly centrist *L'Événement de Jeudi*. The best investigative journalism is in the weekly satirical paper *Le Canard Enchaîné*. *Charlie Hebdo* is a sort of *Private Eye* or *Spy Magazine* equivalent.

Monthlies include the young and trendy – and cheap – *Nova*, with excellent listings of cultural events; the glossy *Paris Capitale*, with fashion, culture and listings; and *Actuel*, which is good for current events. Every month, *Le Monde* publishes the beautifully designed *Le Monde Diplomatique* – good, serious stuff – and there are, of course, all the French versions of *Vogue*, *Elle*, *Marie-Claire*, as well as *Paris-Match* for gossip about stars and the royal families.

"Moral" **censorship** of the press is rare. On the newsstands you'll find pornography of every shade, as well as covers featuring drugs, sex, blasphemy and bizarre forms of grossness alongside knitting patterns and DIY. You'll also find French **comics** – *bandes dessinées* – which often indulge these interests and are wonderful.

TV and Radio

French TV broadcasts six channels, three of them public, along with a good many more cable and satellite channels (see Chapter 19), which include CNN and the BBC World Service. If you've got a radio, you can tune into English-language news on the BBC World Service on 648kHz or 198kHz long wave from midnight to 5am (and Radio 4 during the day). BBC Radio 5 Live can be picked up on 693kHx. The Voice of America transmits on 90.5, 98.8 and 102.4FM. For radio news in French, there's the state-run France Inter (87.8FM), Europe 1 (104.7FM), or round-the-clock news on France Infos (105.5FM).

Business Hours and Holidays

Most shops, businesses, information services, museums and banks in Paris stay open all day. The exceptions are the smaller shops and enterprises. Basic hours of business are from 8 or 9am to 6.30 or 7.30pm. Sunday and Monday are standard closing days, though you can always find boulangeries and food shops that do stay open – on Sunday normally until noon. The standard banking hours are 9am–4/5pm, closed Saturday and Sunday; for more details, see p.276.

Museums open between 9 and 10am and close between 5 and 6pm. Summer times may differ from winter times; if they do, both are indicated in the listings. Summer hours usually extend from mid-May or early June to mid-September, but sometimes they apply only during July and August, occasionally even from Palm Sunday to All Saints' Day. Don't be caught out by **closing days** – usually Tuesday or Monday, sometimes both. **Admission charges** can be a bit off-putting, though some museums offer reductions if you're under 26 or over 60. **Churches** and **cathedrals** are almost always open all day, with charges only for the crypt, treasuries or cloister, and little fuss is made about how you're dressed.

One other factor can disrupt your plans. There are thirteen **national holidays** (*jours fériés*), when most shops and businesses, though not museums or restaurants, are closed. They are:

January 1
Easter Sunday
Easter Monday
Ascension Day (forty days after Easter)
Whitsun (seventh Sunday after Easter, plus the Monday)
May 1
May 8 (VE Day)
July 14 (Bastille Day)
August 15 (Assumption of the Virgin Mary)
November 1 (All Saints' Day)
November 11 (1918 Armistice Day)
Christmas Day

Festivals and Events

With all that's going on in Paris, festivals – in the traditional "popular" sense – are no big deal. But there is an impressive array of arts events and, not to be missed for the politically interested, an inspired internationalist jamboree at the Fête de l'Humanité.

The tourist office produces a biannual *Saisons de Paris – Calendrier des Manifestations*, which gives details of all the mainstream events; otherwise, check the listings and other Paris magazines (see p.36).

Many Parisian *quartiers* like Belleville and Montmartre have *portes ouvertes* (open doors) weeks when artists' studios are open to the public and some festivities are laid on – keep an eye open for posters and flyers.

January

La Grande Parade de Montmartre (January 1): New Year's Day parade from place Pigalle to place Jules-Joffrin.

La Mairie de Paris vous invite au concert: a week of two concert tickets for the price of one

Festival Mondial du Cirque de Demain: international circus festival at the Cirque d'Hiver Bouglione (☎01.44.61.06.00).

February

Foire à la Feraille de Paris: antiques and bric-a-brac fair in the Parc Floral de Paris (☎01.40.62.95.95).

La Mairie de Paris vous invite au cinéma "18H – 18F": a week of 18F cinema tickets for 6pm showings.

Salon de l'Agriculture (end of February to beginning of March): the biggest agricultural show at the Parc des Expositions (☎01.49.09.60.00).

March

Salon de Mars: international antiques, primitive and contemporary art fair by the Eiffel Tower (☎01.44.94.86.80).

Banlieues Bleus (mid-March to mid-April): international jazz festival in the towns of Seine-Saint-Denis (Blanc-Mesnil, Drancy, Aubervilliers, Pantin, St-Ouen, Bobigny); info on ☎01.43.85.66.00.

Festival International Films des Femmes (end of March/beginning of April): women's film festival at Créteil; information from Maison des Arts, place Salvador-Allende, 9400 Créteil (☎01.49.80.38.98).

Festival d'Art Sacré de la Ville de Paris (end of March to beginning of April): concerts and recitals of church music in Paris churches and concert halls (☎01.45.61.54.99). Also in November/December (see below).

Foire du Trône (end of March to end of May): funfair located in the 12e, Pelouse de Reuilly and Bois de Vincennes.

April

Poisson d'Avril (April 1): April Fools' Day with spoofs in the media and people sticking paper fishes on the backs of unsuspecting fools.

Marathon International de Paris: the Paris Marathon departs from Place de la Concorde, arrives at the Hippodrome de Vincennes 42km later.

Festival Exit: international festival of contemporary dance, performance and theatre at at Créteil; information from Maison des Arts, place Salvador-Allende, 9400 Créteil (☎01.45.13.19.19).

Foire de Paris (end April/beginning of May): food and wine fair at the Parc des Expositions, Porte de Versailles (☎01.49.09.60.00).

May

Mai 1er (May 1st): May Day with marches and festivities in eastern Paris and around place de la Bastille.

La Mairie de Paris vous invite au théâtre: a week of two theatre tickets for the price of one.

Finale de la Coupe de France: French football championships final at the Parc des Princes (☎01.44.31.73.00).

Internationaux de France de Tennis (last week of May and first week of June): the French Open tennis championships at Roland Garros (☎01.47.43.48.00).

June

Finale du Championnat de France de Rugby: French rugby championships final at the Parc des Princes (☎01.48.74.84.75).

Fête de la Musique (June 21): Live bands and free concerts throughout the city (☎01.40.03.94.70).

Feux de la Saint-Jean (around June 21): fireworks for St-Jean's Day at the Parc de la Villette and quai St-Bernard.

Gay Pride: Gay and Lesbian Pride march (☎01.43.57.21.47).

Féte du Cinéma (end of June): three days of 10F cinema tickets after you have paid one full-price entry.

Course des Garçons de Café (late June/early July). Waiters race through the streets of Paris carrying trays laden with alcohol. Depart from and arrive at the Hôtel de Ville, 1er (☎01.46.33.89.89).

Halle That Jazz (end of June to beginning of July): jazz festival at Grande Halle de la Villette (☎01.40.03.75.75).

Foire St-Germain (June to July): concerts, antique fairs, poetry and exhibitions in the 6e (☎01.40.46.75.12).

July

La Goutte d'Or en Fête (first week): music festival of rap, reggae, raï with local and international performers (☎01.42.62.11.13).

Bastille Day (July 14th and evening before): the 1789 surrender of the Bastille is celebrated in official pomp, with parades of tanks down the Champs-Élysées, firework displays and concerts. At night there is dancing in the streets around place de la Bastille to good French bands.

Arrivée du Tour de France Cyclistes (third or fourth Sunday) the Tour de France cyclists cross the finishing line in the av des Champs-Élysées.

Paris Quartier d'Été: music, cinema, dance and theatre events around the city (☎01.44.83.64.40).

Festival de Cinéma en Plein Air (July 15–Aug 15): open air cinema at Parc de la Villette (☎01.40.03.75.00).

Festival Musique en l'Île (July to September): classical music festival (☎01.44.62.70.90).

September

Fête de l'Humanité (second weekend): sponsored by the French Communist Party, this annual three-day event just north of Paris at La Courneuve attracts people in their tens of thousands and of every political persuasion. Food and drink (all very cheap), and music and crafts from every corner of the globe, are the predominant features, rather than political platforms. Each French regional CP has a vast restaurant tent with its specialities; French and foreign bands play on an open-air stage; and the event ends on Sunday night with an impressive firework display. (Mº La Courneuve, then bus #177 or special shuttle from *RER*). Info on ☎01.49.22.72.72.

Nouveau Festival International de Danse de Paris (end of September to beginning of October): state-of-the-art international dance festival based at the Théâtre du Châtelet (☎01.40.28.28.40).

Festival d'Automne (end of September to end of December): theatre and music festival including companies from Eastern Europe, America and Japan; multilingual productions; lots of avant-garde and multimedia stuff, most of it very exciting (☎01.42.96.96.94).

October

Fêtes des Vendanges (first or second Saturday): the grape harvest festival in the Montmartre vineyard, at the corner of rue des Saules and rue St-Vincent (☎01.42.62.21.21).

Foire Internationale d'Art Contemporain (FIAC): international contemporary art show by the Eiffel Tower (☎01.49.53.27.00).

Prix de l'Arc de Triomphe: horse flat racing with high stakes at Longchamp (☎01.49.10.20.30).

November

Festival d'Art Sacré de la Ville de Paris (end of November to end of December): concerts and recitals of church music in Paris churches and concert halls (☎01.45.61.54.99).

Mois de la Photo: photographic exhibitions are held in museums, galleries and cultural centres throughout the city (☎01.43.59.41.78).

Lancement des Illuminations des Champs-Élysées (end of November): jazz bands, the Republican Guard and an international star turning on the Christmas lights down the Champs-Élysées.

Concours International de Danse de Paris (end of November/beginning of December): prestigious dance competition at the Opéra Comique (☎01.45.22.28.74).

December

Le Nouvel An (December 31): New Year's Eve – fireworks, drinking and kissing, notably on the Champs-Élysées.

Women's Paris

Paris is an easy city for women to feel comfortable in. The areas you're likely to frequent at night will be full of people; the last métro home is rarely empty; streets are well lit; and Parisians are rather more inclined than Brits or Americans to get involved if scenes get heavy. That's not to say that unpleasant things don't happen, but there's no reason to feel less safe here than you would in any other large European city.

Young women can expect a certain amount of harassment (see below) but also plenty of opportunities for being pleasantly chatted up.

Political correctness is completely alien to the French, partly because it doesn't work in the French language and partly because philosophically and culturally it's a nonsense to them. Attitudes to seduction and sex are much more ingrained than in Anglo-Saxon cultures, though the balance of power between the sexes is no better – some would say worse. You may well be shocked by the sexism of advertising images but at the same time impressed by the confidence and individualism of so many French women.

Sexual Harassment

Much of the eyeing-up and comments that you're likely to experience can be ignored and will not lead to serious annoyance. However, lack of familiarity with linguistic and cultural clues can

sometimes make it difficult to judge a situation correctly. If your French isn't good enough, how do you tell if he's gabbling at you because you left your purse behind in a shop, or is inciting you to swear at him in English and be cuffed round the head for the insult? The answer is that you can't, but there are some pointers.

A "*Bonjour*" or "*Bonsoir*" on the street is almost always a pick-up line: if you return the greeting, you've left yourself open to a persistent monologue and a difficult brush-off job. On the other hand, it's not unusual to be offered a drink in a bar if you're on your own and *not* to be pestered afterwards, even if you accept. This is rarer in Paris than elsewhere in the country, but don't assume that any overture by a Frenchman is a predatory come-on. It's perfectly possible to chat and even flirt, then say goodbye without any hassle at all.

Safe Sex, Periods and Pregnancy

A warning: Paris has the highest incidence of AIDS of any city in Europe; people who are HIV positive are just as likely to be heterosexual as homosexual. **Condoms** (*préservatifs*) are readily available in supermarkets, chemists, clubs, and from dispensers.

Because of the high exchange rate it will be cheaper to bring **tampons** (*tampons*) and sanitary towels (*serviettes hygiéniques*) with you; they are of course available in all supermarkets and chemists. If you get period pains (*douleurs de règles – règles* means "periods") chemists will be able to supply effective painkillers.

Pregnancy test kits (*tests de grossesse*) are sold by chemists; if you need the morning-after pill (the RU624), you will have to go to a hospital (see p.23).

Sexual Assault

The police do not have a good reputation for dealing with violence against women. If you are the victim of rape or any violent crime it's advisable to contact your consulate before going to the police. If you can't get hold of them, or if you want to be sure of speaking only to another woman, there is a freephone **rape crisis number**:

Feminism in France

During the Socialist government's first term in the early 1980s, Yvette Roudy's new **Women's Ministry** spent five years getting long-overdue equal pay and opportunity measures through parliament. Some funding was given to women's groups, but the main emphasis was on legislation, including the provision of socialized health coverage for abortion. A law against degrading, discriminatory or violence-inciting images of women in the media was, however, thrown out by the National Assembly.

Meanwhile, the *MLF* (*Mouvement de Libération des Femmes* – **Women's Liberation Movement**) had been declared by the media to be dead and buried. There were no more Women's Day marches, no major demonstrations, no direct action. Feminist bookshops and cafés started closing, publications reached their last issue, and polls showed that young women leaving school were only interested in men and babies. As the Socialist policies ran out of steam, cuts in public spending and traditional ideas about the male breadwinner sent more and more women back to their homes and hungry husbands.

Under Chirac and the Gaullists, the *Ministère des Droits des Femmes* (Ministry of Women's Rights) was renamed as the *Ministère des Droits de l'Homme* (Ministry of the Rights of Man). The full title of the ministry included "the feminine condition" and "the family", but the irony of the implacably male gender-bias of the French language went generally unremarked. The first woman prime minister, **Edith Cresson** (1991–92), had a disastrous time in office, but was rarely attacked on grounds of gender. Feminist *députés* in parliament did all they could to keep women's issues prominent, but received no support from their colleagues and little from the movement outside.

Feminist intellectuals – always the most prominent section of the French women's movement – have continued their *seminaires*, erudite publications and university Feminist Studies courses, while at the other end of the scale, women's refuges and rape crisis centres are still maintained, with some funding from the ministry. The *MLF* is occasionally seen on the streets, but disorganized and in much diminished numbers.

More recently, a key mobilizing issue has again been **abortion**, with French women fearing the influence of the powerful US anti-abortion lobby on European public opinion. When a French company applied for a licence for the abortion pill RU486, French pro-lifers initially forced them to withdraw it, threatening its employees with violence, even death. The male Minister for Health, however, declared RU486 to be "the moral property of women". It has since been used by tens of thousands of women for terminations that are far safer and simpler than those by surgical methods. How much the minister was influenced by the needs of the French pharmaceutical industry rather than the needs of women is a matter of opinion, but it was a significant victory nevertheless.

Feminists continue to be active in unions and political parties; male bastions in the arts and media have been under attack; in business and local government leading roles have been taken by a few women; and there has even been talk of the possibility of a woman president in the future. Women have also been very visible in the street protests against the government, though gone are the days when International Women's Day would see crowds of women marching.

☎08.00.05.95.95 (*SOS Viol*). It's staffed by members of the *Collectif Féministe Contre le Viol*, 9 Villa d'Este, off bd Masséna, 13e (Mº Porte d'Ivry; Mon–Fri 10am–6pm; ☎01.45.82.73.00). There are also the **women's refuges**: *Centre Flora Tristan* (☎01.47.36.96.48) and *Halte Aide aux Femmes Battues* (☎01.43.48.20.40). English-speakers are rare, but you will at least get sympathy and an all-women environment, whereas going to the police may well be a further trauma.

SOS Help (☎01.47.23.80.80; 3–11pm) is a general **English-language helpline** and can provide information about English-speaking doctors, lawyers, etc.

Feminist Contacts and Information

French culture remains stuck with myths about femininity that disable women to a far greater extent than in Britain, Holland or the USA. There is, however, a strong network for Parisian lesbians, and havens for non-lesbian feminists do exist, such as those listed below.

Maison des Femmes

8 Cité Prost, off rue Chanzy, 11e (Mº Faidherbe-Chaligny; ☎01.43.48.24.91, recorded info ☎01.43.79.61.91). Mon 5–8pm, Wed 3–8pm, Fri 5–10pm; Fri café 8pm–midnight.
A women's meeting place run by *Paris Féministe*, who produce a monthly bulletin and organize a range of events and actions. Many women's organizations use the *Maison* as a base, including *Maries-Pas-Claires* (young feminists), *Elle Sont Pour* and *Association Féministe pour une Politique Alternative;* solidarity groups; the European network for women's rights, *Coordination Européenne des Femmes;* women's aid and rape crisis; lesbian groups; artists and intellectuals.

This is by far the best place to come if you want to make contact with the women's movement. Don't be put off by the back-alley entrance, and though English speakers can't be guaranteed, you can count on a friendly reception. There's a cafeteria, *Hydromel,* run by *MIEL* (*Mouvement d'Information et d'Expression des Lesbiennes*), which serves drinks and dinner most Friday evenings; a salon de thé, *Amandine's* (Sat 5–8pm); a library (Wed 6–8pm); plus open days with exhibitions and concerts or discos, workshops and self-defence classes, discussions and film shows.

Bibliothèque Marguerite Durand

3rd floor, 79 rue Nationale, 13e (Mº Tolbiac; ☎01.45.70.80.30). Tues–Sat 2–6pm.
The first official feminist library in France, this carries the widest selection of contemporary and old periodicals, news clippings files, photographs, posters and etchings, documentation on current organizations, as well as books on every aspect of women's lives, past and present. It's a very pleasant place to sit and read, and admission is free. In order to consult publications you need to fill out a form and produce identification – the staff are very helpful.

Ligue du Droit des Femmes

54 av de Choisy, 13e (Mº Porte de Choisy/Maison Blanche; ☎01.45.85.11.37).
Organization founded by Simone de Beauvoir which campaigns for women's rights and against discrimination and sexist imagery.

Media

There is no national feminist magazine or paper in France; instead nearly every group produces its own publication. Some are stapled, photocopied hand-outs issued at random intervals; others are regular, well-printed serials, with many of them linked to particular political parties.

• **L'Annuaire,** biannual directory of feminist, lesbian and gay groups, venues and publications produced by the lesbian cultural research organization *ARCL;* 70F from *Maison des Femmes* and women's bookshops; available for reference at the Bibliothèque Marguerite-Durand.

• **Lesbia,** a monthly lesbian magazine, is the best general magazine for all feminists.

• **Paris Féministe** (see *Maison des Femmes,* above) is a monthly carrying detailed listings for events and groups in Paris.

• **Paris Plurielle** is a women's radio programme on 106.3MHz each Tuesday 7–8.30pm.

Other Addresses

Lesbian organizations are listed under "Gay and Lesbian Paris", below. Feminist, lesbian or sympathetic commercial enterprises are listed in the relevant chapters of this book: these include bookshops in *Shops and Markets* (Chapter 17); cafés in *Eating and Drinking* (Chapter 13); clubs in *Music and Nightlife* (Chapter 18); cinema in *Film, Theatre and Dance* (Chapter 19); and *hammams* in *Daytime Amusements and Sports* (Chapter 15).

Gay and Lesbian Paris

Paris is one of Europe's major centres for gay men. There are numerous bars, clubs, restaurants, saunas and shops. In the central street of the Marais, rue Ste-Croix-de-la-Bretonnerie, every other address is gay, and the first gay café with pavement tables recently opened up on rue des Archives. Lesbians have much less choice here commercially, but there are networks of feminist groups and specific publications that cater for the well-organized lesbian community (see above).

The high spots of the calendar are the annual **Gay Pride** parade and festival and the **Bastille Day Ball**. Gay Pride is normally held on the Saturday closest to the summer solstice. It starts from the Bastille, and is a major carnival for both lesbians and gays. The Bastille Day Ball (July 13 10pm–dawn) is a wild open-air dance on the quai de la Tournelle, 5e (M° Pont Marie), and is free for all to join in.

For a long time the emphasis of the gay community in Paris tended towards providing the requisites for a hedonistic lifestyle, rather than any very significant political campaigning. With the legal age of consent set at 15, and discrimination and harassment non-routine, protest was not a high priority.

Matters have changed, here as elsewhere, since the advent of AIDS (*SIDA* in French). The resulting homophobia, though not as extreme as in Britain or middle America, has nevertheless increased the suffering in the group statistically most at risk. A group of gay doctors and the association *AIDES* (*Association pour l'Entraide et l'Information SIDA*) have consistently provided sympathetic counselling and treatment, and the gay press has done a great deal to disseminate the facts about AIDS and to provide hope and encouragement.

A second factor has been the success of the gay community in the Marais; a recent backlash has been manifest in the form of increasing complaints against bars and clubs over noise and infraction of licensing laws, with the police taking speedy and sometimes heavy-handed action.

In general, however, the French consider sexuality to be a private matter. On the whole, gays tend to be discreet outside specific gay venues, parades and the prime gay area between the Hôtel de Ville, the Bastille and Arts et Métiers. Gay-bashing is very uncommon.

Contacts and Information

ARCL (Archives, Recherches et Cultures Lesbiennes), postal address: BP 362, 75526, Paris Cedex 11; answerphone ☎01.43.56.11.49; contact at the *Maison des Femmes* (see below), Fri 7–10pm. *ARCL* publish a yearly directory of lesbian, gay and feminist addresses in France (see above under *Feminist Media*) and a tri-monthly bulletin for members. They organize frequent meetings around campaigning, artistic and intellectual issues.

Centre Gai et Lesbienne, 3 rue Keller, 11e (M° Ledru-Rollin; ☎01.43.57.21.47). The main information centre for the gay, lesbian, bisexual and transexual community in Paris (open daily 2–8pm, café Sun 2–7pm; lesbian evening Fri 8–10pm, bisexuals meet first or second Mon of month). The centre publishes a free map/guide to gay and lesbian Paris, *Le Plan Officiel*, and a monthly magazine, *3 Keller*. It's also the meeting place for numerous campaigning, identity, health, arts and intellectual groups. It may be moving because of redevelopment, but the number will stay the same; other contacts, such as *Les Mots à la Bouche* bookshop in the Marais, will have the new address.

David & Jonathan, 92bis rue Picpus, 12e (M° Michel-Bizot; ☎01.43.42.09.49; Fri 6–8pm). Gay Christian organization.

GAGE, c/o *Les Mots à la Bouche* – see below (☎01.48.03.20.12). Gay and lesbian students' group, meeting every Wednesday at the *Duplex* bar, 25 rue Michel-le-Comte, 3e (M° Rambuteau; 8pm–midnight).

Gay Pride, organized by the *Centre Gai et Lesbienne* (see above).

Maison des Femmes, 8 Cité Prost, off rue Chanzy, 11e (M° Faidherbe-Chaligny; ☎01.43.48.24.91). Mon 5–8pm, Wed 3–8pm, Fri 5–10pm; Fri café 8pm–midnight. Run by *Paris Féministe* (see p.51), this is the base for *ARCL, MIEL – Mouvement d'Information et d'Expression des Lesbiennes* (leftist, feminist lesbians) – and other lesbian groups. *MIEL* runs the Friday café and has an information and message phone line, *Canal MIEL* ☎01.43.79.61.91.

Minitel 36.15 GAY is the minitel number to dial for information on groups, contacts, messages, etc; or you can call on premium line ☎01.36.25.00.24.

Media

Chambre avec Vues, 79 rue Vieille du Temple, 4e (Mº St-Paul). Mon–Sat 11am–11pm, Sun 3–7pm. Run by the same management as *Les Mots à la Bouche* (see below) this bookshop sells a variety of literature, including some lesbian titles, and is good for books and guides in English.

FG (Fréquence Gaie), 98.2 FM. 24hr gay and lesbian radio station with music, news, chats, information on groups and events, etc.

Gageure. Small monthly mag for gay students, produced and distributed by *GAGE* (see above).

Gai Pied publishes the annual *Guide Gai*, which is the most comprehensive gay guide to France, carrying a good selection of lesbian and gay addresses, with an English section.

Homosphere. Free gay and lesbian paper with small ads, lonely hearts, services, etc.

Lesbia. The most widely available lesbian publication, available from most newsagents. Each monthly issue features a wide range of articles, listings, reviews, lonely hearts and contacts.

Les Mots à la Bouche, 6 rue Ste-Croix-de-la-Bretonnerie, 4e (Mº Hôtel-de-Ville). The main gay and lesbian bookshop, with exhibition space and meeting rooms.

3 Keller and **Le Plan Officiel**. *Centre Gai et Lesbienne*'s publications (see above).

SOS

Association des Médecins Gais (gay doctors organization), 45 rue Sedaine, 11e (Mº Bréguet-Sabin; ☎01.48.05.81.71; Sat 2–4pm, Wed 6–8pm).

SOS Écoute Gaie (helpline), ☎01.44.93.01.02; daily 6pm to 10pm.

Other Addresses

Gay, lesbian or sympathetic commercial enterprises are listed in the relevant chapters of this book: bookshops in *Shops and Markets* (Chapter 17); bars in *Eating and Drinking* (Chapter 13); tea dances in *Daytime Amusements and Sports* (Chapter 15); clubs in *Music and Nightlife* (Chapter 18). Paris has a great many gay organizations; we've listed only the most prominent here.

Racism

France has a deservedly bad reputation for racist attitudes and behaviour. If you are Arab or look as if you might be, your chances of avoiding unpleasantness are very low. Hotels claiming to be booked up, police demanding your papers, and abuse from ordinary people are all horribly frequent. In addition, being black, of whatever ethnic origin, can make entering the country difficult. Changes in passport regulations have put an end to outright refusal to let some British holidaymakers in, but customs and immigration officers can still be obstructive and malicious. In North African-dominated areas of Paris such as the Goutte d'Or, identity checks by the police are common and not pleasant. The clamp-down on illegal immigration (and much tougher laws), along with the Algerian-based terrorist attacks in the city, have resulted in a significant increase in police stop-and-search operations. Carrying your passport at all times is a good idea.

There are many **antiracist organizations** including *SOS Racisme*, 1 rue Cail, 10e (Mº La Chapelle; ☎01.42.05.44.44/01.42.05.69.69). Though it doesn't represent the majority of immigrants and their descendants in France (for rioting kids in the Paris suburbs, it's an irrelevant middle-class outfit), *SOS Racisme* has done a great deal over the last few years to raise consciousness amongst young white French people. If you speak French, they will give you support should you be the victim of a **racist assault** (phone first, as opening times vary). The police are unlikely to be sympathetic – your consulate may be more helpful.

Trouble and the Police

Petty theft is bad in the crowded hang-outs of the capital, as in most major cities; the métro and Les Halles are notorious pickpocket grounds. It makes sense to take the normal precautions: not flashing wads of notes or travellers' cheques around; carrying your bag or wallet securely; and never letting cameras and other valuables out of your sight. But the best security is having a good insurance policy, keeping a separate record of cheque numbers, credit card numbers and phone numbers for cancelling them (see p.41), and the relevant details of all your valuables.

Cars with foreign number plates are standard prey. Vehicles are rarely stolen, but tape-decks and luggage left in cars make tempting targets. Good insurance is the only answer, but even so, try not to leave any valuables in plain view. If you have an **accident** while driving, officially you have to fill in and sign a **constat à l'aimable** (jointly agreed statement); car insurers are supposed to give you this with the policy, though in practice few seem to have heard of it. For **non-criminal driving offences** such as speeding, the police can impose an on-the-spot fine.

If you need to **report a theft**, go along to the commissariat de police of the *arrondissement* in which the theft took place, where they will fill out a *constat de viol*. The first thing they'll ask for is your passport, and vehicle documents if relevant. Although the police are not always as co-opera-tive as they might be, it is their duty to assist you if you've lost your passport or all your money.

Emergency number to call for police ☎ 17

Should you be **arrested** on any charge, you have the right to contact your consulate (see box over-leaf). People caught **smuggling or possessing drugs**, even a few grammes of marijuana, are liable to find themselves in jail, and consulates will not be sympathetic. This is not to say that hard-drug con-sumption isn't a visible activity: there are scores of kids dealing in *poudre* (heroin) in Paris, and the authorities are unable to do much about it.

Free legal advice over the phone (in French) is available from *SOS Avocats* (☎01.43.29.33.00; Mon–Fri 7.30–9pm; closed Aug).

The Police

French police (in popular argot, *les flics*) are barely polite at the best of times, and can be extremely unpleasant if you get on the wrong side of them. In Paris, the city police force has an ugly history of cockups, including sporadic shootings of innocent people and brutality against "suspects" – often just ordinary teenagers and black people. You can be stopped at any time and asked to produce ID. If that does happen to you, it's highly inadvisable to be difficult or facetious. The police can also be rather sensitive on political issues: a group of Danish students wearing *"Chirac Non!"* T-shirts against the French nuclear tests in the Pacific were surrounded at the Gare du Nord, accompanied in force to their hotel and forced to change.

The **two main types of police** – the *Police Nationale* and the *Gendarmerie Nationale* – are for all practical purposes indistinguishable. The **CRS** (*Compagnies Républicaines de Sécurité*), on the other hand, are an entirely different proposi-tion. They are a mobile force of paramilitary heav-ies, used to guard sensitive embassies, "control" demonstrations, and generally intimidate the populace on those occasions when the public authorities judge that it is stepping out of line. Armed with guns, CS gas and truncheons, they have earned themselves a reputation for brutali-ty over the years, particularly at those moments when the tensions inherent in the long civil war of French politics have reached boiling point.

Foreign Consulates in Paris

Australia
4 rue Jean-Rey, 15^e
(M° Bir-Hakeim)
☎ 01.49.59.33.00

Canada
35 av Montaigne, 8^e
(M° Franklin-D-Roosevelt)
☎ 01.44.43.29.00

Denmark
77 av Marceau, 16^e
(M° Étoile)
☎ 01.44.31.21.21

Ireland
4, rue Rude, 16^e
(M° Charles-de-Gaulle/Étoile)
☎ 01.45.00.20.87

Netherlands
7–9 rue Eblé, 7^e
(M° St-François-Xavier)
☎ 01.43.06.61.88

New Zealand
7e rue Léonardo-de-Vinci, 16^e
(M° Victor-Hugo)
☎ 01.45.00.24.11

Norway
28 rue Bayard, 8^e
(M° Franklin-D-Roosevelt)
☎ 01.47.23.72.78

Sweden
17 rue Barbet-de-Jouy, 7^e
(M° Varenne)
☎ 01.44.18.88.00

UK
9 av Hoche, 8^e
(M° Courcelles)
☎ 01.42.66.38.10

US
2 rue St-Florentin, 1er
(M° Concorde)
☎ 01.43.12.22.22

Work and Study

Specialists aside, most Britons and North Americans who manage to work and live in Paris do so on luck, brazenness and willingness to live in pretty grotty conditions. An exhausting combination of bar and club work, freelance translating, data processing, typing, busking, providing novel services like home-delivery fish'n'chips, teaching English or computer programming, dancing or modelling are some of the ways people get by. Great if you're into self-promotion and living hand-to-mouth, but if you're not, it might be wise to think twice.

France has a **minimum wage** (the *SMIC*), which is currently around 41F an hour. Employers, however, are likely to pay lower wages to temporary foreign workers who don't have easy legal resources. By law, however, all EU nationals are entitled to exactly the same pay, conditions and trade union rights as French nationals. It's also worth noting that if you're a full-time non-EU student in France (see overleaf), you can get a non-EU **work permit** for the following summer so long as your visa is still valid.

Finding a job in a **French language school** is best done in advance. In Britain, jobs are often advertised in the *Guardian*'s "Educational Extra" and in the *Times Educational Supplement*. Late summer is usually the best time. You don't need fluent French to get a post, but a TEFL (Teaching English as a Foreign Language) qualification will almost certainly be required. If you apply in advance, most schools will fix up the necessary

papers for you. EU nationals don't need a work permit, but getting a *carte de séjour* and social security can still be tricky should employers refuse to help. It's quite feasible to find a teaching job once you're already in France, but you may have to accept semi-official status and no job security. For the addresses of schools, look under "*Écoles de Langues*" in the *Professions* directory of the phone book. Offering private lessons (via university notice boards or classified ads), you'll have lots of competition, and it's hard to reach the people who can afford it, but it's always worth a try.

For **temporary work** check the ads in the *Paris Free Voice* and *France USA Contacts* (see p.44) and keep an eye on the notice boards at the Anglophone churches: the American Church *in Paris* (65 quai d'Orsay, 7e; Mº Invalides); St George's English Church (7 rue Auguste-Vacquerie, 16e; Mº Charles-de-Gaulle/Étoile); St Michael's Anglican Church (5 rue d'Aguesseau, 8e; Mº Madeleine) and the American Cathedral (23 av George V, 8e; Mº Alma-Marceau). You could also try the notice boards located in the offices of *CIDJ* at 101 quai Branly, 15e (Mon–Sat 10am–6pm; Mº Bir-Hakeim) and *CROUS*, 39 av Georges Bernanos, 5e (Mº Port-Royal), both youth information agencies which advertise a number of temporary jobs for foreigners. Other possible sources include the "Offres d'Emploi" in *Le Monde*, *Le Figaro* and the *International Herald Tribune*, and notice boards at English bookshops.

Some people have found jobs **selling magazines** on the street and **leafleting** just by asking people already doing it for the agency address. The American/Irish/British **bars and restaurants** sometimes have vacancies. You'll need to speak French, look smart and be prepared to work very long hours. Obviously, the better your French, the better your chances are of finding work.

Although **working as an au pair** is easily set up through any number of agencies (lists are available from French embassies or consulates and there are lots of ads in *The Lady* in the UK), this sort of work can be total misery if you end up with an unpleasant employer, with conditions, pay and treatment the next worst thing to slav-

---

French Bureaucracy: a Warning

French officialdom and bureaucracy can damge your health. That Gallic shrug and "*Ce n'est pas possible*" is not the result of training programmes in making life difficult for foreigners: they drive most French citizens mad as well. Sorting out social security, long-stay visas, job contracts, bank accounts, tenancy agreements, university enrolment or any other financial, legal or state matter, requires serious commitment. Your reserves of patience, diligence, energy

(both physical and mental) and equanimity in the face of bloody-mindedness and Catch-22s will be tested to the full. Expect to spend days repeatedly visiting the same office and considerable sums on official translations of every imaginable document. Before you throw yourself into the Seine in despair, remember that others are going through it too, and sharing the frustration may well help: the American Church (see p.57) is the place for such contacts.

---

ery. If you're determined to try – and it can be a very good way of learning the language – it's better to apply once in France, where you can at least meet the family first and check things out.

Claiming Benefit in Paris

Any British or EU citizen who has been signing on for **unemployment benefit** for a minimum period of four weeks at home, and intends to continue doing so in Paris, needs a letter of introduction from their own social security office, plus an E303 certificate of authorization (be sure to give them plenty of warning to prepare this). You must register within seven days with the *Agence Nationale pour l'Emploi (ANPE)*, whose offices are listed under *Administration du Travail et de l'Emploi* in the Yellow Pages or *ANPE* in the White Pages.

It's possible to claim benefit for up to three months while you look for work, but it can often take that amount of time for the paperwork to be processed (also see warning above). Information about social security is available on freephone ☎05.34.25.70 or from *Les Reseignements sur la Sécurité Sociale*, 69bis rue de Dunkerque, 9e (☎42.80.63.67). Pensioners can arrange for their **pensions** to be paid in France, but cannot, unfortunately, receive French state pensions.

Studying

It's relatively easy to be a student in Paris. Foreigners pay no more than French nationals (around 1300F a year) to enrol in a course, but there's also the cost of supporting yourself (say around 3300F all in). Your *carte de séjour* and – for EU nationals – social security will be assured, and you'll be eligible for subsidized accommodation, meals and all the student reductions. Few people want to do undergraduate degrees abroad, but for higher degrees or other diplomas, the range of options is enormous. Strict entry requirements, including an exam in French, apply only for undergraduate degrees.

Generally, French universities are much less formal than British ones and many people perfect their fluency in the language while studying. For full details and prospectuses, go to the Cultural Service of any French embassy or consulate (see p.20 for the addresses).

Embassies and consulates can also give details of language courses, at the Sorbonne, Alliance Française, etc, which are often combined with lectures on French "civilization" and usually very costly. You'll find ads for lesser language courses in the *Paris Free Voice* and on the notice boards detailed above.

Directory

AIRLINES *Air France*, 119 av des Champs-Élysées, 8ᵉ (info ☎01.44.08.24.24, reservations ☎01.44.08.22.22); *Air Inter*, 119 av des Champs-Élysées, 8ᵉ (☎01.45.46.90.00); *British Airways*, 12 rue Castiglione, 1ᵉʳ (reservations ☎01.48.62.22.80, info Orly airport ☎01.49.75.15.15).

ALARM ☎36.88 or with a digital phone dial *55* then the time in four figures (eg 0715 for 7.15am) then #. To annul, dial #55* then the time, then # (costs around 3.70F).

BBC WORLD SERVICE 648kHz or 198kHz long wave midnight to 5am. Also on television via satellite. For more details, see p.44.

CONTRACEPTIVES Condoms (*préservatifs* or *capotes*) can be bought at chemists, supermarkets, clubs and bars. From pharmacies you can also get spermicidal cream and jelly (*dose contraceptive*), plus suppositories (*ovules, suppositoires*), and (with a prescription) the pill (*la pillule*), a diaphragm or IUD (*le sterilet*).

CUSTOMS With the Single European Market you can bring in and take out most things as long as you have paid tax on them in an EU country, and they are for personal consumption. Customs may be suspicious if they think you are going to resell goods (or break the chassis of your car). Limits still apply to drink and tobacco bought in duty free shops: 200 cigarettes or 250g tobacco or 50 cigars; 1 litre spirits or 2 litres fortified wine, or 2 litres sparkling wine; 2 litres table wine; 50gm perfume and 250ml toilet water. There are no border controls between France and Germany, Spain, the Netherlands and Portugal (all signatories to the Schengen Agreement along with Belgium and Luxembourg with whom France currently insists on border checks).

ELECTRICITY 220V out of double, round-pin wall sockets. Electricity and gas are supplied by *EDF–GDF* (*Electricité de France* ☎01.40.42.22.22 and *Gaz de France* ☎01.47.54.20.20; Mon–Fri 8.30am–6pm), who should be contacted concerning bills, gas problems or blackouts in an apartment building. For problems in individual flats, contact one of the emergency repair numbers listed in the *Pages Jaunes* (Yellow Pages).

EMERGENCY REPAIRS General agencies dealing with gas, electricity, plumbing, car repairs, etc are listed under *SOS, Allo* or *Assistance–Dépannage* in the Yellow Pages.

KIDS/BABIES Visiting Paris with children poses few travel problems. They're allowed in all bars and restaurants, most of which will cook simpler food on request. Hotels charge by the room – there's a small supplement for an additional bed or cot. You'll have no difficulty finding disposable nappies, baby foods and milk powders. The *SNCF* (French Railways) charges half-fare for kids aged 4–11, and the *RATP* (Paris transport) charges half-fares for 4–10s; under-4s travel free. If you have children in pushchairs and are planning to use the métro, be warned that there are frequent flights of steps. For keeping children entertained see Chapter 16.

LEFT LUGGAGE Left luggage lockers at train stations are all closed at the time of writing as an anti-terrorist security measure; only the manual left luggage office at the Gare de Lyon is open.

LEGAL ADVICE *SOS Avocats* offer free legal advice, in French, over the phone ☎01.43.29.33.00; Mon–Fri 7.30–9pm, closed Aug).

LOST BAGGAGE Airports: Orly (☎01.49.75.04.53 or ☎01.41.75.40.38 for *Air France*); Charles de

Gaulle (☎01.48.62.10.46 or ☎01.48.64.92.92 for *Air France*).

LOST PROPERTY *Bureau des Objets Trouvés*, Préfecture de Police, 36 rue des Morillons, 15e; ☎01.45.31.98.11 (Mº Convention). Mon, Wed & Fri 8.30am–5pm, Tues & Thurs 8.30am–8pm, except in July & Aug. For property lost on public transport, phone the *RATP* on ☎01.40.06.75.27.

PETROL 24-hour filling stations: 336 rue St-Honoré, 1er; place de la Bourse, 2e; 42 rue Beaubourg, 3e; 36 rue des Fossés-St-Bernard, 5e; 6 bd Raspail, 7e; 118 av des Champs-Élysées and place de la Madeleine, 8e; 1 bd de la Chapelle, 2 rue Louis-Blanc, 166 rue du Faubourg St-Martin, 152 rue Lafayette, 10e; 55 quai de la Rapée, 12e; Porte d'Ivry and Porte d'Italie, 13e; Porte d'Orléans and av du Maine (nr junction with av Gal-Leclerc), 14e; rue Linois and 95 bd Lefebvre, 15e; Porte de St-Cloud and 24 av Paul-Doumer, 16e; Porte de Champerret and Porte de Clichy, 17e; Porte de la Chapelle, 18e; Porte de Pantin, 19e; and av de la Porte de Vincennes, 20e.

PUBLIC TRANSPORT *RATP* information on ☎08.36.68.77.14 (premium rate).

SMOKING Laws requiring restaurants to have separate smoking and non-smoking areas are widely ignored. Non-smokers may well find themselves eating elbow to elbow alongside smokers, and waiters are not that likely to be sympathetic. Smoking is not allowed on public transport, including surburban trains, or in cinemas. Most office reception areas are non-smoking. But smoking is still a socially acceptable habit in France and tobacco is cheap in comparison with Britain, though the tax has increased recently. A packet of *Gauloises* costs around 12F, an American brand around 18.50F; note that you can only buy tobacco in *tabacs*: *Le Pigalle*, 22 bd de Clichy, 18e (Mº Pigalle) is open till 4.30am.

STUDENT INFORMATION *CROUS*, 39 av Georges-Bernanos, 5e (☎01.40.51.36.00; Mº Port-Royal).

TALKING CLOCK ☎36.99.

TELEGRAMS By phone. Internal – ☎36.55; external – ☎08.00.33.44.41 (all languages).

TIME France is one hour ahead of Britain, six hours ahead of Eastern Standard Time, and nine hours ahead of Pacific Standard Time. Daylight saving operates from the end of March to the end of September, so during October the time is briefly the same as in Britain. The dates of the time changes are announced in the media – watch out if you have planes or trains to catch around those periods. The European Commission should come to a decision on standardizing summer hours in 1997.

TOILETS are usually to be found downstairs in bars, along with the phone. Hole-in-the-ground squats with no paper still exist in cheaper establishments.

TRAFFIC/ROAD CONDITIONS For Paris traffic jams listen to 105.1 FM (FIP) on the radio; for the *boulevard périphérique* and main routes in and out of the city, ring ☎01.48.99.33.33.

TRAVELLING ON Buses to all European destinations: *Eurolines*, 28 av de Gal.-de-Gaulle, Bagnolet (Mº Gallieni; ☎01.49.72.51.51). Hitching agency: *Allostop-Provoya*, 8 rue Rochambeau (square Montholon), 8e (Mº Cadet/Poissonnière; ☎04.53.20.42.42; Mon–Fri 9am–7.30pm, Sat 9am–1pm & 2–6pm).

VAT (Value Added Tax) standard rate in France is 20.6 percent; it's higher for luxury items and lower for essentials, but there are no exemptions (books and children's clothes are therefore a lot more expensive than in the UK).

WEATHER For information on specific locations in France and round the world, phone ☎01.45.56.71.71. For recorded info on the Paris region, phone ☎01.39.65.80.80.

WHAT TO TAKE Because of the strength of the French franc, nearly everything (toothpaste, tampons, razor blades, clothes, stationery, alcohol apart from wine, etc) is more expensive in France, so pack what you can carry. In addition, it's worth taking passport photos for transport passes and youth cards, phone numbers for credit card cancellation, and, of course, this book.

YOUTH INFORMATION *CIDJ* (*Centre d'Information et de Documentation de la Jeunesse*), 101 quai Branly, 15e (Mº Bir-Hakeim; ☎01.44.49.12.00; Mon–Sat 10am–6pm).

The City

The Layout of the City

G eography, history and function have combined to give Paris a remarkably coherent and intelligible structure. The city lies in a basin surrounded by hills. It is very nearly circular, confined within the *boulevard périphérique*, which follows the line of the most recent, nineteenth-century fortifications. Through its middle, the **River Seine** flows east to west in a satisfying arc. At the hub of the circle, in the middle of the river, lies the island from which all the rest grew: the **Île de la Cité** (covered in Chapter 2). Here, the city's oldest religious and secular institutions – the cathedral and the royal palace – stand right beside the river, which was itself both the city's *raison d'être* and its lifeline.

The royal palace of the **Louvre** lies on the north or **Right Bank** (*rive droite*) of the Seine, as the river flows. To the northwest runs the longest and grandest vista of the city – **La Voie Triomphale** (Chapter 3) – used by kings, emperors and presidents for the expression of royal and state power. It comprises the Tuileries gardens, the Champs-Élysées, the Arc de Triomphe, and La Grande Arche de la Défense, among other gestures of self-aggrandizement. To the north and east of that, clamped in an arc around the river, you'll find the commercial and financial quarters necessary to the everyday life of the state (covered in Chapter 4): the stock exchange, the Bank of France, the fashion and leather trades, jewellers, remnants of the medieval guilds, and what remains of the fruit, veg and meat market, the equivalent of London's Covent Garden, that was based in **Les Halles**. Just to the east of it, the **Marais** (Chapter 5) became the first really prestigious address for leading courtiers and businessmen; with the **Bastille**, it is now one of the liveliest areas of the city.

The south bank of the river, on the other hand, the so-called **Left Bank** (*rive gauche*; Chapter 6), developed quite differently. It owes its existence to the cathedral school of Notre-Dame, which spilled over from the Île de la Cité onto the south bank, and became the university of the Sorbonne, attracting scholars and students from all over the medieval world. Ever since then, it has been the traditional domain of the intelligentsia, of academics, writers, artists, the cinema and the liberal professions.

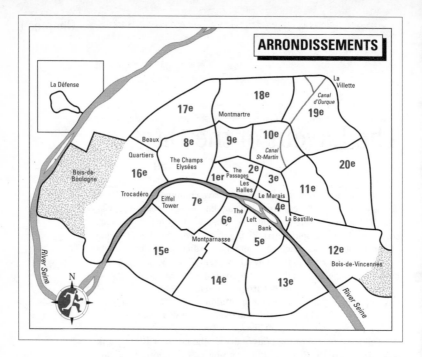

The city is divided into twenty *arrondissements*, whose arrangement provides a pretty accurate guide to its structure and historical development. Centred on the Louvre, they spiral outwards in a clockwise direction. The inner hub of the city comprises *arrondissements* 1er to 6e, and it is here that most of the major sights and museums are to be found. The outer or higher-number *arrondissements* were mostly incorporated into the city in the nineteenth century. Those to the east accommodated mainly the poor and the working-class, while the western ones held the aristocracy and the new rich. Most of them were outlying villages that were gradually swamped as industrialization and colonization brought growing wealth and labour-hunger to the city. Some, such as **Belleville**, **Montmartre** and **Passy**, have succeeded in retaining something of their separate village identity.

These historical divisions according to function and population substantially retain their validity to this day. The Right Bank still connotes business and commerce, the Left Bank arts and letters; west means bourgeois and smart, east means working-class, immigrant and scruffy. In recent years, however, such neat arrangements have been increasingly disturbed as rising property values drive out the poor and open their traditional *quartiers* to gentrification.

One thing Paris is not particularly well endowed with is **parks**. The largest, the **Bois de Boulogne** and the **Bois de Vincennes**, at the western and eastern limits of the city, do possess the odd small pockets of interest, but are largely anonymous sprawls. More enjoyable recreational spaces in Paris are the small squares and *places*, the *quais* along the banks of the Seine, and the bits of unexpected greenery encountered as you wander the streets. For a real break from the bustle of the city, it is best to try an out-of-town excursion, to the *château* of Vaux-le-Vicomte, for example, or the forest of Fontainebleau (see Chapter 20).

Orientation

Paris is strictly confined within the 78-square-kilometre limits of its *boulevard périphérique*; at its widest point it is only about 12km across, which, at a brisk pace, is not much more than two hours' walk. This marvellous compactness means that there is very little dross and tedium, and no lifeless and interminable residential areas. On the contrary, any walk across the city is very much action-packed. You move in a trice from villagey Montmartre to the sleaze of Barbès, from the high-powered elegance of the Faubourg-St-Honoré to the frenetic and downmarket commercialism of Les Halles. You exchange vast subterranean shopping and entertainment complexes for chaotic and colourful *quartiers*, where West African textiles and teapots from the Maghreb are piled high behind narrow counters; you leave the maelstrom of the Right Bank expressway to find yourself alone by the brown waters of the Seine.

If you don't feel like walking, nothing could be easier than the excellent **public transport** system, detailed on p.30. Above ground,

---

Our chapter accounts are based on historic and thematic divisions of the city. Hence we refer to particular *quartiers* and to the erstwhile villages (Belleville, Batignolles, Auteuil, etc) rather than to particular *arrondissements*, except where these define a clearly contained area, such as the 13^e and 15^e. Though we do suggest the occasional walk, our aim has been to avoid imposing priorities or itineraries, allowing you to discover the areas of the city in your own way.

There are, however, certain monuments that it makes sense to describe together. So La Voie Triomphale, the historic axis from the Louvre to the Arc de Triomphe, is treated in one chapter (3), while areas to either side of it are mentioned in Chapter 4 in a section on the fashion business. Equally, Trocadéro, on the north bank of the river in the 16e, is grouped together with the Eiffel Tower and the Invalides, on the south bank (Chapter 7), because together they create another monumental vista.

For the outer areas of the city the chapters are divided simply into southern, northern, eastern and western Paris, beginning with the most obvious destinations or focal points within those areas.

---

the city is served by a network of **buses**, each vehicle and each stop carrying a clear map of the route. Below ground, Paris is criss-crossed with **métro** lines (see map on pp.34–35), as well as the extra-quick **RER** trains (map on p.31). Stops are very frequent, so you are seldom more than a few minutes' walk away from the near-est station. The same tickets are valid on both métro and *RER*, and the cost of travel within the city and closest suburbs is flat-rate.

Chapter 2

Île de la Cité

T he Île de la Cité is where Paris began. The earliest settlements were sited here, as was the small Gallic town of Lutetia, overrun by Julius Caesar's troops in 52 BC. A natural defensive site commanding a major east–west river trade route, it was an obvious candidate for a bright future. The Romans garrisoned it and laid out one of their standard military town plans, overlapping onto the Left Bank. While it never achieved any great political importance, they endowed it with an administrative centre that became the palace of the Merovingian kings in 508 AD, then of the counts of Paris, who in 987 became kings of France. So from the very beginning the Île has been close to the administrative heart of France.

Today the lure of the island lies in its tail end – the **square du Vert-Galant**, **the quais**, **place Dauphine** and the **cathedral of Notre-Dame** itself. Haussmann demolished the central section in the nineteenth century, displacing some 25,000 people and virtually breaking the island's back by constructing four vast edifices in bland Baronial-Bureaucratik, which were largely given over to housing the law. He also perpetrated the litter-blown space in front of the cathedral by razing the medieval houses that clustered close about it, though that at least has the virtue of allowing a full-frontal view of the edifice.

Details of the Seine river boats are given on p.301.

Pont-Neuf and the quais

If you arrive on the island by the **Pont-Neuf**, which despite its name is the city's oldest bridge (and the first to be constructed without the traditional medieval complement of houses on it), you'll see a statue of **Henri IV**, the king who commissioned it in 1607. It was during his reign that the first attempts were made to coordinate town planning in Paris.

Behind his statue, a flight of steps goes down to the **quais** and the **square du Vert-Galant**, a small tree-lined green enclosed within the triangular stern of the island. The name *Vert-Galant*, meaning a

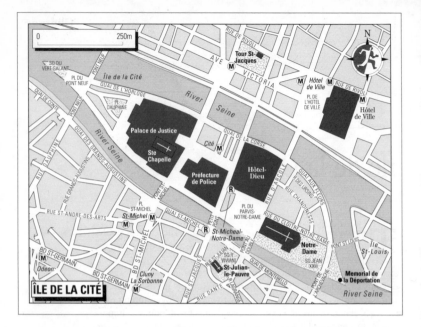

Île de la Cité: listings

RESTAURANTS

Au Rendez-vous des Camionneurs, 72 quai des Orfèvres, 1ᵉʳ. Mᵒ St-Michel.

CAFÉS AND BARS

Taverne Henri IV, 13 place du Pont-Neuf, 1ᵉʳ. Mᵒ Pont-Neuf.

These establishments are reviewed in Chapter 13, Eating and drinking, beginning on p.230.

"green" or "lusty" gentleman, is supposed to celebrate Henri IV's success with women.

The prime spot to occupy is the extreme point beneath a weeping willow – haunt of lovers, sparrows and sunbathers. On the north quay is the dock for the tourist river boats, *Bateaux-Vedettes du Pont-Neuf.*

Sainte-Chapelle and the Conciergerie

On the other side of the bridge, across the street from the king, seventeenth-century houses flank the entrance to the sanded, chestnut-shaded **place Dauphine**, one of the city's most secluded and exclusive squares, where Simone Signoret lived until her death in 1985.

Henri IV

Henri IV was, first of all, King of Navarre in the Pyrenees, a bastion of
Protestantism. On becoming King of France in 1589, he was obliged to
convert to Catholicism out of deference to the sensibilities of the majority
of his new subjects. "Paris is worth a Mass", he is reputed to have said,
somewhat cynically.

Henri's great aim was to reconstruct and reconcile France, and it was
he who guaranteed the civil rights of the Protestants in 1598. When they
were abrogated a hundred years later by Louis XIV under the pressure of
the Counter-Reformation, the Protestants scattered across the globe, from
London's Spitalfields to the New World. As many of them were highly
skilled craftsmen, their departure was a blow to the economy – as was the
death and exile of so many Communards two hundred years later, who in
their turn were also largely the working-class elite.

The far end of the square is blocked by the dull mass of the **Palais de
Justice**, which swallowed up the palace that was home to the French
kings until Étienne Marcel's bloody revolt in 1358 frightened them
off to the greater security of the Louvre. In earlier times it served as
the Roman governors' residence.

The only part of the older complex that remains in its entirety is
Louis IX's **Sainte-Chapelle** (daily April–Sept 9.30am–6.30pm,
Oct–March 10am–5pm, closed bank holidays; 32F/15F, combined
ticket with Conciergerie 45F; M° Cité), built to house a collection of
holy relics he had bought at extortionate rates from the bankrupt
empire of Byzantium. It stands in a courtyard to the left of the main
entrance (bd du Palais), looking somewhat squeezed by the proxim-
ity of the nineteenth-century law courts – which, incidentally, anyone
is free to sit in on. Though much restored, the chapel remains one of
the finest achievements of French Gothic (consecrated in 1248).
Very tall in relation to its length, it looks like a cathedral choir lopped
off and transformed into an independent building. The most radical
feature is its fragility: the reduction of structural masonry to a minimum to make way for a huge expanse of stunning **stained glass**. The
impression inside is of being enclosed within the wings of myriad
butterflies – the predominant colours are blue and red, and, in the
later rose window, grass-green and blue.

It pays to get to the Ste-Chapelle as early as possible. It attracts
hordes of tourists, as does the **Conciergerie** (April–Sept
9.30am–6pm, Oct–March 10am–4.30pm, closed bank holidays;
28F/15F, combined ticket with Ste-Chapelle 45F), Paris' oldest
prison, where Marie-Antoinette and in their turn the leading figures
of the Revolution were incarcerated before execution. The chief
interest of the Conciergerie is the enormous late Gothic **Salle des
Gens d'Arme**, canteen and recreation room of the royal household
staff. You miss little if you don't see Marie-Antoinette's cell and various other macabre mementos of the guillotine's victims.

Sainte-
Chapelle
and the
Conciergerie

For the loveliest view of what the whole ensemble once looked like, you need to get the postcard of the June illustration from the fifteenth-century Book of Hours known as *Les Très Riches Heures du Duc de Berry*, the most mouthwatering of all medieval illuminated manuscripts. It shows the palace with towers and chimneys and trelliswork rose garden, with the Ste-Chapelle touching the sky in the right-hand corner. The Seine laps the curtain wall where now the quai des Orfèvres (goldsmiths) runs. In the foreground, pollarded willows line the Left Bank, while barefoot peasant girls rake hay into stooks and their menfolk scythe light-green swathes up the rue Dauphine. No sign of the square du Vert-Galant: it was just a swampy islet then, not to be joined to the rest of the Cité for another hundred years and more.

The original of
Les Très
Riches Heures
*is in the Musée
Condé outside
Paris – see
p.382.*

Place Lépine and Pont d'Arcole

If you continue along the north side of the island from the Conciergerie you come to **place Lépine**, named for the police boss who gave Paris' coppers their white truncheons and whistles. There is an exuberant **flower market** here six days a week, with **birds and pets** – cruelly caged – on Sunday.

Next bridge but one is the **Pont d'Arcole**, named after a young revolutionary killed in an attack on the Hôtel de Ville in the 1830 rising (see p.412), and beyond that the only bit of the Cité that survived Haussmann's attentions. In the streets hereabouts once flourished the cathedral school of Notre-Dame, forerunner of the Sorbonne.

*Abélard and
Héloïse are
buried in the
Père-Lachaise
cemetery – see
p.180.*

Around the year 1200, one of the teachers was **Peter Abélard**, of Héloïse fame (see below). A philosophical whiz kid and cocker of snooks at the establishment intellectuals of his time, he was very popular with his students and not at all with the authorities, who thought they caught a distinct whiff of heresy. Forced to leave the cathedral school, he set up shop on the Left Bank with his disciples and, in effect, founded the University of Paris. Less successful, though much better known, is the story of his love life. While living near the rue Chanoinesse, behind the cathedral, he fell violently in love with his landlord's niece, Héloïse, and she with him. She had a baby, uncle had him castrated, and the story ended in convents, lifelong separation and lengthy correspondence.

Notre-Dame

The **Cathédrale de Notre-Dame** itself (Sun–Fri 8am–7pm, Sat 8am–12.30pm & 2–7pm; Mº St-Michel) is so much photographed that, seeing it even for the first time, the edge of your response may be somewhat dulled by familiarity. Yet it is truly impressive, that great H-shaped west front, with its strong vertical divisions counterbalanced by the horizontal emphasis of gallery and frieze, all centred on the rose window – a solid, no-nonsense design that confesses its Romanesque ancestry. For a more fantastical kind of Gothic, look rather at the **north transept façade** with its crocketed gables and huge fretted window-space.

Notre-Dame was begun in 1160 under the auspices of Bishop de Sully and completed around 1245. In the nineteenth century, Viollet-le-Duc carried out extensive renovation work, including remaking most of the statuary – the entire frieze of Old Testament kings, for instance, damaged during the Revolution by enthusiasts who took them for the kings of France – and adding the steeple and baleful-looking gargoyles, which you can see close-up if you brave the ascent of the **towers** (daily April–Sept 10am–6pm, Oct–March 10am–5pm; 31F/6F, or 45F combined admission with the *crypte archéologique* – see below). Ravaged by weather and pollution, the façade's beauty may still be partially masked by scaffolding put up for further restoration work.

The original statues are in the Musée National du Moyen-Age on p.285.

Inside, the immediately striking feature, if you can ignore the noise and movement, is the dramatic contrast between the darkness of the nave and the light falling on the first great clustered pillars of the choir, emphasizing the special nature of the sanctuary. It is the end walls of the transepts that admit all this light, nearly two-thirds glass, including two magnificent **rose windows** coloured in imperial purple. These, the vaulting, the soaring shafts reaching to the springs of the vaults, are all definite Gothic elements, yet, inside as out, there remains a strong sense of Romanesque in the stout round pillars of the nave and the general sense of four-squareness. Free guided tours (1hr–1hr 30min) take place in French every weekday at noon and Saturday at 2pm, and in English on Wednesday at noon. There are free organ concerts every Sunday at 5 or 5.30pm, plus four masses on Sunday morning and one at 6.30pm. The **trésor** (daily 9.30am–6pm; 15F/10F) is not really worth the entry fee.

Before you leave, walk round to the public garden at the east end for a view of the **flying buttresses** supporting the choir, and then along the riverside under the south transept, where you can sit – in springtime with the cherry blossom drifting down. And say a prayer of gratitude that the city authorities had the sense to throw out President "Paris-must-adapt-itself-to-the-automobile" Pompidou's scheme for extending the quayside expressway along here.

Out in front of the cathedral, in the square separating it from Haussmann's police HQ, is what appears to be (and smells like) the entrance to an underground toilet. It is, in fact, a very well-displayed and interesting museum, the **crypte archéologique** (daily April–Sept 10am–5.30pm, Oct–March 10am–4.30pm; 28F/15F, or 45F combined admission with the towers) – see above, in which are revealed the remains of the church that predated the cathedral, as well as streets and houses of the Cité dating as far back as the Roman era.

Kilomètre zéro and Le Mémorial de la Déportation

On the pavement by the west door of Notre-Dame cathedral is a spot known as **kilomètre zéro**, from which all main road distances in France are calculated. For the Île de la Cité is the symbolic heart of the country, or at least of the France that in the school books fights wars, undergoes revolutions and launches space rockets.

It is fitting that the island should also be the symbolic tomb of the 200,000 French men and women who died in the Nazi concentration camps during World War II – Resistance fighters, Jews, forced labourers. Their moving memorial, **Le Mémorial de la Déportation**, is a kind of bunker-crypt, barely visible above ground, at the extreme eastern tip of the island. Stairs scarcely shoulder-wide descend into a space like a prison yard. A single aperture overlooks the brown waters of the Seine, barred by a grill whose spiky ends evoke the torments of the torture chamber. Above, nothing is visible but the sky and, dead centre, the spire of Notre-Dame. Inside, the walls of the tunnel-like crypt are studded with thousands of points of light representing the dead. Floor and ceiling are black and it ends in a black raw hole, with a single naked bulb hanging in the middle. Either side are empty barred cells. "They went to the other ends of the Earth and they have not returned. 200,000 French men and women swallowed up, exterminated, in the mists and darkness of the Nazi camps." Above the exit are the words "Forgive. Do not forget . . .".

Chapter 3

Along La Voie Triomphale

T he city's most monumental axis, **La Voie Triomphale** or Triumphant Way, runs from the **Louvre** palace in a dead straight line along the central alley of the **Tuileries** gardens, across **place de la Concorde**, up the av des **Champs-Élysées**, through the **Arc de Triomphe**, then along av de la Grande Armée to the city boundary at Porte Maillot and on all the way out through the suburb of Neuilly to the business skyscrapers of La Défense. Along its nine-kilometre length are monumental constructions erected over the centuries by kings and emperors, presidents and corporations, to propagate French power and prestige.

The tradition of self-aggrandizement dies hard. President Mitterrand, whose *grands projets* for the city outdid even Napoléon's, stamped his mark at either end of La Voie Triomphale, with the glass pyramid entrance to the much-expanded Louvre and an immense marble-clad cubic arch at La Défense. Though plans exist for further extension westward, Mitterrand's *Grande Arche* and the Louvre effectively enclose the historic axis between them. The two great constructions echo each other in scale and geometry, with both aligned at the same slight angle away from the axis – a detail that, given the distance involved, has to be appreciated conceptually rather than visually.

This chapter deals with the stretch from the Arc de Triomphe to the Louvre and the Palais Royal, plus the surrounding streets; for La Défense, see p.205.

The Arc de Triomphe and the Champs-Élysées

The best view of this grandiose and simple geometry of kings to capital is from the top of the **Arc de Triomphe**, Napoléon's homage both to the armies of France and to himself (summer Tues–Sat 9.30am–11pm, Sun & Mon 9.30am–6.30pm, winter Tues–Sat 10am–10.30pm, Sun & Mon 10am–6pm; 32F/21F for under-25s,

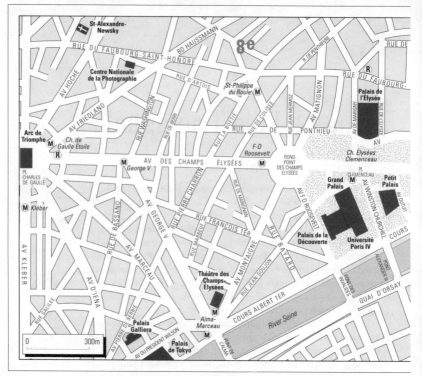

15F for under-17s, free for under-12s; access from stairs on north cnr av des Champs-Élysées; M° Charles-de-Gaulle/Étoile). The emperor and his two royal successors spent ten million francs between them on this edifice, which victorious foreign armies would later use to humiliate the French. After the Prussians' triumphal march in 1871, the Parisians lit bonfires beneath the arch and down the Champs-Élysées to eradicate the stain of German boots.

From 1941 to 1944 Hitler's troops paraded daily around the swastika-decked monument – de Gaulle's arrival at the scene, come Liberation, was probably less effective than the earlier ashes and flames. In 1989 the French humiliated themselves with their grand parade of nations to mark the Bicentennial of the French Revolution. The symbol chosen for France was the locomotive, which features in Émile Zola's novel *La Bête Humaine*, about a railway worker who murders his wife.

Assuming there are no bizarre theatricals or armies in sight (on Bastille Day, the President proceeds down the Champs-Élysées accompanied by tanks, guns and flags), your attention is most likely to be caught, not by the view, but by the mesmerizing traffic movements directly below you around place Charles-de-Gaulle, the world's first organized roundabout, still better known as **place de l'Étoile**.

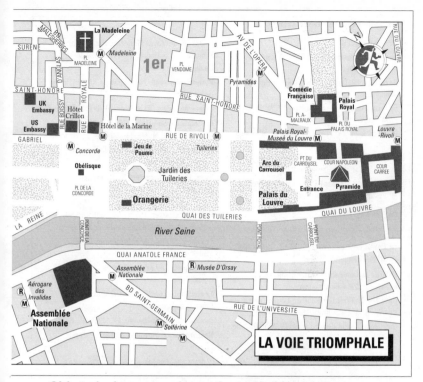

The map shows:

- LA VOIE TRIOMPHALE

Map labels: RUE MALESHERBES, La Madeleine, PL. MADELEINE, Madeleine (M), AV DE L'OPÉRA, RUE DU LOUVRE, SURÈNE, 1er, PL. VENDOME, D'ANGLAS, SAINT-HONORÉ, RUE ROYALE, Pyramides (M), RUE SAINT-HONORÉ, Comédie Française, Palais Royal, UK Embassy, Hôtel Crillon, RUE BOISSY, PL A-MALRAUX, PL DU PALAIS ROYAL, US Embassy, Hôtel de la Marine, RUE DE RIVOLI (M), Palais Royal-Musée du Louvre (M), Louvre-Rivoli (M), GABRIEL, Concorde (M), Jeu de Paume, Tuileries, Arc du Carrousel, PT DU CARROUSEL, COUR NAPOLÉON, COUR CARRÉE, Obélisque, Jardin des Tuileries, Entrance, Pyramide, PL DE LA CONCORDE, Orangerie, Palais du Louvre, QUAI DES TUILERIES, QUAI DU LOUVRE, LA REINE, PONT DE LA CONCORDE, River Seine, PONT ROYAL, PONT DU CARROUSEL, QUAI ANATOLE FRANCE, Assemblée Nationale (M), Musée D'Orsay (R), Aérogare des Invalides (R)(M), BD SAINT-GERMAIN, RUE DE L'UNIVERSITÉ, Assemblée Nationale, Solférine (M)

Of the twelve fat avenues making up the star (*étoile*), much the busiest is the **avenue des Champs-Élysées**, which disgorges and gobbles a phenomenal number of vehicles. Recently, however, the side lanes where cars used to prowl in search of parking spaces have been removed, giving pedestrians an equal share of the avenue's width. At Christmas this is where the fairy lights are draped, and where cars converge on December 31 to hoot in the New Year.

The glamour of the Champs-Élysées, particularly its upper end, may not be quite what it was, dominated as it is nowadays by airline offices, car showrooms, fast food outlets and bright, light shopping arcades. But there's still the *Lido* cabaret, *Fouquet's* high-class bar and restaurant which hosts the César film awards each year, and plenty of cinemas and outrageously priced cafés to bring the punters in. Further down, the perfumier *Guerlain* occupies an exquisite 1913 building at no. 68; the *belle époque* façade of the former *Claridge Hotel*, at no. 74, has been given a facelift; and the *Travellers Club* still glories in the mid-nineteenth-century opulence of the *Hôtel de la Païva*, at no. 25. Newer arrivals, mostly transatlantic, continue the avenue's connection with the entertainment industries: *Virgin Megastore*, a Disney shop and the *Planet*

Hollywood restaurant. At the Renault showrooms (no. 49–53, free) is a display of cars, bikes and vans from the earliest days.

The stretch between the Rond-Point roundabout, whose *Lalique* glass fountains disappeared during the German occupation, and place de la Concorde is bordered by chestnut trees and municipal flowerbeds, pleasant enough to stroll among, but not sufficiently dense to muffle the squeal of accelerating tyres. The gigantic building with overloaded Neoclassical exteriors, glass roofs and exuberant flying statuary rising above the greenery to the south is the **Grand Palais**, created with its neighbour, the **Petit Palais**, for the 1900 *Exposition Universelle*. They house museums and the city's major cultural exhibition space (restricted until 1998 by restoration work on the largest wing of the Grand Palais).

On the north side, combat police guard the high walls of the presidential **Élysée palace** and the line of ministries and embassies ending with the US in prime position on the corner of place de la Concorde. On Thursdays and at weekends you can see a stranger manifestation of the self-images of states in the **postage stamp market** at the corner of avs Gabriel and Marigny.

Place de la Concorde and the Tuileries

The graceful gradients of the Champs-Élysées, like a landing flight-path, finish up in the east at **place de la Concorde**, where more crazed traffic makes crossing over to the middle a death-defying task.

As it happens, some 1300 people did die here between 1793 and 1795, beneath the Revolutionary guillotine: Louis XVI, Marie-Antoinette, Danton and Robespierre among them. The centrepiece of the *place*, chosen like its name to make no comment on these events, is an obelisk from the temple of Luxor, offered as a favour-currying gesture by the viceroy of Egypt in 1829. It serves merely as a pivotal point for more geometry: the alignment of the French parliament, the Assemblée Nationale, on the far side of the Seine, with the church of the Madeleine, at the end of rue Royale, to the north. The Neoclassical Hôtel Crillon – the ultimate luxury address for visitors to Paris – and its twin, the Hôtel de la Marine, flank the entrance to rue Royale, which, needless to say, meets the Voie Triomphale at a precise right angle.

Full accounts of the artwork in the Orangerie are included in the Museums chapter, on p.286.

The symmetry of the Voie Triomphale continues into the formal layout of the **Tuileries gardens**, disrupted only by bodies lounging on the grass, kids chasing their boats round the ponds, and gays cruising on the terrace overlooking the river. The two buildings flanking the garden at the Concorde end are the **Orangerie**, by the river, and the **Jeu de Paume**, by rue de Rivoli.

The Tuileries Gardens

The first garden to take the place of the medieval warren of tilemakers (*tuileries* in French) was that of Catherine de Médicis (her Palais des Tuileries, which ran along what is now the underpass av du Gal-Lemonnier, was burnt down by the Communards in 1870). She had formal vegetable gardens, a labyrinth and a chequerboard of flowerbeds laid out in the 1570s, to be admired by guests at her sumptuous parties. A hundred years later, Le Nôtre created the schema that exists to this day, of a central axis, *terrasses*, and round and octagonal pools; the sculptures from Versailles and Marly appeared here under Louis XV. During the eighteenth century, the Tuileries were where flash Parisians came to preen and party, and in 1783 a hot air balloon was launched from the gardens, the height and breadth of the overgrown trees no doubt adding a certain *frisson* to the event. The first serious replanting was carried out after the Revolution – a 200-year-old plane tree with a three-metre circumference survives near the octagonal pool. In the nineteenth century, rare species were added to the garden, by then dominated by chestnut trees.

Dryness, disease and parasites, vandalism, lack of care and pollution have taken their toll on the trees of the Tuileries. A long and laborious project is now underway, with the aim of having three thousand healthy trees (of which five hundred will be newly planted) by the year 2000.

Place de la Concorde and the Tuileries

Long home to the state's Impressionist collection, the Jeu de Paume is now a beautifully light space used for temporary shows of contemporary art, usually major retrospectives of established artists, but also, every autumn, more cutting-edge stuff by artists invited for the **Festival d'Automne** (Tues noon–9.30pm, Wed–Fri noon–7pm, Sat & Sun 10am–7pm, closed Mon; 35F/25F). Workers doing the refit claimed to have found an eighteenth-century tennis ball in the rafters – a wild shot from the building's earliest days as a royal tennis court.

The Orangerie's collection of Impressionists includes several of Monet's *Water Lilies*. The gallery is going to be extended and will once again have an *orangerie* with orange and lemon trees as it did in the eighteenth and nineteenth centuries.

The Tuileries gardens themselves are not greatly exciting at the moment, with many areas cordonned off for the huge task of replanting, relandscaping and redecorating with newly cast statues, to be completed, they say, by the end of 1997. At the Louvre end, new box hedges fan out from the central walkway in suitably formal fashion. The odd old tree survives, and Malliol statues of chunky female nudes pose as if under hypnosis.

The Louvre

The *Grand Louvre* project was conceived by Mitterrand when he became president in 1981. He was following in the footsteps of François I, Catherine de Médicis, Louis XIV, Napoléon, and all the other kings, queens and emperors who have added to and altered Philippe-Auguste's original fortress, built to defend the city in 1200.

The world-famous collections of the Louvre are covered in our Museums chapter, on p.276.

Twice in its history the Louvre has nearly been razed to the ground. Bernini, hired by Louis XIV's minister, Colbert, to redesign the palace, wanted to start from scratch, but lost the commission. In the mid-eighteenth century, with the court firmly established at Versailles, the Louvre was taken over by artists and squatters, with a hundred different families living round the Cour Carrée. Louis XV's immediate response to such *lèse-majesté* was to call for the building's destruction, but he was dissuaded by his officials, thereby allowing it to become the scene of his son's humiliation at the hands of revolutionaries in 1790.

Despite various alterations and additions up to 1988, the building is surprisingly homogeneous, although, barring the breathtaking Cour Carrée with its Renaissance grace and Three Musketeers associations, not particularly pretty. Nevertheless, it possesses a grandeur, symmetry and Frenchness entirely suited to this most historic of Parisian edifices.

Then came the **Pyramid**, bang in the centre of the palace in the Cour Napoléon, an extraordinary leap of daring and imagination. The creation of Chinese-born architect Ieoh Ming Pei, it has no connection with its surroundings other than as a symbol of symmetry. And it is a lovely thing, a huge glass pyramid surrounded by a pool and fountains and three smaller pyramids. The view you get as you come out of the Cour Carrée through the Pavillon de l'Horloge is stunning, and at night, illuminated, the Pyramid is pure magic. In years to come it could even rival the Eiffel Tower, a hundred years its senior, as the symbol of the city. It has to be said, though, that the distorted view through the glass of the Pavillon de l'Horloge and the two Napoléon III wings is rather unpleasant, and the poor, pinkish-gold Arc du Carrousel, between the Louvre and the Tuileries, is now forlornly upstaged.

The next part of the *Grand Louvre* project was the **Richelieu wing** on the north side, former home of the Finance Ministry. Its two courtyards have been glassed over and are visible from windows in the Passage Richelieu linking place du Palais-Royal and the Cour Napoléon. You get a better view of Cousteau's famous horses, the *Chevaux de Marly*, and Puget's monumental figures from this public passage than you do from within the museum itself. This *grand projet* is far from finished. All the façades of the palace are being cleaned, the lead replaced on the roofs, and the statues restored. Work is likely to continue for several years.

The other major development is underground – a vast space stretching from the Hall Napoléon, the main entrance to the museum, beneath the Pyramid, to beyond the Arc du Carrousel. Known as the "Espaces Carrousel du Louvre", its central crossroads, place de la Pyramide Inversée, is fed with daylight through a smaller, inverted model of the Pyramid.

From the Hall Napoléon, shops, restaurants, exhibition spaces – and bits of the old fortress's outer defences – make up the cold, classy and commercial "Carrousel du Louvre" gallery. Beyond are several auditoriums and conference halls, car and bus parking areas, and new premises for the Louvre's research department, unique in the world for having its own particle accelerator to examine subatomic bits of works of art and archeological finds.

Before this subterranean complex was created, archeologists excavating here discovered Stone Age tools, remnants of an Iron Age farm growing lentils, peas, fruit and cereals, a house dating from 300 BC and a fourteenth-century manor house complete with wall-paintings and garden.

The Palais Royal

With cars and coaches now banished to the Louvre's new underground car park, **place du Palais-Royal** has become a space for roller bladers, pavement artists and performers. On the north side of the *place*, the **Palais Royal**, originally Richelieu's residence, houses various government and constitutional bodies as well as the

The Palais Royal

Comédie Française, where the classics of French theatre are performed.

The palace gardens to the north were once the gastronomic, gambling and amusement hotspot of Paris. There was even a *café mécanique*, where you sat at a table, sent your order down one of its legs, and were served via the other. The prohibition on public gambling in 1838 put an end to the fun, but the flats above the empty cafés remained desirable lodgings for the likes of Cocteau and of Colette, who died here in 1954.

Folly has returned to the *palais* itself, however, in the form of black and white pillars in different sizes standing above flowing water in the main courtyard. The artist responsible, Daniel Buren, was commissioned in 1982 by Jack Lang, the socialist Minister of Culture. His Chirac-ian successor's decision to let the work go ahead caused paroxysms amongst self-styled guardians of the city's heritage and set an interesting precedent. After a legal wrangle, the court ruled that artists had the right to complete their creations.

Kids use the monochrome Brighton Rock lookalikes as an adventure playground, the best game being to use magnets on strings to fish out coins thrown into the water. Grown-ups perch on the pillars eating their lunch-time sandwiches or reading the paper. Though Buren's work has had many detractors, it has turned what used to be a car park into a popular pedestrian space.

Chapter 4

Right Bank Commerce, the Passages and Les Halles

I n the narrow streets of the 1er and 2e *arrondissements*, between the Louvre and the **Grands Boulevards**, the grandiose financial, cultural and political state institutions are surrounded by well-established commerce centred on the rag trade, newspapers, sex and well-heeled shopping. The most appealing features here are the nineteenth-century **passages** – shopping arcades long predating the concept of pedestrian precincts, with glass roofs, tiled floors and unobtrusive entrances. In contrast, the major department stores are next to the river and up in the 9e *arrondissement*, just north of the gaudy original opera house. For the seriously rich, the boutiques at the western end of the 1er and the streets to either side of the Champs-Élysées, display the wares of every top couturier, jeweller, art dealer and furnisher.

This is the area of Paris that has changed least in the last few decades: a mix of the monumental – the **Bourse**, **Banque de France**, **Bibliothèque Nationale**, the **Madeleine** and **Opéra**; the traditional, typified by the Grands Boulevards with their banks, brasseries and entertainment houses; and the intimate, represented by the passages. It is both very chic and seedy. The great exception is **Les Halles**, once the food market of Paris, which no former trader would recognize. Of all the changes to the city in the last 25 years, the transformation of Les Halles is the least inspired, though it does provide some much-needed greenery and attracts the crowds.

The Grands Boulevards, the Opéra and Madeleine

The **Grands Boulevards** run from the **Madeleine** to République, then down to the Bastille. The western section, from the Madeleine to Porte St-Denis, follows the rampart built by Louis XIII. When its defensive

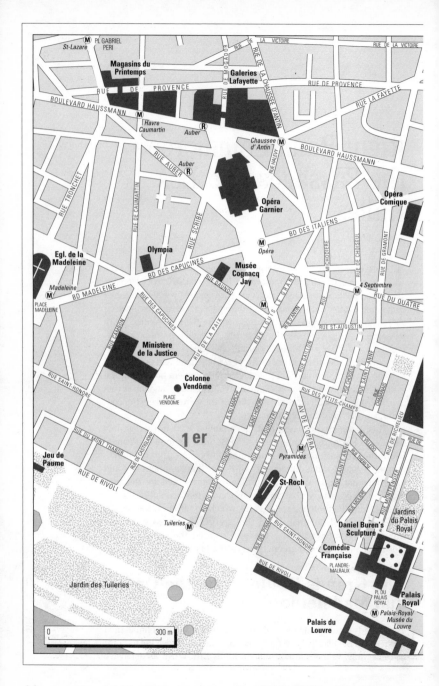

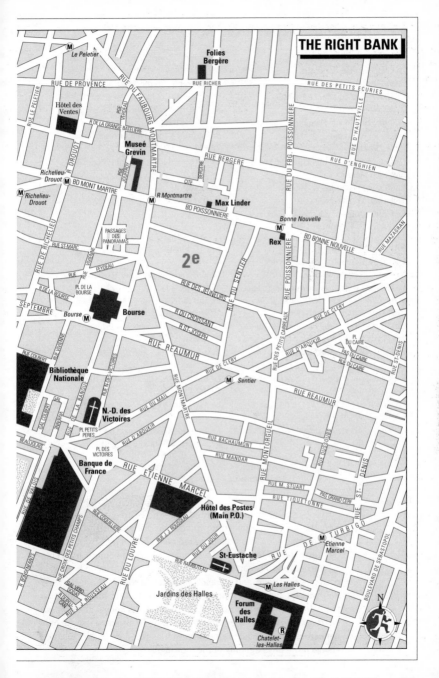

THE RIGHT BANK

Le Peletier

RUE DE PROVENCE

Hôtel des
Ventes

Folies
Bergère

RUE RICHER

RUE DES PETITS ECURIES

Museé
Grevin

RUE BERGERE

RUE D'ENGHIEN

Richelieu-
Drouot

BD MONT MARTRE

Richelieu-
Drouot

R Montmartre

BD POISSONNIERE

Max Linder

Bonne Nouvelle

BD BONNE NOUVELLE

Rex

PASSAGES
DES
PANORAMAS

RUE ST-MARC

2e

RUE DES JEUNEURS

RUE DU SENTIER

SEPTEMBRE

PL DE LA
BOURSE

R DE LA BOURSE

Bourse

Bourse

RUE REAUMUR

R DU CROISSANT

R ST-JOSEPH

RUE DE CLERY

PL
DU CAIRE

RUE DU CAIRE

PAS DU CAIRE

RUE COLBERT

Bibliothèque
Nationale

RUE DE CLERY

Sentier

RUE REAUMUR

N.-D. des
Victoires

PL PETITS
PERES

RUE BACHAUMONT

PL DES
VICTOIRES

Banque de
France

RUE MANDAR

RUE ETIENNE MARCEL

RUE M. STUART

PAS GRAND CERF

RUE TIQUETONNE

Hôtel des Postes
(Main P.O.)

RUE DE TURBIGO

Etienne
Marcel

St-Eustache

RUE RAMBUTEAU

Jardins des Halles

Les Halles

Forum
des
Halles

Chatelet-
les-Halles

N

Right Bank Commerce and the Passages: listings

RESTAURANTS

La Champmeslé, 4 rue Chabanais, 2ᵉ. Mᵒ Pyramides.

Chartier, 7 rue du Faubourg-Montmartre, 9ᵉ. Mᵒ Montmartre.

Country Life, 6 rue Daunou, 2ᵉ. Mᵒ Opéra.

Dilan, 13 rue Mandar, 2ᵉ. Mᵒ Les Halles/Sentier.

Drouot, 103 rue de Richelieu, 2ᵉ. Mᵒ Richelieu-Drouot.

Foujita, 41 rue St-Roch, 1ᵉʳ. Mᵒ Tuileries/Pyramides.

Le Grand Colbert, passage Colbert, rue Vivienne, 2ᵉ. Mᵒ Bourse.

Le Grand Véfour, 17 rue de Beaujolais, 1ᵉʳ. Mᵒ Pyramides/Bourse.

L'Incroyable, 26 rue de Richelieu, 1ᵉʳ. Mᵒ Palais-Royal.

Au Petit Riche, 25 rue Le Peletier, 9ᵉ. Mᵒ Richelieu-Drouot.

Restaurant Végétarien Lacour, 3 rue Villedo, 1ᵉʳ. Mᵒ Pyramides.

La Taverne du Nil, 9 rue du Nil, 2ᵉ. Mᵒ Sentier.

Le Vaudeville, 29 rue Vivienne, 2ᵉ. Mᵒ Bourse.

CAFÉS AND BARS

L'Arbre à Cannelle, 57 passage des Panoramas, 2ᵉ. Mᵒ Rue-Montmartre.

Le Bar de l'Entracte, cnr rue Montpensier & rue Beaujolais, 1ᵉʳ. Mᵒ Palais-Royal/Musée-du-Louvre.

Aux Bons Crus, 7 rue des Petits-Champs, 1ᵉʳ. Mᵒ Palais-Royal.

Le Café, 62 rue Tiquetonne, 2ᵉ. Mᵒ Les Halles/Étienne-Marcel.

Du Croissant, cnr rue du Croissant & rue Montmartre, 2ᵉ. Mᵒ Montmartre.

Le Grand Café Capucines, 4 bd des Capucines, 9ᵉ. Mᵒ Opéra.

Juveniles, 47, rue de Richelieu, 2ᵉ. Mᵒ Palais-Royal.

Kitty O'Shea's, 10 rue des Capucines, 2ᵉ. Mᵒ Opéra.

Lina's Sandwiches, 8 rue Marbeuf, 8ᵉ. Mᵒ Alma-Marceau.

La Muscade, Galerie de Montpensier, 1ᵉʳ. Mᵒ Palais-Royal/Musée du Louvre.

Le Panini, cnr passage des Princes & rue Richelieu, 2ᵉ. Mᵒ Richelieu-Drouot.

Riva Sandwichs, 4 rue du Quatre-Septembre, 2ᵉ. Mᵒ Bourse.

Le Rubis, 10 rue du Marché-St-Honoré, 1ᵉʳ. Mᵒ Pyramides.

Le Tambour, 41 rue Montmartre, 2ᵉ. Mᵒ Sentier.

La Taverne Kronenbourg, 24 bd des Italians, 9ᵉ. Mᵒ Opéra.

These establishments are reviewed in Chapter 13, Eating and drinking, beginning on p.242.

purpose became redundant with the offensive foreign policy of Louis XIV, the walls were pulled down and the ditches filled in, leaving a wide promenade. This was given the name *boulevard* from the military term for the level part of a rampart. In the mid-eighteenth century, the boulevard became a fashionable place to be seen on horseback or in one's carriage, and gradually on which to reside. The eastern section was far more entertaining, with street theatre, mime, juggling, puppets, waxworks and cafés of ill repute. It was known as the *boulevard du Crime*, and inevitably targeted by Haussmann, whose huge new crossroads – place l'Opéra as well as place de la République – changed the physiognomy of the thoroughfare.

In the nineteenth century, the café clientele of the **boulevard des Italiens** set the trends for all of Paris, in terms of manners, dress and what one could gossip about in public. The Grands Boulevards were cobbled; Paris' first horse-drawn omnibus rattled from the Madeleine to the Bastille. From the bourgeois intellectuals in the west to the artisan fun-lovers to the east, this thoroughfare had its finger on the city's pulse. Even forty years ago, a visitor to Paris would, as a matter of course, have gone for a stroll along the Grands Boulevards to see *"Paris vivant"*. And today, for all the desperate traffic pollution and Burger-lands and grills, there are still theatres and cinemas (including the *Max Linder* and *Rex* – an extraordinary building inside and out, see p.356), the waxworks, and numerous brasseries and cafés, which, though not the most fashionable, innovative or amusing, still belong to the tradition of the Grands Boulevards, immortalized in the film *Les Enfants du Paradis*.

It was at 14 **boulevard des Capucines**; in 1895, that Paris first put on a film, or animated photography, as the Lumière brothers' invention was called. An earlier artistic revolution took place at no. 35, where the first **Impressionist exhibition** was shown in Nadar's studio to an outraged art world. As one critic said of Monet's *Impression: Soleil Levant*, "it was worse than anyone had hitherto dared to paint". That was in 1874, just a year before the completion of the city's most preposterous building – the **Opéra de Paris,** now known as the **Opéra Garnier**. Its architect, Charles Garnier, looks suitably foolish in a golden statue on the rue Auber side of his edifice, which so perfectly suited the by-then defunct court of Napoléon III. Excessively ornate and covering three acres, it provided ample space for aristocratic preening, ceremonial pomp and the social intercourse of opera-goers, for whom the performance itself was very much a secondary matter. In order not to mask the vista of the building, the av de l'Opéra, built at the same time, was left deliberately bereft of trees.

By day you can visit the splendidly grand and gilded **interior** (daily 10am–5pm; 30F/18F), including the auditorium – as long as there are no rehearsals (best chance between 1 & 2pm) – whose ceiling is the work of Chagall. The visit includes the **Bibliothèque-Musée de l'Opéra**, containing model sets, dreadful nineteenth-cen-

The Grands Boulevards, the Opéra and Madeleine

Nureyev and the Opéra Garnier

Rudolf Nureyev was director of the Paris Ballet here from 1983 to 1989, and the Opéra presented his last production, *La Bayadère*, with the Kirov, a few months before his death. At his funeral, in January 1993, the steps of the opera house were strewn with white flowers as his coffin was carried up to the foyer, and the orchestra played his favourite piece by Bach. This was Nureyev's home, the venue for his first performance in the West, and the place in which he took refuge after defecting from the Soviet Union in 1961. He is buried in the Russian Orthodox cemetery outside Paris in St-Geneviève-du-Bois.

tury paintings, and rather better temporary exhibitions on operatic themes. The classic horror movie, *The Phantom of the Opera*, was set, though never filmed, here; a real underground stream lends credence to the tale.

To the north of the Opéra, on the barren bd du Haussmann, are two of the city's department stores: **Magasins du Printemps** and **Galeries Lafayette** (opposite the Paris branch of *Marks & Spencer*). Though they still possess their proud, *fin-de-siècle* glass domes, much of the beauty of their interiors has been hacked away.

Southwest of the Opéra, the **church of the Madeleine** is an obese Napoleonic structure on the classical temple model, ordered by the emperor as yet another monument to the glory of his army. A popular venue for society weddings, it provides a perspective across place de la Concorde. Along the east side of the church, a **flower market** lays out its wares every day except Monday, and there's a luxurious **Art Nouveau loo** by the métro at the junction of place and bd de la Madeleine. But it is for rich gourmets and window-gazers that the place de la Madeleine holds the most appeal. In the northeast corner, at *Fauchon's*, are two blocks of the best food display in Paris, and, down the west side, you'll find the smaller *Hédiard's*, as well as caviar, truffle and spirit specialists.

Extensive listings of Parisian food shops can be found on p.329.

Boulevard des Italiens, running south of bd Haussmann from the Opéra to Richelieu-Drouot, has a fine selection of banking buildings. The *Crédit Lyonnais* (which broke records in 1994 for losing money) has its head branch at no. 19, with a huge gold clock surrounded by gigantic women in flowing disarray. Golden balconies and hunting friezes from the 1840s restaurant *Maison Dorée*, at no. 20, have been preserved by the *Banque Nationale Populaire*, and are on display next door to its sleek 1930s main building at no. 16.

The Passages, Palais-Royal garden and Bibliothèque Nationale

Conceived by town planners in the nineteenth century to give pedestrians protection from mud and horse-drawn vehicles, the **Passages** are enjoying a new lease of life as havens from today's far more dangerous traffic. For decades they were left to crumble and decay, and it was only very recently that the charms of walking on beautiful floors in a watery light, secluded from the mayhem of the city's streets, were rediscovered. Many, though by no means all, have now been renovated and returned to their original chic and immaculate state – with mega-premiums on their leases. Their entrances, however, remain easy to miss, and where you emerge at the other end can be quite a surprise. Many are closed at night and on Sundays.

The most homogeneous and aristocratic of the *passages*, with painted ceilings and panelled shop fronts divided by black marble

The
Passages,
Palais-Royal
garden and
Bibliothèque
Nationale

columns, is **Galerie Véro-Dodat** (between rue Croix-des-Petits-Champs and rue Jean-Jacques Rousseau; Mº Palais-Royal/Musée-du-Louvre), named after the two pork butchers who set it up in 1824. It is still a little dilapidated, with peeling paint on many of the shop fronts, and the recession sealed the fate of several old businesses. But at no. 26, Monsieur Capia still keeps a collection of antique dolls in a shop piled high with miscellaneous curios.

The **Banque de France** lies a short way northeast of Galerie Véro-Dodat. Rather than negotiating its massive bulk to reach the *passages* further north, it's more pleasant to walk through the **garden of the Palais Royal** via place de Valois. **Galerie de Valois**, the arcade on the east side of the garden, has an exquisite purple-panelled *parfumerie, Les Salons du Palais Royal Shiseido*, at no. 142. Rue de Montpensier, running alongside the gardens to the west, is connected to rue de Richelieu by several tiny *passages*, of which Hulot brings you out at the statue of Molière on the junction of rues Richelieu and Molière. A certain charm also lurks about rue de Beaujolais, bordering the northern end of the gardens, with its corner café looking on the Théâtre du Palais-Royal, glimpses into *Le Grand Véfour* restaurant, and more short arcades leading up to rue des Petits-Champs.

On the other side of rue des Petits-Champs, just to the left as you come from rue de Beaujolais, looms the forbidding wall of the **Bibliothèque Nationale**, the French equivalent of the British Museum library, soon to have an additional home in the 13e (see p.152). Visiting its temporary exhibitions (closed Mon) will give you access to some of the more beautiful parts of the building, the **Galerie Mazarin** in particular, and you can also pay to see a display of coins and ancient treasures (Mon–Sat 1–5pm; 20F/12F). There's no restriction on entering the library, nor on peering into the atmospheric reading rooms. Researchers take their cigarette and sandwich breaks in a courtyard on rue Vivienne, in a corner of which stands a statue of Jean-Paul Sartre, his mind clearly unaware of his feet.

The library owns **Galerie Colbert**, one of two very upmarket *passages* linking rue Vivienne with rue des Petits-Champs. Gorgeously lit by bunches of bulbous lamps, Galerie Colbert hosts free temporary exhibitions of the library's treasures, and also contains an expensive 1830s-style brasserie, *Le Grand Colbert*, to which senior librarians and rich academics retire for lunch. The flamboyant décor of Grecian and marine motifs in the larger **Galerie Vivienne** establishes the perfect ambience in which to buy Jean-Paul Gaultier gear, or you can browse in the antiquarian bookshop, *Librairie Jousseaume*, which dates back to the *passage*'s earliest days.

Three blocks west of the Bibliothèque Nationale is a totally different style of passage. Just like a regular high street, the **passage Choiseul**, between rue des Petits-Champs and rue St-Augustin (and

The
Passages,
Palais-Royal
garden and
Bibliothèque
Nationale

connected to rue Ste-Anne by passage Ste-Anne), has take-away food, cheap clothes shops, stationers and bars, plus a few arty outlets along its chequerboard tiled length of almost 200m.

For a combination of old-fashioned chic and workaday you need to explore the **passage des Panoramas**, the grid of arcades north of the Bibliothèque Nationale, beyond rue St-Marc, though they are still in need of a little repair and there are no fancy mosaics for your feet. Most of the eateries make no pretence at style, but one old brasserie, *L'Arbre à Cannelle*, has fantastic carved wood panelling, and there are still bric-a-brac shops, stamp dealers and an upper-crust printshop with its original 1867 fittings. It was around the Panoramas, in 1817, that the first Parisian gas lamps were tried out.

In **passage Jouffroy**, across bd Montmartre, a M. Segas sells walking canes and theatrical antiques opposite a shop displaying every conceivable fitting and furnishing for a doll's house. Near the romantic *Hôtel Chopin*, Paul Vulin spreads his second-hand books along the passageway, and *Ciné-Doc* serves cinephiles. Crossing rue de la Grange-Batelière, you enter **passage Verdeau**, where a few of the old postcard and camera dealers still trade alongside smart new art galleries and purveyors of expensive pens, *Stylos Sénanques*.

At the top of rue Richelieu, the tiny **passage des Princes**, with its beautiful glass ceiling, stained glass decoration and twirly lamps, has finally been restored, but any potential charm has been lost in the fast food chains and mundane shops. Its erstwhile neighbour, the passage de l'Opéra, described in surreal detail by Louis Aragon in *Paris Peasant*, was eaten up by the completion of Haussmann's boulevards – a project that demolished scores of old *passages*.

While in this area, you could also take a look at what's up for auction at the Paris equivalent of *Christie's* and *Sotheby's*, the **Hôtel Drouot** (9 rue Drouot; Mo Le Pelletier/Richelieu-Drouot). Details of the auctions are announced in listings magazines such as *Pariscope*, under the heading "*Ventes aux Enchères*", and in the press. To spare any fear of unintended hand movements landing you in the bankruptcy courts, you can wander round looking at the goods before the action starts (11am–6pm on the eve of the sale, 11am–noon on the day itself).

Returning to the 2e *arrondissement*, close to métro Étienne-Marcel, the three-storey **Grand-Cerf**, between rue St-Denis and rue Dessoubs, is stylistically the best of all the *passages*. The wrought-iron work, glass roof and plain-wood shop fronts have all been cleaned, but it's not the liveliest and has yet to attract its full complement of clients. As you exit from the passage du Grand-Cerf at rue Dessoubs you're faced with a mural entitled *La Ville Imaginaire*, inspired by Robert Mallet-Stevens. Fortunately this urban vision is not what's intended for the Montorgueil-St-Denis *quartier*, which is now pedestrianized, its streets recobbled and fitted out with bollards, new rubbish bins and street signs.

Mallet-Stevens, a Cubist architect and contemporary of Le Corbusier, designed the entire rue Mallet-Stevens; see p.201.

Clothes, Sex, the Stock Exchange and News

Mass-produced clothing is the business of **place du Caire**, the centre of the rag-trade district. The frenetic trading and deliveries of cloth, the food market on **rue des Petits-Carreaux**, and the general toing and froing make a lively change from the office-bound *quartiers* further west. Beneath an extraordinary pseudo-Egyptian façade of grotesque Pharaonic heads (a celebration of Napoléon's conquest of Egypt), an archway opens onto a series of arcades, the **passage du Caire**. These, contrary to any visible evidence, are the oldest of all the *passages* and entirely monopolized by wholesale clothes shops.

The garment business gets progressively more upmarket westwards from the trade area. The upper end of **rue Étienne-Marcel**, and Louis XIV's **place des Victoires**, adjoined to the north by the appealingly asymmetrical **place des Petits-Pères**, are centres for designer clothes, with window displays to deter all those without the necessary funds. The boutiques on **rue St-Honoré** and its Faubourg extension beyond rue Royale have the established names, and are paralleled across the Champs-Élysées by those on **rue François-1er**, where Dior occupies at least four blocks on the corner with av Montaigne. *Pierre Marly*, the optician's at 380 rue St-Honoré, contains a small museum dedicated to its craft (see p.293), and *Hermès*, at 24 rue du Faubourg-St-Honoré, displays a small collection of its original saddlery items. The **place Vendôme**, with Napoléon high on a column clad with recycled Austro-Russian cannons, caters for the same wallet. Here you have all the fashionable accessories for *haute*

Notable buildings in the 1er, 2e and 8e arrondissements

• **124 rue Réamur**, 2e, just east of rue Montmartre. M° Sentier.
Almost entirely metal with Art Nouveau curves, these industrial premises were probably the first to make a feature of structure by revealing riveted steel girders on the façade. Attributed to Georges Chedane, 1905.

• **Théâtre des Champs-Élysées**, 15 av Montaigne, 8e. M° Alma-Marceau.
Gold and gleaming white marble plus sculptures by Bourdelle cover this concrete creation of Auguste Perret and Henry van de Velde from 1913.

• **Mural**, cnr Penthièvre and av Delcassé, 8e. M° St-Philippe-du-Roule/Miromesnil.
If you look north down av Matignon from rue du Faubourg-St-Honoré, you'll see a nineteenth-century apartment block painted by J. C. Decaux above two large clocks and rolling billboards.

• **Tour Jean Sans Peur**, 20 rue Étienne-Marcel, 2e. M° Étienne-Marcel.
A fortified tower built in 1408 on Philippe Auguste's city walls.

• **34 avenue Matignon**, 8e M° Miromesnil.
Green Atlases sculpted by Babinel hold up the glass frontage. Designed by Fernier, 1992.

couture – jewellery and perfumes – plus the original *Ritz*, various banks, and the Law and Order ministry.

After clothes, bodies are the most evident commodity on sale in the 1er and 2e *arrondissements*. Rue St-Denis has been the red-light district of Paris for centuries, and attempts by the 2e *arrondissement mairie* to rid the street of its pimps and prostitutes have been to no avail; despite pedestrianizing the area between rues Étienne-Marcel and Réaumur (to stop kerb-crawling) and encouraging cafés like the English *Frog and Rosbif* to move in among the porn outlets, weary women still wait in every doorway between peepshows, striptease joints and sex video shops. Around rue Ste-Anne, business is gay, transvestite and under-age. It's also a notorious spot for heroin hustlers. Such are the libertarian delights of Paris streetlife.

In the centre of the 2^e stands the **Bourse**, the Paris stock exchange, which finally caught up with information technology in the late 1980s (long after the real financial sharks had decamped elsewhere to do their deals). Guided visits, which attempt to equate the business here with London, Tokyo or New York, are not worth the 30F admission fee. A far more convincing impression of efficiency and dynamism is given by the antennae-topped building of the French news agency, *AFP*, which overshadows the Bourse from the south. Rue Réaumur, running east from here, used to be the Fleet Street of Paris, but now only *Le Figaro*'s central offices remain, on the junction of rue Montmartre and rue du Louvre, alongside a mural of tulips laid across newspaper cuttings.

Rues Montmartre, Mongorgueil and Turbigo, leading south from rue Réaumur, begin to concentrate on food as they approach Les Halles. Strictly not for vegetarians, the shops and stalls here feature wild boar, deer and feathered friends, alongside *pâté de foie gras* and caviar. Also on sale is equipment for professional chefs (see p.332).

Les Halles

In 1969 the main **Les Halles market** was moved out to the suburbs after more than eight hundred years in the heart of the city. There was widespread opposition to the destruction of Victor Baltard's nineteenth-century pavilions, and considerable disquiet at what renovation of the area would mean. The authorities' excuse was the *RER* and métro interchange they had to have below. Digging began in 1971, and the hole was only finally filled at the end of the 1980s. Hardly any trace remains of the working-class quarter, with its night bars and bistros for the market traders. Nowadays, rents rival the 16e, and the all-night places serve and profit from salaried and speed-popping types. Les Halles is constantly promoted as the hotspot of Paris, where the cool and famous congregate. In fact, anyone with any sense and money hangs out in the traditional bourgeois

LES HALLES TO BEAUBOURG

quartiers to the west – many of the people mulling about here are up from the suburbs with little or no cash to spend.

From Châtelet-Les Halles *RER*, you surface only after ascending from levels -4 to 0 of the **Forum des Halles** centre, which stretches underground from the Bourse du Commerce rotunda to rue Pierre-Lescot. The overground section comprises aquarium-like arcades of shops, enclosed by glass buttocks, with white steel creases sliding down to an imprisoned patio. To temper all this commerce, poetry, arts and crafts pavilions top two sides in a simple construction – save for the mirrors – that just manages to be out of sync with the curves and hollows below.

Les Halles

*Further details
of the subter-
ranean
delights of the
Forum can be
found in
Chapter 15.*

The gardens have begun to outgrow their protective wire cages and the green space is providing a welcome if crowded respite. On the north side, in front of St-Eustache, the statue of a giant head and hand suggests the dislocation of this place. Beneath the garden, amidst the shops, there's scope for various diversions – swimming, games of billiards, discovering Paris through videos, movie-going, and photography and hologram exhibitions.

After a spate of multi-levels, air-conditioning and artificial light, however, it's a relief to enter the high Gothic and Renaissance space of St-Eustache. From its pulpit, during the Commune, a woman "preached" the abolition of marriage; and in the Chapelle St-Joseph, a naive fresco, entitled *Le départ des fruits et légumes du coeur de Paris, le 28 février 1969*, depicts the area's more recent history.

For an antidote to steel and glass troglodytism, you can join the throng around the **Fontaine des Innocents**, and admire the water cascading down its perfect Renaissance proportions. Clowns imitating your movements for the amusement of everyone else are a regular hazard – or a delight, when you're not the victim.

*Music listings
for the area
around place
du Châtelet
can be found
in Chapter 18.*

There are always hundreds of people around the Forum, filling in time, hustling, or just loafing about. Pickpocketing and sexual harassment are pretty routine; the law plus canine arm are often in evidence, and at night it can be quite tense. The streets on the eastern side have plenty of cafés for breaks from the shoving crowds, while the area southwards to **place du Châtelet** teems with jazz bars,

---

Les Halles to Beaubourg: listings

RESTAURANTS

Aux Deux Saules, 91 rue St-Denis, 1er. M° Châtelet-Les Halles.

La Fresque, 100 rue Rambuteau, 1er. M° Étienne-Marcel/Les Halles.

L'Ostrea, 4 rue Sauval, 1er. M° Louvre-Rivoli/Châtelet.

Le Petit Ramoneur, 74 rue St-Denis, 1er. M° Châtelet-Les Halles.

Au Pied de Cochon, 6 rue Coquillière, 1er. M° Châtelet-Les Halles.

La Tour de Montlhéry (Chez Denise), 5 rue des Prouvaires, 1er. M° Louvre-Rivoli/Châtelet.

CAFÉS AND BARS

À la Cloche des Halles, 28 rue Coquillière, 1er. M° Châtelet-Les Halles/Louvre.

Le Cochon à l'Oreille, 15 rue Montmartre, 1er. M° Châtelet-Les Halles/Étienne-Marcel.

L'Eustache, 37 rue Berger, 1er. M° Les Halles.

Palabres, 44 rue St-Honoré, 1er. M° Louvre-Rivoli/Châtelet.

Au Père Tranquille, cnr of rues Pierre-Lescot and des Pécheurs, 1er. M° Châtelet-Les Halles.

Au Pomelle, 19 rue du Roule, 1er. M° Louvre-Rivoli.

Self-Service de La Samaritaine, *Magasin 2*, rue de la Monnaie, 1er. M° Pont-Neuf.

Le Sous-Bock, 49 rue St-Honoré, 1er. M° Châtelet-Les Halles.

Au Trappiste, 4 rue St-Denis, 1er. M° Châtelet.

These establishments are reviewed in Chapter 13, Eating and drinking, p.244.

South of Les Halles

There's a labyrinth of tiny streets to explore between the Fontaine des Innocents and place du Châtelet, once the site of a notorious fortress prison, now a maelstrom of Parisian traffic overlooked by two grand theatres, the **Théâtre Musicale de Paris** and the **Théâtre de la Ville**. On the quayside, whose name (*Mégisserie*) refers to the treatment of skins in medieval times when this was an area of abattoirs, there are now plants and miserable pets for sale. Further along the riverfront, towards the Louvre, the three blocks of **La Samaritaine** (Mon & Tues, Fri & Sat 9.30am–7pm, Wed 9.30am–10.30pm, Thurs 9.30am–10pm) recall the days when art, not marketing psychology, determined the decoration of a department store. The building, now completely restored, was built in 1903 in pure Art Nouveau style, with gold, green, and glass exteriors, and, inside, brightly painted wrought-iron staircases and balconies against huge backdrops of ceramic floral patterns. Best of all is the view from the roof (take the lift to floor nine in *Magasin 2* and then walk up two flights) – the most central high location in the city.

Chapter 5

Beaubourg, the Marais, Île St-Louis and the Bastille

The **Centre Beaubourg** (or Pompidou Centre), a few blocks away from Les Halles across bd Sébastopol, was a radical architectural breakthrough for its period – the 1970s – and is an enduring, popular focus for the Right Bank of the city. The **quartier Beaubourg** is full of art galleries and cafés, and is as lively as Les Halles by day and night.

The **Marais**, to the east, and the **Île St-Louis** are the loveliest areas of central Paris. The aristocratic mansions, medieval lanes, Jewish quarter and plethora of small, appealing restaurants, shops and cafés have no major thoroughfares to disturb them.

The **Bastille** used to belong in spirit and in style to the working-class districts of eastern Paris. Since the building of the new opera house, however, it has become as fashionable a *quartier* as the Marais, and very much one of Paris' central hotspots.

The interior spaces may be changed as the building undergoes extensive restoration work.

Beaubourg

For years after its opening in 1977, the **Centre Beaubourg** – the **Georges Pompidou National Art and Culture Centre** – was notorious as Paris' most outrageous building. The novel concept of architects Renzo Piano and Richard Rogers was to put all the infrastructure on the outside, leaving maximum space for the interior. Painted in bright colours and with no monumental entrance – just a large, sloping plaza for buskers, magicians, clowns and anyone else to use as their stage – it was designed, in Rogers' words, as "horizontal streets in the air". Talking about the building in 1994, he said, "It's actually a reflection of 1968. I wouldn't have said this in 1971 when we did it, but looking back, I realize how much a reflection it was of my belief in being able to create a people's place. Our report presented it as 'a place for all peoples, all creeds, all colours; a place for old and young'. We searched out things that were not specifically in the brief, areas for old people to be warm and read the newspaper and so on. We designed so that activities could overlap. We thought breadth of choice was very much part of a people's institution."

Geared for 6000 visitors a day, it has seen more in the region of 25,000 – proof of its outstanding success as a non-elitist cultural centre. But the overload of visitors and corrosion in the exterior steel has taken its toll. Major renovation work is underway on both the exterior and interior of the Centre, and the plaza itself is being revamped. Parts of the building are being closed off, and the whole complex is almost certain to be shut from October 1997.

Beaubourg

Inside the Centre

The Centre is open every weekday except Tuesday from noon to 10pm, and at weekends from 10am to 10pm; admission is free except for charges to the exhibitions and art museum. The top floor of the Centre is the venue for big exhibitions lasting several months; other spaces for temporary exhibitions are dedicated to architecture, industrial design, graphic arts and single artists. The **Musée d'Art Moderne** (see p.285) takes up the fourth floor and part of the third; the **Bibliothèque Publique d'Information** (BPI), where you can consult books, tapes, videos and international newspapers for free, spreads from the ground floor to the second. There's a cinema, a cyber café, art shops for posters, books and postcards, play areas for children . . . enough, in fact, to keep you busy for several days.

The **escalator** is usually one long queue, but you should ride up this glass intestine at least once. As the circles of spectators on the plaza recede, a horizontal skyline appears: the Sacré-Coeur, St-Eustache, the Eiffel Tower, Notre-Dame, the Panthéon, the Tour St-Jacques with its solitary gargoyle, and La Défense menacing in the distance. From the platform at the top you can look down on the château-style chimneys of the Hôtel de Ville, with their flowerpot off-spring sprouting all over the lower rooftops.

Quartier Beaubourg and the Hôtel de Ville

The **visual entertainments** around Beaubourg are engagingly diverse. There's the clanking gold *Défenseur du Temps* clock in the Quartier de l'Horloge; a *trompe-l'œil*, as you look west along rue Aubry-le-Boucher from Beaubourg; a nine-digit timepiece counting down by milliseconds to the year 2000 on the right-hand side of the centre; and colourful sculptures and fountains by Niki Tinguely and Nicky de St-Phalle in the pool in front of **Église St-Merri**. This water-work pays homage to Stravinsky and shows scant respect for passers-by; beneath it lies *IRCAM*, a research centre for contemporary music, whose overground extension by Renzo Piano is being extended.

The activites of IRCAM are described on p.351.

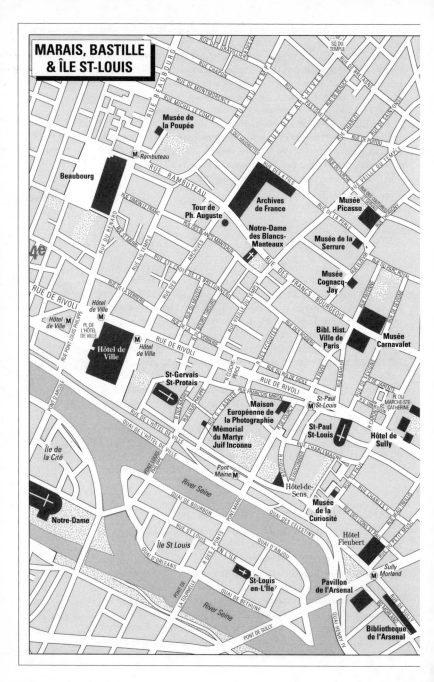

MARAIS, BASTILLE & ÎLE ST-LOUIS

RUE DES GRAVILLIERS
SQ DU TEMPLE
RUE CHAPON
RUE DE BRETAGNE
RUE DE MONTMORENCY
RUE BEAUBOURG
RUE DU TEMPLE
RUE MICHEL LE COMTE
RUE DES ARCHIVES
RUE PASTOURELLE
RUE DE BEAUCE
RUE CHARLOT
RUE DE SAINTONGE
RUE DE POITOU

Musée de la Poupée

RUE DES HAUDRIETTES

M. Rambuteau

RUE RAMBUTEAU

Beaubourg

RUE DES 4 FILS
RUE DU PERCHE
RUE DE LA PERLE
RUE DE BRETAGNE
RUE VIEILLE DU TEMPLE
RUE DES COUTURES ST-GERVAIS
RUE DEBELLEYME
RUE DE THORIGNY

RUE SIMON LE FRANC
Tour de Ph. Auguste
RUE DES BLANCS MANTEAUX
Archives de France
Musée Picasso
Notre-Dame des Blancs-Manteaux
Musée de la Serrure

RUE DU RENARD
RUE ST-MERRI
RUE DU TEMPLE
ARCHIVES
RUE STE-CROIX DE LA BRETONNERIE
RUE DES FRANCS BOURGEOIS
RUE PAYENNE
RUE ELZEVIR
RUE DU PARC ROYAL

4e

Musée Cognacq-Jay

RUE DE RIVOLI
RUE DE LA VERRERIE
RUE DE LA VERRERIE
Hôtel de Ville
RUE DU TEMPLE
RUE DES GUILLEMITES
RUE VIEILLE DU TEMPLE
RUE DES ROSIERS
RUE DE SÉVIGNÉ

Hôtel de Ville M

RUE PONT LOUIS PHILIPPE
RUE MOUSSY
RUE DES ÉCOUFFES
RUE PAVÉE
RUE MALHER
Bibl. Hist. Ville de Paris
Musée Carnavalet

PL DE L'HÔTEL DE VILLE
Hôtel de Ville M
RUE DE RIVOLI
R. CLOCHE PERCE
RUE DU ROI DE SICILE
R. DE SÉVIGNÉ

Hôtel de Ville
RUE DE RIVOLI
St-Gervais St-Protais
RUE FRANÇOIS MIRON
RUE FRANCE
RUE DE TURENNE
PL DE LA BASTILLE
PL DU MARCHÉ-STE-CATHERINE
RUE DE JARENTE
R.D. ORMESSON

PONT D'ARCOLE
RUE DES BARRES
RUE PONT LOUIS PHILIPPE
RUE DE FOURCY
St-Paul M *St-Louis*
RUE CARON
RUE DE SÉVIGNÉ
RUE ST-ANTOINE

QUAI DE L'HÔTEL DE VILLE
Maison Européenne de la Photographie
Mémorial du Martyr Juif Inconnu
St-Paul St-Louis
RUE DE JOUY
RUE CHARLEMAGNE
Hôtel de Sully
R. DE TURENNE
R. ST-PAUL

Île de la Cité

RUE DE L'AVE MARIA
RUE DES JARDINS ST-PAUL
RUE CHARLEMAGNE
Hôtel Fieubert
RUE CHARLES V
RUE BEAUTREILLIS
RUE ST-PAUL
RUE DU PETIT MUSC

PONT LOUIS PHILIPPE
Pont Mairie M
Hôtel-de-Sens

River Seine
QUAI DE BOURBON
PONT MARIE
QUAI DES CÉLESTINS
Musée de la Curiosité

Notre-Dame

RUE ST-LOUIS
Île St Louis
RUE DES 2 PONTS
EN L'ILE
QUAI D'ANJOU
RUE CHARLES V
RUE DES LIONS ST-PAUL

QUAI D'ORLÉANS
RUE ST-LOUIS EN L'ILE
St-Louis en-L'Île
QUAI DE BÉTHUNE
Pavillon de l'Arsenal
Sully Morland M
BD MORLAND

PONT DE LA TOURNELLE
PONT DE SULLY
River Seine
QUAI HENRI IV
Bibliothèque de l'Arsenal

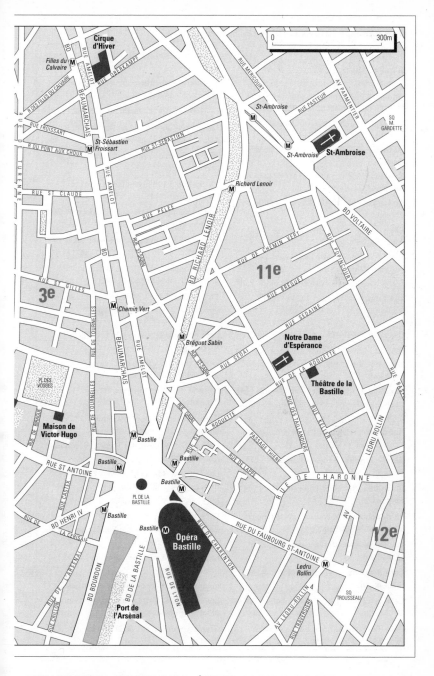

The Marais, Bastille and Île St-Louis: listings

RESTAURANTS

L'Ambroisie, 9 place Vosges, 4e. Mo Chemin-Vert/St-Paul.

Aquarius 1, 54 rue Ste-Croix-de-la-Bretonnerie, 4e. Mo St-Paul/Rambuteau.

Auberge de Jarente, 7 rue Jarente, 4e. Mo St-Paul.

Bofinger, 3–7 rue de la Bastille, 3e. Mo Bastille.

La Canaille, 4 rue Crillon, 4e. Mo Sully-Morland/Bastille.

Le Castafiore, 51 rue St-Louis-en-l'Île, 4e. Mo Pont-Marie.

Chez Jenny, 39 bd du Temple, 3e. Mo Filles-du-Calvaire.

Chez Nénesse, 17 rue Saintonge, 3e. Mo Arts-et-Métiers.

L'Excuse, 14 rue Charles-V, 4e. Mo St-Paul.

Les Fous d'en Face, 3 rue du Bourg-Tibourg, 4e. Mo Hôtel-de-Ville.

CAFÉS AND BARS

L'Apparemment Café, 18 rue des Coutures-St-Gervais, 3e. Mo St-Sébastien-Froissart.

Bar Central, 33 rue Vieille-du-Temple (cnr rue Ste-Croix-de-la-Bretonnerie), 4e. Mo St-Paul.

Bar des Ferrailleurs, 18 rue de Lappe, 11e. Mo Bastille.

Bar de Jarente, 5 rue de Jarente, 4e. Mo St-Paul.

Berthillon, 31 rue St-Louis-en-l'Île, 4e. Mo Pont-Marie.

Le Bouchon du Marais, 15 rue François-Miron, 4e. Mo St-Paul.

Ma Bourgogne, 19 place des Vosges, 3e. Mo St-Paul.

Café Beaubourg, 43 rue St-Merri, 4e. Mo Rambuteau.

Café de l'Industrie, 16 rue St-Sabin, 11e. Mo Bastille.

Café des Phares, 7 place de la Bastille (west side), 4e. Mo Bastille.

Goldenberg's, 7 rue des Rosiers, 4e. Mo St-Paul.

Le Gourmet de l'Île, 42 rue St-Louis-en-l'Île, 4e. Mo Pont-Marie.

Le Grizli, 7 rue St-Martin, 4e. Mo Châtelet.

Le Marais-Cage, 8 rue de Beauce, 3e. Mo Arts-et-Métiers/Filles-du-Calvaire.

Piccolo Teatro, 6 rue des Écouffes, 4e. Mo St-Paul.

Pitchi-Poï, 7 rue Caron (cnr place du Marché-Ste-Catherine), 4e. Mo St-Paul.

Le Quincampe, 78 rue Quincampoix, 3e. Mo Étienne-Marcel/Rambuteau/*RER* Châtelet.

Le Ravaillac, 10 rue du Roi-de-Sicile, 4e. Mo St-Paul.

Thai Elephant, 43–45 rue de la Roquette, 11e. Mo Bastille/Richard-Lenoir.

La Truffe, 31 rue Vieille-du-Temple, 4e. Mo St-Paul.

Café de la Plage, 59 rue de Charonne, 11e. Mo Bastille.

Le Coude Fou, 12 rue du Bourg-Tibourg, 4e. Mo Hôtel-de-Ville.

Cyberia, Centre Pompidou. Mo Rambuteau.

Dame Tartine, 2 rue Brise-Miche, 4e. Mo Rambuteau/Hôtel-de-Ville.

L'Ébouillanté, 6 rue des Barres, 4e. Mo Hôtel-de-Ville.

Les Enfants Gâtés, 43 rue des Francs-Bourgeois, 4e. Mo St-Paul.

L'Enoteca, 25 rue Charles-V, 4e. Mo St-Paul.

Épices et Délices, 53 rue Vieille-du-Temple, 4e. Mo St-Paul.

La Fontaine, 1 rue de Charonne, 11e. Mo Bastille.

Fouquet's, 130 rue de Lyon, 12e. Mo Bastille.

Les Fous de l'Île, 33 rue des Deux-Ponts, 4e. Mo Pont-Marie.

Grand Appetit, 9 rue de la Cerisaie, 4e. Mo Bastille.

Havanita Café, 11 rue de Lappe, 11e. M° Bastille.

Iguana, 15 rue de la Roquette (cnr rue Daval), 11e. M° Bastille.

Pause Café, 41 rue de Charonne (cnrr rue Keller), 11e. M° Ledru-Rollin.

La Perla, 26 rue François-Miron (cnr rue du Pont-Louis-Philippe), 4e. M° St-Paul.

Au Petit Fer à Cheval, 30 rue Vieille-du-Temple, 4e. M° St-Paul.

Le Petit Marcel, 63 rue Rambuteau, 3e. M° Rambuteau.

Le Pick-Clops, 16 rue Vieille-du-Temple, 4e. M° Hôtel-de-Ville.

Le Quetzal, 10 rue de la Verrerie (cnr rue Moussy), 4e. M° St-Paul.

Le Rouge Gorge, 8 rue St-Paul, 4e. M° St-Paul.

Sacha Finkelsztajn, 27 rue des Rosiers & 24 rue des Écouffes, 4e. Both M° St-Paul.

Le St-Régis, 92 rue St-Louis-en-l'Île, 4e. M° Pont-Marie.

SanZSanS, 49 rue du Faubourg-St-Antoine, 11e. M° Bastille.

Les Taillandeurs, 22 rue des Taillandeurs, 11e. M° Ledru-Rollin.

La Tartine, 24 rue de Rivoli, 4e. M° St-Paul.

Le Taxi Jaune, 13 rue Chapon, 3e. M° Arts-et-Métiers.

Le Temps des Cerises, 31 rue de la Cerisaie, 4e. M° Bastille.

Le Trumilou, 84 quai Hôtel-de-Ville 4e. M° Pont-Marie.

Le Volcan de Sicile, 62 rue du Roi-de-Sicile, 4e. M° Hôtel-de-Ville.

Web Bar, 32 rue de Picardie, 3e. M° Filles-du-Calvaire.

Yahalom, 22–24 rue des Rosiers, 4e. M° St-Paul.

Le Zinc, 4 rue Caron, 4e. M° St-Paul.

These establishments are reviewed in Chapter 13, Eating and drinking, p.247.

Commercial art galleries in the quartier Beaubourg, where you can browse to your heart's content for free, are concentrated north of rue Aubry-le-Boucher on **rue Quincampoix**, a narrow picturesque street offering respite from the Beaubourg crowds. Just over rue Renard to the east, in a sixteenth-century mansion on rue St-Merri, the *Galerie Maeght*, run by the Maeght Foundation in St-Paul-de-Vence, sells works by Miró, Picasso, Giacometti and contemporaries, plus its own beautifully printed art books.

Rue Renard runs down to **place de l'Hôtel de Ville**, where the oppressively gleaming and gargantuan mansion is the seat of the city's local government and one whole floor the private apartment of the mayor. An illustrated history of this edifice, always a prime target in riots and revolutions, is displayed along the platform of the Châtelet métro on the Neuilly–Vincennes line.

Those opposed to the establishments of kings and emperors created their alternative municipal governments at this building in 1789, 1848 and 1870. The poet Lamartine proclaimed the Second Republic here in 1848, and Gambetta the third in 1870. But, with the defeat of the Commune in 1871, the conservatives, in control once again, concluded that the Parisian municipal authority had to go, if order, property, morality and the suppression of the working class were to be maintained. For the next hundred years, Paris was ruled directly by the national government.

Beaubourg

The next head of an independent municipality after the leaders of the Commune was **Jacques Chirac**, who became mayor in 1977. He ran Paris as his own fiefdom, with scant regard for other councillors. He even retained the mayorship while he was prime minister – a power base unequalled in French politics – and when he became president, he more or less nominated his successor, Jean Tiberi.

But whatever the political stakes, whatever the personal motives, Paris all too obviously enjoys dynamic local government: a shaming and glaring contrast to the shabby disenfranchizement of London.

The Marais

The **Marais** today comprises most of the 3^e and 4^e **arrondissements**. Yet until the thirteenth century, when the Knights Templar set up house in its northern section, now known as the **quartier du Temple**, and began to drain the land, it was an uninhabitable riverside swamp – *marais* is the French for "swamp". The grand and aristocratic character that has become its hallmark was not acquired until around 1600, when the area became the object of royal patronage, especially after the construction of the place des Vosges – or place Royale, as it then was – by Henri IV in 1605.

Its apogee was relatively short-lived, for the aristocracy began to move away after the king removed his court to Versailles in the latter part of the seventeenth century, leaving their mansions to the trading classes, who were in turn displaced during the Revolution. Thereafter, the masses moved in. The mansions were transformed into multi-occupied slum tenements. Their fabric decayed and the streets degenerated into unserviced squalor – and stayed that way until the 1960s.

Since then, however, gentrification has proceeded apace, and the quarter is now a sought-after enclave for media, arty and gay Parisians. Renovated mansions, their grandeur concealed by the narrow streets, have become museums, libraries, offices and chic flats, flanked by shops selling designer clothes, house and garden accoutrements, works of art and one-off trinkets. Nonetheless, having largely escaped the depredations of modern development as well as the heavy-handed attentions of Baron Haussmann, the Marais remains one of the most seductive districts of Paris – old, secluded, as unthreatening by night as it is by day, and with as many alluring shops, bars and places to eat as you could wish for.

Through the middle, dividing it in two, runs the interminable **rue de Rivoli** and its continuation to Bastille, rue St-Antoine. South of this line is the quartier St-Paul-St-Gervais, the riverside, the Arsenal, and the Île St-Louis. To the north, more homogeneous as well as more fun to walk around, are most of the shops and museums, **place des Vosges**, the **Jewish quarter** and the quartier du Temple. Every street boasts an abundance of colour and detail: magnificent *portes cochères* (huge double carriage gates) with elaborate handles and knockers, stone and iron bollards that protected pedestrians from ruthless carriage drivers, cobbled courtyards, elegant iron railings and gates, sculpted house fronts, Chinese sweatshops, chichi boutiques, ethnic grocers – a wealth of interest.

The Marais hôtels and place des Vosges

The main lateral street of the northern part of the Marais, which also forms the boundary between the 3e and 4e *arrondissements*, is the **rue des Francs-Bourgeois**. Jack Kerouac translated it as "the street of the outspoken middle classes", which may be a fair description of the contemporary residents, though the name in fact means "people exempt from tax", in reference to the penurious inmates of a medieval almshouse that once stood on the site of no. 34.

At its western end, the street begins with the eighteenth-century magnificence of the **Palais Soubise**, which houses the *Archives de France*. Opposite, at the back of a driveway for the *Crédit Municipal* bank, stands a pepperpot tower which formed part of the **city walls**; these were built by King Philippe-Auguste early in the thirteenth cen-

---

Place des Vosges

Royal patronage of the area goes back to the days when a royal palace, the *Hôtel des Tournelles*, stood on the north side of what is now the **place des Vosges**. It remained in use until 1559, having served also as the residence of the Duke of Bedford when he governed northern France in the name of England in the 1420s.

In 1559, Henri II, whose queen was Catherine de Médicis, concluded the treaty of Cateau-Cambrésis, thereby ending his wars with the Holy Roman Empire. To cement the treaty he married his son to the Duke of Savoy and his daughter to Philip II of Spain in a double wedding whose celebrations took place near the place des Vosges. The finale was a jousting tournament, in which the king took part. He won two bouts, wearing the colours of his mistress, Diane de Poitiers, who watched, seated beside his wife. He then challenged the Duke of Montgomery, captain of his guards, who accidentally struck him in the eye. The king died in agony ten days later.

Montgomery fled to England but returned after some years to take part in the Wars of Religion on the Protestant side. He was captured and, in violation of the terms of his surrender, put to death by Catherine de Médicis. She also had the *Hôtel des Tournelles* demolished, and the space thus vacated became a huge **horse market**, trading between one and two thousand horses every Saturday. So it remained until Henri IV decided on the construction of his place Royale.

Since then its name has changed many times, reflecting the fluctuating fortunes of different political tendencies. It stayed place Royale until 1792, when it became, first, Fédérés, then Indivisibilité, then Vosges in 1800 (see opposite). It was changed back to Royale with the Restoration of the monarchy in 1814, to Vosges in 1831, Royale again through the Second Empire up to the Third Republic in 1870, then back to republican Vosges, which it has remained.

---

tury to link up with his new fortress, the Louvre. Further along, past several more imposing façades and the peculiarly public *lycée* classrooms at no.28, you can enter the courtyard of the **Hôtel d'Albret** (no. 31). This eighteenth-century mansion is home to the cultural department of the mayor of Paris. Ironically, the dignified façade is blocked by a revolting sculptural column, a 1989 Bicentennial work by Bernard Pagès, resembling thorns and red and blue sticky tape.

The next landmarks on the street, at the junction with rues Payenne and Pavée, are two of the Marais' grandest **hôtels**, the sixteenth-century **Carnavalet** and *Lamoignon*, housing, respectively, the Musée Carnavalet and the Bibliothèque Historique de la Ville de Paris. Next to the Lamoignon, on rue Pavée – so called because it was among the first Paris streets to be paved, in 1450 – was the site of the **La Force prison**, where many of the Revolution's victims were incarcerated, including the Princesse de Lamballe, who was lynched along with many others in the massacres of September 1792. Her head was presented on a stake to her friend Marie-Antoinette.

Details of the Musée Carnavalet are given on p.295.

Voltaire's widowed niece, with whom he carried on a secret and passionate affair – "I kiss your cute little arse," he wrote to her, "and all the rest of you" – also lived in this street.

On the other side of rue des Francs-Bourgeois, rue Payenne leads up to the lovely gardens and houses of **rue du Parc-Royal** and on to **rue Thorigny**. Here, the magnificent classical façade of the seventeenth-century **Hôtel Salé**, built for a rich salt-tax collector, conceals the **Musée Picasso**.

The Musée Picasso is described on p.287

Continuing along rue des Francs-Bourgeois, you'll come across the **place des Vosges** on your right, a masterpiece of aristocratic elegance and the first example of planned development in the history of Paris. It is a vast square of symmetrical brick and stone mansions built over arcades. Undertaken in 1605 at the inspiration of **Henri IV**, it was inaugurated in 1612 for the wedding of Louis XIII and Anne of Austria; it is Louis' statue – or, rather, a replica of it – that stands hidden by chestnut trees in the middle of the grass and gravel gardens. Originally called place Royale (see opposite), it was renamed Vosges in 1800 in honour of the *département*, which was the first to pay its share of the expenses of the Revolutionary wars.

Through all the vicissitudes of history, the *place* has never lost its cachet as a smart address. Among the many celebrities who made their homes here was **Victor Hugo**; his house, at no. 6, where he wrote much of *Les Misérables*, is now a museum. Today, more than ever, expensive high heels tap through the arcades pausing at art, antique and fashion shops, while toddlers, octogenarians, schoolchildren, and workers on their lunch breaks sit or play in the garden, the only green space of any size in the locality.

The Maison de Victor-Hugo is described on p.297.

From the southwest corner of the *place*, a door leads through to the formal château garden, *orangerie*, and exquisite Renaissance façade of the **Hôtel de Sully**. You can visit the temporary exhibitions mounted here by the *Caisse Nationale des Monuments Historiques et des Sites*, or just pass through, nodding at the sphinxes on the stairs, to rue St-Antoine.

A short distance back to the west along rue St-Antoine, almost opposite the sixteenth-century **church of St-Paul**, which was inaugurated by Cardinal Richelieu, is another square. A complete contrast to the imposing formality of the place des Vosges, the tiny **place du Marché-Ste-Catherine** is a perfect example of that other great French architectural talent: an unerring eye for the intimate, the small-scale, the apparently accidental, and the irresistibly charming.

The Jewish quarter: rue des Rosiers

As the tide of chichification seeps remorselessly northwards up the Marais – at the time of writing the advance guard of galleries and design offices has washed past rues du Poitou and Pastorelle – the only remaining islet of genuine local, community life is in the city's main Jewish quarter, still centred around **rue des Rosiers**, just as it was in the twelfth century. Although the *hammam* is now a trendy café, and many of the little grocers, bakers, bookshops and original cafés are under pressure (for a long time local flats were kept empty, not for property speculation but to try to stem the middle-class invasion), the smells and sounds and the people on the streets are still largely Jewish. There is a distinctly Mediterranean flavour to the *quartier*, testimony to the influence of the **North African Sephardim**, who, since the end of the World War II, have sought refuge here from the uncertainties of life in the French ex-colonies. They have replenished Paris' Jewish population, depleted when its Ashkenazim, having excaped the pogroms of Eastern Europe, were rounded up by the Nazis and the French police and transported back east to concentration camps.

Don't leave the area without wandering the surrounding streets: rue du Roi-de-Sicile, the minute **place Bourg-Tibourg** off rue de Rivoli, **rue des Écouffes**, **rue Ste-Croix-de-la-Bretonnerie**, **rue Vieille-du-Temple**, and **rue des Archives**, where a medieval cloister, the Cloître des Billettes, at nos. 22–26, hosts free exhibitions of art and crafts (daily 10am–8pm). On the other side of rue de Rivoli, at 17 rue Geoffroy l'Asnier, the **Centre de Documentation Juive Contemporaine** (daily except Sat 10am–1pm & 2–5/6pm; 15F) mounts exhibitions concerned with all genocides and oppression of peoples, and guards the sombre Memorial to the Unknown Jewish Martyr.

The Quartier du Temple

The **northern part of the Marais** is ethnic, local, old-fashioned, working-class, and gradually being "discovered" by those who wax lyrical and nostalgic about the little workshops and traditional cafés

The Quartier du Temple

The Knights Templar

The military order of the **Knights Templar** was established in Jerusalem at the time of the Crusades to protect pilgrims to the Holy Land. Its members quickly became exceedingly rich and overweeningly powerful, with some nine thousand *commanderies* spread across Europe. They acquired land in the *marais* in Paris around 1140, and began to build. After the loss of Palestine in 1291, this fortress property, which covered the area now bounded by rues du Temple, Bretagne, Picardie and Béranger and constituted a separate town without the city walls, became their international headquarters, as the seat of their Grand Master.

They came to a sticky end, however, early in the fourteenth century, when King Philippe le Bel, alarmed at their power and in alliance with Pope Clement V, had them tried for sacrilege, blasphemy and sodomy. Fifty-four of them were burnt, including, in 1314, the Grand Master himself, in the presence of the king. Thereafter the order was abolished.

The Temple buildings continued to exist until the Revolution, with about four thousand inhabitants: a mixed population, consisting of artisans not subject to the city's trade regulations, debtors seeking freedom from prosecution, and some rich residents of private *hôtels*. Louis XVI and the royal family were imprisoned in the keep in 1792 (see box opposite). It was finally demolished in 1808 by Napoléon, determined to eradicate any possible focus for royalist nostalgia.

and the "realness" of the people. As you get beyond the cluster of art galleries and brasseries that have sprung up around the Picasso museum, or, over to the west, across rue Michel-le-Comte, the aristocratic stone façades of the southern Marais give way to the more humble, though no less attractive, stucco, paint and thick-slatted shutters of seventeenth- and eighteenth-century streets. Some bear the names of old rural French provinces: **Beauce**, **Perche**, **Saintonge**, **Picardie**. Ordinary cafés and shops occupy the ground floors, while rag-trade leather workshops and printers – though these are getting fewer – operate in the interior of the cobbled courtyards.

Robespierre lived in the **rue de Saintonge**, at no. 64, demolished in 1834. In adjacent **rue Charlot**, at no. 6, you can watch a wind-instrument maker and repairer at work on his precious charges. Opposite, in the dead-end **ruelle de Sourdis**, one section of street has remained unchanged since its construction in 1626. Further along, on the corner of **rue du Perche**, a little classical façade on a leafy courtyard hides the Armenian church of Ste-Croix, testimony to the many Armenians who sought refuge here from the Turkish pogroms of World War I. Further still, on the left and almost to the busy rue de Bretagne, is the easily missed entrance to the **Marché des Enfants-Rouges**, one of the smallest and least-known markets in Paris. Over rue de Bretagne, rue de Picardie leads up to the **Carreau du Temple**.

Nothing remains of the Knights Templar's installations beyond the name of "Temple", although some of the fortifications survived until the Revolution, notably the keep. Now the only direct heirs of the old traditions are the markets and workshops; for the Temple was always a tax-free zone for non-guild craftsmen and a prosecution-free zone for debtors. The Carreau itself, which is a fine *halles*-like structure, shelters a daily clothes market with a heavy preponderance of leather gear. **Rue de la Corderie**, a pretty little street on the north side, opening into an otherworldly *place*, has a couple of pleasant cafés under the trees.

These streets have a genteel and somewhat provincial air about them, but one block to the east it is a different story. **Rue du Temple**, itself lined with many beautiful houses dating back to the seventeenth century (no. 41, for instance, the *Hôtel Aigle d'Or*, is the last surviving coaching inn of the period), is the dividing line, full of fascinating little businesses trading in fashion accessories: chains, buckles, bangles and beads – everything you can think of. The streets to the east of it are narrow, dark, and riddled with passages, the houses half-timbered and bulging with age. Number 3 **rue Volta** is thought to be the oldest house in Paris, built around 1300. Practically every house is a Chinese wholesale business, many of them trading leather – and, on the face of it at least, not very friendly. This was Paris' original **Chinatown**, fed by thousands of immigrant workers brought in to fill the factories while French men were being sent off to die in the trenches of the World War I. In 1865, at **44 rue des Gravilliers**, a

---

The Temple and Louis XVI

Louis XVI, Marie-Antoinette, their two children and immediate family were imprisoned in the keep of the Knights Templar's ancient fortress in August 1792 by the Revolutionary government. By the end of 1794, when all the adults had been executed, the two children – a teenage girl and the nine- or ten-year-old dauphin, now, in the eyes of royalists, Louis XVII – remained there alone, in the charge of a family called Simon. Louis XVII was literally walled up, allowed no communication with other human beings, not even his sister, who was living on the floor above. He died in 1795, a half-crazed imbecile, and was buried in a public grave.

At least that is what appeared to be his fate. A number of clues, however, point to hocus-pocus. The doctor who certified the child's death kept a lock of his hair, but it was later found not to correspond with the colour of the young Louis XVII's hair, as remembered by his sister. MmeSimon confessed on her deathbed that she had substituted another child for Louis XVII. And a sympathetic sexton admitted that he had exhumed the body of this imbecile child and reburied it in the cloister of the Église Ste-Marguerite in the Faubourg St-Antoine (see p.191), but when this body was dug up it was found to be that of an eighteen-year-old.

So what really happened? A plausible theory is that the real Louis XVII died early in 1794. But since Robespierre needed the heir to the throne as a hostage with which to menace internal and foreign royalist enemies, he had Louis disposed of in secret and substituted the idiot.

Taking advantage of this atmosphere of uncertainty, 43 different people subsequently claimed to be Louis XVII.

---

tanner, an engraver and a bronze-worker opened the Paris office of the First International, set up by Karl Marx in London in the previous year; the office was on the ground floor in the courtyard.

South: the Quartier St-Paul-St-Gervais and the Pavillon de l'Arsenal

In the southern section of the Marais, **below rues de Rivoli** and St-**Antoine**, the crooked steps and lanterns of rue Cloche-Perce, the tottering timbered houses of **rue François-Miron**, the medieval *Acceuil des Jeunes en France* buildings behind the church of St-**Gervais**-St-**Protais**, and the smell of flowers and incense on **rue des Barres,** all provide the opportunity to indulge in Paris picturesque. The late Gothic St-Gervais-St-Protais, disappointingly battered and severe from the outside, is more interesting inside, with some lovely stained glass and an eighteenth-century organ. Between rues Fourcy and François-Miron, the *Hôtel Hénault de Cantoube*, with its two-storey *crypte*, has become the **Maison Européenne de la Photographie** (see p.289), hosting excellent exhibitions.

Shift eastwards to the next tangle of streets and you'll find modern, chichi flats in the "**Village St-Paul**", with clusters of expensive antique shops in the courtyards off **rue St-Paul**. This part of the Marais suffered a postwar hatchet job, and, although seventeenth- and eighteenth-century magnificence is still in evidence (there's even a stretch of the city's defensive wall dating from the early thirteenth century in the *lycée* playground on rue des Jardins St-Paul), it lacks the architectural cohesion of the Marais to the north. The fifteenth-century **Hôtel de Sens** (now a public library), on the rue de Figuier, looks bizarre in its isolation.

*St Paul's
museum of
magic is
detailed on
p.293.*

On rue du Petit-Musc there is an entertaining combination of 1930's modernism and nineteenth-century exuberance in the *Hôtel Fieubert* (now a school). Diagonally opposite, at 21 bd Morland, the **Pavillon de l'Arsenal** is an excellent addition to the city's art of self-promotion, signalled by a sculpture of Rimbaud with his feet in front of his head, entitled *The Man with his Soles in Front*. The aim of the Pavillon (Tues–Sat 10.30am–6.30pm, Sun 11am–7pm; free) is to present the city's current **architectural projects** to the public and show how past and present developments have evolved as part and parcel of Parisian history. To this end they have a permanent exhibition of photographs, plans and models, including one of the whole city, with a spotlight to highlight a touch-screen choice of 30,000 images. The temporary exhibitions are equally impressive, and the best thing about the whole display is to see schools, industrial units and hospitals treated with the same respect as La Villette and La Grande Arche.

The **southeast corner of the 4ᵉ arrondissement**, jutting out into the Seine, has its own distinct character. It's been taken up since the last century by the Célestins barracks and previously by the Arsenal,

which used to overlook a third island in the Seine. Boulevard
Morland was built in 1843, covering over the arm of the river that
formed the Île de Louviers. The mad poet Gérard de Nerval escaped
here as a boy and lived for days in a log cabin he made with wood
scavenged from the island's timberyards. In the 1830s, his more
extrovert contemporaries – Victor Hugo, Liszt, Delacroix, Alexandre
Dumas and co – were using the library of the former residence of
Louis XIV's artillery chief as a meeting place. While the literati dis-
cussed turning art to a Revolutionary form, the locals were on the
streets giving the authorities reason to build more barracks.

The Île St-Louis

Unlike its larger neighbour, the Île de la Cité (see p.67), the Île St-
Louis has no monuments or museums (apart from a house – 6 quai
d'Orléans – devoted to the Romantic Polish poet Adam Mickiewicz;
Thurs 2–6pm or by appointment on ☎01.43.54.35.61, free), just high
houses on single-lane streets, a school, a church, and assorted restaurants and cafés. This island gained popularity as a Bohemian hang-
out a decade or so later than the Île de Louviers (see above): the
Hashashins club met every month at the **Hôtel Lauzun**, 17 quai
d'Anjou, and Baudelaire lived for a while in the attic. Nowadays you
only get to have your home on the island if you're the Aga Khan, the
Pretender to the French throne, or an ex grand duke of Russia.

For most visitors, the Île St-Louis is best remembered for its
exceptional **sorbets**, chez *M. Berthillon*, at 31 rue St-Louis-en-l'Île
(closed Mon & Tues). Nothing can rival the taste of iced passion or
kiwi fruit, guava, melon or a number of other flavours; the flavour of
even ripe, fresh-picked fruit is but a shadow in comparison.

If you're looking for absolute seclusion, head for the **southern
quais**, clutching a triple-sorbet cornet as you descend the various
steps, or climb over the low gate on the right of the garden across bd
Henri-IV to reach the best sunbathing spot in Paris. And even when
Berthillon and his six concessionaries are closed, the island and its
quais have their own very distinct charm.

The Bastille

The column surmounted by the "Spirit of Liberty" on **place de la
Bastille** was erected to commemorate not the surrender of the **prison**
with its last seven occupants in 1789, but the July Revolution of
1830, which saw the autocratic Charles X replaced with the "Citizen
King" Louis-Philippe (see p.412). When he in turn fled in the more
significant 1848 Revolution, his throne was burnt beside the column
and a new inscription added. Four months after the birth of the
Second Republic in that year, the workers took to the streets. All of

The Bastille

The only visible remains of the Bastille prison were transported to square Henri-Galli at the end of bd Henri-IV.

eastern Paris was barricaded, with the fiercest fighting on rue du Faubourg-St-Antoine. The rebellion was quelled with the usual massacres and deportation of survivors, and it is of course the 1789 Bastille Day, symbol of the end of feudalism in Europe, that France celebrates every year on July 14. The importance of place de la Bastille as a rallying point for political protestors remains even today.

The Bicentennial of the French Revolution in 1989 was marked by the inauguration of a new opera house on place de la Bastille, the **Opéra-Bastille**. Mitterrand's pet project was the subject of the most virulent sequence of rows and resignations, and the finished building is proving inordinately expensive to run. Filling almost the entire block between rues de Lyon, Charenton and Moreau, it has shifted the focus of place de la Bastille, so that the column is no longer the pivotal point; in fact, it's easy to miss it altogether when dazzled by the night-time glare of lights emanating from the Opéra. One critic has described it as a "hippopotamus in a bathtub", and you can see his point. The architect, Carlos Ott, was concerned that his design should not bring an overbearing monumentalism to place de la Bastille. The different depths and layers of the semicircular façade do give a certain sense of the building stepping back, but self-effacing it is not. Time, use and familiarity have more or less reconciled it to its surroundings, and people happily sit on its steps, wander into its shops and libraries, and camp out all night for the free performance on July 14. When a giant condom was pulled over the Column of Liberty for AIDS awareness, old traditions and contemporary styles were truly wedded.

For a congenial snack next door to the market, try the down-to-earth wine bar Le Baron Rouge; see p.273.

The opera's construction destroyed no small amount of low-rent housing, and the **quartier de la Bastille** is now trendier than Les Halles. But as with most speculative developments, the pace of change is uneven: old tool shops and ironmongers still survive alongside cocktail haunts and sushi bars; and laundries and cobblers flank electronic notebook outlets. You'll find art galleries clustered around rue Keller and the adjoining stretch of rue de Charonne; indie music shops and gay, lesbian and hippie outfits on rues Keller and des Taillandiers; and, on rue de Lappe, one survivor of that very Parisian tradition: of *bals musettes*, or dance halls of 1930s "*gai Paris*", frequented between the wars by Piaf, Jean Gabin and Rita Hayworth. The most famous, *Balajo*, was founded by one Jo de France, who introduced glitter and spectacle into what were then seedy gangster dives, enticing Parisians from the other side of the city to savour the rue de Lappe lowlife.

The Centre Gai et Lesbienne, *3 rue Keller, is detailed on p.52.*

The rue de Lappe can still be as dodgy a place to be at night as it was in prewar days. Nowadays, though, bouncers at clubs like *Balajo* and the *Chapelle des Lombards*, a heavy drugs scene and an uneasy mix of local residents have combined to deprive the street of the soul that ten years ago endeared it to Parisians from all walks of life.

For moving beyond the Bastille further into the 11e and 12e *arrondissements*, see Chapter 10.

Chapter 6

The Left Bank

The term **Left Bank** (*rive gauche*) connotes Bohemian, dissident, intellectual – the radical student type, whether eighteen years of age or eighty. As a topographical term it refers particularly to their traditional haunts, the warren of medieval lanes round the **boulevards St-Michel** and **St-Germain**, known as the **Quartier Latin** because that was the language of the university sited there right up until 1789. In modern times its reputation for turbulence and innovation has been renewed by the activities of painters and writers like Picasso, Apollinaire, Breton, Henry Miller, Anaïs Nin and Hemingway after World War I; Camus, Sartre, Juliette Greco and the Existentialists after World War II; and the political turmoil of 1968, which escalated from student demonstrations and barricades to factory occupations, massive strikes and the near-overthrow of de Gaulle's presidency. This is not to say that the whole of Paris south of the Seine is the exclusive territory of revolutionaries and avant-gardists. It does, however, have a different and distinctive feel and appearance, noticeable as soon as you cross the river. And it's here, still, that the city's myth-makers principally gather: the writers, painters, philosophers, politicians, journalists, designers – the people who tell Paris what it is.

Quartier Latin

The pivotal point of the **Quartier Latin** is **place St-Michel**, where the tree-lined bd St-Michel begins. It has long lost its radical penniless chic, preferring harder commercial values. The cafés and shops are jammed with people, mainly young and (in summer) largely foreign; the fountain in the *place* is a favourite meeting, not to say pick-up, spot. **Rue de la Huchette** – the Mecca of beats and bums in the post-World War II years, with its theatre still showing Ionesco's *Cantatrice Chauve* nearly fifty years on – is given over to Greek restaurants of indifferent quality and inflated prices, as is the adjoining rue Xavier-Privas, with the odd couscous joint thrown in.

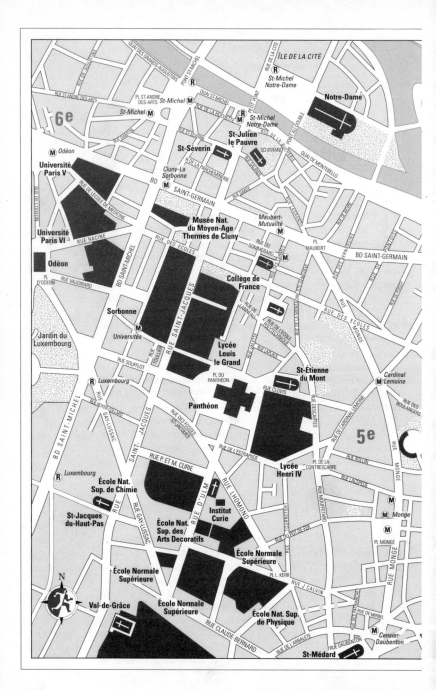

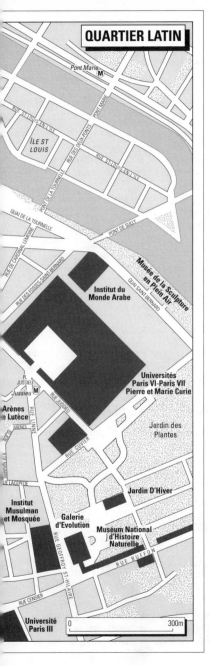

Quartier Latin: listings

RESTAURANTS

Aleka, 187 rue St-Jacques, 5ᵉ. *RER* Luxembourg.

Auberge des Deux Signes, 46 rue Galande, 5ᵉ. Mᵒ St-Michel.

Bambon, 4 rue des Fossés-St-Marcel, 5ᵉ. Mᵒ Censier-Daubenton.

Bistro de la Sorbonne, 4 rue Toullier, 5ᵉ. Mᵒ Luxembourg.

Brasserie Balzar, 49 rue des Écoles, 5ᵉ. Mᵒ Maubert-Mutualité.

Au Buisson Ardent, 25 rue de Jussieu, 5ᵉ. Mᵒ Jussieu.

Chez Léna et Mimile, 32 rue Tournefort, 5ᵉ. Mᵒ Censier-Daubenton.

Chez René, 14 bd St-Germain, 5ᵉ. Mᵒ Maubert-Mutualité.

Chieng-Maï, 12 rue Frédéric-Sauton, 5ᵉ. Mᵒ Maubert-Mutualité.

Le Grenier de Notre-Dame, 18 rue de la Bûcherie, 5ᵉ. Mᵒ Maubert-Mutalité.

Inagiku, 14 rue Pontoise, 5ᵉ. Mᵒ Maubert-Mutualité.

Koutchi, 40 rue du Cardinal-Lemoine, 5ᵉ. Mᵒ Cardinal-Lemoine.

Mavrommatis, 42 rue Daubenton, 5ᵉ. Mᵒ Censier-Daubenton.

La Méthode, 2 rue Descartes, 5ᵉ. Mᵒ Cardinal-Lemoine.

Perraudin, 157 rue St-Jacques, 5ᵉ. *RER* Luxembourg.

Le Petit Prince, 12 rue Lanneau, 5ᵉ. Mᵒ Maubert-Mutualité.

La Petite Légume, 36 rue Boulangers, 5ᵉ. Mᵒ Jussieu.

Les Quatre et Une Saveurs, 72 rue du Cardinal-Lemoine, 5ᵉ. Mᵒ Cardinal-Lemoine.

Le Refuge du Passé, 32 rue du Fer-à-Moulin, 5ᵉ. Mᵒ Les Gobelins.

Student restaurants at 8bis rue Cuvier, 5ᵉ (Mᵒ Jussieu); 39 av G-Bernanos, 5e (Mᵒ Port-Royal); 31 rue Geoffroy-St-Hilaire, 5ᵉ (Mᵒ Censier-Daubenton); and 10 rue Jean-Calvin, 5ᵉ (Mᵒ Censier-Daubenton). *cont.*

Tashi Delek, 4 rue des Fossés-St-Jacques, 5e. Mo Luxembourg.

CAFÉS AND BARS

Le Bâteau Ivre, 40 rue Descartes, 5e. Mo Cardinal-Lemoine.

Café des Arts, cnr place Contrescarpe & rue Lacépède, 5e. Mo Monge.

Café de la Mosquée, 39 rue Geoffroy-St-Hilaire, 5e. Mo Monge.

Café Notre-Dame, cnr quai St-Michel & rue St-Jacques, 5e. Mo St-Michel.

Café Oz, 184 rue St-Jacques, 5e. Mo Luxembourg.

Connolly's Corner, cnr rues Patriarches & Mirbel, 5e. Mo Monge/Censier-Daubenton.

Les Fontaines, 9 rue Soufflot, 5e. Mo Luxembourg.

La Fourmi Ailée, 8 rue du Fouarre, 5e. Mo Maubert-Mutualité.

La Gueuze, 19 rue Soufflot, 5e. Mo Luxembourg.

Net Coffee, 25 rue Lacépède, 5e. Mo Monge.

Le Piano Vache, 8 rue Laplace, 5e. Mo Cardinal-Lemoine.

Les Pipos, 2 rue de l'École-Polytechnique, 5e. Mo Maubert-Mutualité/Cardinal-Lemoine.

Polly Magoo, 11 rue St-Jacques, 5e. Mo St-Michel/Maubert-Mutualité.

Le Verre à Pied, 118bis rue Mouffetard, 5e. Mo Monge.

Le Violon Dingue, 46 rue de la Montagne-Ste-Geneviève, 5e. Mo Maubert-Mutualité.

These establishments are reviewed in Chapter 13,
Eating and drinking, *beginning on p.251.*

Connecting it to the riverside is the city's narrowest street, **rue du Chat-qui-Pêche**, alarmingly evocative of what Paris must have looked like at its medieval worst.

Rue St-Jacques and medieval churches

Things improve as you move away from the boulevard. At the end of rue de la Huchette, **rue St-Jacques** is aligned on the main street of Roman Paris, its name derived from the medieval pilgrimage to the shrine of St Jacques (St James) in Santiago de Compostela, northern Spain. For the millions who set out from the church of St-Jacques (only the tower remains), just across the river, this bit of hill was their first taste of the road.

A short distance to the right, the mainly fifteenth-century **church of St-Séverin** (Mon–Thurs 11am–7.30pm, Fri & Sat 9am–10.30pm, Sun 9am–8pm) is one of the city's most elegant. Built in the Flamboyant Gothic style, it contains some splendidly virtuoso chiselwork in the pillars of the choir, as well as stained glass by the modern French painter Jean Bazaine.

Rue de la Parcheminerie, to the north, is where medieval scribes and parchment sellers used to congregate, hence its name. It's worth cricking your neck to look at the decorations on the façades, including that of no. 29, where the Canadian *Abbey Bookshop* continues the bookish tradition. Back towards the river, **square Viviani**, with its welcome patch of grass and trees, provides the most flattering of all views of Notre-Dame. The ancient, listing tree propped on a concrete pillar by the church wall is reputed to be Paris' oldest, brought over from Guyana in 1680. The church itself, mutilated and disfigured, is **St-Julien-le-Pauvre**. The same age as Notre-Dame, it used to be the venue for university assemblies until some rumbustious students tore it apart in the 1500s. It's a quiet and intimate place, ideal for a moment's soulful reflection. For the last hundred years it has belonged to a Greek Catholic sect, hence the unexpected iconostasis screening the sanctuary. The hefty slabs of stone by the well at the entrance are all that remain of the Roman thoroughfare now overlain by rue St-Jacques.

The river bank and Institut du Monde Arabe

Round to the left on rue de la Bûcherie, the English bookshop **Shakespeare and Co.** is haunted by the shades of James Joyce and other great expatriate literati, though only by proxy, as Sylvia Beach, publisher of Joyce's *Ulysses*, had her original shop on rue de l'Odéon.

More books, postcards, prints, sheet music, records and assorted goods are on sale from the **bouquinistes**, who display their wares in green, padlocked boxes hooked onto the parapet of the **riverside quais** – which, in spite of their romantic reputation, are not much fun to walk along hereabouts because of the traffic. Continuing upstream as far as the tip of the Île St-Louis, you come to the **Pont de Sully**, from which there's a dramatic view of the apse and steeple of Notre-Dame, and the beginning of a riverside garden dotted with pieces of modern sculpture, known as the **Musée de Sculpture en Plein Air**.

At the end of the Pont de Sully, in the angle between quai St-Bernard and rue des Fossés-St-Bernard, shaming the hideous factory of the Paris-VI university next door, stands the **Institut du Monde Arabe** (daily except Mon 10am–6pm). Designed principally by Jean Nouvel, its elegant glass and aluminium mass is cleft in two, the riverfront half bowed and tapering to a knife-like prow, while the broad southern façade, comprising thousands of tiny light-sensitive shutters, employs hi-tech ingenuity to mimic the *moucharabiyah* – the traditional Arab latticework balcony.

The museum of the Institut du Monde Arabe is described on p.288.

Housed within the institute is a museum of Islamic art and artefacts, space for temporary exhibitions, a library, facilities for research, debate and publishing, and an audiovisual centre. This last, the *Espace Image et Son* (Tues–Sun 1–6pm), is located in the basement and stores thousands of slides, photographs, films and recordings, which you can access yourself. Film previews are shown, and in the *Salle d'Actualités* you can watch current news broadcasts from around the Arab world. When you need a rest, take the fastest lifts in

Paris up to the ninth floor for expensive Lebanese eats or just a mint tea, and enjoy a brilliant view over the Seine that stretches from La Grande Arche to Buttes-Chaumont.

Place Maubert and the Sorbonne

Walking back along bd St-Germain towards bd St-Michel, past rue de Pontoise with its Art Deco swimming pool and primary school, you come to **place Maubert** (good market Tues, Thurs and Sat am), at the foot of the **Montagne Ste-Geneviève**, the hill on which the Panthéon stands and the best strolling area this side of bd St-Michel. The best way in is either from the *place* or from the crossroads of bds St-Michel and St-Germain, where the walls of the third-century **Roman baths** are visible in the garden of the **Hôtel de Cluny**. A sixteenth-century mansion resembling an Oxford or Cambridge college, the *hôtel* was built by the abbots of the powerful Cluny monastery as their Paris pied-à-terre. It now houses the very beautiful **Musee Nationale du Moyen-Age**. There is no charge for entry to the quiet shady courtyard.

The Musée Nationale du Moyen-Age is described on p.285.

The grim-looking buildings on the other side of rue des Écoles are the **Sorbonne**, **Collège de France** – where Foucault, specialist in sex and madness, taught – and **Lycée Louis-le-Grand**, which numbers Molière, Robespierre, Pompidou and Victor Hugo among its graduates, and Sartre among its teachers. All these institutions are major constituents of the brilliant and mandarin world of French intellectual activity. You can have a look around the Sorbonne courtyard without anyone objecting. The **Richelieu chapel**, dominating the uphill end and containing the tomb of the great cardinal, was the first Roman-influenced building in seventeenth-century Paris and set the trend for subsequent developments. Nearby, the traffic-free **place de la Sorbonne**, with its lime trees, cafés and student habitués, is a lovely place to sit.

The Panthéon and St-Étienne-du-Mont

Further up the hill, the broad rue Soufflot provides an appropriately grand perspective on the domed and porticoed **Panthéon**. Louis XV's thank-you to Sainte Geneviève, patron saint of Paris, for curing him of illness, it was transformed by the Revolution into a mausoleum for the great. Imposing enough at a distance, the building is cold and uninteresting close to, and deadly inside (April–Sept 9.30am–6.30pm, Oct–March 10am–5.30pm; closed public holidays, 32F/21F). However, if you head towards the Luxembourg gardens, you'll find several cafés to warm the cockles of your heart, including the beer specialist *La Gueuze*.

More interesting than the Panthéon is the mainly sixteenth-century church of **St-Étienne-du-Mont**, on the corner of rue Clovis (daily 8am–noon & 2–7.30pm), whose façade combines Gothic,

Renaissance and Baroque elements. The interior, if not exactly beautiful, is highly unexpected. The space is divided into three aisles by
free-standing pillars connected by a narrow catwalk, and flooded
with light by an exceptionally tall clerestory. Again, unusually – for
they mainly fell victim to the destructive anti-clericalism of the
Revolution – the church still possesses its rood screen, a broad low
arch supporting a gallery reached by twining spiral stairs. There is
also some good seventeenth-century glass in the cloister. Further
down rue Clovis, a huge piece of Philippe-Auguste's **twelfth-century city walls** emerges from among the houses.

South of place du Panthéon, between rues Gay-Lussac and
Lhomond, are more academic institutions: the École Normale
Supérieure, a *grande école* that trains teachers and theorists and
bred structuralism in the 1970s; the Curie and oceanographic institutes; and the *grandes écoles* for chemistry, physics and decorative
arts. Entry to the *grandes écoles* is by exam following two years of
preparation after the equivalent of A levels or a high-school diploma,
the *baccalauréat*. Started by Napoléon to provide professionally
trained engineers and technicians, they represent the elite of French
educational establishments.

There is not much point in going further south on rue St-Jacques.
The area is dull and lifeless once you are over the Gay-Lussac intersection, though Baroque enthusiasts might like to take a look at the
seventeenth-century church of **Val-de-Grâce**, with its pedimented
front and ornate cupola copied from St Peter's in Rome. Round the
corner, on bd de Port-Royal, there are several brasseries and another big **market**.

East of the Panthéon: Mouffetard and Contrescarpe

More enticing wandering is to be had in the villagey streets east of
the Panthéon. **Rue de la Montagne-Ste-Geneviève** climbs up from
place Maubert across rue des Écoles to the gates of what used to be
the **École Polytechnique**, the grandest of the *grandes écoles* (see
above) for entry to the top echelons of state power. The school has
decamped to the suburbs, leaving its buildings to become the
Ministry of Research and Technology – a trip down memory lane for
many of its staff, no doubt. There's a sunny little café outside the gate
and several restaurants in rue de l'École-Polytechnique, facing the
Ministry.

From here, **rue Descartes** runs into the tiny and once-attractive
place de la Contrescarpe. An erstwhile arty hang-out, where
Hemingway wrote – in the café *La Chope* – and Georges Brassens
sang, it is now a tourist hotspot. Just to the east, on rue Lacépède, is
a municipal crèche, built in 1985, whose lovely curved frontage was
inspired by the shape of a pregnant woman's belly.

The medieval **rue Mouffetard** begins here, a cobbled lane winding downhill to the church of **St-Médard**, once a country parish beside the now-covered River Bièvre. On the façade of no. 12 is a curious painted glass sign from the Golliwog era, depicting a Negro in striped trousers waiting on his mistress, with the unconvincing legend, "*Au Nègre Joyeux*". At no. 64, a shoe shop run by Georges the Armenian sells genuine Basque espadrilles and the last of the French wooden clogs (or *sabots*). But most of the upper half of the street is given over to eating places, mainly Greek and little better than those of rue de la Huchette. Like any place devoted to the entertainment of tourists, it has become soulless and tacky, though the bottom half, with its sumptuous fruit and veg stalls, still maintains an authentic local ambience, and no. 30 has an extraordinary façade like the tapestry of a forest scene. On place des Patriarches, one block east, an old market hall has been replaced by a beautiful 1980s construction, containing low-cost flats and a gym, harking back to the style of its predecessor while being unashamedly modern.

The Paris mosque and Jardin des Plantes

A little **further east**, across rue Monge, are some of the city's most agreeable surprises. Down rue Daubenton, past a delightful Arab shop selling sweets, spices and gaudy tea-glasses, you come to the crenellated walls of the **Paris mosque**, topped by greenery and a great square minaret. You can visit the sunken garden and patios with their polychrome tiles and carved ceilings (9am–noon & 2–6pm; closed Fri & Muslim holidays), but not the prayer room. There is also a *hammam*, open to all, a tearoom and restaurant, and a shop selling clothes, birdcages and hubble-bubbles.

The Muséum National de l'Histoire Naturelle is described on p.298.

Opposite the mosque on rue Geoffroy-St-Hilaire, the hideous building belonging to the **Muséum National de l'Histoire Naturelle** was supposed to have been demolished to make way for a portico leading up to the new *Galerie d'Évolution*, housed in a vast glass-domed, metal-framed building contemporary with the Eiffel Tower. Its time will no doubt come, but for the moment you have to admire the new gallery from within the Jardin des Plantes.

There's an entrance to the **Jardin des Plantes** (summer 7.30am–7.45pm, winter 8am–dusk; free) at the corner of rues Geoffroy-St-Hilaire and Buffon, alongside the museum shop selling wonderful books and postcards; other entrances are further north on the corner with rue Cuvier, the main gate on rue Cuvier itself, and on quai St-Bernard. Attractions in the gardens include a small, cramped **zoo** (Mon–Sat summer 9am–6pm, winter 9am–5pm, Sun 9am–6.30pm all year; 25F/15F), botanical gardens and hothouses, as well as museums of paleontology, mineralogy and evolution. Improvements are underway – particularly with regard to the overgrown mazes and trees that block the view across the river from the pergola – and it's a pretty enough space of greenery in which to while away the middle of a day. By the rue Cuvier entrance stands a fine Cedar of Lebanon, planted in 1734 and raised from seed sent over from the Botanical Gardens in Oxford, plus a slice of an American sequoia more than 2000 years old, with the birth of Christ and other historical events marked on its rings. It was in the nearby physics labs that two unwitting ancestors of the *force de frappe* (the French nuclear deterrent) were discovered: radioactivity by Henri Becquerel in 1896, and radium by the Curies, two years later. Pierre Curie, incidentally, ended his days under the wheels of a brewer's dray on rue Dauphine.

A short distance away, with entrances on rue de Navarre, rue des Arènes and through a passage on rue Monge, is Paris' other Roman remain, the **Arènes de Lutèce**, an unexpected and peaceful backwater hidden from the street. This partly restored amphitheatre has a *boules* pitch in the centre, benches, gardens and a kids' playground behind.

St-Germain

The northern half of the 6e *arrondissement*, asymmetrically centred on **place St-Germain-des-Près**, is the most picturesque, animated and stimulating square kilometre in the entire city. It's got the money, elegance and sophistication, but also an easy-going tolerance and simplicity that comes from a long association with mould-breakers and trend-setters in the arts, philosophy, politics and sciences. The aspiring and expiring are equally at home.

Across Pont des Arts

The most dramatic approach to St-Germain is to cross the river from the Louvre by the **Pont des Arts**, taking in the classic upstream view of the Île de la Cité, with barges moored at the quai de Conti, and the Tour St-Jacques and Hôtel de Ville breaking the skyline of the Right Bank.

The dome and pediment at the end of the bridge belong to the **Institut de France**, seat of the Académie Française, an august body of writers and scholars whose mission is to safeguard the purity of the French language. Recent creations include the excellent word *baladeur* for "Walkman", but rearguard actions against Anglo-Saxon terms in the sciences, information technology and management have been hopelessly ineffective.

This is the grandiose bit of the Left Bank riverfront. To the left is the **Hôtel des Monnaies**, redesigned as the Mint in the late eighteenth century. To the right is the **École des Beaux-Arts**, the School of Fine Art, whose students throng the *quais* on sunny days, sketch pads on knee.

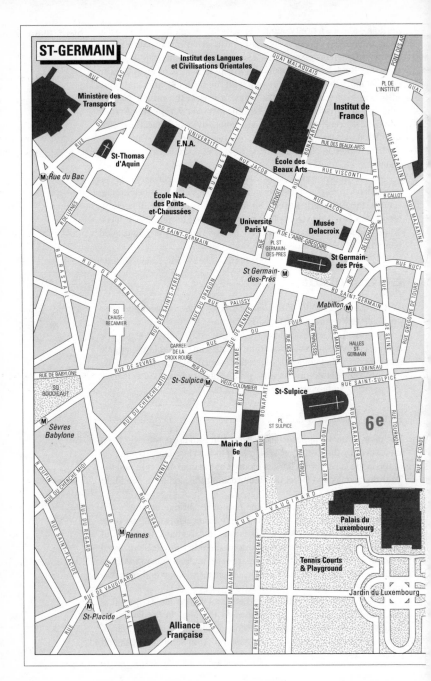

ST-GERMAIN

Institut des Langues et Civilisations Orientales

QUAI MALAQUAIS

RUE BAC

RUE DE L'UNIVERSITÉ

RUE DES SAINTS PÈRES

PL DE L'INSTITUT

QUAI

Ministère des Transports

Institut de France

St-Thomas d'Aquin

E.N.A.

RUE DE SEINE

RUE MAZARINE

RUE DES BEAUX-ARTS

BONAPARTE

M Rue du Bac

RUE LIONE

École des Beaux Arts

RUE VISCONTI

R CALLOT

École Nat. des Ponts-et-Chaussées

RUE JACOB

RUE ST-BENOIT

RUE DE L'ÉCHAUDÉ

RUE DE SEINE

RUE MAZARINE

BD RASPAIL

RUE DE GRENELLE

Université Paris V

R DE L'ABBE-GREGOIRE

PL ST GERMAIN-DES-PRÉS

Musée Delacroix

St Germain-des-Prés

RUE BUCI

St Germain-des-Prés **M**

BD SAINT-GERMAIN

RUE DE SEINE

RUE GRÉGOIRE DE TOURS

BD SAINT-GERMAIN

RUE B. PALISSY

Mabillon **M**

SQ CHAISE-RECAMIER

RUE DES SAINTS PÈRES

RUE DU DRAGON

RUE DE RENNES

RUE DU FOUR

RUE PRINCESSE

RUE DES CANETTES

RUE MABILLON

HALLES ST-GERMAIN

CARREF. DE LA CROIX ROUGE

RUE DE SÈVRES

RUE DU CHERCHE-MIDI

RUE MADAME

RUE DU VIEUX-COLOMBIER

RUE LOBINEAU

RUE SAINT-SULPICE

RUE DE BABYLONE

St-Sulpice **M**

St-Sulpice

SQ BOUCICAUT

M Sèvres Babylone

RUE BONAPARTE

PL ST SULPICE

RUE SERVANDONI

RUE GARANCIÈRE

RUE TOURNON

RUE DE CONDE

6e

R DUPIN

RUE DU CHERCHE MIDI

RUE DU REGARD

BD RASPAIL

Mairie du 6e

RUE FEROU

RUE DE RENNES

RUE D'ASSAS

M Rennes

RUE DE VAUGIRARD

RUE GUYNEMER

Palais du Luxembourg

RUE SAINT-PLACIDE

RUE DE VAUGIRARD

RUE MADAME

RUE GUYNEMER

RUE D'ASSAS

Tennis Courts & Playground

Jardin du Luxembourg

M St-Placide

Alliance Française

St-Germain: listings

RESTAURANTS

Aux Charpentiers, 10 rue Mabillon, 6e. Mº Mabillon.

Jacques Cagna, 14 rue des Grands-Augustins, 6e. Mº Odéon/St-Michel.

Lipp, 151 bd St-Germain, 6e. Mº St-Germain-des-Près.

La Maison de la Lozère, 4 rue Hautefeuille, 6e. Mº St-Michel.

La Maroussia, 9 rue de l'Éperon, 6e. Mº Odéon.

Le Muniche, 7 rue St-Benoît, 6e. Mº St-Germain-des-Près.

Orestias, 4 rue Grégoire-de-Tours, 6e. Mº Odéon.

Le Petit Mabillon, 6 rue Mabillon, 6e. Mº Mabillon.

Le Petit Saint-Benoît, 4 rue Saint-Benoît, 6e. Mº St-Germain-des-Près.

Le Petit Vatel, 5 rue Lobineau, 6e. Mº Mabillon.

Le Petit Zinc, 11 rue Saint-Benoît, 6e. Mº St-Germain-des-Près.

Polidor, 41 rue Monsieur-le-Prince, 6e. Mº Odéon.

Le Procope, 13 rue de l'Ancienne-Comédie, 6e. Mº Odéon.

Restaurant des Arts, 73 rue de Seine, 6e. Mº St-Germain-des-Près.

Restaurant des Beaux-Arts, 11 rue Bonaparte, 6e. Mº St-Germain-des-Près.

La Rôtisserie d'en Face, 2 rue Christine, 6e. Mº Odéon/St-Michel.

Student restaurants at 55 rue Mazet, 6e (Mº Odéon) & 92 rue d'Assas, 6e (Mº Port-Royal/Notre-Dame-des-Champs).

CAFÉS AND BARS

Le 10, 10 rue de l'Odéon, 6e. Mº Odéon.

L'Alsace à Paris, 9 place St-André-des-Arts, 6e. Mº St-Michel.

L'Assignat, 7 rue Guénégaud, 6e. Mº Pont-Neuf.

Le Bonaparte, cnr rue Bonaparte & place St-Germain, 6e Mº St-Germain-des-Près.

cont.

St-Germain: listings (continued)

Café de la Mairie, place St-Sulpice, 6ᵉ. Mᵒ St-Sulpice.

Chez Georges, 11 rue des Canettes, 6ᵉ. Mᵒ Mabillon.

À la Cour de Rohan, Cour du Commerce, off rues St-André-des-Arts & Ancienne-Comédie, 6ᵉ. Mᵒ Odéon.

Les Deux Magots, 170 bd St-Germain, 6ᵉ. Mᵒ St-Germain-des-Près.

L'Écluse, 15 quai des Grands-Augustins, 6ᵉ. Mᵒ St-Michel.

Le Flore, 172 bd St-Germain, 6ᵉ. Mᵒ St-Germain-des-Près.

Le Mazet, 60 rue St-André-des-Arts, 6ᵉ. Mᵒ Odéon.

La Paillote, 45 rue Monsieur-le-Prince, 6ᵉ. *RER* Luxembourg/Mᵒ Odéon.

La Palette, 43 rue de Seine, 6ᵉ. Mᵒ Odéon.

La Pinte, 13 carrefour de l'Odéon, 6ᵉ. Mᵒ Odéon.

Pub Saint-Germain, 17 rue de l'Ancienne-Comédie, 6ᵉ. Mᵒ Odéon.

La Table d'Italie, 69 rue de Seine, 6ᵉ. Mᵒ Mabillon/St-Germain-des-Près.

La Taverne de Nesle, 32 rue Dauphine, 6ᵉ. Mᵒ Odéon.

Au Vieux Colombier, 65 rue des Rennes, 6ᵉ. Mᵒ St-Sulpice.

These establishments are reviewed in Chapter 13,
Eating and drinking, *beginning on p.255.*

The riverside

The riverside part of the *quartier* is cut lengthways by **rue St-André-des-Arts** and **rue Jacob**. It is full of bookshops, commercial art galleries, antique shops, cafés and restaurants. Poke your nose into courtyards and side streets. The houses are four to six storeys high, seventeenth- and eighteenth-century, some noble, some stiff, some bulging and skew, all painted in infinite gradations of grey, pearl and off-white. Broadly speaking, the further west, the posher they get.

Historical associations are legion. Picasso painted *Guernica* in rue des Grands-Augustins. Molière started his career in rue Mazarine. Robespierre et al. split ideological hairs at the *Le Procope* in rue de l'Ancienne-Comédie. In rue Visconti, Racine died, Delacroix painted, and Balzac's printing business went bust. In parallel rue des Beaux-Arts, Oscar Wilde died, Corot and Ampère – father of amps – lived, and crazy poet Gérard de Nerval walked a lobster on a lead.

If you're looking for lunch, **place** and **rue St-André-des-Arts** offer numerous places to snack, but this is still very much tourist territory and you would do better to look further afield. There is, for instance, a brilliant **food market** in rue de Buci, up towards bd St-Germain. Before you get to it, there's a little *passage* on the left, **Cour du Commerce St André**, between a *crêperie* and *Le Mazet* café. Marat had his printing press here, and Dr Guillotin perfected his machine by lopping off sheep's heads in a loft next door. Since the, *Le Procope*, was done up for the Bicentennial, with portraits of

Voltaire and Robespierre on its back façade, a revolutionary theme has enveloped the *passage*. A couple of smaller courtyards open off it, revealing a stretch of Philippe-Auguste's wall.

St-Germain

An alternative corner for midday food or quiet is around rue de l'Abbaye and rue de Furstemberg, where **Delacroix's old studio**, at 6 place Furstemberg, overlooks a secret garden and has been converted into a museum.

The Musée Delacroix is described on p.291.

This is also the beginning of some very **upmarket shopping territory** – in rue Jacob, rue de Seine and rue Bonaparte, in particular. On the wall of no. 56 rue Jacob, a plaque commemorates the signature of the Treaty of Independence between Britain and the US on September 23, 1783, by Benjamin Franklin, David Hartley and others. There are also cheap eating places at this end of the street, serving the university medical school by the intersection with rue des Saints-Pères.

Place St-Germain-des-Près

Place St-Germain-des-Prés, the hub of the *quartier*, is only a stone's throw away, with the *Deux Magots* café on the corner, and *Flore* just down the street. Both are renowned for the number of philosophico-politico-poetico-literary backsides that have shined their seats, like the snootier *Brasserie Lipp*, across the boulevard, longtime haunt of the more successful practitioners of these trades; admission to its hallowed portals has become somewhat easier since the decease of the crotchety old proprietor. All these establishments are expensive and extremely crowded in summer. A place on the *terrasse* will inevitably involve you in the attentions of buskers and street performers.

The tower opposite *Les Deux Magots* belongs to the **church of St-Germain**, all that remains of an enormous Benedictine monastery. There has been a church on the site since the sixth century. Inside, the pure Romanesque lines are still clear beneath the deforming paint of nineteenth-century frescoes, while in the corner of the churchyard by rue Bonaparte, a little Picasso head of a woman is dedicated to the memory of the poet Apollinaire.

St-Sulpice to the Odéon

South of boulevard St-Germain, the streets round St-Sulpice are calm and classy. **Rue Mabillon** is pretty, with a row of old houses set back below the level of the modern street. Among its two or three restaurants is the old-fashioned *Aux Charpentiers*, property of the Guild of Carpenters, decorated with models of rafters and roof-trees. On the left are the **halles St-Germain**, incorporating a swimming pool, gym, auditorium and new commercial complex, built on the site of a fifteenth-century market. Rue Lobineau, which runs along its south side, has a tempting *pâtisserie* at no. 2.

Rue Mabillon abuts on rue St-Sulpice, which leads through to the front of the enormous **church of St-Sulpice**. Erected around the turn of the eighteenth century, this is an austerely classical edifice, with a Doric colonnade surmounted by an Ionic, and Corinthian pilasters in the towers – the only finished one serves as a nesting site for kestrels. The interior, containing some Delacroix frescoes in the first chapel on the right, is not to everyone's taste. But, softened by the chestnut trees and fountain of the square, the ensemble is peaceful and harmonious. To the south, rue Férou – where a gentleman called Pottier composed the revolutionary anthem, the *Internationale*, in 1776 – connects with **rue de Vaugirard**, Paris' longest street, and the **Luxembourg gardens** (see below).

On the sunny north side is the **place St-Sulpice** is the popular *Café de la Marie*, but the main attraction here is **Yves Saint Laurent Rive Gauche**, the most elegant fashion boutique on the Left Bank, on the corner of the ancient **rue des Canettes**. Further along the same side of the *place* there's Saint Laurent for men, and then it's Consume, Consume all the way, with your triple-gilt uranium-plated credit card, down rues Bonaparte, Madame, de Sèvres, de Grenelle, du Four, des Saints-Pères . . . . Hard to believe now, but smack in the middle of all this, at the carrefour de la Croix Rouge, there was a major barricade in 1871, fiercely defended by Eugène Varlin, one of the Commune's leading lights. He was later betrayed by a priest, half-beaten to death and shot by government troops on Montmartre hill.

For more on the Commune, see pp.162 & 413.

These days you're more likely to be suffering from till-shock than shell-shock. You may feel safer in rue Princesse at the small, friend-ly and well-stocked American bookshop, *The Village Voice*, where you can browse through the latest literature and journals. Or you could retreat to the less stylish eastern edge of the *quartier*, around bd St-Michel, where the university is firmly implanted, its attendant bookshops displaying scientific and medical tomes, and skeletons and instruments of torture. But there is really no escape from ele-gance in these parts, as you'll see in rue de Tournon and rue de l'Odéon, both leading up towards the Luxembourg gardens, the lat-ter taking in the Doric portico of the **Théâtre de l'Odéon** en route.

The Luxembourg palace and gardens

It was Marie de Médicis, Henri IV's widow, who had the **Jardin** and **Palais du Luxembourg** built to remind her of the Palazzo Pitti and Giardino di Boboli of her native Florence. The palace forms yet another of those familiar Parisian backdrops that no one pays much attention to, though there would be outrage if they were to disap-pear, not least from the members of the French senate who have their seat here. Opposite the gates, scarcely noticeable on the end wall of the colonnade of no. 36 rue de Vaugirard, is a metre rule, set up during the Revolution to guide the people in the introduction of the new metric system.

The **gardens** are the chief lung and recreation ground of the Left Bank, with tennis courts, pony rides, a children's playground, *boules* pitch, yachts to rent on the pond and, in the wilder southeast corner, a miniature orchard of elaborately espaliered pear trees. With its strollers and mooners and garish *parterres*, it has a distinctly Mediterranean air on summer days, when the most contested spot is the shady Fontaine de Médicis, in the northeast corner.

In the last week of September an "Expo-Automne" takes place in the Orangerie (entrance from 19 rue de Vaugirard, opposite rue Férou) where fruits– including the Luxembourg's own wonderful pears– and floral decorations are sold.

Chapter 7

Trocadéro, Eiffel Tower and Les Invalides

A
s you stand on the terrace of the **Palais de Chaillot** (place du Trocadéro) and look across the river to the **Tour Eiffel** and **École Militaire,** or let your gaze run from the ornate 1900 Pont Alexandre III along the grassy Esplanade to the **Hôtel des Invalides,** the vistas are absolutely splendid. But once you have said to yourself, "How magnificent!", that's it, more or less. This is town planning on the despotic scale, an assertion of power that takes no account of the small-scale interests and details of everyday lives.

The **7e arrondissement**, to which the Left Bank sections of these nineteenth- and twentieth-century urban landscapings belong, has the greatest concentration of ministries, embassies and official residences in Paris. The **Assemblée Nationale** is here, in the Palais Bourbon facing place de la Concorde across the river, and the entrance to the city's **sewers.** But corners of more amenable life do exist – in **rue Babylone**, and in the streets between the Invalides and the Champs de Mars. There is also the best-used decommissioned railway station, the **Musée d'Orsay**, on the river bank towards St-Germain.

Of all the mega-monuments of this area, the best is, undoubtedly, the Eiffel Tower. No matter how many pictures, photos, models or glimpses from elsewhere in the city you may have seen, it is still, when you get up close, an amazing structure.

The Palais de Chaillot

The **Palais de Chaillot** was built in 1937 like a latterday pharaoh's mausoleum, on a site that has been a ruler's favourite since Catherine de Médicis constructed one of her playpens there in the early sixteenth century. Today's monster is home to several interesting museums (see pp.292, 294 & 296) and the *Théâtre National Populaire* company, founded by Jean Vilar. The enormous theatre, where diverse but usually radical productions are staged, lies under the *terrasse*. This is the place to plant yourself, hassled by souvenir vendors, for the view across to the Eiffel Tower and École Militaire. The **Palais de Tokyo**, contemporary with Chaillot and no less hideous, is a short way east on the Right Bank. It houses one of the city's great modern art museums, the **Musée d'Art Moderne de la Ville de Paris**, and is about to become home to the new **Palais du Cinéma**. From here you can reach the Eiffel Tower via the Passerelle Debilly footbridge and quai Branly.

The Palais de Chaillot, Eiffel Tower, École Militaire

The Eiffel Tower

When completed in 1889, the **Tour Eiffel** was, at 300 metres, the tallest building in the world. Its 7000 tonnes of steel, in terms of pressure, sit as lightly on the ground as a child in a chair. Reactions to it were violent:

> *[We] protest with all our force, with all our indignation, in the name of unappreciated French taste, in the name of menaced French art and history, against the erection, in the very heart of our capital, of the useless and monstrous Eiffel Tower. . . Is Paris going to be associated with the grotesque, mercantile imaginings of a constructor of machines?*

The Musée d'Art Moderne de la Ville de Paris and the Palais du Cinéma are reviewed on p.285.

Eiffel himself thought it was beautiful. "The first principle of architectural aesthetics", he said, "prescribes that the basic lines of a structure must correspond precisely to its specified use. . . To a certain extent the tower was formed by the wind itself." Needless to say, it stole the show at the 1889 Exposition, for which it had been constructed.

In 1986 the external night-time floodlighting was replaced by a system of illumination from within the tower's superstructure, so that it now looks at its magical best after dark, as light and fanciful as a filigree minaret. Going to the top by lift (Sept–June 9.30am–11pm, July & Aug 9.30am–midnight) costs 56F (20F and 40F respectively for the first two levels) – so that it is only really worth the expense on an absolutely clear day. If you take the stairs (access to levels 1 and 2 only), the cost is 12F. The only reductions are for children under 12. Tickets allow free entry to the audiovisual show about the Tower on the first level.

Around the École Militaire

Stretching back from the legs of the Tower, the long rectangular gardens of the **Champs de Mars** lead to the eighteenth-century buildings of the **École Militaire**, now the Staff College, originally founded in 1751 by Louis XV for the training of aristocratic army officers. No prizes for guessing who the most famous graduate was. A less illustrious but better loved French soldier has his name remembered in a neighbouring street and square: Cambronne. He commanded the last surviving unit of Napoléon's Imperial Guard at Waterloo. Although surrounded and reduced to a bare handful of men, when called on to surrender by the English he shouted back into the darkness one

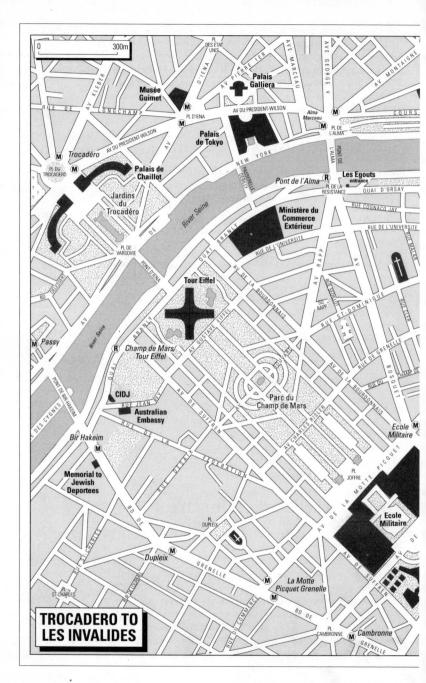

TROCADERO TO
LES INVALIDES

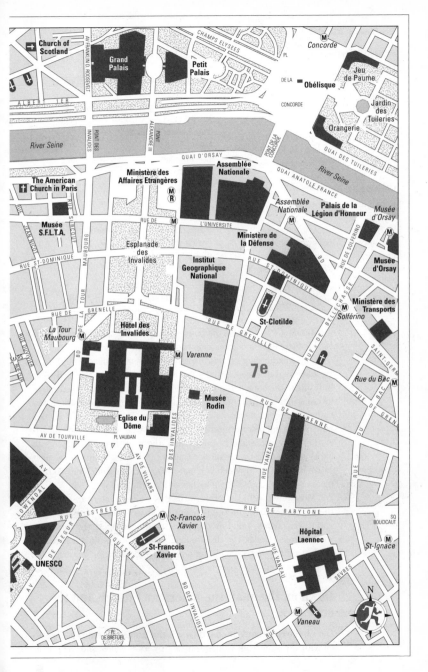

word: *"Merde"* – (Shit!)– the commonest French swear word, known euphemistically ever since as *le mot de Cambronne*.

The surrounding *quartier* may be expensive and sought after as an address, but physically it's uninspiring – just like the UNESCO building at the back of the École Militaire. Controversial at the time of its construction in 1958, these days it looks somewhat pedestrian, and badly weathered. Open to the public (Mon–Fri 9am–6pm), it does have some interesting internal spaces, as well as a number of artworks, both inside and in the garden, the most noticeable being an enormous mobile by Alexander Calder. The finest feature is a quiet Japanese garden, to which you can repair on a summer's day to read a paper bought from the well-stocked kiosk in the foyer.

Most unexpected, therefore, in this rather austere *quartier* is the wedge of **early nineteenth-century streets** between av Bosquet and the Invalides. Chief among them is the market street **rue Cler**, whose cross-streets, rue de Grenelle and rue St-Dominique, are full of classy little shops, including a couple of *boulangeries* with their original painted glass panels.

Down on the quai: the American Church and the sewers

Out on the river bank at quai d'Orsay, the **American church**, together with the American College in nearby av Bosquet (no. 31), provides a focus for the well-organized life of the large American community. The notice board is plastered with job and accommodation offers and requests, and the people are friendly and helpful in all kinds of ways.

Other quayside attractions include the **sewers**, *les égouts* (Mon–Wed, Sat & Sun May–Oct 11am–5pm, Nov–April 11am–4pm; closed Thurs & Fri; last ticket an hour before closing; 25F/20F), the entrance to which is 50m east of the Pont de l'Alma and Quai d'Orsay junction. Your nose will tell you all you need to know, if not the cadaverous pallor of the superannuated sewermen who wait on you. The guidebooks always bill this as an outing for kids; I doubt it. The visit consists of an unilluminating film, a small museum and a very brief look at some tunnels with a lot of smelly water swirling about. Cloacal appetites will derive much more satisfaction from **Victor Hugo's description** in *Les Misérables*: twenty pages on the value of human excrement as manure (25 million francs' worth down the plughole in the 1860s), and the history of the sewer system, including the sewage flood of 1802 and the first perilous survey of the system in 1805, whose findings included a piece of Marat's winding sheet and the skeleton of an orang-utan.

The film show is a laugh for its evasive gentility. It opens with misty sunrises, portraits of monarchs, and a breathless voice saying, "Paris, do you remember when you were little?", before relating how three million *baguettes*, 1000 tonnes of fruit, 100 tonnes of fish and so on make their daily progress through the guts of the city and end up here. As for the museum, serious students of urban planning could find some interesting items, if they were only allowed the time to look. In fact, you might be better off staying in the museum and skipping the tour. Among other things there is an appropriate memorial to Louis Napoléon: an inscription beginning, "In the reign of His Majesty Napoléon III, Emperor of the French, the sewer of the rue de Rivoli . . .".

Notable buildings in the 7e arrondissement

• **29 avenue Rapp.** *RER* Pont de l'Alma.
A really over-the-top Art Nouveau number with bulls' heads, turbaned women and revolting colour changes. Designed by Lavirotte, 1901.

• **Square Rapp**, off av Rapp. *RER* Pont de l'Alma.
A bizarre ensemble: more Lavirotte at no. 43, a trellis *trompe l'œil* and the Société Théosophique de France.

• **12 rue Sédillot.** *RER* Pont de l'Alma.
Art Nouveau and Art Deco elements in superb dormers and wrought iron grills and balconies.

• **Conservatoire de Musique**, 7 rue Jean-Nicot. M° Invalides.
Christian Portzamparc playing with a half-peeled tube of a tower and a window to its right that has some unspecific musical association.

Les Invalides

The **Esplanade des Invalides**, striking due south from **Pont Alexandre III**, is a more attractive and uncluttered vista than Chaillot–École Militaire. The wide façade of the **Hôtel des Invalides**, topped by its distinctive dome, resplendent with new gilding to celebrate the Bicentenary of the Revolution, fills the whole of the further end of the Esplanade. It was built on the orders of Louis XIV as a home for invalided soldiers. Under the dome are two churches: one for the soldiers, the other intended as a mausoleum for the king but now containing the mortal remains of Napoléon. The Hôtel (*son et lumière* in English, April–Sept) houses the vast **Musée de l'Armée**.

Both churches are cold and dreary inside. The **Église du Dôme**, in particular, is a supreme example of architectural pomposity. Corinthian columns and pilasters abound. The dome – pleasing enough from the outside – is covered with paintings and flanked by four round chapels displaying the tombs of various luminaries. Napoléon's sarcophagus, of smooth red porphyry, is sunk into the floor and enclosed within a gallery whose friezes, displaying execrable taste and grovelling piety, are captioned with quotations of awesome conceit from the great man himself: "Co-operate with the plans I have laid for the welfare of peoples"; "By its simplicity my code of law has done more good in France than all the laws which have preceded me"; "Wherever the shadow of my rule has fallen, it has left lasting traces of its value."

The Musée de l'Armée is described on p.294.

East towards St-Germain

Immediately east of the Invalides is the **Musée Rodin**, on the corner of rue de Varenne, housed in a beautiful eighteenth-century mansion which the sculptor leased from the state in return for the gift of all his work at his death. The garden, planted with sculptures, is quite as pretty as the house, with a pond and flowering shrubs and a superb view of the Invalides dome rising above the trees.

The Musée Rodin is fully described on p.287.

The rest of the street, and the parallel rue de Grenelle, is full of aristocratic mansions, including the **Hôtel Matignon**, the prime minister's residence. At the further end, rue du Bac leads into rue de Sèvres, cutting across **rue de Babylone**, another of the *quartier's* livelier streets, which begins at Sèvres-Babylone with the city's oldest department store, **Au Bon Marché**, renowned for its food halls, and ends with the crazy, rich man's folly **La Pagode**, the city's most exotic cinema (see p.356) and one of its most pleasant *salons de thé*.

Newspapers reporting on French foreign policy use "the quai d'Orsay" to refer to the Ministère des Affaires Étrangères, which sits between the Esplanade des Invalides and the Palais Bourbon, home of the **Assemblée Nationale**. Napoléon, never a great one for democracy, had the riverfront façade of the Palais Bourbon done to match the pseudo-Greek of the Madeleine. The result is an entrance that suggests very little illumination within.

The same could perhaps be said of the **Musée d'Orsay**, a few blocks eastward on the riverfront, whose stone façade disguises a huge vault of steel and glass. Once inside, however, illumination is all-pervasive – from the vault and from the greatest collection of Impressionist paintings. The building was inaugurated as a railway station in time for the 1900 World Fair, and continued to serve the stations of southwest France until 1939. The theatre troupe *Reynaud-Barrault*, in their squatting phase, staged several productions here. Orson Welles used it as the setting for his film of Kafka's *Trial*, filling the high, narrow corridors with filing cabinets to create a nightmarishly claustrophobic setting. De Gaulle used it to announce his coup d'état of May 19, 1958 – his messianic return to power to save the *patrie* from disintegration over the Algerian liberation war.

Notwithstanding this illustrious history, it was only saved from a hotel developer's bulldozer by the colossal wave of public indignation and remorse at the destruction of Les Halles. The job of redesigning it as a museum was given to the Italian architect Gae Aulenti in the late 1980s.

Les Invalides

You'll find a full account of the Musée d'Orsay on p.280.

Chapter 8

Montparnasse and the Southern Arrondissements

Montparnasse serves to divide the lands of the well-heeled opinion-formers and power-brokers of St-Germain and the 7ᵉ from the amorphous populations of the three southern *arrondissements*. Overscale developments from the 1950s to the present day have scarred some parts of this southern side of the city, but new spaces have also opened up, and some of the contemporary smaller scale developments are delightful. Here are pockets of Paris that have been allowed to evolve in a happily patchy way – **Pernety** and **Plaisance** in the 14ᵉ, the **rue du Commerce** in the 15ᵉ, and the **Butte-aux-Cailles** *quartier* in the 13ᵉ. These are genuinely pleasant places to explore, and well off the beaten tourist tracks.

Montparnasse

In the eighteenth-century, the pile of spoil from the Denfert-Rochereau quarries, on what is now the corner of bd du Montparnasse and bd Raspail, was named Mont Parnasse (Mount Parnassus) by drunken students who liked to declaim poetry from the top of it. **Montparnasse**, stretching from the railway station to the Observatory, kept its associations with art, bohemia and left-leaning intellectuals, attracting the likes of Verlaine and Baudelaire in the nineteenth century, and Trotsky, Picasso, Man Ray, Chagall, Hemingway, Sartre and Simone de Beauvoir in the twentieth.

Boulevard du Montparnasse runs southeast from rue de Sèvres to Port Royal, passing through the area around the station – a mix of workers' barracks and old-fashioned streets dominated by the gigantic **Tour Montparnasse**. Most of the celebrated **literary cafés** are on the stretch of the boulevard between place du 18-Juin-1940 and bd Raspail, and many of their habitués are buried in **Montparnasse ceme-tery**, between the station and Denfert-Rochereau. To the east of the cemetery is the Paris Observatory, connected to the Jardin du

Montparnasse: listings

RESTAURANTS
Chez Maria, 16 rue du Maine, 14e. M^o
Montparnasse.
La Coupole, 102 bd du Montparnasse, 14e.
M^o Vavin.

CAFÉS AND BARS
La Closerie des Lilas, 171 bd du
Montparnasse, 6e. M^o Port-Royal.
Le Dôme, 108 bd du Montparnasse, 6e. M^o
Vavin.
Mustangs, 84 bd du Montparnasse, 14e.
M^o Montparnasse.
La Pause Gourmande, 27 rue Campagne-
Première, 14e. M^o Raspail.

La Mamma, 46 rue Vavin, 6e. M^o Vavin.
L'Ostréade, 11 bd Vaugirard, 15e. M^o
Montparnasse.

Le Rosebud, 11 bis rue Delambre, 14e. M^o
Vavin.
La Rotonde, 105 bd du Montparnasse, 6e.
M^o Vavin.
Le Select, 99 bd du Montparnasse, 6e. M^o
Vavin.
Tea and Tattered Pages, 24 rue Mayet, 6e.
M^o Duroc.

These establishments are reviewed in Chapter 13, Eating and drinking, *beginning on p.259.*

Luxembourg by the av de l'Observatoire, which crosses the eastern end of bd de Montparnasse and the beginning of bd de Port-Royal en route.

Around the station

Montparnasse was once the great arrival and departure point for boat travellers across the Atlantic, whether impoverished emigrants or passengers on luxury cruises, and for Bretons seeking work in the capital. On place Bienvenue, in front of the modern station, you can still find Breton bands busking. Yet, as a dramatic introduction or farewell to the capital, the scene is hardly auspicious. Despite a new fishbowl glass frontage with curved bits of blue and grey steel, the station fails to impose, mainly because its prospect of the city is blocked by the colossal Tour Montparnasse. This has become one of the city's principal and least-liked landmarks – most tolerable at night, when the red corner lights give it a certain elegance. At 200m, it held the record as Europe's tallest office building until it was overtaken by the tower at London Docklands' Canary Wharf. You can take a tour for less than it costs to go to the top of the Eiffel Tower (summer 9.30am–11.30pm, winter 9.30am–10.30pm; 42F/26F; entrance on the north side), or you could spend the same amount on a drink in the 56th-storey bar – the lift ride is free – where you get a tremendous view westward over the city, especially at sunset.

In front of the tower, on **place du 18-Juin-1940**, is an enormous, largely subterranean shopping complex, on the front of which a plaque records that this was the spot where General Leclerc of the Free French forces received the surrender of von Choltitz, the German general commanding Paris, on August 25, 1944. Under orders from Hitler to destroy the city before abandoning it, von Choltitz luckily dis-

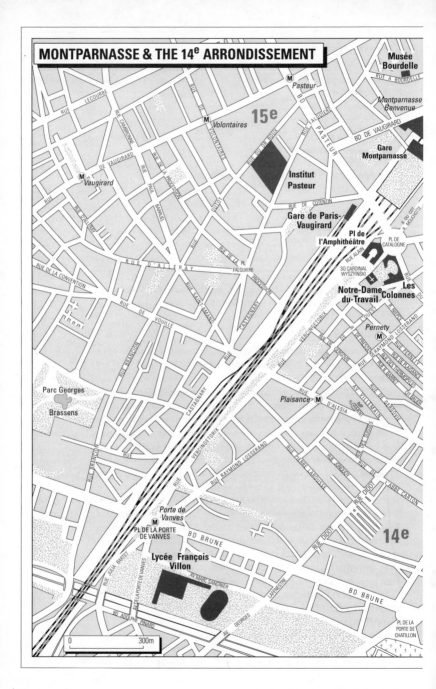

MONTPARNASSE & THE 14ᵉ ARRONDISSEMENT

Musée Bourdelle

RUE A BOURDELLE

RUE LECOURBE

Ⓜ Pasteur

BD PASTEUR

Montparnasse Benvenue

RUE DE CAMBRONNE

Ⓜ Volontaires

15e

BD DE VAUGIRARD

Gare Montparnasse

RUE DE VAUGIRARD

RUE DU DR ROUX

Institut Pasteur

Ⓜ Vaugirard

RUE PAUL BARRUEL

RUE DE LA PROCESSION

RUE DE COTENTIN

Gare de Paris-Vaugirard

RUE DE VAUGIRARD

R. DU COT
PL MOUSTIE

PL DE CATALOGNE

Pl de l'Amphithéâtre

RUE D'ALLERAY

RUE DE LA CONVENTION

RUE SAINT-AMAND

RUE DE LA PL FALGUIÈRE

RUE PROCESSION

RUE ALAIN
SQ CARDINAL WYSZYŃSKI

Les Colonnes

Notre-Dame du-Travail

RUE DE VOUILLÉ

RUE CASTAGNARY

RUE DE CRESSILLY

RUE PERNETY

Pernety Ⓜ

RUE RAYMOND LOSSERAND

RUE DES THERMOPYLES

RUE DE PLAISANCE

RUE DE GERGOVIE

RUE DE BAUER

RUE BRANCION

Parc Georges Brassens

RUE

Plaisance › Ⓜ

AV VILLEMAIN

D'ALÉSIA

RUE DU MOULIN

RUE VERCINGÉTORIX

RUE RAYMOND LOSSERAND

RUE PIERRE LAROUSSE

RUE DE DIDOT

RUE JONQUOY

RUE D

ABBÉ CARTON

RUE BRANCION

Ⓜ Porte de Vanves

PL DE LA PORTE DE VANVES

BD BRUNE

RUE DIDOT

14e

RUE JULIA BARTET

AV DE LA PORTE DE VANVES

Lycée François Villon

AV MARC SANGNIER

LAFENESTRE

BD BRUNE

BD ADOLPHE PINARD

AV GEORGES

PL DE LA PORTE DE CHATILLON

| 0 | 300m |

134

THE CITY: CHAPTER 8

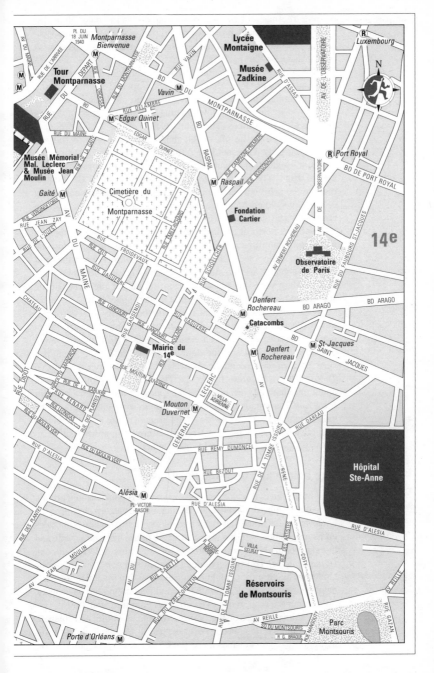

obeyed. The name of the *place* commemorates the date, (June 18, 1940), when de Gaulle broadcast from London, calling on the people of France to continue the struggle in spite of the armistice signed with the Germans by Marshal Pétain.

A memorial to Leclerc, combined with a **museum** dedicated to the Resistance leader, Jean Moulin, has been opened overlooking the newly created and soulless Jardin Atlantique, all built on a raised platform over the railway lines behind the station, surrounded by hideous high rise offices (Tues–Sun 10am–5.40pm; 17.50F/9F; simplest access from the lift on bd du Vaugirard, opposite the *Air France* bureau). Very much an official interpretation of events, the museum's highlight is a panoramic, breathless slide show of the summer of 1944. The museum gives rather short shrift to US involvement in the proceedings, a stance echoed in the fortieth anniversary celebrations, when American visitors to Paris were shocked at the absence of the Stars and Stripes from the tanks parading the streets.

One block north of bd du Vaugirard, on rue Antoine-Bourdelle, a garden of sculptures invites you into the **Bourdelle museum**, the artist's old atelier (see p.291). At the end of the street and to the right on rue Falguière are the stunning offices of *Le Monde* newspaper. The building veers up and away from the line of the street in the smoothest of curves, like the hull of a fantasy spaceship.

To the east of the station, the market on bd Edgar-Quinet provides down-to-earth clientele for cafés in the surrounding streets, in marked contrast to renowned establishments a stone's throw away on bd du Montparnasse. **Rue de la Gaité**, where Trotsky lived, is a slice of turn-of-the-century theatreland, with the newly restored *Théâtre Montparnasse* facing the *Théâtre Gaité-Montparnasse*, and a fair share of porn outlets and junkies. At no. 17, *La Comedia Italienne* has cupids and *commedia della'arte* characters on its violent pink exterior, while the *Rive Gauche*, at no. 8, has an equally spectacular frontage. The street is featured in a mural that's visible as you look south from bd Edgar-Quinet.

The boulevard du Montparnasse

Most of the life of the Montparnasse *quartier* is concentrated around place du 18-Juin-1940 and along the immediate eastern stretch of the boulevard. Like other Left Bank *quartiers*, Montparnasse still trades on its association with the wild characters of the interwar artistic and literary boom. Many were habitués of the cafés *Select*, *Coupole*, *Dôme*, *Rotonde* and *Closerie des Lilas*, all still going strong on the boulevard along with six multi-screen cinemas and several more in the neighbouring streets. It stays up late, and negotiating the pavements, never mind the road, requires careful concentration at all times.

The animated part of the boulevard ends at **boulevard Raspail**, where Rodin's *Balzac* broods over the traffic, though literary curiosity might take you down as far as the **Closerie des Lilas**, on the corner of the tree-lined avenue connecting the Observatory and Luxembourg gardens in a classic grand Parisian vista. Hemingway used to come here to write, and Marshal Ney, one of Napoléon's most glamorous generals, was killed by a royalist firing squad on the pavement outside in 1815. He's still there, waving his sword, immortalized in stone. Close by, dwarfed by apartment buildings at 100bis rue d'Assas, is the house and garden of the Russian sculptor **Ossip Zadkine**, now a museum of his work and one of the most delightful oases in the city.

Montparnasse

The Musée Zadkine is detailed on p.293.

South along bd Raspail at no. 261, about 500m from bd du Montparnasse, is the **Fondation Cartier pour l'Art Contemporain** (Tues–Sun noon–8pm, Thurs till 10pm, closed Mon; 30F/20F), a stunning glass and steel construction designed by Jean Nouvel in 1994. A glass wall following the line of the street is attached by steel tubes to the building behind, leaving a space for trees to grow. All kinds of contemporary art – installations, videos, multi-media – often by American artists little known in France, are shown in temporary exhibitions that use the light and the very generous spaces to maximum advantage.

Montparnasse cemetery and the catacombs

Just off to the southern side of bd Edgar-Quinet is the main entrance to the **Montparnasse cemetery** (Mon–Fri 8am–6pm, Sat 8.30am–6pm, Sun 9am–6pm), a gloomy spot containing ranks of miniature temples, dreary and bizarre, and plenty of illustrious names. To the right of the entrance, by the wall, is the unembellished grave of Jean-Paul Sartre, who lived out the last few decades of his life just a few metres away on bd Raspail.

Notable buildings around boulevard Montparnasse and the Montparnasse cemetery

• **26 rue Varin**, 6e. Mo Vavin.
A block of flats in white and blue tiles, with terraced balconies filled with exuberant gardens in the air. Built by Henri Sauvage in 1912.

• **Rue Schoelcher and rue Froidevaux**. Mo Raspail/Denfert-Rochereau.
An excellent selection of nineteenth- and twentieth-century styles, of particular note being 5, 5bis and 11 rue Schoelcher, 11 and 23 rue Froidevaux, this last a 1930s block of artists' studios, with huge windows for northern light and fabulous ceramic mosaics.

• **266 boulevard Raspail**, 14e. Mo Raspail/Denfert-Rochereau.
An interior design school with a marked Beaubourg influence: external stairs and blue pipe columns in front, plus the 1990s delight of glass and metal shuttering.

• **31 rue Campagne-Première**, 14e. Mo Raspail.
A myriad of earthernware tiles cover the concrete structure of these desirable 1912 *appartements* with huge windows.

Down av de l'Ouest, which follows the western wall of the cemetery, you'll find the **tombs** of Baudelaire (who has a more impressive ceno-taph by rue Émile-Richard, on av Transversale), the painter Soutine, Dadaist Tristan Tzara, sculptor Zadkine, and the Fascist Pierre Laval, a member of Pétain's government who, after the war, was executed for treason, while in the throes of death from suicide. As an antidote, you can pay homage to Proudhon, the anarchist who coined the phrase "Property is theft!"; he lies in Division 1, by the Carrefour du Rond-Point.

In the southwest corner of the cemetery is an old windmill, one of the seventeenth-century taverns frequented by the carousing, versi-fying students who gave the Montparnasse district its name.

Across rue Émile-Richard, in the eastern section of the cemetery, lie the mathematician Poincaré, car-maker André Citroën, Guy de Maupassant, César Frank, and the celebrated victim of turn-of-the-century French anti-semitism, Captain Dreyfus. Right in the northern corner is a tomb with a sculpture by Brancusi – *Le Baiser* – which makes a far sadder statement than the dramatic and passionate scenes of grief adorning so many of the graves here. And, for the bizarre, by the wall along av du Boulevard (parallel to bd Raspail) you can see the inventor of a safe gas lamp, Charles Pigeon, in bed next to his sleeping wife, reading a book by the light of his lamp.

If you are determined to spend your time among the deceased, you can descend into **the catacombs** (Tues–Fri 2–6pm, Sat & Sun 9–11am & 2–4pm; 27F/19F) in nearby **place Denfert-Rochereau**, formerly place d'Enfer – "Hell Square". (The entrance is on the east side of the approach to av Général-Leclerc; don't go down in fancy new shoes – it's wet and gungy underfoot.) These are abandoned quarries stacked with millions of bones cleared from the old charnel houses in 1785, claustrophobic in the extreme, and cold to boot. Some years ago a group of punks and art students developed a macabre taste for this as the ultimate party location, but the over-seeing authorities soon put an end to that.

As well as interesting architecture around the cemetery (see box on p.137), there are quiet little streets to the south, between av du Maine and place Denfert-Rochereau, plus clothes and craft shops and a busy food market on rue Daguerre. Before and during the war, Sartre and Simone de Beauvoir kept separate rooms in the hotel at no. 24 rue Cels; a plaque gives a quote from each on the subject of their togetherness.

From Denfert-Rochereau, bd Arago leads east to the **Observatoire de Paris**, where there's a garden (April–Aug 1–7pm, Sept to mid-Oct 1–4pm) in which to sit and admire the dome. From the 1660s, when the Observatory was constructed, to 1884, all French maps had the zero meridian running through the middle of this building. After that date, they reluctantly agreed that 0° longitude should pass through a village in Normandy, which happens to be due south of Greenwich. Visiting the Observatoire is a complicated procedure and all you'll see are old maps and instruments.

Commerce and convention: the 15^e

Between the Montparnasse train tracks and the river lies the largest, most populated and characterless *arrondissement*, the 15e. It was in **rue du Commerce** that George Orwell worked as a dishwasher in a White Russian restaurant in the late 1920s, described in his *Down and Out in Paris and London*. Although there are still run-down and poor areas, an ever-widening stretch back from **the riverfront** is plush high-rise with underground parking, serviced lifts and electronic security. A **new park** has appeared on the old Citroën works down in the southwest corner, while over towards the rail lines the **Parc Georges-Brassens** is now well established on the former abattoir site.

The riverbank section

The western edge of the 15^e *arrondissement* fronts the Seine from the Eiffel Tower to beyond Pont du Garigliano. It would be almost totally unrecognizable to anyone returning from a thirty-year absence.

Just off Pont de Bir-Hakeim, at the beginning of bd de Grenelle, in a rather undignified enclosure sandwiched by high-rise buildings, a plaque commemorates the notorious **rafle du Vel d'Hiv**: the Nazi and French-aided round-up of 13,152 Parisian Jews in July 1942. Nine thousand of them, including four thousand children, were interned here at the now-vanished cycle track for a week before being carted off to Auschwitz. Thirty adults were the only survivors.

The quaysides are pretty inaccessible, but one place to walk is the **Allée des Cygnes,** a narrow island in midstream joining the Pont de Grenelle and the double-decker road and rail bridge, Pont de Bir-Hakeim. It's a strange place – one of Samuel Beckett's favourites – with just birds and trees and, at the downstream end, a scaled-down version of the **Statue of Liberty**. This was one of the four preliminary models constructed between 1874 and 1884 by sculptor Auguste Bartholdi, with the help of Gustave Eiffel, before the finished article (originally intended for Alexandria in Egypt) was presented to New York. Contemporary photos show the final version, assembled in Bartholdi's rue de Chazelles workshop, towering over the houses of the 17e like a bizarre female King Kong.

The river bank down to Pont Mirabeau is marred by a sort of mini-Défense development of half-cocked futuristic towers bearing pretentious galactic names like Castor and Pollux, Vega and Orion, rising out of a litter-blown pedestrian platform some 10m above ground level.

Three major streets fan into the *arrondissement* from Rond-Point du Pont-Mirabeau. Between rue Émile-Zola (demarcation line for the expensive tower block sector) and the long rue de la Convention lie the buildings of the **Imprimerie Nationale**, the national printworks. Their shop (Mon–Fri 9am–6pm) on rue Paul-Hervieu displays some of their publications – beautifully bound art books, musical scores,

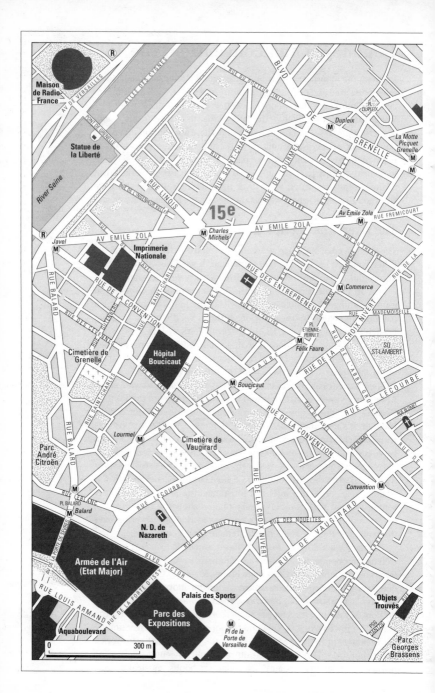

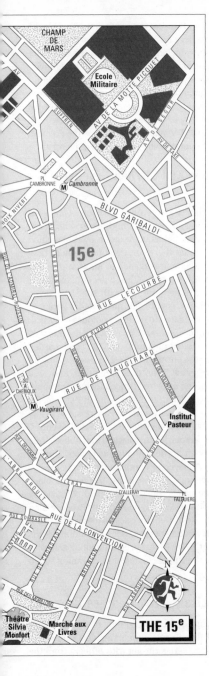

THE 15e

The 15e: listings

RESTAURANTS

Da Attilio, 21 rue Cronstadt, 15e. Mo Convention/Porte de Vanves.

Le Bistrot d'André, 232 rue St-Charles, 15e. Mo Baltard.

Le Clos Morillons, 50 rue Morillons, 15e. Mo Porte-de-Vanves.

Le Commerce, 51 rue du Commerce, 15e. Mo Émile-Zola.

Sampieru Corsu, 12 rue de l'Amiral-Roussin, 15e. Mo Cambronne.

Student restaurant at 156 rue Vaugirard, 15e. Mo Pasteur.

CAFÉS AND BARS

Travel Café, 2 rue d'Alleray, 15e. Mo Vaugirard.

These establishments are reviewed in Chapter 13, Eating and drinking, *on p.260.*

the *Rights of Man* on vellum, and current tax regulations. Two blocks east on rue St-Charles is a pocket of street life – rare for this side of the 15e – with small food shops, including a branch of the upmarket *Hédiard* and an excellent *boulangerie* on the corner with rue Javel.

Where the yuppie apartment blocks end at Rond-Point du Pont-Mirabeau, yuppie offices begin, notably the gleaming white, smooth hulk of the TV company *Canal +*. At this point, the quayside road diverts underground – to the fury of Parisian cyclists who now have to make a two-kilometre detour. The reason for this was the creation of the new Parc André-Citroën, on the site of the old car factory.

The Parc André-Citroën and Citroën-Cévennes quartier

For transport through the 15e, 14e and 13e arrondisse-ments, bus #62 plies a useful route along rues Convention, Alésia and Tolbiac.

The best thing about the **Parc André-Citroën** (Mon–Fri 7.30am–7pm, Sat & Sun 9am–7pm) are the hothouses – big glass boxes with mimosa, fish-tailed palms and other sweet-smelling shrubbery. The worst thing is that there's more concrete here than greenery, including the absurdist extravagance of an arch over the *RER* lines by the river, which is not a bridge, just a decorative device.

The layout of the park is extremely formal, with split levels, terraces, monumental plant holders, small enclosures, and a series of rather unsuccessful gardens dedicated to different colours – in April, the red garden is full of white apple and pear blossom, the only flower in the blue garden is a violent pink tulip, and the black garden is full of green helibore. Near the entrance closest to Pont-Mirabeau, you can at least walk on the grass, if on plastic matting, and on a cloud-scudding day the top of the mirrored office block to the south merges into the sky. The oddest thing is that no-one in Paris seems to know about this park, so it's virtually empty.

Across rue Balard is the totally new **quartier du Citroën-Cévennes**, with pedestrian streets, sports centres, youth clubs and the **Bibliothèque St-Charles**, a children's library on rue de la Montagne-d'Aulas. You can imagine Gutenberg – the German inventor of printing, remembered in a neighbouring street name – wearing a hat shaped like this peculiar black building with slanting metallic bands. Built in 1990 and designed by Franck Hammoutene, it has windows on only one side and inside around a circular courtyard in which a cherry tree struggles up towards the light.

In the middle of the new developments is a slice of traditional Paris – the **Grenelle cemetery**. In France, however influential and with however many politicians in their pockets, developers cannot touch a burial ground.

From the École Militaire to Parc Georges-Brassens

If you start walking in **avenue de la Motte-Picquet**, by the **École Militaire**, you'll get the full flavour of the **quartier du Commerce**. That's the staid end, where brasseries throng with officers from the

École, and 150 expensive antique shops in the rather dreary **Village Suisse** (all open Thurs–Mon) display Louis Quinze and Second Empire. The nature of the *quartier* changes at **boulevard de Grenelle**, where the métro runs on iron piers above the street. Seedy hotels rent rooms by the month, and the corner cafés offer cheap *plats du jour*. **Rue du Commerce** begins here, a lively, old-fashioned high street – once you're past the *Burger King* and *Uniprix* – full of small shops and peeling, shuttered houses. Scale and architecture give it a sunny, friendly atmosphere. The best-known cheap eating establishment is *Le Commerce*, at no. 51, and there are other restaurants and interesting shops in the surrounding streets.

Towards the end of the street is **place du Commerce**, with trees and a bandstand in the middle – a model of old-fashioned, petty-bourgeois respectability. Cafés and *pâtisseries* proliferate as rue du Commerce ends at place Étienne-Pernet, where cottagey houses still exist on the west side of the *place*. If you follow rue des Entrepreneurs east, past a beautiful apartment building at no. 109, you come to the surprisingly generous green space of **square Lambert**, with fountains and lawns overlooked by the prison-like premises of a *lycée* (top-stream secondary school).

If you carry on south, rue de la Croix-Nivert brings you to the **Porte de Versailles** where, at an informer's signal, government troops first entered the city in their final assault on the Commune on May 21, 1871. Today it is the site of several large **exhibition halls** that host the *foires* – the Agricultural Show, Ideal Home Exhibition and the like. To the west, along bd Victor, are good discount clothes shops and the wonderful 1930s École Nationale Supérieure de Techniques Avancées, decorated with reliefs of "advanced technologies". Behind the headquarters of the French Air Force, to which the school is attached, is *Aquaboulevard*, the city's largest **leisure centre**, whose main attraction is an artificial tropical lagoon complete with beaches, exotic plants and giant water chutes (see p.304).

Discount clothes shops are reviewed on p.327.

More traditional relaxation – and for free – is on hand at **parc Georges-Brassens**, whose main entrance, on rue des Morillons, is flanked by two bronze bulls. The old Vaugirard abattoir was transformed into this park in the 1980s, and the original clock tower remains, surrounded by a pond. It's a delight, especially for children – there is a garden of scented herbs and shrubs designed principally for the blind (best in late spring), puppets and rocks and merry-go-rounds for the kids, a mountain stream with pine and birch trees, beehives and a tiny terraced vineyard. The corrugated pyramid with a helter-skelter-like spiral is a theatre, the *Silvia-Montfort*.

Book lovers should take a look in the sheds of the old horse market between the park and rue Briançon where, every Saturday and Sunday morning, dozens of **book dealers** set out their genuinely interesting stock. The success of the park has rubbed off on **rue des**

La Ruche

After the World Fair ended, the wine pavilion was bought by Alfred Boucher, sculptor of public monuments and friend of Rodin, and re-erected here in an altruistic gesture of help for struggling artists. Very soon La Ruche, or the Beehive, became home to Fernand Léger, Modigliani (briefly), Chagall, Soutine, Ossip Zadkine and many others, mainly Jewish refugees from pogroms in Poland and Russia. Boucher, somewhat overwhelmed by the unconventional work and behaviour of his protégés, commented goodnaturedly: "I'm like a hen who finds she has laid ducks' eggs."

Léger, evoking the poverty, recalls how he was invited to lunch one day by four Russian residents who had just made a few francs selling cat pelts. The meal was the cats, dismembered and fricassé-ed in vodka. "It burnt your mouth and it stank," he noted, "but it was better than nothing."

The writer Blaise Centrars was a regular visitor, as were Apollinaire and Max Jacob, who provided a link with the Picasso gang across the river in Montmartre, and there was much cross-fertilization going on in the cafés too, especially *La Rotonde*, at 105 bd du Montparnasse. But at *La Ruche* itself the French were in a minority; you were much more likely to hear Yiddish, Polish, Russian or Italian spoken.

It is still something of a Tower of Babel these days, with Irish, American, Italian and Japanese artists in residence, although, as an Italian mosaicist who has been there since the 1950s said, there is no longer the Bohemian camaraderie and festivity of the old days. The buildings were saved from the bulldozers in 1970 by a campaign led by Marc Chagall, since which physical conditions have improved.

Morillons and **rue Briançon**; new restaurants and tearooms have opened, and old cafés have livened up.

On the east side of the park, in a secluded garden in passage Dantzig, off rue Dantzig, stands an unusual polygonal building known as **La Ruche**. It was designed by Eiffel and started life as the wine pavilion for the 1900 trade fair (see box). Although not strictly open to the public, residents are quite happy to let you wander around.

If you're heading towards Montparnasse from Parc Georges-Brassens, take bus #89 rather than slogging it on foot. Not a lot happens in this eastern stretch of the 15e. To the north, between rue du Docteur-Roux and rue Falguière, is the **Pasteur Institute**, renowned for its founder, (who more or less invented modern biology), and for its research into AIDS.

*For details of
the Pasteur
Museum, see
p.298.*

The 14e below Montparnasse

The 14e is one of the best of the outer *arrondissement*s. While the area beside the train tracks immediately south of Gare Montparnasse has changed dramatically, old-fashioned networks of streets still exist in the **Pernety** and **Plaisance** *quartiers*, and between avs Réné-Coty and Général-Leclerc. In the early years of the century, so many outlawed Russian revolutionaries lived in the 14e that the Tsarist police ran a special Paris section to keep tabs on them. The 14e was also a favourite address for artists, who could live in seclusion in its many *villas* (mews) built in the 1920s and 1930s. There is still a thriving artistic community here, though only the very successful can afford the *villas* these days. Down in the southeast corner there's plenty of green space, in the **Parc Montsouris** and in the **Cité Universitaire**, home to more revolutionaries in their student days.

Pernety, Plaisance and down to the perimeter

Had it not been for the efforts of the local campaign group "Vivre dans le 14e", there might have been an expressway flanked by tower blocks all the way down the western edge of the *arrondissement* to the *boulevard périphérique*. Instead, the old **rue Vercingétorix** has become a walkway and cycle track past gardens, kids' play areas, *boules* pitches and tennis courts.

This is not at all what you'd expect if you approach from **place de Catalogne**, where the Catalan architect Ricardo Bofill has created one of his gargantuan Wagnerian complexes of amphitheatres and colonnades bedecked with classical features stripped of any structural purpose. They're an improvement on the supremely gross office blocks that bridge the train lines between bd Pasteur and place de Catalogne, and the titled disc fountain in the square is quite fetching. But it's a relief to find yourself in front of **Notre-Dame du Travail**, designed for humans rather than imaginary giants.

This church was built at the turn of the century to cater for a congregation swollen by the men employed in building the Eiffel Tower and the surrounding exhibition palaces for the Exposition Universelle.

The stone came from the Cloth Pavilion and the slender metal columns of the interior from the Palace of Industry, while the bell hails from Sebastopol – a present to the local people from Napoléon III.

No trace remains of the flats where these skilled builders would have lived on rue Vercingétorix or rue de l'Ouest (birthplace of comic actor/director Jacques Tati); nor of the working-class population that would have outnumbered the present residents of Pernety and Plaisance by two to one. But wander westwards through the streets between rue Raymond-Losserand and rue des Plantes and you'll find pockets where the physical fabric, if not the social make-up, hasn't changed since Notre-Dame du Travail was built. And artists still love this part of town.

Cité Bauer has adorable little houses with gardens; neighbouring rue des Thermopyles has its secluded courtyards; and below rue d'Alésia, more quiet mews lead off from rue Didot. Giacometti's old ramshackle studio and home still stands on the corner of rue du Moulin Vert and rue Hippolyte-Maindron. At the end of Impasse Floriment, behind a petrol station on rue d'Alésia and holding out against development threats, a bronze relief of Georges Brassens smoking his pipe – created by a contemporary local artist – adorns the tiny house where Brassens lived and wrote his songs from 1944–66. At 3 rue Jonquoy, sculptors, musicians and painters from all round the world are given space to live and work in the **Musée Adzak** (see p.290), built by the English artist Roy Adzak in the 1980s. And it was by a artist living in this neighbourhood that I. M. Pei, the architect of the Louvre's pyramid, was introduced to Paris.

Across av du Maine, on the corner of rues Boulard and Mouton-Duvernet (Mº Mouton-Duvernet), a market dedicated to the arts has been established (Sun 10.30am–dusk), where all the stalls are run by the artists or craftworkers themselves.

Cinema has one of its best Parisian homes at *L'Entrepôt*, 7–9 rue Francis-de-Pressensé, with spaces for talks, meals and drinks, and even a garden where they sometimes light incense in the trees on summer nights. **Rue Raymond-Losserand**, the main street of Pernety and Plaisance, is full of crowded bars, though new smart hotels are edging in. A mural of books faces north at the junction with av Villemain, while a Chagallesque painting of horses, doves, elephants and hunters adorns the garden wall on the corner with rue d'Alésia. Further down rue Raymond-Losserand, the superbly proud and ugly building at no. 168 is the ancient Plaisance electricity substation.

Rue d'Alésia, the main east–west route through the 14e, has a small **food market** every Thursday and Sunday between Plaisance métro and rue Didot, but is best known for its good-value **clothes shops**, many selling discounted couturier creations. These congregate towards place Victor & Hélène Basch, where there's another delightful example of an old-style mews, the Villa d'Alésia.

At the weekend it's worth heading out to the southern edge of the *arrondissement*, past the characterless flats on bd Brune, for one of the city's best **junk markets**. Starting at daybreak (see p.338), it spreads along the pavements of avs Marc-Sangnier and Georges-Lafenestre, petering out at its western end in place de la Porte-de-Vanves, where the city fortifications used to run until the 1920s.

The 14^e below Montparnasse

South from Denfert-Rochereau

From Denfert-Rochereau to Parc Montsouris, most of the space is taken up by *RER* lines, reservoirs and **Ste-Anne's psychiatric hospital**, where the great political philosopher Louis Althusser was incarcerated after murdering his wife. His autobiography, which was written in Ste-Anne's but came out posthumously in 1992 because as a patient he had no right to publish, suggests that he would have preferred to have been tried and sent to prison. The plea of madness was, under French law, not a mitigating circumstance, but a total denial that a crime had taken place. His wife and victim, Hélène, had supported him through fits of severe mental illness for over thirty years. Some say she had had enough and threatened to leave him – a tragic story that was mercilessly exploited by the right-wing French press.

At the junction of rue d'Alésia and av Réné-Coty, steep steps lead up into rue des Artistes and one of the most isolated spots in the city. At the end of the street, brambles grow over the fencing round the Montsouris reservoir. Dali, Lurgat, Miller, Durrell and other artists found homes around here in the cobbled cul-de-sac of **Villa Seurat**, off rue de la Tombe-Issoire. Lenin and his wife, Krupskaya, lived across the street at 4 rue Marie-Rose.

South of the reservoir are more secluded cobbled streets and mews. The **square du Montsouris** leads off av Reille, close by one of Corbusier's earliest Parisian commissions, the studio at no. 53 for his painter friend Ozenfant, who styled the Hispano-Suiza cars of the 1920s. The roof has been altered, but not the Corbusier trademark of horizontal slices of windows. All manner of styles – even mock Norman farmhouse – can be spied along the verdant and secretive square du Montsouris, whose other entrance is on rue Nansouty. There are more *villas* off this street; Georges Braque lived at no. 6 in the one named after him.

Parc Montsouris was a favourite walking place of Lenin's, and no doubt of all the local artists, too. Its peculiarities include a meteorological office, a marker of the old meridian line, near bd Jourdan, and, by the southwest entrance, a kiosk run by the French Astronomy Association. Alas, the most surprising structure, a beautiful reproduction of the Bardo palace in Tunis, built for the 1867 Exposition Universelle, burnt down in half an hour in the early 1990s, just after restoration work had finished. But it is still a good place to stroll, with its unlikely contours, winding paths and the cascade above the lake. Even the *RER* tracks cutting right through it fail to dent its charm – though park police, whistling at you for being on the grass, might.

The 14ᵉ
below
Montparnasse

On the other side of bd Jourdan, several thousand students from over one hundred different countries live in the curious array of buildings of the **Cité Universitaire**. The central Maison Internationale resembles the Marlinspike of *Tintin* books, while the diverse styles of the others reflect the variety of nations and peoples willing to subsidize foreign study. Armenia, Cuba, Indo-China and Monaco are neighbours at the western end; Japan, Brazil, Italy, India and Morocco gather together at the other; Cambodia is guarded by startling stone creatures next to the *boulevard périphérique*; Switzerland (designed by Le Corbusier during his stilts phase) and the US are the most popular for their relatively luxurious rooms; and the Collège Franco-Britannique is a red-brick monster.

The atmosphere is still far from international, but there are films, shows and other events (check the notice boards in the Maison Internationale), and you can eat cheaply in the cafeterias if you have a student card.

The 13ᵉ

The tight-knit community on and around **rue Nationale**, between bd Vincent-Auriol and the inner ring road, never had much to hope for in the postwar days. But they were able to make do with their crowded, rat-ridden, ramshackle slums because much of life could be lived on the street – in the shops and cafés (of which there were 48 on rue Nationale alone). Paris was another place, rarely ventured into. Come the 1950s and 1960s, however, the city planners, here as elsewhere, came up with their usual solution to the housing problem – getting rid of the slums to make way for tower blocks. Today's community lives in flats that are hygienic, secure and costly to run, the next-door neighbour is a stranger, and only a couple of cafés remain on rue Nationale. The architectural gloom of the southeastern half of the *arrondissement* is only alleviated by the gormandize of the **Chinese quarter**, the admirable **Dunois jazz venue** (see p.349), and one or two clever new buildings.

West of av d'Italie and av des Gobelins – site of the famous tapestry works – there remains the almost untouched *quartier* of the **Butte-aux-Cailles**, and little streets and cul-de-sacs of prewar houses and studios.

The eastern edge of the 13ᵉ, along the riverfront, is in the throes of mammoth development centred around the new **Bibliothèque de France** (see p.152). Eventually everything from the Gare d'Austerlitz out to the *périphérique* will be transformed and known as the "Seine Rive Gauche" (see p.153).

Butte-aux-Cailles and the old quartiers

Between rue de Tolbiac and the stretch of bd Auguste-Blanqui where the food market is held, from place d'Italie to beyond Corvisart

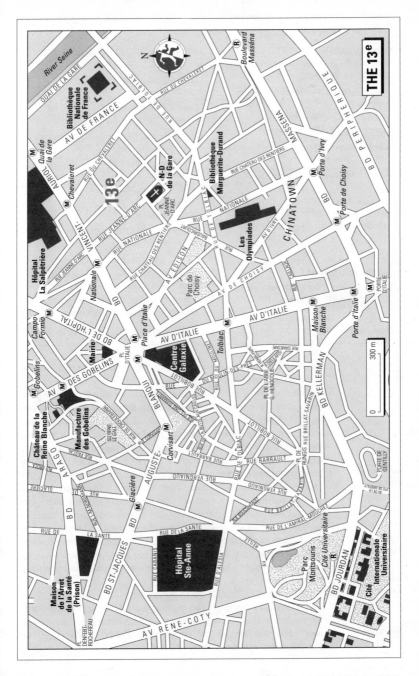

métro, rises a hill – the *butte* – on which the quails – *cailles* – of the *quartier*'s name must once have roamed.

The five-storey houses on **rue Butte-aux-Cailles** are typical of pre-1960s Paris, and though many of the flats have shared loos and no bathrooms, the rents are not cheap. It's a pleasantly animated street, recently recobbled and furnished with lampposts, where you can find book, wine and food shops, a newsagents, a community action centre, and one of the green Art Nouveau municipal drinking fountains donated to the city by the nineteenth-century British art collector Sir Richard Wallace. New bars and restaurants open up without putting old ones out of business: there's a co-operative jazz bar, *La Folie en Tête*, at no. 33, and a restaurant, *Le Temps des Cerise*, at no. 18–20, plus nine other places to eat and drink, most of which stay open till the early hours. In addition to these are the establishments on the streets between rue Butte-aux-Cailles and bd August-Blanqui, to which there's a short cut by a path and steps from rue des Cinq-Diamants.

South of rue de Tolbiac, small houses with fancy brickwork, decorative tiles and timbers, crazy paving walls and near-vertical roofs have remained intact: between rues Boussingault and Brillat-Savarin, near place de Rungis, and on place de l'Abbé-G-Henocque, rue Dieulafoy and rue Henri-Pape.

Le Temps de Cerise *was a famous song of the late 1870s, popular for referring to the heady days of the recently defeated Commune, at a time when it was not possible to talk openly.*

Place d'Italie, the Gobelins workshops and La Salpêtrière

Place d'Italie, the central junction of the 13e, is one of those Parisian roundabouts that takes half an hour to cross. On its north side is the ornate *mairie* of the *arrondissement*, while to the south the huge white edifice with a tangled coloured wire appendage houses a new cinema. In the 1848 revolution, the *place* was barricaded and the scene of one short-lived victory of the Left. A government general and his officers were allowed through the barricades, only to be surrounded and dragged off to the police station, where the commander was persuaded to write an order of retreat and a letter promising three million francs for the poor of Paris. Needless to say, neither was honoured and reprisals were heavy. Many of those involved in the uprising were tanners, laundry-workers or dye-makers, with their workplace the banks of the River Bièvre. This area was covered over in 1910 (creating rues Berbier-du-Mets and Croulebarbe) as a health hazard, the main source of pollution being the dyes from the **Gobelins tapestry workshops**, at 42 av des Gobelins, which had operated here for some four hundred years. Tapestries are still being made by the same, painfully slow methods, now featuring cartoons by contemporary painters (guided visits Tues–Thurs 2 & 2.45pm; 37F/30F; Mᵒ Les Gobelins).

Hidden just north of Gobelins is an exquisite fairytale octagonal tower and gateway hemmed in by workshops and lockups. This is all that remains of the **Château de la Reine Blanche**, where the young Charles VI of France supposedly went mad after a riotous party in 1393 when he was nearly burnt alive. The château was rebuilt in the sixteenth century, from which the remaining structures date. You can take a look through a gateway on rue des Gobelins or through the courtyard at 4 rue Gustave-Geffroy.

A stone's throw away, between rues Berbier and Corvisart, is a big public garden – nothing very special, but worth knowing if you need a snooze or place to picnic.

The ornate, bourgeois buildings between bds St-Marcel and Vincent-Auriol are dominated by the immense **Hôpital de la Salpêtrière**, built under Louis XIV to dispose of the dispossessed, and later used as a psychiatric hospital (today it's a general hospital). Jean Charcot, who believed that susceptibility to hypnosis proved hysteria, staged his theatrical demonstrations here, with Freud one of his fascinated witnesses. If you ask very nicely in the Bibliothèque Charcot (block 6, red route), the librarian may show you a book of photographs of the desperate female victims of these experiments.

A more positive statement on women is provided by the building at 5 rue Jules-Breton, which declares in large letters on its façade, "In humanity, woman has the same duties as man. She must have the same rights in the family and in society."

Tolbiac and Chinatown

The restaurants of Chinatown are detailed on p.261.

The area between rue de Tolbiac, av de Choisy and bd Masséna is the **Chinatown of Paris**, with no concessions to organic matter unless it's to be ingested. From rue de Tolbiac, just east of rue Baudricourt, steps and escalators lead up to a concrete platform known as *"Les Olympiades"*, where the tower blocks hide a clutch of brilliant Asiatic restaurants and sundry arcades with Chinese high-street businesses – travel agents, video libraries, hairdressers and bowling alleys – where few transactions are carried out in French. As you step out into av d'Ivry, you'll find the **Tang-Frères supermarket** and a larger **covered market**, where birds circle above the mind- and stomach-boggling goods. Chinese, Laotian, Cambodian, Thai and Vietnamese shops and restaurants fill av d'Ivry and av de Choisy all the way down to the city limits, many of them in shopping mazes on the ground floors of tower blocks.

If this is all too materialistic for you, head into the underground service road, rue du Disque, just by the escalators up to *Les Olympiades* at 66 av d'Ivry. Red and gold lanterns announce the entrance to a Buddhist temple. Community activities as well as worship go on here, and no-one will mind your presence.

Back on rue de Tolbiac, on the corner with rue Nationale, there's a wonderful municipal library in a steel-framed, curved building with a giant, semi-transparent photograph on the rue Nationale side. It houses the **Bibliothèque Marguerite Durand**, the first official feminist library in France (see p.51), and has newspapers and a video auditorium.

If you prefer to relax outside, the parc de Choisy, on the north side of rue de Tolbiac, has outdoor ping-pong tables with concrete nets, archery targets, and birds and trees. There are more good modern buildings near here: Christian de Portzamparc's public housing estate on rue des Hautes-Formes, and, at 106 rue du Château-des-Rentiers, a ten-storey block of public flats whose façade, on rue Jean-Colly, has a map of the *quartier* in coloured tiles, with pipes to show the métro lines.

Serious Le Corbusier fans could make the long slog down rue Cantagrel, where his Salvation Army building, blackened by traffic fumes, stands at no. 12. Alternatively take bus #62 east along rue de Tolbiac towards the Seine, and you'll come to the most recent monumental construction of the city, the new national library, the last of Mitterrand's *grands projets*.

The Bibliothèque Nationale de France

The four enormous L-shaped glass towers of the **Bibliothèque Nationale de France**, overlooking the Seine between Pont de Bercy and Pont de Tolbiac, looked lovely in the original models. Unfortunately, Dominique Perrault's design failed to take into account the effect of light on printed matter, so blinds had to be added, lending an orange hue and an office block appearance to what was supposed to suggest open books and accessibility of knowledge. In addition, the scale is so vast that when viewed from the river the towers bear no obvious relation to each other. But once you mount the wooden steps surrounding the library, the perspective changes. Now you're looking down into a sunken pine wood with glass walls that filter light into the floors below your feet, and the towers seem somehow closer than the 250m length and 130m width that separate their corners. This vast space, though open on all sides, feels enclosed, cut off from everything beyond, like being at the edge of a volcano crater. It's a startlingly original concept.

The sense of isolation deepens as you descend into the library (all the public spaces are below ground). Even with all the building works going on nearby, not a whisper of external sound penetrates; that goes for the birds in the wood as well. To reach the lowest level, where researchers can access every book, periodical and audio-visual material ever published or produced in France, you travel down steep escalators beneath the towers whose walls are hung with a metal mesh like chain mail. From what seems like a dungeon in the bowels of the earth you pass into daylight – at ground level in relation to the trees. A rich russet carpet muffles footfalls; metallic lamps, air-conditioning cylinders and more fireproof mesh shine silver while the desks, chairs and shelves are made of pale, warm, comforting wood. Mezzanines divide but don't partition off this study space that occupies the entire building's length. It feels strangely cosy, like a luxuriously converted monastery.

Visiting the library

Assuming plans haven't changed by the time the library opens at the end of 1996, admission to the site will be via steps from Quai de la Gare (a short walk downstream from M° Quai-de-la-Gare), with entrances to the building itself between the towers at either end. A belvedere on the eighteenth floor of the southeast tower will have paying entry, as will all exhibitions and the libraries themselves. Access to the ground floor library will only be granted to bona fide researchers (you can make an appointment with a librarian on the spot to state your case). The library above, where less rare books can be consulted from open shelves, can be used by anyone aged over 18 (a two-day pass will cost around 20F). There will also be shops and restaurants, though the latter may be exclusively for pass-holders. The wood is off limits to everyone.

Seine Rive Gauche

The grand plans for the three new *quartiers* that are supposed to make up **Seine Rive Gauche** – Austerlitz, from the station to bd Vincent-Auriol; Tolbiac, around the library; and Masséna, out to the perimeter – are in big financial trouble. In theory, Tolbiac would be finished by 1997; in 1998 the new Météor *RER* line would be completed, along with an extension of the métro from Gare d'Austerlitz; and, eventually, with the Austerlitz and Masséna quarters completed in the second decade of the twenty-first century, 15–20,000 people would become smart Seine Rive Gauche residents, with another 60,000 working here. But no-one's buying the flats, and office space and prices have dropped by almost fifty percent. Meanwhile, the cost of building the thirty-hectare platform over the railway lines looks set to undermine the whole profitability of the development. Parisian tax-payers may start squealing if the eighty percent of the loans to the development company, guaranteed by the Ville de Paris, start to be called in. Everything about the development smacks of property boom that has gone bust.

. . .Which is probably no bad thing. There's something very disconcerting about the attempt to create a new, and enormous, district from scratch; eradicating all past traces of the area, so that every park, street and building belongs to just one period of approximately twenty years. Perhaps now diversity will win out over monolithic mono-culture, reprieving, amongst other buildings, the gigantic old **mills** just south of Pont de Tolbiac. Occupied by musicians, anarchists, oddballs and artists, these are lovely, old, messy buildings, full of character, which recall the history of this long-ignored industrial corner of the city.

Chapter 9

Montmartre and Northern Paris

Montmartre lies in the middle of the largely petit bourgeois and working-class 18^e *arrondissement*, respectable round the slopes of the hill (or Butte Montmartre), distinctly less so around **Pigalle** on the northern edge of the 9^e *arrondissement* and towards the **Gare du Nord** and **Gare de l'Est** into the 10^e *arrondissement*, where the colourful bazaar-like shops and depressing slums of the **Goutte d'Or** crowd along the train tracks. On its northern edge, across the so-called "plain of Montmartre", lies the extensive **St-Ouen flea market**. To the west, between av de **Clichy** and the St-Lazare train lines, is the little-explored **Batignolles** *quartier*.

Montmartre

At 130m, the **Butte Montmartre** is the highest point in Paris. All the various theories as to the origin of its name have a Roman connection: it could be a corruption of *Mons Martyrum*, "the Martyrs' hill" – the martyrs being St Denis and his companions; on the other hand, it might have been named *Mons Mercurii*, in honour of a Roman shrine to Mercury; or possibly *Mons Martis*, after a shrine to Mars.

In spite of being one of the city's chief tourist attractions, the Butte manages to retain the quiet, almost secretive, air of its rural origins. Only incorporated into the city in the mid-nineteenth century, it received its first major influx of population from the poor displaced by Haussmann's rebuilding programme. Its **heyday** was from the last years of the century to World War I, when its rustic charms and low rents attracted crowds of artists. Although that traditional community of workers and artists has largely been supplanted by a more chic and prosperous class of Bohemians, the *quartier*'s physical appearance has changed little, thanks largely to the warren of **plaster-of-Paris quarries** that perforate its bowels and render the ground too unstable for new building.

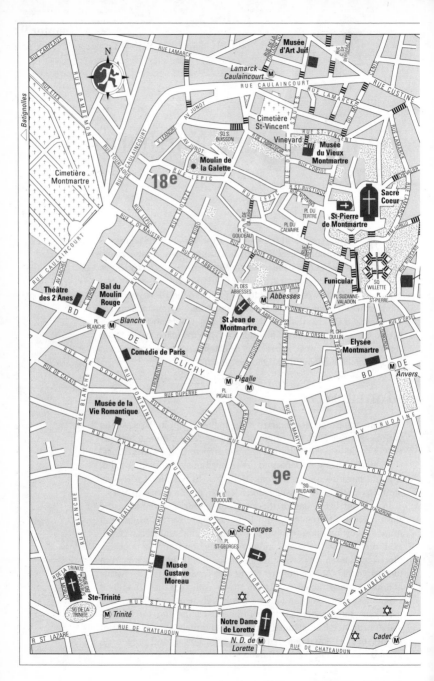

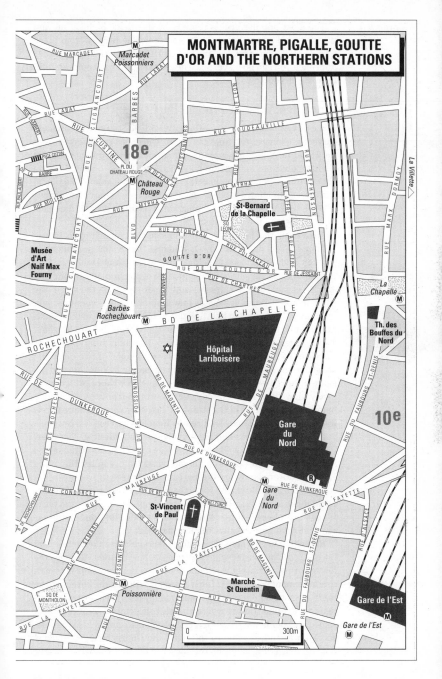

The **most popular access** route is via the rue de Steinkerque and the steps below the Sacré-Cœur (the funicular railway from place Suzanne-Valadon is covered by the *Carte Orange*). But for **a quieter approach** you can go up via place des Abbesses or rue Lepic, and still have the streets to yourself.

Place des Abbesses to the Butte

Place des Abbesses is postcard-pretty, with one of the few complete surviving Guimard Art Nouveau métro entrances (transferred from the Hôtel de Ville); the glass porch as well as the railings and the slightly obscene orange-tongued lanterns. The bizarre-looking church of St-Jean de Montmartre, on the downhill side of the *place*, had the distinction of being the first concrete church in France (1904), its internal structure remarkably pleasing despite the questionable taste of the decoration.

East from the *place*, at the Chapelle des Auxiliatrices in rue Yvonne-Le-Tac, Ignatius Loyola founded the **Jesuit** movement in 1534. It is also supposed to be the place where **Saint Denis**, the first Bishop of Paris, had his head chopped off by the Romans around 250 AD. He is said to have carried it until he dropped, on the site of the cathedral of St-Denis, in what is now a traditionally Communist suburb north of the city. Just beyond the end of the street, in the beautiful little place **Charles-Dullin**, the *Théâtre de l'Atelier* is still going strong after nearly two centuries. To continue from place des Abbesses to the top of the Butte, there is a choice of two quiet and attractive routes. You can either climb up **rue de la Vieuville** and the stairs in rue Drevet to the minuscule **place du Calvaire**, which has a lovely view back over the city, or go up **rue Tholozé**, then right below the **Moulin de la Galette** – the last survivor of Montmartre's forty-odd windmills, immortalized by Renoir – into rue des Norvins.

The Salvador Dali museum is located at 11 rue Poulbot, adjacent to place du Calvaire; see p.291.

Artistic associations abound hereabouts. Zola, Berlioz, Turgenev, Seurat, Degas and Van Gogh lived in the area. Picasso, Braque and Juan Gris invented Cubism in an old piano factory in the tiny place Émile-Goudeau, known as the **Bateau-Lavoir** (see box opposite); it still provides studio space for artists, though the original building burnt down some years ago. On the corner of bd de Clichy and place Blanche, Toulouse-Lautrec's inspiration, the **Moulin Rouge**, still survives, albeit a mere shadow of its former self.

Rue Lepic begins here, its winding contours recalling the lane that once served the plaster quarry wagons. A busy market occupies the lower part of the street, but once above rue des Abbesses it reverts to a mixture of tranquil and furtive elegance. Round the corner above rue Tourlaque a flight of steps and a muddy path sneak between gardens to **avenue Junot**, where the still delectable actress, Anouk Aimée, has her home. To the left is the secluded and exclusive cul-de-sac **Villa Léandre**, while to the right, the Cubist house of Dadaist poet Tristan Tzara stands on the corner of another exclusive enclave

Picasso at the Bateau-Lavoir

Picasso came here in 1904 and stayed for the best part of a decade working (he painted *Les Demoiselles d'Avignon* here) and sharing loves, quarrels, febrile discussions, opium trips and diverse escapades with Braque, Juan Gris, Modigliani, Max Jacob, Apollinaire and others both famous and obscure. It was on the square that he had his first encounter with the beautiful Fernande Olivier, thrusting a kitten into her hand as she passed by. "I laughed," she said, "and he took me to see his studio." Fernande became his model and lover.

Although what you see today is a reconstruction, it still has the same aspect on the street side, and little has changed in the square itself.

of houses and gardens, the **Hameau des Artistes**. Higher up the street, offering the best view of the Moulin de la Galette, the **square Suzanne-Buisson** provides a gentle haven for young and old alike, with a sunken *boules* pitch overlooked by a statue of St Denis clutching his head to his breast.

Further on, **rue des Saules** tips steeply down the north side of the Butte past the terraces of the tiny **Montmartre vineyard**; its annual harvest of about 1500kg of grapes produces in the region of 1500 bottles of wine. To the right, **rue Cortot** cuts through to the water tower, whose distinctive form, together with that of the Sacré-Cœur, is one of the landmarks of the city's skyline.

At 12 rue Cortot, a pretty old house with a grassy courtyard was occupied at different times by Renoir, Dufy, Suzanne Valadon and her mad son, Utrillo. It is now the **Musée de Montmartre** (Tues–Sun 11am–6pm; 25F/15F), whose disappointing exhibits (nearly all the works by major artists are reproductions) attempt to recreate the atmosphere of Montmartre's pioneering heyday. It does, however, have interesting temporary exhibitions, as well as a magnificent view from the back over the vineyard and the northern reaches of the city.

Next to the vineyard on **rue St-Vincent** is a patch of totally overgrown ground that looks like a vacant building lot. It is, in fact, the **garden of the museum**, officially left wild since 1985, to allow a space for the natural development of Paris' native flora and fauna (April–Oct Mon 4–6pm, except during school and public hols, and Sat 2–6pm; free; further information from *Paris Espace Nature*, ☎01.43.28.47.63). Berlioz lived just beyond it with his English wife, in the corner house on the steps of rue du Mont-Cenis, whence there is a breathtaking view northwards along the canyon of the steps, as well as back up towards place du Calvaire. The steps are perfect sepia-romantic Montmartre: a double handrail runs down the centre, with the lampposts between. The streets below are among the quietest and least touristy in Montmartre.

Place du Tertre and the Sacré-Cœur

The heart of Montmartre, the **place du Tertre**, photogenic but totally bogus, is jammed with tourists, overpriced restaurants and

Montmartre "artists" doing quick portraits while you wait. Its trees, until recently under threat of destruction for safety reasons by overzealous officialdom, have been saved by the well-orchestrated protests of its influential residents.

Between place du Tertre and the Sacré-Cœur, the **church of St-Pierre** – the oldest in Paris, along with St-Germain-des-Près – is all

---

Montmartre, Pigalle, Goutte d'Or and the northern stations: listings

RESTAURANTS

L'Alsaco, 10 rue Condorcet (at the extreme eastern end), 9e. Mo Poissonnière.

L'Assiette, 78 rue Labat, 18e. Mo Château-Rouge.

Auberge Bourbonnaise, 45 rue St-Georges, 9e. Mo St-Georges.

Baalbeck, 16 rue de Mazagran, 10e. Mo Bonne-Nouvelle.

La Casserole, 17 rue Boinod, 18e. Mo Simplon/Marcedet-Poissonniers.

Chez Arthur, 25 rue du Faubourg-St-Denis, 10e. Mo Strasbourg-St-Denis.

Chez Ginette, 101 rue Caulaincourt, 18e. Mo Lamarck-Caulaincourt.

Chez Jean, 52 rue Lamartine, 9e. Mo Notre-Dame-de-Lorette/Cadet.

Chez Paula, 26 rue Letort, 18e. Mo Joffrin, Porte-de-Clignancourt.

Aux Deux-Théâtres, 18 rue Blanche (cnr rue Pigalle), 9e. Mo Trinité.

L'Enchotte, 11 rue de Chabrol, 10e. Mo Gare-de-l'Est.

Flo, 7 cours des Petites-Écuries, 10e. Mo Château-d'Eau.

Fouta Toro, 3 rue du Nord, 18e. Mo Marcadet-Poissonniers.

Au Grain de Folie, 24 rue La Vieuville, 18e. Mo Abbesses.

Haynes, 3 rue Clauzel (cnr rue des Martyrs), 9e. Mo St-Georges.

L'Homme Tranquille, 81 rue des Martyrs, 18e. Mo Abbesses.

Julien, 16 rue du Faubourg-St-Denis, 10e. Mo Strasbourg-St-Denis.

KOH, 12 rue de la Fidelité, 10e. Mo Gare-de-l'Est.

Le Maquis, 69 rue Caulaincourt, 18e. Mo Lamarck-Caulaincourt.

Marie-Louise, 52 rue Championnet, 18e. Mo Simplon.

Le Moulin à Vins, 6 rue Burq, 18e. Mo Abbesses.

À la Pomponnette, 42 rue Lepic, 18e. Mo Blanche/Abbesses.

Au Port de Pidjiguiti, 28 rue Étex, 18e. Mo Guy-Môquet.

Le Relais de la Butte, 12 rue Ravignan, 18e. Mo Abbesses.

Le Relais Savoyard, 13 rue Rodier (cnr rue de l'Agent-Bailly), 9e. Mo Notre-Dame-de-Lorette/Anvers/Cadet.

Le Restaurant, 32 rue Véron, 18e. Mo Abbesses.

Le Réveil du Dixième, 35 rue au Château-d'Eau, 10e. Mo Château-d'Eau.

La Table d'Anvers, 2 place d'Anvers, 9e. Mo Anvers.

Terminus Nord, 23 rue de Dunkerque, 10e. Mo Gare-du-Nord.

Au Virage Lepic, 61 rue Lepic, 18e. Mo Blanche/Abbesses.

CAFÉS AND BARS

Le Dépanneur, 27 rue Fontaine, 9e. Mo Pigalle.

Aux Négociants, 27 rue Lambert (cnr rue Custine), 18e. Mo Château-Rouge.

La Petite Charlotte, 24 rue des Abbesses, 18e. Mo Abbesses.

Le Refuge, cnr rue Lamarck and the steps of rue de la Fontaine-du-But, 18e. Mo Lamarck-Caulaincourt.

Le Sancerre, 35 rue des Abbesses, 18e. Mo Abbesses.

These establishments are reviewed in Chapter 13, Eating and drinking, on p.265.

---

that remains of a Benedictine convent that occupied the Butte Montmartre from the twelfth century on. Though much altered, it still retains its Romanesque and early Gothic feel. The four ancient columns inside the church, two by the door and two in the choir, are leftovers from the Roman shrine that stood on the hill, while the cemetery dates from Merovingian times.

Crowning the Butte is the **Sacré-Cœur**, a graceless and vulgar pastiche, whose white pimply domes are an essential part of the Paris skyline. Construction was started in the 1870s on the initiative of the Catholic Church to atone for the "crimes" of the Commune (see box overleaf). The thwarted opposition, which included Clemenceau, eventually got its revenge by naming the space at the foot of the monumental staircase **square Willette**, after the local artist who turned out on inauguration day to shout, "Long live the devil!".

The best thing about the Sacré-Cœur is the **view from the top** (summer 9am–7pm, winter 9am–6pm; 15F). It is almost as high as the Eiffel Tower, and you can see the layout of the whole city – a wide, flat basin ringed by low hills, with stands of high-rise blocks in the southeastern corner, on the heights of Belleville, and at La Défense in the west. In the hazy distance, the tall flat faces of the suburban workers' barracks rise like slabs of tombstone.

To the south and east of the Sacré-Cœur, the slopes of the Butte drop much more steeply down towards bd Barbès and the Goutte d'Or (see below). Directly below are the gardens of square Willette, milling with tourists. If you want to avoid the crowds, there's the stepped rue Utrillo and rue Paul Albert, which joins rue Ronsard along the edge of the gardens. The circular **Halles St-Pierre** on rue Ronsard (Tues–Sat 10am–10pm, Sun & Mon 10am–6pm) hosts changing exhibitions and the **Musée d'Art Naïf Max Fourny**, with works from all over the world. There's also an auditorium for film, theatre, music and dance, a bookshop and a cheap cafeteria with the day's papers to read. It's a great place, totally ignored by the tourists being disgorged from their coaches only metres away.

Outside, in **rue Ronsard**, masked by overhanging greenery, are the now-sealed entrances to the quarries where plaster of Paris was extracted, and which were used as refuges by the revolutionaries of 1848.

The Montmartre cemetery

West of the Butte, near the beginning of rue Caulaincourt in place Clichy, lies the **Montmartre cemetery** (Mon–Fri 8am–5.30pm, Sat 8am–8.30pm, Sun 8am–9pm). Tucked down below street level in the hollow of an old quarry, it is a tangle of trees and funerary pomposity, more intimate and less melancholy than Père-Lachaise or Montparnasse.

The illustrious dead include Zola, Stendhal, Berlioz, Degas, Feydeau, Offenbach, Dalida and François Truffaut. There is also a

The cemeteries of Père-Lachaise and Montparnasse are detailed on pp.187 and 137.

The Paris Commune

On March 18, 1871, in the **place du Tertre**, Montmartre's most illustrious mayor and future prime minister of France, **Georges Clemenceau**, flapped about trying to prevent the bloodshed that gave birth to the Paris Commune and the ensuing civil war with the national government.

On that day, Adolphe Thiers' government dispatched a body of troops under General Lecomte to take possession of 170 guns, which had been assembled at Montmartre by the National Guard in order to prevent them falling into German hands. Although the troops seized the guns easily in the dark before dawn, they had forgotten to bring any horses to tow them away. That gave Louise Michel, the great woman revolutionary, time to raise the alarm.

A large and angry crowd gathered, fearing another restoration of empire or monarchy such as had happened after the 1848 Revolution. They persuaded the troops to take no action and arrested General Lecomte, along with another general, Clément Thomas, whose part in the brutal repression of the 1848 republican uprising had won him no friends among the people.

The two generals were shot and mutilated in the garden of **no. 36 rue du Chevalier-de-la-Barre**, behind the Sacré-Cœur. By the following morning, the government had decamped to Versailles, leaving the Hôtel de Ville and the whole of the city in the hands of the National Guard, who then proclaimed the Commune.

Divided among themselves and isolated from the rest of France, the Communards only finally succumbed to government assault after a week's bloody street-fighting between May 21 and 28. No-one knows how many of them died; certainly no fewer than 20,000, with another 10,000 executed or deported. By way of government revenge, Eugène Varlin, one of the founder members of the First International and a leading light in the Commune, was shot on the selfsame spot where the two generals had been killed just a few weeks before.

It was a working-class revolt, as the particulars of those involved clearly demonstrate, but it hardly had time to be as socialist as subsequent mythologizing would have it. The terrible cost of repression had long-term effects on the French working-class movement, both in terms of numbers lost and psychologically. For, thereafter, not to be revolutionary seemed like a betrayal of the dead.

For more details on the German siege of Paris and on the Commune, see p.413.

large Jewish section by the east wall. The entrance is on av Rachel under rue Caulaincourt, next to an antique cast-iron poor-box (*Tronc pour les Pauvres*).

Next to the cemetery, with its entrance on rue Carpeaux, the **Hôpital Bretonneau** – a curious assembly of brick and iron-frame pavilions condemned to demolition due to subsidence – has been given a temporary reprieve by being loaned to an organization called *Usines Ephémères*, whose *raison d'être* is to recuperate old buildings for use as studios and performance spaces by young artists and musicians, both French and foreign. Its original lease has been extended, so there will continue to be free shows and exhibitions.

Batignolles to Clichy

East of Montmartre cemetery, in a district bounded by the St-Lazare train lines, marshalling yards, and av de Clichy, is the "village" of **Batignolles**. Its heart is rue des Batignolles and it is sufficiently conscious of its uniqueness to have formed an association for the preservation of its *caractère villageois*. The poet Verlaine was brought up here, while Stéphane Mallarmé lived on bd des Batignolles. At the northern end of the street, the attractive semicircular **place du Dr F. Lobligeois** frames the colonnaded church of **Ste-Marie-des-Batignolles**, its entrance modelled on the Madeleine; behind the church the tired and trampled greenery of **square Batignolles** stretches back to the big rail marshalling yards. On the corner of the *place*, the modern *L'Endroit* bar attracts the bourgeois kids of the neighbourhood until 2am.

From rue des Batignolles, rue Legendre and rue des Dames lead southeast across the train lines to **rue de Lévis** and one of the city's most flamboyant and appetizing food and clothes markets, held every day except Monday.

To the northeast, the long **rue des Moines** leads towards Guy-Môquet, with a covered market on the corner of rue Lemercier. This is the working-class Paris of the movies: all small, animated, friendly shops, four- or five-storey houses in shades of peeling grey, and brown-stained bars, where men drink standing at the "zinc".

Across av de Clichy, round **rue de la Jonquière**, the quiet streets are redolent of petit bourgeois North African respectability, interspersed with decidedly upper-crust enclaves. The latter are typified by the film-set perfection of the **Cité des Fleurs**, a residential lane of magnificent private houses and gardens that would not look out of place in London's Chelsea.

From Guy-Môquet, it's a short walk to rue Lamarck, which will take you up to Montmartre, or back along av de St-Ouen to rue du Capitaine-Madon, leading through to the wall of the Montmartre cemetery. In the heart of this cobbled alley, with washing strung at the windows, the ancient *Hôtel Beau-Lieu* still survives. Ramshackle and peeling, on a tiny courtyard full of plants, it epitomizes the kind-hearted, instinctively arty, sepia Paris that every romantic visitor secretly cherishes. Most of the guests have been there years.

From av de St-Ouen, the so-called *plaine* of Montmartre stretches respectably eastwards until it reaches the slummy district lining the railway tracks heading north to Lille and Belgium from the Gare du Nord. There is little of note to see, besides a long street market at the western end of rue Ordener, an attractive and lively little sector round the *mairie* of the 18e, especially the food shops round the rue du Poteau and rue Duhesme junction. It is here that the *"Mont"* in *"Montemartre"* begins to make particular sense, for the north side of the Butte is very much steeper than the south and looms quite dramatically above the contrasting *plaine*.

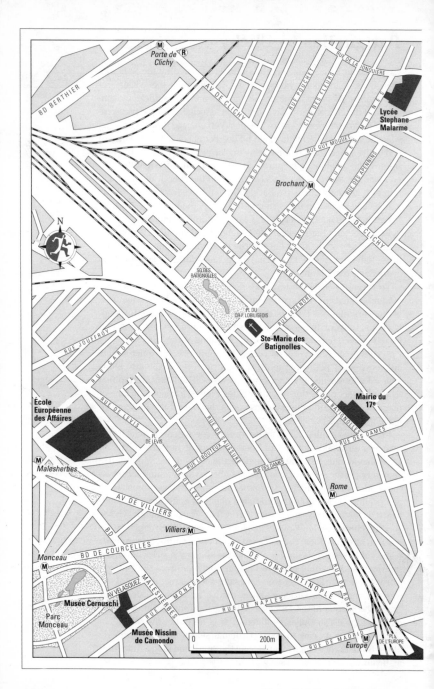

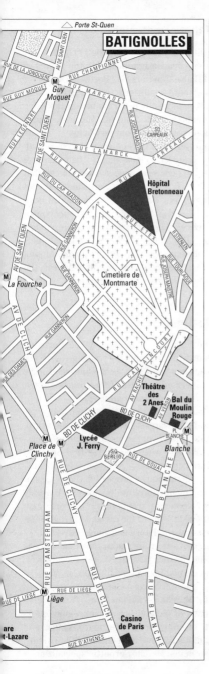

Batignolles: listings

RESTAURANTS

Joy in Food, 2 rue Truffaut, 17e. Mº Place-Clichy.

CAFÉS AND BARS

Bar Belge, 75 av de St-Ouen, 17e. Mº Guy-Môquet.

L'Endroit, 67 place F-Lobligeois, 17e. Mº Rome/La Fourche.

These establishments are reviewed in Chapter 13, Eating and drinking, *beginning on p.266.*

The Batignolles and dog cemeteries

Right at the frontier of the 17e and Clichy, under the *périphérique*, lies the little-visited **Cimetière des Batignolles**, with the graves of André Breton, Verlaine and Blaise Cendrars (Mº Porte-de-Clichy).

A great deal curiouser, and more lugubrious, is the **dog cemetery** on the banks of the Seine at Asnières. It is accessible on the same métro line, about fifteen minutes' walk from Mº Mairie-de-Clichy along bd Jaurès, then left at the far end of Pont de Clichy.

Privately owned, the **Cimetière des Chiens** (mid-March to mid-Oct 10am–noon & 3–7pm, mid-Oct to mid-March 10am–noon & 2–5pm, closed Tues & holidays) occupies a tree-shaded ridgelet that was once an island in the river. It is full of tiny graves decked with plastic flowers. Most of them, going back to 1900, belong to dogs and cats, many with epigraphs of the kind: "To Fifi, the only consolation of my wretched existence". There is a surprising preponderance of Anglo-Saxon names – Boy, Pussy, Dick, Jack: a tribute perhaps to the peculiarly English sentimentality about animals. Among the more exotic cadavers are a Muscovite bear, a wolf, a lioness, the 1920 Grand National winner, and the French Rintintin, vintage 1933.

The flea market of St-Ouen

In spite of the "St-Ouen" in its name, it is actually the **Porte de Clignancourt** – the old gateway to the Channel – which gives access to the market of St-Ouen, and not the Porte de St-Ouen itself. The market is located on the northern edge of the 18e *arrondissement*, now hard up against the *boulevard périphérique.*

Officially open from 7.30am to 7pm – unofficially, from 5am – the **puces de St-Ouen** claims to be the largest flea market in the world, the name "flea" deriving from the state of the second-hand mattresses, clothes and other junk sold here when the market first operated in the free-fire zone outside the city walls.

Nowadays, however, it is predominantly a proper – and very expensive – antiques market, selling mainly furniture but also such trendy "junk" as old café counters, telephones, traffic lights, posters, jukeboxes and petrol pumps, with what is left of the rag-and-bone element confined to the further reaches of **rue Fabre** and **rue Lécuyer**.

First impressions as you arrive from the métro are that there is nothing for sale but jeans and leather jackets. There are, however, seven official markets within the complex: Marché **Biron**, selling serious and expensive antique furniture; Marché **Cambo**, next to Biron, also with expensive furniture; Marché **Vernaison** – the oldest – which has the most diverse collection of old and new furniture and knickknacks; Marché **Paul-Bert**, offering modern furniture, china, etc; Marché **Malik**, with mostly clothes, some high-class couturier stuff, and a lot of uninteresting new items; Marché **Serpette**, specializing in

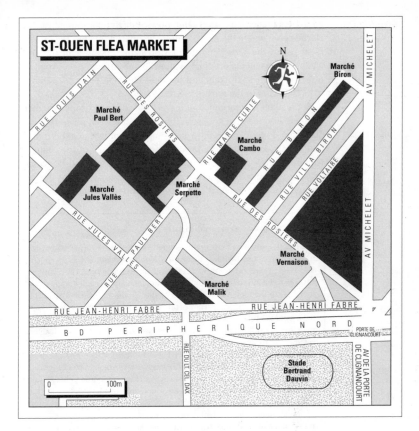

ST-OUEN FLEA MARKET

Marché Biron

Marché Paul Bert

RUE LOUIS DAIN

RUE DES ROSIERS

RUE MARIE CURIE

Marché Cambo

RUE BIRON

RUE VILLA BIRON

RUE VOLTAIRE

AV MICHELET

Marché Jules Vallès

Marché Serpette

RUE JULES VALLÈS

RUE PAUL BERT

RUE DES ROSIERS

Marché Vernaison

AV MICHELET

Marché Malik

RUE JEAN-HENRI FABRE

RUE JEAN-HENRI FABRE

PORTE DE CLIGNANCOURT

BD PERIPHERIQUE NORD

RUE DU LT. COL. DAX

AV DE LA PORTE DE CLIGNANCOURT

Stade Bertrand Dauvin

0   100m

1900–1930; and Marché **Jules-Vallès**, which is the cheapest, most junk-like and most likely to throw up an unexpected treasure.

It can be fun to wander around, but it's foolish to expect any bargains. In some ways the streets of St-Ouen beyond the market are just as interesting for the glimpse they give of a tempo of living long vanished from the city itself. Should hunger overtake you, there is a touristy *restaurant-buvette* in the centre of Marché Vernaison, *Chez Louisette*, where the great gypsy jazz guitarist, Django Reinhardt, sometimes played. But for more dependable and cheaper eating, it's best to go to one of the brasseries on av Michelet, just outside the market, or back on bd Ornano.

Pigalle

From place Clichy in the west to Barbès-Rochechouart in the east, the hill of Montmartre is underlined by the sleazy **boulevards of Clichy** and **de Rochechouart**, the centre of the roadway often occupied by bumper-car pistes and other funfair sideshows. At **the Barbès end**, where the métro clatters by on iron trestles, the crowds teem round the *Tati* department stores, the cheapest in the city, while the pavements are thick with Arab and African street vendors offering watches, trinkets and textiles. The best place to watch is from the stairs to the Barbès métro.

At the **place Clichy** end, tour buses from all over Europe feed their contents into massive hotels. In the middle, between **place Blanche** and **place Pigalle**, sex shows, sex shops and prostitutes, both male and female, keep alive the tawdry, tarnished image of the Naughty Nineties. You won't find the golden-hearted whores and Bohemian artists of popular tradition here, but, as with any red-light district, tour guides seem to feel it's an essential stop on the tourist trail.

Cabarets and sex: around Pigalle

For many foreigners, Paris is still synonymous with a use of the stage perpetuated by those mythical names the *Moulin Rouge*, *Folies Bergères* and *Lido*. These **cabarets**, which flash their presence from the Champs-Élysées to bd Montmartre, predate the film industry, though it appears as if the glittering Hollywood musicals of the 1930s were their inspiration rather than their offspring. They define an area of pornography that would have trouble titillating a prudish Anglo-Saxon, and, though the audience is mainly male, the whole event is to live sex shows what glossy fashion reviews are to "girlie" mags. Apart from seeing a lot of bare breasts, your average coached-in tourist may well feel he has not got what he paid (rather excessively) for – all the more easy prey for the pimps of Pigalle.

The *Lido*, for example, takes breaks from multi-coloured plumage and illuminated distant flesh to bring on a conjuror to play tricks with the clothes and possessions of the audience. Then back come the computer-choreographed "Bluebell Girls", in a technical *tour de force* of light show, music and a moving stage transporting the thighs and breasts to more faraway exotica – the sea, a volcano, ice or Pacific island. The scale is far too spectacular to be a dirty mac's night out.

The *Moulin Rouge* is of the same ilk with its "Doriss Girls", and still trades on its Toulouse-Lautrec painted fame as the place for "the most celebrated can-can in the world". The oldest cabaret, the *Folies Bergères*, closed down in 1992, but reopened in 1993 with a new pastiche show starring a drag artist as the lead chorus "girl".

At the *Crazy Horse*, the theatrical experience convinces the audience that they are watching art and the prettiest girls in Paris. In the ranks of defences for using images of female bits to promote, sell, lure and exploit, Frenchmen are particular in putting "art and beauty" in the front line. In upholding the body suspendered and pouting, weak and whimpering, usually nude and always immaculate, they claim to protect the femininity, beauty and desirability of the Frenchwoman as she would wish it herself.

Moving from the glamour cabarets to the **"Life Sex"** and **"Ultra-Hard Life Sex"** venues (never "Live Sex" for some reason) is to leave the world of elegant gloss and exportable Frenchness for a world of sealed-cover porn that knows no cultural borders.

It is an area in which respectability and sleaze rub very close shoulders. On **place Pigalle** itself, huge anatomical blow-ups (unveiled only after dark in deference to the residents' sensibilities) assail the senses on the very corner of one of the city's most elegant private *villas*, **avenue Frochot**. In the adjacent streets – **rues de Douai, Victor-Massé**, and **Houdon** – specialist music shops (this is *the* area for instruments and sound systems) and grey house façades are interspersed with tiny ill-lit bars where "hostesses" lurk in complicated tackle, ready to snatch at passing prey.

South of Pigalle

The rest of the 9e *arrondissement*, which stretches south of Pigalle, is rather dull, with the exception of some blocks of streets round **place St-Georges**, where Thiers, president of the Third Republic, lived in a house that is now a library (rebuilt after being burnt by the Commune). In the centre of the *place* stands a statue of the nineteenth-century cartoonist Gavarni, who made a speciality of lampooning the mistresses that were *de rigueur* for bourgeois males of the time. This was the mistresses' *quartier* – they were known as *lorettes*, after the nearby church of Notre-Dame-de-Lorette.

Place Toudouze and **rues Clauzel, Milton** and **Rodier** are worth a look. Renovation has revealed some beautiful and elegantly ornamented façades. **Rue St-Lazare**, between the St-Lazare station and the hideous church of Ste-Trinité, is a welcome swathe of activity amid the residential calm. Close by is the bizarre and little-visited museum dedicated to the works of the Symbolist painter **Gustave Moreau** (see p.292), opposite rue de la Tour-des-Dames, where two or three gracious mansions and gardens recall the days when this was the very edge of the city.

The Goutte d'Or and the northern stations

Continuing east from Pigalle, bd Rochechouart becomes bd de la Chapelle, along the north side of which, between **boulevard Barbès** and the **Gare du Nord** railway lines, stretches the poetically named, crumbling and squalid quarter of the **Goutte d'Or**. The name – the "Drop of Gold" – derives from the vineyard that occupied this site in medieval times. Since World War I, however, when large numbers of North Africans were imported to replenish the ranks of Frenchmen dying in the trenches, it has gradually become an immigrant ghetto.

In the late 1950s and early 1960s, during the Algerian war, few middle-class Parisians would have dreamt of entering the *quartier*, not just for its reputation for score-settling, prostitution and drugs, but because of the clandestine activity of the Algerian National

Liberation Front (FLN). In fact, the new residents of the *quartier* had far better reason to fear the respectable "law-abiding" French.

Many of the buildings remain in a lamentable state of decay. While artists, writers and others have moved in, attracted by the only affordable property left in the city, a major programme of pulling down, rebuilding and cleaning up is underway. As the physical backdrop changes, so inevitably does the character of the *quartier*. Much of **rue de la Goutte-d'Or** itself is new, including a lovely nursery school on the corner with rue Islettes. For the moment, however, rue de la Goutte-d'Or and its tributary lanes – especially to the north: rue Myrha, rue Léon, the Marché Dejean, rue Polonceau (with its basement mosque at no. 55), and the cobbled alley and gardens of **Villa Poissonnière** – remain distinctly North African and poor.

Washing hangs from every balcony and tiny shops sell snazzy cloth and jewellery as well as traditional *djellabas*. The windows of the *pâtissiers* are stacked with trays of equally brightly coloured cakes and pastries. Sheeps' heads grin from the slabs of the halal butchers. The grocers shovel their wares from barrels and sacks, and the plangent sounds of Arab music echo evocatively from the record shops. In the playground of square Léon, there's authorized graffiti tagging and three brilliant murals. It's a funny place to sit, as the play areas are cordoned off with high, mauve-painted grills. The cafés and bars of the Goutte d'Or tend to be too small and intimate to appeal to outsiders, but you'd certainly be able to find a good mint tea.

The stations and faubourgs

On the **south side of boulevard de la Chapelle** lie the big northern stations, the **Gare du Nord** (serving the Channel ports and places north) and **Gare de l'Est** (serving northeastern and eastern France and Eastern Europe), with the major traffic thoroughfares, bd de Magenta and bd de Strasbourg, both bustling, noisy and not in themselves of much interest.

To the right of the Gare de l'Est as you face the station, a high wall encloses the gardens of **square Villemin**, which once belonged to the Couvent des Récollets – the near wreck of a building along rue du Faubourg-St-Martin. The same campaign groups that saved the gardens for public use (entrance on rue des Récollets), including a 200-day occupation to stop the bulldozers, are now focusing on the convent. Various projects are in the air and local people fear the building will deteriorate beyond the point of repair. However, given their success with the gardens, they may well win this one, too.

On rue de Nancy, a little street off rue du Faubourg-St-Martin, is one of the three remaining makers of brass musical instruments in France. Antoine Courtois moved to no. 8 in 1856 – the same business had made the cavalry trumpets for Napoléon's army.

The liveliest part of the quarter is the **rue du Faubourg-St-Denis**, full, especially towards the lower end, of *charcuteries*, butchers, greengrocers and foreign delicatessens, as well as a number of restaurants, including *Brasserie Julien* and *Brasserie Flo*, the latter in an old-world stableyard, the cour des Petites-Écuries.

The Goutte d'Or and the northern stations

Brasserie Julien *and* Brasserie Flo *are reviewed on p.268.*

Spanning the end of the street is the **Porte St-Denis**, a triumphal arch built in 1672 on the Roman model to celebrate the victories of Louis XIV. Feeling secure behind Vauban's extensive frontier fortifications, Louis demolished Charles V's city walls and created a swathe of leafy promenades, where the Grands Boulevards now run. In place of the city gates he planned a series of triumphal arches, of which this and the neighbouring **Porte St-Martin**, at the end of rue du Faubourg-St-Martin, were the first.

The whole area between the two *faubourg* ("suburbs") through to the provincial **rue du Faubourg-Poissonnière** is honeycombed with *passages* and courtyards. China and glass enthusiasts should take a walk along **rue de Paradis**, whose shops specialize in such wares, with the *Baccarat* firm's **Musée du Cristal** at no. 30 (see p.293), tucked away behind the classical façade of Louis XV's *cristallerie*. Close by, at no. 18, the magnificent mosaic and tiled façade of Monsieur Boulanger's *Choisy-le-Roi* tileworks shop is now the entrance to an art gallery, *Le Monde d'Art* (Mon 2–7pm, Tues–Sat 1–7.30pm). You can go inside and admire more exuberant ceramics featuring peacock tails and flamingoes on the stairs and floors.

Across bd Bonne-Nouvelle are the *passages* of place du Caire and rue St-Denis leading down to Les Halles (see Chapter 4).

Chapter 10

Eastern Paris

P aris east of the **Canal St-Martin** has always been a working class area, from the establishment of the Faubourg St-Antoine as the workshop of the city in the fifteenth century, to the colonization of the old villages of Belleville, Ménilmontant, and Charonne by the French rural poor in the mid-nineteenth century. These were the populations that supplied the manpower for the great rebellions of the last century: the insurrections of 1830, 1832, 1848, and 1851, and the short-lived Commune of 1871, which divided the city in two, with the centre and west battling to preserve the status quo against the oppressed and radical east. Even in the 1789 Revolution, when Belleville, Ménilmontant and Charonne were still just villages, the most progressive demands came from the artisans of the Faubourg St-Antoine.

Until quite recently, in the demonology of bourgeois Parisians, nothing was to be more feared than the "*descente de Belleville*": the descent from the heights of Belleville of the revolutionary mob, imaginary knives clenched between their teeth. It was in order to contain this threat that so much of the Canal St-Martin, a natural line of defence, was covered over by **Baron Haussmann** in 1860.

Today, precious little stands in remembrance of these events. The *Mur des Fédérés* in **Père-Lachaise cemetery** records the death of 147 Communards; the Bastille column and its inscription commemorate 1830 and 1848; a few streets bear the names of the people's leaders. But nothing you now see in the 11e, for instance, suggests its history as the most fought-over *arrondissement* in the city.

Indeed, the physical backdrop itself is also slowly disappearing. Narrow streets and artisans' houses still survive in **Belleville**, **Ménilmontant**, and off the Canal St-Martin, but many of the crumbling, dank, damp and insanitary houses have now been demolished. Earlier rebuilding produced shelving-unit apartment blocks, but in recent years the new constructions have shown far more imagination and sensitivity.

Though some of the new is public housing, redevelopments have inevitably shifted old populations out and encouraged new arty and media intelligentsia in, with the result that the old character of the city's most Parisian areas is gradually being effaced. It doesn't happen overnight, however, and they continue to provide some of the most fascinating urban landscapes in the city. Belleville remains the most extraordinary mix of races and cultures, and **rue du Faubourg-St-Antoine** is still full of cabinet-makers and joiners. Only **La Villette**, up in the city's northeast corner in the 19ᵉ, and **Bercy**, along the Seine in the 12ᵉ, have been totally transformed.

Place de la République and the Canal St-Martin

Abutting three *arrondissements* – the 3ᵉ, 10ᵉ and the 11ᵉ – the grimly barren **place de la République** is one of the largest roundabouts in Paris. It was designed as a pivotal point in Haussmann's counter-insurgency road scheme. An army barracks dominated the north side, and still does. Seven major streets radiate from the *place*, cutting through the then-inflammable neighbourhoods of working-class Paris to make this the most blatant example of Napoléon III's political town-planning. In order to build it, Haussmann destroyed a number of popular theatres, including the *Funambules* of *Les Enfants du Paradis* fame, and Daguerre's unique diorama.

The motivation for covering over the **Canal St-Martin** from Bastille to rue du Faubourg-du-Temple with the bd Richard-Lenoir was similar. Completed in 1825, the canal was built as a short cut for the river traffic to lop off the great western loop of the Seine around Paris. Spanned by six swing-bridges, which could easily be jammed open, it formed a splendid natural defence for the rebellious quarters of eastern Paris.

The streets to either side of bd Richard-Lenoir have a fine selection of eating places and make for pleasant wandering. Some possibilities to incorporate into a walk are the iced-cake looks of the **Cirque d'Hiver** (the circus) just by Filles-du-Calvaire métro; a multi-layered mural of literature on rue Nicolas-Appert (east of the boulevard between Mº Richard-Lenoir and Mº Bréguet-Sabins); or the gilt and mirrored *boulangerie* selling Viennese, French and English bread on the corner of rue du Chemin-Vert and rue Popincourt (Mº St-Ambroise).

Canal St-Martin

The **southern stretch** of the revealed canal is the most attractive. Plane trees line the cobbled *quais*, and elegant high-arched footbridges punctuate the spaces between the locks, where you can still watch the occasional barge slowly rising or sinking to the next level. The canalside houses are solid bourgeois-looking residences of the mid-nineteenth century. Although small back-street workshops and

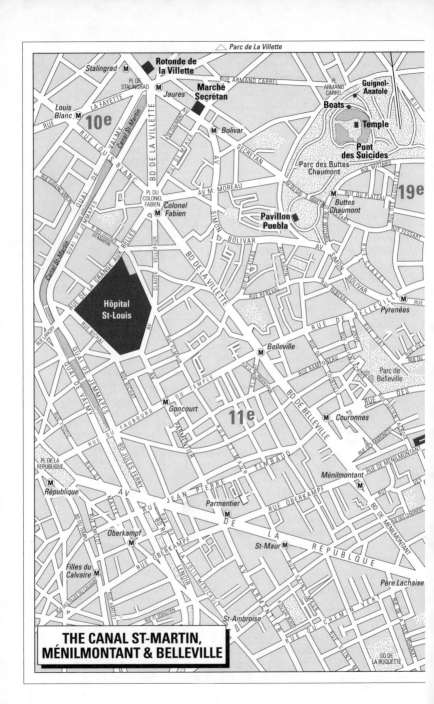

THE CANAL ST-MARTIN,
MÉNILMONTANT & BELLEVILLE

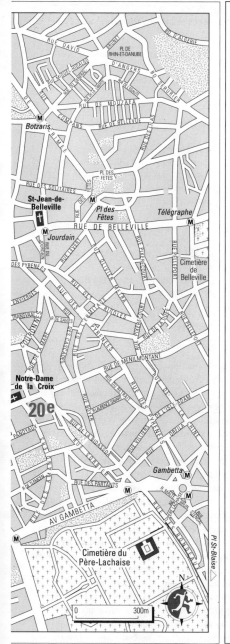

Canal St-Martin, République, Belleville, Ménilmontant, Charonne and Père Lachaise: listings

RESTAURANTS

Anjou-Normandie, 13 rue de la Foli-Méricault, 11e. Mo St-Ambroise.

Astier, 44 rue Jean-Pierre Timbaud, 11e. Mo Parmentier.

Aucune Idée, 2 place St-Blaise, 20e. Mo Porte-de-Bagnolet/Gambetta.

À la Courtille, 1 rue des Envierges, 20e. Mo Pyrénées.

Chez Jean, 38 rue Boyer (near cnr with rue de Ménilmontant), 20e. Mo Gambetta/Ménilmontant.

Égée, 19 rue de Ménilmontant, 20e. Mo Ménilmontant.

La Fontaine aux Roses, 27 av Gambetta, 20e. Mo Père-Lachaise.

Au Gigot Fin, 56 rue de Lancry (nr canal), 10e. Mo Jacques-Bonsergent.

L'Homme Bleu, 57 rue Jean-Pierre-Timbaud, 11e. Mo Parmentier.

Lao Siam, 49 rue de Belleville, 19e. Mo Belleville.

Louis Valy, 49 rue Orfila, 20e. Mo Gambetta/Pelleport.

Le Pacifique, 35 rue de Belleville, 20e. Mo Belleville.

Au Pavillon Puebla, Parc des Buttes-Chaumont, 19e. Mo Buttes-Chaumont.

Pho-Dong-Huong, 14 rue Louis-Bonnet, 11e. Mo Belleville.

Le Polonia, 3 rue Chaumont, 19e. Mo Jaurès.

Le Président, 19 rue Louis-Bonnet, 11e. Mo Belleville.

Au Rendez-Vous de la Marine, 114 quai de la Loire, 19e. Mo Jaurès.

Aux Rendez-Vous des Amis, 10 av Père-Lachaise, 20e. Mo Gambetta.

Restaurant de Bourgogne, 26 rue des Vinaigriers, 10e. Mo Jacques-Bonsergent.

Le Royal Belleville, 19 rue Louis-Bonnet (floor below *Le Président*; see above), 11e. Mo Belleville.

cont.

businesses still exist, gentrification and modernization are well advanced. The idea of canal frontage has clearly put a light in the developers' eyes, although you can at least be thankful it has not been turned into the motorway envisaged by President Pompidou.

Ancient corners do still exist. Down the steps to **rue des Vinaigriers**, the shoemakers' union, *Fédération Nationale des Artisans de la Chaussure*, has its headquarters behind a Second Empire shop front whose fluted wooden pilasters are crowned with capitals of grapes and a gilded Bacchus. Across the street, the surely geriatric *Cercle National des Garibaldiens* still has a meeting place, and at no. 35 *Poursin* has been making brass buckles since 1830.

On the other side of the canal, in the rustic-sounding **rue de la Grange-aux-Belles**, the name *Le Pont-Tournant* (The Swing-Bridge) café recalls the canal's more vigorous youth. Traditionally, the bargees came from the north, whence the name of the **Hôtel du Nord** at 102 quai de Jemappes, made famous by Marcel Carné's film starring Arletty and Jean Gabin. For a long time there was talk of transforming it into a movie museum, but now, with its façade restored, it has been incorporated into a block of modern apartments.

Local residents are very active in defence of their neighbourhood – the **square Villemin** gardens abutting the canal just above rue des

---

The Montfaucon gallows

Long ago, rue de la Grange-aux-Belles was a dusty track leading uphill, past fields, on the way to Germany. Where no. 53 now stands, a path led to the top of a small hillock. Here, in 1325, on the king's orders, an enormous gallows was built, consisting of a plinth 6m high, on which stood sixteen stone pillars 10m high. These were joined by chains, from which malefactors were hanged in clusters. They were left there until they disintegrated, by way of an example, and they stank so badly that when the wind blew from the northeast they infected the nostrils of the far-off city.

This practice continued until the seventeenth century. Bones and other remains from the pit into which they were thrown were found during the building of a garage in 1954.

Récollets (see p.170) being one successful instance. A local magazine, *La Gazette du Canal*, publicizes local campaigns and gives addresses of cafés, restaurants and events in the area.

Just across the canal is one of the finest and least-visited buildings in Paris, the early seventeenth-century **Hôpital St-Louis**, built in the same style as the **place des Vosges** (see p.100). Although it still functions as a hospital, you can walk through into its quiet central courtyard to admire the elegant brick and stone façades and steep-pitched roofs.

At the back of the hospital, on rue Juliette-Dodu, an unprepossessing building houses one of the key centres in world research into human genetics. The **Centre des Études du Polymorphisme Humain** was financed by the art business of its founder's wife and studies DNA from forty families – French, Venezuelan, Amish and Mormon.

Place de Stalingrad and Bassin de la Villette

Both banks of the canal along the northern section to La Villette have now been thoroughly sanitized. The one major improvement is the restoration of the **place de Stalingrad**, which has been sanded and grassed.

To the north of the square, the Roman-inspired building with a Doric portico and pediments surmounted by a rotunda is the **Rotonde de la Villette**, whose stonework has been scrubbed clean. This was one of the toll houses designed by the architect Ledoux as part of Louis XVI's scheme to tax all goods entering the city. At that time, every road out of the city had a customs post or *barrière* linked by a six-metre-high wall, known as "*Le Mur des Fermiers-Généraux*" – a major irritant in the run-up to the French Revolution.

One of the side effects of the general cleanup has been to enhance the elegant aerial stretch of métro, supported on Neoclassical iron and stone pillars, which backs the toll house. Looking back from further up the **Bassin de la Villette**, it provides a focus for an impressive new monumental vista.

Place de la
République
and the
Canal St-
Martin

Recobbled, and with its dockside buildings converted into offices
for **canal boat trips** (see p.301), the Bassin has lost all vestiges of its
former status as France's premier port. The old portside restaurant
Au Rendez-Vous de la Marine is still going, however, and on
Sundays and holidays people stroll along the *quais*, play *boules*, fish
or canoe and row in the dock. At rue de Crimée, a **hydraulic bridge**
(1885) marks the end of the dock and the beginning of the **Canal de
l'Ourcq**. To the east, the burrowing slums of the rue de Flandres are
coming down, and it's all a bit of a wasteland from here up to the
junction of canals, where a rearing megachain hotel, as ugly as they
come, faces the architectural cacophony across the water of Paris'
most extravagant high-tech park, the Parc de la Villette.

Parc de la Villette

All the **meat** for Paris use to come from **La Villette**. Slaughtering
and butchering, and industries based on the meat markets' by-prod-
ucts, provided plenty of jobs for its dense population, whose recreation time was spent betting on cockfights, skating or swimming,
and eating in the numerous local restaurants famed for their fresh
meat. In the 1960s, vast sums of money were spent modernizing La
Villette, including the building of a gigantic new abattoir. Yet, just as
it was nearing completion, the emergence of new refrigeration techniques rendered the centralized meat industry redundant. The only
solution was to switch course entirely: billions continued to be
poured into La Villette, with the revised aim of creating a **music, art
and science complex** that would stun the world with Parisian brilliance.

The end result, the **Parc de la Villette**, stuns not so much with brilliance as with brain fatigue. There is so much going on here, most of
it highly stimulating and entertaining, but it's all so disparate and dis-
connected, with such a clash of architectural styles, that the problem
is knowing where to start – it's rather like a miniature material equivalent of the Internet. According to the park's creators, this is all
intentional, and philosophically justified (see box). Yet there is
something vaguely menacing about the setting. The 900-metre

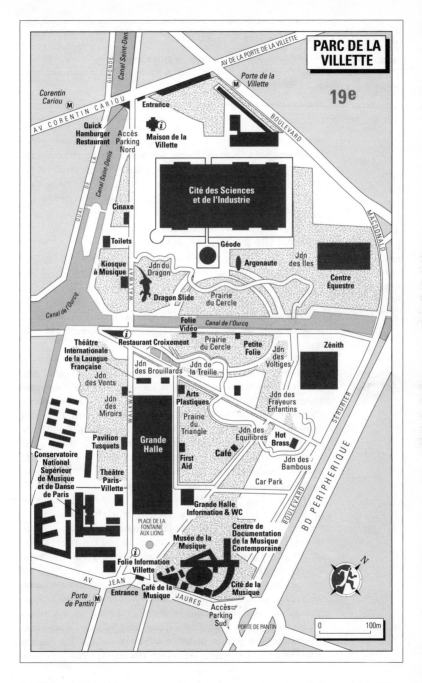

PARC DE LA VILLETTE

19e

Corentin Cariou Ⓜ

AV DE LA PORTE DE LA VILLETTE

Porte de la Villette Ⓜ

AV CORENTIN CARIOU

GIRONDE

Canal-Saint-Denis

Entrance

BOULEVARD

Quick Hamburger Restaurant

Accès Parking Nord

ⓘ Maison de la Villette

Canal-Saint-Denis

QUAI DE LA

Cinaxe

Cité des Sciences et de l'Industrie

MACDONALD

Toilets

Géode

Kiosque à Musique

Jdn du Dragon

Argonaute

Jdn des Îles

Centre Équestre

Canal de l'Ourcq

WALKWAY

Dragon Slide

Prairie du Cercle

Folie Vidéo

Canal de l'Ourcq

ⓘ Restaurant Croixement

Prairie du Cercle

Petite Folie

Jdn des Voltiges

Zénith

Théâtre Internationale de la Laungue Française

Jdn des Brouillards

Jdn de la Treille

Jdn des Vents

Jdn des Miroirs

WALKWAY

Arts Plastiques

Jdn des Frayeurs Enfantins

SERURIER

Pavilion Tusquets

Grande Halle

Prairie du Triangle

Jdn des Equilibres

Hot Brass

Conservatoire National Supérieur de Musique et de Danse de Paris

Théâtre Paris-Villette

First Aid

Café

Jdn des Bambous

Car Park

BD PERIPHERIQUE

Grande Halle Information & WC

PLACE DE LA FONTAINE AUX LIONS

Musée de la Musique

Centre de Documentation de la Musique Contemporaine

BOULEVARD

ⓘ Folie Information Villette

AV JEAN

Café de la Musique

Cité de la Musique

Porte de Pantin Ⓜ

Entrance

JAURES

Accès Parking Sud

PORTE DE PANTIN

N

0   100m

straight **walkway**, with its wavy shelter and complicated metal bridge across the Canal de l'Ourcq, seems to insist that you cover the park from end to end, and there's something too dogmatic about the arrangement of the bright red **follies** like chopped-off cranes, each slightly different but all spaced exactly 120m apart. And the Cité des Sciences is alarming for its sheer bulk.

Details of the museums, music venues and exhibition spaces are provided in Chapters 14 and 18.

Visiting the park

The Parc de la Villette (daily 6–1am; free, except some of the gardens) is accessible from M° Porte-de-la-Villette, at the northern end by av Corentin-Cariou and the Cité des Sciences; from the canal de l'Ourcq's quai de la Marne to the west (see p.178); or from M° Porte-de-Pantin, on av Jean-Jaurès, at the southern entrance by the Cité de la Musique and Grande Halle. There are information centres by both entrances and by the canal bridge.

The best defence against being totally overwhelmed by the park is to come here for a specific purpose rather than just an idle stroll. And there are a wealth of attractions to choose from. The abandoned abattoir has been turned into the **Cité des Sciences et de l'Industrie**, one of the world's finest science museums. High-tech film experiences are on offer at the **Cinaxe** and at the **Géode**, the bubble of reflecting steel dropped from an intergalactic *boules* game to land beside the **"Argonaut" submarine** beached between the Cité and the Canal de l'Ourcq. Rock concerts are staged at the inflatable **Zenith** venue, and there's jazz at **Hot Brass** in one of the park's bright red follies. Or you might opt to join the crowds lounging on the acres of grass known as "prairies" for a movie in the open air. At the recently completed **Cité de la Musique** you can hear Pierre Boulez' latest experimental compositions, or visit the **music museum**. Plays are performed in the nineteenth-century **Théatre Paris-Villette**, dwarfed between the western half of the Cité de la Musique and the elegant old iron-framed beef market hall, the **Grande Halle**, venue for large-scale art and trade shows. Additional draws for children include the **dragon slide** of recycled drums and pipes; **gardens** of "mirrors", "mists", "winds and dunes" and "islands"; other areas with trampolines, sounds, bamboos and vines; and a prairie where a giant bicycle appears half buried in the ground.

Deconstructivism

The Parc de la Villette was conceived by Bernard Tschumi as a futuristic "activity" park which would dispense with the eighteenth- and nineteenth-century notion of parks and gardens as places of gentle and well-ordered relaxation. What, in fact, is going on here is a landscaping expression of deconstructivism. This, more or less, is the idea that the only way to approach artistic creation is to back off from the old-fashioned idea of unity, meaning and purpose, to "deconstruct" the work into its disparate elements, thereby opening up all possible interpretations.

In contrast, the Cité des Sciences and the Grande Halle belong firmly to the "modernist" tradition with their clear rectangular shapes and their function dictating the building's appearance. The form of the Cité comes from the concrete hulk of the abandoned abattoir; the great walls and steel lattice are tellingly similar to the nineteenth-century market hall.

There is nothing modernist about the Cité de la Musique, but nor is it about fragmentation and multiple interpretations. The forms of the buildings make abstract artistic statements about the function; shapes and patterns reappear and evolve in different parts of the buildings. Christian de Portzamparc is creating a new language of architecture, one in which the experience of moving within the spaces goes beyond the functional need of, for example, a corridor or a reception area.

The Cité des Sciences and the Cité de la Musique

The park's dominant building, the Cité des Sciences, is an enormous construction – four times the size of Beaubourg. Despite the transparency of its giant glass walls hanging beneath a dark blue lattice of steel, it is a fortress, from which walkways accelerate out towards the Géode across a moat that is level with the underground floors. Once you are inside, however, the experience is quite the reverse. The three themes of water (around the building), vegetation (the three greenhouses using the glass walls) and light (with which the building is flooded, from vast skylights as well as the glass façade), realized by architect Adrien Fainsilber, work admirably.

The waves and funnels, irregular polygons and non-parallel lines of the two complexes making up the Cité de la Musique are based on a completely different mindset, though you might find the façade of the *Paris Music and Dance Conservatory* (on the left, as you look from av Jean-Jaurès) no less threatening, initially, than the Cité des Sciences. If you regard it with its use in mind, however, it begins to make abstract sense: windows in sequences like musical notation; the wavy roof which, according to the architect, Christian de Portzamparc, is like a Gregorian chant, but could equally suggest the movement of a dancer or a conductor's baton; and the crescendo of the rising curves of the façade.

The wedge-shaped complex to the right contains the public spaces, which include the *Musée de la Musique*, the very chic *Café de la Musique*, a music and dance information centre, and a concert hall whose ovoid dome rises like a perfect soufflé from the roof line.

Parc de la
Villette

A glass-roofed arcade surrounds the auditorium with pale blue sloping walls that give out deep relaxation sounds. Other walls are coloured and textured like abstract paintings. From within, this is a beautifully sensual building, and very unexpected from the one harsh semi-exterior element of a girdered "arrow" pointing down to the entrance arch pretending to be another red folly.

Belleville, Ménilmontant and Charonne

The old villages of **Belleville**, **Ménilmontant** and **Charonne**, only incorporated into the city in 1860, are strung out along the western slopes of a ridge that rises steadily from the Seine at Bercy to an altitude of 128m near Belleville's place des Fêtes, the highest point in Paris after Montmartre. The quickest and easiest way to see them is to take a trip on the #26 **bus** from the Gare du Nord, getting on and off at strategic points along the **avenue de Simon-Bolivar** and **rue des Pyrénées**, which between them run the whole length of the ridge to Porte de Vincennes.

At the northern end of the Belleville heights, a shortish walk from La Villette, is the **parc des Buttes-Chaumont** (M° Buttes-Chaumont/Botzaris; bus #26, stop Botzaris/Buttes-Chaumont). It was constructed under the guidance of Haussmann in the 1860s to camouflage what until then had been a desolate warren of disused quarries, rubbish dumps and miserable shacks. The sculpted, beak-shaped park stays open all night and, equally rarely for Paris, you're not cautioned off the grass.

At its centre, a huge rock upholds a delicate Corinthian temple. You can cross the lake that surrounds it, via a suspension bridge, or take the shorter Pont des Suicides. This, according to Louis Aragon, the literary grand old man of the French Communist Party,

before metal grills were erected along its sides, claimed victims even from passers-by who had had no intention whatsoever of killing themselves but were suddenly tempted by the abyss . . . And just see how docile people turn out to be: no one any longer jumps off this easily negotiable parapet.

Le Paysan de Paris

Perhaps the attraction for suicides and roving Commie writers is the unlikeliness of this park, with its views of the Sacré-Coeur and beyond, its grotto of stalactites, and the fences of concrete moulded to imitate wood – for that matter, its very existence, in this erstwhile working-class corner of the city. There are enticements, too, for kids and other lovers of life (see p.312).

Claude Chappe and the rue du Télégraphe

The **rue du Télégraphe** is named in memory of Claude Chappe's invention of the optical telegraph. Chappe first tested his device here in September 1792, in a corner of the Belleville cemetery. When word of his activities got out, he was nearly lynched by a mob that assumed he was trying to signal to the king, who was at that time imprisoned in the Temple (see p.105). Eventually two lines were set up, from Belleville to Strasbourg and the east, and from Montmartre to Lille and the north. By 1840 it was possible to send a message to Calais in three minutes, via 27 relays, and to Strasbourg in seven minutes, using 46 relays.

Belleville

East of the parc des Buttes-Chaumont, between rue de Crimée and place Rhin-et-Danube, dozens of cobbled and gardened *villas* lead off from rue Miguel-Hidalgo, rue du Général-Brunet, rue de la Liberté, rue de l'Égalité and rue de Mouzaïa. It is so light and airy here, you wonder why places like Auteuil and Passy should ever have seemed so much more desirable. Heading south, the first main street you meet is the **rue de Belleville**. Close to its highest point is the **place des Fêtes**, still with a market, though no longer festive. Once the village green, it is now totally unrecognizable under concrete tower blocks and shopping parades, a terrible monument to the unimaginative redevelopment of the 1960s and 1970s. But things improve as you descend the steepening gradient towards rue des Pyrénées. Round the church of St-Jean-de-Belleville, among the *boulangeries* and *charcuteries*, you could be in the busy main street of any French provincial town. Below rue des Pyrénées, just before the mural of a detective on the left, the neo-realist artist Ben has sculpted a trompe l'œil of a sign being erected which says "Words must be mistrusted".

Below rue des Pyrénées, bits of old Belleville remain – very, very dilapidated – alongside the new. On the wall of no. 72 a plaque commemorates the birth of the legendary chanteuse, Édith Piaf, although she was in fact found abandoned as a baby on the steps here.

A little lower, the cobbled **rue Piat** climbs past the beautiful wrought-iron gate of the jungly **Villa Otoz** to the newly created **Parc de Belleville**. From the terrace at the junction with rue des Envierges, there is a fantastic view across the city, especially at sunset. At your feet the small park descends in a series of terraces and waterfalls, a total success compared with the nondescript development of a decade ago. Inevitably this has brought the establishment of one or two rather chic eating and drinking places.

*The restau-
rants of
Belleville are
detailed on
p.270.*

Continuing straight ahead, a path crosses the top of the park past a minuscule vineyard and turns into steps that drop down to **rue des Couronnes**. Some of the adjacent streets are worth a wander for a feel of the changing times – rue de la Mare, rue des Envierges, rue des Cascades – with two or three beautiful old houses in overgrown gardens, alongside new housing that follows the height and curves of the streets and recently reopened *passages* between them.

Between the bottom of the park and bd de Belleville, the squalid, rotting housing, combined with a teeming street life, has been almost erased, despite the concerted efforts of the local organization for the defence of Belleville, which fought hard for restoration rather than demolition and for preserving the little cafés, restaurants and shops that gave the *quartier* its animation. Rue Ramponeau has an historic record of resistance: at the junction with rue de Tourtille the very last barricade of the Commune was defended single-handedly for fifteen minutes by the last fighting Communard, before he melted away – to write a book about it all.

It is also in these streets and on the boulevard that the strong ethnic diversity of Belleville becomes apparent. Rue Ramponeau, for example, is still full of – though for how long it's hard to say – kosher shops, belonging to Sephardic Jews from Tunisia. Around the crossroads of rue du Faubourg-du-Temple and bd de Belleville there are

---

La descente de la Courtille

The name "*Courtille*" comes from *courti*, a Picard dialect word for "garden". The heights of Belleville were known as *La Haute Courtille* in the nineteenth century, while the lower part around rue du Faubourg-du-Temple and rue de la Fontaine-au-Roi was *La Basse Courtille*. Both were full of boozers and dance halls, where people flocked from the city on high days and holidays.

The wildest revels of the year took place on the night of Mardi Gras, when thousands of masked people turned out to celebrate the end of the *carnaval*. Next morning – Ash Wednesday – they descended in drunken procession from Belleville to the city, in up to a thousand horse-drawn vehicles: *la descente de la Courtille*.

The bygone eastern villages

Before redevelopment, the superb hillside location combined with cobbled lanes, individual gardens, numerous stairways, and local shops and cafés perfectly integrated with human-scale housing, gave the area a unique charm – quite the equal of Montmartre, but without the touristy commercialism.

For a picture of what it was like, there is no more evocative record than Willy Ronis's atmospheric photographs in *Belleville Ménilmontant* (see *Contexts*, p.425). But there is still on-the-ground evidence, in addition to the little cul-de-sacs of terraced houses and gardens north of rue des Pyrénées. There are alleys so narrow that nothing but the knife-grinder's tricycle could fit down them, like **passage de la Duée**, 17 rue de la Duée, and little detached houses, like 97 rue Villiers-d'Adam. You can also see the less romantic side of life in the grim neo-Gothic fortress housing estates of 140 rue de Ménilmontant, built in 1925 for the influx of rural populations after World War I, and the 1913 Villa Stendhal, off rue Stendhal. In marked contrast is the housing right over to the east, near the Porte de Bagnolet, provided for workers in 1908 and almost unmatched in the city. From place Octave-Chanute, wide stone steps bordered by lanterns lead up to a miraculous little sequence of streets of terraced houses and gardens, some with Art Nouveau glass porches, fancy brickwork and the shade of lilac and cherry trees.

dozens of Chinese restaurants and a scattering of eateries owned by East Europeans (descendants of refugees from nineteenth-century pogroms in Russia and Poland, and the twentieth-century atrocities of the Nazis), Turks and Greeks. On the boulevard, especially during the Tuesday and Friday morning market, you see women from Mali, Gambia and Zaire, often wearing local dress, and men in burnouses, who look as if they still had the arid ridges of the High Atlas in their mind's eye. All this diversity is reflected in the produce on sale.

The boulevard is now lined with dramatic new architecture, employing jutting triangles, curves, and the occasional reference to the roof lines of nineteenth-century Parisian blocks.

The combination of old and new continues in Basse Belleville, in the large triangle of streets below bd de Belleville, bounded by rue du Faubourg-du-Temple (the most lively) and av de la République. Zany high-tech metal and glass at 117 rue Faubourg-du-Temple coexists with small unchanged business premises in the Cour des Bretons. Goods still cost around half the price that they do in shops in the centre of the city, despite a number of increasingly fashionable restaurants. Here there is still a good mix of French and immigrant, workshop, residence and commerce. And the houses are built on the traditional pattern, with *passages* and courtyards burrowing within courtyards.

Ménilmontant

Like Belleville, **Ménilmontant** aligns itself along one long, straight, steep street, the rue de Ménilmontant. It has always been less dilapidated than Belleville. Though it has its black spots, it is somehow more respectable.

For half its length, the **rue de Ménilmontant** is a busy, multi-racial shopping street, full of traditional, small shops and snack bars, the continuation of the equally busy rue Oberkampf. The upper reaches, above rue Sorbier, are quieter. Looking back from here, you find yourself dead in line with the rooftop of the Centre Beaubourg, a measure of how high you are above the rest of the city.

Like Belleville, the area closest to bd Belleville has been almost completely demolished and rebuilt – on a small scale, around court-yards with open spaces for kids to play. Centred around rue des Amandiers, it's all a bit squeaky-clean and unweathered as yet, and the café count has dropped to near zero. **Rue Eliza-Berry** turns into steps alongside the extraordinary *France Telecom* building, topped with great bunches of masts and facing a lovely small park on rue Sorbier.

If you cross the park, take a right, then a left into rue Boyer, you'll find the splendid mosaic and sculpted constructivist façade of **La Bellevilloise** at no. 25, built for the *PCF* in 1925 to celebrate fifty years of work and science. Saved from demolition by a preservation order, it is now home to a theatre school.

A short way before it, a delightful lane of village houses and gardens, **rue Laurence-Savart**, climbs up to rue du Retrait and rue des Pyrénées opposite the poetically named alley of sighs, the "*passage des Soupirs*".

There is more melancholy poetry near the northeast corner of the Père-Lachaise cemetery, where the last crumbling houses of the **rue des Partants** (the street of the departers) offer the most poignantly evocative streetscape in the *quartier*. But only the **street names** echo the long-vanished orchards and rustic pursuits of the villagers: *Amandiers* (almond trees), *Pruniers* (plum trees), *Mûriers* (mulberry trees), *Pressoir* (wine press).

Rue des Pyrénées, the main cross-route through this *quartier*, is itself redolent of the provinces, getting busier as it approaches place Gambetta. The post office at no. 248 has a big ceramic wall-piece by the sculptor Zadkine. Close by place Gambetta, on rue Malte-Brun, is the big glass frontage of the **Théâtre National de la Colline**, built in 1987 to replace the dingy old cinema that used to house the theatre. You can **snack** in its cafeteria and pick up the beautifully produced and illustrated brochures on current productions.

Charonne

If you like unexpected and unvisited corners of cities, take a walk from the av du Père-Lachaise entrance to the cemetery along rue des Rondeaux, the street that follows the cemetery wall, with a very desirable residence for exhibitionists at no. 26.

Cross rue des Pyrénées by the bridge in rue Renouvier, turn right on rue Stendhal (Villa Stendhal is opposite – see p.185), past the underground reservoir that serves as a gigantic header tank for the stopcocks that wash the city's gutters, and go down the steps at the

end to rue de Bagnolet. Alternatively, take rue Lisfranc off rue
Stendhal and left on rue des Prairies, then left again on rue de
Bagnolet. It's a longer way round, but **rue des Prairies** has excellent
examples of sensitive and imaginative infill. The new buildings have
a pleasing variety of designs and colours, with bright tiling and ochre
shades of cladding.

In place St-Blaise is the perfect little church of **St-Germain-de-
Charonne**. It has changed little since it served a village, and its
Romanesque belfry not at all, since the thirteenth century. Unique
among Paris' churches, with the exception of St-Pierre in
Montmartre, it has its own graveyard, in which several hundred murdered Communards were buried after being accidentally disinterred
during the construction of a reservoir in 1897. Otherwise, charnel
houses were the norm, with the bones emptied into the catacombs as
more space was required. It was not until the nineteenth century that
public cemeteries appeared on the scene, the most famous being
Père-Lachaise (see below).

*For more on
the catacombs
and under-
ground Paris,
see p.138.*

Opposite the church, the old cobbled village high street, **rue St-
Blaise**, is one of the most picturesque in Paris, or was, until it was
prettified further, the face-lift eradicating the charm it once had.
Beyond place des Grès, the argument for infill, for preserving and
creating the new, is clear. Everything has been rebuilt; it is hard and
harsh and the few cafés are full of young men aggressively jolting at
arcade games.

Rue de Vitruve, however, which crosses rue St-Blaise at place des
Grès, has a great new swimming pool and the Artignan youth hostel
to the north; and to the south, at no. 39, a school, built in 1982.
Designed by Jacques Bardet, the school's rectangular mass is broken
up by open-air segments, enclosed only by the structural steel lattice
of the building over which plants are supposed to spread – though
there's very little sign of them yet. But the best thing is hidden round
the corner, visible as you approach from rue des Pyrénées – a huge
sculptured **salamander** and its footprints mounted on the window-
less side of a building on rue R-A-Marquet. Engraved above the street
sign are the words: "A legend is told that a salamander, after passing
by the square where it would have left a long trail, set off towards rue
R-A-Marquet and stopped to rest on a corner of rue Vitruve."

Père-Lachaise cemetery

The **cimetière Père-Lachaise** (daily 7.30am–6pm; M°
Gambetta/Père-Lachaise/Alexandre-Dumas) is like a miniature city
devastated by a neutron bomb: a great number of dead, empty houses and temples of every size and style, and exhausted survivors, some
congregating aimlessly, some searching persistently for their
favourite famous dead in an arrangement of numbered divisions that
is neither entirely haphazard nor strictly systematic.

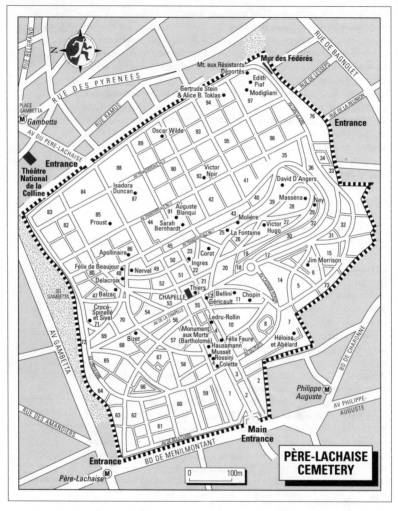

Père-Lachaise cemetery was opened in 1804, after an urgent stop had been put to further burials in the then-overflowing city cemeteries and churchyards. It was an incredibly successful piece of land speculation. Nicolas Frochot, the urban planner who bought the land, persuaded the civil authorities to have **Molière**, **La Fontaine**, **Abélard** and **Héloïse** reburied in his new cemetery. To be interred in Père-Lachaise quickly became the ultimate status symbol for the rich and successful. Ironically, Frochot even sold a plot to the original owner for considerably more money than the price he had paid for the entire site. Even today, the rates are still extremely high.

Some of the most celebrated dead have unremarkable tombs, while those whose fame died with them, or who were nonentities to start with, have the most expressive monuments. Swarms flock to ex-Doors lead singer **Jim Morrison's tomb** in Division 6. Once graffiti-covered and wreathed in marijuana fumes, it has been completely refurbished, its neighbours scrubbed clean as well, and put under police guard to ensure it stays that way. *Femme fatale* **Colette**'s tomb, close to the main entrance in division 4, is very plain, though always covered in flowers. The same is true for the divine **Sarah Bernhardt**'s (division 44) and the great chanteuse **Edith Piaf**'s (division 97). **Marcel Proust** lies in his family's conventional tomb (division 85), which honours the medical fame of his father.

Père-
Lachaise
cemetery

In contrast, one **Jean Pezon**, a lion-tamer, is shown riding his pet lion, which ate him (division 86). In division 92, nineteenth-century journalist **Victor Noir** – shot for daring to criticize a relative of Napoléon III – lies flat on his back, fully clothed, his top hat fallen by his feet. His prostrate figure has been a magnet, not for anti-censorship campaigners, but for infertile women rubbing themselves against him as a sexual charm. Close by, a forgotten and unlamented French diplomat must turn in his grave with envy – he provided himself with an enormous tapering phallus, admirably higher than the trees around it in division 48. In division 71, two men lie together hand in hand – not a gay couple (as far as anyone knows), but a pair of balloonists who went so high they died from lack of oxygen.

Other bed scenes include **Félix Faure** (division 4), French president, who died in the arms of his mistress in the Élysée palace in 1899. Draped in a French flag like a sheet, his head is raised and his hand seems to be groping the flagpole as if it might be his lover. **Géricault** reclines on cushions of stone (division 12), paint palette in hand, his neck and bony face taut with concentration. Close by is the relaxed figure of **Jean Carriès**, a model-maker, in felt hat and overalls, holding one of his figures in the palm of his hand. For a more fearsome view of death, there's the tomb of a French judge, **Raphaël Roger**, in division 94, where a figure, cowled from head to foot, stands sentinel beneath a pointed arch; or the poet in division 6, bursting out of his granite block.

Painter **Corot** (division 24) and novelist **Balzac** (division 48) both have superb busts, Balzac looking particularly satisfied with his life. **Chopin** (division 11) has a willowy muse weeping for his loss. The most impressive of the individual tombs is **Oscar Wilde**'s, for which Jacob Epstein sculpted a strange Pharaonic winged messenger. The inscription is a grim verse from *The Ballad of Reading Gaol.*

Approaching Oscar Wilde's grave from the centre of the cemetery, you pass the tomb of **Auguste Blanqui** (division 91), after whom so many French streets are named. Described by Karl Marx as the nineteenth century's greatest revolutionary, he served his time in jail – 33 years in all – for political activities that spanned the 1830 Revolution to the Paris Commune.

Père-
Lachaise
cemetery

Below Blanqui's and Wilde's graves – along with Victor Noir, Edith Piaf and Raphaël Roger – you'll find in division 96 the grave of **Modigliani** and his lover **Jeanne Herbuterne**, who killed herself in crazed grief a few days after he died in agony from meningitis. **Laura Marx**, Karl's daughter, and her husband **Paul Lafargue**, who committed suicide together in 1911, also lie in this southeast corner of the cemetery (division 76).

But it is the monuments to the collective, violent deaths that have the power to change a sunny outing to Père-Lachaise into a much more sombre experience. In division 97, you'll find the memorials to **victims of the Nazi concentration camps**, to executed **Resistance fighters** and to those who were never accounted for in the genocide of World War II. The sculptures are relentless in their images of inhumanity, of people forced to collaborate in their own degradation and death.

Finally, there is the **Mur des Fedérés** (division 76), the wall where the last troops of the Paris Commune were lined up and shot in the final days of the battle. The man who ordered their execution, **Adolphe Thiers**, lies in the centre of the cemetery in division 55.

Defeat is everywhere: the oppressed and their oppressors are interred with the same ritual, in the same illustrious spot; the relative riches and fame as unequal among the tombs of the dead as they are in the lives of the living.

A good map of the cemetery is available for 10F in the newsagent and flower shop on av Père-Lachaise and at outlets near the main entrance on bd de Ménilmontant. You'll find that the rue de la Réunion and around place Gambetta are the best places to seek out **sustenance**.

Down to the Faubourg St-Antoine

Heading back to Bastille from Père-Lachaise, **rue de la Roquette** and **rue de Charonne** are the principal thoroughfares. There's nothing particularly special about the numerous passages and ragged streets that lead off into the lower 11ᵉ *arrondissement*, except that they are utterly Parisian, with the odd detail of a building, the obscurity of a shop's speciality, the display of vegetables in a simple greengrocer's, the sunlight on a café table, or the graffiti on a Second Empire street fountain to charm an aimless wanderer. And the occasional reminder of the sheer political toughness of French working-class tradition, as in the plaque on some flats in rue de la Folie-Regnault commemorating the first FTP (Francs-Tireurs Partisans) Resistance group, which used to meet here until it was betrayed and its members executed in 1941. Square de la Roquette was the site of an old prison, where 4000 members of the Resistance were imprisoned in 1944. The low, foreboding gateway on rue de la Roquette has been preserved in their memory.

The closer you get to the Bastille, the more chunks are missing – demolition areas of several blocks at a time. It's depressing, but so too is the northeast corner of the 11e, where the buildings are crumbling and the poverty very much in evidence. South of rue de Charonne, between rue St-Bernard and impasse Charrière, stands the rustic-looking **church of Ste-Marguerite**, with a garden beside it dedicated to the memory of Raoul Nordling, the Swedish consul who persuaded the retreating Germans not to blow up Paris in 1944.

The church itself (Mon–Sat 8am–noon & 3–7.30pm, Sun 8.30am–noon & 5–7.30pm) was built in 1624 to accommodate the growing population of the *faubourg*, which was about 40,000 in 1710 and 100,000 in 1900. The sculptures on the transept pediments were made by its first full-blown parish priest. Inside it is wide-bodied, low and quiet, with a very local and un-urban feel, as if it were still out in the fields. The stained-glass windows record a very local history: the visit of Pope Pius VII in 1802, in Paris for Napoléon's coronation; the miraculous cure of a Madame Delafosse in the rue de Charonne on May 31, 1725; the fatal wounding of Monseigneur Affre, the archbishop of Paris, in the course of a street battle in the *faubourg* on June 25, 1848; the murder of sixteen Carmelite nuns at the Barrière du Trône in 1794 (presumably, more revolutionary anti-clericalism); the *quartier*'s dead in World War I.

In the now disused cemetery of Ste-Marguerite, the story goes – though no-one has been able to prove it – lies the body of Louis XVII, the 10-year-old heir of the guillotined Louis XVI, who died in the Temple prison (see box on p.105). The cemetery also received the dead from the Bastille prison.

From square R-Nordling, rue de la Forge-Royale – with the *Casbah* nightclub magnificently decorated in North African style at no. 18 – takes you down to rue du Faubourg-St-Antoine. Or you can continue down rue de Charonne and hit the stretch of Faubourg-St-Antoine that has a series of courtyards, mews and alleyways, providing quiet havens for the Bastille traffic. No. 56, for example, has ivy and roses curtaining three shops, window boxes on every storey, and lemon trees in tubs tilted on the cobbles.

After Louis XI licensed the establishment of craftsmen in the fifteenth century, the *faubourg* became the principal working-class *quartier* of Paris, cradle of revolutions and mother of street-fighters. From its beginnings, the principal trade associated with it has been **furniture-making**, and this was where the classic styles of French furniture – Louis Quatorze, Louis Quinze, Second Empire – were developed. The maze of interconnecting yards and *passages* are still full of the workshops of the related trades: marquetry, stainers, polishers, inlayers etc, many of which are still producing those styles.

To the east, rue du Faubourg-St-Antoine ends at place de la Nation, along with bd Voltaire that cuts diagonally right across the 11e *arrondissement* and the continuation of bd de Ménilmontant.

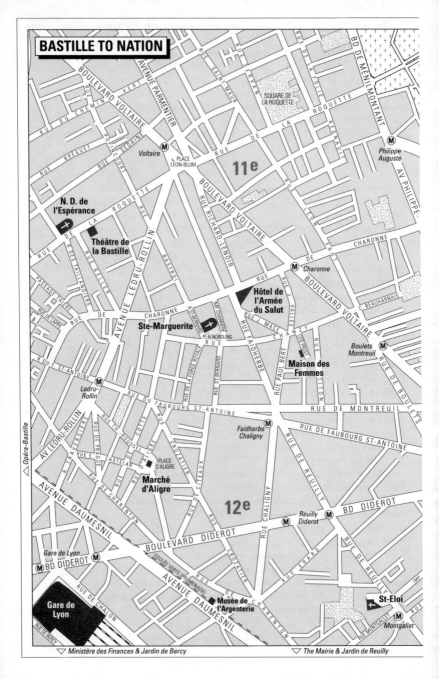

BASTILLE TO NATION

11e

12e

N. D. de
l'Espérance

Théâtre de
la Bastille

Ste-Marguerite

Hôtel de
l'Armée
du Salut

Maison des
Femmes

Marché
d'Aligre

Gare de
Lyon

Musée de
l'Argenterie

St-Eloi

SQUARE DE
LA ROQUETTE

Voltaire

Philippe
Auguste

Charonne

Boulets
Montreuil

Ledru-
Rollin

Faidherbe
Chaligny

Reuilly
Diderot

Montgallet

PLACE
LÉON-BLUM

PL. R-NORDLING

PLACE
D'ALIGRE

BOULEVARD VOLTAIRE
AVENUE PARMENTIER
BOULEVARD VOLTAIRE
RUE SAINT-MAUR
RUE ST MAUR
RUE SERVAN
RUE DE LA ROQUETTE
RUE DE LA FOLIE REGNAULT
BD DE MÉNILMONTANT
RUE DE LA ROQUETTE
AV PHILIPPE-AUGUSTE
RUE BRÉGUET
RUE DU CHEMIN VERT
RUE POPINCOURT
RUE SEDAINE
RUE KELLER
RUE DE LA ROQUETTE
RUE BASFROI
BOULEVARD VOLTAIRE
RUE RICHARD-LENOIR
AVENUE LEDRU-ROLLIN
RUE DES TAILLANDIERS
PASSAGE THIÉRÉ
RUE DE LAPPE
RUE DE CHARONNE
RUE DE CHARONNE
RUE KELLER
RUE DE LA FORGE ROYALE
RUE ST-BERNARD
RUE N CHARRIÈRE
RUE BERNARD
RUE J MACÉ
CITÉ PROST
RUE CHANZY
RUE FAIDHERBE
RUE DE
CHARONNE
RUE PAUL-BERT
RUE TITON
RUE DE MONTREUIL
RUE DE BOULETS
C. BEAUHARNAIS
RUE ST-ANTOINE
RUE DU FAUBOURG ST-ANTOINE
RUE DE FAUBOURG ST-ANTOINE
RUE DE MONTREUIL
RUE DE REUILLY
RUE DE REUILLY
AV LEDRU-ROLLIN
RUE TRAVERSIÈRE
RUE TH. ROUSSEL
RUE DE PRAGUE
RUE E. CASTELAR
RUE DE COTTE
RUE D'ALIGRE
RUE CROZATIER
RUE DE CITEAUX
RUE CHALIGNY
BOULEVARD DIDEROT
RUE DE CHARENTON
RUE E.E. DE PRAGUE
AVENUE DAUMESNIL
BD DIDEROT
BD DIDEROT
RUE ERARD
RUE DE REUILLY
RUE MONTGALLET
Gare de Lyon
RUE DE CHALON
COULÉE VERTE (PROMENADE)
AVENUE DAUMESNIL
RUE DE CHARENTON
RUE DE BERCY

Opéra-Bastille

△ Ministère des Finances & Jardin de Bercy   ▽ The Mairie & Jardin de Reuilly

Cimetière du Père-Lachaise

BOULEVARD DE

RUE DE BAGNOLET

Alexandre Dumas

20e

CHARONNE

AUGUSTE

RUE ALEXANDRE DUMAS

BOULEVARD

AV PHILIPPE-AUGUSTE

Avron

RUE DE MONTREUIL

BOULEVARD VOLTAIRE

DE CHARONNE

PLACE DE Nation
Triomphe de la République
AV DU TRÔNE
Nation LA NATION

COURS DE VINCENNES

RUE DE

BD DE PICPUS

AVENUE DU BEL AIR

R. DES COLONNES DU TRÔNE

PICPUS

MOUSSET

DU SERGENT BAUCHAT

AVENUE DE ST-MANDE

N

0   300 m

▽ Pl. Félix Eboué

To the Faubourg St-Antoine and the northern 12e arrondissement: listings

RESTAURANTS

Les Amognes, 243 rue du Faubourg-St-Antoine, 11e. Mo Faidherbe-Chaligny.

Le Bistrot du Peintre, 116 av Ledru-Rollin, 11e. Mo Faidherbe-Chaligny.

Chardenoux, 1 rue Jules-Vallès, 11e. Mo Charonne.

Les Cinq Points Cardinaux, 14 rue Jean-Macé, 11e. Mo Faidherbe-Chaligny/Charonne.

Les Demoiselles de Charonne, 44 rue Léon-Frot, 11e. Mo Charonne.

L'Ébauchoir, 43-45 rue de Cîteaux, 12e. Mo Faidherbe-Chaligny.

La Gourmandise, 271 av Daumesnil, 12e. Mo Porte-Dorée.

La Mansouria, 11 rue Faidherbe-Chaligny, 11e. Mo Faidherbe-Chaligny.

Palais de la Femme, 94 rue de Charonne, 11e. Mo Charonne/Faidherbe-Chaligny.

CAFÉS AND BARS

Le Baron Rouge, 1 rue Théophile-Roussel (cnr place d'Aligre market), 12e. Mo Ledru-Rollin.

Jacques-Mélac, 42 rue Léon-Frot, 11e. Mo Charonne.

Le Penty Bar, cnr place d'Aligre and rue Emilio-Castellar, 12e. Mo Ledru-Rollin.

These establishments are reviewed in Chapter 13, Eating and drinking, on p.272.

Down to the Faubourg St-Antoine

The *place* is adorned with the Triumph of the Republic bronze, and, at the start of the Cours de Vincennes, the bizarre ensemble of two medieval monarchs, looking very small and sheepish in pens on the top of two high columns. During the Revolution, when the old name of place du Trône became place du Trône-Renversé, ("the overturned throne"), more people were guillotined here than on the more notorious execution site of place de la Concorde.

The 12ᵉ arrondissement

South of the Ledru-Rollin métro station on rue du Faubourg-St-Antoine, a small tangle of streets survives between the Bastille Opera, place d'Aligre and the major building works around the **Gare du Lyon**. The *boulangerie* on the corner of rues Charenton and Emilio-Castelar has beautiful painted glass panels – and good bread. On rue d'Aligre you can buy tagine pots, olives from the barrel, spices and cheap clothes. **Place d'Aligre**, centre of opposition to the demolition of the Opera House, has a raucous market (daily except Mon) with food in and around the covered *halles* and secondhand clothes and junk, as well as cheap and friendly cafés.

To the south, along av Daumesnil, the main artery of the 12ᵉ, runs the old railway viaduct, which has, at long last, been turned into a pedestrial promenade and cycle track known as the **Coulée Verte**. Planted with roses, camellias, viburnum and rosemary, and with prime views of chaotic chimneypots, it runs all the way from the junction with rue Ledru-Rollin to the Jardin de Reuilly and on out to Vincennes (see p.196). The arches underneath, their brickwork scrubbed clean, are now known as the **Viaduct des Arts** (see p.322) and include the copper and silver workshops of the **Musée de l'Argenterie** (see p.291).

A short way south of av Daumesnil is the gorgeous nineteenth-century extravaganza of the Gare du Lyon, hemmed in on its southern flank by building works for an interchange on the new Metéor underground line, and by the office blocks of quai de la Rapée. This stretch of the river has long been a business quarter, but in the last ten years or so the whole quayside right out to the *périphérique* has gradually been subjected to an increasing number of major developments. Among these is the new and rather elegant road bridge (with cycle track), Pont Charles de Gaulle, under construction between Pont d'Austerlitz and Pont de Bercy.

Just downstream of the Pont de Bercy is the **Ministère des Finances**, built in 1988 after the treasury staff had finally agreed to move out of the *Richelieu* wing of the Louvre. It stretches like a giant loading bridge from above the river (where higher bureaucrats and ministers arrive by boat) to rue de Bercy, a distance of some 400m. Kafka would have loved it, and contemporary Czechs would probably imagine the hand of Stalin on it. The best view of the monster is from the Charles-de-Gaulle–Nation métro line as it crosses the Pont de Bercy.

From the métro – which also gives good views of the new National Library on the opposite bank – you can see, on the east side of bd de Bercy, the **Palais Omnisports de Bercy**. Built in 1983, its concrete bunker frame, clad with sloping lawns, covers a vast arena used for sporting and cultural events. Beyond it used to be the old Bercy warehouses, where for centuries the capital's wine supplies were unloaded from river barges. This has now been turned into a very welcome green space, the **Parc de Bercy**, with various sculptural oddities, neat flowerbeds with box hedges, an *orangerie*, a "Pavillon" for contemporary art expos (Wed–Sun, noon–6pm; free), and one house preserved from the old days. In the course of demolition and excavation, archeologists unearthed the remains of Neolithic dug-out boats, dwellings and other bits and pieces dating back to around 4000 BC, adding an extra dimension to the city's history.

New buildings surround the park, from the ugly megahotels rearing up beside the Palais Omnisports to the line of steel and reflecting glass offices at the eastern end. On the north side, on rue Paul-Belmondo, is the now closed **American Centre**, designed by one of America's most fashionable architects, Frank O. Gehry. Constructed from zinc, glass and limestone, it resembles a falling pack of cards – according to Gehry, the inspiration was Matisse's collages done "with a simple pair of scissors".

All this new grand-scale development of Bercy is to match the emerging "Seine Rive Gauche" (see p.153) on the opposite bank. Planners envisage the whole of eastern Paris as the new ultramodern, high-tech zone of the city, between the two "poles" of La Villette and the Seine Rive Gauche. For the moment, however, Bercy is cut off from the rest of the 12e *arrondissement* by the rail tracks of the Gare du Lyon and the Gare de Paris-Bercy (the motorail station). You can walk under the lines along bd de Bercy or rue Proudhon, but it's not much fun. The only bus is the #62 from Pont de Tolbiac and place Lachambeaudie to place Félix-Eboué, and all the new building works may disrupt its route.

North of the tracks, on the eastern intersection of av Daumesil and rue de Charenton, stands the ebullient *mairie* of the 12e, with a particularly splendid rear side on rue Bignon. A short way down rue Charenton, at no. 119–120, a block built in 1911 has sculpted figures of a tired miner, sailor, industrial worker and farm labourer holding up the heavy weight of the window bays.

The traditional work in this area used to be at the freight station of Reuilly to the north of the *mairie*. This has now become the **Jardin de Reuilly**, a large circle of grass that you can walk, sleep or play on, with water gardens, a kids' playground, and statues baring their rears to av Daumesil There's a sundial with the hours marked on the

The 12ᵉ arrondissement

ground (and, in typical French fashion, details of the calculation methods, the movements of the earth, the history of sundials and so on engraved on it), and a lovely wooden footbridge that crosses over the park to the pedestrian **allée Vivaldi**. Though not very exciting architecturally, this leads on, through a tunnel beneath rue de Reuilly, to the continuation of the Coulée Verte, now running below the level of the surrounding streets, in the old railway cutting.

Rue de Reuilly meets Daumesnil at place Félix-Eboué, graced with some very smug lions. A short way east along av Daumesnil, an extremely narrow brickwork façade, topped by the tallest bell tower in Paris, conceals the vast cupola – filling the whole block behind the street – of the **Église du Saint-Esprit**. It was built in 1931 in memory of the colonial missionaries. The Roman Catholic Church was worried by the possible reaction of the anticlerical, communist sympathies of the local residents, hence the disguise of its enormous dimensions. Between rues Tourneux and Fecamp, one block down from the church, one of the city's grim 1920s housing estates has been cleaned up and restored.

Another peculiar church, St-Éloi, built in 1968, lies north of the Jardin de Reuilly on place M. de Fontenay, off rue de Reuilly (M° Montgallet). Its ground plan is a right-angled triangle with the altar positioned at one of the non-right-angled corners, and it feels like an industrial building. Both outside and inside are clad with lacquered aluminium leaves, in honour of St Éloi, patron saint of jewellers and iron-workers who lived in this area in the seventh century.

Close by the church, on the other side of rue de Reuilly, is one of the most perfect mews in Paris, the **impasse Mousset**. Roses, clematis, wisteria and honeysuckle wind across telegraph lines and up the whitewashed walls of tiny houses. A rusted hotel sign advertising wines and liqueurs as well as beds still hangs from one of the houses. You can hear children playing in hidden gardens; there are no designer offices here, just homes, the odd artist's studio and a small, still busy, printworks.

Vincennes

Beyond the 12ᵉ *arrondissement*, across the *boulevard périphérique*, lies the **Bois de Vincennes**. Besides the Bois de Boulogne, this is the only large green space that the city has to offer and hence a favourite family Sunday outing. Unfortunately it's so crisscrossed with roads that countryside sensations don't stand much of a chance, but it has some pleasant corners: the Parc Floral, the recently opened Château de Vincennes on the northern edge, the arboretum and the two lakes.

To reach the Bois de Vincennes from the 12ᵉ, you can take bus #86 from rue du Faubourg-St-Antoine, or more directly bus #46,

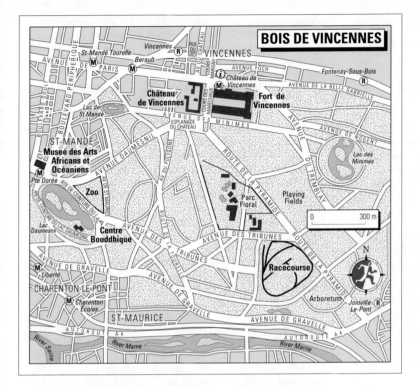

BOIS DE VINCENNES

which runs along rue de Reuilly and the last stretch of av Daumesnil. On the other side of Porte Dorée, bus #46 passes the **Musée des Arts Africains et Océaniens,** with its 1930s colonial façade of jungles, hard-working natives and the place names of the French Empire representing the "overseas contribution to the capital". The bus next stops at the **Parc Zoologique** (daily summer 9am–6pm, winter 9am–5.30pm; 40F/20F), which was one of the first zoos to replace cages with trenches and give the animals room to exercise themselves. The entrance is at 53 av de St-Maurice (M° Porte-Dorée).

The bizarre collection of the Musée des Arts Africains et Océaniens is detailed on p.287.

You can spend an afternoon **boating** on Lac Daumesnil (just by the zoo), or rent a bike from the same place and take some stale *baguette* over to the ducks on Lac des Minimes, on the other side of the wood (also reached by bus #112 from Château-de-Vincennes métro). In the southeast corner (rue de la Pyramide, Mon–Fri 9.30am–6.30pm; free; *RER* Joinville-le-Pont) you can wander amongst 2000 trees of over 800 different species that have been cultivated in the Arboretum.

The fenced enclave on the southern side of Lac Daumesnil is a **Buddhist centre** with a Tibetan temple, Vietnamese chapel and international pagoda, and all occasionally visitable (information on ☎01.40.04.98.06). As far as real woods go, the *bois* opens out and flowers once you're east of av de St-Maurice. *Boules* competitions are popular – there's usually a collection of devotees between route de la Tourelle and av du Polygone.

The **Parc Floral** (summer 9.30am–8pm, winter 9.30am–5/6pm; summer 10F/5F, winter 5F/2.50F, over-65s and under-6s free; bus #112 or short walk past the château from M° Château de Vincennes) is one of the best gardens in Paris. Flowers are always in bloom in the *Jardin des Quatres Saisons*; you can picnic beneath pines while the kids play on slides, flying foxes and climbing frames, then wander through concentrations of camellias, cacti, ferns, irises and bonsaï trees. Between April and September there are art and horticultural exhibitions, free jazz and classical music concerts, and numerous activities for children (see Chapter 16) including a mini-golf of Parisian monuments.

In summer, the Parc Floral hosts any number of fun things to do for kids; see p.312.

To the east of the Parc Floral is the **Cartoucherie de Vincennes**, an old ammunitions factory, now home to four theatre companies including the radical *Théâtre du Soleil* (see p.358).

On the northern edge of the *bois*, the **Château de Vincennes** (daily 10am–5/6pm; guided visits with choice of long circuit 32F/21F or short circuit 22F/14F), royal medieval residence, then state prison, porcelain factory, weapons dump and military training school, is still undergoing restoration work started by Napoléon III. The fourteenth-century keep is currently closed for a five-year repair job; what you can visit (on both circuits) is the Flamboyant Gothic **Chapelle Royale**, completed in the mid-sixteenth century and decorated with superb Renaissance stained-glass windows around the choir.

Chapter 11

Western Paris

T he **Beaux Quartiers** of western Paris are essentially the 16e and
17e *arrondissements*. The 16e is aristocratic and rich; the 17e,
or at least the southern part of it, bourgeois and rich, embody-
ing the staid, cautious values of the nineteenth-century manufacturing
and trading classes. The northern half of the 16e, towards place Victor-
Hugo and place de l'Étoile, is leafy and distinctly metropolitan in feel.
The southern part, round the old villages of **Auteuil** and **Passy**, has an
almost provincial air, and is full of pleasant surprises for the walker. One
good focus for a walk is the **Musée Marmottan**, in av Raphael, which
has a marvellous collection of late Monets. The district also boasts a
number of interesting examples of turn-of-the-century and early **twentieth-century architecture**, especially those pieces by Hector Guimard,
designer of the swirly green Art Nouveau métro stations, and by Le
Corbusier and Mallet-Stevens, architects of the first "Cubist" buildings.

Auteuil

The ideal place to start an architectural exploration of the Beaux
Quartiers is the **Église d'Auteuil** métro station. Around this area are
several of Hector Guimard's **Art Nouveau** buildings: at 34 rue
Boileau, 8 av de la Villa-de-la-Réunion, 41 rue Chardon-Lagache, 142
av de Versailles, and 39 bd Exelmans.

The house at 34 rue Boileau was one of Guimard's first commissions in 1891. A high fence, creepers and a huge satellite dish obscure
much of the view, but you can see some of the decorative tile-work
under the eaves and around the doors and windows. Close by, at no.
40, the Algerian embassy with Islamic motifs stands at the corner of a
leafy *villa* called the Hameau Boileau. Further down on this fascinating street, just before you reach bd Exelmans, the house at no. 62 successfully combines 1970s Western architecture with the traditional
Vietnamese elements of a pagoda roof and earthenware tiles. If you
continue along rue Boileau beyond bd Exelmans, you'll find a series
of charming *villas* backing onto the Auteuil cemetery.

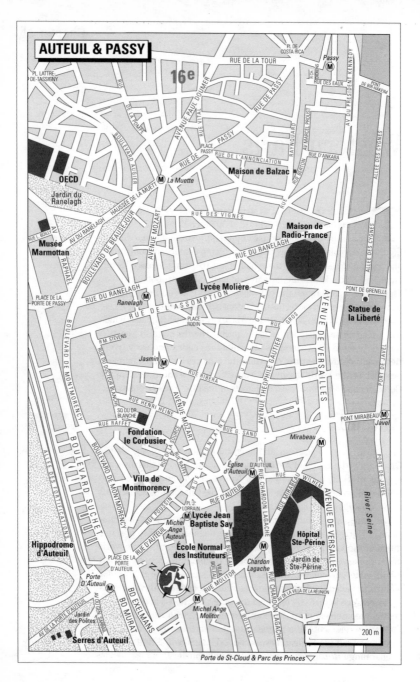

AUTEUIL & PASSY

16e

PL. LATTRE-
DE-TASSIGNY

PL. DE
COSTA RICA

RUE DE LA TOUR

Passy Ⓜ

RUE DES EAUX

RUE DE LA POMPE

RUE VITAL

AVENUE PAUL DOUMER

BOULEVARD AIGIER

HAUSSÉE DE LA MUETTE

RUE DE PASSY

RUE DE PASSY

RUE DE L'ANNONCIATION

PLACE
PASSY

RAYNOUARD

RUE BERTON

AV. MARCEL PROUST

RUE D'ANKARA

AV. DU PRESIDENT KENNEDY

PONT
DE BIR-HAKEIM

OECD

Jardin du
Ranelagh

La Muette Ⓜ

Maison de Balzac

AV. DU RANELAGH

BOULEVARD DE BEAUSEJOUR

AVENUE MOZART

RUE DES VIGNES

Maison de
Radio-France

ALLÉE DES CYGNES

Musée
Marmottan

RUE RAPHAEL

RUE I. BOILLY

RUE DU RANELAGH

RUE DU RANELAGH

Lycée Molière

RUE FONTAINE

RUE GROS

PONT DE GRENELLE

Statue de
la Liberté

PLACE DE LA
PORTE DE PASSY

BOULEVARD DE MONTMORENCY

Ranelagh Ⓜ

RUE DE L'ASSOMPTION

PLACE
RODIN

AVENUE DE VERSAILLES

R.M. STEVENS

RUE DU DOCTEUR BLANCHE

Jasmin Ⓜ

RUE RIBERA

AVENUE THÉOPHILE GAUTIER

PORT DE JAVEL

RUE HENRI HEINE

AVENUE MOZART

RUE G. SAND

PONT MIRABEAU Ⓜ
Javel

SQ DU DR.
BLANCHE

RUE RAFFET

Mirabeau Ⓜ

Fondation
le Corbusier

RUE DE LA SOURCE

RUE FONTAINE

Église
d'Auteuil

PL
D'AUTEUIL

RUE MIRABEAU

PORT DE JAVEL

Villa de
Montmorency

RUE RAFFET

RUE D'AUTEUIL

RUE CHARDON LAGACHE

RUE WILHEM

AVENUE DE VERSAILLES

River Seine

ALLÉE DES FORTIFICATIONS

BOULEVARD DE MONTMORENCY

RUE POUSSIN

PL. J.
LORRAIN

Michel
Ange
Auteuil Ⓜ

Lycée Jean
Baptiste Say

Hôpital
Ste-Périne

Hippodrome
d'Auteuil

BOULEVARD SUCHET

PLACE DE LA
PORTE
D'AUTEUIL

École Normal
des Instituteurs

RUE BOILEAU

Chardon
Lagache

Jardin de
Ste-Périne

RUE CHARDON LAGACHE

Porte
D'Auteuil Ⓜ

BD MURAT

RUE MOLITOR

Jardin
des Poètes

AV. DE LA PORTE D'AUTEUIL

AV. DU GEN SARRAIL

BD EXELMANS

VILLA
BOILEAU

RUE BOILEAU

Michel Ange
Molitor Ⓜ

DE LA VILLA DE LA RÉUNION

Serres d'Auteuil

N

0   200 m

Porte de St-Cloud & Parc des Princes ▽

The Guimard block at 142 av de Versailles (1905) has the typically
bulging, heaving effect of Art Nouveau buildings, which at worst can
make you feel almost seasick. It's just by the Exelmans crossroads (on
bus #72's route) and a short way from Villa de la Réunion. If you're
heading back up to Église-d'Auteuil from here, you can cut across the
surprisingly large **Jardin de Ste-Périne**, once the rural residence of
the monks of Ste Geneviève's abbey, established here in 1109. The
entrances are opposite 135 av de Versailles and alongside the hospital
on rue Mirabeau, just north of the rue Chardon-Lagache junction.

For more of the life of the *quartier*, follow the old village high
street, **rue d'Auteuil**, from the métro exit to **place Lorrain**, which
hosts a Saturday market. In rue Poussin, just off the *place*, carriage
gates open onto **Villa Montmorency**, a typical 16ᵉ *villa*, in the sense
of a sort of private village of leafy lanes and English-style gardens.
Gide and the Goncourt brothers of Prix fame lived in this one.

Behind it, in a cul-de-sac on the right of rue du Dr-Blanche, are **Le
Corbusier's first private houses** (1923), the Villa Jeanneret and the
Villa La Roche, now the *Fondation Le Corbusier* (Mon–Thurs
10am–12.30pm & 1.30–6pm, Fri till 5pm; closed Aug). They are
built in strictly Cubist style, very plain, with windows in bands. The
only extravagance is the raising of one wing of the Villa La Roche on
piers, and its curved frontage. It looks commonplace enough now,
but what a contrast to all that had gone before! Further along rue du
Dr-Blanche, the tiny rue Mallet-Stevens was built entirely by Robert
Mallet-Stevens (see p.88), also in Cubist style. No. 12, where Mallet-
Stevens had his offices, has been altered, along with other houses in
the street, but you can still see the architectural intention – familiar
enough today – of sculpting the entire street space as a unity. To continue on to the **Musée Marmottan**, a subway under the disused
Petite Ceinture rail line brings you out by av Raphael.

Returning to place Lorrain, **rue de la Fontaine**, running from the
place to the *Radio-France* building, has Guimard buildings at nos.

Aueteuil

14, 17, 19, 21 and 60. No. 14 is the most famous: the "Castel Béranger" (1898), with exuberant Art Nouveau decoration and shapes in the bay windows, the roofline and the chimney. No. 60 is worth a look too, and at no. 65 there's a huge block of artists' studios by Henri Sauvage (1926) with a fascinating colour scheme, influenced by Cubism.

Poets, greenhouses and the Musée Albert Kahn

East of Porte d'Auteuil are two gardens: the **Jardin des Poètes** (M° Porte d'Auteuil, sortie bd Murat, entrance on av du Général Sarrail; 9am–6pm; free) and the **Jardin des Serres d'Auteuil** (main entrance at 3 av de la Porte d'Auteuil, daily l0am–5/6pm, or you can enter from the Jardin des Poètes; 5F/2.50F). You can't escape the traffic noise completely, but the Jardin des Poètes is extremely tranquil. Famous French poets are remembered by a verse (of a mostly pastoral nature) engraved on small stones surrounded by little flowerbeds. A statue of Victor Hugo by Rodin, almost obscured by a laurel bush, stands in the middle of this very informal garden. Approaching the Auteuil garden and its greenhouses (*serres*) from the Jardin des Poètes, you pass the delightful potting sheds with rickety wooden blinds that every Parisian park has hidden somewhere. Then you're into a formal garden, beautifully laid out around the big old-fashioned metal frame greenhouses. There may be a special exhibition on – azaleas in April, for example – in which case there'll be an extra entrance fee for the greenhouses. Check first in *Pariscope*.

Directly beyond the Jardin des Serres d'Auteuil is the Stade Roland Garros, venue for the French tennis championships. To the south is the main football and rugby stadium, the Parc des Princes.

The **Musée Départemental Albert Kahn** (☎01.46.04.52.80; Tues–Sun 11am–6/7pm; 22F/15F) is at 14 rue du Port (M° Pont-St-Cloud/Boulogne), in the neighbouring suburb of Boulogne-Billancourt. It consists of a very pretty garden and a small museum dedicated to temporary exhibitions of "*Les Archives de la Planète*" – photographs and films collected by the banker and philanthropist Albert Kahn between 1909 and 1931 to record human activities and ways of life that he knew would soon disappear for ever. His aim in the garden was to combine English, French, Japanese and other styles to demonstrate the possibility of a harmonious, peaceful world. It is an enchanting place, with rhododendrons and camellias under blue cedars, a rose garden and an espaliered orchard, a forest of Moroccan pines and streams with Japanese bridges beside pagoda tea houses, Buddhas and pyramids of pebbles. A palm hothouse has been turned into a very chic *salon de thé*, serving such delights as pear liqueur and *marrons glacés* sorbet. Beside the exit on rue des Abondances there's a *boulangerie* that serves good sandwiches for half the price of the garden's *salon de thé*.

Passy

Passy too offers scope for a good meandering walk, from place du Trocadéro (cemetery enthusiasts can take a look at the **Cimetière de Passy**, containing the graves of Manet and Berthe Morisot) to Balzac's house, and up rue de Passy to the Marmottan museum.

If you start in **rue Franklin**, take a left after place de Costa-Rica and go down the steps into square Alboni, a patch of garden enclosed by tall apartment buildings as solid as banks. Here the métro line emerges from what used to be a vine-covered hillside for the Passy stop – more like a country station – before rumbling out across the river by the Pont de Bir-Hakeim.

Below the station, in **rue des Eaux**, Parisians used to come to take the Passy waters, and today the street is enclosed by a canyon of moneyed apartments, which dwarf the eighteenth-century houses of **square Charles-Dickens**. In one of them, burrowing back into the cellars of a vanished monastery, the **Musée du Vin** puts on a disappointing display of viticultural odds and bobs (*dégustation*, if you need it). Its vaults connect with the ancient quarry tunnels – not visitable – from which the stone for Notre-Dame was hewn.

If you continue along the foot of the Passy hill, on av Marcel-Proust, you arrive in the cobbled **rue d'Ankara** at the gates of an eighteenth-century château half-hidden by greenery and screened by a high wall. It's a brave punter who will march resolutely up to the gate and peer in with the confident air of the connoisseur. And you'd better make it convincing, for all the time your nose is pressed between the bars at least four armed guards are watching you intently, fingers on the trigger. This is the Turkish Embassy, and there's not even a parked car to obstruct the field of fire. It was once a clinic where the pioneering Dr Blanche tried to treat the mad Maupassant and Gérard de Nerval, among others; before that it was the home of Marie-Antoinette's friend, the Princesse de Lamballe.

From the gates, **rue Berton**, a cobbled path with its gas lights still in place, follows round the ivy-covered garden wall. By an old green-shuttered house, a boundary stone bears the date 1731, and apart from the Embassy security, nothing in this tiny backwater seems to have changed since that time. The house was **Balzac's** (Tues–Sun 10am–noon & 2.30–5.40pm; 17.5F/9F free Sun) in the 1840s, and contains memorabilia and a library. The entrance is from rue Raynouard, down a flight of steps into a dank garden overshadowed at one end by a singularly unattractive block of flats built, and lived in, by the architect Auguste Perret, father of French concrete.

Across the street, in the very heart of Passy, **rue de l'Annonciation**, where once you could have had your Bechstein

There's more about the Maison de Balzac on p.296.

Passy

repaired or your furniture lacquered, is being violated by developers. At the further end, at **place de Passy**, you join the old high street, **rue de Passy**, which leads past a parade of eye-catching boutiques to **métro La Muette**, from where Chaussée-de-la-Muette leads into the Ranelagh gardens (with a rather engaging sculpture of La Fontaine with the eagle and fox) and the Musée Marmottan.

Bois de Boulogne

Activities for children in the Bois de Boulogne are covered on p.311.

The **Bois de Boulogne**, running all the way down the west side of the 16e, is supposedly modelled on London's Hyde Park, in a very French interpretation. It offers all sorts of facilities: the **Jardin d'Acclimatation**, with lots of attractions for kids; the excellent **Musée National des Arts et Traditions Populaires** (p.295); the **Parc de Bagatelle**, with beautiful displays of tulips, hyacinths and daffodils in early April, irises in May, waterlilies and roses at the end of June; a **riding** school; **bike rental** at the entrance to the Jardin d'Acclimatation; **boating** on the Lac Inférieur; and **race courses** at Longchamp and Auteuil. The best, and wildest, part for walking is towards the southwest corner.

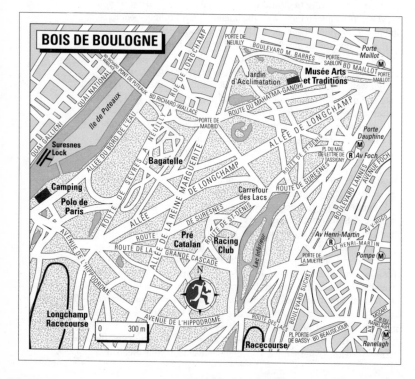

When the Bois de Boulogne opened in the eighteenth century, it was popularly said that *"Les mariages du bois de Boulogne ne se font pas devant Monsieur le Curé"* – "Unions cemented in the Bois de Boulogne do not take place in the presence of a priest." Today's after-dark unions are no less disreputable – but don't be tempted to go in for any night-time sightseeing. This can be a very dangerous place.

Bois de Boulogne

Around the Étoile

Twelve avenues make up the star of the **Étoile**, or place Charles-de-Gaulle, with the Arc de Triomphe at its centre (see Chapter 3). The northern 16e and eastern 17e *arrondissements*, through which the avenues fan out, are cold and soulless, and the huge apartments here are empty much of the time as their owners – royal, exiled royal, ex-royal or just extremely rich – move between their other residences dotted about the globe.

The best avenue to start wandering down – apart from the Champs-Élysées – is the northerly av de Wagram. Devotees of Art Nouveau can stop in front of no. 34, Jules Lavirotte's design of 1904, to see if they can honestly persist in saying the style is beautiful. Less taxing aesthetic judgements are called for in front of the flower market and cafés of place des Ternes, the first big junction on av de Wagram, where rue du Faubourg-St-Honoré begins. If you take this street and then the second left – you're in the 8e *arrondissement* now – you can admire the five gold onion domes of the Cathédrale Alexandre-Nevski, at 6 rue Daru, before turning right on rue de Courcelles, which brings you to the enormous gilded gates of the av Hoche entrance to **Parc Monceau**. The park has a roller-skating rink and kids' play facilities, but basically it's a formal garden with antique colonnades and artificial grottoes. Half the people who command the heights of the French economy spent their infancy there, promenaded in prams by proper nannies. In av Velasquez, on the far side, the **Musée Cernuschi** houses a small collection of ancient Chinese art (see p.291) bequeathed to the state by the banker Cernuschi, who nearly lost his life for giving money to the Commune.

More interesting, and not many blocks to the south of the park, at 158 bd Haussmann, is the lavishly ornamented and newly restored palace of the nineteenth-century banker and art-lover Edouard André. Now known as the **Musée Jacquemart-André** (see p.292), it houses his impressive private collection and a fabulous *salon de thé* that is surely destined to become a meeting place of the elegant and discreet.

La Défense

La Défense, accessible by *RER* line A and métro line 1, has been elevated to one of the top places of pilgrimage for visitors to Paris by **La Grande Arche**. This beautiful and astounding structure, a 112-metre

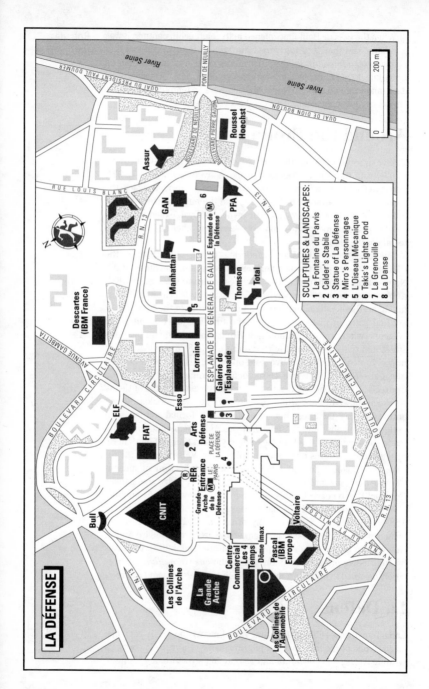

LA DÉFENSE

SCULPTURES & LANDSCAPES:
1 La Fontaine du Parvis
2 Calder's Stabile
3 Statue of La Défense
4 Miro's Personnages
5 L'Oiseau Mécanique
6 Takis's Lights Pond
7 La Grenouille
8 La Danse

hollow cube clad in white marble, stands 6km out from the Arc de Triomphe at the far end of the Voie Triomphale, from which it stands at a slight angle. Suspended within its hollow, which could enclose Notre-Dame with ease, are open lift shafts and a "cloud" canopy. Designed by the Danish architect Johann Otto von Spreckelsen, who died before it was completed, La Grande Arche is a pure and graceful example of design wedded to innovative engineering, on a par with the Eiffel Tower and in marked contrast to other recent Parisian monuments. The building was originally intended for the 1989 Bicentennial, but squabbles between Chirac and Mitterrand over its use delayed the project. It now houses a government ministry, international businesses, an information centre on the European Union, "*Sources d'Europe*" (Mon–Fri 10am–6pm) and, in the roof section, the *Fondation Internationale des Droits de l'Homme*, which stages exhibitions and conferences on issues related to human rights.

A ride up to the roof costs 40F/30F (daily 9/10am–6/7pm). From here as well as having access to the exhibitions, you can admire Jean-Pierre Raynaud's "Map of the Heavens" marble patios and, on a clear day, scan from the marble path on the *parvis* below you to the Arc de Triomphe, and beyond to the Louvre.

Around the complex

Back on the ground, with La Grande Arche behind you, an extraordinary monument to twentieth-century capitalism stands before and above you. To your right is the latest addition: another galactic *boule* lobbed from the realms of higher technology, come to displace La Villette's *Géode* as the world's largest cinema screen. It's the Dôme-Imax, in the same building complex as a new automobile museum.

Details of shows at the Dôme-Imax are on p.357.

In front of you, along the axis of the Voie Triomphale, an assortment of towers – token apartment blocks, offices of ELF, Esso, IBM, banks, and other businesses – compete for size, dazzle of surface and ability to make you dizzy. Finance made flesh, they are worth the trip out in themselves.

Mercifully, too, **bizarre artworks** lighten the nightmarish mood. **Joan Miró**'s giant wobbly creatures bemoan their misfit status beneath the biting edges and curveless heights of the buildings. Opposite is **Alexander Calder**'s red iron offering – a stabile rather than a mobile – while in between the two, a black marble metronome shape releases a goal-less line across the *parvis*. **Torricini**'s huge **fat frog** screams to escape to a nice quiet pond. A statue commemorating the **defence of Paris** in 1870 (for which the district is named) perches on a concrete plinth in front of a coloured plastic waterfall and fountain pool, while nearer the river, disembodied people clutch each other round endlessly repeated concrete flowerbeds.

Art Défense, alongside Agam's waterworks, displays models and photographs of the artworks, with a map to locate them and a guide for 15F (daily 10am–6pm), as well as temporary exhibitions (daily except Tues noon–7pm). The **CNIT building,** next to La Grande Arche, looks a bit like a covered stadium with businesses instead of seats. The pitch, all gleaming granite, is softened by slender bamboo trees; all the serious activity takes place beyond the far goal, where every major computer company has an office. There's also a *FNAC*, and overpriced cafés and brasseries. Less damaging to the pocket, if unhealthy for the soul, is the **Quatre-Temps** commercial centre, the biggest of its ilk in Europe, across the *parvis*, opposite. To minimize the encounter, enter from the left-hand doors, and you'll find *crêperies*, pizzerias and cafés without having to leave ground level.

New skyscrapers are still being built, but the glut of unrented office space, along with recession-led fears of new investment, have begun to bite. Plans for a *tour sans fin* – a "tower without end" – by Jean Nouvel, which would have a needle point disappearing into the clouds, have had to be put on hold indefinitely.

Île de la Jatte and Île de Chatou

Below La Défense, the **Île de la Jatte** floats in the Seine just off rich and leafy Neuilly, an ideal venue for a romantic riverside walk. From the Pont de Levallois, near the métro, a flight of steps descends to the tip of the island. Formerly an industrial site, it is now part public garden (Mon–Fri 8.30am–6pm, Sat & Sun 10am–8pm) and part stylish new housing development. What remains of the island's erstwhile rustic character is to be found along the tree-lined bd de Levallois, where a line of Heath Robinson houses and workshops quietly moulders away. On the right, a former *manège* has become the smart *Café de la Jatte*, while beside the bridge the pricey *Guinguette de Neuilly* restaurant still flourishes.

It was from the Île de Chatou that Vlaminck set off for the 1905 Salon des Indépendents with the truckload of paintings that led critics to coin the term "Fauvism".

A long narrow island in a loop of the Seine further downstream, the **Île de Chatou** was once a rustic spot where Parisians came on the newly opened rail line to row, dine and flirt at the riverside *guinguettes* (eating and dancing establishments). The one *guinguette* to survive, just below the Pont de Chatou road bridge, is the **Maison Fournaise**. This was a favourite haunt of Renoir, Monet, Manet, Van Gogh, Seurat, Sisley and Courbet, half of whom were in love with the proprietor's daughter, Alphonsine. One of Renoir's best-known canvases, *Le Déjeuner des Canotiers*, shows his friends lunching on the balcony. Vlaminck and his fellow-Fauves, Derain and Matisse, were also habitués.

Derelict for many years, the *Maison Fournaise* has recently reopened, restored and refurbished, as a very agreeable **restaurant** (see p.274). The outbuildings have been renovated too and house a small museum of memorabilia from this artistic past (Wed–Sun 11am–5pm; permanent exhibition 15F, temporary exhibition 25F). It's a great site, with a huge plane tree shading the river bank and a view of the barges racing downstream on the current.

Gustave Flourens

One of the boldest and most colourful of the Commune's commanders met his death on the Île de Chatou – Gustave Flourens, commander of the Red Belleville battalions. Although far from being a proletarian himself, Flourens was a flamboyant champion of freedom, who had already taken part in Crete's attempts to throw off the Turkish yoke in the 1860s – whence his preferred uniform and arm, a Grecian kilt and *yataghan*. Impatient with the inertia of his colleagues, he led an attack on the government forces at Versailles. He continued, when others fell back. Surrounded and outnumbered, he was captured and had his head split in twain.

The downstream end of the island is now a park, tapering away into a tree-lined tail hardly wider than the path. The upstream end is wild, overgrown and rather spooky, though its few rather louche and certainly illegal residents have now been evicted for good.

Access to the island is from the Rueil-Malmaison *RER* stop. Take the Sortie av Albert-1er, go left out of the station and right along the dual carriageway onto the bridge – a ten-minute walk. Bizarrely, there's a twice-yearly **ham and antiques fair** on the island, which is fun to check out (March and Sept).

Paris: Listings

Accommodation

The hotels and hostels of Paris are often heavily booked, so it's wise to reserve a place well in advance, if you can. If not, there are two agencies to turn to for help: the tourist board's Bureaux d'Accueil, and the youth-orientated Accueil des Jeunes en France (AJF). The former charges a small commission (from 20F for a hotel; 8F for a hostel): its function is to bale you out of last-minute difficulty rather than find the most economical deal. The AJF guarantees to find you a room – in a hostel (around 110F B&B) if you arrive early enough, or in a hotel (240F upwards). You pay for the accommodation, plus a 10F fee, and receive vouchers to take to the establishment. The best area for budget priced hotels is the 11e. There are bargains in the 17e as well, but they are a lot further from the centre, where cheapies fill up quickly and need reserving well in advance. Not all hotels accept credit cards – you may have to send an international money order with your reservation.

Bureaux d'Accueil

Office du Tourisme, 127 av des Champs-Élysées, 8e; ☎01.49.52.53.54, fax 01.49.52.53.00 (Mº Charles-de-Gaulle/Étoile). 9am–8pm throughout the year except off season, Sun, hols and May 1; off season, Sun and hols 11am–6pm.

Gare d'Austerlitz, arrival point for main line platforms bd de l'Hôpital, 13e;

☎01.45.84.91.70. Mon–Fri 8am–3pm, Sat 8am–1pm.

Gare de l'Est, arrival hall bd de Strasbourg, 10e; ☎01.46.07.17.73. Summer Mon–Sat 8am–9pm, off season Mon–Sat 8am–8pm.

Gare de Lyon, exit from main line platforms 20 bd Diderot, 12e; ☎01.43.43.33.24. Summer Mon–Sat 8am–9pm, off season Mon–Sat 8am–8pm.

Gare Montparnasse, arrival point for main line platforms place R-Dautry, 15e; ☎01.43.22.19.19. Summer Mon–Sat 8am–9pm, off season Mon–Sat 8am–8pm.

Gare du Nord, arrival point for international trains 18 rue de Dunkerque, 10e; ☎01.45.26.94.82. Summer Mon–Sat 8am–9pm, off season Mon–Sat 8am–8pm.

Tour Eiffel, Champ de Mars, 7e; ☎01.45.51.22.15 (RER Champs-de-Mars/Tour Eiffel). May–Sept 11am–6pm.

24-hour information in English: ☎01.49.52.53.56.

Each year, the Paris hoteliers' organization publishes a list of the most heavily booked periods for accommodation, which is available from French Government Tourist Offices (see p.37). The list is based on the dates of the salons or trade fairs; September and October are invariably the worst months, otherwise dates vary slightly from year to year. It is worth checking them out when planning a trip.

Accommodation

Accueil des Jeunes en France

Beaubourg, 119 rue St-Martin, opposite Centre Beaubourg, 4e; ☎01.42.77.87.80 (Mº Châtelet-Les Halles). All year Mon–Sat 10am–6.30pm. This office can also be used as a forwarding address for mail.

Gare du Nord, Nouvelle gare banlieue; ☎01.42.85.86.19. June–Sept 10am–6.30pm.

Hotels

If you value your independence and have a preferred location, there's obviously more scope in booking a hotel yourself than using the official reservation services.

There are a great many in all price categories, with a still considerable, if dwindling, number of small **family-run hotels with budget-priced rooms**.

The hotels listed in this section have been arranged by *arrondissement* and divided into the following **seven price categories**:

①	up to 160F
②	160–220F
③	220–300F
④	300–400F
⑤	400–500F
⑥	500–600F
⑦	over 600F

The prices given are for the cheapest double rooms normally available in high season. Most hotels have a selection of rooms at different prices; where there are very few rooms in the lower category or where the range in any one establishment is particularly large, we have used more than one symbol; eg ①–② or ②–⑤. Note that a new **municipal tax** is now payable, from 1F to 5F a night.

Most of the hotels in the second-cheapest category are perfectly adequate – the sheets are clean, you can wash decently, and there isn't a brothel on the floor below. There won't be much luxury, however. Price seems to relate chiefly to location, condition of paintwork, glitziness of the reception area, and the pres-

> If you're seriously interested in a long stay on a low budget, then it's worth checking out the various basic and starless hotels you'll see as you go about the streets, especially in less central districts. Many only let rooms by the month, often catering for immigrant workers, at very low prices.

ence or absence of a lift. Most small Paris hotels are in converted old buildings, with faded décor, dark stairs, cramped rooms and views onto an internal courtyard.

We've assumed that most visitors come to Paris to see the city and will treat their hotel simply as a convenient and inexpensive place to lay their head. Where we think conditions are at the limit of what most people will accept, we say **"basic"**. In this edition, in view of the unfavourable pound–franc exchange rate, we have included more of these hotels than before, describing some as very basic or primitive. These are perfectly viable for hardened budget-travellers, but we would not recommend them to women on their own or to people who are at all fastidious about their comforts.

All hotels are obliged to display **room prices** somewhere prominent – usually in the entrance or by the reception desk. Certain **standard terms recur**. *Eau courante (EC)* means a room with washbasin only, *cabinet de toilette (CT)* means basin and bidet. In both cases there will be communal toilets on the landing and probably a communal shower as well. *Douche/WC* and *Bain/WC* mean that you have a shower or bath as well as toilet in the room. A room with a *grand lit* (double bed) is invariably cheaper than one with *deux lits* (two separate beds). Out of season it is possible to "negotiate" a reduction of up to 10 percent of the advertised rate, perhaps more, depending on your length of stay. You should at least be able to haggle away the charge for a shower on the landing in the cheaper places. Have a go!

Breakfast (*petit déjeuner* or *PD*) is sometimes included (*compris*) in the

room price and sometimes extra (*en sus*)
– the amount varies between about 25F
and 45F per person. Though it isn't supposed to be obligatory, some hotels may
make a sour face when you decline to
give it. Always make it clear whether you
want breakfast or not when you take the
room. It's usually a fairly indifferent continental affair, and you'll get a fresher,
cheaper one at the local café.

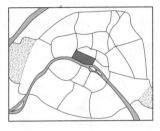

1er Arrondissement

Hôtel Henri IV, 25 place Dauphine, 1er;
☎01.43.54.44.53 (Mº Pont-Neuf/Cité).
An ancient and well-known cheapie in
the beautiful place Dauphine at the sharp
end of the Île de la Cité. Nothing more
luxurious than *cabinet de toilette* and
now very run-down. Essential to book. ②.

Hôtel de Lille, 8 rue du Pélican, 1er;
☎01.42.33.33.42 (Mº Louvre/Les
Halles/Palais-Royal).
Very small, very basic, but clean. ②.

Hôtel de la Vallée, 84 rue St-Denis, 1er;
☎01.42.36.46.99 (Mº Étienne-
Marcel/Châtelet).
Great location, absolutely smack in the
middle of Les Halles. Perfectly adequate
rooms. ②.

Hôtel Vauvilliers, 6 rue Vauvilliers, 1er;
☎01.42.36.89.08 (Mº Châtelet-Les
Halles/Louvre).
Need to book well in advance for this
well-established cheapie. ②.

Hôtel St-Honoré, 85 rue St-Honoré, 1er;
☎01.42.36.20.38, fax 01.42.21.44.08
(Mº Châtelet-Les Halles/Louvre).
Conveniently close to the heart of things
and recently done up, but still admirably
low-priced. ②–③.

Hôtel Lion d'Or, 5 rue de la Sourdière,
1er; ☎01.42.60.79.04, fax 01.42.60.09.14
(Mº Tuileries).
Spartan, but clean, friendly and very central. ③.

Hôtel Washington Opéra, 50 rue de
Richelieu, 1er; ☎01.42.96.68.06 (Mº
Palais-Royal).
Pleasant and comfortable, with good
deals for 4 people sharing. ④.

Agora, 7 rue Cossonerie, 1er;
☎01.42.33.46.02, fax 01.42.33.80.99
(Mº Châtelet-Les Halles).
Charming, peaceful hotel with individually styled rooms. ⑥.

Ducs d'Anjou, 1 rue Ste-Opportune, 1er;
☎01.42.36.92.24, fax 01.42.36.16.63
(Mº Châtelet).
A carefully renovated old building overlooking the endlessly crowded place Ste-
Opportune, the focus for Les Halles
nightlife. ⑥.

Tonic Hôtel du Louvre, 12–14 rue du
Roule, 1er; ☎01.42.33.00.71, fax
01.40.26.06.86 (Mº Louvre/Rivoli).
Expensive for a 2-star but not for the
location nor for the steam baths and
jacuzzis in each bathroom. ⑥.

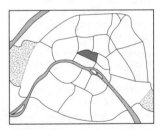

2e Arrondissement

Hôtel de France, 11 rue Marie-Stuart, 2e;
☎01.42.36.35.33 (Mº Châtelet-Les
Halles/Sentier).
Don't be put off by the exterior. Bargain
prices, clean, and a great location. ②.

Hôtel Tiquetonne, 6 rue Tiquetonne, 2e;
☎01.42.36.94.58 (Mº Étienne-Marcel).
Old-fashioned, well-maintained cheapie
on a pedestrian street, but close to the
red-light stretch of rue St-Denis. ③.

Accommodation

*The price
categories
used in this
chapter are as
follows:
① up to 160F
② 160–220F
③ 220–300F
④ 300–400F
⑤ 400–500F
⑥ 500–600F
⑦ over 600F.
For a fuller
explanation,
see opposite.*

Accommodation

Les Noailles, 9 rue Michodière, 2e; ☎01.47.42.92.90, fax 01.49.24.92.71 (Mº Opéra/Quatre-Septembre). Contemporary styling with traditional pleasures of garden and *terrasse*. ⑦.

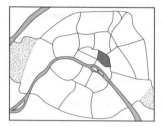

3e Arrondissement

Hôtel du Marais, 16 rue de Beauce, 3e; ☎01.42.72.30.26 (Mº Arts-et-Métiers/Filles-du-Calvaire). The genuine article: a prewar Paris cheapie, complete with brown spiral stairs, iron handrail, tiled floors and Turkish loos. Primitive but clean, with very nice *patron* who runs a similarly old-fashioned bar downstairs. Quiet medieval street. ①.

Hôtel du Séjour, 36 rue du Grenier-St-Lazare, 3e; ☎01.48.87.40.36 (M° Rambuteau/Étienne-Marcel). A decent cheapie a short walk from Beaubourg. ①–②.

Paris France Hôtel, 72 rue de Turbigo, 3e; ☎01.42.78.64.92, fax 01.42.71.99.43 (M° République). On a noisy road but in an animated *quartier* off the beaten track. ③.

Hôtel Picard, 26 rue de Picardie, 3e; ☎01.48.87.53.82, fax 01.48.87.02.56 (Mº Arts-et-Métiers/Filles-du-Calvaire). Clean establishment run by a very accommodating Pole, in a great location overlooking the Carreau du Temple. Ten percent reduction if you produce your *Rough Guide*. ③.

Hôtel de Saintonge, 16 rue de Saintonge, 3e; ☎01.42.77.91.13, fax 01.48.87.76.41 (Mº Filles-du-Calvaire). In a sixteenth-century house on the edge of the Marais, near the Picasso Museum. A soothing place to stay. ⑤.

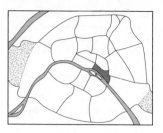

4e Arrondissement

Hôtel Moderne, 3 rue Caron, 4e; ☎01.48.87.97.05 (Mº St-Paul/Bastille). Much better than the first impression of the staircase would suggest, and the price is amazing for this area. ①.

Grand Hôtel du Loiret, 8 rue des Mauvais-Garçons, 4e; ☎01.48.87.77.00, fax 01.48.04.96.56 (Mº Hôtel-de-Ville). Simple small rooms, but very good value for the price. ②.

Castex Hôtel, 5 rue Castex, 4e; ☎01.42.72.31.52, fax 01.42.72.57.91 (Mº Bastille/Sully-Morland). Renovated building in a quiet street on the edge of the Marais. ③.

Hôtel de Nice, 42bis rue de Rivoli, 4e; ☎01.42.78.55.29, fax 01.42.78.36.07 (M° Hôtel-de-Ville). Very pretty rooms, and a *salon* where guests socialize (no TVs in the rooms). ④.

Hôtel Sévigné, 2 rue Mahler, 4e; ☎01.42.72.76.17 (Mº St-Paul). Very comfortable, pleasant hotel frequented by foreigners, and consequently overbooked. ④.

Hôtel Central Marais, 33 rue Vieille-du-Temple, 4e; ☎01.48.87.56.08, fax 01.42.77.06.27 (Mº Hôtel-de-Ville). The only gay and lesbian hotel in Paris. ⑤.

Grand Hôtel Jeanne d'Arc, 3 rue de Jarente, 4e; ☎01.48.87.62.11, fax 01.48.87.37.31 (Mº St-Paul). Clean, quiet and attractive. Necessary to reserve. ⑤.

Hôtel du Septième Art, 20 rue St-Paul, 4e; ☎01.42.77.04.03, fax 01.42.77.69.10 (Mº St-Paul/Pont-Marie).

Decorated with posters and photos from old movies, with stairs and bathrooms in black-and-white-movie style. Pleasant and comfortable rooms, each equipped with a safe. ⑤.

Grand Hôtel Mahler, 5 rue Mahler, 4e; ☎01.42.72.60.92, fax 01.42.72.25.37 (M⁰ St-Paul).
Right in the heart of the Marais; breakfast in a recently renovated seventeenth-century vaulted wine cellar. ⑥.

Hôtel de Lutèce, 65 rue St-Louis-en-l'Île, 4e; ☎01.43.26.23.52, fax 01.43.29.60.25 (M⁰ Pont-Marie).
Small but exquisite rooms on the most desirable island in France. ⑦.

Hôtel St-Louis Marais, 1 rue Charles-V, 4e; ☎01.48.87.87.04, fax 01.48.87.33.26 (M⁰ Sully-Morland).
A very comfortable restored seventeenth-century mansion. ⑦.

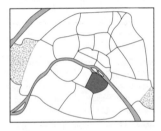

5e Arrondissement

Hôtel du Commerce, 14 rue de la Montagne-Ste-Geneviève, 5e; ☎01.43.54.89.69, fax 01.43.54.89.69 (M⁰ Maubert-Mutualité).
Popular if somewhat gloomy cheapie run by a charming old lady. Nothing over 140F despite its location in the heart of the Latin Quarter. Communal washing and toilets. No reservations, so turn up early in the morning. ①.

Hôtel Médicis, 214 rue St-Jacques, 5e; ☎01.43.54.14.66 (M⁰ Luxembourg).
Very primitive, but the prices are unbeatable. It's popular with hard-up backpackers, and the owners are charming. ①–②.

Hôtel Port-Royal, 8 bd Port-Royal, 5e; ☎01.43.31.70.06 (M° Gobelins).

A real bargain – clean, attractive and friendly. It's at the rue Mouffetard end of the boulevard, close to the métro. ②–③.

Hôtel St-Jacques, 35 rue des Écoles, 5e; ☎01.43.26.82.53, fax 01.43.25.65.50 (M⁰ Maubert-Mutualité/Odéon).
Reasonable anchorage in the heart of the district. ②–④.

Hôtel Esmeralda, 4 rue St-Julien-le-Pauvre, 5e; ☎01.43.54.19.20, fax 01.40.51.00.68 (M⁰ St-Michel/Maubert-Mutualité).
A delightful place: an ancient house on square Viviani, with a superb view of Notre-Dame. Most rooms are 350–500F, though there are several much cheaper ones. ②–⑤.

Hôtel des Alliés, 20 rue Berthollet, 5e; ☎01.43.31.47.52, fax 01.45.35.13.92 (M⁰ Censier-Daubenton).
Simple and clean, and bargain prices. ③.

Hôtel des Carmes, 5 rue des Carmes, 5e; ☎01.43.29.78.40, fax 01.43.29.57.17 (M⁰ Maubert-Mutualité).
Established, good-value tourist hotel. ③.

Hôtel Le Central, 6 rue Descartes, 5e; ☎01.46.33.57.93 (M⁰ Maubert-Mutualité/Cardinal-Lemoine).
Clean, decent accommodation in a typically Parisian old house on top of the Montagne Ste-Geneviève, overlooking the gates of the former École Polytechnique. One of a dying breed. ③.

Hôtel Marignan, 13 rue du Sommerard, 5e; ☎01.43.54.63.81 (M⁰ Maubert-Mutualité).
One of the best bargains in town, totally sympathetic to the needs of rucksack-toting foreigners. Laundry (10F) and ironing facilities, plus a room to eat your own food in – plates provided. Even the maid speaks English. No reservations, so turn up early. Rooms for 2, 3 and 4 people. For 3, you'll pay around 370F. ③.

Hôtel Gay-Lussac, 29 rue Gay-Lussac, 5e; ☎01.43.54.23.96 (M⁰ Luxembourg).
Friendly, no-frills establishment with an adjoining café-bar. Excellent value for the area – close to Luxembourg gardens. No credit cards. Book at least a week in advance. ③–④.

Accommodation

The price categories used in this chapter are as follows:
① *up to 160F*
② *160–220F*
③ *220–300F*
④ *300–400F*
⑤ *400–500F*
⑥ *500–600F*
⑦ *over 600F.*
For a fuller explanation, see p.214.

Accommodation

Hôtel du Progrès, 50 rue Gay-Lussac, 5e; ☎01.43.54.53.18 (M° Luxembourg/Port-Royal.
No frills and old-fashioned, but well-situated and fine for a cheap stay. Free showers for rooms without them. ③–④.

Grand Hôtel Oriental, 2 rue d'Arras, 5e; ☎01.43.54.38.12, fax 01.40.51.86.78 (M° Jussieu/Cardinal-Lemoine/Maubert-Mutualité).
Recently refurbished like so many of the old cheapies, but still quite a bargain for this locality – and nice people, too. ④.

Grand Hôtel St-Michel, 19 rue Cujas, 5e; ☎01.46.33.33.02 (M° Odéon/Cluny).
Comfortable hotel in a great location between the Panthéon and the Luxembourg gardens. ④–⑤.

Familia Hôtel, 11 rue des Écoles, 5e; ☎01.43.54.55.27, fax 01.45.29.61.77 (M° Cardinal-Lemoine/Maubert-Mutualité/Jussieu).
Friendly hotel in the heart of the *quartier*. ④–⑤.

Hôtel Mont-Blanc, 28 rue de la Huchette, 5e; ☎01.43.54.22.29, fax 01.46.34.14.56 (M° St-Michel).
Another face-lift and higher prices, but a great if noisy location a stone's throw from Notre-Dame. ⑤.

Hôtel de la Sorbonne, 6 rue Victor-Cousin, 5e; ☎01.43.54.58.08, fax 01.40.51.05.18 (M° Luxembourg).
An attractive old building in the heart of things, but quiet, comfortable and close to the Luxembourg gardens. ⑤.

Hôtel des Grandes Écoles, 75 rue du Cardinal-Lemoine, 5e; ☎01.43.26.79.23, fax 01.43.25.28.15 (M° Cardinal-Lemoine).
A beautiful, recently decorated hotel in old buildings in the heart of the Latin Quarter, enclosing a lovely courtyard garden. Book well ahead. A few cheaper singles, but most ⑤–⑥.

Hôtel des Trois Collèges, 16 rue Cujas, 5e; ☎01.43.54.67.30, fax 01.46.34.02.99 (M° Luxembourg).
Light, airy and modernized. ⑤–⑥.

Agora St-Germain, 42 rue des Bernardins, 5e; ☎01.46.34.13.00, fax 01.46.34.75.05 (M° Maubert-Mutualité).
A very comfortable and well-appointed hotel. ⑦.

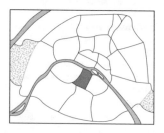

6e Arrondissement

Hôtel de Nesle, 7 rue de Nesle, 6e; ☎01.43.54.62.41 (M° St-Michel).
Characterful former hippy haven. No reservations, so get there before 10am. ②.

Hôtel St-Michel, 17 rue Gît-le-Coeur, 6e; ☎01.43.26.98.70 (M° St-Michel).
Simple, but perfectly adequate. Great location in a very attractive old street close to the river. ③–④.

Hôtel Delhy's, 22 rue de l'Hirondelle, 6e; ☎01.43.26.58.25 (M° St-Michel).
Just off place St-Michel. An old house in a tiny street – spotlessly maintained, but a little overpriced. ④–⑤.

Hôtel du Dragon, 36 rue du Dragon, 6e; ☎01.45.48.51.05, fax 01.42.22.51.62 (M° St-Germain-des-Près/Sèvres-Babylone).
Fairly basic, but clean, friendly and in a great location. Closed Aug. ④–⑤.

Hôtel Récamier, 3bis place St-Sulpice, 6e; ☎01.43.26.04.89 (M° St-Sulpice/St-Germain-des-Près).
A comfortable, old-fashioned hotel offering few concessions to modernity or fashion. Superb location. ④–⑥.

Grand Hôtel des Balcons, 3 rue Casimir-Delavigne, 6e; ☎01.46.34.78.50, fax 01.46.34.07.27 (M° Odéon).
An attractive and comfortable hotel, complete with Art Nouveau entrance, in a lovely location near the Odéon and Luxembourg gardens. ⑤.

Hôtel Michelet Odéon, 6 place de l'Odéon, 6e; ☎01.46.34.27.80, fax

01.46.34.55.35 (Mº Odéon/Luxembourg). Another fantastic location. ⑤.

Welcome Hotel, 66 rue de Seine, 6ᵉ; ☎01.46.34.24.80, fax 01.40.46.81.59 (Mº Odéon).
Adequate rooms in a great but rather noisy location by the Buci street market. ⑥.

Hôtel de l'Angleterre, 44 rue Jacob, 6ᵉ; ☎01.42.60.34.72, fax 01.42.60.16.93 (Mº St-Germain-des-Près).
Classy and elegant, this was once the British Embassy. Later, Hemingway lived in room 14. ⑦.

Hôtel des Marronniers, 21 rue Jacob, 6ᵉ; ☎01.43.25.30.60, fax 01.40.46 83.56 (Mº St-Germain-des-Près).
This 3-star costs more than our usual prices, but is a delightful place with a dining room overlooking a secret garden. Good for special occasions. No credit cards. ⑦.

Hôtel de l'Odéon, 13 rue St-Sulpice, 6ᵉ; ☎01.43.25.70.11, fax 01.43.29.97.34 (Mº St-Sulpice/Odéon).
Old-fashioned luxury – flowers, twin beds, antique furniture. ⑦.

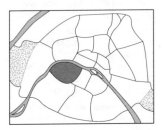

7ᵉ Arrondissement

Hôtel de la Paix, 19 rue du Gros-Caillou, 7ᵉ; ☎01.45.51.86.17 (Mº École-Militaire).
Simple, clean and a great bargain. Very close to the Eiffel Tower. ①–④.

Grand Hôtel Lévèque, 29 rue Cler, 7ᵉ; ☎01.47.05.49.15, fax 01.45.50.49.36 (Mº École-Militaire/Latour-Maubourg).
Clean and decent; nice people, who speak some English. Good location smack in the middle of the rue Cler market. Book a month ahead. ②–④.

Hôtel Eiffel Rive-Gauche, 6 rue du Gros-Caillou, 7ᵉ; ☎01.45.51.11.77 (Mº École-Militaire).
A great little hotel practically underneath the Eiffel Tower. ③–④.

Hôtel Rapp, 8 av Rapp, 7ᵉ; ☎01.45.51.42. 28, fax 01.43.59.50.70 (Mº Alma-Marceau).
A little dingy and charmless, but close to the Seine and the Palais Chaillot. Some singles at ③; most ④.

Hôtel du Centre, 24bis rue Cler, 7ᵉ; ☎01.47.05.52.53, fax 01.40.62.95.66 (Mº École-Militaire).
An old-fashioned, no-frills establishment in a posh and attractive neighbour-hood. Reserve a fortnight in advance. ④.

Hôtel Malar, 29 rue Malar, 7ᵉ; ☎01.45.51.38.46, fax 01.45.55.20.19 (Mº Latour-Maubourg/Invalides).
Small, with slightly pokey rooms, but in a very attractive street close to the river. ④.

Royal Phare Hôtel, 40 av de la Motte-Picquet, 7ᵉ; ☎01.47.05.57.30, fax 01.45.51.64.41 (Mº École-Militaire).
A bit impersonal, but very convenient and with some good views. Close to rue Cler and its sumptuous market. ④.

Hôtel du Champs-de-Mars, 7 rue du Champs-de-Mars, 7ᵉ; ☎01.45.51.52.30, fax 01.45.51.64.34 (Mº École-Militaire).
Completely refurbished. Comfortable but slightly small rooms in a very attractive neighbourhood. ④–⑤.

Hôtel du Palais Bourbon, 49 rue de Bourgogne, 7ᵉ; ☎01.45.51.63.32, fax 01.45.55.20.21 (Mº Varenne).
A handsome old building in a sunny street by the Musée Rodin. Rooms are spacious and light. ④–⑥.

Hôtel Muguet, 11 rue Chevert, 7ᵉ; ☎01.47.05.05.93, fax 01.45.50.25.37 (M° École-Militaire/Latour-Maubourg).
A newly renovated oldie in a quiet street between the Eiffel Tower and Invalides. ⑤.

Hôtel de Beaune, 29 rue de Beaune, 7ᵉ; ☎01.42.61.24.89, fax 01.49.27.02.12 (Mº Bac).

Accommodation

The price categories used in this chapter are as follows:
① up to 160F
② 160–220F
③ 220–300F
④ 300–400F
⑤ 400–500F
⑥ 500–600F
⑦ over 600F.
For a fuller explanation, see p.214.

Accommodation

A very pretty hotel in an ideal location close to St-Germain and the Musée d'Orsay. ⑤–⑥.

Le Pavillon, 54 rue St-Dominique, 7e; ☎01.45.51.42.87, fax 01.45.51.32.79 (Mº Invalides/Latour-Maubourg).
A tiny former convent set back from the tempting shops of the rue St-Dominique in a leafy courtyard. A lovely setting, but the rooms are a little pokey for the price. ⑤–⑥.

Hôtel de la Tulipe, 33 rue Malar, 7e; ☎01.45.51.67.21, fax 01.47.53.96.37 (Mº Latour-Maubourg).
Patio for summer breakfast and drinks. Beamy and cottagey. But, as with all hotels in this area, you are paying for the location rather than great luxury. ⑤–⑥.

Hôtel Solférino, 91 rue de Lille, 7e; ☎01.47.05.85.54, fax 01.45.55.51.16 (Mº Solférino/*RER* Musée-d'Orsay).
Attractive place near the Musée d'Orsay and river, featuring an old-fashioned cage-lift. ⑥–⑦, with a few much cheaper rooms.

Hôtel Bersoly's St-Germain, 28 rue de Lille, 7e; ☎01.42.60.73.79, fax 01.49.27.05.55 (Mº Bac).
Small but exquisite rooms, each named after an artist. Impeccable service. ⑥–⑦.

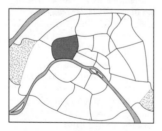

8e Arrondissement

Hôtel d'Artois, 94 rue la Boétie, 8e; ☎01.43.59.84.12 (Mº St-Philippe-du-Roule).
One of the cheapest in this smartest part of town, with unusually gracious and spacious rooms. A very good bargain. ③–⑤.

Hôtel de la Paix, 22 rue Roquépine, 8e; ☎01.42.65.14.36, fax 01.42.65.14.36 (Mº St-Augustine).
A bit gloomy, but in a very Parisian fashion, ④.

Hôtel de l'Élysée, 12 rue des Saussaies, 8e; ☎01.42.65.29.25, fax 01.42.65.64.28 (Mº St-Philippe-du-Roule).
Chandeliers and four-posters – classic luxury. ⑦.

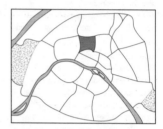

9e Arrondissement

Hôtel des Trois Poussins, 15 rue Clauzel, 9e; ☎01.48.74.38.20 (Mº St-Georges/Anvers).
Old-fashioned and simple, but rather charming. Located in a quiet, attractive street at the foot of Montmartre, close to convenient bus and métro lines. ②–③.

Hôtel des Arts, 7 Cité-Bergère, 9e; ☎01.42.46.73.30, fax 01.48.00.94.42 (Mº Montmartre).
A charming and friendly hotel and one of the cheaper ones in this quiet alley close to the *Grands Boulevards*. ④.

Hôtel de Beauharnais, 51 rue de la Victoire, 9e; ☎01.48.74.71.13 (Mº Le Peletier/Havre-Caumartin).
Louis Quinze, First Empire . . . every room decorated in a different period style. ④.

Hôtel Imperial, 45 rue de la Victoire, 9e; ☎01.48.74.10.47, fax 01.44.63.02.47 (Mº Le Peletier/Chaussée-d'Antin).
Young, efficient manager speaking excellent English. Fairly nondescript but adequate rooms. ④.

Mondial Hôtel, 21 rue Notre-Dame-de-Lorette, 9e; ☎01.48.78.60.47, fax 01.42.81.95.58 (Mº St-Georges).

Acceptable, if uninspired, by the lovely place St-Georges. Rooms for 4 under 500F. ④.

Parrotel Paris-Montholon, 11bis rue Pierre-Sémard, 9ᵉ; ☎01.48.78.28.94, fax 01.42.80.11.15 (Mᵒ Poissonnière).
Rooms are a little small and dark, but functional and reasonably priced. ④.

Hôtel des Croisés, 63 rue St-Lazare, 9ᵉ; ☎01.48.74.78.24, fax 01.49.95.04.43 (Mᵒ Trinité).
Low on mod cons but great on style: a hotchpotch of different periods. Good value. ④–⑤.

Hôtel des Champs-Élysées, 2 rue Artois, 9ᵉ ☎01.43.59.11.42, fax 01.45.61.00.61 (Mᵒ Franklin-D-Roosevelt/St-Philippe-du-Roule).
Old-fashioned hospitality and excellent value for the area. ⑤.

Hôtel Chopin, 46 passage Jouffroy, 9ᵉ; ☎01.47.70.58.10, fax 01.42.47.00.70 (Mᵒ Richelieu-Drouot).
Entrance on bd Montmartre, near rue du Faubourg-Montmartre. A splendid, characterful period building in the old *passage*. Rooms are acceptable. ⑤.

Hôtel du Léman, 20 rue Trévise, 9ᵉ; ☎01.42.46.50.66, fax 01.48.24.27.59 (Mᵒ Montmartre).
Tiny rooms, but a delightful address. ⑤–⑥.

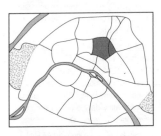

10ᵉ Arrondissement

Hôtel Moderne du Temple, 3 rue d'Aix, 10ᵉ; ☎01.48.08.09.04, fax 01.42.41.72.17 (Mᵒ République/Goncourt).
Bargain cheapie, Czech-run, just the job for a low budget. ①–②.

Hôtel Savoy, 9 rue Jarry, 10ᵉ; ☎01.47.70.03.72 (Mᵒ Gare-de-l'Est/Château-d'Eau).

Pokey and basic with no maintenance, but very cheap. ①–②.

Hôtel du Brabant, 18 rue des Petits-Hôtels, 10ᵉ; ☎01.47.70.12.32 (Mᵒ Poissonnière/Gare-du-Nord/Gare-de-l'Est).
Six floors of gloomy but manageable rooms in an ancient, liftless building. ①–③.

Hôtel Palace, 9 rue Bouchardon, 10ᵉ; ☎01.40.40.09.45 01.42.06.59.32, fax 01.42.06.16.90 (Mᵒ Strasbourg-St-Denis).
Gloomy corridors but acceptable rooms in a busy, colourful and central district near the Porte St-Martin. Popular with backpackers. Nice, helpful owners. A good deal. ①–③.

Hôtel du Jura, 6 rue de Jarry, 10ᵉ; ☎01.47.70.06.66 (Mᵒ Gare-de-l'Est/Château-d'Eau).
Primitive, but friendly and decent. ②.

Grand Hôtel d'Amiens, 88 rue du Faubourg-Poissonnière, 10ᵉ (nr junction with rue La-Fayette); ☎01.48.78.71.48 (Mᵒ Poissonnière).
Worn stairs and no frills, but clean and reasonably spacious rooms. ②–③.

Hôtel Jarry, 4 rue Jarry, 10ᵉ; ☎01.47.70.70.38 (Mᵒ Gare-de-l'Est/Château-d'Eau).
First impression is gloomy, but the rooms are OK. Fresher than the other cheapies in this street. ②–③.

Hôtel Mazagran, 4 rue Mazagran, 10ᵉ; ☎01.48.24.25.26, fax 01.42.47.17.96 (Mᵒ Bonne-Nouvelle).
Agreeable accommodation in a quiet but central street close to the Turkish quarter. ③–④.

Nord-Est Hôtel, 12 rue des Petits-Hôtels, 10ᵉ; ☎01.47.70.07.18, fax 01.42.46.73.50 (Mᵒ Poissonnière/Gare-du-Nord/Gare-de-l'Est).
Rooms are clean and modern, though characterless, which is a disappointment after the exquisite garden in front of the hotel ④.

Hôtel St-Louis, 8 rue Buisson-St-Louis, 10ᵉ; ☎01.42.49.18.85, fax 01.42.06.08.74 (Mᵒ Belleville).
Very pleasant modern building. ③.

Accommodation

The price categories used in this chapter are as follows:
① up to 160F
② 160–220F
③ 220–300F
④ 300–400F
⑤ 400–500F
⑥ 500–600F
⑦ over 600F.
For a fuller explanation, see p.214.

Accommodation

Hôtel Parisiana, 21 rue de Chabrol, 10e; ☎01.47.70.68.33, fax 01.48.00.00.67 (Mº Gare-de-l'Est).
Reasonable, though a little worn. ④.

Hôtel-Résidence Magenta, 35 rue Yves-Toudic, 10e; ☎01.42.40.17.72, fax 01.42.02.59.66 (Mº République/Jacques-Bonsergent).
Friendly, clean, attractive hotel with patio breakfast area. The top 2 rooms, 61 and 62, are particularly nice. ④–⑥.

Adix Hôtel, 30 rue Lucien-Sampaix, 10e; ☎01.42.08.19.74, fax 01.42.08.27.28 (Mº Jaques-Bonsergent).
In a pleasant street close to the St-Martin canal. Reasonable value for money. ⑤.

Belta Hôtel Résidence, 46 rue Lucien-Sampaix, 10e; ☎01.46.07.23.87, fax 01.42.09.87.27 (Mº Gare-de-l'Est).
Good location on the St-Martin canal bank. Totally renovated in bland airport style, but comfortable. ⑦.

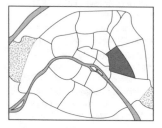

11e Arrondissement

Hôtel de Vienne, 43 rue de Malte, 11e; ☎01.48.05.44.42 (Mº République/Oberkampf).
Very pleasant, good-value cheapie, and nice people. Don't be put off by the crumbling façade. Closed Aug. ①–②, with some cheaper singles.

Hôtel de la Nouvelle France, 31 rue Keller, 11e; ☎01.47.00.40.74 (Mº Brèguet-Sabin).
An old-fashioned and basic hotel. ②.

Cosmo's Hotel, 35 rue Jean-Pierre Timbaud, 11e; ☎01.43.57.25.88 (Mº Parmentier).
Clean and decent, with good restaurants nearby. ②–③.

Mary's Hotel, 15 rue de Malte, 11e; ☎01.47.00.81.70, fax 01.47.00.58.06 (Mº République).
No frills, but clean and run by courteous people. ②–③.

Hôtel de Nevers, 53 rue de Malte, 11e; ☎01.47.00.56.18, fax 01.43.57.77.39 (Mº République/Oberkampf).
You couldn't find better value than this clean, decent hotel run by a very sympathetic proprietor. Excellent breakfasts. ②–③.

Hôtel des Arts, 2 rue Godefroy-Cavaignac, 11e; ☎01.43.79.72.57 (Mº Voltaire).
Not much charm, but hospitable, and acceptable at the price. ②–④.

Plessis-Hôtel, 25 rue du Grand-Prieuré, 11e; ☎01.47.00.13.38 (Mº République/Oberkampf).
Friendly and good value. ②–④.

Grand Hôtel Amelot, 54 rue Amelot, 11e; ☎01.48.06.15.19 (Mº St-Sébastien-Froissart).
Not the best location, but reasonable rooms and good value. ③.

Pax Hotel, 12 rue de Charonne, 11e; ☎01.47.00.40.98, fax 01.42.28.57.81 (Mº Ledru-Rollin/Bastille).
A reasonable establishment if you want to be in the centre of the Bastille's nightlife. Can be noisy. ③.

Hôtel Beaumarchais, 3 rue Oberkampf, 11e; ☎01.43.38.16.16, fax 01.43.38.32.86 (Mº Filles-du-Calvaire/Oberkampf).
All rooms come with bathrooms and a complimentary daily copy of *Libération* newspaper. Pleasant. ④.

Garden Hôtel, 1 rue du Général-Blaise, 11e; ☎01.47.00.57.93, fax 01.47.00.45.29 (Mº St-Ambroise).
Comfortable and newly renovated – located on the pleasant square Parmentier. ④.

Hôtel du Nord et de l'Est, 49 rue de Malte, 11e; ☎01.47.00.71.70, fax 01.43.57.51.16 (Mº République/Oberkampf).
Clean and comfortable accommodation. ④.

Hôtel St-Martin, 12 rue Léon-Frot, 11e;
☎01.43.71.09.14 (Mº Boulets-
Montreuil).
Dull neighbourhood, but a nice, friendly
hotel with all the mod cons. ④.

Méridional, 36 bd Richard-Lenoir, 11e;
☎01.48.05.75.00, fax 01.43.57.42.85
(Mº Brèguet-Sabin).
Attractive, with light rooms and a garden.
⑤–⑥.

Accommodation

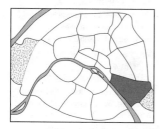

12e Arrondissement

Hôtel de Reims, 26 rue Hector-Malot,
12e; ☎01.43.07.46.18 (Mº Gare-de-
Lyon/Ledru-Rollin).
On a quiet street with access to the
"Coulée Verte" promenade and close to
the place d'Aligre market. Closed Aug.
②.

Grand Hôtel Doré, 201 av Daumesnil
12e; ☎01.43.43.66.89, fax
01.43.43.65.20 (Mº Daumesnil).
Not very central, but smart for the price.
③.

Hôtel du Midi, 31 rue Traversière, 12e;
☎01.43.07.88.68 (Mº Ledru-Rollin).
Very pleasant accommodation close to
the Gare du Lyon. ④.

Hôtel des Pyrénées, 204 rue du
Faubourg-St-Antoine, 12e;
☎01.43.72. 07.46, fax 01.43.72.98.45
(Mº Faidherbe-Chaligny).
Comfortable and quiet behind its posh
reception area. ④.

Hôtel Saphir, 35 rue de Citeaux, 12e;
☎01.43.07.77.28, fax 01.43.46.67.45
(Mº Faidherbe-Chaligny).
On a quiet street off Faubourg
St-Antoine. No special charms, but
comfortable. ④.

13e Arrondissement

Hôtel Tolbiac, 122 rue de Tolbiac, 13e;
☎01.44.24.25.54, fax 01.45.85.43.47
(Mº Tolbiac).
On a noisy junction, but all rooms are
very pleasant, with loos and showers;
breakfast is only 15F. In July & Aug you
can rent small studios by the week. ②.

Hôtel de la Place des Alpes, 2 place
des Alpes, 13e; ☎01.42.35.14.14, fax
01.45.86.30.06 (Mº Place-d'Italie).
Agreeable enough for the price. ③.

Résidence Les Gobelins, 9 rue des
Gobelins, 13e; ☎01.47.07.26.90, fax
01.43.31.44.05 (Mº Les Gobelins).
Delightful, popular establishment that
must be booked well in advance. ⑤.

Hôtel du Vert-Galant, 41 rue
Croulebarbe, 13e; ☎01.44.08.83.50, fax
01.44.08.83.69 (Mº Les Gobelins).
In a quiet, verdant backwater, above a
renowned Basque restaurant. Cosy
rooms, and a vine climbing up the wall
from the garden. ⑤.

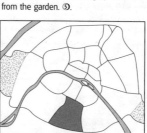

14e Arrondissement

Ouest Hotel, 27 rue de Gergovie, 14e;
☎01.45.42.64.99, fax 01.45.42.46.65
(Mº Pernety).
Basic but perfectly acceptable, in a very
pleasant part of town. ②.

*The price
categories
used in this
chapter are as
follows:
① up to 160F
② 160–220F
③ 220–300F
④ 300–400F
⑤ 400–500F
⑥ 500–600F
⑦ over 600F.
For a fuller
explanation,
see p.214.*

Accommodation

Hôtel Le Lionceau, 22 rue Daguerre, 14e; ☎01.42.22.53.53, fax 01.44.10.72.49 (Mº Denfert-Rochereau).
Decent-sized rooms and decorated with murals throughout. On the pedestrian market street. ③.

Virginia Hotel, 66 rue du Père-Corentin, 14e; ☎01.45.40.70.90, fax 01.45.40.95.21 (Mº Porte-d'Orléans).
Quiet part of town some way from the centre, but very good value; rooms for 4 at 460F. ③.

Hôtel de la Loire, 39bis rue du Moulin-Vert, 14e; ☎01.45.40.66.88, fax 01.45.40.89.07 (Mº Alésia/Plaisance).
Attractive hotel on a very quiet street, with breakfast served in a little garden. ④.

Hôtel du Parc Montsouris, 4 rue du Parc-Montsouris, 14e; ☎01.45.89.09.72, fax 01.45.80.92.72 (Mº Porte-d'Orléans/*RER* Cité-Universitaire).
Modern, a bit impersonal, but in a lovely tiny street right by the park. ④.

Comfort Hotel Losserand, 76 rue Raymond-Losserand, 14e; ☎01.40.52.12.40, fax 01.40.52.12.41 (Mº Pernety).
Part of a chain and business-orientated, but with stylish rooms and a dependable level of service and comfort. ⑤.

Hôtel Istria, 29 rue Campagne-Première, 14e; ☎01.43.20.91.82, fax 01.43.22.48.45 (Mº Raspail).
Beautifully decorated, with legendary artistic associations: Duchamp, Man Ray, Aragon, Mayakovsky and Rilke all stayed here. ⑥.

15e Arrondissement

Mondial Hôtel, 136 bd de Grenelle, 15e; ☎01.45.79.73.57, fax 01.45.79.58.65 (Mº La Motte-Picquet).

Despite its rather grim appearance, this hotel is friendly and decent, with large rooms and good views. Right under the raised métro. ③.

Hôtel Fondary, 30 rue Fondary, 15e; ☎01.45.75.14.75, fax 01.45.75.84.42 (Mº Émile-Zola).
Quiet and agreeable location in one of the more animated areas of the 15e. ④.

Hôtel King, 1 rue de Chambéry, 15e; ☎01.45.33.99.06, fax 01.42.50.02.34 (Mº Porte-de-Vanves/Convention).
Quiet and pleasant, conveniently close to parc Georges-Brassens. ④.

Hôtel Pasteur, 33 rue du Docteur-Roux, 15e; ☎01.47.83.53.17, fax 01.45.66.62.39 (Mº Pasteur).
A small garden, and rooms that are comfortable and well-equipped for the price. ④.

Hôtel Tour Eiffel Dupleix, 11 rue Juge, 15e; ☎01.45.78.29.29, fax 01.45.78.60.00 (Mº Dupleix).
Recently renovated, with tasteful rooms and a tiny garden in which to breakfast. ⑤–⑥.

Hôtel Wallace, 89 rue Fondary, 15e; ☎01.45.78.83.30, fax 01.40.58.19.43 (Mº Émile-Zola).
Unpretentious and charming place with a pretty garden in the courtyard. ⑦.

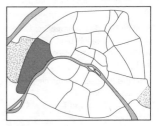

16e Arrondissement

Hôtel Keppler, 12 rue Keppler, 16e; ☎01.47.20.65.05, fax 01.47.23.02.29 (Mº George-V/Kléber).
Rooms a little small, but spotless, quite comfortable, and just a few steps from the Champs-Élysées. ⑤.

Hameau de Passy, 48 rue Passy, 16e;
☎01.42.88.47.55, fax 01.42.30.83.72
(Mº Muette).
Tucked away in a mews – utterly
peaceful and with faultless service.
⑤–⑥.

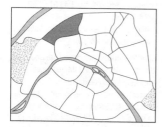

Accommodation

17e Arrondissement

Hôtel Gauthey, 5 rue Gauthey, 17e;
☎01.46.27.15.48 (Mº Brochant).
Basic but clean. ①.

Hôtel Savoy, 21 rue des Dames, 17e;
☎01.42.93.13.47 (Mº Place-
Clichy/Rome).
Typical unmodernized Paris cheapie;
basic, but decent. ①.

Hôtel Avenir-Jonquière, 23 rue de la
Jonquière, 17e; ☎01.46.27.83.41 (Mº
Guy-Môquet).
Clean, friendly establishment offering bar-
gain accommodation. ②.

Hôtel des Batignolles, 26–28 rue des
Batignolles, 17e; ☎01.43.87.70.40 (Mº
Rome/Place-Clichy).
A quiet and very reasonable establishment in a neighbourhood that prides
itself on its village character. Triples for
370F. ②–④.

Résidence Lévis, 16 rue Lebouteux, 17e;
☎01.47.63.86.38, fax 01.40.53.00.92
(Mº Villiers).
Only 10 rooms, but very nice, clean and
quiet, in a small side street off the rue
de Lévis market. ④–⑤.

Hôtel du Roi René, 72 place Félix-
Lobligeois, 17e; ☎01.42.26.72.73, fax
01.42.63.74.99 (Mº Rome/Villiers).
A mid-priced hotel in a very nice location
by a mini-Greek temple and public garden. ⑤.

18e Arrondissement

Hôtel du Commerce, 34 rue des Trois-
Frères, 18e; ☎01.42.64.81.69 (Mº
Abbesses/Anvers).
Very basic and dirt-cheap; for the hard-
ened dosser only. ①.

Hôtel Versigny, 31 rue Letort, 18e;
☎01.42.59.20.90, fax 01.42.59.32.66
(Mº Jules-Joffrin).
Unmodernized and basic – fine if you're
tough and want a cheap sleep. ①–②.

Hôtel Caulaincourt, 2 square Caulaincourt
(by 63 rue Caulaincourt), 18e;
☎01.46.06.42.99, fax 01.46.06.48.67 (Mº
Lamarck-Caulaincourt).
One of the nicest, cleanest and friend-
liest of the cheaper hotels – magnificent
view from room 16. ①–③.

Hôtel New Montmartre, 7 rue Paul-Albert,
18e; ☎01.46.06.03.03, fax 01.46.06.73.28
(Mº Anvers/Château-Rouge).
Just east of the Sacré-Cœur; light and
roomy. ②.

Hôtel du Puy de Dôme, 180 rue
Ordener (av St-Ouen end), 18e;
☎01.46.27.78.55, fax 01.42.29.13.67
(Mº Guy-Môquet).
On the north side of Montmartre, close
to a big street market and the métro. A
pleasant, cheap and friendly hotel, being
steadily renovated. ②.

Idéal Hôtel, 3 rue des Trois-Frères, 18e;
☎01.46.06.63.63, fax 01.42.64.97.01
(Mº Abbesses).
Marvellous location on the slopes of
Montmartre. Basic, but clean, friendly and
used to backpackers. ②–③.

Style Hôtel, 8 rue Ganneron (av Clichy
end), 18e; ☎01.45.22.37.59, fax
01.45.22.81.03 (Mº Place-Clichy).

*The price
categories
used in this
chapter are as
follows:*
① up to 160F
② 160–220F
③ 220–300F
④ 300–400F
⑤ 400–500F
⑥ 500–600F
⑦ over 600F.
*For a fuller
explanation,
see p.214.*

Accommodation

Wooden floors, marble fireplaces, a secluded internal courtyard, nice people – great value. ②–③.

Hôtel André Gill, 4 rue André-Gill, 18e; ☎01.42.62.48.48, fax 01.42.62.77.92 (Mº Pigalle/Abbesses).
In a quiet alley on the slopes of Montmartre. Pretty characterless, but clean and comfortable. ③–④.

La Résidence Montmartre, 10 rue Burcq, 18e; ☎01.46.06.51.91, fax 01.42.52.82.59 (Mº Abbesses).
A smart and comfortable hotel. ⑥.

Timotel, 11 place Émile-Goudeau, 18e; ☎01.42.55.74.79, fax 01.42.55.71.01 (Mº Abbesses/Blanche).
Rooms are modern, comfortable and freshly decorated in a non-descript chain-hotel way. The location, however, is unbeatable, on the beautiful shady square where Picasso had his studio in 1900, with views across the whole city. ⑥.

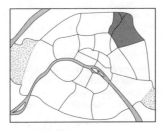

19e Arrondissement

Hôtel Rhin et Danube, 3 place Rhin-et-Danube, 19e; ☎01.42.45.10.13, fax 01.42.06.88.82 (Mº Danube).
Way out of the centre on the airy heights of Belleville, and geared to self-catering. Good value. ④.

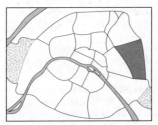

20e Arrondissement

Ermitage Hôtel, 42bis rue de l'Ermitage, 20e; ☎01.46.36.23.44 (Mº Jourdain).
A clean and decent cheapie, close to the leafy, provincial rue des Pyrénées. ②–③.

Mary's, 118 rue Orfila (at the rue Pelleport end), 20e; ☎01.43.61.51.68 (Mº Pelleport).
A little far out, but simple, clean, friendly and good value. ②–③.

Hôtel Nadaud, 8 rue de la Bidassoa, 20e; ☎01.46.36.87.79 (Mº Gambetta, exit Place Martin-Nadaud).
A great little place close to Père-Lachaise cemetery. No luxury, but comfortable, clean, attentive and friendly. Closed Aug. ②–③.

Hôtel Tamaris, 14 rue des Maraîchers, 20e; ☎01.43.72.85.48 (Mº Porte-de-Vincennes).
Simple, clean, attractive, and run by nice people. Extremely good value. Close to métro and terminus of bus route 26 from Gare du Nord. ②–③.

Hôtel Pyrénées-Gambetta, 12 av du Père-Lachaise, 20e; ☎01.47.97.76.57, fax 01.47.97.17.61 (Mº Gambetta).
Perfect for anyone passionate about Père-Lachaise cemetery. Unpretentious and very pleasant. ③–⑤.

Hostels, Foyers and Campsites

Youth Hostels

The cheapest youth accommodation is to be found in the hostels run by the **French Youth Hostel Association**, for which you need International YHA membership (no age limit), and those connected with the **MIJE** (*Maison Internationale de la Jeunesse et des Étudiants*) and **UCRIF** (*Union des Centres de Rencontres Internationaux de France*). Current costs for bed and breakfast are: youth hostels 110–171F, *MIJE* hostels 120–168F, and *UCRIF* hostels between 120F and 175F. The determining factor is whether you have an individual or shared room. There is no effective age limit at either.

CENTRAL YOUTH HOSTELS

There are four **youth hostels** in or very close to Paris proper, and it's advisable to book ahead in summer (send a cheque or postal order to cover the cost of the first night). All charge 110F, including breakfast..

D'Artagnan, 80 rue Vitruve, 20e; ☎01.40.32.34.53, fax 01.42.32.34.55 (Mº Porte-de-Bagnolet).
A pleasant modern building in Charonne, on the edge of the city.

Jules Ferry, 8 bd Jules-Ferry, 11e; ☎01.43.57.55.60, fax 01.40.21.79.92 (Mº République).
In the lively, colourful area at the foot of the Belleville hill. When full, they will help you find a bed elsewhere for the same price.

Léo Lagrange, 107 rue Martre, Clichy; ☎01.41.27.26.90, fax 01.42.70.52.53 (Mº Maine-de-Clichy).
Also has some individual (171F) and double rooms (128F).

SUBURBAN YOUTH HOSTELS

Several hostels exist on the outskirts of Paris, often in rather inconvenient locations. The *Cité des Sciences*, just northeast of the city, is the closest suburban hostel.

Cité des Sciences, 24 rue des Sept-Arpents 93310, Le Pré-St-Gervais; ☎01.48.43.24.11, fax 01.48.43.26.82 (Mº Hoche).

Points d'Accueil Jeunesse, allée des Matelots, route de St-Cyr, 7800 Versailles ☎01.30.21.84.85 (*RER ligne C* to Versailles-Chantiers, then bus P). Open mid-June to mid-Sept. 16–26s only.

Other hostels are at 3 rue Marcel-Duhamel, Arpajon; ☎01.64.90.28.85 (*RER ligne C4* to Arpajon); and 125 av Villeneuve-St-Georges, Choisy-le-Roi; ☎01.48.90.92.30 (*RER ligne C* from St-Michel to Choisy-le-Roi, 10min from place St-Michel; or bus #182 direction Villeneuve-Triage, station "Auberge de Jeunesse"). 91F with breakfast, or 68F for 2 plus a tent in the campsite.

Foyers

The **MIJE**'s **foyers**, which cannot be booked in advance and where the maximum length of stay is seven days, are:

Le Fauconnier, 11 rue du Fauconnier, 4e; ☎01.42.74.23.45 (Mº St-Paul/Pont-Marie).

Le Fourcy, 6 rue de Fourcy, 4e; ☎01.42.74.23.45 (Mº St-Paul).

François Miron, 6 rue François-Miron, 4e (Mº Hôtel-de-Ville). Annexe of above.

Maubuisson, 12 rue des Barres, 4e; ☎01.42.74.23.45 (Mº Pont-Marie/Hôtel-de-Ville).

The *foyers* above are superbly and very centrally situated, occupying historic buildings in the Marais. Other **foyers** include:

Cité Universitaire, bd Jourdan, 14e; ☎01.44.16.44.00 (*RER* Cité-Universitaire). Mon–Fri 9am–5pm.
The student campus can provide a list of the different *maisons* or *fondations* that let out rooms during the summer holidays, some April–Sept. These include the *Maison des États-Unis* (☎01.45.89.35.79) and the *Collège Franco-Britannique* (☎01.44.16.24.00). Costs vary from around 145F to 170F a night. Sometimes there is a minimum length of stay, around 5 nights.

Maison des Étudiants, 18 rue Jean-Jacques-Rousseau, 1er; ☎01.45.08.02.10 (Mº Palais-Royal).
Available for travellers June 15–Aug 30; minimum stay 3 nights. B&B in double room costs 100F; 200F in a single.

Résidence Bastille, 151 av Ledru-Rollin, 11e; ☎01.43.79.53.86 (Mº Ledru-Rollin/Bastille/Voltaire).

UCRIF has at its disposal a number of hostels in or close to Paris, for which there is no advance booking. *UCRIF* advises you either to phone individual hostels on arrival in Paris or to go along to the main office at 27 rue de Turbigo, 2e; ☎01.40.26.57.24, fax 01.40.26.58.20; Mon–Fri 10am–6pm. All the following provide canteen meals for around 50F.

Accommodation

The price categories used in this chapter are as follows:
① up to 160F
② 160–220F
③ 220–300F
④ 300–400F
⑤ 400–500F
⑥ 500–600F
⑦ over 600F.
For a fuller explanation, see p.214.

Accommodation

Bureau de Voyages de la Jeunesse (BVJ) Centre International de Paris/Les Halles, 5 rue du Pélican, 1er; ☎01.42.36.88.18, fax 01.42.33.40.53 (Mº Louvre/Châtelet-Les Halles/Palais-Royal).

(BVJ) Centre International de Paris/Louvre, 20 rue Jean-Jacques-Rousseau, 1er; ☎01.42.36.88.18, fax 01.42.33.40.53 (Mº Louvre/Châtelet-Les Halles).

(BVJ) Centre International de Paris/Opéra, 11 rue Thérèse, 1er; ☎01.42.36.88.18, fax 01.42.33.40.53 (Mº Pyramides/Palais-Royal).

(BVJ) Centre International de Paris/Quartier Latin, 44 rue des Bernardins, 5e; ☎01.42.36.88.18, fax 01.42.33.40.53 (Mº Maubert-Mutualité).

Centre d'Accueil et d'Animation Paris 20e, 46 rue Louis-Lumière, 20e; ☎01.43.61.24.51 (Mº Porte-de-Bagnolet/Porte-de-Montreuil).

Centre International de Séjour de Paris (CISP) Kellermann, 17 bd Kellermann, 13e; ☎01.44.16.37.38 (Mº Porte-d'Italie).

(CISP) Maurice Ravel, 6 av Maurice-Ravel, 12e; ☎01.44.75.60.00, fax 01.43.44.45.30 (Mº Porte-de-Vincennes).

Foyer International d'Accueil de Paris Jean Monnet, 30 rue Cabanis, 14e; ☎01.45.89.89.15, fax 01.45.81.63.91 (Mº Glacière).

Maison des Clubs UNESCO de Paris, 43 rue de la Glacière, 13e; ☎01.43.36.00.63, fax 01.45.35.05.96 (Mº Glacière).

Further possibilities include more hostel-type accommodation, notably:

Aloha Hostel, 1 rue Borromé, 15e; ☎01.42.73.03.03, fax 01.42.73.14.14 (Mº Volontaires).
Same management as *Three Ducks Hostel*, below. Oct–March 87F, April–Sept 97F. Arrive by 9am to book.

Association des Étudiants Protestants de Paris (Protestant Student Association), 46 rue de Vaugirard, 6e; ☎01.43.33.23.30, fax 01.46.34.27.09

(Mº Luxembourg/Mabillon/St-Sulpice). Friendly but pretty basic, for people aged 18–26 of all nationalities and creeds. No advance booking; turn up or phone on the day – early. Maximum stay 5 weeks. Current cost is 10F membership (valid for subsequent visits) and 75–95F, depending on size of dormitory, for B&B, plus 150F deposit.

Auberge International des Jeunes Ste-Marguérite, 10 rue Trousseau, 11e; ☎01.47.00.62.00, fax 01.47.00.33.16 (Mº Bastille/Ledru-Rollin).
No card necessary. B&B March–Oct 91F, Nov–Feb 81F.

CROUS, Académie de Paris, 39 av Georges-Bernanos, 5e; ☎01.40.51.36.00 (Mº Port-Royal).
This is the organization that controls student accommodation in Paris and lets free space during university vacations.

Maison Internationale des Jeunes, 4 rue Titon, 11e; ☎01.43.71.99.21, fax 01.43.71.78.58 (Mº Faidherbe-Chaligny). For 18–30s. Operates like a youth hostel, but does not require YHA membership. 110F B&B.

Three Ducks Hostel, 6 place Étienne-Pernet, 15e; ☎01.48.42.04.05, fax 01.48.42.99.99 (Mº Émile-Zola).
A private youth hostel with no age limit, though guests are mainly young and noisy. The whole place has been totally renovated, and offers kitchen facilities as well as a bar with the cheapest beer in town. Essential to book ahead between May and Oct: send the price of the first night. Lock-out 12am–5pm, curfew at 2am. 75F Oct–March, 97F April–Sept; some rooms for couples.

Woodstock Hostel, 48 rue Radier, 9e; ☎01.48.78.87.76 (Mº Anvers/St-Georges).

Young and Happy Hostel, 80 rue Mouffetard, 5e; ☎01.45.35.09.53, fax 01.47.07.22.24 (Mº Monge/Censier-Daubenton).
Turn up between 8am and 10am to book. Noisy, basic and studenty. 97F B&B.

Another hostel in the *Three Ducks* stable, with its own bar. A great location in a pretty, untouristy street near Montmartre. 75F.

For Women Only

Résidence Orfila, 65 rue Orfila, 20e; ☎01.46.36.82.80 (Mº Gambetta/Pelleport).
Nominal age limit 24, but not applied to foreign travellers. Current cost, including breakfast and dinner (obligatory), is 150F in single room, 130F in double, or 680F and 580F respectively for 7 days, including breakfast and dinner Mon–Fri. A month's stay is even more advantageous. Kitchen facilities available. Minimum stay 3 nights.

Foyer des Jeunes Filles, 234 rue Tolbiac, 13e; ☎01.44.16.22.22, fax 01.43.71.78.58 (Mº Glacière).
18–30s only. Excellent facilities. 120F.

For sundry **other addresses** try the **CIDJ** office's information files at 101 quai Branly, 15e (Mº Bir-Hakeim).

Résidence Naples, 22 rue de Naples, 8e; ☎01.45.22.23.49, fax 01.42.94.81.24 (Mº Europe/Villiers).
Minimum stay 3 nights; no age limit. 100F B&B in a 2-, 3- or 4-bed room, 120F in a single. There are often vacancies, even in term time.

Résidence Blomet, 168 rue Blomet, 15e; ☎01.45.33.48.21, fax 01.45.33.70.32 (Mº Convention).
Minimum stay 3 nights. 150F for a single room, 130F for a double – including breakfast and dinner. Worth trying even in term time.

Camping

WIth the exception of the one in the Bois de Boulogne, most of Paris' **camp-** sites are some way out of town. For other possibilities, contact the tourist office.

Camping du Bois de Boulogne, Allée du Bord-de-l'Eau, 16e; ☎01.45.24.30.00. (Mº Porte-Maillot/bus #244 to Route des Moulins). April–Oct; camping shuttle bus 10F.
Much the most central campsite, next to the River Seine in the Bois de Boulogne, and usually booked out in summer. 60–80F for a tent. The ground is pebbly, but the site is well-equipped and has a useful information office.

Camping du Parc de la Colline (slightly further east than the above), Route de Lagny, 77200 Torcy; ☎01.60.05.42.32 (*RER ligne A4* to Torcy, then bus #421 to stop Le Clos) March 15–Oct 15..

Camping du Parc-Étang (southwest of Paris), Base de Loisirs, 78180 Montigny-le-Bretonneux; ☎01.30.58.56.20 (*RER ligne C* St-Quentin-en-Yvelines. Métro connections for *RER ligne C* at Invalides/St-Michel/Gare-d'Austerlitz) April–end Sept.

Bed and Breakfast

Finally, there remains the possibility of **bed and breakfast** in private houses. Two organizations to contact are:

France Lodge, 5 rue du Faubourg-Montmartre, 9e; ☎01.42.46.68.19, fax 01.42.46.65.61 (Mº Rue-Montmartre). From 120F, plus 85F annual membership.

Bed & Breakfast 1 Connection, 73 rue Notre-Dame-des-Champs, 6e; ☎43.25.70.39, fax 01.40.47.69.20 (Mº Vavin).
3 days minimum stay; 325F upwards for 2, plus 50F reservation per person.

Accommodation

Chapter 13

Eating and Drinking

As in the rest of France, Parisian cooking has art status, the top chefs are stars, and dining out is a national pastime, whether it's at the bistro on the corner or at a famed house of haute cuisine. In recent years, prices at the top end of the market have come down – with some superb-value midday menus on offer – while the quality at the bottom end, particularly in the tourist hotspots, has sunk. Our advice to gourmets is to snack it out for a few days, then go for a blowout (but don't forget that wine with a 220F menu can easily send the bill to 400F).

Paris is also renowned for its foreign cuisine. There are numerous excellent Thai, Chinese and Vietnamese establishments, and you will find restaurants of Caribbean, Middle Eastern, Central African and

---

Choosing a Café

The most enjoyable cafés in Paris are often ordinary, local places, but there are particular areas which café-lizards head for. **Boulevards Montparnasse** and **St-Germain** on the Left Bank are especially favoured. There you'll find the *Select, Coupole, Closerie des Lilas, Deux Magots* and *Flore* – the erstwhile hang-outs of Apollinaire, Picasso, Hemingway, Sartre, de Beauvoir and most other literary/intellectual figures of the last six decades. Most are still frequented by the big, though not yet legendary, names in the Parisian world of arts and letters, cinema, fashion, politics and thought, as well as by their hangers-on and other lesser mortals.

The location of other lively **Left Bank café concentrations** is determined by the geography of the university. Science students gravitate towards the cafés in rue Linné, by the Jardin des Plantes. The humanities gather in the place de la Sorbonne and rue Soufflot. And all the world – especially non-Parisians – finds its way to the place St-André-des-Arts and the downhill end of bd St-Michel.

The Bastille is another good area to tour – now livelier than ever as the new Opéra and rocketing property values bring headlong development. The same is true of **Les Halles**, though the latter's trade is principally among transient out-of-towners up for the bright lights.

As to cost, obviously, addresses in the smarter or more touristy *arrondissements* set prices soaring. The Champs-Élysées and rue de Rivoli, for instance, are best avoided, at double or triple the price of a café in Belleville, La Villette or the lower 14e. As a rule of thumb, if you are watching the budget, avoid the main squares and boulevards. Cafés a little removed from the thoroughfares are invariably cheaper.

Western and Eastern European origin, along with Kurdish, Afghan, Japanese and even Tibetan.

Like other Latin Europeans, the French seldom separate the major pleasures of eating and drinking. Drinking is never an end in itself, as it so often is for Anglo-Saxons, and drink other than wine is referred to as *apéritifs* and *digestifs*. There are in consequence thousands of establishments in Paris where you can both eat and drink. In order to simplify matters, we have divided them into two broad categories: **Restaurants** and **Cafés and Bars**. The former is fairly unambiguous. "Cafés and Bars", on the other hand, includes places which offer anything from a sandwich to a full-blown meal, or no food at all.

You will find the listings which follow arranged in alphabetical order under the same geographical headings as are used in Chapters 2 to 11. By way of an introduction, we have included a description of the kinds of food and drink you might expect to find in the various kinds of establishment, as well as some indication of the conventions which surround eating and drinking in France.

Following that list are boxes on vegetarian (p.235), ethnic (p.261), and late-night (p.271) restaurants in Paris.

Cafés and Bars

In our "Cafés and Bars" category in the listings which follow, we've included cafés, café-bars, café-brasseries, *salons de thé*, *bistrots à vin*, cocktail-type bars, and beer cellars/pubs. Of these, the last two are the only ones where you may not find anything to eat.

Some **brasseries** are more restaurant than café (see p.233), have little to distinguish them from cafés and café-bars. The principal difference is that anything with "brasserie" in the title will serve proper meals in addition to the usual range of sandwiches, snacks, alcoholic and non-alcoholic drinks. **Salons de thé** and **bistrots à vin**, on the other hand, do have a distinctive identity, which is not adequately conveyed by the stan-

dard English translations, tearoom and wine bar; for details, see overleaf.

There's really no difference between **cafés** and **bars**. Although the number of them in Paris is said to be decreasing rapidly, you still see them everywhere: big ones, small ones, scruffy ones, stylish ones, snobby ones, arty ones. They line the streets and cluster around crossroads and squares. **Cybercafés** have also arrived on the scene, charging from 10F to 20F for a 15min connection to the Internet.

Many bars and cafés advertise **les snacks** or *un casse-croûte* (a bite) with pictures of omelettes, fried eggs, hot dogs or various sandwiches displayed on the pavement outside. But, even when they don't, they will usually make you a half or a third of a *baguette* (French bread stick), buttered or filled with cheese or meat (*une tartine/au beurre/au jambon*, etc). This, or a croissant, with hot chocolate or coffee, is generally the best way to eat **breakfast** – and cheaper than the rate charged by most hotels. (Brasseries also are possibilities for cups of coffee, eggs, snacks and other breakfast- or brunch-type food.)

If you **stand at the counter**, which is always cheaper than sitting down, you may see a **basket of croissants** or some hard-boiled eggs (they're usually gone by 9.30 or 10am). The drill is to help yourself – the waiter will keep an eye on how many you've eaten and bill you accordingly.

Coffee is invariably espresso and very strong. *Un café* or *un express* is black; *une noisette* has a touch of milk; *un crème* is milky; and *un grand café* or *un grand crème* is a large cup. In the morning you could also ask for *un café au lait* – espresso in a large cup or bowl filled up with hot milk. *Un déca*, decaffeinated coffee, is very widely available. Drinkers of **tea** (*thé*), nine times out of ten, have to settle for *Lipton's* tea-bags. To have milk with it, ask for *une goutte de lait*. **Hot chocolate** (*chocolat chaud*) is a better bet and can be had in any café.

Many cafés, you will find, also offer reasonably priced **lunches**. These usually

Eating and Drinking

Eating and Drinking

consist of salads, the more substantial kind of snack such as *croque-monsieurs* or *croque-madames* (both of which are variations on the grilled-cheese sandwich), a **plat du jour** (chef's daily special), or a **formule**, which is a limited or no-choice set menu.

Full price lists have to be displayed in every bar or café by law, usually without the fifteen percent service charge added, but detailing separately the prices for consuming at the bar (*au comptoir*), sitting down (*la salle*), or on the terrace (*la terrasse*) – all progressively more expensive. You pay when you leave, unless your waiter is just going off shift, and you can sit for hours over just one cup of coffee.

ALCOHOLIC AND NON-ALCOHOLIC DRINKS

All cafés and bars serve a full range of alcoholic and non-alcoholic drinks throughout the day. Although on the whole there is much less drunkenness than in Britain, it is still common to see people starting their day with a beer, cognac or *coup de rouge* (glass of red wine). A *café cogna* is the popular combination of a cup of espresso and a glass of cognac.

On the **soft drink** front, bottled fruit juices and the universal standard canned lemonades, Cokes (*Coca*) and clones are available. You can also get freshly squeezed orange and lemon juice (*orange/citron pressé*). Particularly French are the various **sirops**, diluted with water to make cool, eye-catching drinks with traffic-light colours, such as *menthe* (peppermint) and *grenadine* (pomegranate). Bottles of **spring water** (*eau minérale; pétillante* for sparkling, *plate* for still) are widely drunk, from the best-selling Badoit to the most obscure spa product.

Characteristically French **apéritifs** are the aniseed drinks – *pastis*, in French – *Pernod* and *Ricard*. Like Greek *ouzo*, they turn cloudy when diluted with water and ice cubes (*glaçons*) – very refreshing and inexpensive. Two other drinks designed to stimulate the appetite are *Pineau* (cognac and grape juice) and *kir* (white wine with a dash of blackcurrant syrup – or champagne for a *kir royal*).

Beers are the familiar Belgian and German brands, plus home-grown ones from Alsace. Draught (*à la pression,* usually *Kronenbourg*) is the cheapest drink you can have next to coffee and wine. Ask for *un demi* (one-third of a litre). For a wider choice of draughts and bottles you need to go to the special beer-drinking establishments, or English-Irish-style pubs found in abundance in Paris.

Wine

Wine – *vin* – is drunk at just about every meal or social occasion. Red is *rouge*, white *blanc*, or there's *rosé*. *Vin de table* or **vin ordinaire** – table wine – is always cheap and generally drinkable.

AC (Appellation d'Origine Contrôlée) wines are another matter. They can be excellent value at the lower end of the price scale, where favourable French taxes keep prices down to 15–25F a bottle, but move much above it and you're soon paying serious prices for serious bottles.

Restaurant mark-ups of *AC* wines can be outrageous. Popular *AC* wines found on most restaurant lists include Côtes du Rhône (from the Rhône valley), St-Émilion and Médoc (from Bordeaux), Beaujolais and very upmarket Burgundy.

The **basic wine terms** are *brut*, very dry; *sec*, dry; *demi-sec*, sweet; *doux*, very sweet; *mousseux*, sparkling; *méthode champenoise*, mature and sparkling. There are grape varieties as well, but the complexities of the subject take up volumes.

A glass of wine at a bar is simply *un verre de rouge* or *un verre de blanc*. If it is an *AC* wine you may have the choice of *un ballon* (a large round glass).

Eating and Drinking

Tisanes

Tisanes or *infusions* are the generic terms for **herb teas**. Every café serves them. They are particularly soothing after overeating or overdrinking, as well as for stomach upsets. The more common ones are *verveine* (verbena), *tilleul* (lime blossom), *menthe* (mint) and *camomille*.

A light summertime option is shandy (*une panachée*).

As for the harder stuff, there are dozens of **eaux de vie** (brandies distilled from fruit) and **liqueurs**, in addition to the classic cognacs or *Armagnac*. Among less familiar names, try *Poire William* (pear brandy), *Marc* (a spirit distilled from grape pulp), the *grappa*-like Basque *Izarra*, or just point to the bottle with the most attractive colour. Measures are generous, but they don't come cheap: the same applies for imported spirits like whisky, always called *scotch*.

Salons de Thé

Salons de thé are a relatively new-fangled invention, cropping up characteristically in both established upper-class haunts and newly gentrified parts of town. More refined than anything suggested by "tearoom", they serve everything from light midday meals, brunches, salads and quiches to rich confections of cake and ice-cream. The oldest is *Angélina's*, with its marble cake-frosting exterior. More exotic and relaxed are *La Pagode* and *La Mosquée*, in the two least Parisian of the city's buildings.

Bistrots à Vins

Bistrots à vins, unlike *salons de thé*, are an ancient institution, traditionally working-class sawdust-on-the-floor drinking haunts.

Some genuine *bistrots* still exist, such as *La Tartine*, *Le Rubis* and *Le Baron Rouge*, unpretentious and catering for everyone. The newer generation, however, who ironically owe their existence in large part to the English influence, have a distinctly yuppified flavour, and are far from cheap. Most serve at least a limited range of dishes or *plats*, often deriving from a particular regional *cuisine*, and specialize in the less usual and less commercial wines, again often from a particular region. Some, like *Le Baron Rouge*, sell good, inexpensive wine from the barrel, if you bring your own containers. The basic idea is to enable you to try wines by the glass.

Restaurants

In terms of quality and price, there's nothing to choose between restaurants (*auberges* or *relais*, as they sometimes call themselves) and brasseries. The dis-

---

Snacks and Picnics

For those occasions when you don't want – or can't face – a full meal, Paris offers numerous **street stalls** and stand-up **sandwich bars**. In addition to the indigenous *frites* (French fries), *crêpes*, *galettes* (wholewheat pancakes), *gauffres* (waffles) and fresh sandwiches, there are Tunisian snacks like *brik à l'oeuf* (a fried pastry with an egg inside), *merguez* (spicy North African sausage), Greek *souvlaki* (kebabs), Middle Eastern *falafel* (deep-fried chickpea balls with salad), Japanese titbits, and all manner of good things from eastern European delicatessens.

For **picnics** and takeaway food, head for either a **charcuterie** proper or the delicatessen counter in a good supermarket. Although specializing in pork-based preparations like salami and ham, most *charcuteries* also stock a wide range of cold cuts, *pâtés*, *terrines*, ready-made salads and fully prepared main courses. These are not exclusively meaty, either: artichokes *à la grecque*, stuffed tomatoes and *paellas* are common. You buy by weight, by the slice (*tranche*) or by the carton (*barquette*).

Eating and Drinking

tinction is that brasseries, which often resemble cafés, serve quicker meals and at most hours of the day, while restaurants tend to stick to the **traditional mealtimes** of noon until 2pm, and 7pm until 9.30 or 10.30pm.

The latest time at which you can walk into a restaurant and order is usually about 9.30 or 10pm, although once ensconced you can often remain well into the night. (Hours − last orders − are stated in the listings below, and unusually or specifically **late-night places** are included in the box on p.271.) After 9pm or so, some restaurants serve only *à la carte* meals, which invariably work out more expensive than eating the set menu. For the more upmarket places, it's wise to make **reservations** − easily done on the same day. When hunting, avoid places that are half-empty at peak time, and treat the business of sizing up different menus as an enjoyable appetizer in itself.

Prices

You should find a display of prices and what you get for them posted outside every restaurant. There is usually a choice between one or more **menus fixes**, where the number of courses for the stated price is fixed and the choice accordingly limited. There are numerous fixed-price menus **under 80F**, particularly at lunchtime, providing staple dishes of varying quality.

At that price, menus will be three courses with a choice of four to six entrées, three main courses, and three or four desserts. They will be fairly standard dishes, such as steak and chips (*steak frites*), chicken and chips (*poulet frites*), or various preparations of offal. Look for the *plat du jour*, which may be a regional dish and more appealing. You will also find **formules**, usually choices of a main dish plus starter or dessert.

The more you pay, the greater the choice. **Menus between 150F and 200F** offer a significantly more interesting range of dishes, including, probably, some regional and other specialities, and once **over 200F** you should get some serious gourmet satisfaction. Eating **à la carte**, of course, gives you access to everything on offer, plus complete freedom to construct your meal as you choose. But it will cost a great deal more. The *à la carte* prices we give are for an average three-course meal with half a bottle of wine. One simple and perfectly legitimate ploy is to have just one course instead of the expected three or more. There is no minimum charge.

Wine (*vin*) or a drink (*boisson*) may be included, though it is unlikely on menus under 100F. When ordering house wine (*vin ordinaire*), ask for *un pichet* (a small jug); they come in quarter- (*un quart*) or half-litres (*un demi*). A bottle of wine can easily add 80F to the bill.

Chain Restaurants

There are a number of French **restaurant chains** with addresses all over the city. Service is usually quick and there's no need to book, but they are not the best places in which to experience the ritual of a leisurely French meal.

The best is **L'Amanguier**, open daily till midnight, with a wide-choice 110F menu and an 88F *formule*. At 20 bd Montmartre, 9e; 46 bd Montparnasse, 15e; 51 rue du Théâtre, 15e; and 43 av des Ternes, 17e, 110 rue de Richelieu, 2e.

La Criée specializes in seafood and fish and is also dependable, offering menus at 119F with wine and 79F without: 31 bd Bonne-Nouvelle, 2e; 15 rue Lagrange, 5e; 54 bd du Montparnasse, 15e. Open till 1am.

Batifol, with 17 establishments throughout Paris, is fine but not very exciting (120F *à la carte*), and **Hippopotamus** (13 addresses), though a lot cheaper, is not particularly good. **Le Bistro Romain** has gone downhill and is desperately trying to wean back its old clientele with cheaper menus.

Service compris or s.c. means the **service charge** is included in the price of the fixed menu. Service non compris, s.n.c., or service en sus means it isn't, and you need to calculate an additional fifteen percent. The bill for a fixed-price menu will always include the service charge, so there is no need to leave a tip.

Student Restaurants

Students of any age are eligible to apply for tickets for the **university restaurants** under the direction of CROUS de Paris. A list of addresses, which includes numerous cafeterias and brasseries, is available from their offices at 39 av Georges-Bernanos, 5e (☎01.40.51.36.00; Mon–Fri 9am–5pm; Mº Port-Royal). The tickets, however, have to be obtained from the particular restaurant of your choice (opening hours generally 11.30am–2pm & 6–8pm). They will cost you 21.10F if you can produce an International Student Card; 26.40F otherwise.

Chapter 2: Île de la Cité

CAFÉS AND BARS

Taverne Henri IV, 13 place du Pont-Neuf, 1er (Mº Pont-Neuf). Mon–Fri noon–10pm, Sat noon–4.30pm; closed Sun & Aug. One of the good older wine bars, opposite Henri IV's statue. Yves Montand used to come here when Simone Signoret lived in the adjacent place Dauphine. Full of lawyers from the Palais de Justice. The food is good but a bit pricey for a full meal. Plates of meats and cheeses around 70F, sandwiches 30F, wine 25–50F a glass.

RESTAURANTS

Au Rendez-Vous des Camionneurs, 72 quai des Orfèvres, 1er: ☎01.43.54.88.74 (Mº St-Michel). Daily noon–2pm, 7–11.30pm. Crowded, traditional establishment serving snails, steaks and scallops. Two midday **menus** under 100F; evening menu 120F.

Eating and Drinking

Paris for Vegetarians

Vegetarians will find that French chefs have not yet grasped the idea that tasty and nutritious meals do not need to be based on meat or fish. Consequently, the chances of finding vegetarian main dishes on the menus of regular restaurants are not good. However, it is possible to have a vegetarian meal at even the most meat-oriented brasserie by choosing dishes from among the starters (crudités, for example, are nearly always available) and soups, or by asking for an omelette.

But you'll be far better off going to a vegetarian restaurant. There are not many, but the numbers are slowly increasing as ideas of health and vegetarian diet catch on (the moral/ecological motive is very rare amongst Parisians). All the establishments listed below are reviewed in the pages that follow.

Eating and Drinking

FOODS AND DISHES

Basics

Pain	Bread	*Sel*	Salt	*Couteau*	Knife
Beurre	Butter	*Sucre*	Sugar	*Cuillère*	Spoon
Oeufs	Eggs	*Vinaigre*	Vinegar	*Table*	Table
Lait	Milk	*Bouteille*	Bottle	*L'addition*	The bill
Huile	Oil	*Verre*	Glass		
Poivre	Pepper	*Fourchette*	Fork		

Snacks

Crêpe	Pancake (sweet)	*Omelette . . .*	Omelette . . .
au sucre	with sugar	*nature*	plain
au citron	with lemon	*aux fines herbes*	with herbs
au miel	with honey	*au fromage*	with cheese
à la confiture	with jam	*Salade de . . .*	Salad of . . .
aux oeufs	with eggs	*tomates*	tomatoes
à la crème	with chestnut	*betteraves*	beetroot
de marrons	purée	*concombres*	cucumber
Galette	Buckwheat (savoury) pancake	*carottes rapées*	grated carrots

Un sandwich/	A sandwich . . .	**Other fillings/salads**	
une baguette . . .		*Anchois*	Anchovy
jambon	with ham	*Andouillette*	Tripe sausage
fromage	with cheese	*Boudin*	Black pudding
saucisson	with sausage	*Coeurs de palmiers*	Palm hearts
à l'ail	with garlic	*Fonds d'artichauts*	Artichoke
au poivre	with pepper		hearts
pâté	with pâté	*Hareng*	Herring
(de campagne)	(country-style)	*Langue*	Tongue
croque-monsieur	Grilled cheese & ham sandwich	*Poulet*	Chicken
		Thon	Tuna
croque-madame	Grilled cheese & bacon, sausage, chicken or an egg	**And some terms**	
		Chauffé	Heated
panini	Flat toasted Italian sandwich	*Cuit*	Cooked
		Cru	Raw
Oeufs	Eggs	*Emballé*	Wrapped
au plat	fried	*A emporter*	Takeaway
à la coque	boiled	*Fumé*	Smoked
durs	hard-boiled	*Salé*	Salted/spicy
brouillés	scrambled	*Sucré*	Sweet

Soups (soupes)

Bisque	Shellfish soup	*Velouté*	Thick soup, usually made with fish or poultry
Bouillabaisse	Marseillais fish soup		
Bouillon	Broth or stock		
Bourride	Thick fish soup	**Starters (hors d'œuvres)**	
Consommé	Clear soup	*Assiette anglaise*	Plate of cold meats
Pistou	Parmesan, basil & garlic paste added to soup	*Crudités*	Raw vegetables with dressings
Potage	Thick vegetable soup	*Hors d'oeuvres*	Combination of the
Rouille	Red pepper, garlic & saffron mayonnaise with fish soup	*variés*	above, plus smoked or marinated fish

Fish (poisson), seafood (fruits de mer) and shellfish (crustaces or coquillages)

Anchois	Anchovies	*Moules (marinière)*	Mussels (with shallots in white wine sauce)
Anguilles	Eels		
Barbue	Brill		
Bigourneau	Periwinkle	*Oursin*	Sea urchin
Brème	Bream	*Palourdes*	Clams
Cabillaud	Cod	*Praires*	Small clams
Calmar	Squid	*Raie*	Skate
Carrelet	Plaice	*Rouget*	Red mullet
Claire	Type of oyster	*Saumon*	Salmon
Colin	Hake	*Sole*	Sole
Congre	Conger eel	*Thon*	Tuna
Coques	Cockles	*Truite*	Trout
Coquilles St-Jacques	Scallops	*Turbot*	Turbot
Crabe	Crab		
Crevettes grises	Shrimps		

Fish: dishes and terms

Crevettes roses	Prawns
Daurade	Sea bream
Eperlan	Smelt or whitebait
Escargots	Snails
Flétan	Halibut
Friture	Assorted fried fish
Gambas	King prawns
Hareng	Herring
Homard	Lobster
Huîtres	Oysters
Langouste	Spiny lobster
Langoustines	Saltwater crayfish (scampi)
Limande	Lemon sole
Lotte	Burbot
Lotte de mer	Monkfish
Loup de mer	Sea bass
Louvine, loubine	Similar to sea bass
Maquereau	Mackerel
Merlan	Whiting

Aïoli	Garlic mayonnaise served with salt cod & other fish
Béarnaise	Sauce made with egg yolks, white wine, shallots & vinegar
Beignets	Fritters
Darne	Fillet or steak
La douzaine	A dozen
Frit	Fried
Fumé	Smoked
Fumet	Fish stock
Gigot de mer	Large fish baked whole
Grillé	Grilled
Hollandaise	Butter & vinegar sauce
A la meunière	In a butter, lemon & parsley sauce
Mousse/ mousseline	Mousse
Quenelles	Light dumplings

Meat (viande) and poultry (volaille)

Agneau (de pré-salé)	Lamb (grazed on salt marshes)	*Contrefilet*	Sirloin roast
		Coquelet	Cockerel
Andouille, andouillette	Tripe sausage	*Dinde, dindon*	Turkey
		Entrecôte	Ribsteak
Boeuf	Beef	*Faux filet*	Sirloin steak
Bifteck	Steak	*Foie*	Liver
Boudin blanc	Sausage of white meats	*Foie gras*	Fattened (duck/ goose) liver
Boudin noir	Black pudding	*Gigot (d'agneau)*	Leg (of lamb)
Caille	Quail	*Grillade*	Grilled meat
Canard	Duck	*Hâchis*	Chopped meat or mince hamburger
Caneton	Duckling		(cont')

Eating and Drinking

Meat and poultry (continued)

Langue	Tongue	*Poulet*	Chicken
Lapin, lapereau	Rabbit, young rabbit	*Poussin*	Baby chicken
Lard, lardons	Bacon, diced bacon	*Ris*	Sweetbreads
Lièvre	Hare	*Rognons*	Kidneys
Merguez	Spicy, red sausage	*Rognons blancs*	Testicles
Mouton	Mutton	*Sanglier*	Wild boar
Museau de veau	Calf's muzzle	*Tête de veau*	Calf's head (in jelly)
Oie	Goose	*Tournedos*	Thick slices of fillet
Onglet	Cut of beef	*Tripes*	Tripe
Os	Bone	*Veau*	Veal
Porc	Pork	*Venaison*	Venison

Meat and poultry: dishes and terms

Aile	Wing	*Médaillon*	Round piece
Blanquette de veau	Veal in cream & mushroom sauce	*Mijoté*	Stewed
		Museau	Muzzle
Boeuf bourguignon	Beef stew with burgundy, onions & mushrooms	*Pavé*	Thick slice
		Rôti	Roast
		Sauté	Lightly cooked in butter
Canard à l'orange	Roast duck with an orange-and-wine sauce	*Steak au poivre (vert/rouge)*	Steak in a black (green/red) pepper corn sauce
Carré	Best end of neck, chop or cutlet	*Steak tartare*	Raw chopped beef, topped with a raw egg yolk
Cassoulet	A casserole of beans & meat		
Civit	Game stew	**For Steaks**	
Confit	Meat preserve	*Bleu*	Almost raw
Coq au vin	Chicken with wine, onions & mushrooms, cooked till it falls off the bone	*Saignant*	Rare
		A point	Medium
		Bien cuit	Well done
		Très bien cuit	Very well cooked
Côte	Chop, cutlet or rib	*Brochette*	Kebab
Cou	Neck		
Cuisse	Thigh or leg	**Garnishes and sauces**	
Daube, estouffade, hochepôt, navarin and *ragoût*	All are types of stew	*Beurre blanc*	Sauce of white wine & shallots, with butter
		Chasseur	White wine, mushrooms & shallots
En croûte	In pastry	*Diable*	Strong mustard seasoning
Épaule	Shoulder		
Farci	Stuffed	*Forestière*	With bacon & mushroom
Au feu de bois	Cooked over wood fire		
Au four	Baked	*Fricassée*	Rich, creamy sauce
Garni	With vegetables	*Mornay*	Cheese sauce
Gésier	Gizzard	*Pays d'Auge*	Cream & cider
Grillé	Grilled	*Piquante*	Gherkins or capers, vinegar & shallots
Magret de canard	Duck breast		
Marmite	Casserole	*Provençale*	Tomatoes, garlic, olive oil & herbs

Vegetables (légumes), herbs (herbes) and spices (épices), etc

Eating and Drinking

Ail	Garlic	*rouges*	kidney
Algue	Seaweed	*beurres*	butter
Anis	Aniseed	*Laurier*	Bay leaf
Artichaut	Artichoke	*Lentilles*	Lentils
Asperges	Asparagus	*Maïs*	Corn
Avocat	Avocado	*Menthe*	Mint
Basilic	Basil	*Moutarde*	Mustard
Betterave	Beetroot	*Oignon*	Onion
Carotte	Carrot	*Pâte*	Pasta or pastry
Céleri	Celery	*Persil*	Parsley
Champignons,	Mushrooms of	*Petits pois*	Peas
cèpes,	various kinds	*Piment*	Pimento
chanterelles		*Pois chiche*	Chickpeas
Chou (rouge)	(Red) cabbage	*Pois mange-tout*	Snow peas
Chou-fleur	Cauliflower	*Pignons*	Pine nuts
Ciboulettes	Chives	*Poireau*	Leek
Concombre	Cucumber	*Poivron*	Sweet pepper
Cornichon	Gherkin	*(vert, rouge)*	(green, red)
Échalotes	Shallots	*Pommes (de terre)*	Potatoes
Endive	Chicory	*Primeurs*	Spring vegetables
Épinards	Spinach	*Radis*	Radishes
Estragon	Tarragon	*Riz*	Rice
Fenouil	Fennel	*Safran*	Saffron
Flageolet	White beans	*Salade verte*	Green salad
Gingembre	Ginger	*Sarrasin*	Buckwheat
Haricots	Beans	*Tomate*	Tomato
verts	string (French)	*Truffes*	Truffles

Vegetables: dishes and terms

Beignet	Fritter	*Jardinière*	With mixed diced
Farci	Stuffed		vegetables
Gratiné	Browned with cheese	*Sauté*	Lightly fried in butter
	or butter	*À la vapeur*	Steamed
À la	Sautéed in butter	*Je suis*	I'm a vegetarian.
parisienne	(potatoes); with white	*végétarien(ne).*	
	wine sauce & shallots	*Il y a quelques*	Are there any
Parmentier	With potatoes	*plats sans viande?*	non-meat dishes?

Fruits (fruits) and nuts (noix)

Abricot	Apricot	*Fraises (de bois)*	Strawberries (wild)
Amandes	Almonds	*Framboises*	Raspberries
Ananas	Pineapple	*Fruit de la passion*	Passion fruit
Banane	Banana	*Groseilles*	Redcurrants &
Brugnon, nectarine	Nectarine		gooseberries
Cacahouète	Peanut	*Mangue*	Mango
Cassis	Blackcurrants	*Marrons*	Chestnuts
Cérises	Cherries	*Melon*	Melon
Citron	Lemon	*Myrtilles*	Bilberries
Citron vert	Lime	*Noisette*	Hazelnut
Figues	Figs	*Noix*	Nuts
			(cont')

Eating and Drinking

Fruits and nuts (continued)

Orange	Orange	*Raisins*	Grapes
Pamplemousse	Grapefruit		
Pêche (blanche)	(White) peach	**Fruit: terms**	
Pistache	Pistachio	*Beignets*	Fritters
Poire	Pear	*Compôte de . . .*	Stewed . . .
Pomme	Apple	*Coulis*	Sauce
Prune	Plum	*Flambé*	Set aflame in alcohol
Pruneau	Prune	*Frappé*	Iced

Desserts (desserts or entremets) and pastries (pâtisserie)

Barquette	Small boat-shaped flan	*Île flottante/ oeufs à la neige*	Soft meringues floating on custard
Bavarois	Refers to the mould, could be mousse or custard	*Macarons*	Macaroons
		Madeleine	Small sponge cake
		Marrons	Chestnut purée &
Bombe	A moulded ice-cream dessert	*Mont Blanc*	cream on a rum-soaked sponge cake
Brioche	Sweet, high yeast breakfast roll	*Mousse au chocolat*	Chocolate mousse
		Palmiers	Caramelized puff pastries
Charlotte	Custard & fruit in lining of almond fingers	*Parfait*	Frozen mousse, sometimes ice-cream
Coupe	A serving of ice-cream	*Petit Suisse*	A smooth mixture of cream & curds
Crème Chantilly	Vanilla-flavoured & sweetened whipped cream	*Petits fours*	Bite-sized cakes/ pastries
Crème fraîche	Sour cream	*Poires Belle Hélène*	Pears & ice-cream in chocolate sauce
Crème pâtissière	Thick eggy pastry-filling		
Crêpe	Pancake	*Sablé*	Shortbread biscuit
Crêpe suzette	Thin pancake with orange juice & liqueur	*Savarin*	A filled, ring-shaped cake
		Tarte	Tart
Fromage blanc	Cream cheese	*Tartelette*	Small tart
Galette	Buckwheat pancake	*Truffes*	Truffles, chocolate or liqueur variety
Gênoise	Rich sponge cake	*Yaourt, yogourt*	Yoghurt
Glace	Ice-cream		

Cheese (fromage)

There are over 400 types of French cheese, most of them named after their place of origin. *Chèvre* is goat's cheese. *Le plateau de fromages* is the cheeseboard, and bread – but not butter – is served with it.

Addressing the waiter or waitress

Always call the waiter or waitress *Monsieur* or *Madame* (*Mademoiselle* if a young woman), never *garçon*, no matter what you've been taught in school.

Chapter 3: Along La Voie Triomphale

CAFÉS AND BARS

Angélina, 226 rue de Rivoli, 1er (Mº Tuileries). Daily 9am–7pm; closed Aug. A long-established gilded cage, where the well-coiffed sip the best hot chocolate in town. *Pâtisseries* and other desserts of the same high quality. Not cheap.

La Boutique à Sandwiches, 12 rue du Colisée, 8e (Mº St-Philippe-du-Roule). Mon–Sat 11.45am–11.30pm; closed Aug. Not the best sandwiches in the world, but certainly cheap for this part of town, plus there's *raclette* and *steak frites* for under 80F at the counter.

Café de la Comédie, 153 rue Rivoli, 1er (Mº Palais-Royal/Musée-du-Louvre). Tues–Sun 10am–midnight. Small café opposite the Comédie Française, complete with a mirror painted with theatrical scenes at the back.

Café Marly, Cour Napoléon du Louvre, 93 rue de Rivoli, 1er (Mº Palais-Royal/Musée-du-Louvre). Daily to 2am. Inside the Louvre, with tables beneath the colonnade overlooking the Pyramid; very chic, very classy and very expensive.

Café Véry, Jardin des Tuileries, 1er (Mº Concorde). Daily 11am–midnight. The best of an ever-increasing number of snack bars in the gardens. Ice-creams, sandwiches, cold beers, etc.

E. Fahy Patissier, 165 rue du Faubourg-St-Honoré, 8e (Mº St-Philippe-du-Roule/George-V). Open weekdays at midday. A *boulangerie* selling sandwiches, tarts, quiches, ready-made salads to take away or eat in a corner at the back.

Fauchon, 24 place de la Madeleine, 8e (Mº Madeleine). Mon–Sat 9.45am–6.30pm. Narrow and uncomfortable counters at which to gobble wonderful *pâtisseries*, *plats du jour* and sandwiches – at a price.

Le Fouquet's, 99 av des Champs-Élysées, 8e (Mº George-V). Daily till 1.30am. Such a well-established watering hole for stars of the stage and screen, politicians, newspaper editors

and advertising barons, that it's now been classified as a *Monument Historique*. You pay dearly to sit in the deep leather armchairs and, as for the restaurant, don't expect any change from 300F.

Le Griffonier, 6 rue des Saussaires, 8e (Mº Champs-Élysées). Mon–Fri 8am–9pm. Well-paid office types in this small wine bar with a good selection of Loire wines at 21–20F a glass.

Osaka, 163 rue St-Honoré, 1er (Mº Palais-Royal). Daily noon–2pm & 7–10pm. Japanese snack bar with meals for 60F. More expensive sushi, sushimi and tempura bar on the left.

Restorama, Le Carrousel du Louvre, 1er (Mº Louvre). Daily 9am–9pm. One vast underground fast-food eating hall served by over a dozen different outlets: *rôtisseries*, hamburgers, pizzas, Tex-Mex, Chinese, Lebanese, Japanese, *crêperies*, salad bars . . . easy to eat for under 40F. Access from place du Carrousel or the Louvre Pyramid.

RESTAURANTS

Aux Amis du Beaujolais, 28 rue d'Artois, 8e; ☎01.45.63.92.21 (Mº George-V/St-Philippe-du-Roule). Mon–Sat noon–3pm & 6.30–9pm; closed middle two weeks of July. If you can fathom the hand-written menu, you'll find good traditional French dishes of stews and sautéed steaks, and Beaujolais. Around 150F.

Barry's, 9 rue Duras, 8e (Mº Champs-Élysées/Clemenceau). Mon–Sat 11am–3pm. Salads, snacks and sandwiches for under 30F in a tiny street behind the Élysée palace.

Le Dauphin, 167 rue St-Honoré, 1er; ☎01.42.60.40.11 (Mº Palais-Royal/Musée-du-Louvre). Daily noon–2.30pm & 7–11.30pm; June–Oct till 12.30am. A genuine *bistrot* with menus at 79F & 135F. Seafood platter for 167F. Excellent *lapereau* (young rabbit) *à la grand-mère* and *magnet de canard*.

Dragons Élysées, 11 rue de Berri, 8e; ☎01.42.89.85.10 (Mº George-V). Daily till

See p.271 for a list of cafés and restaurants that stay open late.

Some of Paris' top gourmet restaurants are listed on p.274.

Eating and Drinking

See p.235 for a list of vegetarian restaurants in Paris.

Our glossary of French food and dishes begins on p.236.

11.30pm. The Chinese-Thai cuisine encompasses dim sum, curried seafood and baked mussels, but the overriding attraction is the extraordinary décor. Beneath a floor of glass tiles water runs from pool to pool inhabited by exotic fish. Water even pours down part of one wall, and on the ceiling pinpoints of light imitate stars. And all this amid the usual *chinoiserie* of red lanterns and black furniture. 75F menu, 200F Thai seafood menu, *carte* 250F.

L'Élysées Bar Restaurant, 134 rue du Faubourg-St-Honoré, 8e (Mº St-Philippe-du-Roule). Tues–Sat noon–2.30pm & 7–9.30pm. Tables outside for *gigot d'agneau* (72F) and *steak tartare frites* (73F).

La Fermette Marbeuf 1900, 5 rue Marbeuf, 8e; ☎01.47.23.31.31 (Mº Franklin-D-Roosevelt). Daily until 11.30pm. Try to eat in the tiled and domed inner room, where the original Art Nouveau décor has been restored. A rather well-heeled clientele, foreign as well as French, but not stuffy. A good inclusive menu for 175F; *carte* up to 350F.

Le Jardin du Royal Monceau, Hôtel Royal Monceau, 35 av Hoche, 8e (Mº Charles-de-Gaulle/Étoile). Daily noon–2.30pm & 7–11pm. Seriously good food in a luxury hotel. *A la carte* will set you back 500F or more, but there's a midday menu for 280F.

Planet Hollywood, 78 av Champs-Élysées, 8e; ☎01.53.83.78.27 (Mº George-V). Mon–Fri 11.30am–1am, Sat 11am–1am. Parisians adore this Californian import. The entrance is a marketing franchise; you descend to the bar and restaurant, where models of filmstars and props plus soundtracks provide a Hollywood ambience. Expensive American and French food; bar drinks 35F.

Prince de Galles, 33 av George-V, 8e; ☎01.47.23.55.11 (Mº George-V). Daily noon–2.30pm & 7–10.30pm. A blow-out place for Sun lunch, with a choice of three entrées, three main courses and three puds in very classy surroundings

for under 200F – so long as you only drink water.

Le Relais du Sud-Ouest, 154 rue St-Honoré, 1er; ☎01.42.60.62.01 (Mº Palais-Royal/Musée-du-Louvre). Mon–Sat till 10.30pm. An ancient map of the southwest of France hangs on the wall; there's an old kitchen range, and traditional southwest specialities are served at candlelit tables. Good value on the 85F menu.

Restaurant Le Café St-Honoré, 95 rue St-Honoré, 1er; ☎01.42.86.08.72. (Mº Louvre-Rivoli). Mon–Sat till 9.30pm. Small, old-style resto serving traditional French food. Menus at 160F and 200F.

Yvan, 1bis rue J-Mermoz, 8e; ☎01.43.59.18.40 (Mº Franklin-D-Roosevelt). Mon–Fri noon–2.30pm & 7pm–midnight, closed Sat lunchtime & Sun. Fish specialities and pigeon with polenta attract a stylish clientele. Extremely good food and menus from 168F.

Chapter 4: Right Bank Commerce, the Passages and Les Halles

Grands Boulevards, the Opéra and Madeleine

CAFÉS AND BARS

Le Grand Café Capucines, 4 bd des Capucines, 9e (Mº Opéra). A favourite all-nighter with over-the-top *belle époque* décor and excellent seafood. Boulevard prices mean 20F for an espresso.

Kitty O'Shea's, 10 rue des Capucines, 2e (Mº Opéra). Noon–1.30am. An Irish pub with excellent *Guinness* and *Smithwicks*. A favourite haunt of Irish expats. The *John Jameson* restaurant upstairs serves high-quality, pricey, Gaelic food, including seafood flown in from Galway.

La Taverne Kronenbourg, 24 bd des Italiens, 9e (Mº Opéra). Daily till 3am. Silver chandeliers, clocks, bells and old shop signs decorate this otherwise typical boulevard brasserie. *Plats du jour* from 76F, menu 140F.

RESTAURANTS

Chartier, 7 rue du Faubourg-Montmartre, 9e; ☎01.47.70.86.29 (Mº Montmartre). Mon–Sat till 11pm. Brown linoleum floor, dark-stained woodwork, brass hat-racks, clusters of white globes suspended from the high ceiling, mirrors, waiters in long aprons – the original décor of a turn-of-the-century soup kitchen. Worth seeing and, though crowded and rushed, the food is not bad at all. Under 100F.

Country Life, 6 rue Daunou, 2e; ☎01.42.97.48.51 (Mº Opéra). Mon–Sat 11.30am–2.30pm only. Vegetarian soup, *hors d'œuvres*, lasagne and salad for under 70F. Menu details gluten and soya contents. No alcohol, no smoking.

Drouot, 103 rue de Richelieu, 2e; ☎01.42.96.68.23 (Mº Richelieu-Drouot). Daily noon–3pm & 6.30–10pm. Same management as *Chartier*; Admirably cheap food served at a frantic pace, in Art Deco surroundings. Menu around 80F.

Au Petit Riche, 25 rue Le Peletier, 9e; ☎01.47.70.68.68 (Mº Richelieu-Drouot). Mon–Sat till 12.15am; closed second half of Aug. A long-established restaurant with a mirrored 1900s interior. Prompt and attentive service, good food. Very much a business hang-out. Menu at 160F.

Passages, Palais-Royal Garden & Bibliothéque National

CAFÉS AND BARS

L'Arbre à Cannelle, 57 passage des Panoramas, 2e (Mº Rue-Montmartre). Mon–Sat till 6.30pm. Exquisite wooden panelling, frescoes and painted ceilings; puddings, flans and *assiettes gourmandes* for 54–70F.

Le Bar de l'Entracte, on the corner of rue Montpensier and rue Beaujolais, 1er (Mº Palais-Royal/Musée-du-Louvre). Mon–Sat 10am–2am. Theatre people, bankers and journalists come for quick snacks of *gratin de pomme de terre* and Auvergnat ham in this almost traffic-free spot. Fills up to bursting during the inter-vals at the Palais-Royal theatre just down the road.

Aux Bons Crus, 7 rue des Petits-Champs, 1er (Mº Palais-Royal). Mon–Fri 11am–10pm, Sat 11am–6pm. A relaxed workaday place that has been serving good wines and cheese, sausage and ham for over eighty years. Wine from 10F a glass; plate of cold meats from 30F.

Juveniles, 47 rue de Richelieu, 2e (Mº Palais-Royal). Mon–Sat noon–midnight. Very popular tiny wine bar run by a Brit. Wine from 68F a bottle; *plats du jour* around 68F.

La Muscade, Galerie de Montpensier, 1er (Mº Palais-Royal/Musée-du-Louvre). Daily noon–9pm. Smart café in the Palais Royal gardens where the hot chocolates, fruit and herb teas and cakes are superb (served 3–6.15pm).

Le Panini, cnr passage des Princes and rue Richelieu, 2e (Mº Richelieu-Drouot). Completely uninspired décor but who cares when you can sit at the counter and have a strong coffee with a chocolate and a macaroon for just 6F.

RESTAURANTS

Le Grand Colbert, passage Colbert, rue Vivienne, 2e; ☎01.42.86.87.88 (Mº Bourse). Daily noon–2pm & 7.30pm–1am; closed mid-July to mid-Aug. In the same high style as the *passage* in which it's situated. Solid French cooking – *canard confit* and *andouillette* – and a 160F menu including wine.

Le Grand Véfour, 17 rue de Beaujolais, 1er; ☎01.42.96.56.27 (Mº Pyramides/Bourse). Mon–Fri 12.30–2pm & 7.30–10pm, Sat 7.30–10pm. The carved wooden ceilings, frescoes, velvet hangings and late eighteenth-century chairs haven't changed since Napoléon brought Josephine here. Considering the luxuriance of the *cuisine*, the lunchtime menu for 305F is a cinch. Go *à la carte* and the bill could top 800F.

L'Incroyable, 26 rue de Richelieu, 1er; ☎01.42.96.24.64 (Mº Palais-Royal).

Eating and Drinking

Eating and Drinking

Some of Paris' top gourmet restaurants are listed on p.274.

Tues–Thurs lunchtime & 6.30–9pm, Sat & Mon lunch only; closed Sun & two weeks at Christmas. Hidden in a tiny *passage*, this very pleasant restaurant serves decent meals for 65F at midday and 75F in the evening.

Restaurant Végétarien Lacour, 3 rue Villedo, 1er; ☎01.42.96.08.33 (Mº Pyramides). Mon–Sat noon–2.15pm. Vegetarian lunches for under 50F.

Le Vaudeville, 29 rue Vivienne, 2e; ☎01.40.20.04.62 (Mº Bourse). Daily till 2am. A lively late-night brasserie where it's often necessary to queue. Good food, attractive marble-and-mosaic interior. *A la carte* from 150F. 115F menu after 10pm.

Clothes, Sex, the Stock Exchange and News

CAFÉS AND BARS

Le Café, 62 rue Tiquetonne, 2e (Mº Les Halles/Étienne-Marcel). Daily 10am–2am. On the junction with rue Étienne-Marcel; quiet and secluded with people playing chess and old maps adorning the walls. *Plats du jour* 45–55F.

Du Croissant, cnr rue du Croissant and rue Montmartre, 2e (Mº Montmartre). On July 31, 1914, the Socialist and pacifist leader Jean Jaurès was assassinated in this café for his anti-war activities. The table he was sitting at still remains.

Lina's Sandwiches, 8 rue Marbeuf, 8e (Mº Alma-Marceau); also at 50 rue Étienne-Marcel, 2e (Mº Étienne-Marcel) and 27 rue St-Sulpice, 6e (Mº St-Sulpice). Mon–Sat 9am–7pm. Excellent sandwiches; plus salads, soups, brownies and breakfasts – ideal for a designer- or window-shopping break.

Riva Sandwichs, 4 rue du IV-Septembre, 2e (Mº Bourse). Mon 11am–8pm, Tues–Sat 11am–midnight. Cybercafé with cheap coffee and snacks in clinical pale green décor.

Le Rubis, 10 rue du Marché-St-Honoré, 1er (Mº Pyramides). Mon–Fri 7am–10pm, Sat 8am–4pm; closed mid-Aug. One of the oldest wine bars, with a reputation

for excellent wines, snacks and *plats du jour*. Very small and very crowded. Glasses of wine from 5.50F.

Le Tambour, 41 rue Montmartre, 2e (Mº Sentier). Open 24 hours daily. A local habitués' café, with photos above the bar of old Les Halles traders. Coffee not brilliant.

RESTAURANTS

La Champmeslé, 4 rue Chabanais, 2e (Mº Pyramides). Daily 6pm–2am. Lesbian bar, with two rooms reserved for women, and one room for mixed company. Cocktails (from 45F), picture/photo exhibitions, and Thurs night cabaret.

Dilan, 13 rue Mandar, 2e; ☎01.42.21.14.88 (Mº Les Halles/Sentier). Daily noon–2pm & 7.30–11pm; closed Sat & Sun midday. An excellent-value Kurdish restaurant. Beautiful starters, stuffed aubergines (*babaqunuc*), fish with yoghurt and courgettes (*kanarya*). Midday menu 60F.

Foujita, 41 rue St-Roche, 1er; ☎01.42.61.42.93 (Mº Tuileries/Pyramides). Mon–Sat noon–2.15pm & 7.30–10pm; closed mid-Aug. One of the cheaper but best Japanese restaurants, as proven by the numbers of Japanese eating here. Quick and crowded; soup, sushis, rice and tea for 71F at lunchtime; plate of sushis or sushimis for under 100F.

La Taverne du Nil, 9 rue du Nil, 2e; ☎01.42.33.51.82 (Mº Sentier). Sun–Fri till 11pm, closed Sun lunchtime & Aug. Very good Lebanese food; delicious lamb kebabs and *mezze*. Menus from 60F to 182F.

Les Halles

CAFÉS AND BARS

A la Cloche des Halles, 28 rue Coquillière, 1er (Mº Châtelet-Les Halles/Louvre). Open till 8.30pm, closed Sat eve & Sun. The bell hanging over this little wine bar is the one that used to mark the end of trading in the market halls. Though today's noise is from traffic on this busy corner, you are assured of some very fine wines.

Le Cochon à l'Oreille, 15 rue Montmartre, 1er (Mº Châtelet-Les Halles/Étienne-Marcel). Mon–Sat 7am–5pm. This classic little café, with raffia chairs outside and scenes of the old market in ceramic tiles inside, opens early for the local fishmongers and meat traders.

L'Eustache, 37 rue Berger, 1er (Mº Les Halles). Daily till 2am. A traditional brasserie, in marked contrast to the trendy *Le Comptoir* next door, with line jazz in the evening on weekends. *Plats du jours* 60–80F.

Palabres, 44 rue St-Honoré, 1er (Mº Louvre-Rivoli/Châtelet). Daily 8am–8pm. Light and attractive *salon de thé*, decorated with South American "palaver" (*palabre*). Soup and savoury *tarte* for 40F.

Au Père Tranquille, on the corner of rues Pierre-Lescot and des Pécheurs, 1er (Mº Châtelet-Les Halles). Daily till 2am. One of the big Les Halles cafés, overlooking the favoured stage where clowns make fools of passers-by against the backdrop of the horrid mirror structures. Expensive.

Au Pomelle, 19 rue du Roule, 1er (Mº Louvre-Rivoli). Tiny old-fashioned bar with a low zinc counter and newspapers on wooden batons.

Self-Service de la Samaritaine, Magasin 2, rue de la Monnaie, 1er (Mº Pont-Neuf). Mon–Sat 9.30am–7pm, Thurs in summer 9.30am–9pm. In the number two *magasin*. The view over the Seine is probably

more of an attraction than the food, though that isn't bad for the price (around 80F menu midday only).

Le Sous-Bock, 49 rue St-Honoré, 1er (Mº Châtelet-Les Halles). Daily 11am–5am. Hundreds of bottled beers (around 33F a pint) and whiskies to sample, plus simple, inexpensive food. Mussels a speciality (45–60F). Frequented by night owls. Happy hour 3–7pm.

Au Trappiste, 4 rue St-Denis, 1er (Mº Châtelet). Daily 11am–2am. Numerous draught beers include *Jenlain*, France's best-known *bière de garde*, Belgian *Blanche Riva* and *Kriek* from the *Mort Subite* (Sudden Death) brewery – plus mussels and *frites* for 69F and various *tartines*.

RESTAURANTS

Aux Deux Saules, 91 rue St-Denis, 1er; ☎01.42.36.46.57 (Mº Châtelet-Les Halles). Daily till 1am. Cheap if unexciting dishes. A leftover from the days of the market; the tile work representing this is its best feature.

La Fresque, 100 rue Rambuteau, 1er; ☎01.42.33.17.56 (Mº Étienne-Marcel/Les Halles). Daily till midnight; closed Sun midday. Nicely dingy with the old décor of a snail merchant's hall appearing through the gloom. 65F midday menu with wine. *Carte* 120F.

L'Ostrea, 4 rue Sauval, 1er; ☎01.40.26.08.07 (Mº Louvre-Rivoli/Châtelet). Till 11pm; closed Sat lunchtime, Sun & Aug. Pretty fish and

Eating and Drinking

See p.261 for a list of the various ethnic restaurants in Paris.

Chartier

One hundred years old in March 1996, *Chartier* was first opened in 1896 by Camille and Frédéric Chartier. Their idea was to provide affordable meals for those who could not manage regular restaurant prices. It was a roaring success, coinciding as it did with the arrival in Paris of tens of thousands of people escaping the poverty and hardship of life in the hills of the Massif Central: the *bougnats*, as they were called, in imitation of their accents and the fact that so many of them were involved in the charcoal industry – *charbougna*. It spawned some thirty similar establishments, but the original *Chartier* is the only one to have survived. And little changes at *Chartier*: same staff and same customers for years and years. The current owner has been in residence for fifty years, and he is only the fourth since 1896.

Eating and Drinking

seafood restaurant. *Plateau de fruits de mer* for two 350F; *moules* from 65F.

Le Petit Ramoneur, 74 rue St-Denis, 1er; ☎01.42.36.39.24 (Mº Châtelet-Les Halles). Mon–Fri until 9.30pm; closed end Aug. Elbow-rubbing cheapie in good *bistrot* tradition, with cheap wine that's better than table wine. Crowded, but a welcome and genuine relief in Les Halles. 68F menu including wine.

Au Pied de Cochon, 6 rue Coquillière, 1er; ☎01.42.36.11.75 (Mº Châtelet-Les Halles). Open 24 hours. For extravagant middle-of-the-night pork chops and oysters. Menus from 119F, *carte* up to 300F.

La Tour de Montlhéry (Chez Denise), 5 rue des Prouvaires, 1er; ☎01.42.36.21.82 (Mº Louvre-Rivoli/Châtelet). Till midnight; closed Sat evening & Sun. An old-style Les Halles *bistrot* serving substantial food; always crowded and smoky; *carte* from 200F.

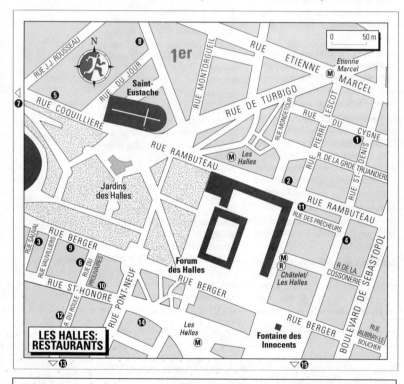

RESTAURANTS

1 Aux Deux Saules
2 La Fresque
3 L'Ostrea
4 Le Petit Ramoneur
5 Au Pied de Cochon
6 La Tour de Montlhéry (Chez Denise)

CAFÉS AND BARS

7 A la Cloche des Halles
8 Le Cochon à l'Oreille
9 L'Eustache
10 Palabres
11 Au Père Tranquille
12 Au Pomelle

13 Self-Service de la Samaritaine
14 Le Sous-Bock
15 Au Trappiste

Chapter 5: Beaubourg, the Marais, Île St-Louis and the Bastille

Beaubourg and Hôtel de Ville

CAFÉS AND BARS

Café Beaubourg, 43 rue St-Merri, 4e (Mº Rambuteau). Until 1am Mon–Thurs & Sun till 1am, Sat till 2am. An intellectuals' haunt designed by Christain de Partzamparc and overlooking Beaubourg's piazza; expensive, rather sour service, and very stylish loos.

Cyberia, Centre Pompidou, 43. Mon & Wed–Fri noon–10pm, Sat & Sun 10am–10pm. Cybercafé within Beaubourg, above the ticket office. 30F for 30min connection.

Dame Tartine, 2 rue Brise-Miche, 4º (Mº Rambuteau/Hôtel-de-Ville). Daily noon–11.30pm. Overlooking the Stravinsky pool, serving particularly delicious open toasted sandwiches (27–40F). Inside, decorated with kids' pictures.

Le Petit Marcel, 63 rue Rambuteau, 3e (Mº Rambuteau). Mon–Sat till 2am. Speckled tabletops, mirrors and Art Nouveau tiles, cracked and faded ceiling and about eight square metres of drinking space. Friendly barman and "local" atmosphere.

RESTAURANTS

Les Fous d'en Face, 3 rue du Bourg-Tibourg, 4e; ☎01.48.87.03.75 (Mº Hôtel-de-Ville). Daily till midnight. Delightful little restaurant and wine bar serving wonderful marinated salmon and scallops. Midday menu under 100F, otherwise *carte* 200F upwards.

Le Grizli, 7 rue St-Martin, 4e; ☎01.48.87.77.56 (Mº Châtelet). Mon–Sat till 11pm. Turn-of-the-century *bistrot* serving superb food with specialities from the Pyrenees. 110F midday menu, 145F evening.

Le Quincampe, 78 rue Quincampoix, 3e; ☎01.40.27.01.45 (Mº Étienne-

Marcel/Rambuteau/*RER* Châtelet). Till 10.45pm, closed Mon pm & Sun. Moroccan restaurant where you can eat around a real fire in the *salon* at the back; pleasant atmosphere and high quality food; tagines 60–70F, *pastilla* 80F.

The Marais

CAFÉS AND BARS

L'Apparemment Café, 18 rue des Coutures-St-Servais, 3e (Mº St-Sébastien-Froissart). Daily till 2am. Chic but cosy café resembling a series of comfortable sitting-rooms, with quiet corners and deep sofas. Cocktails from 50F.

Bar Central, 33 rue Vieille-du-Temple (cnr rue Ste-Croix-de-la-Bretonnerie), 4e (Mº St-Paul). Daily noon–2am. One of the most popular gay bars in the Marais.

Bar de Jarente, 5 rue de Jarente, 4e (Mº St-Paul). A lovely old-fashioned café-bar remaining nonchalantly indifferent to the shifting trends that surround it.

Le Bouchon du Marais, 15 rue François-Miron, 4e; ☎01.48.87.44.13 (Mº St-Paul). Mon–Sat 10am–3pm & 7.30pm–2am. A small relaxed wine *bistrot* serving the patron's own wines from Touraine. Sandwiches as well as meals. 70F–180F.

Le Coude Fou, 12 rue du Bourg-Tibourg, 4e (Mº Hôtel-de-Ville). Daily noon–4pm & 6pm–midnight; Happy Hour 5–7pm weekdays; closed Sun lunchtime. A popular, rather pricey wine bar, which serves some good and unusual wines, *charcuterie* and cheese.

L'Ébouillanté, 6 rue des Barres, 4e (Mº Hôtel-de-Ville). Tues–Sun noon–10pm, 9pm in winter. Tiny *salon de thé* in a picturesque street behind the church of St-Gervais, with reasonable prices and simple fare – chocolate cakes and *pâtisseries* as well as savoury dishes. *Plats du jour* for 60F.

Les Enfants Gâtés, 43 rue des Francs-Bourgeois, 4e (Mº St-Paul). Daily noon–8pm. Deep armchairs, painting exhibitions and snacks such as goat's cheese and tarragon tart (40F).

Eating and Drinking

See p.235 list of vegetarian restaurants in Paris.

See p.271 for a list of cafés and restaurants that stay open late.

Eating and Drinking

Our glossary of French food and dishes begins on p.236.

L'Enoteca, 25 rue Charles-V, 4e; ☎01.42.78.91.44 (Mº St-Paul). Open noon–2pm & 7pm–midnight. A very pleasant and fashionable Italian *bistrot à vins*. *Plats* between 60F and 70F.

Épices et Délices, 53 rue Vieille-du-Temple, 4e (Mº St-Paul). Daily till midnight. Restaurant and *salon de thé* with very pleasant service and food. Aubergine *gratin* 80F. 85F evening menu.

Ma Bourgogne, 19 place des Vosges, 3e (Mº St-Paul). Daily until 12.30am or 1am in summer. A quiet and pleasant arty café with tables under the arcades on the northwest corner of the square. Best in the morning when the sun hits this side of the square. Serves somewhat pricey meals too.

La Perla, 26 rue François-Miron (cnr rue du Pont-Louis-Philippe), 4e (Mº St-Paul). Daily noon–2am. A spacious trendy corner café specializing in things Mexican. The tequila cocktails are especially good (average price 48F). Snacks from around 40F, and meals too, though these are best avoided.

Au Petit Fer à Cheval, 30 rue Vieille-du-Temple, 4e (Mº St-Paul). Mon–Fri 9am–2am, Sat–Sun 11am–2am; food noon–midnight. Very attractive small *bistrot*/bar with trad décor. Good wine, excellent *gigot d'agneau à romarin* for 62F and other good-value *plats*.

Le Pick-Clops, 16 rue Vieille-du-Temple (cnr rue du Roi-de-Sicile), 4e (Mº Hôtel-de-Ville). Daily until 2am. An attractive, easy-going bar, popular with the youngish and hippish.

Le Quetzal, 10 rue de la Verrerie (cnr rue Moussy), 4e (Mº St-Paul). Daily until 3am. A fashionable and stylish gay bar, with space for dancing.

Le Rouge Gorge, 8 rue St-Paul, 4e (Mº St-Paul). Mon–Sat noon–1am. The young and enthusiastic clientele sip familiar wines and snack on *chèvre chaud* and smoked salmon salad, or tuck into more substantial fare (*plats du jour* around 60F) while listening to jazz or classical music.

Sacha Finkelsztajn, 27 rue des Rosiers, 4e (Wed–Sun 9.30am–1.30pm & 3–7.30pm) and 24 rue des Écouffes, 4e (Mon & Thurs–Sun 9.30am–1.30pm & 3–7.30pm). Both Mº St-Paul. Marvellous for takeaway snacks and goodies: gorgeous East European breads, cakes, *gefilte* fish, aubergine purée, tarama, *blinis* and *borscht*.

La Tartine, 24 rue de Rivoli, 4e (Mº St-Paul). Wed–Mon until 10pm; closed Aug. The genuine 1900s article, which still cuts across class boundaries in its clientele. A good selection of affordable wines, plus excellent cheese and *saucisson* with *pain de campagne*.

Le Trumilou, 84 quai Hôtel-de-Ville 4e; ☎01.42.77.63.98 (Mº Pont-Marie). Daily till 11pm. The Parisian equivalent of a diner. Pigs' trotters, Lyonnais sausage, and wonderful sweet chestnut charlotte. 70F and 85F menus.

Le Volcan de Sicile, 62 rue du Roi-de-Sicile, 4e (Mº Hôtel-de-Ville). Flooded with sunshine at midday, this is *the* café to sit and sip on the corner of the exquisite and minuscule place Tibourg.

Yahalom, 22–24 rue des Rosiers, 4e (Mº St-Paul). Kosher *falafel* 23F; *plats du jour* 45F.

Le Zinc, 4 rue Caron, 4e (Mº St-Paul). Daily 11am–2am, Sun 8.30am–6pm. A small modern bar run by a rugby and Guinness fan. Food costs 60–80F.

RESTAURANTS

L'Ambroisie, 9 place des Vosges, 4e; ☎01.42.78.51.45 (Mº Chemin-Vert/St-Paul). Daily till 10.30pm; closed first three weeks in Aug plus Sun & Mon during school holidays. Scoring 18 out of 20 in the gourmet's bible *Gault et Millau*, this is exquisite food in an exquisite location, costing 600F upwards. Booking imperative.

Aquarius 1, 54 rue Ste-Croix-de-la-Bretonnerie, 4e; ☎01.48.87.48.71 (Mº St-Paul/Rambuteau). Mon–Sat noon–10pm; closed Sun & last fortnight in Aug. Austere and penitential vegetarian restaurant: no alcohol, no smoking, and a leavening of Rosicrucianism. Menu at 53F.

Auberge de Jarente, 7 rue Jarente, 4e; ☎01.42.77.49.35 (Mº St-Paul). Tues–Sat noon–2.30pm & 7–10.30pm; closed Aug. A hospitable and friendly Basque restaurant, serving first-class food: *cassoulet*, hare stew, king prawns in whisky, *magret de canard*, and *piperade* – the Basque omelette. Menus at 117 F, 132F with wine, and 185F.

L'Excuse, 14 rue Charles-V, 4e; ☎01.42.77.98.97 (Mº St-Paul). Noon–2pm & 7.30–11pm; closed Sun & mid-Aug. The cuisine is *nouvelle*-ish, as refined and elegant as the very pretty décor. Midday weekday menu at 120F, evening 165F, *carte* from 290F. A good place for a quiet but stylish date.

Goldenberg's, 7 rue des Rosiers, 4e; ☎01.48.87.20.16 (Mº St-Paul). Daily until 2am. The best-known Jewish restaurant in the capital; its *borscht*, *blinis*, potato strudels, *zakouski*, and other Central European dishes are a treat. Around 200F.

Piccolo Teatro, 6 rue des Écouffes, 4e; ☎01.42.72.17.79 (Mº St-Paul). Wed–Sun noon–3pm & 7–11pm; closed Aug. Great vegetarian restaurant, with one of the best lunch menus at 54F and 75F, evening at 99F and 115F.

Pitchi-Poï, 7 rue Caron (cnr place du Marché-Ste-Catherine), 4e; ☎01.42.77.46.15 (Mº St-Paul). Noon–3pm & 7.30–11pm. Excellent Polish/Jewish cuisine in a lovely location with sympathetic ambience. 150F, kids menu 73F, choice of delicious *hors d'œuvres* from 62F.

Le Ravaillac, 10 rue du Roi-de-Sicile, 4e; ☎01.42.72.85.85 (Mº St-Paul). Noon–3pm & 7–10.30pm; closed Sun, Mon lunchtime & Aug. Long-established Polish restaurant. Specialities include meat *perushkis*, beef Stroganoff, and *choucroute*. Excellent quality for the price – around 130F.

La Truffe, 31 rue Vieille-du-Temple, 4e; ☎01.42.71.08.39 (Mº St-Paul). Daily

noon–4pm & 7.30–11pm. A vegetarian restaurant specializing in mushrooms, as well as lentil and cheese dishes and delicious fruit tarts; also organic choices. 51F midday menu, evenings from 120F.

Quartier du Temple

CAFÉS AND BARS

Le Taxi Jaune, 13 rue Chapon, 3e (Mº Arts-et-Métiers). Mon–Sat until 11pm. An ordinary café made special by the odd poster, good taped rock and new wave music, and interesting food. Lunchtime menu at 68F with wine, evening menu 89F, cocktails 35F. Offers the occasional concert.

Web Bar, 32 rue de Picardie, 3e (Mº Filles-du-Calvaire). Daily 11.30am–3am. A pared-down trendy Internet café, with fashionable art on the walls. Opposite the Temple market.

RESTAURANTS

Chez Jenny, 39 bd du Temple, 3e; ☎01.42.74.75.75 (Mº Filles-du-Calvaire). Daily till 1am. 1930s Alsatian brasserie serving superb *choucroute* (though the fish one is a bit odd) and different daily specialities including *backeoffe* (a meat casserole) on Wed. Two courses plus drink *formule* 99F; kids' menu 49F; *carte* expensive.

Chez Nénesse, 17 rue Saintonge, 3e; ☎01.42.78.46.49 (Mº Arts-et-Métiers). Mon–Fri noon–2pm & 7.45–10.15pm; closed Aug. Steak in bilberry sauce and figs stuffed with cream of almonds are two of the unique delights of this restaurant, along with home-made chips on Thurs lunchtimes. Under 100F midday, over 200F for dinner.

Le Marais-Cage, 8 rue de Beauce, 3e; ☎01.48.87.31.20 (Mº Arts-et-Métiers/Filles-du-Calvaire). Noon–2.15pm & 7–10.30pm; closed Sat lunchtime, Sun & Aug. Friendly and popular West Indian restaurant; good food, especially seafood. Menus at 160F (including wine) and 130F (weekday lunchtime, wine included).

Eating and Drinking

See p.261 for a selection of the various ethnic restaurants in Paris.

See p.235 for a list of vegetarian restaurants in Paris.

Eating and Drinking

Île St-Louis

CAFÉS AND BARS

Berthillon, 31 rue St-Louis-en-l'Île, 4e (M° Pont-Marie). Wed–Sun 10am–8pm. Long queues for these excellent ice-creams and sorbets (20F a triple), which are made and sold here on the Île St-Louis. Also available at *Lady Jane* and *Le Flore-en-l'Île*, both on quai d'Orléans, as well as at four other island sites listed on the door.

Les Fous de l'Île, 33 rue des Deux-Ponts, 4e (M° Pont-Marie). Light lunches in bookish surroundings for around 50–60F, tea and cakes till 7pm and dinner until 11pm; closed Mon.

Le St-Régis, 92 rue St-Louis-en-l'Île, 4e (M° Pont-Marie). An unpretentious brasserie opposite the Pont St-Louis, with views of Notre-Dame. *Plats du jour* from 57F; 63F *formule*.

RESTAURANTS

Le Castafiore, 51 rue St-Louis-en-l'Île, 4e; ☎01.43.54.78.62 (M° Pont-Marie). Daily till 10.30pm. Italian specialities. Very pleasant *patron*. Menu 90F before 8pm, 160F after.

Le Gourmet de l'Île, 42 rue St-Louis-en-l'Île, 4e; ☎01.43.26.79.27 (M° Pont-Marie). Wed–Sun noon–2pm & 7–10pm. A bargain four-course menu for 130F, including wonderful stuffed mussels.

Bastille

CAFÉS AND BARS

Bar des Ferrailleurs, 18 rue de Lappe, 11e (M° Bastille). Tues–Sun 5pm–2am. Dark and stylishly sinister, with rusting metal décor.

Café de l'Industrie, 16 rue St-Sabin, 11e (M° Bastille). Noon–2am. Rugs on the floor around solid old wooden tables, miscellaneous objects on the walls, and a young, unpretentious crowd enjoying the lack of chrome, minimalism or Philippe Starck. One of the best Bastille addresses. *Plats du jour* from 45F.

Café des Phares, 7 place de la Bastille (west side), 4e (M° Bastille). Every Sunday at 11am a public philosophy debate is held in the back room here, run by Nietzsche specialist Marc Sautet, who also offers private philosophical consultations. Some academic colleagues say he's incapable of coherence; others see these sessions as the first revolutionary move since May 1968. Either way, it's good theatre.

Café de la Plage, 59 rue de Charonne, 11e (M° Bastille). Mon–Sat 8pm–2am. A multi-racial clientele and as many women as men in this low-ceilinged, friendly, youthful and often very crowded bar. Jazz club downstairs.

La Fontaine, 1 rue de Charonne, 11e (M° Bastille). Gentrified, as are all the cafés hereabouts, but not too self-conscious or expensive. On the corner of rue du Faubourg-St-Antoine, by the fountain.

Fouquet's, 130 rue de Lyon, 12e (M° Bastille). Till midnight; closed Sat & Sun midday. A smart and expensive café-restaurant underneath the new Opéra, sister establishment to the Champs-Élysées *Fouquet's*. But with perfect French courtesy they will leave you undisturbed for hours with a 15F coffee. Menu, including wine, at 165F.

Grand Appetit, 9 rue de la Cerisaie, 4e (M° Bastille). Mon–Thurs noon–7pm, Fri & Sun noon–2pm; closed Sat. Vegetarian meals served by dedicated eco-veggies at the back of a shop.

Havanita Café, 11 rue de Lappe, 11e (M° Bastille). Daily till 2am. Large, comfortable Cuban-style bar with battered old leather sofa. Cocktails from 48F; Happy Hour 5–8.30pm.

Iguana, 15 rue de la Roquette (cnr rue Daval), 11e (M° Bastille). Mon–Sat 10am–4am. A place to be seen in. Décor of trellises, colonial fans, and a brushed bronze bar. The clientele studies *récherché* art reviews, and the coffee's excellent.

Pause Café, 41 rue de Charonne (cnr rue Keller), 11e (M° Ledru-Rollin). Tues–Sat 8am–2am, Sun till 9pm. A fashionable Bastille café, down among the galleries.

SanZSanS, 49 rue du Faubourg-St-Antoine, 11e (Mº Bastille). Mon–Sat 8.30am–2am, Sun 11am–2am. Gothic decor of red velvet, oil paintings and chandeliers, with a young clientele in the evening. Drinks reasonably priced; main courses for around 50F.

Les Taillandeurs, 22 rue des Taillandeurs, 11e (Mº Ledru-Rollin). Daily lunchtime only. Scruffy old-timer with 52F menu including wine.

Le Temps des Cerises, 31 rue de la Cerisaie, 4e (Mº Bastille). Mon–Fri until 8pm; food at midday only; closed Aug. It's hard to say what's so appealing about this café, with its dirty yellow décor, old posters and prints of *vieux Paris*, save that the *patronne* knows most of the clientele, who are young, relaxed and not the dreaded *branchés*. 68F menu. See p.150 for a note on the origin of the name.

RESTAURANTS

Bofinger, 3–7 rue de la Bastille, 3e; ☎01.42.72.87.82 (Mº Bastille). Daily until 1am. A well-established and popular turn-of-the-century brasserie, with stunning original décor, serving the archetypal fare of sauerkraut and seafood. Menu at 169F including wine, otherwise over 200F. *Bistro de Bofinger* (☎01.42.72.05.23; noon–3pm & 7pm–midnight), opposite, is under the same management, and serves lighter dishes, with *plats du jour* from 75F.

La Canaille, 4 rue Crillon, 4e; ☎01.42.78.09.71 (Mº Sully-Morland/Bastille). Mon–Sat lunchtime & 7.30pm–midnight. Bar in front, restaurant behind, decorated with revolutionary posters invoking rather more durable old-fashioned values than the usual contemporary fast-buck stuff. The food is simple, traditional and well cooked. Delightful, friendly atmosphere. There are 85F and 125F evening menus, and *à la carte* at 140F.

Thai Elephant, 43–45 rue de la Roquette, 11e; ☎01.47.00.42.00 (Mº Bastille/Richard-Lenoir). Daily till midnight; closed Sat midday. Superb Thai restaurant in tropical forest decor. Worth every centime. 150F midday menu; otherwise over 250F.

Chapter 6: The Left Bank

Quartier Latin

CAFÉS AND BARS

Le Bâteau Ivre, 40 rue Descartes, 5e (Mº Cardinal-Lemoine). Closed Mon. Happy Hour is 4–8pm at this small bar just clear of the Mouffetard tourist hotspot.

Café des Arts, cnr place Contrescarpe and rue Lacépède, 5e (Mº Monge). Prettier cups and cheaper coffee than its touristy neighbour *La Chope*.

Café de la Mosquée, 39 rue Geoffroy-St-Hilaire, 5e (Mº Monge). Mon–Thurs, Sat & Sun 10am–9.30pm; closed Aug. In fine weather you can drink mint tea and eat sweet cakes beside a fountain and assorted fig trees in the courtyard of this Paris mosque – a delightful haven of calm. The interior of the *salon* is beautifully Arabic with cats curled up on the seats. You can have meals in the adjoining restaurant.

Café Notre-Dame, cnr quai St-Michel and rue St-Jacques, 5e (Mº St-Michel). With a view right across to the cathedral. Lenin used to drink here.

Café Oz, 184 rue St-Jacques, 5e (Mº Luxembourg). Daily 11am–2am. An all-Australian pub, very crowded, serving midday food at 40–60F.

Connolly's Corner, cnr rues Patriarches and de Mirbel, 5e (Mº Monge/Censier-Daubenton). Noon–2am, Sat 4pm–2am. An Irish bar with darts, *Smithwicks* and not a lot of space, but plenty of atmosphere. Very smoky.

Les Fontaines, 9 rue Soufflot, 5e (Mº Luxembourg). Mon–Sat noon–3pm & 7.30–10.30pm. A brasserie serving huge seafood salads, roast rabbit in mustard sauce and chicken fricassee with *morilles* mushrooms. Up to 200F for a full meal; lunchtime *plats* around 55F.

Eating and Drinking

The cafés and restaurants of the Quartier Latin are keyed on our special map over the page.

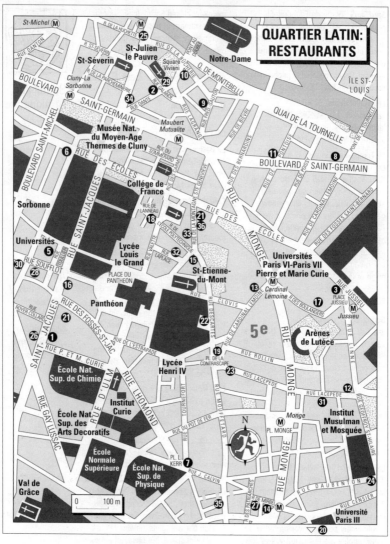

La Fourmi Ailée, 8 rue du Fouarre, 5e (Mº Maubert-Mutualité). Noon–7pm; closed Tues. Simple, light fare – including weekend brunch – in this feminist bookshop-cum-*salon-de-thé*. Around 60F for tea and a cake.

La Gueuze, 19 rue Soufflot, 5e (Mº Luxembourg). Mon–Sat noon–2am.

Comfy surroundings – lots of wood and stained glass. Kitchen specials are *pier-rades*: dishes cooked on hot stones. Numerous bottles and several draughts, including cherry beer. Close to the university, with lots of student habitués.

Net Coffee, 25 rue Lacépède, 5e (Mº Monge). All-Australian café for those who

Quartier Latin: Restaurants (see opposite)

RESTAURANTS

1 Aleka
2 Auberge des Deux Signes
3 Bambou
4 Bistro de la Sorbonne
5 Brasserie Balzar
6 Au Buisson Ardent
7 Chez Léna et Mimile
8 Chez René
9 Chieng-Maï
10 Le Grenier de Notre-Dame
11 Inagiku
12 Au Jardin des Pâtes
13 Koutchi
14 Mavrommatis
15 La Méthode
16 Perraudin
17 La Petite Légume
18 Le Petit Prince
19 Les Quatre et Une Saveurs
20 Le Refuge du Passé
21 Tashi Delek

CAFÉS AND BARS

22 Le Bâteau Ivre
23 Café des Arts
24 Café de la Mosquée
25 Café Notre-Dame
26 Café Oz
27 Connolly's Corner
28 Les Fontaines
29 La Fourmi Ailée
30 La Gueuze
31 Net Coffee
32 Le Piano Vache
33 Les Pipos
34 Polly Magoo
35 Le Verre à Pied
36 Le Violon Dingue

Eating and Drinking

can't sit still without being wired up to the Internet.

Le Piano Vache, 8 rue Laplace, 5e (Mº Cardinal-Lemoine). Noon–6pm & 9pm–2am. Venerable student bar with canned music and relaxed atmosphere.

Les Pipos, 2 rue de l'École-Polytechnique, 5e (Mº Maubert-Mutualité/Cardinal-Lemoine). 8am–9pm; closed Sun & three weeks in Aug. Old carved wooden bar and sculpted chimney piece, its own wines, and a long-established position opposite the gates of the former *grande école*. Wine at 12–20F a glass; *plats* for 54–60F.

Polly Magoo, 11 rue St-Jacques, 5e (Mº St-Michel/Maubert-Mutualité). A scruffy all-nighter frequented by chess addicts.

Le Verre à Pied, 118bis rue Mouffetard, 5e (Mº Monge). Closed Sun afternoon, Mon & mid-July to Aug. An old-fashioned café-bar with cheap drinks.

Le Violon Dingue, 46 rue de la Montagne-Ste-Geneviève, 5e (Mº Maubert-Mutualité). Mon & Wed–Sun 6pm–1am. Happy Hour 6–9pm. A long, dark, student pub that's noisy and friendly.

RESTAURANTS

Aleka, 187 rue St-Jacques, 5e; ☎01.44.07.02.75 (*RER* Luxembourg). 10am–midnight; closed noon Sat & Sun, and Aug. Fresh and simple combinations

– *brochettes*, rice, salads, followed by *crêpes* – sometimes served by the champion roller-skating sons of the proprietors. *Plats* under 80F; Greek wines and *ouzo*.

Auberge des Deux Signes, 46 rue Galande, 5e; ☎01.43.25.00.46 (Mº St-Michel). Closed Sat midday, Sun & Aug. A medieval setting and, for once, an interesting choice on the *menus fixes* at 150F (lunchtime only) and 230F.

Bambou, 4 rue des Fossés-St-Marcel, 5e; ☎01.45.87.14.14 (Mº Censier-Daubenton). Closed Sat noon, Sun, and Mon eve. Light and tasty cuisine from southeast Asia. Around 100F *à la carte*; menus from 55F at lunchtime.

Bistro de la Sorbonne, 4 rue Toullier, 5e; ☎01.43.54.41.49 (Mº Luxembourg). Mon–Sat until 11pm. Help-yourself starters and salads, good ices and *crêpes flambées*. Copious portions. Crowded and attractive student ambience. 70F lunchtime menu, including wine and service; 95F in eve.

Brasserie Balzar, 49 rue des Écoles, 5e; ☎01.43.54.13.67 (Mº Maubert-Mutualité). Daily until 12.30am; closed Aug. A traditional literary-bourgeois brasserie, frequented by the intelligentsia of the Latin Quarter. About 180F *à la carte*.

Au Buisson Ardent, 25 rue Jussieu, 5e; 42.54.93.02 (Mº Jussieu). Closed Sat,

Eating and Drinking

See p.271 for a list of cafés and restaurants that stay open late.

See p.261 for a list of the various ethnic restaurants in Paris.

Sun, and Aug. Copious helpings of first-class traditional cooking: mussels, duck, warm goat cheese salad, lamb, etc. 75F menu at lunchtime, 140F in the evening.

Chez Léna et Mimile, 32 rue Tournefort, 5e; ☎01.47.07.72.47 (Mº Censier-Daubenton). Until 11pm; closed Sat noon, and Sun. The south-facing high *terrasse* is the main attraction, and the 190F menu (with wine and coffee included) is excellent. 98F menu at lunchtime on weekdays.

Chez René, 14 bd St-Germain, 5e; ☎01.43.54.30.23 (Mº Maubert-Mutualité). Closed Sat & Sun. A grand old *bistrot* serving the old favourites: coq au vin, boeuf bourguignon. Not cheap: around 150F without wine, except at lunchtime, when the 150F menu includes wine.

Chieng-Maï, 12 rue Frédéric-Sauton, 5e; ☎01.43.25.45.45 (Mº Maubert-Mutualité). Closed Sun. Excellent Thai dishes; 69F at lunchtime, otherwise 120–160F.

Le Grenier de Notre-Dame, 18 rue de la Bûcherie, 5e (Mº Maubert-Mutualité). Daily noon–11.30pm. Some veggies love this place, others hate it. Substantial fare, including couscous, fried tofu, cauliflower cheese. Menus at 75F, 105F and 140F.

Inagiku, 14 rue Pontoise, 5e; ☎01.43.54.70.07 (Mº Maubert-Mutualité). Mon–Sat till 11pm. Authentic Japanese: 4 pieces sushi 65F; 88F midday menu.

Au Jardin des Pâtes, 4 rue Lacépède, 5e; ☎01.43.31.50.71 (Mº Jussieu). Closed Mon. Delicious home-made pasta only, but with all manner of flourishes and garnishings. Around 100F for a full meal.

Koutchi, 40 rue du Cardinal-Lemoine, 5e; ☎01.44.07.20.56 (Mº Cardinal-Lemoine). Closed Sun. An Afghan restaurant, with pretty good prices: 55F menu at lunchtime; 78F in the evening.

Mavrommatis, 42 rue Daubenton, 5e; ☎01.43.31.17.17 (Mº Censier-

Daubenton). Closed Mon. A sophisticated Greek restaurant, whose cooking has been favourably influenced by French attention to detail. Quite expensive – even the lunchtime menu is 120F – but you are definitely tasting Greek food at its best.

La Méthode, 2 rue Descartes, 5e; ☎01.43.54.22.43 (Mº Cardinal-Lemoine). Daily 7–11.30pm. Very friendly family-run resto in a late-sixteenth-century building. Enormous snail starter, duck and home-made *tarte tartin* on 145F menu.

Perraudin, 157 rue St-Jacques, 5e; ☎01.46.33.15.75 (*RER* Luxembourg). Service until 10.15pm; closed Sun, midday on Sat & Mon, last fortnight in Aug. One of the classic *bistrots* of the Left Bank, with lots of atmosphere and solid home cooking. A midday menu at 63F; *carte* around 120F.

Le Petit Prince, 12 rue Lanneau, 5e; ☎01.43.54.77.26 (Mº Maubert-Mutualité). Evenings only, until 12.30am. Good food in a restaurant full of Latin Quarter charm in one of the *quartier*'s oldest lanes. Menus at 89F and 146F.

La Petite Légume, 36 rue Boulangers, 5e (Mº Jussieu). Mon–Sat noon–2.30pm & 7.30–10pm. This is a health-food grocery that doubles as a restaurant, serving quality ingredients in a variety of *plats* for around 65F.

Les Quatre et Une Saveurs, 72 rue du Cardinal-Lemoine, 5e; ☎01.43.26.88.80 (Mº Cardinal-Lemoine). Tues–Sun till 10pm. Inventive high-class vegetarian food. 115F menu includes wine.

Le Refuge du Passé, 32 rue du Fer-à-Moulin, 5e; ☎01.47.07.29.91 (Mº Les Gobelins). Till midnight; closed Sun & midday Mon & Sat. Stuffed full of bric-a-brac and musical instruments, this is a rare home for French *chansons*. Decent food from southwest France. 119F midday menu with wine; 150F evening menu.

Student restaurants at 8bis rue Cuvier, 5e (Mº Jussieu); 39 av G-

Bernanos, 5e (Mº Port-Royal); 31 rue Geoffroy-St-Hilaire, 5e (Mº Censier-Daubenton); and 10 rue Jean-Calvin, 5e (Mº Censier-Daubenton). For the "Resto-U's", above, those with student cards can buy tickets (books of ten/12.30F a meal). Not all serve both midday and evening meals, and times change with each term. Full details can be had from the student organization, *CROUS* (☎01.40.51.36.00). Though the food is not wonderful, it is certainly filling, and you can't complain for the price. Tickets are available in the entrances to the restaurants. Some are less fussy than others about student credentials, and will sell tickets to anyone for 24.60F (in *carnets* of ten).

Tashi Delek, 4 rue des Fossés-St-Jacques, 5e; ☎01.43.26.55.55 (Mº Luxembourg). Lunchtime and evenings until 10.30pm; closed Sun & Aug. An enjoyable Tibetan restaurant – run by refugees – where you can eat for as little as 58F, without wine. There is even yak bitter tea for those immune to altitude sickness.

St-Germain

CAFÉS AND BARS

Le 10, 10 rue de l'Odéon, 6e (Mº Odéon). Daily 5.30pm–2am. The beer here is very cheap, hence its youthful and foreign clientele. Old posters, a juke-box, and a lot of chatting-up.

L'Alsace à Paris, 9 place St-André-des-Arts, 6e; ☎01.43.26.21.48 (Mº St-Michel). A very busy and well-worn brasserie, with menus at 110F, 130F and 180F. Also delicious, cheap *tartes flambées* like thin pizzas that you can take away.

L'Assignat, 7 rue Guénégaud, 6e (Mº Pont-Neuf). Mon–Sat 7.30am–8.30pm; closed July. Zinc counter, bar stools, bar football and young regulars in an untouristy café close to quai des Augustins. 25F for a sandwich and a glass of wine.

Le Bonaparte, cnr rue Bonaparte and place St-Germain (Mº St-Germain-des-Près). Meeting place for the *quartier*'s intellectuals, quieter and less touristy than *Les Deux Magots* or *Le Flore*.

Café de la Mairie, place St-Sulpice, 6e (Mº St-Sulpice). A peaceful, pleasant café on the sunny north side of the square, opposite the church of St-Sulpice.

Chez Georges, 11 rue des Canettes, 6e (Mº Mabillon). Tues–Sat noon–2am; closed July 14–Aug 15. An attractive winebar in the spit-on-the-floor mode, with its old shop front still intact in a narrow street leading off place St-Sulpice. Can get very crowded.

A la Cour de Rohan, Cour du Commerce, off rues St-André-des-Arts and Ancienne-Comédie, 6e (Mº Odéon). Tues–Fri noon–7pm, Sat & Sun 3–7pm; closed Aug. A genteel, chintzy drawing-room atmosphere in a picturesque eighteenth-century alley close to bd St-Germain. Cakes, *tartes*, poached eggs, etc. No smoking. 75–100F menu.

Les Deux Magots, 170 bd St-Germain, 6e (Mº St-Germain-des-Près). Open until 2am; closed Aug. Right on the corner of place St-Germain-des-Près, it too owes its reputation to intellectuals of the Left Bank, past and present. In summertime it picks up a lot of foreigners seeking the exact location of the spirit of French culture, and buskers galore play to the packed terrace.

L'Écluse, 15 quai des Grands-Augustins, 6e (Mº St-Michel). Noon–2am. Forerunner of the new generation of wine bars, with décor and atmosphere in authentic traditional style – just lacking the workmen to spit on the floor. Small and intimate: a very agreeable place to sit and sip. It has spawned several offspring, none of which is as pleasant.

Le Flore, 172 bd St-Germain, 6e (Mº St-Germain-des-Près). Open until 2am; closed July. The great rival and immediate neighbour of *Les Deux Magots*, with a very similar clientele.

Eating and Drinking

See p.271 for a list of cafés and restaurants that stay open late.

Eating and Drinking

Le Mazet, 60 rue St-André-des-Arts, 6e (Mº Odéon). Mon–Thurs 10am–2am, Fri & Sat until 3.30am. A well-known hangout for buskers (with a lockup for their instruments) and heavy drinkers. What about a *bière brûlée* for an evil concoction – it's flambéed with gin.

La Paillote, 45 rue Monsieur-le-Prince, 6e (*RER* Luxembourg/Mº Odéon).

Mon–Sat 9pm till dawn; closed Aug. *The late-night bar for jazz fans, with one of the best collections of recorded jazz in the city. Drinks around 38F.*

La Palette, 43 rue de Seine, 6e (Mº Odéon). Mon–Sat 8am–2am; closed Aug. Once-famous Beaux-Arts student hangout, now more for art dealers and their customers. The service can be uncivil

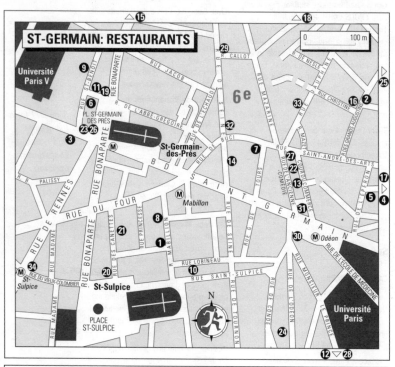

RESTAURANTS			
1	Aux Charpentiers	12 Polider	23 À la Cour de Rohan
2	Jacques Cagna	13 Le Procope	24 Les Deux Magots
3	Lipp	14 Restaurant des Arts	25 L'Écluse
4	La Maison de la Lozére	15 Restaurant des Beaux-Arts	26 Le Flore
5	La Maroussia	16 La Rôtisserie d'en Face	27 Le Mazet
6	Le Muniche		28 La Paillote
7	Orestias	**CAFÉS AND BARS**	29 La Palette
8	Le Petit Mabillon	17 Le 10	30 La Pinte
9	Le Petit St-Benoît	18 L'Alsace à Paris	31 Pub St-Germain
10	Le Petit Vatel	19 L'Assignat	32 La Table d'Italie
11	Le Petit Zinc	20 Le Bonaparte	33 La Taverne de Nesle
		21 Café de la Mairie	34 Au Vieux Colombier
		22 Chez Georges	

and the bill rather expensive, but the *terrasse*, murals and every detail of the décor are superb.

La Pinte, 13 carrefour de l'Odéon, 6e (Mº Odéon). Daily 6.30pm–2am; closed Aug. Boozy, crowded beer cellar, with piano and jazz.

Pub St-Germain, 17 rue de l'Ancienne-Comédie, 6e (Mº Odéon). Open daily 24 hours. 21 draught beers and hundreds of bottles. Huge, crowded and expensive. Hot food at mealtimes, otherwise cold snacks. For a taste of "real" French beer try *ch'ti* (patois for "northerner"), a *bière de garde* from the Pas-de-Calais.

La Table d'Italie, 69 rue de Seine, 6e (Mº Mabillon/St-Germain-des-Près). Italian pasta, snacks, etc, at the counter, plus a grocery selling pasta and other Italian delicatessen products. 98F menu.

La Taverne de Nesle, 32 rue Dauphine, 6e (Mº Odéon). Daily 7am–5am. Vast selection of beers. Full of local night birds. Cocktails from 40F.

Au Vieux Colombier, 65 rue des Rennes, 6e (Mº St-Sulpice). An Art Deco café on the corner of rue du Vieux-Colombier, with enamelled dove medallions, ice-cream cone lights and stained green wooden window frames.

RESTAURANTS

Aux Charpentiers, 10 rue Mabillon, 6e; ☎01.43.26.30.05 (Mº Mabillon). Daily until 11pm; closed hols. A friendly, old-fashioned place belonging to the *Compagnons des Charpentiers* (Carpenters' Guild), with appropriate décor of roof-trees and tie beams. Traditional *plats du jour* are their forte. Around 220F à la carte. Lunchtime menu at 135F.

Jacques Cagna, 14 rue des Grands-Augustins, 6e; ☎01.43.26.49.39 (Mº Odéon/St-Michel). Till 10.30pm; closed Sat lunchtime, Sun three weeks in Aug. Classy surroundings for very classy food – Scottish beef with Périgord truffles and the like for 700F upwards à la carte. But a midday menu for 260F.

Lipp, 151 bd St-Germain, 6e; ☎01.45.48.53.91 (Mº St-Germain-des-Près). Daily until 12.30am; closed mid-July to mid-Aug. A 1900s brasserie, and one of the best-known establishments on the Left Bank; haunt of the very successful and very famous. Rather more welcoming now that its sour old owner has died and been replaced by a nephew. 200–250F. No reservations; be prepared to wait.

La Maison de la Lozère, 4 rue Hautefeuille, 6e; ☎01.43.54.26.64 (Mº St-Michel). Closed Sun & Mon, mid-July to mid-Aug & the last week in Dec. A scrubbed-wood restaurant serving up the cuisine, cheeses, etc, of the Lozère *département*. Menus at 91F (lunchtime only during the week, wine included), 123F and 148F. Excellent omelettes for under 50F.

La Maroussia, 9 rue de l'Éperon, 6e; ☎01.43.54.87.50 (Mº Odéon). Closed Sun, Mon & two weeks in Aug. Polish and Ukrainian dishes – *bigos* (sausage and cabbage stew), *shashlik* (kebabs), salmon *kulibiak* (soup) and *zakouskis* (cold *hors d'œuvres*). 150F menu; 230F *carte*. Music Sat and Wed eves.

Le Muniche, 7 rue St-Benoît, 6e; ☎01.42.61.12.70 (Mº St-Germain-des-Près). Daily noon–2am. A crowded old-style brasserie with an oyster bar, mirrors and theatre posters on the walls and classic French brasserie fare on the menu: seafood, *choucroute*, leg of lamb. Menus at 90F and 148F; *carte* 180F.

Orestias, 4 rue Grégoire-de-Tours, 6e; ☎01.43.54.62.01 (Mº Odéon). Mon–Sat lunchtime & eve until 11pm. A mixture of Greek and French cuisine. Good helpings and very cheap – with a menu at 44F.

Le Petit Mabillon, 6 rue Mabillon, 6e; ☎01.43.54.08.41 (Mº Mabillon). Closed Sun & midday Mon. A little Italian restaurant, justly popular for its good food and reasonable prices. Menu at 75F.

Le Petit St-Benoît, 4 rue St-Benoît, 6e; ☎01.42.60.27.92 (Mº St-Germain-des-Près). Mon–Fri lunchtime & 7–10pm. A

Eating and Drinking

See p.171 for a list of cafés and restaurants that stay open late.

Eating and Drinking

Some of Paris' top gourmet restaurants are listed on p.274.

See p.261 for a list of the various ethnic restaurants in Paris.

simple, genuine and very appealing local for the neighbourhood's chattering classes. Serves solid traditional fare in a brown-stained, aproned atmosphere. Another of the St-Germain institutions. Menu at 128F; otherwise around 200F.

Le Petit Vatel, 5 rue Lobineau, 6e; ☎01.43.54.28.49 (Mº Mabillon). Mon–Sat lunchtime & 7pm–midnight, Sun eve only. A tiny, matey place with good, plain home cooking, including a vegetarian *plat* – for around 60F.

Le Petit Zinc, 11 rue St-Benoît, 6e; ☎01.42.61.20.60 (Mº St-Germain-des-Près). Daily noon–2am. Excellent traditional dishes, especially seafood, in stunning new Art Nouveau premises, complete with white fringed parasols over the pavement tables. Not cheap – menu 168F, seafood platter 440F for two.

Polidor, 41 rue Monsieur-le-Prince, 6e; ☎01.43.26.95.34 (Mº Odéon). Mon–Sat until 1am, Sun until 11pm. A traditional *bistrot*, whose visitors' book, they say, boasts more of history's big names than all the glittering palaces put together. Not as cheap as it was in James Joyce's day, but good food and great atmosphere. Lunches at 55F during the week, and an excellent 100F evening menu.

Le Procope, 13 rue de l'Ancienne-Comédie, 6e; ☎01.43.26.99.20 (Mº Odéon). Daily noon–1am. This was the first establishment to serve coffee in Paris. Over 300 years it has retained its reputation as the place for powerful intellectuals. It is popular with tourists too, which is not surprising as it still offers a good 99F menu (up to 8pm) and 119F with wine included after 11pm. At other times you won't see any change out of 200F.

Restaurant des Arts, 73 rue de Seine, 6e. (Mº St-Germain-des-Près). Mon–Thurs till 9pm, Fri lunchtime only; closed Aug. Menu at 80F. A small, crowded, friendly place with simple, homely meals.

Restaurant des Beaux-Arts, 11 rue Bonaparte, 6e; ☎01.43.26.92.64 (Mº St-Germain-des-Près). Daily lunchtime & evening until 10.45pm. The traditional

hang-out of the art students from the Beaux-Arts across the way. Menu at 75F including wine. The choice is wide, portions generous, and queues long in high season. The atmosphere is generally good, though the waitresses can get pretty tetchy.

Le Rôtisserie d'en Face, 2 rue Christine, 6e; ☎01.43.26.40.98 (Mº Odéon/St-Michel). An annexe to *Jacques Cagna* (see p.257). Excellent grilled meats. 195F or a midday menu at 150F in a rather too businesslike atmosphere.

Student restaurants at 55 rue Mazet, 6e (Mº Odéon) and 92 rue d'Assas, 6e (Mº Port-Royal/Notre-Dame-des-Champs). See under "Quartier Latin", p.254, for details.

Chapter 7: Trocadéro, Eiffel Tower and Les Invalides

CAFÉS AND BARS

Kléber, place du Trocadéro, 16e (Mº Trocadéro). Daily until dawn. Good for cinematic views of the Eiffel Tower catching the first light, or morning mist filling the valley of the Seine.

La Pagode, 57bis rue de Babylone, 7e (Mº St-François-Xavier/Sèvres-Babylone). Daily 4–9.45pm, Sun 2–8pm. A real-life pagoda (see p.356) – one of the most beautiful buildings in Paris in which to have tea. Tables in the Chinese garden in summer.

Restaurant du Musée d'Orsay, 1 rue Bellechasse, 7e (*RER* Musée-d'Orsay/Mº Solférino). Tues, Wed, Fri & Sat 11.30am–2.15pm, 4–5.30pm & 7–9.45pm, Thurs 11.30am–2.15pm & 7–9.45pm, Sun 11.30am–2.15pm & 4–5.30pm. Superb views over the Seine in the museum's magnificent rooftop restaurant. *hors d'oeuvres*, dessert and wine for 75F. Quick and friendly service.

Sancerre, 22 av Rapp, 7e (Mº Alma-Marceau). Wine shop and bar serving glasses of Sancerre from 22F and sandwiches from 16F. Try the rosé (and other Loire wines).

Le Suffren, cnr avs Motte-Piquet and Suffren, 15e (M⁰ École-Militaire/La Motte-Piquet). Big café-brasserie distinguished by serving dark Swiss chocolate with its *café crème*, and being the only obvious place to sit down after walking the length of the École Militaire.

Veggie, 38 rue de Verneuil, 7e. M⁰ Solférino Mon–Fri 10.30am–2.30pm & 4.30–7.30pm. Organic take-away from health-food shop near the Musée d'Orsay.

RESTAURANTS

L'Ami Jean, 27 rue Malar, 7e; ☎01.47.05.86.89 (M⁰ Latour-Maubourg). Mon–Sat lunchtime & 7–10.30pm; closed Sun & Aug. Pleasant ambience, if rather hurried, and good Basque food (paella, pipérade, *poulet basquaise*) for around 130–150F.

Au Babylone, 13 rue de Babylone, 7e; ☎01.45.48.72.13 (M⁰ Sèvres-Babylone). Mon–Sat lunchtime only; closed Aug. Lots of old-fashioned charm and culinary basics like *rôti de veau* and steak, etc, plus wine on the 90F menu.

Le Basilic, 2 rue Casimir-Périer, 7e; ☎01.44.18.94.64 (M⁰ Solférino). Daily noon–2.30pm & 7.30–11.30pm. Very classy with lots of polished brass and a terrace overlooking the apse of Ste-Clotilde church. Specialities such as lamb from Sisteron in salt and basil will set you back 88F. Count on 250F for a full meal.

Le Bourdonnais, 113 av La Bourdonnais, 7e; ☎01.47.05.47.06 (M⁰ École-Militaire). Daily till 11pm. A gem of a restaurant and a high-class one at that. A la carte costs upwards of 400F, but there's a superb midday menu including wine for 240F, and an evening menu at 320F.

Café de Mars, 11 rue Augereau, 7e; ☎01.47.05.05.91 (M⁰ École-Militaire). Closed Sun eve. A fashionable American-style café close to the Eiffel Tower and frequented by Americans – the American College is nearby. *Plats du jour* at 50F and a 68F menu at lunchtime. Brunch on Sat & Sun for around 130F.

Chez Germaine, 30 rue Pierre-Leroux, 7e; ☎01.42.73.28.34 (M⁰ Duroc,/Vaneau). Closed Sun, Sat eve & Aug. A simple, tiny and unbelievably cheap restaurant, with a 60F menu, including wine. The *carte* costs up to about 90F.

Au Pied de Fouet, 45 rue de Babylone, 7e; ☎01.47.05.12.27 (M⁰ St-François-Xavier/Sèvres-Babylone). Mon–Fri 12–2pm & 7–8.50pm, Sat 12–2pm; closed Aug. Good food and a great little place. Little is the operative word: there are just four tables and no reservations. Around 80–90F.

Thoumieux, 79 rue St-Dominique, 7e; ☎01.47.05.49.75 (M⁰ Latour-Maubourg). Daily lunchtime & 7–11.30pm. A large and popular establishment in this rather smart district, with traditional brasserie service. A menu at 67F, usually offal, another at 160F, otherwise you have to be careful to get away with less than 180F.

La Varangue, 27 rue Augereau, 7e; ☎01.47.05.51.22 (M⁰ École-Militaire). Closed Sat eve & Sun. A simple and relaxed sort of place with the emphasis on salads, greens and desserts. Menu at 96F or a two-course *formule* for 74F including wine or cider.

Chapter 8: Montparnasse and the Southern Arrondissements

Montparnasse

CAFÉS AND BARS

La Closerie des Lilas, 171 bd du Montparnasse, 6e (M⁰ Port-Royal). 10am–1am. The smartest, artiest, classiest one of all, with excellent cocktails for around 60F in the bar. The tables are name-plated after celebrated habitués (Verlaine, Mallarmé, Lenin, Modigliani, Léger, Strindberg). The restaurant is very expensive, but you can eat at the brasserie for under 140F, and there's a resident pianist.

Le Dôme, 108 bd du Montparnasse, 6e (M⁰ Vavin). Tues–Sun until 1am. Next

Eating and Drinking

Some of Paris' top gourmet restaurants are listed on p.274.

Eating and Drinking

See p.235 for a list of vegetarian restaurants in Paris.

See p.271 for a list of cafés and restaurants that stay open late.

door to *La Coupole*, and another of Sartre's haunts. Cinema pics decorate each alcove; beautiful and expensive.

La Pause Gourmande, 27 rue Campagne-Première, 14e (Mº Raspail). Mon–Fri. Delicious salads and savoury and sweet *tartes* from 38F.

Mustangs, 84 bd du Montparnasse, 14e (Mº Montparnasse-Bienvenue). Daily 9am–4am. Young crowd and happy atmosphere. A good place to finish up the evening after nightclubbing in St-Germain. Tex-Mex food, cocktails and beers. Happy Hour Mon–Fri 4–7pm: frozen margaritas recommended.

Le Rosebud, 11bis rue Delambre, 14e (Mº Vavin). Daily till 3am. Cheaper cocktails than on the boulevard (around 45F). The clientele usually makes an amusing spectacle.

Le Rotonde, 105 bd du Montparnasse, 6e (Mº Vavin). Another of the grand old Montparnasse establishments frequented by Lenin and Trotsky in their time.

Le Select, 99 bd du Montparnasse, 6e (Mº Vavin). Daily until 3am. The least spoilt and most traditional of the Montparnasse cafés.

Tea and Tattered Pages, 24 rue Mayet, 6e (Mº Duroc). Daily 11am–7pm. Rather a long way from anywhere, and looks like a shop from the outside. But inside you can have tea and cakes, speak English and browse through a very good selection of cheap second-hand English books.

RESTAURANTS

Chez Maria, 16 rue du Maine, 14e; ☎01.43.20.84.61 (Mº Montparnasse). Daily 8.30pm–1am. Zinc bar, candlelight, posters, paper tablecloths – an intimate gloom that appeals to arty theatre creatures after hours. Very pleasant. Around 170F.

La Coupole, 102 bd du Montparnasse, 14e; ☎01.43.20.14.20 (Mº Vavin). Daily 7.30–10.30am for breakfast, then noon–2am. The largest and perhaps the most famous and enduring arty-chic

Parisian hang-out for dining, dancing and debate. It has been lavishly renovated by the prince of Paris' turn-of-the-century brasseries, Jean-Paul Bucher of *Flo* and *Julien* fame . . . but it ain't the same, say the old habitués. Some complain that the lighting is now too bright, that the intimacy has gone and the food has deteriorated; others say the opposite. Either way its future is assured, even if it's for who has eaten there rather than who's to be seen tonight. One definite improvement is an after 11pm menu at 119F including wine. *Carte* and coffee 170–310F. Dancing 3–7pm weekends (Sat 60F, Sun 80F) and 9.30pm–4am Fri & Sat (90F).

La Mamma, 46 rue Vavin, 6e; ☎01.46.33.17.92 (Mº Vavin). Daily till 1am. Affordable and good Italian restaurant. 60F menu; pizzas from 34F.

L'Ostréade, 11 bd Vaugirard, 15e; ☎01.43.21.87.41 (Mº Montparnasse). Daily till 11pm. A seafood brasserie with *tapas* on a 85F *formule*, and excellent oysters. Around 175F for a full whack.

The 15e Arrondissement

CAFÉS AND BARS

Travel Café, 2 rue d'Alleray, 15e (Mº Vaugirard). Mon–Sat 9am–6pm. Global connections in this tiny and friendly cybercafé and travel shop. Bagels, *paninis* and salads for under 40F.

RESTAURANTS

Le Bistrot d'André, 232 rue St-Charles, 15e; ☎01.45.57.89.14 (Mº Baltard). Till 9.30pm, closed Sun eve. A reminder of the old Citroën works before the Parc André-Citroën was created, with pictures and models of the classic French car. Great puds; midday menu 59F, otherwise around 120F.

Da Attilio, 21 rue Cronstadt, 15e; ☎01.40.43.91.90 (Mº Convention/Porte-de-Vanves). Mon–Sat till 9.30pm. Close to the Parc Georges Brassens. Unprepossessing décor and run-of-the-mill food, but very friendly service and a

Eating and Drinking

Ethnic Restaurants In Paris

Our selection of the **ethnic restaurants** of Paris can only scratch the surface of what's available. **North African** places can be found throughout the city; apart from rue Xavier-Privas in the Latin Quarter, where the trade is chiefly tourists, the heaviest concentration is the Little Maghreb district along bd de Belleville. **Indo-Chinese** restaurants are also widely scattered, with notable concentrations around av de la Porte-de-Choisy in the 13ᵉ and in the Belleville Chinatown. The **Greeks** are tightly corralled, in rue de la Huchette, rue Xavier-Privas and along rue Mouffetard, all in the 5ᵉ and, frankly, a rip-off.

AFGHAN

Koutchi, 40 rue du Cardinal-Lemoine, 5ᵉ. Afghan. p.254.

AFRICAN AND NORTH AFRICAN

Le Berbère, 50 rue de Gergovie, 14ᵉ. North African. p.263.

Entoto, 143–145 rue Léon-Maurice-Nordmann, 13ᵉ. Ethiopian. p.264.

Fouta Toro, 3 rue du Nord, 18ᵉ. Senegalese. p.265.

La Mansouria, 11 rue Faidherbe-Chaligny, 11ᵉ. Moroccan. p.273.

L' Homme Bleu, 57 rue Jean-Pièrre-Timbaud, 11ᵉ. Berber. p.269.

N'Zadette M'Foua, 152 rue du Château, 14ᵉ. Congolese. p.263.

Au Port de Pidjiguiti, 28 rue Étex, 18ᵉ. Co-operative, run by a village in Guinea-Bissau. p.266.

La Quincampe, 78 rue Quiucampoix, 3ᵉ. Moroccan. p.247.

CARIBBEAN

Le Marais-Cage, 8 rue de Beauce, 3ᵉ. p.249.

EAST EUROPEAN

La Maroussia, 9 rue de l'Éperon, 6ᵉ. Polish and Ukrainian. p.257.

Pitchi-Poï, 7 rue Caron, 4ᵉ. Polish/Jewish. p.249.

Le Polonia, 3 rue Chaumont, 19ᵉ. Polish. p.272.

Le Ravaillac, 10 rue du Roi-de-Sicile, 4ᵉ. Polish. p.249.

GREEK

Égée, 19 rue de Ménilmontant, 20ᵉ. p.270.

Mavrommatis, 42 Daubenton. 5ᵉ. p.254.

Orestias, 4 rue Grégoire-de-Tours, 6ᵉ. p.257.

ITALIAN

Da Attilio, 21 rue Cronstadt, 15ᵉ. p.260.

Le Castafiore, 51 rue St-Louis-en-L'Île, 4ᵉ. p.250.

L'Enoteca, 25 rue Charles-V, 4ᵉ. p.248.

La Mamma, 46 rue Vavin, 6ᵉ. p.260.

Le Petit Mabillon, 6 rue Mabillon, 6ᵉ. p.257.

INDO-CHINESE

Bambou, 4 rue des Fossés-St-Marcel, 5ᵉ. Southeast Asia. p.253.

Chieng-Maï, 12 rue Fréderic-Santa, 5ᵉ. Thai. p.254.

Dragons Élysées, 11 rue de Berri, 8ᵉ. Chinese-Thai. p.241.

Lao Siam, 49 rue de Belleville, 19ᵉ. Thai and Laotian. p.270.

Lao-Thai, 128 rue de Tolbiac, 13ᵉ. Thai and Laotian. p.264.

Le Pacifique, 35 rue de Belleville, 20ᵉ. Chinese. p.270.

Pho-Dong-Huong, 14 rue Louis-Bonnet, 11ᵉ. Chinese. p.270.

(continued overleaf)

Eating and Drinking

See p.235 for a list of vegetarian restaurants in Paris.

Ethnic Restaurants in Paris (continued)

Phuong Hoang, Terrasse des Olympiades, 52 rue du Javelot, 13e. Vietnamese, Thai and Singaporean. p.264.

Le Royal Belleville and **Le Président**, 19 rue Louis-Bonnet, 11e. Chinese. p.272.

Taï Yen, 5 rue de Belleville, 20e. Thai. p.272.

Thai Elephant, 43–45 rue de la Roquette, 11e. p.257.

Thuy Huong, Kiosque de Choisy, 15 av de Choisy, 13e. Chinese and Cambodian. p.264.

JAPANESE
Foujita, 41 rue St-Roch, 1er. p.244.
Inagiku, 14 rue Pontoise, 5e. p.254.
Osaka, 163 rue St-Honoré, 1er. p.241.

JEWISH
Goldenberg's, 7 rue des Rosiers, 4e. p.249.
Pitchi-Poï, 7 rue Caron, 4e. p.249.

KURDISH
Dilan, 13 rue Mandar, 2e. p.244.

LEBANESE
Au Saveurs du Liban, 11 rue Eugène-Jumin, 19e. p.269.
Baalbeck, 16 rue Mazagran, 10e. p.267.
La Taverne du Nil, 9 rue du Nil, 2e. p.244.

TIBETAN
Tashi Delek, 4 rue des Fossés-St-Jacques, 5e. p.255.

---

great atmosphere. Different Italian specialities each day; *plats du jour* 50F.

RESTAURANTS

Le Clos Morillons, 50 rue Morillons, 15e; ☎01.48.28.04.37 (Mº Porte-de-Vanves). Mon–Fri 12.15–2.15pm & 8–10.15pm, Sat 8–10.30pm. Rabbit stuffed with aubergines, veal in lemon and almond purée, and some alluring fish dishes. Menus at 165F and 270F.

Le Commerce, 51 rue du Commerce, 15e; ☎01.45.75.03.27 (Mº Émile-Zola). Daily noon–3pm & 6.30–midnight. A two-storey restaurant that has been catering for *le petit peuple* for over a hundred years. Still varied, nourishing and cheap. Midday menu 100F; *plats du jour* 55–65F; 88F and 114F *formules*; *carte* around 145F.

Sampieru Corsu, 12 rue de l'Amiral-Roussin, 15e (Mº Cambronne). Mon–Fri lunchtimes & 7–9.30pm. Decorated with the posters and passionate declarations of international socialism, this restaurant has as its purpose the provision of meals for the homeless, the unem-

ployed, the low-paid. The principle is that you pay what you can and it is left to your conscience how you settle the bill. The minimum requested is 36F for a three-course meal with wine. However poor you might feel, as a tourist in Paris you should be able to pay more. The restaurant only survives on the generosity of its supporters, and it's a wonderful place.

Student restaurant at 156 rue Vaugirard, 15e (Mº Pasteur). See pp.235 and 254, for details.

The 14e Arrondissement

CAFÉS AND BARS

L'Entrepôt, 7–9 rue Francis-de-Pressensé, 14e (Mº Pernety). Mon–Sat 2–11.30pm. Cinema with a spacious café. Midday menu 58F; evening menus 95F and 125F.

Le Rallye, 6 rue Daguerre, 14e (Mº Denfert-Rochereau). Tues–Sat until 8pm; closed Aug. A good place to recover from the catacombs or Montparnasse cemetery. The patron offers a bottle for tasting; gulping the lot would be considered bad form. Good cheese and *saucisson*.

RESTAURANTS

Aquarius 2, 40 rue Gergovie, 14e; ☎01.45.41.36.88 (Mº Pernety). Mon–Sat noon–3pm & 7–10.30pm. Imaginative vegetarian meals served with proper Parisian bustle. 60F menu midday.

Le Berbère, 50 rue de Gergovie, 14e; ☎01.45.42.10.29 (Mº Pernety). Daily, lunchtime & evenings until 10pm. A very unprepossessing place décor-wise, but serves wholesome, unfussy and cheap North African food. Couscous from 60F.

Bergamote, 1 rue Niepce, 14e; ☎01.43.22.79.47 (Mº Pernety). Tues–Sat lunchtime & evenings until 11pm; closed Aug. A small and sympathetic *bistrot* in a quiet, ungentrified street off rue de l'Ouest. Only about ten tables; you need to book weekends. There are 61F and 100F *formules* at lunchtime; 125F in the evening; *carte* around 160F.

N'Zadette M'Foua, 152 rue du Château, 14e; ☎01.43.22.00.16 (Mº Pernety). Mon–Sat until 1am. A small and tasty Congolese restaurant, with dishes such as *maboké* (meat or fish baked in banana leaves). Reservations required at weekends. Around 120F.

Pavillon Montsouris, 20 rue Gazan, 14e; ☎01.45.88.38.52 (RER Cité-Universitaire). Daily 12.15–2.30pm & 7.45–10.30pm. A special treat for summer days. Sit on the terrace overlooking the park, and choose from a menu featuring truffles, *foie gras* and the divine *pêche blanche rôtie à la glace vanille*. Menus at 90F (except in summer) and 255F.

Phineas, 99 rue de l'Ouest, 14e; ☎01.45.41.33.50 (Mº Pernety). Mon–Sat 9am–11pm; closed Mon midday. A gallery-restaurant specializing in plates of food arranged into funny faces. Several veggie dishes and a friendly atmosphere. A good one for kids, and it's easy to eat for less than 100F.

La Régalade, 49 av Jean-Moulin, 14e; ☎01.45.45.68.58 (Mº Alésia). Till mid-

night; closed Sat lunchtime, Sun, Mon & mid-July to last week of Aug. You need to book several days in advance for this very high-class and good value restaurant. Around 170F.

Au Rendez-Vous des Camioneurs, 34 rue des Plantes, 14e; ☎01.45.40.43.36 (Mº Alésia). Mon–Fri lunchtime & 6–9.30pm; closed Aug. No lorry drivers any more, but good food for under 100F; menu at 60F. Wise to book.

La Route du Château, 123 rue du Château, 14e; ☎01.43.20.09.59 (Mº Pernety). Mon lunchtimes only, Tues–Sat lunchtimes & evenings until 12.30am; closed Aug. An old-fashioned *bistrot* atmosphere, with linen tablecloths and a rose on your table. The food is beautifully prepared and cooked – try the thin slice of rump steak (well over 150F). Menus at 82F and 145F.

Student restaurants at 13/17 rue Dareau (Mº St-Jacques) and in the *Cité-Universitaire* (RER Cité Universitaire). See pp.235 and 254 for details.

L'Univers, 73 rue d'Alésia (cnr rue Marguerin), 14e; ☎01.43.27.17.71 (Mº Alésia). Solid cooking under 100F. Excellent-value Sancerre rosé.

The 13e Arrondissement

CAFÉS AND BARS

Le Diapason, 15 rue Butte-aux-Cailles, 13e (Mº Place d'Italie/Corvisart). A more staid alternative to *Le Merle Moqueur*. Happy Hour 6–8pm.

La Folie en Tête, 33 rue Butte-aux-Cailles, 13e (Mº Place-d'Italie/Corvisart). Mon–Sat 5am–2am. Cheap beer, sandwiches and occasional concerts & solidarity events from some of the people who used to run *Le Merle Moqueur* and *Le Temps des Cerises*. A very warm and laid-back address.

Le Merle Moqueur, 11 rue Butte-aux-Cailles, 13e (Mº Place-d'Italie/Corvisart). 9pm–1am. Still going strong and still popular, with live rock some nights.

Eating and Drinking

See p.271 for a list of cafés and restaurants that stay open late.

Eating and Drinking

Our glossary of French food and dishes begins on p.236.

RESTAURANTS

Auberge Etchegorry, 41 rue Croulebarbe, 13e; ☎01.44.08.83.51 (Mº Gobelins). Mon–Sat till 10.30pm. A former *guinguette* on the banks of the Biévre, this Basque restaurant has preserved an old-fashioned atmosphere of relaxed convivility, and the food's good too. Menus from 130F.

Bol en Bois, 35 rue Pascal, 13e; ☎01.47.07.27.24 (Mº Gobelins). Mon–Sat noon–2.30pm & 7–10pm. Macrobiotic veg tempura and fish restaurant in a street being taken over by veggie/Buddhist concerns. 115F "Zen" menu. Generous portions.

Chez Gladines, 30 rue des Cinq-Diamants, 13e; ☎01.45.80.70.10 (Mº Corvisart). Tues–Sun 7.30am–2am. This small corner *bistrot* is always welcoming. Excellent wines and dishes from the southwest. The mashed/fried potato is a must and goes best with *magret de canard*. Around 120F for a full meal.

Chez Grand-Mère, 92 rue Broca, 13e; ☎01.47.07.13.65 (Mº Gobelins). Mon–Sat till 10.15pm. Excellent *terrines*, rabbit in mustard sauce, and stuffed trout. 69F midday menu; evening menus 109F and 149F including wine.

Chez Paul, 22 rue Butte-aux-Cailles, 13e; ☎01.45.89.22.11 (Mº Place-d'Italie/Corvisart). Daily till midnight. Elegant *bistrot* serving traditional French country food. From 150F.

Entoto, 143–145 rue Léon-Maurice-Nordmann, 13e; ☎01.45.87.08.51 (Mº Glacière). Tues–Sat 7.30–10pm. An Ethiopian restaurant where you can share plates, using *indjera* (bread) rather than knives and forks. Veggie and meat dishes, some of them spiced with very hot pepper called *mitmita*. Around 150F.

Le Jean-Baptiste-Clément, 11 rue Butte-aux-Cailles, 13e; ☎01.45.80.27.22 (Mº Place d'Italie/Corvisart). Daily till 1am. Kebabs chargrilled at your table. 85F menu before 10pm.

Le Languedoc, 64 bd Port-Royal, 5e; ☎01.47.07.24.47 (Mº Gobelins). Thurs–Mon till 10pm; closed Aug. Just in the 5e, but closer to the Gobelins than the Latin Quarter. A traditional checked tablecloth *bistrot* with an illegible menu on which you might decipher frogs' legs, snails, *museau de boeuf*, etc. Good value for a 105F menu including wine.

Lao-Thai; 128 rue de Tolbiac, 13e; ☎01.44.24.28.10 (Mº Tolbiac). Mon & Tues, Thurs–Sun 11.30am–2.30pm & 7–11pm. Big glass-fronted resto on a busy interchange. Finely spiced Thai and Laotian food, with coconut, ginger and lemongrass flavours. Around 120F.

Phuong Hoang, Terrasse des Olympiades, 52 rue du Javelot, 13e; ☎01.45.84.75.07 (Mº Tolbiac: take the escalator up from rue Tolbiac). Mon–Fri noon–1pm & 7–11.30pm. Like most of its neighbours this is a family business and the quality varies depending on which uncle, nephew or niece is at the stove that day. Vietnamese, Thai and Singapore specialities on lunch menus at 50F and 70F; *carte* 100–150F. If it's full or doesn't take your fancy, try *Le Grand Mandarin* or *L'Oiseau de Paradis* nearby.

Student restaurant 105 bd de l'Hôpital, 13e (Mº St-Marcel). See p.254.

Le Temps des Cerises, 18–20 rue Butte-aux-Cailles, 13e; ☎01.45.89.69.48 (Mº Place-d'Italie/Corvisart). Mon–Fri noon–2pm & 7–11pm, Sat 7–11pm. A well-established workers' co-op with elbow-to-elbow seating and a different daily choice of imaginative dishes. 118F menu.

Thuy Huong and **Tricotin**, Kiosque de Choisy, 15 av de Choisy, 13e; ☎01.45.86.87.07/01.45.84.74.44 (Mº Porte-de-Choisy). Noon–2.30pm & 7–10.30pm; closed Thurs. *Thuy Huong* is in the inner courtyard of this Chinese shopping centre and is more of a café. *Tricotin* has two restaurants, visible from the avenue; no. 1 specializes in Thai dishes, no. 2 in the other Asiatic cuisines. Not easy to work out what's on the menu (*méduse*, by the way, is jellyfish), but you can depend on the *dim sum*, the duck dishes and the Vietnamese rice pancakes. Around 100F, or 70F at *Thuy Huong*.

Chapter 9: Montmartre and Northern Paris

Montmartre

CAFÉS AND BARS

Aux Négociants, 27 rue Lambert (cnr rue Custine), 18e; ☎01.46.06.15.11 (Mº Château-Rouge). Lunchtime Mon–Fri & eves till 10pm on Tues, Wed & Thurs; closed Sat, Sun, public holidays & Aug. An intimate and friendly *bistrot à vins* with a selection of well-cooked *plats* and good wines: around 140F for a full meal. The clientele is vaguely arty-intellectual. Wise to book.

La Petite Charlotte, 24 rue des Abbesses, 18e (Mº Abbesses). Tues–Sun till 8pm. Crêpes, *pâtisseries* and 58F *formule* on sunny tables.

Le Refuge, cnr rue Lamarck and the steps of rue de la Fontaine-du-But, 18e (Mº Lamarck-Caulaincourt). A gentle café stop with a long view west down rue Lamarck to the country beyond.

Le Sancerre, 35 rue des Abbesses, 18e (Mº Abbesses). Daily 7am–2am. As the southern slopes of Montmartre have become cleaner and more gentrified, this café and its neighbours have become a fashionable hang-out for the young and trendy of all nationalities.

RESTAURANTS

L'Assiette, 78 rue Labat, 18e; ☎01.42.59.06.63 (Mº Château-Rouge). Closed Wed & Sat midday. A bit out of the way, but very friendly, with an extraordinarily good-value 86F menu, delicious *champignons forestières*, chocolate charlotte, and a surprising beetroot sorbet starter.

La Casserole, 17 rue Boinod, 18e; ☎01.42.54.50.97 (Mº Simplon/Marcadet-Poissonniers). Closed Sun, Mon & Aug. Good and copious helpings – a wide variety of game in season. The place is festooned with knick-knacks: jolly atmosphere. Menu at 130F; 70F at lunchtime in the week.

Chez Ginette, 101 rue Caulaincourt, 18e; ☎01.46.06.01.49 (Mº Lamarck-Caulaincourt). Lunchtime and eves until 11.30pm; closed Sun & Aug. Good, uncomplicated food (*blanquette de veau, boeufgros sel*, etc) in a traditional "Parisian" environment, with live piano and dancing. Noisy and fun. *Carte* around 130F; lunchtime menu at 65F. Wise to book, especially at weekends.

Chez Paula, 26 rue Letort, 18e; ☎01.42.23.86.41 (Mº Joffrin/Porte-de-Clignancourt). A genuine local, with straightforward home cooking. Lunchtime menu at 48F, evening at 69F. Rather out of the way unless you're staying in the neighbourhood. Close to the colourful rue du Poteau market.

Fouta Toro, 3 rue du Nord, 18e; ☎01.42.55.42.73 (Mº Marcadet-Poissonniers). 7.30pm–1am; closed Tues. A tiny, crowded, welcoming Senegalese diner in a very scruffy alley northeast of Montmartre. No more than 70F all in. Be prepared for a wait unless you come at the 8pm opening time, or after about 10.30pm.

Au Grain de Folie, 24 rue La Vieuville, 18e; ☎01.42.58.15.57 (Mº Abbesses). 12.30–2.30pm & 7–11.30pm. Tiny, simple, cheap and friendly, with just the sort of traditional atmosphere that you would hope for from Montmartre. Vegetarian. Soup and tart 60F, menu 100F.

L'Homme Tranquille, 81 rue des Martyrs, 18e; ☎01.42.54.56.28 (Mº Abbesses). Eves only, 7–11.30pm; closed Sun, Mon & Aug. Simple and pleasant *bistrot* ambience, with posters and nicotine-coloured paint. Imaginative French dishes include chicken in honey, coriander and lemon. Menu at 118F.

Le Maquis, 69 rue Caulaincourt, 18e; ☎01.42.59.76.07 (Mº Lamarck-Caulaincourt). Mon–Sat lunchtime & eves until 10pm. Lunchtime menu at 63F (with wine, but no dessert); *carte* around 180F. A gently elegant and courteous place.

Marie-Louise, 52 rue Championnet, 18e; ☎01.46.06.86.55 (Mº Simplon).

Eating and Drinking

See p.271 for a list of cafés and restaurants that stay open late.

Eating and Drinking

Lunchtime & eves until 9.30pm; closed Sun, Mon & Aug. A place with a well-deserved reputation. A bit of a trek north, but very much worth the journey for a special meal, for the traditional French cuisine is excellent. Menu at 130F, otherwise around 180F.

Le Moulin à Vins, 6 rue Burq, 18e; ☎01.42.52.81.27 (Mº Abbesses). 6pm-12.30am (bar 2am), lunchtime Wed–Thurs only; closed Sun, Mon & three weeks in Aug. Wine bar with interesting selection of wines to accompany the cheese, *charcuteries* or *plats* such as *coq au vin* – around 140F.

A la Pomponnette, 42 rue Lepic, 18e; ☎01.46.06.08.36 (Mº Blanche/Abbesses). Lunchtime, and eves until 9.30pm; closed Sun, Mon lunchtime & Aug. A genuine old Montmartre *bistrot*, with posters, drawings, zinc-top bar, nicotine stains, etc. The food is excellent, but will cost you 200–250F *à la carte*; good menu including wine at 150F.

Au Port de Pidjiguiti, 28 rue Étex, 18e; ☎01.42.26.71.77 (Mº Guy-Môquet). Lunchtime, and eves until 11pm; closed Mon & Jan. Very pleasant atmosphere and excellent food for about 100F; lunchtime menu at 88F. It is run by a village in Guinea-Bissau, whose inhabitants take turns in staffing the restaurant; the proceeds go to the village. Good-value wine list.

Le Relais de la Butte, 12 rue Ravignan, 18e; ☎01.42.23.94.64 (Mº Abbesses). Tues–Sun until 11pm. A quaint building in a beautiful spot on the corner of the little square where Picasso's Bateau-Lavoir studio used to be. Menus at 105F and 150F (*carte* only at lunchtime) – there's a touch of cheese in practically everything, but it is very good. Extremely crowded on summer eves.

Au Virage Lepic, 61 rue Lepic, 18e; ☎01.42.52.46.79 (Mº Blanche/Abbesses). Eves only, 7pm-2am; closed Tues & mid-July for six weeks. Simple traditional fare in a noisy, friendly atmosphere created by the singers – in the French/Parisian idiom. The place is small and smoky and there's no escape. Very enjoyable. Around 100F.

Le Restaurant, 32 rue Véron, 18e; ☎01.42.23.06.22 (Mº Abbesses). Closed Sun & Mon lunchtimes. An attractive corner restaurant offering light and unexpected tastes. A good value *formule* for 70F at lunchtime and a 120F menu for dinner.

Batignolles

CAFÉS AND BARS

Bar Belge, 75 av de St-Ouen, 17e (Mº Guy-Môquet). Tues–Sun 3.30pm–1am. Belgian beers and *moules frites* for 60F, *coq au vin* 70F and *poulet aux cèpes* 65F.

L'Endroit, 67 place Félix-Lobligeois, 17e; ☎01.42.29.50.00 (Mº Rome/La Fourche). Daily noon–2am. A smartish late-night bar serving the local youth. Drinks from about 60F.

RESTAURANTS

Joy in Food, 2 rue Truffaut, 17e; ☎01.43.87.96.79 (Mº Place-Clichy). Mon–Sat lunchtime, also eves Tues, Fri & Sat. Minuscule veggie, with its mind on higher things: open meditation sessions at 8pm Wed. Good food, inexpensive and attractive atmosphere. 71–100F.

Pigalle

CAFÉS AND BARS

Le Dépanneur, 27 rue Fontaine, 9e; ☎01.40.16.40.20 (Mº Pigalle). Open 24 hours. A relaxed and fashionable all-night bar in black and chrome, just off place Pigalle.

RESTAURANTS

L'Alsaco, 10 rue Condorcet (at the extreme eastern end), 9e; ☎01.45.26.44.31 (Mº Poissonnière).

Closed Sat lunchtime, Sun & Aug. A real Alsatian *winstub* serving the traditional dishes and wines of Alsace. 85F menu in the eve, and a massive one at 168F; *carte* 100–140F.

Auberge Bourbonnaise, 45 rue St-Georges, 9e; ☎01.48.78.40.30 (Mº St-Georges). Closed Sat lunchtime, Sun, Mon eve and three weeks in Aug. Menus at 78F and 120F will give you a good, if unexciting, meal at this pretty corner restaurant with lace curtains at its windows and 100-year-old paintings on its walls.

Chez Jean, 52 rue Lamartine, 9e; ☎01.48.78.62.73 (Mº Notre-Dame-de-Lorette/Cadet). Closed Sat lunchtime & Sun. The rather *rustique* exterior belies the refined and interesting cuisine within. The 155F menu includes quail salad, bisque of shellfish, *râble* of rabbit, and apple tart with mango sorbet. The *carte* costs more like 200F.

Aux Deux-Théâtres, 18 rue Blanche (cnr rue Pigalle), 9e; ☎01.45.26.41.43 (Mº Trinité). Daily till 12.30am. A distinctly bourgeois but welcoming and friendly place, whose 165F menu includes coffee and wine – a bottle for two. The entrées and desserts are particularly good. And it is open Sun.

Haynes, 3 rue Clauzel (cnr rue des Martyrs), 9e; ☎01.48.78.40.63 (Mº St-Georges). Mon–Sat 7.30pm–midnight. A black-American restaurant serving generous quantities of rich and heavy dishes from the southern states. It's been going since the 1940s and is now run by widow Haynes. The décor is vaguely reminiscent of a grotto, but the atmosphere is warm, and there is often good live music (piano and singer, guitar and bass). It is certainly something different in Paris. Around 160F, with wine.

Le Relais Savoyard, 13 rue Rodier (cnr rue Agent-Bailly), 9e; ☎01.45.26.17.18 (Mº Notre-Dame-de-Lorette/Anvers/Cadet). Closed Sun & Aug. You enter what looks like a very ordinary local bar. At the back is the dining room, where you can get a very good three-course meal for 72F. The *carte* is around 130–140F, and there is a more sophisticated menu at 115F.

La Table d'Anvers, 2 place d'Anvers, 9e; ☎01.48.78.35.21 (Mº Anvers). This is one of the city's really top restaurants, whose chef is renowned for his creativity, daring to combine the most improbable elements. Lunchtime menus at 180F and 340F give a good taste of his skills. Evening menus at 250F and 550F; *à la carte* would cost over 600F.

Eating and Drinking

The Stations and Faubourgs

RESTAURANTS

Baalbeck, 16 rue de Mazagran, 10e; ☎01.47.70.70.02 (Mº Bonne-Nouvelle). Mon–Sat lunchtime & 8pm–midnight. Much liked by the moneyed refugees, this Lebanese restaurant has dozens of appetizers. For 555F you can have a representative selection for four, with *arak* to drink. Belly-dancing and sticky Levantine/Turkish cakes too. Very busy, so reserve or go early.

Chez Arthur, 25 rue du Faubourg-St-Denis, 10e; ☎01.42.08.34.33 (Mº Strasbourg-St-Denis). Lunchtime Mon–Fri, eves Tues–Sat. An easy-going, attractive restaurant, popular with theatre-goers and actors. Good classic cuisine; menu at 120F.

L'Enchotte, 11 rue de Chabrol, 10e; ☎01.48.00.05.25 (Mº Gare-de-l'Est). Closed Sat lunch, Sun, hols and second half of Aug. A relaxed, friendly wine bar opposite the St-Quentin market, with

---

At the south end of rue du Faubourg-St-Denis, in rue d'Enghien and rue de l'Échiquier, there are numerous – mainly Turkish, Kurdish and Indian – snack bars and restaurants. They are much frequented by the members of those communities, so you can be sure of the quality of the food.

Eating and Drinking

Some of Paris' top gourmet restaurants are listed on p.274.

cheese and *charcuteries at* around 50–70F. 65F menu at lunchtime, supplemented in the eves by menus at 90F and 120F.

Flo, 7 cours des Petites-Écuries, 10ᵉ; ☎01.47.70.13.59 (Mº Château-d'Eau). Daily until 1.30am. Handsome old brasserie, all dark-stained wood, mirrors and glass partitions, in attractive courtyard off rue du Faubourg-St-Denis. You eat elbow-to-elbow at long tables, served by waiters in ankle-length aprons. Excellent food and atmosphere. Fish, *choucroute* and seafood (platter for 198F) are among the specialities. From around 200F; really good value menus at 109F midday, 185F evenings, with a 109F *formule* after 11pm. Wine is included in the price of all menus.

Julien, 16 rue du Faubourg-St-Denis, 10ᵉ. ☎01.47.70.12.06 (Mº Strasbourg-St-Denis). Daily until 1.30am. Part of the same enterprise as *Flo*, with an even more splendid décor. Same good Alsatian – vaguely Germanic – cuisine; same prices and similarly crowded. From around 230F, with a 109F menu including wine at lunchtime and after 11pm.

KOH, 12 rue de la Fidelité, 10ᵉ; ☎01.42.46.02.13 (Mº Gare-de-l'Est). Daily until 6am. This is where the late-night workers and party-goers head for a feed when everyone else is thinking of breakfast. Generous helpings of good food: *plats* around 70F. Pretty quiet before midnight.

Le Réveil du Dixième, 35 rue du Château-d'Eau, 10ᵉ; ☎01.42.71.77.59 (Mº Château-d'Eau). A welcoming, unpretentious wine bar open lunchtimes from Mon–Sat, and Tuesday eve until 9.30pm. Glasses of wine and regional *plats* or a menu at 150F including wine.

Terminus Nord, 23 rue de Dunkerque, 10ᵉ; ☎01.42.85.05.15 (Mº Gare-du-Nord). Daily until 12.30am. A magnificent 1920s brasserie where a full meal costs around 250F, but you could easily satisfy your hunger with just a main

course – an excellent steak, for example – and still enjoy the décor for considerably less money. 109F menu after 11pm.

Chapter 10: Eastern Paris

République and the Canal St-Martin

CAFÉS AND BARS

Chez Imogéne, cnr rue Jean-Pièrre-Timbaud and rue du Grand-Prieuré, 11ᵉ (Mº Oberkampf). Mon–Sat till 10.30pm. Cheap and cheerful *crêperie* with 49.50F midday menu including drink.

Le Clown Bar, 114 rue Amelot, 11ᵉ; ☎01.43.55.87.35 (Mº Filles-du-Calvaire). Closed Sat lunchtime, Sun & Aug. An attractive and increasingly popular wine bar with *plats du jour* for 58–65F.

La Divette de Valmy, 71 quai de Valmy, 10ᵉ (Mº Jacques-Bonsergent). An ordinary café-brasserie at the foot of one of the arching canal bridges. A lovely spot in the afternoon sun.

L'Opus, 167 quai de Valmy, 10ᵉ; ☎01.40.38.09.57 (Mº Château-Landon). Mon–Sat 8pm–4am. A stylish modern-chintzy atmosphere in a barn-like space used as British officers' mess during World War I. Live music every evening: country, salsa, African – no longer the classical only of the early days. Drinks 60–80F average, plus 50F surcharge for the music.

RESTAURANTS

Anjou-Normandie, 13 rue de la Foli-Méricault, 11ᵉ; ☎01.47.00.30.59 (Mº St-Ambroise). Till 9pm; closed Sat, Sun & Mon eves. Fresh ingredients, and renowned for its patés and *andouillettes*. Lunchtime two-course *formule* for 68F; menus at 130F and, with fish, 165F. Best to book.

Astier, 44 rue Jean-Pièrre-Timbaud, 11ᵉ; ☎01.43.57.16.35 (Mº Parmentier). Mon–Fri until 10pm; closed Aug, fortnight in May & fortnight at Christmas. Very successful and popular. Simple décor, unstuffy atmosphere, and food renowned for its freshness and refinement. Essential to book. Menu at 135F.

Au Gigot Fin, 56 rue de Lancry (close to the canal), 10e; ☎01.42.08.38.81. Lunchtime & eves until 10pm; closed Sat lunchtime & Sun. Another very Parisian old-timer, like the *Bourgogne*, with solid country fare, and specializing in lamb. Midday menu at 60F and 80F, evening menus 110F and 175F.

L'Homme Bleu, 57 rue Jean-Pièrre-Timbaud, 11e (M° Parmentier). Mon–Sat till 10pm. Very affordable and pleasant Berber restaurant. Popular with students.

Au Rendez-Vous de la Marine, 114 quai de la Loire, 19e; ☎01.42.49.33.40 (M° Jaurès). Lunchtime & eves until 10pm; closed Sun, Mon & Aug. A busy successful old-time restaurant on the east bank of the Bassin de la Villette, renowned for its meat and desserts. A really good meal for around 150F. Need to book.

Restaurant de Bourgogne, 26 rue des Vinaigriers, 10e; ☎01.46.07.07.91 (M° Jacques-Bonsergent). Lunchtime & eve until 10pm; closed Sat eve, Sun & Aug. Homely old-fashioned restaurant with midday menu at 53F and evening menu at 58F. Still has a strong local character despite the changing nature of the area.

Au Trou Normand, 9 rue Jean-Pièrre-Timbaud, 11e; ☎01.48.05.80.23 (M° Filles-du-Calvaire/Oberkampf/République). Mon–Fri lunchtime & eve until 9.30pm, Sat open eve only; closed Aug. A small, totally unpretentious and very attractive. local *bistrot* serving good traditional food at knock-down prices. Dinner around 80F.

Au Val de Loire, 149 rue Amelot, 11e. ☎01.47.00.34.11 (M° République). Noon–2.30pm & 6.30–9.45pm; closed Sun & Aug. Simple, good food in a rather dingy street. Menus at 58F and 105F. A real bargain.

La Villette

CAFÉS AND BARS

Café de la Musique, 213 av Jean-Jaurés, 19e (M° Porte-de-Pantin). Daily till 2am. Part of the new *Cité de la Musique*; a typical subtle space by the *Cité* architect Portzamparc exuding sophistication, discretion and comfort.

RESTAURANTS

Aux Saveurs du Liban, 11 rue Eugène-Jumin, 19e (M° Porte-de-Pantin). Mon–Sat to 9.30pm. Tiny and very good value Lebanese restaurant not far from the Parc de la Villette, with sandwiches from 18F to take away.

Belleville, Menilmontant, Charonne and Père Lachaise

CAFÉS AND BARS

Le Baratin, 3 rue Jouye-Rouve, 20e (M° Pyrénées). Tues–Fri 11am–1am, Sat 6pm–1am. Friendly, unpretentious *bistrot à vins* in a run-down area with a good mix of people. Fine selection of lesser-known wines and whiskies. Midday menu 65F; *à la carte* 150F.

Le Blue Billard, 111–113 rue St-Maur, 11e (M° St-Maur/Parmentier). Daily 11am–2am. Blue-carpeted bar and billiard tables in a glass-roofed ex-factory. Popular with the neighbourhood's younger generation and arty types.

Café Charbon, 109 rue Oberkampf, 11e (M° St-Maur/Parmentier). Daily 9am–2am. A very successful and attractive resuscitation of a turn-of-the-century café. Particularly popular with the younger, fashionable crowd who are moving into these old working-class districts. Nice *plats du jour* 40-60F at lunchtime. DJ Thurs, Fri, Sat eves, and a rather younger clientele.

Cithea, 114 rue Oberkampf, 11e (M° Parmentier). Daily 5pm–2am. Bar and venue next door for Afro funk, funk reggae, world beat, jazz fusion etc on Thurs, Fri & Sat nights. Cocktails 40F. No admission charge for the music, but busy.

Eating and Drinking

See p.235 for a list of vegetarian restaurants in Paris.

Eating and Drinking

See p.271 for a list of cafés and restaurants that stay open late.

Some of Paris' top gourmet restaurants are listed on p.274.

Les Envierges, 11 rue des Envierges, 20e (Mº Pyrénées). Wed–Fri noon–midnight, Sat & Sun noon–8pm. Another *bistrot à vins.* purveying good-quality, lesser-known wines to connoisseurs. An attractive bar – though more a place to taste and buy wine than eat – in a great location above the Parc de Belleville.

La Flèche d'Or, 102bis rue de Bagnolet (cnr rue des Pyrénées), 20e (Mº Porte-de-Bagnolet/Alexandre-Dumas – a 15min walk in either case). A large, lively café attracting the biker, arty, post-punkish Parisian young. The décor is *très destroy*, ie railway sleepers and a sawn-off bus front hanging from the ceiling, and the building itself is the old Bagnolet station on the *petite ceinture* railway that encircled the city until around thirty years ago. Food available.

Tabac-Charonne, 120 rue de Bagnolet., 20e (Mº Porte-de-Bagnolet). Beautiful old café in Charonne village, with fading painted panels.

Le Vieux Belleville, 12 rue des Envierges, 20e; ☎01.44.62.92.66 (Mº Pyrénées). 7am–11pm; closed Sun. An old-fashioned café, simple and attractive. Meals around 120F. *Plats du jour* 49-65F.

RESTAURANTS

Aucune Idée, 2 place St-Blaise, 20e; ☎01.40.09.70.67 (Mº Porte-de-Bagnolet/Gambetta). Closed Sun eve, Mon & two weeks in Aug. Opposite the Charonne parish church, on the corner of the very pretty rue St-Blaise. It looks modern chichi, but the food is copious and good and the atmosphere very pleasant. 75F at lunch; 155F eves; 299F or so *à la carte*.

Chez Jean, 38 rue Boyer (near cnr with rue de Ménilmontant), 20e; ☎01.47.97.44.58 (Mº Gambetta/Ménilmontant). Mon–Fri lunchtime & eves till 10.30pm; closed Sat midday, Sun & first half of Aug. A charming, friendly, intimate place, with a small but carefully chosen menu. 54F midday menu; 120F *à la carte*.

A la Courtille, 1 rue des Envierges, 20e; ☎01.46.36.51.59 (Mº Pyrénées). Lunchtime, and eves until 11.30pm. Slightly stark modern interior, but good traditional cuisine in an unbeatable situation overlooking the delightful new Parc de Belleville. Get a pavement table on a summer evening and you'll have the best restaurant view in Paris. Midday menus 70F and 100F; *à la carte* 200F.

Égée, 19 rue de Ménilmontant, 20e; ☎01.43.58.70.26 (Mº Ménilmontant). Noon–2.30pm & 7.30–11.30pm. Greek and Turkish specialities served with home-made bread. Lunch menu at just 45F; *à la carte* more like 120F.

La Fontaine aux Roses, 27 av Gambetta, 20e; ☎01.46.36.74.75 (Mº Père-Lachaise). Till 10pm; closed Sun lunchtime, Mon & Aug. Small, beautiful restaurant with first-rate menus: midday 110F, evenings 165F, both including *kir royale*, wine and coffee.

Lao Siam, 49 rue de Belleville, 19e; ☎01.40.40.09.68 (Mº Belleville). Daily till 11pm. Extremely good Thai and Laotian food, popular with locals. Around 120F.

Louis Valy, 49 rue Orfila, 20e; ☎01.46.36.73.60 (Mº Gambetta/Pelleport). Lunchtime only; closed Sun & Aug. Generous helpings of good terrines, meat dishes and cheeses, and a very convivial atmosphere. Menu at 140F.

Le Pacifique, 35 rue de Belleville, 20e; ☎01.42.49.66.80 (Mº Belleville). Daily 11am–1am. A huge Chinese eating house with variable culinary standards, but low prices. 120F *à la carte*.

Au Pavillon Puebla, Parc des Buttes-Chaumont, 19e; ☎01.42.08.92.62 (Mº Buttes-Chaumont). Tues–Sat noon–10pm. Luxury cuisine in an old hunting lodge (enter by the rue Botzaris/av Bolivar gate to the park). Poached lobster, stuffed baby squid, duck with *foie gras*, and spicy oyster raviolis are some of the *à la carte* delights. Around 400F *à la carte*; midday menus at 180F; evening menus 230F.

Pho-Dong-Huong, 14 rue Louis-Bonnet, 11e; ☎01.43.57.42.81 (Mº Belleville).

Late-night Paris

For bars and brasseries in Paris to stay open after midnight is not unusual; the list below comprises cafés and bars open after 2am, and restaurants open beyond midnight.

Eating and Drinking

CAFÉS AND BARS

Connolly's Corner, cnr rues Patriarches and de Mirbel, 5ᵉ. Until 4am. p.251.

Le Dépanneur, 27 rue Fontaine, 9ᵉ. All-nighter. p.266.

Le Grand Café Capucines, 4 bd des Capucines, 9e. All-nighter. p.242.

Iguana, 15 rue de la Roquette, 11ᵉ. Until 4am. p.250.

Kléber, place du Trocadéro, 16ᵉ. Until dawn. p.259.

Le Mazet, 6 rue St-André-des-Arts, 6ᵉ. Until 2am, Fri & Sat until 3.30am. p.256.

Mustangs, 84 bd Montparnasse, 14ᵉ. Till 4am. p.260.

L'Opus, 167 quai de Valmy, 10ᵉ. Until 4am. p.268.

La Paillote, 45 Monsieur-Le-Prince, 6ᵉ. Until dawn. p.256.

Polly Magoo, 11 rue St-Jacques, 5ᵉ. All-nighter. p.253.

Pub St-Germain, 17 rue de l'Ancienne-Comédie, 6ᵉ. 24 hours. p.257.

Le Rosebud, 11bis rue Delambre, 14ᵉ. Until 3am. p.260.

Le Select, 99 bd du Montparnasse, 6ᵉ. Until 3am. p.260.

Le Sous-Bock, 49 rue St-Honoré, 1ᵉʳ. Until 5am. p.245.

Le Tambour, 41 rue Montmartre, 2ᵉ. 24 hours. p.244.

La Taverne Kronenbourg, 24 bd des Italiens, 9ᵉ. Until 3am. p.242.

La Taverne de Nesle, 32 rue Dauphine, 6ᵉ. Until 5am. p.257.

RESTAURANTS

Aux Deux-Théâtres, 18 rue Blanche, 9ᵉ. Till 12.30 am. p.267.

Baalbeck, 16 rue Mazagran, 10ᵉ. Until midnight. p.267.

Bofinger, 3–7 rue de la Bastille, 3ᵉ. Until 1am. p.251.

La Coupole, 102 bd du Montparnasse, 14ᵉ. Until 2am. p.260.

Aux Deux Saules, 91 rue St-Denis, 1ᵉʳ. Until 1am. p.245.

L'Enoteca, 25 rue Charles-V, 4ᵉ. Till midnight. p.248.

Flo, 7 cours des Petites-Écuries, 10ᵉ. Until 1.30am. p.268.

Fouta Toro, 3 rue du Nord, 18ᵉ. Until 1am. p.265.

Chez Gladines, 30 rue des Cinq-Diamants, 13ᵉ. Until 2am. p.264.

Goldenberg's, 7 rue des Rosiers, 4ᵉ. Until 2am. p.249.

Le Grand Colbert, passage Colbert, rue Vivienne, 2ᵉ. Until 1am. p.243.

Julien, 16 rue du Faubourg-St-Denis, l0ᵉ. Until 1.30am. p.268.

KOH, 12 rue de la Fidelité, 10ᵉ. Until 6am. p.268.

Lipp, 151 bd St-Germain, 6ᵉ. Until 12.30am. p.257.

Chez Maria, 16 rue du Maine, 14ᵉ. Until 1am. p.260.

Le Muniche, 22 rue Guillaume-Apollinaire, 6ᵉ. Until 2am. p.297.

Le Pacifique, 35 rue de Belleville, 20ᵉ. Until 1am. p.270.

Le Petit Prince, 12 rue Lanneau, 5ᵉ. Until 12.30am. p.254.

Le Petit Zinc, 11 rue St-Benoît, 6ᵉ. Until 2am. p.258.

Au Pied de Cochon, 6 rue Coquillière, 1ᵉʳ. 24 hours. p.246.

Planet Hollywood, 78 av des Champs-Elysées, 8ᵉ. Until 1am. p.242.

Polidor, 41 rue Monsieur-le-Prince, 6ᵉ. Until 1am. p.258.

(continued overleaf)

Eating and Drinking

Late-night Paris (continued)

Le Procope 13 rue de l'Ancienne-Comédie, 6e. Until 1am. p.258.

La Route du Château, 123 rue du Château, 14e. Until 12.30am. p.263.

Le Royal Belleville/Le Président, 19 rue Louis-Bonnet, 11e. Until 2am. p.272.

Terminus Nord, 23 rue de Dunkerque, 10e. Until 12.30am. p.268.

Taï Yen, 5 rue de Belleville, 20e. Until 1am. p.272.

Le Vaudeville, 29 rue Vivienne, 2e. Until 2am. p.244.

Wed–Mon noon–10.30pm. Spotlessly clean Vietnamese resto, where all dishes are under 50F and come with piles of fresh green leaves. Spicy soups, crispy pancakes, but slow service.

Le Polonia, 3 rue Chaumont, 19e; ☎01.42.40.38.97 (Mº Jaurès). Lunchtime & eves until 10.30pm; closed Sun eve, Mon & Aug. Don't be put off by the grubby exterior – underneath hotel of the same name. Inside there's a jovial Polish welcome and good Polish dishes for as little as 50F, though 100–120F is more realistic.

Aux Rendez-Vous des Amis, 10 av Père-Lachaise, 20e; ☎01.47.97.72.16 (Mº Gambetta). Lunchtime only, noon–2.30pm; closed Sun & mid-July to mid-Aug. Unprepossessing surroundings for very good, simple and satisfying family cooking – at around 80F; menu at 59F.

Le Royal Belleville, 19 rue Louis-Bonnet, 11e (☎01.43.38.22.72), and **Le Président** (☎01.47.00.17.18), the floor above – entrance on rue du Faubourg-du-Temple (Mº Belleville). Daily 11am–2am. A dramatic blood-red double staircase leads up to *Le Président*, the more expensive of these two cavernous Chinese restaurants. You go for the atmosphere and décor rather than the food, though the spring rolls and rum banana fritters are acceptable. The Thai dishes at *Le Président* are not very special. Between 100F and 150F.

Taï Yen, 5 rue de Belleville, 20e; ☎01.42.41.44.16 (Mº Belleville). 11.30am–1am. You can admire the koi carps like embroidered satin cushions idling round their aquarium while you

wait for the copious soups and steamed specialities. 60F menu; 100F *à la carte*.

Le Zéphyr, 1 rue Jourdain, 20e; ☎01.46.36.65.81 (Mº Jourdain). Mon–Sat till 11.30pm. A rather trendy but relaxed 1930s-style *bistrot* with menus at 69F and 110F including wine and coffee.

To the Faubourg St-Antoine

CAFÉS AND BARS

Jacques-Mélac, 42 rue Léon-Frot, 11e; ☎01.43.70.59.27 (Mº Charonne). 9am–10.30pm; closed Mon eve, weekends & Aug. Some way off the beaten track (between Père-Lachaise and place Léon-Blum) but a highly respected and very popular *bistrot à vins*, whose patron even makes his own wine – the solitary vine winds round the front of the shop (harvest celebrations in the second half of Sept; said to be great fun). The food (*plats* around 45F), wines and atmosphere are great, but you can't book, so it pays to get there early.

RESTAURANTS

Les Amognes, 243 rue du Faubourg-St-Antoine, 11e; ☎01.43.72.73.05 (Mº Faidherbe-Chaligny). Tues–Sat noon–2.30pm & 7.30–10.30pm; closed two weeks in Aug. Excellent, interesting food in a very popular place. Need to book. A menu at 180F; otherwise well over 250F.

Le Bistrot du Peintre, 116 av Ledru-Rollin, 11e; ☎01.47.00.34.39 (Mº Faidherbe-Chaligny). Mon–Sat till midnight, Sun till 9pm. Small tables jammed together beneath Art Nouveau frescoes and wood panelling. Traditional Parisian *bistrot* food with *plats du jour* at 60F; full meal from 130F.

Chardenoux, 1 rue Jules-Vallès, 11e; ☎01.43.71.49.52 (Mº Charonne). Mon–Fri noon–2.30pm & 8–10pm; closed Aug. An authentic oldie, with engraved mirrors dating back to 1900. Still serving solid meaty fare like calf kidneys grilled in mustard. Upwards of 200F.

Les Cinq Points Cardinaux, 14 rue Jean-Macé, 11e; ☎01.43.71.47.22 (Mº Faidherbe-Chaligny/Charonne). Mon–Fri noon–2pm & 7–10pm; closed Aug. An excellent, simple, old-time *bistrot*, still mainly frequented by locals and decorated with the old tools of their trades. Prices under 60F for lunch; around 100F in the evening. The snails in basil and the profiteroles are worth trying.

Les Demoiselles de Charonne, 44 rue Léon-Frot, 11e; ☎01.40.09.03.93 (Mº Charonne). Lunchtime only; closed Sat & Sun. Delicious old-fashioned home cooking. Menu at 85F, plus cheaper *formules*.

La Mansouria, 11 rue Faidherbe-Chaligny, 11e; ☎01.43.71.00.16 (Mº Faidherbe-Chaligny). Lunchtimes and eves until 11.30pm; closed Sun, Mon lunchtime, and a fortnight in Aug. An excellent and elegant Moroccan restaurant. Superb couscous and tagines. Around 170f.

Palais de la Femme, 94 rue de Charonne, 11e; ☎01.43.71.11.27 (Mº Charonne/Faidherbe-Chaligny). Daily 11.30am–2pm & 6.30–8pm. A good self-service restaurant in the women's hostel, run separately and open to all. Solid meals for less than 60F.

The 12e Arrondissement

CAFÉS AND BARS

Le Baron Rouge, 1 rue Théophile-Roussel (cnr place d'Aligre market), 12e (Mº Ledru-Rollin). 10am–2pm & 5–9.30pm; closed Sun eve & Mon. Another popular local bar, as close as you'll find to the spit-on-the-floor stereo-type of the old movies. As well as the wines – you can fill your own containers from the barrel for around 16F per litre – it serves a few snacks of cheese, *foie gras*, and *charcuterie* to the shoppers and workers of the Aligre market.

Le Penty Bar, cnr place d'Aligre and rue Emilio-Castellar, 12e. Small, old-fashioned café making no concessions to 1990s sanitation and still charging only 5F for a sit-down cup of coffee.

RESTAURANTS

L'Ébauchoir, 43–45 rue de Cîteaux, 12e; ☎01.43.42.49.31 (Mº Faidherbe-Chaligny). Mon–Sat until 11pm. Good *bistrot* fare in a sympathetic atmosphere; midday menu including wine for 70F; *carte* 150F upwards. Best to book for the evening.

La Gourmandise, 271 av Daumesnil, 12e; ☎01.43.43.94.41 (Mº Porte-Dorée). Till 10.30pm; closed Mon midday, Sun & first half Aug. Superb and original food (a mango charlotte, for example), with a good menu at 140F.

Chapter 11: Western Paris

Auteuil and Passy

CAFÉS AND BARS

Le Coquelin Aîné, 67 rue de Passy, 16e (Mº Muette). Tues–Sat 9am–6.30pm. An elegant café on place Passy, meeting place of gilded youth and age. Excellent salads, *tartes*, cakes, at a price – this is not for paupers. 110F menu noon–2.30pm.

RESTAURANTS

Aéro-Club de France, 6 rue Galiléo, 16e; ☎01.47.20.42.51 (Mº Boissière). Lunchtime only; closed Sat, Sun & Aug. Open to all, this massive upmarket canteen serves very nourishing and tasty fillers at 71F, 88F and 103F; you get an extra course with each increase in price. Pretty good value.

Eating and Drinking

See p.261 for a list of the various ethnic restaurants in Paris.

Eating and Drinking

See p.271 for a list of cafés and restaurants that stay open late.

Les Chauffeurs, 8 chaussée de la Muette, 16e; ☎01.42.88.50.05 (Mº Muette). Daily noon–2.30pm & 7.30–10pm. A relaxed, easy-going brasserie/café that takes its food seriously. You can't beat the 65F menu (not available Sun) for this part of the world.

The 17e Arrondissement

RESTAURANTS

Musée Jacquemart-André, 158 bd Haussmaun, 8e; ☎01.45.62.11.59 (Mº St-Philippe-du-Roule/Miromesnil). Daily 11am–6pm. A sumptuously appointed *salon de thé* in a nineteenth-century *palazzo*, with salads at 60–80F and a lunchtime *formule* at 78F. You do not need a museum ticket to use it.

Natacha, 35 rue Guersant, 17e; ☎01.45.74.23.86 (Mº Porte-Maillot). Lunchtime and eves until 11pm (11.30pm on Sat); closed Sun, Sat noon & Aug 10–20. A bit out of the way, beyond the place des Ternes, but a great bargain. For 80F at midday or 100F in the evening, you can help yourself to *hors d'oeuvres* and wine, with three other very respectable courses to follow. Not surprisingly, it pulls in the crowds. Best to be early.

Sangria, 13bis rue Vernier, 17e; ☎01.45.74.78.74 (Mº Porte-de-Champerret). As at *Natacha*, for 75F at midday and 85F in the evening you can help yourself to starters and wine in addition to enjoying three other courses. Also very popular and crowded, and just has the edge over *Natacha*.

Île de Chatou

RESTAURANTS

Restaurant Fournaise, Île de Chatou; ☎01.30.71.41.91 (*RER ligne A2* to Rueil-Malmaison, then a 10min walk along the dual carriageway to the bridge). Lunchtime, and eves until 10pm; closed Sun eve in winter. There is a menu at 150F; the *carte* is more like 200–250F. The food is good, but the location is the real attraction (see p.208). The restaurant, now beautifully restored, was a favourite haunt of the Impressionists and is the subject of Renoir's painting *Le Déjeuner des Canotiers*. The verandah, which features in the painting, is still there, shaded by a magnificent riverside plane tree. A real treat for a lunchtime in spring, or dinner on a warm summer night.

Over the Top . . . The Gourmet Restaurants of Paris

If you're feeling slightly crazed – or you happen on a winning lottery ticket – there are, of course, some really spectacular Parisian restaurants. For *nouvelle cuisine* at its very best *Robuchon* (59 av Raymond-Poincaré, 16e; ☎01.43.59.12.27), *Lucas Carton* (9 place de la Madeleine, 8e; ☎01.42.65.22.90), and *Taillevent* (15 rue Lamenais, 8e; ☎01.44.95.15.01) are said to be the pinnacles of gastronomic experience and not just for bills that can reach 10,000F for two. For pride of place, if not so much for *plats*, there's *Jules Vernes*, on the second floor of the Eiffel Tower (☎01.45.55.61.44). Unfortunately, the moment's madness that might inspire you to eat in any of these restaurants would most likely come months too late for you to make reservations.

Museums and Galleries

You may find there is sufficient visual stimulation to be gained from just wandering the streets of Paris, without feeling the need to explore the city's galleries and museums. It's certainly questionable whether the Louvre, for example, can compete in pleasure with the Marais, the quais or parts of the Latin Quarter. But if established art appeals to you at all, the Paris collections are not to be missed.

The most popular are the various **museums of modern art**: in the Beaubourg Pompidou Centre, Palais de Tokyo and Musée Picasso, and, for the brilliantly represented opening stages, in the **Musée d'Orsay, Orangerie** and **Marmottan**. Since Paris was the well-rocked cradle of Impressionism, Fauvism, Cubism, Surrealism and Symbolism, there's both justice and relevance in such a multitude of works being here. No less breathtaking, going back to earlier cultural roots, are some of the medieval works in the **Musée National du Moyen-Age** (the old Musée Cluny), including the glorious *La Dame à la Licorne* tapestry. Contemporary art is included in several collections, notably **Beaubourg**, and in temporary exhibitions at the **Jeu de Paume** and **Fondation Cartier** (detailed in the main text, Chapters 3 and 8). Photography has a new home at the **Maison Européenne de la Photographie**.

Among the city's extraordinary number of technical, historical, social and applied art museums, pride of place must go to the dazzling **Cité des Sciences**, radical in both concept and architecture – and fun. If any answer were needed to Disneyland Paris, this is it. Entertaining too, if more conventional, is the **Musée National des Arts et Traditions Populaires**, its equivalent for the past. Some of the smaller ones are dedicated to a single person – Balzac, Hugo, Piaf – and others to very particular subjects – spectacles, counterfeits, tobacco. We've detailed all but a very few of the smallest and most highly specialized, such as the freemasonry and lawyers' museums (details can be obtained from the tourist office). A few others, like **Le Corbusier, Montmartre**, the **Pavillon de l'Arsenal**, the **Gobelins, Musée Jean Moulin** and the **Bibliothèque Nationale** have been incorporated in the text in the relevant chapters. **Out-of-town museums** are detailed in Chapter 20, *Day trips from Paris.*

The Big Four – Louvre, Orsay, Cité des Sciences and the Beaubourg: Musée National d'Art Moderne – are described first. The remainder of the city's museums arw grouped into sections on smaller museums; fashion; history and social sciences; performance arts, literature and sport; and science and industry.

Admission prices vary, but all have gone up considerably in the last few years: the Musée Grevin is the most expensive at 50F; the Cité des Sciences

Museums and Galleries

and the Louvre are better value at 45F; the rest range from around 17F to 35F. Some museums offer student reductions for which the only acceptable ID is an ISIC (International Student Identity Card). This can still be refused, however, if you're obviously over 25, despite claims to the contrary. Other museums, such as the Louvre and Orsay, offer the *tarif réduit* to those aged between 18 and 25 and over 60, for which you'll need to show your passport, and free entry for the under-18s.

If you're going to visit a great many museums in a short time, it's worth buying the **Carte Musées et Monuments pass** (70F 1-day; 140F 3-day; 200F 5-day; available from *RER* stations and museums), which is valid for 65 museums and monuments in and around Paris, and allows you to bypass the ticket queues.

The Louvre and most other state-owned museums **close** on Tuesday and some have **half-price admission** on Sunday; the city-owned museums **close** on Monday and some have **free admission** on Sunday. Opening days and hours are all given below.

Lastly, keep an eye out for **temporary exhibitions**, some of which match any of Paris' regular collections. Beaubourg, the Grand Palais and the Grande Halle at La Villette have the major ones, well advertised by posters and detailed in *Pariscope* and the other listings magazines. Many of the museums and commercial galleries host themed exhibitions during the various arts festivals (see p.46–48). The **commercial galleries** (heavily concentrated in the Beaubourg, Bastille and St-Germain areas and detailed in Chapters 5 and 6) are always good for a look-in, which of course you can do without charge.

The Louvre

There's more about the Palais du Louvre itself on p.78

Pyramide, Cour Napoléon, Palais du Louvre, 1er; ☎ 01.40.20.51.51/01.40.20.53.17 (Mº Palais-Royal/Musée-du-Louvre/Louvre-Rivoli). Permanent collection Mon & Thurs–Sun 9am–6pm, Wed till 9.45pm; Richelieu Wing Thurs–Sun 9am–6pm, Mon 9am–9.45pm; Histoire du Louvre rooms and Medieval Louvre Mon & Wed–Sun 9am–9.45pm; Hall Napoléon temporary exhibitions Mon & Wed–Sun 10am–9.45pm; bookshop 9.30am–9.45pm; cafés and restaurant 9.30am–10pm. Everything closed Tues. Tickets valid all day, re-entry allowed; last tickets 45min before closing time. Admission 45F up to 3pm, thereafter and all day Sun 26F; free for under-18s and for everyone on the first Sun of every month. Combined ticket (museum and exhibition) 60F until 3pm; thereafter and all day Sun, 40F. Temporary exhibitions 30F. Under-26s and teachers can buy a ticket called La Carte Louvre Jeunes, which, for 100F, gives access to the museum and its temporary exhibitions for one year.

"You walked for a quarter of a mile through works of fine art; the very floors echoed the sounds of immortality . . . It was the crowning and consecration of art . . . These works instead of being taken from their respective countries were given to the world and to the mind and heart of man from whence they sprung . . ."

William Hazlitt, writing of the Louvre in 1802, goes on, in equally florid style, to proclaim this museum as the beginning of a new age when artistic masterpieces would be the inheritance of all, no longer the preserve of kings and nobility. Novel the Louvre certainly was. The palace, hung with the private collections of monarchs and their ministers, was first opened to the public in 1793, during the Revolution. Within a decade Napoléon had made it the largest art collection on earth with takings from his empire.

However inspiring it might have been then, the Louvre has been a bit of a nightmare over the last few decades, requiring heroic willpower and stamina to find one work of art that you want to see among the 30,000. The new "**Grand Louvre**", which was finally inaugurated by President Mitterrand in the autumn of 1988 and is now more or less complete, has failed to solve the problems.

The Pyramid is now the main entrance, covering a subterranean but day-lit concourse – the **Hall Napoléon** – with lifts and escalators leading into the three wings of the building, each with four floors: the *entresol* (the level reached from the escalators in the *Hall Napoléon*), the *rez-de-chaussée* (ground floor), then the first and second floors. The three wings are *Sully* (around the *Cour Carrée*), *Denon* (the south wing) and *Richelieu* (the north wing). These are then divided into ten numbered areas, subdivided into numbered rooms and colour-coded for the main categories of the collection (see below). The trouble with the Louvre has always been horizontal not vertical orientation and distance, so the access up from the *Hall Napoléon* doesn't get you very far. The signing system, including the giant electronic billboards in the *Hall Napoléon*, and the arrangement of the works, remains as mysterious and frustrating as ever. Most works – but not all – are now in their definitive place, but the insur-

mountable problem is that the Louvre is just too big. When you need a break, you still have to get back down to the ticket concourse to find a cup of coffee.

One bonus from all the building works has been the opportunity to excavate the remains of the **medieval Louvre** – Philippe-Auguste's twelfth-century fortress and Charles V's fourteenth-century palace conversion – under the Cour Carrée. These are now on show along with a permanent exhibition on the history of the Louvre, from the Middle Ages up to the current transformations. The medieval Louvre is all on the *entresol*, *Sully*, and easy to find.

The **seven basic categories** of the museum's collections are: three lots of antiquities, sculpture, painting, applied and graphic arts. Each category spreads over more than one wing (except Egyptian Antiquities – all are in *Sully*) and several floors. The free handbook (in English) gives details. **Oriental Antiquities**

Museums
and
Galleries

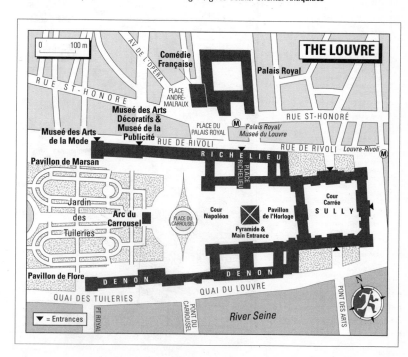

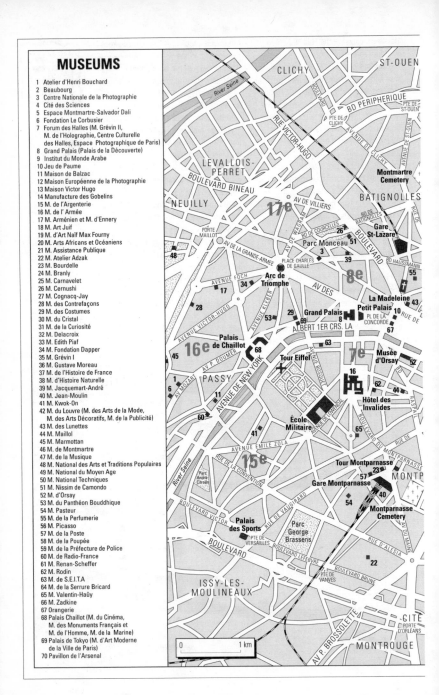

MUSEUMS

1 Atelier d'Henri Bouchard
2 Beaubourg
3 Centre Nationale de la Photographie
4 Cité des Sciences
5 Espace Montmartre-Salvador Dali
6 Fondation Le Corbusier
7 Forum des Halles (M. Grévin II,
   M. de l'Holographie, Centre Culturelle
   des Halles, Espace Photographique de Paris)
8 Grand Palais (Palais de la Découverte)
9 Institut du Monde Arabe
10 Jeu de Paume
11 Maison de Balzac
12 Maison Européenne de la Photographie
13 Maison Victor Hugo
14 Manufacture des Gobelins
15 M. de l'Argenterie
16 M. de l'Armée
17 M. Arménien et M. d'Ennery
18 M. Art Juif
19 M. d'Art Naïf Max Fourny
20 M. Arts Africains et Océaniens
21 M. Assistance Publique
22 M. Atelier Adzak
23 M. Bourdelle
24 M. Branly
25 M. Carnavalet
26 M. Cernuschi
27 M. Cognacq-Jay
28 M. des Contrefaçons
29 M. des Costumes
30 M. du Cristal
31 M. de la Curiosité
32 M. Delacroix
33 M. Edith Piaf
34 M. Fondation Dapper
35 M. Grévin I
36 M. Gustave Moreau
37 M. de l'Histoire de France
38 M. d'Histoire Naturelle
39 M. Jacquemart-André
40 M. Jean-Moulin
41 M. Kwok-On
42 M. du Louvre (M. des Arts de la Mode,
   M. des Arts Décoratifs, M. de la Publicité)
43 M. des Lunettes
44 M. Maillol
45 M. Marmottan
46 M. de Montmartre
47 M. de la Musique
48 M. National des Arts et Traditions Populaires
49 M. National du Moyen Age
50 M. National Techniques
51 M. Nissim de Camondo
52 M. d'Orsay
53 M. du Panthéon Bouddhique
54 M. Pasteur
55 M. de la Perfumerie
56 M. Picasso
57 M. de la Poste
58 M. de la Poupée
59 M. de la Préfecture de Police
60 M. de Radio-France
61 M. Renan-Scheffer
62 M. Rodin
63 M. de S.E.I.T.A
64 M. de la Serrure Bricard
65 M. Valentin-Haüy
66 M. Zadkine
67 Orangerie
68 Palais Chaillot (M. du Cinéma,
   M. des Monuments Français et
   M. de l'Homme, M. de la Marine)
69 Palais de Tokyo (M. d'Art Moderne
   de la Ville de Paris)
70 Pavillon de l'Arsenal

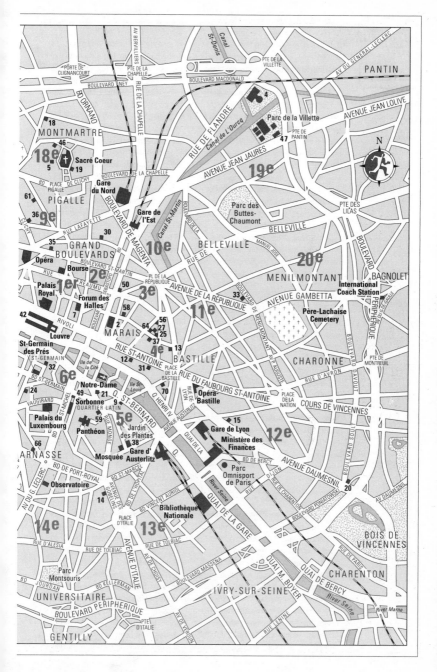

Museums and Galleries

– including the newly presented Islamic Art collection – covers the Sumerian, Babylonian, Assyrian and Phoenician civilizations, plus the art of ancient Persia. **Egyptian Antiquities** contains jewellery, domestic objects, sandals, sarcophagi and dozens of examples of the delicate naturalism of Egyptian decorative technique, such as the wall tiles depicting a piebald calf galloping through fields of papyrus and a duck taking off from a marsh. Some of the major exhibits are: the pink granite *Mastaba Sphinx*, the *Kneeling Scribe* statue (*Sully* ground floor 2 & 5), a wooden statue of *Chancellor Nakhti*, the god *Amon*, protector of Tutankhamun, a bust of *Amenophis IV*, *Sethi I* and the *goddess Hathor*.

The **Greek and Roman Antiquities** include the *Winged Victory of Samothrace* (*Denon* first floor, at the top of the great staircase) and the *Venus de Milo* (*Sully* ground floor 9), biggest crowd-pullers in the museum after the *Mona Lisa*. *Venus*, striking a classic model's pose, is one of the great sex-pots of all time. She dates from the late second century BC. Her antecedents are all on display, too, from the delightful *Dame d'Auxerre* (seventh century BC) and the fifth-century BC bronze *Apollo of Piombino*, still looking straight ahead in the archaic manner, to the classical perfection of the *Athlete of Beneveneto*. In the Roman section are some very attractive mosaics from Asia Minor and luminous frescoes from Pompeii and Herculaneum, which already seem to foreshadow the decorative lightness of touch of a Botticelli still 1000 years and more away.

The **Applied Arts** collection is heavily weighted on the side of vulgar imperial opulence. Beautifully crafted and extravagantly expensive pieces of furniture arouse no aesthetic response whatever; just an appalled calculation of the cost. The same has to be said of the renowned cabinet-maker Boulle's work (active round 1700), immediately recognizable by the heavy square shapes and lavish use of inlays in copper, bronze and pewter, and such ecologically cata-

strophic exuberance as entire doors of tortoiseshell. There are also several acres of tapestry – all of the very first quality and workmanship, but a chore to look at. Relief has to be sought in the smaller, less public items: Marie-Antoinette's travelling case, for example, fitted up with the intricacy of a jigsaw to take an array of bottles, vials and other queenly necessaries. Or the carved Parisian ivories of the thirteenth century: angels with rouged cheeks, and the Virgin pulling a sharp little nipple from her dress to suckle the Babe. Or the Limoges enamels and even earlier Byzantine ivories.

The **Sculpture section** covers the entire development of the art in France from Romanesque to Rodin, all in the new *Richelieu* wing, and Italian and Northern European sculpture in *Denon*, including Michelangelo's *Slaves*, designed for the tomb of Pope Julius II (*Denon* ground floor 10). The huge glass-covered courtyards of the *Richelieu* wing – the Cour Marly with the Marly Horses that once graced place de la Concorde, and the Cour Puget with Puget's *Milon de Crotone* as the centrepiece – are very impressive. But it's a bit too grandiose and overwhelming – the view from the passage Richelieu (see Chapter 3) is better. Upstairs, on the second floor, Napoléon III's apartments of flock wallpaper, matching upholstery and vast chandeliers, are now open to view. You can see why the Finance Ministry was so reluctant to move out.

The largest and most indigestible section by far is the **paintings** section: French from the year dot to mid-nineteenth century, with Italians, Dutch, Germans, Flemish and Spanish represented too. Among them are many paintings so familiar from reproduction in advertisements and on chocolate boxes that it is a surprise to see them on a wall in a frame. And, unless you're an art historian, it is hard to make much sense of the parade of mythological scenes, classical ruins, piteous piety, acrobatic saints and sheer dry academicism. A portrait, a domestic scene, a still life, is a real relief. Walking by with eyes selectively shut is probably the best advice. At least the lighting is much improved, with all the paintings on the first and second floors, and the ceilings designed by a specialized CAD programme to maximize and unify the natural light.

The early Italians (*Denon* first floor 5 & 7) are the most interesting part of the collection, at least up to Leonardo and the sixteenth century. Giotto, Fra Angelico, Uccello's Mantegna, Botticelli, Filippo Lippi, Raphael . . . all the big names are represented. It is partly their period, but there is still an innate classical restraint which is more appealing to modern taste than the exuberance and grandiloquence of the eighteenth and nineteenth centuries. If you want to get near the *Mona Lisa* (*Denon* first floor 5), go first or last thing in the day. No one, incidentally, pays the slightest bit of attention to the other Leonardos right alongside, including the *Virgin of the Rocks*.

Access to the *Hall Napoléon* and its shops, information services, audiovisual shows and so on, is free (so long as the Louvre queues do not preclude access to the Pyramid). You can reach it through passage Richelieu from rue de Rivoli, from the underground car park, or through the Tuileries, taking the spiral staircase down from the base of the pyramid.

The Palais du Louvre houses three other museums – decorative arts, fashion and publicity – listed under "The Rest of the art" and "Fashion and fripperies" on p.285 and p.293.

Musée d'Orsay

1 rue de Bellechasse/quai Anatole-France (for major exhibitions), 7e; 01.40.49.48.84/01.45.49.11.11 (Mº Solférino/RER Musée-d'Orsay). Tues, Wed, Fri & Sat 9/10am–6pm, Thurs 9/10am–9.45pm, Sun 9am–6pm; closed Mon. Admission 36F, 18–25s & over 60s 24F, under-18s free; Sun 24F; guided tours in English by staff lecturer Tues–Sat 11am, Thurs 7pm, 36F.

The conversion of the disused train station, the Gare d'Orsay, into the Musée d'Orsay marked a major advance in the reorganization of the capital's art collections. It houses the painting and sculpture of the immediately pre-modern period, 1848–1914, bridging the gap between the Louvre and the Centre Beaubourg. Its focus is the cobweb-clearing, eye-cleansing collection of **Impressionists** rescued from the cramped corridors of the Jeu de Paume – though not, unavoidably, from the coach parties and gangs of brats. Scarcely less electrifying are the works of the **Post-Impressionists** brought in from the Palais de Tokyo.

The **general layout** is as follows. On the ground floor, the **mid-nineteenth-century sculptors**, including Barye, caster of super-naturalistic bronze animals, occupy the centre gallery. To their right, a few canvases by Ingres and Delacroix (the bulk of whose work is in the Louvre) serve to illustrate **the transition from the early nineteenth century**. Puvis de Chavannes, Gustave Moreau, the Symbolists and early Degas follow, while in the galleries to the left Daumier, Corot, Millet and the Realist school lead onto the **first Impressionist works**, including Manet's *Déjeuner sur l'Herbe*, which sent the critics into apoplexies of rage and disgust when it appeared in 1863. *Olympia* is here, too; equally controversial at the time, for the colour contrasts and sensual surfaces, rather than the content, though the black cat was considered peculiar.

Contemporary controversy has surrounded Courbet's *L'Origine du Monde* (room 7), acquired from the psychoanalyst Lacan, who had it screened behind a curtain in his consulting rooms. The painting centres on a nude female torso: if not the "origin of the world", then certainly the origin of individual human life.

To get the chronological continuation you have to go straight up to the top level, where numerous landscapes and outdoor scenes by **Renoir, Sisley, Pissarro** and **Monet** owe much of their brilliance to the novel practice of setting up easels in the open to catch a momentary light. Monet's *Waterlilies* are

Museums and Galleries

Museums and Galleries

here in abundance, too, along with five of his Rouen cathedral series, each painted in different light conditions.

Le Berceau (1872), by Morisot, the only woman in the early group of Impressionists, is one of the few to have a complex human emotion as its subject – perfectly synthesized within the classic techniques of the movement. A very different touch, all shimmering light and wide brush strokes, is to be seen in Renoir's depiction of a good time being had by all in *Le Moulin de la Galette* – a favourite Sunday afternoon out on the Butte Montmartre.

Room 86 is full of the blinding colours and disturbing rhythms of **Van Gogh**, while **Cézanne**, a step removed from the preoccupations of the mainstream Impressionists, is wonderfully represented in room 39. One of the canvases most revealing of his art is *Still Life with Apples and Oranges* (1895–1900), in which the background abandons perspective while the fruit has an extraordinary reality.

The rest of this level is given over to the various **offspring of Impressionism**. Among a number of pointilliste works by Seurat, (the famous *Cirque*), Signac and various other artists is Rousseau's dream-like *La Charmeuse de Serpent*, of 1907. There's Gauguin, post- and pre-Tahiti, as well as lots of Toulouse-Lautrec at his caricaturial nightclubbing best – one large canvas including a rear view of Oscar Wilde at his grossest.

The middle level takes in Rodin and other **late nineteenth-century sculptors**, several rooms of superb **Art Nouveau** furniture and *objets*, and the sumptuous reception room (room 51) of the station hotel. Vuillard and Bonnard are tucked away here (rooms 71–72), while Klimt and Munch feature in the rooms overlooking the Seine.

The Pavillon Amont, in the far left corner of the building, displays furniture and architectural models from Viollet-le-Duc to Frank Lloyd Wright; while at the far end of the ground floor much attention is devoted to the Opéra Garnier.

The design of the Musée d'Orsay is, without doubt, very clever, and the artworks have been given the best lighting you could wish for. But many people find the space overdesigned, the sequences of galleries on the upper floors too intense, and the ground floor so marbled it feels like a tomb. There is also an enormous amount of indigestible nineteenth-century establishment work, admired at the time but of interest nowadays only to art historians. In general, the collection suffers by simply being too large. Exhaustion dampens the exuberance that so many of the paintings can inspire; returning to a favourite for another look requires a lot of effort, and the surroundings are too sombre and serious. The view over the river through the old station clocks give some relief., however, and there's the *Café des Hauteurs* on the upper level plus a restaurant and tearoom in gilded rooms on the middle level in which to recuperate.

Cité des Sciences et de l'Industrie

Parc de la Villette, 30 av Corentin-Cariou, 19e; ☎01.36.68.29.30 (Mº Porte-de-la-Villette). Tues–Sat 10am–6pm, Sun 10am–7pm; everything closed Mon. Cité pass giving access to Explora and its temporay exhibitions, planetarium, Cinéma Louis-Lumière, Salle Jean-Painlevé and mediathèque screens, aquarium and Argonaute: 45F, reduced tarif 35F, under-7s free; Géode Tues–Sun 10am–8pm; 50F/37F (some films are more), combined ticket with Cité 85F/72F (available from Géode only); Inventorium and Cité des Enfants (see p.316) 15F and 20F extra; Cinaxe 27F/22F.

This is the science museum to end all science museums, and worth visiting for the interior of the building alone: all glass and stainless steel, crow's-nests and cantilevered platforms, bridges and suspended walkways, the different levels linked by lifts and escalators around a huge central space open to the full 40m height of the roof. It may be colossal, but you are more likely to lose yourself mentally rather than physically, and come out after several hours reeling with images and ideas, while possibly none the wiser about DNA, quasars, bacteria reproduction, curved space or rocket launching.

The **permanent exhibition**, called Explora, takes up the top two floors and is divided into sixteen units (pick up a detailed plan from the *Accueil général* Explora on *niveau* 1). These cover different subjects such as sounds, robots, computer science, expression and behaviour, oceans, energy, light, the environment, mathematics, medicine, space, language, etc. The emphasis, as the name suggests, is on exploring; the means used are interactive computers, multimedia displays, videos, holograms, animated models and games. Most of the explanations and instructions are in English as well as French; one exception, unfortunately, is the *Jeux de Lumière* ("light games"), a whole series of experiments to do with colour, optical illusions, refraction, etc. But then you can treat working out what you're supposed to do as an experiment in itself.

A classic example of chaos theory introduces the **maths section**: a wheel of glasses rotating below a stream of water in which the switch between clockwise and anticlockwise motion is unpredictable beyond two minutes. An "inertial carousel" – a revolving drum (2–6pm only) provides a four-minute insight into the strange transformations of objects in motion. In *Expressions et Comportements* you can intervene in stories acted out on videos, changing the behaviour of the characters to engineer a different outcome. Hydroponic plants grow for real in the green bridge across the central space. You can steer robots through mazes; make music by your own movements; try out a flight simulation; watch computer-guided puppet shows and holograms of different periods' visions of the universe; examine microbes magnified millions of times; explore large-scale models of space rockets and space stations and a real Mirage jet fighter; and smell the herbs used in different cultures as alternative remedies. To have your head spun further by a session in the

planetarium (on the top floor; shows at 11am, noon, 2pm, 3pm, 4pm & 5pm), you need to have booked a place when buying your ticket.

There are always several **temporary exhibitions** within *Explora* (and in other spaces throughout the building), plus a major one each year based on an inter-disciplinary theme to which all the natural and social sciences, plus art and literature, can be brought into play. The new networks of digital information is the proposed theme for the end of 1997.

When all this interrogation and stimulation becomes too much, you can relax at one of the two cafés within Explora (by the planetarium and by the *Biologie* section), where the coffee's cheap and you can even smoke.

Back on the ground floor, the **Ciméma Louis-Lumière** shows short stereoscopic films every half hour or so, for which you'll have to queue. There are more films in the **Salle Jean-Bertin** (1hr programmes at 10.15am, 2.15pm & 4.15pm) and more serious documentaries in the **Salle Jean-Painlevé** (*niveau* S1; Sat & Sun 4pm & 5.30pm). In the **Médiathèque** (*niveau* S1 & S2; noon–8pm) you can call up your own choice from over 4000 films at individual consoles, as well as consulting CD-ROMs, educational software, books and magazines. Information on current French and international scientific research is displayed in the **Salle Science Actualités** (S1) next dor to the new **Cité des Métiers** (Tues–Fri 10am–6pm, Sat noon–6pm), which provides free access to information on finding work, changing careers, training, creating your own employment, and working conditions in different countries. It even offers an on-the-spot consultancy with a careers advisor. Finally, on the lowest floor (S2), you can eat and drink beside an **aquarium** filled with Mediterranean sea life.

For details of the **Cité des Enfants**, temporary exhibitions geared to kids, and the **Médiathèque des Enfants** (for all of which you have to be accompanied by a child), plus the **Techno Cité** designed for teenagers, see p.316.

Museums
and
Galleries

Museums and Galleries

A Walkman guide in English is available at the counter in the main hall (around 15F), and includes details of the architecture, explanations for Explora and the soundtrack for the planetarium shows.

The entire building is **accessible by wheelchair** (as is the park, with escalators at the bridge across the canal); the *Médiathèque* has a **Braille** room; many of the *Explora* exhibits have audio explanations; and there are also **signers** (in FSL).

Outside, you can clamber around the **Argonaute**, a real 1957 French military submarine, discover masses of facts about underwater transportation, and view the park through its periscope. The **Géode** shows films shot on the 180-degree Omnimax system (see *Film, theatre and dance* chapter, p.353), while the **Cinaxe** combines 70mm film shot at thirty frames a second with seats that move, so that a bobsleigh ride down the Cresta Run, for example, not only looks unbelievably real, but feels it too.

Beaubourg: Musée National d'Art Moderne

Centre National d'Art et de Culture Georges Pompidou (or Beaubourg), rue St-Martin/rue du Renard, 4ᵉ (Mº Rambuteau/Hôtel-de-Ville). Centre and museum open Mon & Wed–Fri noon–10pm, Sat & Sun 10am–10pm; closed Tues. Free entry to building: Musée National d'Art Moderne 35F; under-24s & Sun 24F; under 18s free, tickets available from main hall (up to 1hr before closing)or from coin-operated machine by museum entrance (no change); temporary exhibitions 27F/20F to 45F/30F; day pass for exhibitions and permanent collections 70F/45F, free for under-16s.

The Musée National d'Art Moderne, on the third and fourth floors of Beaubourg, is second to none. The art is exclusively twentieth century and constantly expanding. Contemporary movements and works dated the year before last find their place here along with the Fauvists, Cubists, Dadaists, Figuratives, Abstractionists and the rest of this century's First World art trends. The lighting and spacing is superb, but only a fraction of the whole collection is hung at any one time.

A huge cut-out by Matisse, *La Tristesse du Roi*, greets you on entry. In a different world, Picasso's *Femme Assise* of 1909 brings in the reduced colours and double dimensions of Cubism, presented in its fuller development by Braque's *L'Homme à la Guitare* (1914) and, later, in Léger's solid balancing act, *Les Acrobates en Gris* (1942–44). All three artists are stunningly well represented.

Marcel Duchamp's games with the status of art objects (the bearded *Mona Lisa*, bottle-racks, etc) are some of the most enjoyable of the **Dada** School. Among **Abstracts**, there's the sensuous rhythm of colour in Sonia Delaunay's *Prismes Électriques* (1914) and a good number of Kandinskys at his most harmonious and playful. Dali disturbs, amuses or irritates with works such as *Six apparitions de Lénine sur un piano* (1931), and there are more Surrealist images from Magritte and de Chirico. A pleasing contrast is the room full of happy and calming Mirós and Calders.

Moving to the **Expressionists**, one of the most compulsive pictures – of 1920s female emancipation as viewed by a male contemporary – is the portrait of the journalist Sylvia von Harden by Otto Dix. In contrast, the gender of the sleeping woman in *Le Rêve* by Matisse has no importance – it is the human body at its most relaxed that the artist has painted.

Jumping forward, to Francis Bacon, you find the tension and the torment of the human body and mind in the portraits, and – no matter that the figure is minute – in *Van Gogh in Landscape* (1957). Squashed-up cars, lines and squares, wrapped-up grand pianos and Warhol's *Electric Chair* (1966) may be on show, while, for a reminder that contemporary art can still hold its roots, there's the classic subject of *Le Peintre et son modèle* by Balthus in 1980–81. Installation art is also included in the contemporary section on the third floor along with a huge collection of videos to consult.

There are temporary exhibitions of photographs, drawings, collages and prints in the **Galerie d'Art Graphique** and within the museum, along with changing exhibitions from its permanent collections. If your grasp of French is sufficient, you can take advantage of the **audiovisual presentations** on the major artistic movements of this century, or the **films**, projected several times daily in the **Salle Garance** on the ground floor, on contemporary art, on current exhibitions or as experimental art in themselves.

The **Grande Galerie**, right at the top of the building, is where the big-time exhibitions are held. They usually last several months, are extremely well publicized, and can, occasionally, be brilliant. Temporary shows on design and engineering are presented by the **Centre de Création Industrielle**, based in the building, and other exhibitions, large and small, fill the galleries on the mezzanines and lower floor, dealing with every diverse aspect of art, architecture, art theory and applied arts. The **day pass** includes guided tour in English of the Musée d'Art Moderne (3.30pm), the Grande Galerie exhibition (2.30pm) and the building itself (Fri–Sun 2.30pm).

Beaubourg also has an excellent cinema (see p.356), a reference library including foreign newspapers open to all, a record library where you can take a music break, a snack bar and restaurant (with seating on the roof), a bookshop, dance and theatre space, a cybercafé, and a kids' workshop (see p.315).

The Rest of the Art

Musée d'Art Moderne de la Ville de Paris

Palais de Tokyo east wing, 11 av du Président-Wilson, 16e; ☎ 01.53.67.40.00 (Mº Iéna/Alma-Marceau). Tues–Fri 10am–5.30pm, Sat & Sun 10am–7pm, Wed till 8.30pm in summer; closed Mon & hols. 27F/19F, under-18s free.

The problem with reviewing Paris' Musée d'Art Moderne is that it is difficult to predict which works will be on display and where, for this gallery suffers from seemingly chronic St Vitus' Dance. But you can rest assured that the museum's schools and trends of **twentieth-century art** will always be richly represented by artists such as Vlaminck, Zadkine, Picasso, Braque, Juan Gris, Valadon, Matisse, Dufy, Utrillo, both Delaunays, Chagall, Modigliani, Léger and many others, as well as by sculpture and painting by contemporary artists.

Among the most spectacular works on permanent show are Robert and Sonia Delaunay's huge whirling wheels and cogs of rainbow colour (which are now displayed in the ground floor corridor); the pale leaping figures of Matisse's *La Danse*; and Dufy's enormous mural, *La Fée Électricité* (done for the Electricity Board), illustrating the story of electricity from Aristotle to the then-modern power station, in 250 lyrical, colourful panels that fill three entire walls.

The upper floors of the gallery are reserved for all sorts of contemporary and experimental work, including music and photography.

On sale in the bookshop are a number of artists' designs, among them a set of Sonia Delaunay's playing cards, guaranteed to rejuvenate the most jaded cardsharp. Next to it is an excellent and reasonably priced snack bar.

Musée National du Moyen-Age

6 place Paul-Painlevé, (off rue des Écoles), 5e; ☎ 01.43.25.62.00 (Mº Cluny-La Sorbonne/St-Michel). Mon & Wed–Sun 9.15am–5.45pm; closed Tues. 28F/18F, under-18s free; half-price Sun. Audio & tactile aids for the visually impaired.

If you have always found tapestries boring, this treasure house of medieval art may well provide the flash of enlightenment. The numerous beauties in the former Musée de Cluny include a marvellous depiction of the grape harvest; a Resurrection embroidered in gold and silver thread, with sleeping guards in

Museums and Galleries

Museums and Galleries

medieval armour; and a whole room of sixteenth-century Dutch tapestries, full of flowers and birds, a woman spinning while a cat plays with the end of the thread, a lover making advances, and a pretty woman in her bath, overflowing into a duck pond.

But the greatest wonder of all is *La Dame à la Licorne* – "The Lady with the Unicorn": six enigmatic scenes featuring a beautiful woman flanked by a lion and a unicorn. Dating from the late fifteenth century, and perhaps made in Brussels, it is quite simply the most stunning piece of art you are likely to see in many a long day. The ground of each panel is a delicate red worked with a thousand tiny flowers, birds and animals. In the centre, on a green island, equally flowery and framed by stylized trees, the young woman plays a portable organ, takes a sweet from a proffered box, makes a necklace of carnations, while a pet monkey, perched on the rim of a basket of flowers, holds one to his nose.

Unfortunately, the lighting and general atmosphere of this museum are a trifle gloomy, and it doesn't yet feature on the list for dramatic renovations, but nevertheless it's a treat (and generally uncrowded).

The Orangerie

Jardins des Tuileries, Place de la Concorde, 1er; ☎ 01.42.97.48.16 (Mº Concorde). Mon & Wed–Sun 9.45am–5.15pm; closed Tues. 27F over 60s, under-25s; Sun 18F.

The Orangerie, on the south side of the Tuileries terrace overlooking place de la Concorde, is one of the museums people tend to forget about, despite its two oval rooms arranged by **Monet** as panoramas for his largest waterlily paintings. In addition, there are works by no more than a dozen other **Impressionist** artists – Matisse, Cézanne, Utrillo, Modigliani, Renoir, Soutine and Sisley among them.

This is a private collection, inherited by the state with the stipulation that it should always stay together. Consequently, none of the pictures were

moved to the Musée d'Orsay, and the Orangerie remains one of the top treats of Paris art museums.

Cézanne's southern landscapes, the portraits by Van Dongen, Utrillo and Derain o˙ Paul Guillaume and Jean Walter, whose taste this collection represents, the massive nudes of Picasso, Monet's *Argenteuil* and Sisley's *Le Chemin de Montbuisson*, are the cherries on the cake of this visual feast. What's more, you don't need marathon endurance to cover the lot and get back to your favourites for a second look.

Musée Marmottan

2 rue Louis-Boilly, off av Raphael, 16e; ☎ 01.42.24.07.02 (Mº Muette). Tues–Sun 10am–5.30pm; closed Mon. 35F/15F.

The Marmottan house itself is interesting, with some splendid pieces of First Empire pomposity: chairs with golden sphinxes for armrests, candelabra of complicated headdresses and twining serpents. There is a small and beautiful collection of thirteenth- to sixteenth-century manuscript illuminations, but the star of the show is the collection of **Monet paintings** bequeathed by the artist's son. Among them is the canvas entitled *Impression, Soleil Levant* (Impression, Sunrise), an 1872 rendering of a misty sunrise over Le Havre, whose title the critics usurped to give the Impressionist movement its name. There's a dazzling collection of canvases from Monet's last years at Giverny. They include several *Nymphéas* (Waterlilies), *Le Pont Japonais, L'Allée des Rosiers* and *La Saule Pleureur*, where rich colours are laid on in thick, excited whorls and lines. To all intents and purposes, these are abstractions – so much more "advanced" than the work of, say, Renoir, Monet's exact contemporary.

Impression, Soleil Levant was stolen from the gallery in October 1985, along with eight other paintings. After a police operation lasting five years and going as far afield as Japan, the paintings were discovered in a villa in southern Corsica, and are back on show – with greatly tightened security measures.

Musée des Arts Africains et Océaniens

293 av Daumesnil, 12e; ☎ 01.44.74.84.80 (Mº Porte-Dorée). Daily except Tues 10am–noon & 1.30–5.30pm, Sat & Sun 12.30–6pm; 28F/18F (36F/26F with exhibition).

This strange museum – one of the least crowded in the city – has an African gold brooch of curled-up sleeping crocodiles on one floor and, in the basement, five live crocodiles in a tiny pit surrounded by tanks of tropical fishes. Imperialism is much in evidence in a gathering of culture and creatures from the old French colonies: hardly any of the black African artefacts are dated, as the collection predates European acknowledgement of history on that continent, and the captions are a bit suspicious, too. These masks and statues, furniture, adornments and tools should be exhibited with paintings by Expressionists, Cubists and Surrealists to see in which direction inspiration went. Picasso and friends certainly came here often. And though casual tourists might not respond with a bit of painting or sculpture, they should find a lot to enjoy.

Musée Picasso

Hôtel Salé, 5 rue de Thorigny, 3e; ☎ 01.42.71.25.21 (Mº St-Paul/Chemin-Vert). Wed 9.15am–10pm, Mon & Thurs–Sun 9.15am–5.15pm; closed Tues. 36F/18–25s 26F, under-18s free; Sun 26F.

The French are justly proud of this 1980s art museum. The grandiloquent seventeenth-century mansion, the *Hôtel Salé*, was restored and restructured at a cost to the government of £3–4m. The spacious, undaunting interior is admirably suited to its contents: the largest collection of Picassos anywhere. A large proportion of the works were personally owned by Picasso at the time of his death, and the state had first option on them in lieu of taxes owed. They include all the different media he used, the paintings he bought or was given by his contemporaries, his African masks and sculptures, photographs, letters and other personal memorabilia.

All of which said, it's a bit disappointing. These are not Picasso's most enjoyable works – the museums of the Côte d'Azur and the Picasso gallery in Barcelona are more exciting. But the collection does leave you with a definite sense of the man and his life in conjunction with his production. This is partly because these were the works he wanted to keep. The paintings of his wives, lovers and families are some of the gentlest and most endearing: the portraits of *Marie-Thérèse* and *Claude Dessinant, Françoise et Paloma*, for example. Throughout the chronological sequence, the photographs are vital in showing this charismatic (and highly photogenic) man seen at work and at play by friends and family.

The portrait of *Dora Maar*, like that of *Marie-Thérèse*, was painted in 1937, during the Spanish Civil War, when Picasso was going through his worst personal and political crises. This is the period when emotion and passion play hardest on his paintings and they are by far the best (though *Guernica* is in Madrid, not here). A decade later, Picasso was a member of the Communist Party – his cards are on show along with a drawing entitled *Staline à la Santé* (Here's to Stalin), and his delegate credentials for the 1948 World Congress of Peace. The *Massacre en Corée* (1951) demonstrates the lasting pacifist commitment in his work.

Temporary exhibitions will bring to the *Hôtel Salé* works from the periods least represented: the Pink Period, Cubism (despite some fine examples here, including a large collection of collages), the immediate postwar period and the 1950s and 1960s.

The modern museological accoutrements are all provided: audiovisuals and films in a special cinema, biographical and critical details displayed in each room, and a library.

Musée Rodin

Hôtel Biron, 77 rue de Varenne, 7e (just to the east of the Invalides); ☎ 01.44.18.61.10

Museums and Galleries

Museums and Galleries

(M° Varenne). Tues–Sun 9.30am–5/5.45pm; closed Mon. 28F/18F, garden only 5F.

This collection represents the whole of Rodin's work. Major projects like *Les Bourgeois de Calais, Le Penseur, Balzac, Orpheus, La Porte de l'Enfer, Ugolini et fils* are exhibited in the garden – the latter forming the centrepiece of the ornamental pond. Indoors (and very crowded) are works in marble like *Le Baiser, La Main de Dieu, La Cathédrale* – those two perfectly poised, almost sentient, hands. There is something particularly fascinating about those works, such as *Romeo and Juliet* and *La Centauresse*, which are only, as it were, half-created, not totally liberated from the raw block of stone.

There is a reasonably priced café in the garden (summer only).

Also open to the public, and worth the trouble if you are interested in Rodin, is the house in which he spent the last years of his life, the **Villa des Brillants**, in the tranquil suburb of Meudon, to the southwest of the city (19 av Rodin, Meudon; ☎01.45.34.13.09; July–Sept Fri–Sun 1–6pm; 15F) *RER ligne C* to Meudon-Val Fleury, then 15min walk along avs Barbusse & Rodin.

Rodin, already famous, acquired the house in 1895 and installed his studio in the first room you encounter as you enter through the veranda. It was in this room that he used to dine with his companion, Rose Beuret, on summer evenings, and here that he married her, after fifty years together, just a fortnight before her death in February 1917. His own death followed in November, and they are buried together on the terrace below the house, beneath a version of *Le Penseur*. The classical façade behind them masks an enormous pavilion containing plaster casts of many of the most famous works.

Musée des Arts Décoratifs

Palais du Louvre, 107 rue de Rivoli, 1er; ☎01.44.55.57.50 (M° Palais-Royal/Musée-du-Louvre). Wed–Sat 12.30–6pm, Sun noon–6pm; closed Mon & Tues. 28F/18F; disabled access.

This is an enormous museum, except by the standards of the building housing it – the Louvre – of which it takes up the Tuileries end of the north wing. It is, however, being reorganized, and alterations will be going on until 1998, with the permanent collections closed some of the time. The contents are the furnishings, fittings and objects of French interiors: beds, blankets, cupboards, tools, stained glass and lampshades – in fact almost anything that illustrates the decorative skills from the Middle Ages to the 1990s.

The meagre contemporary section has recently been added to – principally works by French, Italian and Japanese designers, including, inevitably, Philippe Starck. The rest of the twentieth century is fascinating – a bedroom by Guimard, Jeanne Lanvin's Art Deco apartments, and a salon created by Georges Hoentschel for the 1900 Expo Universelle. You can work your way back through the nineteenth century's fascination with the foreign and love of vivid colouring, to the intricate wood-carving of the eighteenth century, to seventeenth-century marquetry and Renaissance tapestries and ivories.

One section is dedicated to toys throughout the ages, with changing exhibitions. The museum shop, with books, clothes, accessories, playing cards and other amusements, is good, though not cheap.

Institut du Monde Arabe

1 rue Fossés-St-Bernard, 5e; ☎01.40.51.38.38 (M° Jussieu/Cardinal-Lemoine). Tues–Sun 10am–6pm; closed Mon. 25F/20F.

Spread over seven spacious floors, the museum of the Institut du Monde Arabe has something of the atmosphere of a mosque – a rarefied place where you can talk and walk or think and study, at ease in the gracefulness of the building. There is a great deal of information, in the form of interactive videos and sheets (in both French and English) which you can take with you, while the choice of exhibits is extremely select.

Weights and measures, celestial globes, astrolabes, compasses and sun dials, along with the grinding and mixing implements for medicines, illustrate an early period of Arab scientific research between 750 and 1258 AD. There are coins from an even earlier era, and illuminated manuscripts with fairy-tale pictures. Among the half a dozen or so exquisite silk carpets, one, of sixteenth-century Persian origin, has arabesques of flowers and birds with a swirling movement far removed from the static geometries usually associated with oriental carpet design. Ceramics and the tools of calligraphy and cookery are also represented.

On the ground floor are **contemporary paintings and sculpture** from the Arab world. Many of these have an emotional charge lacking in most Western contemporary art. Perhaps it is the political context that makes, for example, the brilliant bands of colour denoting sea, sand and city in Saliba Douaihy's *Beirut-Mediterranean*, painted during the Civil War in Beirut, such a powerful statement. Sami Mohamed Al-Saleh's bronze sculpture *Sabra and Chatila* would represent profound agony in any context, but the reference is there. Not all the paintings, by any means, address political "issues". They represent a wonderful diversity of the main artistic movements currently being explored in the Arab world.

Maison Européenne de la Photographie

5-7 rue de Fourcy, 4e; ☎ 01.44.78.75.00 (Mº St-Paul/Ste-Marie). Wed–Sun 11am–8pm; closed Mon & Tues. 30F/15F.

A gorgeous Marais mansion, the early eighteenth-century *Hôtel Hénault de Cantobre* has been turned into a vast and serene space dedicated to the art of contemporary photography. Temporary shows join the revolving exhibiton of the Maison's permanent collection; young photographers and news photographers get a look in, as well as artists using photography in multi-media creations or installation art. A library and videothèque can be freely consulted and there's a pleasant café.

Musée Maillol

61 rue de Grenelle, 7e; ☎ 01.42.22.59.58 (Mº Rue-du-Bac). Mon & Wed–Sun 11am–6pm. 40F/26F, under-18s free.

The exhibits in this elegant eighteenth-century house belong to Dina Vierny, former model and inspiration to the sculptor Aristide Maillol, whose work adorns the Jardin du Carrousel, by the Louvre. It's a peculiar collection: huge numbers of Maillol's female nudes, which, sculpted or painted, become overbearing en masse; not particularly wonderful drawings by Matisse, Dufy and Bonnard, for whom Dina also modelled; hideous Naïve paintings by Seraphine and Bombois; the odd Picasso, Degas, Gauguin and Kandinsky; Duchamp urinals and bike wheels; a happy spider by Redon (in the furthest corner of the top floor); and Soviet installation art of the 1970s. The most interesting works fall into this last category: Ilya Kabakov's *Communal Kitchen*, based on the rows and grumblings of Soviet families sharing a tiny eating and cooking space; and Vladimir Yankilevski's *The Door*, in which the shape of a downtrodden Soviet man returning to his flat provides the outline, on the other side of the door, for a vision of sky and sea.

There are also temporary exhibitions and a good bookshop, plus the house itself is an attractive space to explore.

Musée-Fondation Dapper

50 av Victor-Hugo, 16e; ☎ 01.45.00.01.50 (Mº Étoile). Daily 11am–7pm during exhibitions. 20F/10F; free Wed.

The art of pre-colonial Africa is presented in superb temporary exhibitions based around a region, a period or a particular aspect of culture. Check *Pariscope*, etc, for details. The library is open to students and researchers.

Grand and Petit Palais

Av W-Churchill, 8e; ☎ 01.44.13.17.17/ 01.44.13.17.30 (Mº Champs-Élysées/ Clemenceau). Grand Palais Mon &

Museums
and
Galleries

Museums and Galleries

Thurs–Sun 10am–8pm, Wed 10am–10pm; prices vary depending on the exhibition, reduced rate Mon; closed Tues; Petit Palais Tues–Sun 10am–5.40pm; closed Mon & hols. 27F/14.50F.

The **Grand Palais** holds major temporary art exhibitions, good ones being evident from the queues stretching down av Churchill. Pariscope and co will have details, and you'll probably see plenty of posters around. Two years of work on the roof and nave is planned, so exhibitions may be limited.

In the **Petit Palais**, whose entrance hall is a brazenly extravagant painted dome, you'll find the Beaux Arts museum, which at first sight seems to be a collection of leftovers, from every period from the Renaissance to the 1920s, after the other main galleries have taken their pick.

However, the Petit Palais does have some gems. Monet's Coucher de Soleil à Lavacourt and Boudin's Coup de Vent au Havre stand out against some rather uninspiring Renoirs, Morisots, Cézannes and Manets. There's the ultimate seductive actress pose of Sarah Bernhardt, painted by Georges Clairin, and you'll also find a sculpture of her many years later, downstairs between galleries Zoubaloff and Dutuit.

Ugly furniture and fantasy jewellery of the Art Nouveau period, effete eighteenth-century furniture, plaster models designed for the Madeleine church in the early nineteenth century, and vast canvases recording Paris street battles during the 1830 and 1848 revolutions, trumpeting the victory of the Tricolour, are other potential attractions of this collection.

Musée Nationale des Arts Asiatiques – Guimet

6 place d'Iéna, 16e (Mº Iéna). Closed until 1999.

Little visited, this features a huge and beautifully displayed collection of Oriental art, from China, India, Japan, Tibet and Southeast Asia. Unfortunately, it is closed until 1999 for renovation and reorganiza-

tion. The intention is to upgrade the museum so that it reflects the growing influence of Far Eastern civilizations. During the closure some of the museum's works will be on display in temporary exhibitions at the Musée du Panthéon Bouddhique (see below).

Musée du Panthéon Bouddhique

19 av d'Iéna, 16e; ☎01.47.23.61.65 (Mº Iéna). Daily 9.45am–5.45pm; closed Tues. 15F/10F.

The permanent collection in this attractive and relatively small museum consists of the Chinese and, particularly Japanese Buddhist painting and sculptures brought back to France by Émile Guimet after his visit in 1876. He came from a family of enormously wealthy industrialists, and was a great collector and patron of the arts. He also espoused the Christian-socialist-egalitarian theories about society, class and government proposed by Founier, Saint-Simon and, in England, Robert Owen. At the back of the museum is an exquisite Japanese garden, with bamboo, water and pussy willows.

Centre National de la Photographie

Hôtel Salomon de Rothschild, 11 rue Berryer, 8e; ☎01.56.76.12.31 (Mº George-V). Daily except Tues noon–7pm. 30F/15F.

Temporary exhibitions in a superb classical mansion. Check Pariscope for details.

Individual artists and smaller museums

Musée-Atelier Adzak

3 rue Jonquoy, 14e; ☎01.45.43.06.98 (Mº Plaisance). Check Pariscope, etc, for exhibition times. Free.

A showcase for the work of the British army artist Roy Adzak, who built the studio with his own hands in the 1980s, this is also a living and working space for artists from all round the world, who are given lodgings in the rabbit warren of rooms behind the studio. It's much less formal than most Parisian art galleries, and very artist-centred. Temporary exhibitions – of painting, drawing, sculpture, prints – are organized by artists belonging to the *Association du Musée Roy Adzak*, which anyone can join.

Musée de l'Argenterie,

109–113 av Daumesnil, 12e;
☎ *01.43.40.20.20 (Mº Gare-de-Lyon). Mon–Sat 10am–7pm. 35F/25F, students 30F.*

The process of creating and repairing copper- and silver-plated items using time-honoured methods is fascinating to watch in this living workshop. Unfortunately, the guided visits, followed by an exhibition of the use of copper in buildings and an excellent film on copper-working, are overlong (90min–2hr, in French only, except for the film). And the desirable copper pots and pans in the shop are prohibitively expensive. There are no set hours for visits; simply turn up and hope there are enough non-French speakers for a much faster tour.

Musée d'Art Juif

42 rue des Saules, 18e; ☎ 01.42.57.84.15 (Mº Lamarck-Caulaincourt). Mon–Thurs & Sun 3–6pm; closed Fri, Sat & Aug. 30F/20F.

Some contemporary art, models of the great synagogues, and numerous objects to do with worship, supplemented by temporary exhibitions.

Atelier d'Henri Bouchard

25 rue de l'Yvette, 16e; ☎ 01.46.47.63.46 (Mº Jasmin). Wed & Sat only, 2–7pm. 25F/15F.

The preserved studio of a sculptor (1875–1960), exhibiting works in bronze, stone, wood and marble.

Musée Bourdelle

16 rue Antoine-Bourdelle, 15e;
☎ *01.45.48.67.27 (Mº Montparnasse/Falguière). Tues–Sun 10am–5.45pm; closed Mon & hols. 27F/19F.*

The work of the early twentieth-century sculptor, including casts, drawings and tools, in his studio-house, and a new extension in which you can see studies for the great works such as the homage to Mickiewicz and *L'Épogée Polonaise*.

Musée Cernuschi

7 av Velasquez, (by east gate of Parc Monceau) 17e; ☎ 01.45.63.50.75 (Mº Monceau/Villiers). Tues–Sun 10am–5.40pm; closed Mon & hols. 27F/19F; disabled access.

A small collection of ancient Chinese art, with some exquisite pieces., but of fairly specialized interest.

Musée Cognacq-Jay

Hôtel Donon, 8 rue Elzévir, 3e;
☎ *01.40.27.07.21 (Mº St-Paul/Chemin-Vert/Rambuteau). Tues–Sun 10am–5.40pm; closed Mon & hols. 17F/9F.*

For lovers of European art of the eighteenth century: Canaletto, Fragonard, Tiepolo and early Rembrandt. Also porcelain, furniture and aristocratic trinkets in a matching setting of wood-panelled rooms.

Espace Montmartre-Salvador Dali

9–11 rue Poulbot (place du Tertre), 18e;
☎ *01.42.64.40.10 (Mº Abbesses). Daily 10am–6pm. 35F/25F.*

An underground museum, all in black with atmospheric sound effects, which shows less well-known, though still very familiar, Dali works: watercolour illustrations for books – *Alice in Wonderland*, Dante's *Inferno* – and small sculptures of soft watches, melting snails and other phantasms from the incomprehensible mind of the self-promoting master. A must for Dali lovers.

Musée Delacroix

6 rue Furstemburg, 6e; ☎ 01.44.41.87.50 (Mº St-Germain-des-Prés). daily 9.45am–5pm; closed Tues. 15F/10F (23F/18F with exhibition).

Delacroix lived and worked here from 1857 till his death in 1863. Some attrac-

Museums and Galleries

Museums and Galleries

tive watercolours, illustrations from *Hamlet*, and a couple of versions of a lion hunt hang in the painter's old studio, with an attractive secret garden on the courtyard side. The museum has just been renovated and slightly enlarged, but there is nothing much in the way of major work.

Musée Nissim de Camondo

63 rue Monceau, 8e; ☎ 01.45.63.26.32 (Mº Villiers/Monceau). Wed–Sun 10am–5pm; closed Mon & Tues. 27F/18F.

It's only worth forking out for the Musée Nissim de Camondo if you share Count Camondo's taste for eighteenth-century French aristocratic luxuries: tapestries, paintings, gilded furniture, and tableware of the porcelain and solid silver variety. The museum is named after the count's son, killed while flying missions for France in World War I.

Musée de l'Holographie

15 Grand-Balcon, niveau -1, Forum des Halles, 1er; ☎ 01.40.33.68.76 (Mº/RER Châtelet-Les Halles). Mon–Sat 10am–7pm, Sun & hols 1–7pm. 33F/26F.

Like most holography museums to date, this one is less exciting than you expect, the fault lying primarily with the state of the art. But one or two of the holograms are more inspired than women winking as you pass, and there are also works where artists have combined holograms with painting. The most impressive technically are the reproductions of museum treasures; just like the originals, you can't touch them.

Musée Jacquemart-André

158 bd Haussmann, 8e; ☎ 01.42.89.04.91 (Mº Miromesnil/St-Philippe-du-Roule). Daily 10am–6pm; closed Mon & Tues. 45F/30F.

The house itself is an extraordinary extravaganza of a palace, built for the nineteenth-century banker's son, Édouard André. Bequeathed to the Institut de France by his widow, it contains their private art collection deployed as they ordained. Tiepolo frescoes grace the staircase and gallery round an interior garden

of palm trees, while his eighteenth-century French contemporaries and his fellow Venetian, Canaletto, hang in the ground floor rooms. The collection contains several Rembrandts and, best of all, fifteenth-and sixteenth-century Italian genius in the works of Botticelli, Donatello, Mantegna, Tintoretto, Titian and Uccello.

There is also a fabulous *salon de thé*, open 11am–6pm, which can be entered without a museum ticket (see p.233).

Musée des Monuments Français

Palais de Chaillot, place du Trocadéro, 16e; ☎ 01.44.05.39.05 (Mº Trocadéro). Mon & Wed–Sun 10am–5.30pm; temporary exhibitions 10.30am–7pm, Wed till 9pm; closed Tues & hols. 32F/21F.

In the east wing of the Palais de Chaillot, the Musée des Monuments Français comprises full-scale reproductions of the most important church sculpture from Romanesque to Renaissance. All the major sites are represented. This is an ideal place to familiarize yourself with the styles and periods of monumental sculpture in France. Also included are repros of the major frescoes.

There is also a programme of lecture tours (*visites-conférences*) to places both in Paris (37F/30F) and outside (320–370F); information on ☎ 01.44.61.21.69.

Musée Gustave Moreau

14 rue de la Rochefoucauld, 9e; ☎ 01.48.74.38.50 (Mº Trinité). Mon & Wed 11am–5.15pm, Thurs–Sun 10am–12.45pm & 2–5.15pm; closed Tues. 20F/13F.

An out-of-the-way, bizarre, overcrowded collection of cluttered, joyless paintings by the Symbolist Gustave Moreau. If you know you like him, go along. Otherwise, give it a miss.

Espace Photographique de Paris

4–8 Grande Galerie, niveau -1, Porte Pont-Neuf, Forum des Halles, 1er (Mº/RER Châtelet-Les Halles). Tues–Fri 1–6pm, Sat & Sun 1–7pm; closed Mon. 10F.

A space for photographic art with changing exhibitions of the greats – Cartier-

Bresson, Brandt, Cameron, etc – as well as the lesser known.

Musée Valentin-Haüy

5 rue Duroc, 7e; ☎ 01.44.49.27.27 (Mº Duroc). Tues & Wed only 2.30–5pm; closed July & Aug. Free.

Not for the blind, but about them – the aids devised over the years as well as art and objects made by blind people.

Musée Zadkine

100bis rue d'Assas, 6e; ☎ 01.43.26.91.90 (Mº Vavin). Tues–Sun 10am–5.40pm; closed Mon & hols. 17F/9F.

In Zadkine's own house and garden – a secret, private garden hidden away among tall apartment blocks. His angular Cubist bronzes are sheltered by the trees or emerge from a clump of bamboos. The rustic cottage, like the garden, is full of his sculptures. A place you want to linger in.

Fashion and Fipperies

Musée des Arts de la Mode et du Textile

Palais du Louvre, 109 rue de Rivoli, 1er (Mº Palais-Royal).

Like everything else in the Palais du Louvre, this fashion museum is being extended, and it should reopen in 1997.

Musée de la Curiosité

11 rue St-Paul, 4e; ☎ 01.42.72.13.26 (Mº St-Paul/Sully-Morland). Wed, Sat & Sun 2–7pm. 45F/30F.

A delightful museum dealing with magic and illusion. A few tricks are explained – the museum does not want to encourage any occult or supernatural beliefs – but conjurors' professional secrets are protected, so don't expect to glean all the answers. Automatas, distorting mirrors and optical illusions, things that float on thin air, a box for sawing people in half – they're all on view with examples from the eighteenth and nineteenth centuries, as well as contemporary magicians' tools.

The best fun is a live demonstration of the art (every 30min from 2.30–6pm) by the highly skilled Monsieur Cadiarc, who speaks excellent English and whose sleight of hand is mesmerizing.

The museum shop sells books on conjuring and magic cards, wands, boxes, scarves, etc. Groups of school-children tend to visit on Wed, so best to visit at weekends.

Musée du Cristal

30bis rue de Paradis, 10e (Mº Gare-de-l'Est/ Château-d'Eau). Mon–Fri 9am–5.30/6pm, Sat 10am–noon & 2–5pm; closed Sun & hols. Free.

The most intricate and beautiful examples of crystal glass from the manufacturers *Baccarat* in a modern building behind a seventeenth-century arcade.

Musée Pierre Marly des Lunettes et Lorgnettes de Jadis

380 rue St-Honoré, 1er (Mº Place-de-la-Concorde/Madeleine). Tues–Sat 9am–1pm & 2–7pm; closed Sun, Mon & Aug. Free.

This superb collection of focusing aids resides in an ordinary optician's shop. The exhibits span pretty much the whole history of the subject, from the first medieval corrective lenses to modern times, taking in binoculars, microscopes and telescopes on the way. Many items are miniature masterpieces: bejewelled, inlaid, enamelled and embroidered – an intricate art that readily accommodated itself to the gimmickry its rich patrons demanded. There are, for example, lenses set in the hinges of fans and the pommels of gentlemen's canes, and one lorgnette case pops open to reveal an eighteenth-century dame sitting on a swing above a waterfall. A special collection consists of pieces that have sat upon the bridges of the famous: Audrey Hepburn, the Dalai Lama, Sophia Loren and ex-president Giscard.

Musée de la Mode et du Costume

Palais Galliera, 10 av Pierre 1er-de-Serbie, 16e; ☎ 01.47.20.85.23 (Mº Iéna/Alma-

Museums
and
Galleries

Museums and Galleries

Marceau). Tues–Sun 10am–5.40pm; closed Mon. 30F.

Clothes and fashion accessories of the rich and powerful, from the eighteenth century to present day, exhibited in temporary thematic exhibitions. They last about six months, and during changeovers (usually in May and Nov) the museum is closed.

Musée de la Poupée

Impasse Berthaud, 3e; ☎ 01.42.72.55.90 (Mº Rambuteau). Wed & Fri–Sun 10am–6pm, Thurs 2–10pm. 30F/25F.

A doll museum with tableaux in which the objects – tiny irons and sewing machines, school books, furniture and pots and pans – are more interesting and finely detailed than the dolls themselves. Almost certain to appeal to small children.

Musée de la Publicité

Palais du Louvre, 107 rue de Rivoli, 1er (Mº Palais-Royal/Musée du Louvre).

Along with the Musée des Arts Décoratifs and Musée de la Mode et du Textile, this collection of publicity posters, adverts and TV and radio commercials, presented in temporary exhibitions, is being reorganized, and is due to reopen in 1997–98.

SEITA

12 rue Surcouf, 7e; ☎ 01.45.56.60.17 (Mº Invalides/Latour-Maubourg). Mon–Sat 11am–7pm; closed Sun & hols. Free.

The state tobacco company has this small and, unfortunately, delightful museum in its offices, presenting the pleasures of smoking, and none of the dangers, with pipes and pouches from every continent – early Gauloises packets, painted tabac signs and, best of all, a slide show of tobacco in paintings from the seventeenth century to now.

History and Social Sciences

Musée de l'Armée

Hôtel des Invalides, 7e; ☎ 01.44.42.37.67 (Mº Invalides/Latour-Maubourg/École-Militaire). Daily 10am–5pm. 35F/25F; no hats to be worn.

France's national war museum is enormous. The largest part is devoted to the uniforms and weaponry of Napoléon's armies. Napoléon's personal items include his campaign tent and bed, and even his dog, stuffed. Later French wars are represented, too, through paintings, maps and engravings. Sections on the two world wars are good, with deportation and resistance covered in addition to the battles. Some of the oddest exhibits are Secret Service sabotage devices – for instance, a rat and a lump of coal stuffed with explosives.

Musée Arménien and Musée d'Ennery

59 av Foch, 16e (Mº Porte-Dauphine). Sun & Thurs only 2–6pm; closed Aug. Free.

On the ground floor, artefacts, art and historical documents of the Armenian people from the Middle Ages to the genocide by the Turks at the start of this century. On the floors above, the personal acquisitions of a nineteenth-century popular novelist: Chinese and Japanese objects including thousands of painted and sculpted buttons.

Musée de l'Homme

Palais de Chaillot, place du Trocadéro, 16e; ☎ 01.44.05.72.72 (Mº Trocadéro). 9.45am–5.15pm; closed Tues & hols. 30F/20F.

Much of the museum has now been renovated and its displays modernized in the best tradition of French museum design. It's a gigantic place, as befits its subject. Anthropology, ethnology, paleontology, along with more recent studies in genetics and linguistics, are dealt with (plus musical instruments with a concert programme) from the year dot, and from Polynesia to the Arctic. You've got to be selective unless you want to camp overnight among the mummified Incas, Menton Man's skeleton, hosts of African masks or Descartes' skull.

Musée National des Arts et Traditions Populaires

6 av du Mahatma-Gandhi, Bois de Boulogne (beside main entrance to Jardin d'Acclimatation, signposted from Les Sablons – 15min walk), 16ᵉ (Mº Les Sablons/Porte-Maillot). Mon & Wed–Sun 9.45am–5.15pm. 22F/15F (32F/23F with exhibition).

If you have any interest in the beautiful and highly specialized skills, techniques and artefacts developed before the age of industrialization, standardization and mass production, then you should find this museum fascinating. Boat-building, shepherding, farming, weaving, blacksmithing, pottery, stone-cutting, games, clairvoyance . . . all well illustrated and displayed. Downstairs, there is a study section with cases and cases of various implements, and cubicles where you can call up explanatory slide shows at the touch of a switch.

Musée de l'Assistance Publique

Hôtel de Miramion, 47 quai de la Tournelle, 5ᵉ; ☎ 01.46.33.01.43 (Mº Maubert). Tues–Sat 10am–5pm; closed Sun, Mon, hols & Aug. 20F/10F.

The history of Paris hospitals from the Middle Ages to the present with pictures, pharmaceutical containers, surgical instruments and decrees relating to public health.

Musée Carnavalet

23 rue de Sévigné, 3ᵉ; ☎ 01.42.72.21.13 (Mº St-Paul). Tues–Sun 10am–5.40pm, Thurs till 8.30pm; closed Mon & hols. 27F/14.50F (35F/25F with exhibitions); disabled access.

A Renaissance mansion in the Marais presents the history of Paris as viewed and lived by royalty, aristocrats and the bourgeoisie. Though it focuses mainly on the era between François I and 1900, there's also a small section spanning Roman times to the Middle Ages. Decorative arts feature strongly, with numerous recreated salons and boudoirs from the time of of Louis XII to Louis XVI.

The rooms for 1789–95 are full of sacred mementos: models of the Bastille, original Declarations of the Rights of Man and the Citizen, Tricolours and liberty caps, sculpted allegories of Reason, crockery with revolutionary slogans, glorious models of the guillotine, and execution orders to make you shed a tear for the royalists as well.

In the rest of the gilded rooms, the display of paintings, maps and models of Paris is too exhaustive to give you an overall picture of the city changing. And unless you have the historical details to hand, it's hard to get intrigued by any one period. Some of the set pieces – the *belle époque* interiors of one of the cafés on the *Grands Boulevards*, and Fouquet the jeweller's shop of the same date – are quite fun, but you can see similar in the real city. That is the problem with this museum – competing with its own subject.

The museum owns an impressive collection of photographs by Brassaï, Atget and Doisneau, but these are only brought out for temporary exhibitions.

Owing to limited funds, not all the rooms are open at the same time: the Second Empire to the twentieth century part is only open 10–11.50am; and the newly restored section on the sixteenth to the eighteenth century is only open 1.10–5.40pm. However, the ticket lasts all day, so you can return.

Musée Grévin I

10 bd Montmartre, 9ᵉ; ☎ 01.42.46.13.26 (Mº Montmartre). Daily 1–7pm (during school hols 10am–6pm); no admissions after 6pm. 50F, under-14s 36F.

The main Paris waxworks are nothing like as extensive as London's, and only worth it if you are desperate to do something with the kids and can afford to throw money around. The ticket includes a ten-minute conjuring act.

Musée Grévin II

Grand Balcon, Forum des Halles, niveau 1, 1ᵉʳ; ☎ 01.40.26.28.50 (Mº/RER Châtelet-Les Halles). Mon–Sat 10.30am–6.45pm, Sun & hols 1–6.30pm. 42F, under-14s 32F.

Museums and Galleries

Museums and Galleries

One up on the wax statue parade of the parent museum, but typically didactic. It shows a series of wax-model scenes of French brilliance at the turn of the century. Each montage is surrounded by doors that open and close automatically to prevent you from skipping any part of the voice-over and animation.

Musée de l'Histoire de France

Archives Nationales, 60 rue des Francs-Bourgeois, 3e; ☎ 01.40.27.60.96 (Mº Rambuteau/St-Paul). Wed–Mon 1.45–5.45pm; closed Tues & hols. 15F/10F.

Some of the authentic bits of paper that fill the vaults of the Archives Nationales: wills, edicts and papal bulls; a medieval English monarch's challenge to his French counterpart to stake his kingdom on a duel; Henry VIII's RSVP to the Field of the Cloth of Gold invite; fragile cross-Channel treaties; Joan of Arc's trial proceedings with a doodled impression of her in the margin; and recent legislation and constitutions. The Revolution section includes the book of samples from which Marie-Antoinette chose her dress each morning, and a Republican children's alphabet where J stands for Jean-Jacques Rousseau and L for labourer. It's scholarly stuff (and no English translations), but the early documents are very pretty, dangling seals and penned in delicate and illegible hands. Note that the collection changes every two to three months.

Musée de la Marine

Palais de Chaillot, place du Trocadéro, 16e; ☎ 01.45.53.31.70 (Mº Trocadéro). Wed–Sun 10am–6pm. Closed Tues. 38F/25F.

Beautiful models of French ships, ancient and modern, war-like and commercial.

Musée de la Préfecture de Police

1bis rue des Carmes, 5e; ☎ 01.44.41.52.50 (Mº Maubert). Mon–Fri 9am–5pm, Sat 10am–5pm; closed Sun & hols. Free.

The history of the Paris police force, as presented in this collection of uniforms, arms and papers, stops at 1944 and is,

as you might expect, all of the "legendary criminals" variety.

Performance arts, literature and sport

Maison de Balzac

47 rue Raynouard, 16e; ☎ 01.42.24.56.30 (Mº Passy/La Muette) Tues–Sun 10am–5.40pm; closed Mon & hols. 27F/19F.

Contains several portraits and caricatures of the writer, plus a library of works by him, his contemporaries and his critics. Balzac lived here between 1840 and 1847, but literary grandees seem to share the common fate of not leaving ghosts.

Musée du Cinéma Henri Langlois

Palais de Chaillot (East Wing on river side, pending new palace arrangements), place du Trocadéro, 16e; ☎ 01.45.53.74.39 (Mº Trocadéro). Guided tours only Wed–Sun at 10am, 11am, 2pm, 3pm & 4pm; closed Mon, Tues & hols. 30F.

The Musée du Cinéma will be modernized and shifted to the new Palais du Cinéma in the Palais de Tokyo at some point in 1997. In the meantime, this tour of costumes, sets, cameras, projectors, etc, from magic lanterns to the latest Depardieu performance, ending with a showing of a rare movie from the archives, is a must for *cinéastes*.

Centre Culturel des Halles

Terrasse du Forum des Halles, 101 rue Rambuteau, 1er (Mº/RER Châtelet-Les Halles). Tues–Sun 11.30am–6.30pm; closed Mon & hols. Prices vary.

Temporary exhibitions, events and workshops of poetry, arts and crafts take cover beneath the queasy strictured structures above the Forum: in the Maison de la Poésie, Pavillon des Arts and Maison des Ateliers.

Musée Kwok-On

57 rue du Théâtre, 15e; ☎ 01.45.75.85.75 (Mº Émile-Zola). Closed until the end of 1997.

Changing exhibitions feature the popular arts of southern Asia, with musical instruments, festival decorations, religious objects, and a wealth of costumes, puppets, masks and stage models for theatre from eleven different countries stretching from Japan to Turkey.

The collection includes such things as figures for the Indonesian and Indian Theatres of Shadows, Peking Opera costumes and storytellers' scrolls from Bengal. The colour is overwhelming and the unfamiliarity shaming – highly recommended.

Musée Édith Piaf

5 rue Créspin-du-Gast, 11e; ☎ *01.43.55.52.72 (Mº Ménilmontant/St-Maur). Admission by appointment only. Mon–Thurs 1–6pm; closed July. Free.*

Édith Piaf was not an acquisitive person. The few clothes, letters, toys, paintings and photographs that she left are almost all here, along with every one of the recordings. The venue is a flat lived in by her devoted friend Bernard Marchois, and it is he who will show you round and tell you stories about her.

Musée de la Musique

Cité de la Musique, Parc de la Villette, 19e. (Mº Porte-de-Pantin). Check Pariscope, etc, for opening hours and prices.

Yet to open at the time of writing, this new museum promises to present the history of music from the end of the Renaissance to the present day, both visually – a collection of 4500 instruments – and aurally, with headsets and interactive displays. Each instrument on display (around 800 at any one time) will be presented in the context of a key work in the history of Eastern music.

The museum space includes an auditorium where there'll be regular concerts of all kinds of music from all over the world, plus spaces for a huge documentation centre, workshops, films and audiovisuals.

Musée Renan-Scheffer/La Vie Romantique

16 rue Chaptal, 9e; ☎ *01.48.74.95.38 (Mº Pigalle/St-Georges). Tues–Sun 10am–5.45pm; closed Mon & hols. 27F/19F.*

The house itself is a delightful surprise: a shuttered provincial villa on a cobbled courtyard at the end of a private alley behind an imposing street front. George Sand used to visit here, and the museum consists mainly of bits and pieces (jewels, lockets with her hair) associated with her. The studio of the painter Scheffer, who owned the house, is also open to the public, though not very interesting.

Musée du Sport Français

Parc des Princes, 24 rue du Commandant-Guilbaud (Mº Porte-de-St-Cloud). Mon–Fri 9.30am–12.30pm & 2–5pm, Sun 10.30am–12.30pm & 2–6pm; closed Sat & hols. 20F/10F.

Books, posters, paintings and sculptures to do with the history of French sport are exhibited here on a rotating basis, along with trophies and boots, caps, rackets and gloves worn by the famous, and the vanity case of the greatest French Wimbledon champion, Suzanne Lenglen.

Maison de Victor-Hugo

6 place des Vosges, 4e; ☎ *01.42.72.10.16 (Mº Bastille/Chemin-Vert). Tues–Sun 10am–5.40pm; closed Mon & hols. 17.50F/9F.*

This museum is saved by the fact that Hugo decorated and drew, as well as wrote. Many of his ink drawings are exhibited, and there's an extraordinary Japanese dining room he put together for his lover's house. That apart, the usual portraits, manuscripts and memorabilia shed sparse light on the man and his work.

Science and industry

La Colline de l'Automobile

1 place du Dôme, La Défense (Mº Grande-Arche-de-la-Défense). Daily noon–7pm. 30F/20F.

Museums and Galleries

Museums and Galleries

A car museum, with 100 models illuminating developments from the earliest times until the present day.

Palais de la Découverte

Grand Palais, av Franklin-D-Roosevelt, 8e; ☎ 01.40.74.81.82 (Mº Champs-Élysées-Clemenceau/Franklin-D-Roosevelt). Tues–Sat 9.30am–6pm, Sun & hols 10am–7pm; closed Mon. 25F/15F.

This, the old science museum, has brightened itself up considerably since the Cité des Sciences came on the scene. It can't really compete, but it does have plenty of interactive exhibits, some very good temporary exhibitions, and an excellent planetarium (15F/10F supplement; check *Pariscope* and co for times).

Musée Branly

21 rue d'Assas, 6e; ☎ 01.49.54.52.00 (Mº St-Placide). Mon–Fri 9am–noon & 2–5pm; closed July & Aug. By appointment only. Free.

In the 1890s Marconi used Branly's invention of an electric wave detector – the first coherer – to set up a startling system of communication that didn't need wires. The coherer in question is exhibited along with other pieces from the physicist's experiments.

Musée de la Contrefaçon

16 rue de la Faisanderie, 16e; ☎ 01.45.01.57.11 (Mº Porte-Dauphine). Mon & Wed 2–4.30pm, Fri 9.30am–noon; closed Tues, Thurs & weekends. 10F/5F.

One of the odder ones – examples of imitation products, labels and brand marks trying to pass themselves off as the "genuine article".

Muséum d'Histoire Naturelle

Jardin des Plantes, 57 rue Cuvier, 5e; ☎ 01.40.79.36.00 (Mº Austerlitz/Jussieu/Monge). Grande Galerie de l'Évolution (1): Mon, Wed & Fri–Sun 10am–6pm, Thurs 10am–10pm (40F/30F/10F); Galerie d'Anatomie Comparée et de Paléontologie: Mon & Wed–Sun 10am–5pm (25F/15F/6F); Galerie de Minéralogie (2): Mon & Wed–Sun 10am–5pm (25F/15F/6F); Galerie de Paléobotanique: Mon & Wed–Sun 10am–5pm; Galerie d'Entomologie: 1–5pm (12F/8F/4F). All closed Tues.

The four musty old galleries have been upstaged by *La Grande Galerie de l'Évolution* in a dramatic transformation of the old nineteenth-century Galerie de Zoologie, overlooking rue Geoffroy-St-Hilaire. Behind the scrubbed stone façade, the magnificent interior, supported by iron columns and roofed with glass, has been adapted to tell the story of evolution and the relations between human beings and nature. On the lower level, submarine light suffuses the space where the murkiest deep ocean creatures are displayed. Above, glass lifts rise silently from the savannah into the higher regions. There are videos and touch-screen databases. The stuffed animals are near enough to touch and lit to look real. Great fun for children. A café overlooking the savannah area serves sandwiches at 25–30F and a light lunch for 59F.

Musée Pasteur

Institut Pasteur, 25 rue du Docteur-Roux, 7e; ☎ 01.45.68.82.82 (Mº Volontaires/Pasteur). Mon–Fri 2–5.30pm; closed weekends & Aug. 15F/8F; pass needed to enter the building – available from the office opposite.

Guided tours (English version available) of the apartment, scientific souvenirs and Byzantine-style mausoleum of Dr Pasteur, the great nineteenth-century chemist-biologist who created the science of microbiology by discovering how fermentation worked (hence the term "pasteurization"). The main non-scientific interest in the museum lies in seeing the sombre interior decoration (plus innovative plumbing) of nineteenth-century Parisian middle-class homes.

Musée de la Poste

34 bd de Vaugirard, 15e; ☎ 01.42.79.23.00 (Mº Montparnasse).

Not just stamps, though plenty of those. The museum covers the history of sending messages, from the earliest times to the present. Currently being refurbished, it should reopen by 1997, and will be well worth a visit.

Musée de Radio-France

116 av du Président-Kennedy, 16e; ☎ 01.42.30.21.80 (Mº Passy/Ranelagh/ Mirabeau). Mon–Sat guided visits at 10.30am, 11.30am, 2.30pm, 3.30pm, 4.30pm; closed Sun & hols. 15F/10F.

Housed in the national TV and radio building, this museum contains a wide assortment of models, machines and documents covering the history of broadcasting.

Musée de la Serrure Bricard

Hôtel Libéral-Bruand, 1 rue de la Perle, 3e; ☎ 01.42.77.79.62 (Mº Chemin-Vert/Rambuteau). Mon–Fri 10am–noon & 2–5pm; closed Sat, Sun & hols. 30F.

This collection of elaborate and artistic locks throughout the ages includes the fit-

tings for Napoléon's palace doors (the one for the Tuileries bashed in by revolutionaries), locks that trapped your hand or shot your head off if you tried a false key, and a seventeenth-century masterpiece made by a craftsman kept under lock and key for four years. The rest of the exhibits are pretty boring, though the setting – in a Marais mansion – is some compensation.

Musée National des Techniques

292 rue St-Martin, 3e; ☎ 01.40.27.22.20 (Mº Réaumur-Sébastopol/Arts-et-Métiers). Tues–Sun 10am–5.30pm; closed Mon & hols. Free while renovation works are in progress.

Interminable works have kept this museum of technology semi-closed for years; 1998 is the current projected completion date. In the meantime, various parts are open, including the laboratory of Lavoisier, the French chemist who first showed that water is a combination of oxygen and hydrogen.

Museums and Galleries

A Daytripper's Guide to Outlying Museums

Chapter 20, *Day trips from Paris*, includes details of several more museums within a day's excursion from central Paris. The following are among the more interesting.

Musée d'Art et d'Histoire at St-Denis. Local archeology and Commune documents; p.375.

Musée Condé and **Musée Vivant du Cheval** at Chantilly. Live horses and lots of paraphernalia, at the château which also contains the magnificent medieval *Très Riches Heures du Duc de Berry*; p.382.

Musée de l'Air et de l'Espace at Le Bourget. Planes and spacecraft from

Lindbergh to *Apollo 13* displayed in Paris' original airport; p.384.

Musée des Antiquités Nationales at St-Germain-en-Laye. Evocative archeological displays, from cave-dwellers onwards; p.385.

Musée de l'Île de France at Sceaux. Local history, from kings to artists; p.386.

Musée National de la Céramique at Sèvres. Ceramics from all over the world as well as the local stuff; p.387.

Chapter 15

Daytime Amusements and Sports

For details on the cinemas of Paris, see Chapter 19.

When it's cold and wet, and you've had enough of peering at museums, monuments, the dripping panes of shop fronts and café vistas, don't despair or retreat back to your hotel. There are saunas to soak in, roller-blading and ice-skating rinks to fall on, music halls inviting you to dance the tango, bowling alleys, billiards, swimming pools and gyms. You can take advantage of the Parisian love of high technology to call up a choice of music and videos on CD-ROM or examine, in old-fashioned style, obscure picture books in medieval libraries.

If you're feeling brave, you could also change your hairstyle, indulge in a total body tonic, take up yoga or take your first steps as a ballerina. You could even learn how to concoct sublime French dishes at a professional cookery school. And when the weather isn't so bad, you can go for a ride in a boat or perhaps even a heli-copter if you've had a successful flutter on the horses in the Bois de Boulogne.

Paris' range of **sports**, both for spectators and participants, is also outlined below. For additional possibilities, check *L'Officiel des Spectacles* (the best of the listings magazines for sports facilities) or, to see which major sporting events may be taking place during your stay, *L'Équipe*, the daily sports newspaper. The highlight of the calendar is, of course, the triumphal arrival of cycling's *Tour de France* in July.

Boat Trips, Balloon and Heli Rides

Seeing Paris by boat is one of the city's most popular and durable tourist experiences – and a lot of fun, if the mood grabs you. Seeing it from the air is even better.

Bateaux-Mouches

From the *quais* or the bridges, after night has fallen, the sudden appearance of a bulging **Bateau-Mouche**, blaring its multi-lingual commentaries and dazzling with its floodlights, can come as a nasty shock to anyone indulging in romantic contemplations. One way of avoiding the ugly sight of these hulking hulls is to get on one yourself. You may not be able to escape the trite narration, but the evening rides certainly give a superb and very glamorous close-up view of the classic Seine-side buildings.

Bateaux-Mouches start from the *Embarcadère du Pont de l'Alma*, on the right bank in the 8ᵉ (reservations ☎01.42.25.96.10, information ☎01.40.76.99.99 Mº Alma-Marceau). The rides, which usually last between an hour and an hour and a quarter, depart at 11am, noon, 2pm, 2.30pm, 3.15pm, every half hour from 4 to 9pm, and at 9.30pm; winter departures at 11am, 2.30pm, 4pm and 9pm only (40F, under-

14s 20F; after 8pm 50F/20F). Make sure you avoid the outrageously priced lunch and dinner trips, for which "correct" dress is mandatory. The main **competitors** to the *Bateaux-Mouches* are *Bateaux Parisiens*, *Bateaux-Vedettes de Paris* and *Bateaux-Vedettes du Pont Neuf*. They're all much of a muchness, and can be found detailed in *Pariscope*, etc, under *Promenades*.

One alternative way of riding on the Seine, which spares you the commentaries, is the *Batobus*, a river transport system operating from May to September between port de la Bourdonnais by the Eiffel Tower and quai de l'Hôtel-de-Ville, stopping at port de Solférino (by the Musée d'Orsay), quai Malaquais (by the Pont des Arts, the footbridge to the Louvre) and quai de Montebello (by Notre-Dame). The service runs from 10am until 7pm, about every three-quarters of an hour, and costs 12F per stop or 60F for a day pass.

Canal Trips

Less overtly tourist fodder than the *Bateaux-Mouches* and their clones are the **canal boat trips**. *Canauxrama* (reservations ☎01.42.39.15.00) chugs up and down between the Port de l'Arsenal (opposite 50 bd de la Bastille, 12e; Mº Bastille) and the Bassin de la Villette (5bis quai de la Loire, 19e; Mº Jaurès) on the Canal St-Martin. Daily departures are at 9.45am and 2.30pm from La Villette and at 9.45am and 2.30pm from the Bastille. At the Bastille end is a long tunnel from which you don't surface till the 10e *arrondissement*. The ride lasts three hours – not a bad bargain for 75F (students 60F, under-12s 45F, under-6s free; no reductions weekends or holiday afternoons). The company also runs day trips along the Canal de l'Ourcq, west as far as Meaux, with a coach back (for around 200F).

A more stylish vessel for exploring the canal is the **catamaran** of *Paris-Canal*, with trips between the Musée d'Orsay (quai Anatole-France by the Pont Solférino, 7e; Mº Solférino) and the Parc de la Villette (*La Folie des Visites*

Guidées, on the canal by the bridge between the Grande Salle and the Cité des Sciences, 19e; Mº Porte-de-Pantin), which also last three hours. The catamaran departs from the Musée d'Orsay at 9.30am daily. Parc de la Villette departures are at 2.30pm. Trips cost 95F, 12–25s 70F (except Sun and holiday afternoons), 4-11s 55F; reservations ☎01.42.40.96.97. One Saturday a month the company runs night-time cruises with a live New Orleans jazz band (around 250F per person, including drinks).

Paris by Helicopter or Balloon

Having seen Paris from the water, the next step up is Paris from the air. A **helicopter tour** above all the city's sights is somewhat pricey, but if whirlygig rides turn you on as much or more than a four-star meal or a stalls seat at the theatre, then a quick loop around La Défense is on: *Héli-France* at the *Héliport de Paris*, 4 av de la Porte-de-Sèvres, 15e (☎01.45.54.95.11, Mon–Fri 8am–8pm, Sat & Sun 9am–6pm; Mº Balard). A thirty-minute trip will set you back about 850F for five passengers.

For an even classier and far more extravagant overview, how about going up in an **air balloon**? *Air Atmosphère Dirigeable Montgolfière* (87bis bd de la République, Boulogne; ☎01.46.09.44.22) will be happy to oblige.

Afternoon Tangos

One less obvious pastime for filling the afternoon hours is a **bal musette**. The dance halls where they take place were the between-the-wars solution in the down-and-out parts of *Gay Paree* to depression, dole and the demise of the Popular Front. They crossed social scales, too, with film stars and jaded aristocrats coming to indulge in a bit of rough. Three or four generations of owners later, only **Balajo** remains in the rue de Lappe, still attracting a partially working-class clientele, and running both afternoon and evening sessions. Turn up on a Friday afternoon and you'll find people

Daytime
Amusements
and Sports

Daytime Amusements and Sports

For details of evening activities at Balajo *and* Chez Gégène, *see p.344.*

dancing to the accordion, cheek-to-cheek, couple squashed against couple. Their clothes aren't smart, their French isn't academy, men dance with women, and everyone drinks.

Less conducive to participation, but potentially entertaining, are the **tea dances**, a much more genteel or camp experience than the *bals musettes*.

Balajo, 9 rue de Lappe, 11e; ☎01.47.00.07.87 (M° Bastille). Afternoons Mon 2–6.30pm, Fri–Sun 2–7pm, reopening at 11pm for the evening session. The original *bal musette* venue. Music, all recorded, is a mixture of waltz, tango, java, disco and rock; admission price – Mon, Fri & Sat 30F, Sun 50F – includes drink.

Carbone 14, 15 rue Henri-Regnault, 14e; ☎01.43.29.79.54 (M° Porte-d'Orléans). Wed–Sun 3.30–8.30pm; 40F including drink & coffee.

Chez Gégène, 162bis quai de Polangis, Joinville-Le-Pont; ☎01.48.83.29.43 (RER Joinville-Le-Pont). Just across the Marne from the Bois de Vincennes. Midday *bals musettes* at weekends from March to Oct, but ring first to check. High-class rétro dancing in a 1900-style *guinguette*.

La Coupole, 102 bd Montparnasse, 14e; ☎01.43.20.14.20 (M° Vavin). Sat, Sun & hols 3–7pm; 70–80F. For the older generation.

La Java, 105 rue du Faubourg-du-Temple, 10e (M° Belleville). Mon & Sun 2–7pm; free. A tea dance for oldies in the oldest of the dance halls. *La Java* is being renovated; times and prices may change.

Le Palace, 8 rue du Faubourg-Montmartre, 9e; ☎01.42.46.10.87 (M° Rue-Montmartre). Gay tea dance every Sun afternoon, 4pm onwards; 40F before 6pm, 69F after; drinks from 50F.

Retro République, 23 rue du Faubourg-du-Temple, 10e; ☎01.42.08.54.06 (M° République). Daily 2–6.30pm; weekdays 30F including drink.

Le Tango, 13 rue au Maire, 3e; ☎01.42.72.17.78 (M° Arts-et-Métiers). Sat 2–6pm, Sun 2–8pm; 60F.

Musical and Visual Discoveries

If you want, you can listen to CDs or watch videos all day in public places. Libraries can offer unexpected delights, too, and you don't have to pay to browse through any of the municipal collections.

FNAC, 4 place de la Bastille, 11e (M° Bastille). Mon–Sat 10am–8pm, Wed & Fri until 10pm. *FNAC's* newest music shop has touch-screen access to a limited but interesting selection of CDs. Once you've donned the headphones, touch the square on the screen reading "*Touchez l'écran*". If you then touch first "*Répérages FNAC*", then "*Variétés Françaises*", then "*Rock*", you'll end up with a list of recent French rock recordings which you can listen to, adjusting the volume or flicking forwards by touching arrows. "*Sommaire*" takes you back to the previous list. Of course you can choose medieval church music, jazz or Pierre Boulez instead – it's very simple, and when the shop isn't crowded you can spend as long as you like for free.

Vidéothèque de Paris, 2 Grande Galerie, Porte St-Eustache, Forum des Halles, 1er; ☎01.44.76.63.44 (RER Châtelet-Les Halles). Tues–Sun 1–8.30pm, Thurs till 10pm. For 30F/25F you can watch any of the four videos or films screened each day, and, in the *Salle Pierre Emmanuel*, make your own selection from 4000 film clips, newsreel footage, commercials, documentaries, soaps, etc, from 1896 to the present day. All the material is connected to Paris in some way, and you can make your choice – on your individual screen and keyboard – via a Paris place name, an actor, a director, a date, and so on. Don't be put off by the laboratory atmosphere or by the idea that this can't be for just anyone to play with. It is, and there are instructions in English at the desk and a friendly "librarian" to help you out. Once you're in the complex you can go back and forth between the projection rooms, the *Salle*

Pierre Emmanuel and a café, open 12.30–6pm. You can also hook up to the Internet.

Virgin Megastore, 52 av des Champs-Élysées, 8ᵉ (Mº George-V). Mon–Sat 10am–midnight, Sun 2pm–midnight. No sophisticated computers here: just grab the headphones of whichever one of the hundred hooked-up CDs takes your fancy, or the headphones for one of the feature film videos being screened, and pretend you're on a transatlantic flight.

Libraries

Bibliothèque André-Malraux, 78 bd Raspail, 6ᵉ (Mº Rennes). Tues, Wed & Fri 10am–7pm, Thurs 1–7pm, Sat 10am–5pm. Books on cinema on the sixth floor.

Bibliothèque Forney, _Hôtel de Sens_, 1 rue du Figuier, 4ᵉ (Mº Pont-Marie). Tues–Fri 1.30–10.30pm, Sat 10am–8.30pm. Medieval building filled with volumes on fine and applied arts.

Bibliothèque Marguerite-Durand, 79 rue Nationale, 13ᵉ (Mº Nationale). A feminist library with books, journals, photos, posters and manuscripts.

Bibliothèque Nationale de France (see Chapter 8, p.152).

Sources d'Europe, base of La Grande Arche, La Défense, 18ᵉ (Mº La Défense). Mon–Fri 11am–5pm. French- and European-sponsored centre, with documents and videos on the EU.

Bibliothéque des Partitions, 12 place Carrée, Porte St-Eustache, Forum des Halles, 1ᵉ (_RER_ Chatelet-Les Halles). Tues–Sat noon–7pm. 26,000 musical scores, mainly classical but also jazz and rock.

Bibliothèque Publique d'Information (BPI), 2nd floor, Centre Pompidou (Beaubourg), 4ᵉ (Mº Rambuteau). Mon & Wed–Fri noon–10pm, Sat & Sun 10am–10pm; free. Everything, including foreign newspapers, and a free language lab, the _Espace Langue_, if you feel like brushing up on your French, Mandarin or Euskara, or watching TV transmission from all around the world.

The Body Beautiful

Parisians are, predictably, keen on twisting, stretching and straining muscles, competing in style rather than on scores. Aerobics, dance workouts and anti-stress fitness programmes are big business, along with the other well-established trends of yoga, tai-chi and martial arts.

Fitness venues

Many **fitness clubs** organize their activities in courses or require a minimum month's or year's subscription (big gym chains like _Garden Gym_ and _Gymnase Club_ are financially prohibitive, and even the exceptions are costly enough to excuse you), but if your last meal has left you feeling you need it, here are some options.

Académie de Danse à Magenta, 62 bd Magenta, 10ᵉ (Mº Gare-de-l'Est). All types of dance, and a free trial.

Getting to Grips with Gastronomy and Wines

Cordon Bleu, at 8 rue Léon-Delhomme, 15ᵉ; ☎01.53.68.22.50 (Mº Vaugirard/Convention), offers cookery demonstrations followed by tastings (morning or afternoon sessions, some in English. 48hr notice; 220F) or day-long hands-on sessions (again some in English, 2 weeks' advance booking required; 750F). You can make your reservations from London (0171/935

3503) or in Canada/US (toll free 1-800-457 CHEF).

Centre d'Information, de Documentation et de Dégustation (CIDD), 30 rue de la Sabliéne, 14ᵉ; ☎01.45.45.32.20/01.43.27.67.21 (Mº Pernéty), has free "Porte-Ouvertes" days with tastings, and runs wine-tasting courses in English (390F for 3hr).

Daytime Amusements and Sports

Centre de Danse du Marais, 41 rue du Temple, 4e; ☎01.42.72.15.42 (Mº Hôtel-de-Ville). 9am–9pm. You can try out rock 'n' roll, folkloric dance classes from the East, tap dancing, modern dance, physical expression or flamenco. You'll find a board advertising all the workshops in the alleyway. Expect to pay around 85F per session.

Centre de Yoga Sivananda Vedanta, 123 bd de Sébastopol, 2e; ☎01.40.26.77.49 (Mº Strasbourg-St-Denis). 11am–9.30pm. First lesson is free.

Club Quartier Latin, 19 rue de Pontoise, 5e; ☎01.43.25.31.99 (Mº Maubert-Mutualité). Mon–Fri 9am–10pm, Sat & Sun 9.30am–7pm. Dance, gym, swimming and squash.

Espace Vit'Halles, place Beaubourg, 48 rue Rambuteau, 3e; ☎01.42.77.21.71 (Mº Rambuteau). Daily 8am-10pm. Fanatics can spend a day doing every kind of tendon-shattering gyration. It's divided into four "work zones": the parquet, gym floor, body-building room, and multi-gym room. *Détente* – "relaxation" – is also provided for with a sauna, *hammam*, solarium and diet bar. For an 80F day pass you can have access to these and one floor session.

Swimming

For straightforward exercise, and for around 23F, you can go swimming in any of Paris' **municipal baths**, but check first in *L'Officiel des Spectacles* for opening times (under *Activités Sportives*) as varying hours are given over to schools and clubs. The following are among the best.

Les Amiraux, 6 rue Hermann-Lachapelle, 18e (Mº Simplon). Municipal pool.

Armand-Massard, 66 bd Montparnasse, 15e (Mº Vavin). Municipal pool.

Bernard-Lafay, 79 rue de la Jonquière, 17e (Mº Guy-Môquet). Municipal pool.

Butte aux Cailles, 5 place Verlaine, 13e (Mº Place-d'Italie). Housed in a 1920s brick building with an Art Deco ceiling,

recently spruced up. One of the most pleasant swims in the city.

Château-Landon, 31 rue du Château-Landon, 10e (Mº Château-Landon). Municipal pool.

Henry-de-Montherlant, 32 bd Lannes, 16e (Mº Porte-Dauphine). Two pools, a terrace for sunbathing, a solarium, and the Bois de Boulogne close by.

Jean Taris, 16 rue de Thouin, 5e (Mº Cardinal-Lemoine). An unchlorinated pool in the centre of the Latin Quarter and a student favourite.

Georges-Vallerey Tourelles, 148 av Gambetta, 20e (Mº St-Fargeau). Municipal pool.

Piscine Susanne Berlioux/Les Halles, 10 place de la Rotonde, *niveau* 3, Porte du Jour, Forum des Halles, 1er (*RER* Châtelet-Les Halles). A 50-m pool with a vaulted concrete ceiling and a glass wall looking through to the tropical garden.

PRIVATELY RUN POOLS

Non-municipal pools are usually twice as expensive or more, but some have their attractions.

Aquaboulevard, 4 rue Louis-Armand, 15e ☎01.40.60.10.00 (Mº Balard/*RER* Bd-Victor). Daily 9am–11pm, Sat & Sun 8am–12pm. An American-style vast multi-sports complex. The pool has wave machines and water slides, and costs 56F weekdays and 77F weekends (50F/59F for children) for a 4-hr session.

Molitor, 2–8 av de la Porte-Molitor 16e (Mº Porte-d'Auteuil). For outside bathing, try this 1930s pool on the edge of the Bois de Boulogne.

Pontoise, 19 rue de Pontoise, 5e (Mº Maubert-Mutualité). Features night sessions from 9pm until midnight Mon–Thurs, and sometimes nude swimming. Rates under 25F.

Roger-Le Gall, 34 bd Carnot, 12e (Mº Porte-de-Vincennes). Most of the extras are reserved for club members, but anyone can swim in the pool (covered in winter and open in summer). 33F/17F.

Hairdressing salons

The range of **hairdressing salons** is as wide – style-wise and price-wise – as you'd expect in this supremely fashion-conscious city.

Alexandre, for women at 3 av Matignon, 8e; ☎01.42.25.57.90 (Mº Franklin-D-Roosevelt). Also for men at 29 rue Marbeuf, 8e; ☎01.42.25.29.41 (Mº Alma-Marceau). The long-established *haut-coif-feur* of Paris could be an intimidating experience unless you're wearing Yves St-Laurent or Gaultier. Wash, cut and blow-dries for women are not that expensive considering the clientele – around 450F – but the men's salon, with saunas, massage, manicure, pedicure, etc, would cost you your beautified arm and leg.

Jacques Dessange, 37 av Franklin-D-Roosevelt, 8e; ☎01.43.59.31.31 (Mº Franklin-D-Roosevelt). And at 13 other addresses. Less classic, but still very smart, this is Charlotte Rampling's favourite cutter; around 450F for women, 350F for men for wash, cut and blow-dry.

Jean-Marc Maniatis, 35 rue de Sèvres, 6e; ☎01.45.44.16.39 (Mº Sèvres-Babylone). Younger and less-established beauties come here for the renowned and meticulous cutting. You can have a free cut by a trainee; phone ☎01.47.20.00.05 to make an appointment.

CHEAPER CUTS – AND SCHOOLS

The more run-of-the-mill Paris hair-dressers may be more appealing. Around Les Halles, the Bastille and St-Germain many salons go for maximum visibility, so you can watch what's being done and take your pick. It's always a gamble anyway, and it could be fun trying out your French in the intimate trivial chitchat that all hair-dressers insist on. Book a couple of days in advance.

Various salons or schools offer low fee or free wash, cut and blow-dries to those bold enough to act as guinea-pigs for new cuts or inexperienced trainees. These include the following:

Les Salons Jean-Claude Biguine, 50 salons around the city; ☎01.44.76.88.10 for addresses. No need to make an appointment. From 110F for men, 150F for women. Good value.

Jean-Louis Déforges Académie, 71 bd Richard-Lenoir, 11e; ☎01.43.55.56.67 (Mº Richard-Lenoir). Mon–Thurs 9.30am, 1.30pm & 3.30pm, Fri 9.30am & 1.30pm. Monsieur Déforges may be wandering around criticizing his trainees, in which case your cut will take much longer. Around 50F.

Jean-Louis David, 5 rue Cambon, 1er; ☎01.42.97.51.71 (Mº Concorde). You need to go to the salon to make an appointment for a free cut by a trainee. Mon–Fri 9.30am–1.30pm & 2.30–5pm.

Centre de Formation Jacques Dessange, 24 rue St-Augustin, 2e; ☎01.47.42.24.73 (Mº 4-Septembre). Mon–Wed, by appointment. 40F. Women only, and you must be prepared to lose at least 4cm of hair.

Hammams

A steam bath and a massage may be as necessary after a trip to the Louvre as after intentional physical exercise. The **hammams**, or Turkish baths, are one of the unexpected delights of Paris. Much more luxurious than the standard Swedish sauna, these are places to linger and chat.

Les Bains d'Odessa, 5 rue d'Odessa, 14e; ☎01.43.20.91.21 (Mº Montparnasse). *Women*: Mon & Thurs–Sat 10.30am–9pm; *men*: Mon, Tues & Thurs–Sat 9.30am–9pm. 83F for steam-bath and sauna; jacuzzi 120F, massage 110F. The oldest *hammam* in the city, which you reach through a courtyard decorated with shells and cupids.

Cleopatra Club, 53 bd de Belleville, 11e; ☎01.43.57.34.32 (Mº Belleville). Tues–Sun 10am–6.30pm. Women only. 80F for a sauna, 130F for massage. Very relaxed *hammam* with beautiful tiling; mint tea served.

Daytime Amusements and Sports

Daytime Amusements and Sports

Hammam de la Mosquée, 39 rue Geoffroy-St-Hilaire, 5e; ☎01.43.31.18.14 (Mº Censier-Daubenton). Hours and days for men and women change, so phone first, but generally women on Mon & Wed 11am–8pm, Thurs 11am–9pm, Sat 10am–8pm; men on Fri 11am–8pm & Sun 10am–8pm; closed Aug. You can order mint tea and honey cakes after your baths, around a fountain in a marble and cedarwood-covered courtyard. It's very good value for 85F (massage 65F extra), and a very unintimidating experience if you've never taken a public bath before.

Participatory Sports

Ice-skating, roller-blading, skateboarding, jogging, bowling, billiards, *boules* - it's all here to be enjoyed.

Skating and Skateboarding

If it's your ankles and shock absorbers you want to exercise, get on the ice at the city's only permanent **ice rink**. The *Patinoire des Buttes-Chaumont* (30 rue Edouard-Pailleron, 19e; ☎01.42.08.72.20; Mº Bolivar) is open Mon, Tues & Thurs 3–9pm, Wed 10am–9pm, Fri 3pm–midnight, Sat 10am–midnight, Sun 10am–6pm. Admission is 30F, 25F for children, plus 16F for skate rental.

From Nov to March a small rink is set up in the Tuileries gardens, (Mº Place-de-la-Concorde) by the Orangerie, Mon, Tues, Thurs & Fri noon–1.30pm & 4–7pm, Wed, Sat & Sun 10am–7pm; 40F/30F including skate hire.

Roller bladers can take advantage of a special disco rink at *La Main Jaune* (place de la Porte-de-Champerret, 17e; Mº Porte-de-Champerret) Wed, Sat & Sun 2.30–7pm, 50F plus 15F skate hire. Fri & Sat disco sessions 10pm–dawn; 80F plus 15F skate hire.

The main official outdoor arena for **roller-blading** and **skateboarding** is the concourse of the Palais de Chaillot (Mº Trocadéro), though Les Halles (around the Fontaine des Innocents), the Beaubourg piazza and place du Palais-Royal are also very popular.

Jogging – and the Marathon

The **Paris Marathon** is held in May over a route from place de la Concorde to Vincennes. If you want to join in and need details and equipment, the best place for information is a shop owned by a dedicated marathon runner, *Marathon* (29 rue de Chazelles, 17e; ☎01.42.27.48.18; Mº Monceau). A shorter race, *"Les 20km de Paris"*, takes place mid-October and begins and ends at the Eiffel Tower.

If you feel compelled to go running or **jogging** by yourself, take great care with the traffic. The Jardin du Luxembourg, Tuileries and Champs de Mars, which are particularly popular with Parisian joggers, all provide decent, varied runs, and are more or less flat. If you want to run hills, head for the Parc des Buttes-Chaumont in the 19e or Parc Montsouris in the 14e for plenty of suitably rugged gradients. If you have easy access to them, the Bois de Boulogne and the Bois de Vincennes are the largest open spaces, though both are cut through by a number of roads.

Cycling

Very few people cycle in Paris, with good reason, although in these days of traffic congestion their numbers are increasing. Several outlets **rent bikes**, by the hour, day, weekend or week. Prices depend on the type of bike, but are usually around 100–150F per day and up to 500F for the week. You will need a credit card or at least 2000F by way of a deposit.

Some companies also organize **bike trips**. To tour the city on two wheels, try *Paris-Vélo, Paris à Vélo C'est Sympa* and *Paris Bike; Paris-Vélo's* night-time tours are especially enjoyable. For sorties into the outlying countryside, phone *Bicy-Club* or *Vélonature* for information about a variety of expeditions.

Bicy-Club, 8 place de la Porte-de-Champerret ☎01.47.66.55.92 (Mº Porte-de-Champerret).

Bois de Boulogne near the Porte de Sablons entrance (Mº Les Sablons). For rides through the wood.

Cycles Laurent, 9 bd Voltaire, 11e; ☎01.47.00.27.47 (Mº République/Oberkampf). Mon–Sat 10am–7pm.

Paris Bike, 83 rue Daguerre, 14e; ☎01.45.38.58.58 (Mº Denfert-Rochereau).

Paris à Vélo C'est Sympa, 9 rue Jacques-Coeur, 4e; ☎01.48.87.60.01 (Mº Bastille). Daily 9.30am–7.30pm. Also at 78 rue de l'Ouest, 14e; ☎01.40.47.08.04 (Mº Pernéty). One of the cheapest – phone first to reserve a bike.

Paris-Vélo, 2 rue du Fer-à-Moulin, 5e (Mº Gobelins). Mon–Sat 10am–12.30pm & 2–7pm.

Vélonature, 5 rue St-Victor, 5e; ☎01.40.46.87.65 (Mº Cardinal-Lemoine/Maubert-Mutualité).

Bowling Alleys

There's nothing particularly Parisian about **bowling** alleys, but they exist and they're popular, should the urge to scuttle skittles take you. Prices vary between 16F and 35F a session, plus 8F for shoe hire.

Bowling-Académie de Billard, 66 av d'Ivry, 13e; ☎01.45.86.55.52 (Mº Tolbiac). Daily 2pm–2am. Entrance by escalators to Olympiades. Attracts an active and young clientele to roll the balls in Chinatown. With bar billiards and pool alongside.

Bowling de Montparnasse, 25 rue Commandant-Mouchotte, 14e; ☎01.43.21.61.32 (Mº Montparnasse-Bienvenue). Daily 10am–2am, Sat till 5am. A complex with sixteen lanes, plus a bar, brasserie, pool tables and video games.

Bowling Mouffetard, Centre-Commercial Mouffetard-Monge, 73 rue Mouffetard, 5e; ☎01.43.31.09.35 (Mº Monge). Daily 11am–2am. The cheapest in town, frequented by students, with bar and billiards.

Bowling de Paris, Jardin d'Acclimatation, Bois de Boulogne 16e; ☎01.40.67.94.00 (Mº Sablons). Daily 11am–2am. Popular with the chic types west of town.

Billiards

Unlike bowling, **billiards** is an original and ancient French game played with three balls and no pockets. Pool, or American billiards as the French call it, is also played. If you want to watch or try your hand (for around 60F per hour plus deposits of around 100F), head for one of the following:

Académie de Clichy-Montmartre, 84 rue de Clichy, 9e (Mº Clichy). Daily 1.30–11.30pm. The chicest billiard hall in Europe, where the players look like they've stepped out of a 1940s movie (or a *Men in Vogue* ad) and the décor is all ancient gilded mirrors, high ceilings and panelled walls.

Blue-Billard, 111 rue St-Maur, 11e (Mº Parmentier). Daily 5pm–2am. Cocktails, chess and backgammon as well as billiards, in arty-intellectual hang-out close to Belleville.

Bowling-Académie de Billard, 66 av d'Ivry, 13e (Mº Tolbiac). Daily 2pm–2am. See under "Bowling Alleys" above.

Bowling Mouffetard, 73 rue Mouffetard, 5e (Mº Monge). See "Bowling Alleys".

Salle des Billards des Halles, *niveau 2*, Porte du Jour, Forum des Halles, 1er (*RER* Châtelet-Les Halles). Mon–Fri 10am–10pm, Sat & Sun 2–10pm. Free.

Boules

The classic French game involving balls, **boules** (or *pétanque*), is best performed (or watched) at the *Arènes de Lutèce* (see p.117) and the Bois de Vincennes. On balmy summer evenings it's a common sight in the city's parks and gardens.

Rock Climbing

The best training wall for **rock climbing** in Paris is at the *Centre Sportif Poissonnier*, 2 rue Jean-Cocteau, 18e; ☎01.42.51.24.68 (Mº Porte-de-Clignancourt). Mon–Fri noon–2pm, Sat & Sun noon–4pm. It's 23m high, with corridors and chimneys. There's another wall in *Aquaboulevard* (see p.308) and one

Daytime Amusements and Sports

Daytime Amusements and Sports

One sport that is not really worth trying in Paris is **horse riding**. You need to have all the gear with you and a licence, the *Carte Nationale de Cavalier*, before you can mount.

for kids in the sports and camping shop, *Au Vieux Campeur*, in rue des Écoles (see Chapter 17).

Other Sports

Tennis, squash, golf, dry-slope skiing, archery, canoeing, fishing, windsurfing, water-skiing and parachuting – you name it, you can do it, in or around the city. Whether you'll want to spend the time and money on booking and renting equipment is another matter. If you're determined, you'll find some details in *L'Officiel des Spectacles*, etc, or you can ring *Allo Sports* on ☎01.42.76.54.54 (Mon–Fri 10.30am–5pm) or pay a visit to the *Direction Jeunesse et Sports* (25 bd Bourdon, 4e; Mon–Fri 10am–5.30pm; Mº Bastille). These are both municipal outfits, so the places they have listed will all be subsidized and cheapish.

Of the private clubs and complexes, *Aquaboulevard*, 4 rue Louis-Armand, 15e (Mº Balard/*RER* Boulevard-Victor) is the newest and biggest, with squash and tennis courts, a climbing wall, golf tees, aquatic diversions, *hammams*, dance floors, shops, restaurants and other money-extracting paraphernalia. Some sample prices are: 68F for the *parc aquatique* (weekdays); 55F for tennis.

Spectator Sports

Paris' best football team, *Paris St-Germain (Paris-SG)*, are currently resurgent in the French league, and the capital retains a special status, too, in the rugby, cycling and tennis worlds. Horse racing is as serious a pursuit as in Britain or North America.

Cycling

The biggest event of the French sporting year is the grand finale of the *Tour de France*, which ends in a sweep along the Champs-Élysées in the third week of July. In theory the last day of the race is a competitive time trial, but most years this amounts to a triumphal procession, the overall winner of the *Tour* having long since been determined. Only very rarely does Paris witness memorable scenes such as those of 1989, when American Greg Lemond snatched the coveted *maillot jaune* (the winner's yellow jersey) on the final day.

Football and Rugby

The *Parc des Princes* (24 rue du Commandant-Guilbaud, 16e; ☎01.42.88.02.76; Mº Porte-de-St-Cloud) is the capital's main stadium for both rugby union and football events, and home ground to the first-division Paris football team *Paris-SG* and the rugby champions, *Le Racing*. In 1998 France will be hosting the World Cup – a new stadium is being built in St-Denis.

Tennis

The French equivalent of Britain's Wimbledon, Roland-Garros, lies between the *Parc des Princes* and the Bois de Boulogne, with the ace address of 2 av Gordon-Bennett, 16e (☎01.47.43.00.47; Mº Porte-d'Auteuil). The French Tennis Open, one of the four major events which together comprise the Grand Slam, takes place in the last week of May and first week of June, and tickets need to be reserved before February. A few are sold each day, but only for the unseeded matches. Unlike Wimbledon, you can't get near the main courts once inside the turnstiles.

Athletics and Other Sports

The *Palais des Omnisports Paris-Bercy (POPB)* at 8 bd Bercy, 12e (☎01.40.02.60.60) hosts all manner of sporting events, including athletics, cycling, handball, dressage and show-jumping, ice hockey, ballroom dancing, judo and motorcross. Keep an eye on the sports pages of the newspapers (except *Le Monde*, which has no sports coverage at all), and you might find something on that interests you. The complex holds 17,000 people, so you've a fair chance of getting a ticket at the door, championships excepted.

Horse Racing

Being a spectator at a horse race could make a healthy change from looking at art treasures. If you want to fathom the **betting system**, any bar or café with the letters *PMU* will take your money on a three-horse bet, known as *le tiercé*. The **biggest races** are the *Prix de la République* and the *Grand Prix de L'Arc de Triomphe*, held on the first and last Sundays in October at Auteuil and Longchamp. The week starting the last Sunday in June sees nine big events, at Auteuil, Longchamp, St-Cloud and Chantilly (see p.381). **Trotting races**, with the jockeys in chariots, run from August to September on the Route de la Ferme in the Bois de Vincennes.

St-Cloud Champ de Courses is in the Parc de St-Cloud off Allée de Chamillard. *Auteuil* is off the route d'Auteuil, and *Longchamp* off the route des Tribunes, both in the Bois de Boulogne. *L'Humanité* and *Paris-Turf* carry details, and admission charges are around 25F.

Daytime
Amusements
and Sports

Chapter 16

Kids' Stuff

For details on Disneyland Paris, see p.392.

Paris is often considered a strictly adult city, with little to engage or entertain energetic kids. Keeping teenagers amused may be as hard in Paris as it is anywhere, but for the younger ones there is a lot on offer, in addition to Disneyland Paris (see Chapter 21).

You shouldn't underestimate the sheer attraction of Paris' vibrant sense of life, with its diversity of sights and sounds so far removed from typical British and American cities. But neither should you expect kids to be enthralled by "doing" the Louvre, Notre-Dame and the Invalides. There are museums and monuments to excite most children, as

well as playgrounds, puppet shows, wonderful shops and high-tech treats. The French are also extremely welcoming to children, so there's never a problem taking them into cafés, bars or restaurants.

If your offspring know that **Disneyland Paris** is just outside the city, you probably won't be able to do anything with them until they've been there. If you can keep its existence a secret, so much the better, but at least take them to the **Cité des Sciences**, at La Villette, for a contrast.

For older kids, a good start to life in Paris is a visit to **Paristoric**, at 11 rue Scribe, 9e; ☎01.42.66.62.06 (M°

Paris With Babies

You will have little problem in getting hold of essentials for **babies**. Familiar brands of baby food are available in the supermarkets, as well as disposable nappies (*couches à jeter*), etc. After hours, you can get most goods from late-night pharmacies.

Getting around with a pushchair poses the same problems as in most big cities. The métro is particularly bad, with its constant flights of stairs (and few escalators), difficult turnstiles and very stiff doors. One particular place to avoid is the Louvre: taking a buggy in there is like trying to pothole with a rucksack.

For emergency medical care, see under "Health and Insurance".

Baby-sitters

The most reliable **baby-sitting** agency is *Ababa*, 8 av du Maine, 15e (☎01.45.49.46.46), which has English speakers; you pay around 31F per hour plus agency fees of 62F and taxis home after 11pm. Other possibilities are *Kid Service* (☎01.47.66.00.52; 30F per hour plus 58F fees), or individual notices at the American Church, 65 quai d'Orsay, 6e (M° Invalides), the *Alliance Française*, 101 bd Raspail, 6e (M° St-Placide), or *CIDJ*, 101 quai Branly, 15e; ☎01.44.49.12.00 (M° Bir-Hakeim). If you know someone who has a phone, you could dial up Babysitting on *"Elletel"* via their Minitel.

Opéra/Chaussée-d'Antin; Nov–March Sun–Thurs 9am–6pm, Fri, Sat & April–Oct 9am–9pm). This 45-minute film (English version) illustrating the history of the city is breathy-voiced and romantic, but informative and fun to watch. Performances are on the hour, every hour.

In this chapter we assess the principal outdoor spaces and indoor attractions Paris can offer your kids, as well as shops specializing in items for children and special events such as theatre performances and circuses.

The most useful **sources of information**, for current shows, exhibitions and events, are the special sections in the listings magazines: "*Pour les jeunes*" in *Pariscope* and the more expensive "*Jeunes*" in *L'Officiel des Spectacles*. The best place for **details of organized activities**, whether sports, courses or local youth clubs, is the *Centre d'Information et de Documentation de la Jeunesse (CIDJ)*, 101 quai Branly, 15ᵉ; ☎01.44.49.12.00 (Mº Bir-Hakeim; Mon–Sat 10am–6pm). The Mairie of Paris also provides information about sports and special events at the *Kiosque Paris-Jeunes*, 25 bd Bourdon, 4ᵉ; ☎01.42.76.22.60 (Mº Bastille; Mon–Fri noon–7pm).

Parks, Gardens and Zoos

Younger kids are well catered for by the **parks and gardens** within the city, though some may find the activities too structured or even twee. The most standard forms of entertainment are puppet shows and *Guignol*, the French equivalent of Punch and Judy. Adventure playgrounds hardly exist, and there aren't, on the whole, any open spaces for spontaneous games of football, baseball or cricket. French sport tends to be thoroughly organized (see Chapter 15).

The real star attractions for young children have to be the **Jardin d'Acclimatation** and the **Parc de la Villette**, though you can also let your kids off the leash at the **Jardin des Plantes**, 57 rue Cuvier, 5ᵉ; ☎01.40.79.30.00 (Mº Jussieu/Monge).

Open from 7.30/8am until dusk, it contains a small zoo (9am–5/6pm; 25F/15F), a playground, hothouses and plenty of greenery. There's a better zoo at the **Bois de Vincennes**, 53 av de St-Maurice, 12ᵉ; ☎01.43.43.84.95 (Mº Porte-Dorée; summer 9am–6pm, winter 9am–5.30pm; 40F/20F, free for children under 6; see p.196).

Jardin d'Acclimatation

In the Bois de Boulogne, by Porte des Sablons; ☎01.40.67.90.82 (Mº Les Sablons/Porte-Maillot). 10F, under-3s free; rides from 10F. Daily 10am–6pm, with special attractions Wed, Sat, Sun & all week during school hols, including a little train to take you there from Mº Porte-Maillot (behind L'Orée du Bois restaurant; every 10min, 1.30–6pm; 5F one way, 10F return).

The garden is a cross between a funfair, a zoo and an amusement park, with temptations ranging from bumper cars, go-karts, pony and camel rides, sea lions, birds, bears and monkeys, to a magical mini-canal ride (*la rivière enchantée*), distorting mirrors, scaled-down farm buildings, and a puppet theatre. Astérix and friends may be explaining life in their Gaulish village, or Babar the world of the elephants – created by archeologists in the **Musée en Herbe**. If not, there'll be some other child-friendly exhibition with game sheets (also in English), workshops and demonstrations of traditional crafts. And if they just want to watch and listen, the **Théâtre du Jardin pour l'Enfance et la Jeunesse** puts on musicals and ballets.

Outside the *jardin*, in the **Bois de Boulogne**, older children can amuse themselves with mini-golf and bowling, or boating on the Lac Inférieur. By the entrance to the *jardin* there's **bike rental** for roaming the wood's cycle trails.

Parc de la Villette

In the 19ᵉ between avs Jean-Jaurès and Corentin-Cariou; ☎01.40.03.75.75 (Mº Porte-de-Pantin/Porte-de-la-Villette). Daily 6am–1am; free.

Kids' Stuff

Kids' Stuff

As well as the *Cité des Sciences*, various satellite attractions (see below), and wide open spaces to run around or picnic in, the **Parc de la Villette** has a series of themed gardens, some specially designed for kids.

Polished steel monoliths hidden amongst the trees and scrub cast strange reflections in *Le Jardin des Miroirs*, while *Le Jardin des Brouillards* has jets and curtains of water at different heights and angles. Formalized shapes of dunes and sails, windmills and inflated mattresses make up *Le Jardin des Vents et des Dunes* (under-12s only and their accompanying adults). Strange music creates a fairy-tale or horror-story ambience in the imaginary forests of *Le Jardin des Frayeurs Enfantines. Le Jardin des Voltiges* has an obstacle course with trampolines and rigging. Small bronze figures lead you through the vines and other climbing plants of *Le Jardin de la Treille*; and *Le Jardin des Bambous* is filled with the sound of running water. On the north side of the canal de l'Ourcq is the Dragon Slide.

Some of the park's "follies" have activities for kids: video editing (over-8s; Mon–Sat 9am–5pm; 100F) in the *Folie Vidéo* and a game-filled crèche for 2–5s year-olds in *La Petite Folie*, both on the south bank of the canal de l'Ourcq; and arts activities for 7- to 10-year-olds in the *Folie des Arts Plastiques*, by the northeast corner of the Grande Halle (details on ☎01.40.03.75.00).

Parc Floral

In the Bois de Vincennes, on rte de la Pyramide; ☎01.43.43.92.95 (Mº Château-de-Vincennes, then bus #112). Daily March–Sept 9.30am–8pm, Oct–Feb 9.30am–5pm; admission 10F, 6- to 10-year-olds 5F plus supplements for some activities, under-6s & over-65s free. A little train tours all the gardens (April–Oct Wed–Sun 10.30am–5pm; 5F).

There's always fun and games to be had at the **Parc Floral**, on the other side of the Bois de Vincennes to the zoo. The excellent playground has slides, swings,

ping-pong and pedal carts; a few paying extras like mini-golf modelled on Paris monuments (from 1.45pm; 25F), an electric car circuit, and pony rides (April–Oct daily 2–6pm); and clowns, puppets and magicians on summer weekends. Most of the activities are free, and in general you'll be far less out of pocket after an afternoon here than at the *Jardin d'Acclimatation*. Also in the park is a children's theatre, the **Théâtre Astral**, which may have mime, clowns or other not-too-verbal shows.

Jardin des Halles

105 rue Rambuteau, 1er ☎01.45.08.07.18 (Mº/RER Châtelet-Les Halles). 7–11-year-olds only; Tues–Sat 10am–6pm, Sun 1–6pm; closed Mon; winter closing 4pm; closed in bad weather; 2.50F per hour.

Right in the centre of town, the **Jardin des Halles** is great if you want to lose your charges for the odd hour. A whole series of fantasy landscapes fill this small but cleverly designed space. On Wednesday, animators organize adventure games; and at all times the children are supervised by professional child-carers. You may have to reserve a place an hour or so in advance. On Saturday mornings you too can go in and play. Several languages are spoken, including English. Opening times vary a bit in the middle of the day, so it might be best to phone ahead.

Other Parks, Squares and Public Gardens

All of these assorted **open spaces** can offer play areas, puppets or, at the very least, a bit of room to run around in, and are open from 7.30 or 8am till dusk. **Guignol and puppet shows** take place on Wednesday and weekend afternoons (and more frequently in the summer holidays).

Buttes-Chaumont, 19e; ☎01.42.40.88.66 (Mº Buttes-Chaumont/Botzaris). Donkey-drawn carts, puppets, grassy slopes to roll down (see p.182).

Champs-de-Mars, 7e; ☎01.48.56.01.44 (Mº École-Militaire). Puppet shows.

Jardin du Luxembourg, 6e;
☎01.43.26.46.47 (M² St-Placide/Notre-Dame-des-Champs/RER Luxembourg). A large playground, pony rides, toy boat rental, bicycle track, roller-blading rink, and puppets (see p.122).

Jardin du Ranelagh, av Ingres, 16º (M² Muette). Donkey-carts, *Guignol*, pony rides, cycle track, roller-blading rink and playground.

Jardin des Tuileries, place de la Concorde/rue Rivoli, 1e (M² Place-de-la-Concorde/Palais-Royal/Musée-du-Louvre). Pony rides, marionettes, ice rink (in winter, funfair in July).

Jardins du Trocadéro, place du Trocadéro, 16e (M² Trocadéro). Roller-blading, skateboarding and aquarium.

Parc Georges-Brassens, rue des Morillons, 15e (M² Convention/Porte-de-Vanves). Climbing rocks, puppets, pony rides, artificial river, playground and scented herb gardens (see p.143).

Parc Monceau, bd de Courcelles, 17e;
☎01.42.67.04.63 (M² Monceau). Roller-blading rink (see p.205).

Parc Montsouris, bd Jourdan, 14e (M² Glacière/RER Cité-Universitaire). Puppet shows by the lake (see p.147).

Funfairs

With the exception of the Tuileries funfair, whose future within the new garden scheme is uncertain, **funfairs** are, alas, few and far between. There's usually a **merry-go-round** at the Forum des Halles and beneath Tour St-Jacques at Châtelet, with carousels for smaller children on place de la République, at the Rond-Point des Champs-Elysées by av Matignon, and at place de la Nation. Very occasionally, rue de Rivoli around M² St-Paul hosts a mini-fairground. There is also a funfair museum, the **Musée des Forains**, which at the time of writing was looking for a new home (for the address and hours, check with the Paris Tourist Office on ☎01.49.52.53.54). It's a treat, with working merry-go-rounds and magic shows as well as fascinating relics from nineteenth-century fairs.

Fantasy Worlds and Theme Parks

Disneyland Paris (see p.392) has now put all Paris' other **fantasy worlds and theme parks** into the shade. And unfortunately it's the only one with direct transport links. But, if you're prepared to make the effort, **Parc Astérix** is better mind-fodder and cheaper than Disney.

Kids' Stuff

Food for Kids

Junk-food addicts no longer have any problems in Paris. *McDonald's, Quick Hamburger* and their clones are to be found all over the city. The French-style *"fast foude"* chain, *Hippopotamus*, is slightly healthier (branches throughout the centre of the city, including 1 bd des Capucines, 2e; ☎01.47.42.75.70; M⁰ Opéra; daily 11am–5am; 47F *menu enfants*). At *Chicago Meatpackers* (8 rue Coquillière, 1er; ☎01.40.28.02.33; M⁰ Les Halles; daily 11.45am–1am; 59F children's menu) a dining room with giant electric trains is reserved for kids. They're given balloons and drawing equipment, and on Wednesday, Saturday and Sunday lunchtimes at 1pm & 2pm (every day during hols) there are mime, music or magic shows.

Other restaurants are usually good at providing small portions or allowing children to share dishes. The *Hammam Café* (4 rue des Rosiers, 4e; ☎01.42.78.04.45; M⁰ St-Paul; 11am–12.30pm; 79F children, 120F adults) serves a special kids' brunch every other Sunday, with wonderful crêpes, cakes and entertainment. Keeping away from ice-creams (rather than finding them) is the main problem in Paris. One thing to remember when ordering a steak, hamburger, etc, is that the French will serve it rare unless you ask for it *"bien cuit"*.

Kids' Stuff

If outer space is the kids' prime interest, then bear in mind the two **planetariums**, in the *Palais de la Découverte* (see p.298) and the *Cité des Sciences* (see p.282). For children who enjoy working things out for themselves, the latter is the best adventure land of all. If their minds are more tuned to basic matters, an excursion into the catacombs or even the sewers might be an idea.

Other possibilities include the various river and canal trips detailed in Chapter 15.

The Catacombs and the Sewers

Horror fanatics and ghouls should get a really satisfying shudder from the **catacombs** at 1 place Denfert-Rochereau, 14ᵉ; ☎01.43.22.47.63; (Tues–Fri 2–6pm, Sat & Sun 9–11am & 2–4pm; closed Mon & hols; 27F/19F; *RER* Denfert-Rochereau), though perhaps you should read p.138 first.

The archetypal pre-teen fixation, on the other hand, can be indulged in the sewers – **les égouts** – at place de la Résistance, on the corner of quai d'Orsay and the Pont de l'Alma; ☎01.47.05.10.29 (Sat–Wed 11am–4/5pm; closed Thurs, Fri & last 3 weeks in Jan; 25F/20F; Mº Alma-Marceau). For further details, see p.129.

Parc Astérix

In Plailly, 38km north of Paris off the A1 autoroute, most easily reached by half-hourly shuttle bus from RER Roissy-Charles-de-Gaulle (ligne B). April–June Mon–Fri 10am–6pm, weekends 10am–7pm; July and Aug daily 10am–7pm; Sept & Oct Wed & weekends only 10am–6pm. (phone to check). Closed mid-Oct to March. Admission is 160F, 3–12s 110F, under-3s free.

A Via Antiqua shopping street, with buildings from every country in the Roman Empire, leads to a Roman town where gladiators play comic battles and dodgem chariots line up for races. There's a legionaries' camp where incompetent soldiers attempt to keep watch, and a wave-manipulated lake which you cross on galleys and long-ships. In the Gaulish village, Getafix mixes his potions, Obelix slavers over boars, Astérix plots further sorties against the occupiers, and the dreadful bard is exiled up a tree. In another area, street scenes of Paris show the city changing from Roman Lutetia to the present-day capital. All sorts of rides are on offer (with long queues for the best ones); dolphins and sea lions perform tricks for the crowds; there are parades and jugglers; restaurants for every budget; and most of the actors speak English (even if they occasionally get confused with the variations on the names). Information about Parc Astérix in the UK is available on ☎01242/236169; in Paris, ☎01.44.62.34.44.

Circus, Film and Theatre

Language being less of a barrier for smaller children, the younger your kids, the more likely they are to appreciate Paris' many special theatre shows and films. There's also mime and the circus, which need no translations.

Circus

Circuses, unlike funfairs, are taken seriously in France. They come under the heading of culture as performance art (and there are no qualms about performing animals).

Some circuses have permanent venues, of which the most beautiful in Paris is the nineteenth-century *Cirque d'Hiver Bouglione* (see below). You'll find details of the seasonal ones under "*Cirques*" in *Pariscope*, etc., and there may well be visiting circuses from Warsaw or Moscow.

Cirque Bormann Diana Moreno. This touring circus sets up at *Les Grands Sablons* at the *Jardin d'Acclimatation*, 16ᵉ (☎01.45.00.23.01), during its two seasons: April–June & Sept–Dec. From 60F.

Cirque d'Hiver Bouglione, 110 rue Amelot, 11ᵉ; ☎01.47.00.12.25. Strolling players and fairy lights beneath the dome welcome circus-goers from Oct to

Jan (and TV and fashion shows the rest of the year).

Cirque National Alexis Gruss. Performs at various venues between Oct and mid-Feb. Phone ☎01.40.36.08.00 for details.

Cirque de Paris, on the corner of av Hoche and av de la Commune-de-Paris, Nanterre; ☎01.47.24.11.70 (*RER* Nanterre-Ville). This dream day out allows you to spend an entire day at the circus (Oct–June Wed, Sun & school hols 10am–5pm; 235F adults, 195F children). In the morning you are initiated into the arts of juggling, walking the tightrope, clowning and make-up. You have lunch in the ring with your artist tutors, then join the spectators for the show, after which, if you're lucky, the lion-tamer will take you round to meet his cats. You can, if you prefer, just attend the show at 3pm (70–155F/45–95F), but if so, you'd better not let the kids know what they have missed.

Theatre

Several **theatres**, apart from the ones in the *Parc Floral* and the *Jardin d'Acclimatation*, specialize in shows for children.

The *Blancs Manteaux* and *Point Virgule* in the Marais, *Au Bec Fin* in the 1er, *Le Dunois* in the 13e, and the *Bateau Théâtre* moored by the Passerelle des Arts, all have excellent reputations, but it's doubtful how much pleasure your children will get unless they're bilingual. Still, it's worth checking in the listings magazines for any magic, mime, dance or music shows.

Full details of Paris theatres are given in Chapter 19.

Cinema

There are many **cinemas** showing cartoons and children's films, but if they're foreign they are inevitably dubbed into French. Listings of the main Parisian cinemas are given in Chapter 19. The pleasure of an Omnimax projection at *La Géode* in La Villette or *Dôme-Imax* at La Défense,

however, is greatly enhanced by not understanding the commentary. The *Cinaxe* projection at La Villette simulates motion to accompany high-definition film (see p.357). Films at the *Louis-Lumière* cinema (also in the *Cité des Sciences* – see below) may be less accessible, but you can ask at the enquiry desk for advice.

Kids' Stuff

Museums

The best treat for children of every age from three upwards is the **Cité des Sciences** in the Parc de la Villette. All the other museums, despite entertaining collections and special activities and workshops for children, pale into insignificance. So beware that, if you visit the *Cité* on your first day, your offspring may decide that's where they want to stay.

Given kids' particular and sometimes peculiar tastes, the choice of other museums and monuments is best left to them, though the **Musée des Enfants** itself, purveying sentimental images of childhood, is certainly one to avoid. On the other hand, don't forget the gargoyles of Notre-Dame, the aquariums at the **Musée des Arts Africains et Océaniens** (see p.287) and beneath the **Palais de Chaillot** (place du Trocadéro, 16e; daily 10am–5.30pm; Mº Trocadéro), and the new **Grande Galerie de l'Évolution** (see p.298). The **Musée de la Poupée** (see p.294) should please children who like dolls; and the **Musée de la Curiosité** (see p.293) should appeal to most kids.

Certain museums have **children's workshops**, giving you the freedom to enjoy the sort of things that bore most children to tears. When they've exhausted **Beaubourg's** free attractions – the performers on the plaza and the building in itself – you can deposit 6- to 14-year-olds in the *Atelier des Enfants* (Mon & Wed–Sun 1.30–5.30pm; 30F; some English-speaking animators), where they can create their own art and play games. The **Musée d'Art Moderne de la Ville de Paris** has special exhibitions and work-

Details of the Dôme-Imax are given on p.357.

Kids' Stuff

The Cité des Sciences et de l'Industrie *is described in full on p.282.*

shops in its children's section (Wed, Sat & Sun; entrance 14 av de New-York). The **Musée d'Orsay** provides worksheets (English promised) for 8- to 12-year-olds that make them explore every aspect of the building; plus the house runs children's workshops (☎01.40.20.52.63 to reserve a place; 22F). Other municipal museums with sessions for kids include the **Musée Carnavalet**, **Musée de la Mode et du Costume**, **Musée des Arts Décoratifs** and the **Petit Palais**; costs are around 25F.

Full details of all the state museums' activities for children, which are all included in the admission charge, are published in *Objectif Musée*, a booklet available from the museums or from the *Direction des Musées de France* (34 quai du Louvre, 1er; closed Tues).

Cité des Sciences et de l'Industrie

Parc de la Villette, 30 av Corentin-Cariou, 19e; ☎01.36.68.29.30 (Mº Porte-de-la-Villette). Tues–Sat 10am–6pm, Sun 10am–7pm; everything closed Mon. Cité pass giving access to Explora & its temporary exhibitions, planetarium, Cinéma Louis-Lumière, Salle Jean-Painlevé and mediathèque screens, aquarium and Argonaute: 45F, reduced tarif 35F, under-7s free; Géode Tues–Sun 10am–8pm: 50F/37F (some films are more), combined ticket with Cité 85F/72F (available from Géode only); Inventorium and Cité des Enfants (see p.282) 15F and 20F extra; Cinaxe 27F/22F.

The **Cité des Enfants**, the Cité's special section for children, divided between 3–5s and 6–12s, is totally engaging. The kids can touch and smell and feel inside things, play about with water, construct buildings on a miniature construction site (complete with cranes, hard hats and barrows), experiment with sound and light, manipulate robots, race their own shadows, and superimpose their image on a landscape. They can listen to different languages by inserting telephones into the appropriate country on a globe, and put together their own television news. Everything, including the butterfly park, is

on an appropriate scale, and the whole area is beautifully organized and managed. If you haven't got a child, it's worth borrowing one to get in here.

A new space on the ground floor, **Techno Cité**, (90min sessions; Tues & Sat 2pm & 4pm; during summer hols Tues–Sat 10.30am, 12.30pm. 2.30pm & 4.30pm; over-11s only) offers hands-on application of technology to industry. You can write a programme for a robotic videotape selector, design a prototype racing bike, manufacture a plastic puzzle and package it using a laser-guided cutter, and set up a control system for an assembly line.

The rest of the museum is also pretty good for kids, often with temporary exhibitions designed for the young, plus there are the cinematic treats (see above), the Argonaut submarine, and the gardens and "follies" of the Parc de la Villette (see above).

Shops

If your offspring belong to the modern breed of sophisticated consumers, then keeping them away from **shops** will be your biggest saving. This can be difficult given the Parisian art of enticing window displays, practised to the full on every other street. Children with an eye for clothes are certain to spy boots, gloves or dresses without which life will not be worth living. Huge cuddly animals, gleaming models, and the height of fashionable sports equipment will beckon them from every turn, not to mention ice-creams, waffles, chips and pancakes. The only goodies you are safe from are high-tech toys, of which France seems to offer a particularly poor selection.

However, the brats may get the better of you, or you may decide to treat them anyway. So here's a small selection of shops to seek out, be dragged into or to avoid at all costs.

Books

The following are among a number of shops stocking a good selection of English books, but be warned: they're expensive.

Brentano's, 37 av de l'Opéra, 2e (Mº Opéra). Mon–Sat 10am–7pm.

Chantelivre, 13 rue de Sèvres, 6e (Mº Sèvres-Babylone). Mon 1–6.50pm, Tues–Sat 10am–6.50pm; closed Mon in Aug. A huge selection of everything to do with and for children, including good picture books for the younger ones, an English section, a play area, and drawing and mime classes.

Galignani, 224 rue de Rivoli, 1er (Mº Tuileries). Mon–Sat 10am–7pm.

W H Smith, 248 rue de Rivoli, 1er (Mº Concorde). Mon–Sat 9.30am–7pm.

Tea and Tattered Pages, 24 rue Mayet, 6e (Mº Duroc). Daily 11am–7pm. The English bookshop and *salon de thé* has a storyteller every Wed 11am–noon, suitable for 3–7-year-olds. ☎01.40.65.94.35 for more details.

Toys and games

As well as the wide assortment of shops listed below, it's worth bearing in mind that if children have enjoyed a museum they'll probably want what's on offer in the museum shops. The boutiques at **Beaubourg** and the **Cité des Sciences** have wonderful books, models, games, scientific instruments and toys covering a wide price range.

Art et Joie, 74 rue de Maubeuge, 9e; ☎01.48.78.27.72 (Mº Poissonnière). Mon–Fri 9.30am–6.30pm, Sat 10am–12.30pm; closed Aug. Everything you need for painting, modelling, graphic design, pottery and every other art and craft.

Le Ciel Est à Tout le Monde, 10 rue Gay-Lussac, 5e; ☎01.46.33.21.50 (Mº Luxembourg); 7 av Trudaine, 9e (Mº Anvers). Tues–Sat 10am–7pm; closed Mon. The best kite shop in Europe also sells frisbees, boomerangs, etc, and, next door, books, slippers, mobiles and traditional wooden toys.

Au Cotillon Moderne, 13 bd Voltaire, 11e; ☎01.47.00.43.93 (Mº Oberkampf). Mon–Fri 9.30am–6.30pm, Sat 10am–12.30pm & 2–6pm; closed Aug.

Celluloid and supple plastic masks of animals and fictional and political characters, plus there are trinkets, festoons and other party paraphernalia.

Les Cousins d'Alice, 36 rue Daguerre, 14e; ☎01.43.20.24.86 (Mº Gaîté/Edgar-Quinet). Tues–Sat 10am–1pm & 3–5pm, Sun 11am–1pm; closed Mon & Aug. *Alice in Wonderland* decorations, toys, games, puzzles and mobiles, plus a general range of books and records.

Deyrolle, 46 rue du Bac, 7e; ☎01.42.22.30.07 (Mº Bac). Mon–Sat 10am–1pm & 2–6.45pm. The best-known taxidermist: insects, butterflies, stuffed animals – from the biggest to the smallest, plus rocks and fossils. Fun to look at.

Magie Moderne, 8 rue des Carmes, 5e; ☎01.43.54.13.63 (Mº Maubert-Mutualité). Tues–Sat 10am–8pm, Sun, Mon & hols 2–8pm. A magician's paradise.

La Pelucherie, 84 av des Champs-Élysées, 8e; ☎01.43.59.49.05 (Mº George-V/Franklin-D-Roosevelt). Mon 10am–7.30pm, Tues–Sat 10am–11pm, Sun & hols noon–8pm. The top cuddly toy consortium. Expensive, but worth a look.

Au Nain Bleu, 406–410 rue St-Honoré, 8e; ☎01.42.60.39.01 (Mº Concorde). Mon–Sat 9.45am–6.30pm; closed Mon in Aug. The Paris equivalent of London's *Hamley's* – a large store completely devoted to toys of all kinds.

Puzzles d'Art, 116 rue du Château, 14e; ☎01.43.22.28.73 (Mº Pernéty). Mon–Fri 8.30am–8pm, Sat 10am–8pm. Exactly what the name says; with workshop on the premises.

Pains d'Épices, 29 passage Jouffroy, 9e; ☎01.47.70.82.65 (Mº Montmartre). Mon 2–7pm, Tues–Sat 10am–7pm. Fabulous doll's house necessities from furniture to wine glasses, and puppets.

Renault – Salles des Expositions, 51–52 av des Champs-Élysées, 8e (Mº Franklin-D-Roosevelt). Mon–Sat 9.30am–6pm. The main Paris showrooms have a collection

Kids' Stuff

Kids' Stuff

of Renault cars from prewar to recent Formula Ones, which you can look at without pretending you want to buy a new one.

Si Tu Veux, 68 galerie Vivienne, 2e; ☎01.42.60.59.97 (Mº Bourse). Mon–Sat 11am–7pm. Well-made traditional toys plus do-it-yourself and ready-made costumes.

Le Train Bleu, 55 rue St-Placide, 6e (Mº St-Placide). Mon 2–7pm, Tues–Sat 10am–7pm. Also at *Centre Beaugrenelle*, 16 rue Linois, 15e (Mº Charles-Michels; Tues–Sun 10am–7.30pm); and 2/6 av Mozart, 16e; ☎01.42.88.34.70 (Mº Ranelagh; Mon 2–7pm, Tues–Sat 10am–7pm). A fairly expensive chain, with the biggest array at St-Placide; good on electric trains, remote control vehicles and other things you don't want to carry home with you.

Virgin Megastore, 52 av des Champs-Élysées, 8e; ☎01.49.53.50.00 (Mº George-V). Mon–Thurs 10am–midnight, Fri & Sat 10am–1am. As well as all the cassettes and CDs to listen to, there's a Nintendo Gameboy to play with, but the Sega Super Entertainment console is not in fact hooked up to a machine.

Clothes

Besides the specialist shops we list here, most of the big department stores and the discount stores have children's sections (see Chapter 17, *Shops and markets*). Of the latter, *Tati* and *Monoprix* are the cheapest places to go for vital clothing purchases.

Agnès B, 2 rue du Jour, 1er; ☎01.40.39.96.88 (Mº/*RER* Châtelet-Les Halles). Mon–Sat 10am–7pm. Very fashionable, desirable and unaffordable, with lovely animal rocking chairs for the kids to sit in and contemplate their image.

Baby Dior, 28 av Montaigne, 8e; ☎01.40.73.55.14 (Mº Alma-Marceau/Frankllin-D-Roosevelt). Mon–Sat 10am–6.30pm. Even more unaffordable, but entertaining – especially the prices.

A Carnaval et Fêtes, 22 rue Ledru-Rollin, 12e; ☎01.43.47.06.08 (Mº Gare-de-Lyon). Tues–Sat 10am–7pm. Need something a little different? Fancy dress galore, gimmicks, masks, accessories and stage make-up all for hire or purchase.

Dipaki, 46 rue de l'Université, 7e; ☎01.42.97.49.89 (Mº Bac). Mon–Sat 10am–6.45pm. Also at 23 other addresses. Dependable, hard-wearing and reasonably priced clothes for up to 14-year-olds.

Junior Gaultier, 7 rue du Jour, 1er; ☎01.44.83.93.97 (Mº/*RER* Châtelet-Les Halles). Mon–Fri 10am–7pm, Sat 11am–7pm. Horror-movie décor to draw the brats in. The clothes are cheaper than the adult range.

Menkes, 12 rue de Rambuteau, 3e; ☎01.40.27.91.81 (Mº Rambuteau). Tues–Sat 10am–12.30pm & 2–7pm. A vibrant selection of Spanish flamenco outfits, sombreros, fans and footwear for boys and girls. Classes also on offer.

Nic et Pouf, 32 rue du Four, 6e; ☎01.45.44.39.58 (Mº St-Germain-des-Près). Mon 2–7pm, Tues–Sat 10.15am–7pm; closed Mon in Aug. All the top-name designers for kiddies. Good stuff, though not cheap.

Du Pareil au Même, 122 rue du Faubourg-St-Antoine, 12e; ☎01.43.44.67.46 (Mº Ledru-Rollin). Daily 10am–7pm. Beautiful kids' clothing at very good prices. Gorgeous floral dresses for around 65F. Branches all over Paris.

Pom d'Api, 13 rue du Jour, 1er; ☎01.42.36.08.87 (Mº/*RER* Châtelet-Les Halles). Mon–Sat 10.30am–7pm. Also at 28 rue du Four, 6e (Mº St-Germain-des-Près; Mon–Sat 10am–7pm); and 6 rue Guichard, 16e (Mº La Muette; Mon–Fri 10am–1pm & 2–7.30pm, Sat 10am–7.30pm). The most colourful, imaginative and well-made shoes for kids in Paris (up to size 40/7, and from 250F), plus exquisite chairs in the shapes of swans and dogs for the little ones to sit on while they try them on.

Unishop, 4 rue Rambuteau, 3e; ☎01.42.78.07.81 (Mº Hôtel-de-Ville). Tues–Sat 10.15am–7pm. Very cheap and cheerful kids' clothes: vibrant selection of zebra leggings, teeny hooded sweat-shirts and floral dresses. Branch also at 42 rue de Rivoli, 4e; ☎01.42.72.62.84 (M° Hôtel-de-Ville).

Au Vieux Campeur, 48 rue des Écoles, 5e; ☎01.43.29.12.32 (M° Cluny-La Sorbonne). Mon 2–7pm, Tues, Thurs & Fri 10.30am–7.30pm, Wed 10.30am–9pm, Sat 10am–7.30pm. The best camping and sporting equipment range in Paris, spread over several shops in the *quartier*. The special attraction for kids is a climbing wall.

Kids' Stuff

Chapter 17

Shops and Markets

Flair for style and design is as evident in the shops of Paris as it is in other aspects of the city's life. Parisians' fierce attachment to their small local traders, especially when it comes to food, has kept alive a wonderful variety, despite the pressures to concentrate consumption in gargantuan underground and multistorey complexes.

Even if you don't plan – or can't afford – to buy, Parisian shops are one of the chief delights of the city. Some of the most entertaining and tempting are those small cluttered affairs which reflect their owners' particular passions. You'll find traders in offbeat merchandise in every *quartier*.

Markets, too, are a grand spectacle. Mouthwatering arrays of food from half the countries of the globe, intoxicating in their colour, shape and smell, assail the senses in even the drabbest parts of town. In Belleville and the Goutte d'Or, North Africa predominates; Southeast Asia in the 13e *arrondissement*. Though the food is perhaps the best offering of

Toy shops, and shops selling children's clothes and books, are detailed in Chapter 16.

the Paris markets, there are also street markets dedicated to second-hand goods (the *marchés aux puces*), clothes and textiles, flowers, birds, books and stamps.

Shops

The most distinctive and unusual shopping possibilities are in the nineteenth-century arcades of the *passages* in the 2e and 9e *arrondissements*, almost all now smartly renovated. On the streets proper, the square kilometre around place St-Germain-des-Près is hard to beat, packed with books, antiques, gorgeous garments, artworks and playthings.

Les Halles is another well-shopped district, with its focus the submarine shopping complex of the Forum des Halles, good for everything from records through to designer clothes. The aristocratic **Marais** and the new trendies' *quartier* of the **Bastille** have filled up with dinky little boutiques, arty and specialist shops and galleries. For window-shopping, the really moneyed Parisian *haute couture* – Hermès and the like – the two traditional areas are av Montaigne, rue François-1er and rue du Faubourg-St-Honoré in the 8e, and av Victor-Hugo in the 16e. The fashionable newer designers, led by the Japanese, are to be found around place des Victoires in the 1er and 2e.

For food and essentials, the cheapest supermarket chain is *Ed l'Épicier*. Other last-minute or convenience shopping is probably best at *FNAC* shops (for books and records) and the big department stores (for everything else).

Art and Design

If you want to get an idea of what is going on in the world of contemporary art, you should take a look at the **commercial art galleries**. They are concentrated in four main areas: in the 8e, especially in and around av Matignon; in the Marais; around the Bastille; and in St-Germain.

There are literally hundreds of galleries, and for an idea of who is being exhibited where, you'll need to consult the booklet *Rive Droite Rive Gauche,* available from the galleries themselves or from more upmarket hotels, or *Pariscope,* which carries details of major exhibitions under "*Expositions*"and "*Galeries*". Entry to the commercial galleries is free to all.

DESIGN

A small selection of places where contemporary and the best of twentieth-century **design** can be seen is listed

below. Also worth checking out are the shops of the art and design museums, and the rue St-Paul with a particularly high concentration of shops specializing in particular periods.

Artistes et Modèles, 3 rue Jacques-Callot, 6e; ☎01.46.33.83.20 (Mº Odéon). Daily 11am–1pm & 2.30–7pm. Small gallery specializing in the work of Italian designer Gætano Pesce. A lot of plastic pieces: furniture, candlesticks, objects for the home. Interesting, and not too extortionate!

Décalage, 33 rue des Francs-Bourgeois, 4e; ☎01.42.77.55.72 (Mº St-Paul). Mon 2–7pm, Tues–Sat 11am–7pm. Beautiful hand-crafted jewellery – unusual, yet reasonably priced. Also, a good range of lights, from antique to contemporary.

Dream On, 31 rue de Charonne, 11e; ☎01.47.00.41.44 (Mº Ledru-Rollin). Mon–Sat 10.30am–7.30pm. Corner shop that specializes in 1960s furniture, including several armchairs taken off the set of *2001: A Space Odyssey.*

En Attendant les Barbares, 50 rue Étienne-Marcel, 2e; ☎01.45.39.59.40 (Mº

Shops and
Markets

Late-night Shopping

The **Drugstores** at 149 bd St-Germain, 6e (Mº St-Germain-des-Près), and 133 av Champs-Élysées, 8e (Mº Charles-de-Gaulle/Étoile), are open for books, newspapers, tobacco and all kinds of gift gadgetry until 2am every night.

In addition, you could try:

Prisunic supermarket, 109 rue de la Boétie, 8e (Mº Franklin-D-Roosevelt). Open till midnight Mon–Sat.

Boulangerie de l'Ancienne-Comédie, 10 rue de l'Ancienne-Comédie, 6e (Mº Odéon). Mon–Sat open 24hrs.

Kiosque, place Charles-de-Gaulle, 8e (Mº Charles-de-Gaulle/Étoile). Newsagents open 24hrs daily.

Tabacs
La Favourite, 3 bd St-Michel, 5e (Mº St-Michel). *Tabac* open daily to 2am.

Old Navy, 150 bd St-Germain, 6e (Mº St-Germain-des-Près). Open till 5am.

Shell Garage, 6 bd Raspail, 7e (Mº Rue-du-Bac). 24-hr food shop and garage.

Petrol stations open all night
There are two dozen or so petrol stations in the city that stay open 24hrs. The following are some central addresses:

Esso, 336 rue St-Honoré, 1er.

Garage St-Bernard, 36 rue des Fossés-St-Bernard, 5e.

Shell, underground car park, place de la Bourse, 2e; 10 rue de Bailleul, 1er; and 6 bd Raspail, 7e.

Shops and Markets

Our Books
section on
p.424
recommends
dozens of
excellent books
about Paris.

Châtelet-Les Halles). Tues–Fri 10.30am–7pm, Mon 10.30am–1pm & 2–7pm, Sat 11am–6.30pm. The style known as neo-Barbarian: Baroque gilding on bizarre experimental forms. Nothing you'd actually trust your weight to, but fun to look at.

Eugénie Seigneur, 16 rue Charlot, 3e; ☎01.48.04.81.96 (Mº République). Mon–Fri 10am–7pm, Sat 10am–1pm & 3–7pm. The place to take your print or original for a highly unique frame.

Galerie Documents, 53 rue de Seine, 6e; ☎01.43.54.50.68 (Mº Odéon). Tues–Sat 10.30am–12.30pm & 2.30–7pm. Best antique posters.

Louvre des Antiquaires, 2 place du Palais-Royal, 1er; ☎01.42.97.27.00 (Mº Palais-Royal/Musée-du-Louvre). Tues–Sun 11am–7pm; closed Sun in July and Aug. An enormous antiques and furniture hypermarket where you can pick up anything from a Mycenean seal ring to an Art Nouveau vase – for a price.

VIA (Valorisation de l'Innovation dans l'Ameublement), 29–37 av Daumesnil, 12e; ☎01.46.28.11.11 (Mº Bastille). Mon–Sat 10.30am–7pm, Sun 11am–6pm. These are the headquarters of *Le Viaduc des Arts* (below), where information is given out to young designers who need support, advice and promotion. It is also a venue for temporary exhibitions of indigenous talent.

Le Viaduc des Arts, 15–121 av Daumesnil, 12e (Mº Bastille). Practically the entire north side of the street is dedicated to an extremely high standard of skilled workmanship and craft. Each arch of this old railway viaduct houses a shop front and workspace for the artists within. Walk the length of the *viaduc* for a show of contemporary metalwork, ceramics, tapestry, sculpture and much more.

Bookshops

Books are not cheap in France – foreign books least of all. But don't let that stop you browsing. The best areas are the Seine *quais* with their rows of stalls

perched against the river parapet and the narrow streets of the Quartier Latin, but don't neglect the array of specialist shops listed below.

ENGLISH-LANGUAGE

Abbey Bookshop/La Librairie Canadienne, 29 rue de la Parcheminerie, 5e (Mº St-Michel). Mon–Sat 10am–7pm. A Canadian bookshop round the corner from *Shakespeare & Co.* with lots of second-hand British and North American fiction; good social and political science sections; knowledgeable and helpful staff . . . and free coffee.

Brentano's, 37 av de l'Opéra, 2e (Mº Opéra). Mon–Sat 10am–7pm. English and American books. Good section for kids.

FNAC Librairie Internationale, 71 bd St-Germain, 6e (Mº Cluny/*RER* St-Michel). 10am–8pm; closed Sun. Literally hundreds of foreign newspapers and magazines and tens of thousands of foreign books.

Galignani, 224 rue de Rivoli, 1er (Mº Concorde). Mon–Sat 10am–7pm. Good range, including children's books.

Shakespeare & Co., 37 rue de la Bûcherie, 5e (Mº Maubert-Mutualité). Noon–midnight every day. A cosy, friendly, famous literary haunt, with the biggest selection of second-hand English books in town. Also poetry readings and such.

Village Voice, 6 rue Princesse, 6e (Mº Mabillon). Mon 2–8pm, Tues–Sat 11am–8pm. Principally poetry and modern literature, both British and American.

W H Smith, 248 rue de Rivoli, 1er (Mº Concorde). Mon–Sat 9.30am–7pm. Wide range of books and newspapers.

GENERAL FRENCH

For general French titles, the biggest and most convenient shop has to be the *FNAC* in the Forum des Halles, though it's hardly the most congenial of places. If you fancy a prolonged session of browsing, the other general bookstores below are probably more suitable.

Le Divan, 39 rue Bonaparte, 6e (Mº St-Germain-des-Près). Mon–Sat 10am–7.30pm.

FNAC, at the Forum des Halles, *niveau 2*, Porte Pierre-Lescot (Mº/*RER* Châtelet-Les Halles). Also at 136 rue de Rennes, 6e (Mº Montparnasse); 26 av des Ternes, 17e (Mº Ternes); and *CNIT*, 2 place de la Défense (Mº La Défense). Mon–Sat 10am–7.30pm. Lots of *bandes dessinées*, guidebooks and maps, among everything else.

Gallimard, 15 bd Raspail, 7e (Mº Sèvres-Babylone). Mon–Sat 10am–7pm. The shop of the great French publisher.

Gibert Jeune, 6 place St-Michel, 5e and 27 quai St-Michel, 5e (both Mº St-Michel). Mon–Sat 9.30am–7.30pm. With lots of sales, some English books and secondhand, too. These are the number-one suppliers of school and university set books. Their chain of shops now stretches up bd St-Michel. For English literature, go to *Joseph Gibert* at no. 26.

La Hune, 170 bd St-Germain, 6e (Mº St-Germain-des-Près). Mon–Sat 10am–midnight. One of the biggest and best.

SECOND-HAND AND ANTIQUARIAN

In addition to the *quais*, you might try:

Albert Petit Siroux, Galerie Vivienne, 2e (Mº Bourse). New and second-hand books, including musty leather-bound volumes on Paris and France. Mon–Sat 11am–7pm.

Gibert Jeune, see above.

Giraud-Badin, 22 rue Guynemer, 6e (Mº Notre-Dame-des-Champs). Mon & Wed–Sat 9am–1pm & 2–6pm; closed Aug. These are books which belong in museum collections – with prices to match.

L'Introuvable, 25 rue Juliette-Dodu, 10e (Mº Colonel-Fabien). Tues–Sat 11am–1pm & 3–7pm. All sorts stocked, but particular specialization is detective, crime, spy and SF stories.

AFRICAN/THIRD WORLD

L'Harmattan, 16 rue des Écoles, 5e; ☎01.43.26.04.52 (Mº Maubert-Mutualité). Mon–Sat 10am–12.30pm & 1.30–7pm. Excellent, very knowledgeable bookshop, especially good for Arab/North African literature (in French). Publisher, too.

Présence Africaine, 25bis rue des Écoles, 5e; ☎01.43.54.13.74 (Mº Maubert-Mutualité). Mon–Sat 10am–7pm. Specialist black African bookshop, with titles ranging from literature to economics and philisophy by Caribbean and North American as well as African writers.

ART AND ARCHITECTURE

Artcurial, 9 av Matignon, 8e; ☎01.42.99.16.16 (Mº Franklin-D-Roosevelt). Mon–Sat 10.30am–7.15pm; closed two weeks in Aug. *The* art bookshop in Paris – French and foreign editions. There is also a gallery, which puts on interesting exhibitions.

Librairie de l'École des Beaux Arts, 13 quai Malaquais, 6e; ☎01.47.03.50.70 (Mº St-Germain-des-Près). Mon–Fri 10am–7pm; closed Aug. The bookshop of the national Fine Art school: own publications, posters, reproductions, postcards, etc.

Librairie du Musée d'Art Moderne de la Ville de Paris, Palais de Tokyo, 11 av du Président-Wilson, 16e (Mº Iéna). Tues–Sun 10am–5.30pm. Specialist publications on modern art, including foreign works.

Librairie du Musée des Arts Décoratifs, 107 rue de Rivoli, 1er (Mº Palais-Royal). Wed–Sun 12.30–6pm. Design, posters, architecture, graphics, etc.

Liliane & Michel Durand-Dessert, 28 rue de Lappe, 11e (Mº Bastille); ☎01.48.06.92.23. Tues–Sat 10am–6pm. Excellent selection of books on contemporary art.

AUTOGRAPHS

Librairie de l'Abbaye, 27 rue Bonaparte, 6e; ☎01.43.54.89.99 (Mº St-Germain-des-Près). Tues–Sat 10am–12.30pm & 2–7pm; closed Aug. Signatures of the famous. Good for a browse.

Shops and Markets

Shops and Markets

COMICS/BANDES DESSINÉES

Album, 60 rue Monsieur-le-Prince, 6e; ☎01.43.26.19.32 (Mº Odéon). Also at 6-8 rue Dante, 5e (Mº Maubert-Mutualité). Tues-Sat 10am-8pm. Vast collection of French, US and oher comics, some of them the rarest editions with original artwork.

Boulinier, 20 bd St-Michel, 6e; ☎01.43.26.76.96 (Mº St-Michel). Mon-Sat 10am-midnight, Sun 2pm-midnight. Renowned for its selection of new and second-hand comics, including many that are difficult to obtain. Good collection of second-hand CDs as well.

La Terrasse de Gutenberg, 9 rue Émilio-Castelar, 12e (Mº Ledru-Rollin). Mon 2.30-8pm, Tues-Sun 10am-7.30pm. Excellent collection of fine and graphic art, including *bandes dessinées*, plus photographs, postcards and general books. Near the Bastille.

COOKERY, GARDENING, CRAFTS

Librairie Gourmande, 4 rue Dante, 6e; ☎01.43.54.37.27 (Mº Maubert-Mutualité). Mon-Sat 10am-7pm, Sun 2.30-7pm. The very last word in books about cooking.

La Maison Rustique, 26 rue Jacob, 6e; ☎01.43.25.67.00 (Mº St-Germain-des-Près). Mon-Sat 10am-7pm. Books – many in English – on all kinds of country and outdoor interests, from gardening to pruning olive trees and identifying wild flowers and birds.

FEMINIST

La Brèche, 9 rue de Tunis, 11e; ☎01.43.67.63.57 (Mº Nation). Mon 2-8pm, Tues-Sat noon-8pm. Feminist books and journals. Run by the *Ligue Communiste Révolutionnaire*.

La Fourmi Ailée, 8 rue du Fouarre, 5e; ☎01.43.29.40.99 (Mº Maubert-Mutualité). Daily noon-7pm. Left-wing bookshop and *salon de thé*, stocking most feminist reviews.

Librarie des Femmes, 74 rue de Seine, 6e; ☎01.43.29.50.75 (Mº Mabillon).

Mon-Sat 10am-7pm. Large bookshop run by Antoinette Fouque's political group.

GAY AND LESBIAN

Les Mots à la Bouche, 6 rue Ste-Croix-de-la-Bretonnerie, 4e; ☎01.42.78.88.30; and **Chambre avec Vues**, 79 rue Vieille du Temple, 4e; (Mº St-Paul). Mon-Sat 11am-11pm, Sun 3-7pm. Two shops under the same management, selling books and magazines on literature, psychology, etc, plus some lesbian titles. They speak English well. *Chambre avec Vues*, the newer shop, is better for books and guides in English.

LEFTIST AVANT-GARDE

Actualités, 38 rue Dauphine, 6e; ☎01.43.26.35.62 (Mº Odéon). Tues-Sat 11am-1pm & 2-7pm. Literature (foreign included), philosophy, *bandes dessinées* (especially US comic books), etc.

Parallèles, 47 rue St-Honoré, 1er; ☎01.42.33.62.70 (Mº Châtelet-Les Halles). Mon-Sat 10am-7pm. The place to go for green, feminist, anti-racist, 57 brands of socialist publications. As well as most of the "underground" press, you can pick up info on current events, demos etc. Good too on music and comics.

PERFORMING ARTS

Les Feux de la Rampe, 2 rue de Luynes, 7e (Mº Bac). Tues-Sat 11am-1pm & 2.30-7pm; closed three weeks in July and Aug 15. Books, scripts, stills, etc.

Librairie Bonaparte, 31 rue Bonaparte, 6e; ☎01.43.26.97.56 (Mº St-Germain-des-Près). Mon-Sat 9am-7pm; closed Aug. Exhaustive stock of books on ballet, theatre, opera, puppets, music hall, *chansonniers* etc.

POETRY

L'Arbre Voyageur, 55 rue Mouffetard, 5e; ☎01.47.07.98.34 (Mº Monge). Tues-Thurs 11am-8pm, Fri & Sat 11am-midnight, Sun 11am-8pm. Poetry from all over the world, plus readings, discussions and exhibitions.

L'Envers du Miroir, 19 rue de Seine, 6e; ☎01.43.54.45.13 (Mº Mabillon). Tues–Sat 2–7pm; closed Aug. Some fine and rare editions of modern poetry, as well as periodicals.

TRAVEL

L'Astrolabe, 46 rue de Provence, 9e; ☎01.42.85.42.95 (Mº Le Peletier). Mon–Sat 9.30am–7pm. Every conceivable map, French and foreign; guidebooks; climbing and hiking guides; sailing, natural history, etc.

Institut Géographique National (IGN), 107 rue La-Boétie, 8e; ☎01.42.56.06.68 (Mº Miromesnil). Mon–Fri 9.30am–7pm, Sat 10.30am–12.30pm & 2–5.30pm. The French Ordnance Survey: the best for maps of France and the entire world, plus guidebooks, *GR* route descriptions, satellite photos, day packs, map holders, etc.

Clothes

There may be no way you can get to see the *haute couture* shows (see the box below), but there's nothing to prevent you trying on fabulously expensive creations by famous **couturiers** in rue du Faubourg-St-Honoré, av François-1er and av Victor-Hugo – apart from the intimidating air of the assistants and the awesome chill of the marble portals. Likewise, you can treat the **younger designers** round place des Victoires and in the Marais and St-Germain area as stops on your sightseeing itinerary. The long-time darling of the glitterati is **Azzedine Alaïa**, for whom the likes of Christy Turlington model for free. He is to fashion what Jean Nouvel is to architecture and Philippe Starck to interior design – together they form the triumvirate of Paris style. **Jean-Paul Gaultier** remains as popular as ever for his anti-fashion fashion, famous model Inès de la Fressange

Shops and Markets

The common signs you see in clothes stores, vente en gros and vente en détail (or vente aux particuliers), mean "wholesale" and "retail", respectively.

The Haute Couture Shows

Invitations to the January and July *haute couture* shows go out exclusively to the elite of the world's fashion editors and to the 2000 or so clients for whom price tags between $10,000 and $100,000 for a dress represent a mere day or week or two's unearned income. *Hello!*, *Ola!* and the like have a field day as the top hotels, restaurants and palace venues disgorge famous bodies cloaked in famous names. Mrs ex-Trump thrills the press by saying husbands come and go but couturiers are worth hanging onto, and every arbiter of taste and style maintains the myth that fashion is the height of human attainment. The truth, of course, is that the catwalks and the clientele are there to promote more mass-consumed luxuries, *prêt-à-porter* (ready-to-wear) lines and perfumes.

During the early 1990s, with the Gulf War keeping Gulf princesses away and the fear of terrorist bombs deterring Americans, fashion-house accountants began to question the cost-effectiveness of *haute couture* collections; fewer clothes were shown and some couturiers switched to producing videos. But the super-rich have weathered the recessions as they always do and are happily flocking to the lavish shows of Givenchy's John Galliano, Chanel's Karl Lagerfeld, Dior's Gianfranco Ferre, Yves St-Laurent, Christian Lacroix, Valentino and Versace. The Carrousel du Louvre has a new subterranean space specially designed for fashion shows, but designers have taken to making their statements in sports stadiums, the Grande Arche de la Défense or, in the case of Jean Paul Gaultier, a draughty, uncomfortable warehouse. Models now command mega-fees – about forty percent of the budget for most shows – and music is as important as visual effects. The requisite minimum of 75 garments has been reduced to 50, but they must still all be hand-sewn.

Shops and Markets

Big Names in Paris Fashion

Prices at Paris' big-name fashion emporia are well into the stratosphere.
The addresses below are those of the main or most conveniently located shops.

Agnès B, 6 rue du Jour, 1er (Mº Châtelet-Les Halles).

Azzedine Alaïa, 7 rue de Moussy, 4e (Mº Hôtel-de-Ville).

Balenciaga, 10 av George-V, 8e (Mº Alma-Marceau).

Balmain, 44 rue François-1er, 8e (Mº George-V).

Cacharel, 5 place des Victoires, 1er (Mº Bourse).

Carven, 6 rond-point des Champs-Élysées, 8e (Mº Franklin-D-Roosevelt).

Castelbajac, 31 place du Marché-St-Honoré, 1er (Mº Pyramides).

Cerruti, 1 & 15 place de la Madeleine, 8e (Mº Madeleine).

Chanel, 31 rue Cambon, 1er (Mº Madeleine).

Chloë, 60 rue du Faubourg-St-Honoré, 8e (Mº Madeleine).

Christian Lacroix, 73 rue du Faubourg-St-Honoré, 8e (Mº Concorde).

Claude Montana, 3 rue des Petits-Champs, 1er (Mº Bourse/Pyramides).

Comme des Garçons, 40–42 rue Étienne-Marcel, 2e (Mº Châtelet-Les Halles).

Courrèges, 40 rue François-1er, 8e (Mº George-V).

Dior, 32 av Montaigne, 8e (Mº Franklin-D-Roosevelt).

Dorothée Bis, 46 rue Étienne-Marcel, 1er (Mº Châtelet-Les Halles).

Emmanuelle Khan, 2 rue de Tournon, 6e (Mº Odéon).

Gianni Versace, 62 rue du Faubourg-St-Honoré, 8e (Mº Concorde).

Giorgio Armani, 6 & 25 place Vendôme, 1er (Mº Opéra).

Givenchy, 8 av George-V, 8e (Mº Alma-Marceau).

Guy Laroche, 30 rue du Faubourg-St-Honoré, 8e (Mº Concorde).

Inès de la Fressange, 14 av Matignon, 8e (Mº Alma-Marceau).

Issey Miyake, 3 place des Vosges, 4e (Mº St-Paul).

Jean-Louis Scherrer, 51 av Montaigne, 8e (Mº Franklin-D-Roosevelt).

Jean-Paul Gaultier, 6 rue Vivienne, 2e (Mº Bourse) & 30 rue du Faubourg-St-Antoine, 12e (Mº Bastille).

Jil Sander, 52 av Montaigne, 8e (Mº Franklin-D-Roosevelt).

Junko Shimada, 54 rue Étienne-Marcel, 1er (Mº Châtelet-Les Halles).

Lanvin, 2 rue du Faubourg-St-Honoré, 8e (Mº Concorde).

Louis Féraud, 88 rue du Faubourg-St-Honoré, 8e (Mº Madeleine).

Karl Lagerfeld, 19 rue du Faubourg-St-Honoré, 8e & 51 rue François-1er, 8e (both Mº Concorde).

Kenzo, 3 place des Victoires, 1er (Mº Bourse).

Myrène de Prémonville, 38 rue de Bac, 7e (Mº Rue-du-Bac).

Nina Ricci, 39 av Montaigne, 8e (Mº Alma-Marceau).

Paco Rabanne, 7 rue du Cherche-Midi, 6e (Mº Sèvres-Babylone).

Pierre Cardin, 59 rue du Faubourg-St-Honoré, 8e (Mº Madeleine).

Ted Lapidus, 35 rue François-1er, 8e (Mº Franklin-D-Roosevelt).

Thierry Mugler, 10 place des Victoires, 2e (Mº Bourse).

Ungaro, 2 av Montaigne, 8e (Mº Alma-Marceau).

Valentino, 17–19 av Montaigne, 8e (Mº Alma-Marceau).

Saint-Laurent, 38 rue du Faubourg-St-Honoré, 8e (Mº Concorde) & 6 place St-Sulpice, 6e (Mº St-Sulpice/Mabillon).

Sonia Rykiel, 175 bd St-Germain, 6e (Mº St-Germain-des-Près).

produces her own lines, and new foreign designers like Jil Sander from Germany are competing with the wares of Japanese stylists.

End-of-line and old stock of the couturiers are sold all year round in discount shops (listed below). For clothes without the fancy labels, the best area is the 6e: round rue de Rennes, rue de Sèvres and, in particular, rue St-Placide and rue St-Dominique in the neighbouring 7e. The **department stores** *Galeries Lafayette* and *Au Printemps* have good selections of designer *prêt-à-porter*; the **Forum des Halles** is chock-a-block with clothes shops but at less competitive prices; and individual **boutiques** are taking over more and more of the Marais and the Bastille around rue de la Roquette.

The Les Halles end of rue de Rivoli has plenty of **chain stores**, including a *Monoprix* supermarket for essentials, or you can get even better bargains in the **rag-trade district** round place du Caire or place de la République, with a *Printemps* on the north side, *Tati* on the south, and the adjacent rues Meslay and Notre-Dame-de-Nazareth full of **shoe** and **clothes** shops respectively. For **jewellery** – gems and plastic – try rue du Temple and rue Montmorency.

The **sales** take place in January and July, with reductions of up to forty percent on designer clothes. This still leaves prices running into hundreds of pounds, but if you want to blow out on something bizarre and beautiful, these are the months to do it. The sales in the more run-of-the-mill shops don't offer significant reductions.

DISCOUNT

The best areas to wander for shops selling end-of-line and last year's models at thirty- to fifty-percent reductions are in rue d'Alésia in the 14e, west of place Victor-Blasch; bd Victor in the 15e between rue Lecourbe and rue Desnouettes (Mo Balard); for shoes rue Meslay in the 3e; and rue St-Placide in the 6e. Before you get too excited, however, remember that twenty percent off

£500 still leaves a hefty bill – not that all items are this expensive. The best times of year to join the scrums are after the new collections have come out in January and October.

Cacharel Stock, 114 rue d'Alésia, 14e, ☎01.45.42.53.04 (Mo Alésia). Mon–Sat 10am–7pm. 40–50 percent off last season's stock. Men, women and kids.

La Clef des Marques, 99 rue St-Dominique, 7e; ☎01.47.05.04.55 (Mo Varenne). Mon noon–7pm, Tues–Fri 10am–noon & 3–7pm, Sat 10am–1pm & 2–7pm. Huge store with wide choice of clothes for men and women.

Le Mouton à Cinq Pattes, 8 & 18 rue St-Placide, 6e; ☎01.45.48.20.29, and

L'Annexe (for men) at no. 48 (Mo Sèvres-Babylone). Mon–Sat 10am–7pm. Popular discount store, with discounts on a wide range of big names.

Stock 2, 92 rue d'Alésia, 14e; ☎01.45.41.65.57 (Mo Alésia). Mon–Sat 10am–7pm. 30 percent off on Daniel Hechter's end-of-line items.

Toutes Griffes Dehors, 76 rue St-Dominique, 7e; ☎01.45.51.68.14 (Mo Latour-Maubourg); 84 rue de Sèvres, 6e (Mo Duroc). Mon 10.30am–noon & 1–7pm, Tues–Sat 10am–noon & 1–7pm. End-of-lines from *Guy Laroche* among others.

SECOND-HAND AND RÉTRO

Rétro means "period clothes", mostly unsold factory stock from the 1950s and 1960s, though some shops specialize in expensive high fashion articles from as far back as the 1920s. Plain second-hand stuff is referred to as *fripe* – not especially interesting compared with London, and dominated by the US combat-jacket style. The best place to look is probably the Porte de Montreuil flea market (see p.338).

L'Apache, 45 rue Vieille-du-Temple, 4e; ☎01.42.71.84.27 (Mo Hôtel-de-Ville). Mon 2–7pm, Tues–Sat 11am–7.30pm. A big selection of 1920–1950s popular fashions.

Derrière les Fagots, 8 rue des Abbesses, 18e; ☎01.42.59.72.53 (Mo Abbesses).

Shops and Markets

Shops and Markets

For shops selling children's clothes, see Chapter 16.

Tues–Sat 11.30am–7.30pm. A gold mine of 1960s clothes and accessories in (on the whole), very good condition. Reasonable prices.

Halle aux Fringues Rétro, 16 rue de Montreuil, 11ᵉ; ☎01.43.73.13.12 (Mº Faidherbe-Chaligny). 10am–7pm; closed Sun & Mon am. Classy 1940s–1960s clothes, hats of all descriptions, and kimonos.

Rag Time, 23 rue du Roule, 1ᵉʳ; 01.42.36.89.36 (Mº Louvre). Mon–Sat 2.30–7.30pm. A veritable museum of superb dresses and high-fashion articles from the 1920s to the 1950s. Some for hire. Expensive.

Réciproque, 89, 93, 95, 101 & 123 rue de la Pompe, 16ᵉ; ☎01.47.04.30.28 (Mº Pompe). Tues–Sat 10am–6.45pm. *Haute couture*: for women at no. 95; accessories and coats for men at no. 101; more accessories and coats for women at no. 123.

Rétro Activité, 38 rue du Vertbois, 3ᵉ; ☎01.42.77.64.43 (Mº Temple). Tues–Sat noon–7pm. Dresses from the 1930s to 1960s, and men's suits from the 1950s and 1960s– unbelievably cheap.

TATI

Tati is in a class by itself, the cheapest-of-cheap clothes stores and always thronged with people. Addresses are: 2–30 bd Rochechouart, 18ᵉ (Mº Barbès-Rochechouart); 140 rue de Rennes, 6ᵉ (Mº St-Placide); and 13 place de la République, 11ᵉ (Mº République).

TRENDY

APC, 3 (*femme*) & 7 (*homme*) rue de Fleurus, 6ᵉ; ☎01.42.22.12.77 (Mº St-Placide). Mon–Sat 10.30am–7pm. Hip collection for the young and stylish.

Bonnie Cox, 38 rue des Abbesses, 18ᵉ; ☎01.42.54.95.68 (Mº Abbesses). Mon–Sun 10.30am–8pm. Young fashion names and recent graduates have their sartorial creations on show here.

Le Garage, 23 rue des Francs-Bourgeois, 4ᵉ; ☎01.48.04.73.72 (Mº St-Paul) & 40 rue du Four, 6ᵉ. Lots of slinky shirts for women only – sexy and smart under one roof.

Kabuki, 25 rue Étienne-Marcel, 1ᵉʳ; ☎01.42.33.55.65 (Mº Étienne-Marcel). Mon–Sat 11am–7pm. For all your *Prada*, *D&G* and *Calvin Klein* needs.

Kiliwatch, 64 rue Tiquetonne, 2ᵉ; ☎01.42.21.17.37 (Mº Étienne-Marcel). Mon 1–7pm, Tues–Sat 10.30am–7pm. Cheap 'n' chic youth streetwear. From purple *Adidas* sporty numbers to zebra-print macs. Also at *Le Shop*, 3–5 rue d'Argout, 2ᵉ; ☎01.40.26.21.45.

Miss China, 4 rue Française, 1ᵉʳ; ☎01.40.41.08.07 (Mº Étienne-Marcel). Beautiful shop creating a *look-chinoise* for Western girls, with exquisite shoes and gags to match. Children's range to open in boutique directly opposite.

Patrick Cox, 62 rue Tiquetonne, 2ᵉ; ☎01.40.26.66.55 (Mº Étienne-Marcel). Mon–Sat 10am–7pm. The chic and friendly Paris outlet of the London-based shoe designer. Clothes to match.

ACCESSORIES

D Lavilla, 47 rue du Faubourg-St-Antoine, 11ᵉ; ☎01.53.33.85.55 (Mº Bastille). Mon–Sat 11am–7pm. Beautiful bags in vibrant colours. Also at 15 rue du Cherche-Midi, 6ᵉ, and 38 rue de Sévigné, 4ᵉ.

Freelance, 30 rue du Four, 6ᵉ; ☎01.45.48.14.78 (Mº Mabillon). Mon–Sat 10am–7pm. Unique shoe store – from orange snakeskin loafers to glow-in-the-dark mules.

Stephane Plassier, 19 bd Raspail, 7ᵉ; ☎01.45.44.62.62 (Mº Rue du Bac). Tues–Sat 11am–7.30pm, Sun & Mon 2.30–7pm. Underwear only for men and women. Also at 2 rue des Blancs-Manteaux, 4ᵉ.

Department Stores and Hypermarkets

Paris' two largest **department stores**, *Printemps* and *Galeries Lafayette*, are right next door to each other near the

St-Lazare station, and between them there's not much they don't have. Less enticing for its wares, perhaps, but a visual knock-out, is the renovated *Samaritaine*. Best for food is *Au Bon Marché*.

In addition, Paris has its share of **hypermarkets** – giant shopping complexes – of which the *Forum des Halles*, in the 1er; the *Centre Maine-Montparnasse*, in the 14e; and the *Quatre-Saisons*, in La Défense, are the biggest.

Bazar de l'Hôtel de Ville (BHV), 52–64 rue de Rivoli, 4e (Mº Hôtel-de-Ville). Daily 9.30am–7pm, Mon &, Wed till 9pm. Only two years younger than the *Bon Marché* and noted in particular for its DIY department and cheap self-service restaurant overlooking the Seine. Less elegant in appearance than some of its rivals, perhaps, but the value for money is pretty good.

Au Bon Marché, 38 rue de Sèvres, 7e (Mº Sèvres-Babylone). Mon–Sat 9.30am–7pm. Paris' oldest department store, founded in 1852. The prices are lower on average than at the more chic *Galeries Lafayette* and *Printemps*, and the tone is more mass-market middle-class. It has an excellent kids' department and a renowned food hall.

Galeries Lafayette, 40 bd Haussmann, 9e (Mº Havre-Caumartin). Mon–Sat 9.30am–6.45pm, Thurs till 9pm. The store's forte is high fashion. Two complete floors are given over to the latest creations by leading designers for men, women and children. Then there's household stuff, tableware, furniture, a host of big names in men's and women's accessories, a huge *parfumerie*, etc – all under a superb 1900 dome.

Au Printemps, 64 bd Haussmann, 9e (Mº Havre-Caumartin). Mon–Sat 9.30am–7pm, Thurs till 10pm. Books, records, a *parfumerie* even bigger than the rival *Galeries Lafayette*'s. Excellent fashion department for women – less so for men.

La Samaritaine, 75 rue de Rivoli, 1er (Mº Rivoli). Daily 9.30am–7pm, Thurs till 10pm. The biggest of the department stores, spread over three buildings, whose boast is to provide anything anyone could possibly want. It aims downmarket of the previous two. *Magasin 3* is wholly devoted to sport. You get a superb view of the Seine from the tenth-floor terrace, which is closed from Oct–March.

Food and Drink

The general standard of **food shops** throughout the capital is remarkably high, both in quality and presentation: a feast for the eyes quite as much as the palate. These listings are for the **specialist places**, many of which are veritable palaces of gluttony, and very expensive. Markets are detailed in a separate section at the end of this chapter.

Food halls to equal that of *Harrods* are to be found at *Fauchon's*, on place de la Madeleine, and the *Grande Épicerie*, in the *Bon Marché* department store – each with exhibits to rival the best of the capital's museums. In addition, there are **one-product specialists** for whom gourmets will cross the city: *Poilâne's* or *Ganachaud's* for bread, *Barthélémy* for cheese, *La Maison de l'Escargot* for snails, *Émile's* for fish.

As for buying food with a view to **economic eating**, you will be best off shopping at the street markets or supermarkets – though save your bread-buying at least for the local *boulangerie* and let yourself be tempted once in a while by the apple *chaussons*, *pains aux raisins*, *pains au chocolat*, *tartes aux fraises* and countless other goodies. Useful **supermarkets** with branches throughout the city are *Félix Potin*, *Prisunic* and *Monoprix*. The cheapest supermarket chain is *Ed l'Épicier* choice, inevitably, is limited, but they do some things very well – jams, for instance.

Next door to the *Tang Frères* emporium in Chinatown (see under "Markets", below) is the *Supermarché Paris Store*, 21 av d'Ivry, 13e (Mº Porte-d'Italie). Open daily 9.30am–7pm, this is one of the best **Chinese supermarkets**, selling

Shops and Markets

Shops and Markets

Any list of food shops in Paris has to have at its head the two **palaces**:

Fauchon, 26 place de la Madeleine, 8ᵉ (Mᵒ Madeleine). Mon–Sat 9.40am–7pm. An amazing range of extravagantly beautiful groceries, fruit and veg, *charcuterie*, wines both French and foreign . . . almost anything you can think of. The quality is assured by blind testing, which all suppliers have to submit to. Just the place for presents of tea, jam, truffles, chocolates, exotic vinegars, mustards and so forth. A self-service, too.

Hédiard, 21 place de la Madeleine, 8ᵉ (Mᵒ Madeleine). Mon–Sat 9.30am–9pm. Since 1854, the aristocrat's grocer, with sales staff as deferential as servants, as long as you don't try to reach down items for yourself. Superlative quality. Among the other branches are those at 126 rue du Bac, 7ᵉ; 106 bd de Courcelles, 17ᵉ; and Forum des Halles, level-1.

everything from teacups to ampoules of royal jelly and ginseng. Other branches are at 12 bd de la Villette, 19ᵉ (Mᵒ Belleville), and 8–10 rue de l'Evangile, 18ᵉ (Mᵒ Marx-Dornoy).

BREAD

La Flûte Gana, 226 rue des Pyrénées, 20ᵉ (Mᵒ Gambetta). Mon–Sat 7.30am–1.30pm & 2.30–8pm. Run by the daughters of Ganachaud. Start the day with a *pain biologique* and you'll live a hundred years, guaranteed.

Ganachaud, 150–154 rue de Ménilmontant, 20ᵉ (Mᵒ Pelleport). Tues 2.30–8pm, Wed–Sat 7.30am–8pm, Sun 7.30am–1.30pm; closed Mon & Aug. Although father Ganachaud has left the business, the new owners continue his recipes, and the bread is still out of this world.

Poilâne, 8 rue du Cherche-Midi, 6ᵉ (Mᵒ Sèvres-Babylone). Mon–Sat 7.15am–8.15pm. More marvellous bread, which is baked to ancient and secret family recipes. These are shared with brother Max, who has shops at 29 rue de l'Ouest, 14ᵉ (Mᵒ Gaîté/Pernety; Mon–Sat 7.15am–8pm); 87 rue Brancion, 15ᵉ (Mᵒ Porte-de-Vanves; Mon–Sat 7.15am–8pm); and 42 place du Marché-St-Honoré, 1ᵉʳ (Mᵒ Pyramides).

Poujauran, 20 rue Jean-Nicot, 7ᵉ (Mᵒ Latour-Maubourg). Tues–Sat 8am–8.30pm; closed Aug. The shop itself is exquisite, with its original painted glass panels and tiles. The bread is excellent – there are several different kinds – and so too are the *pâtisseries*.

CHARCUTERIE

Divay, 50 rue du Faubourg-St-Denis, 10ᵉ (Mᵒ Château-d'Eau). Tues & Thurs–Sat 7.30am–1pm & 4–7.30pm, Wed & Sun 7.30am–1pm; closed Mon. *Foie gras, choucroute, saucisson* and such.

Aux Ducs de Gascogne, 4 rue du Marché-St-Honoré, 1ᵉʳ (Mᵒ Pyramides). Mon–Sat 10am–7pm. Further branches at 112 bd Haussmann, 8ᵉ (Mᵒ St-Augustin; 10am–7pm; closed Sun & Mon am); 111 rue St-Antoine, 4ᵉ (Mᵒ St-Paul; 9.30am–2pm & 3–8pm; closed Sun & Mon am); 21 rue de la Convention, 15ᵉ (Mᵒ Boucicaut; 9.30am–1pm & 4–8pm; closed Sun & Mon am); 41 rue des Gatines, 20ᵉ (Mᵒ Gambetta; 9am–12.45pm & 3–8pm; closed Sun & Mon am). An excellent chain with numerous southwestern products like preserved fruits in Armagnac, *foie gras*, conserves, hams, and so forth.

Ets Bruneau, 6 rue Montmartre, 1ᵉʳ (Mᵒ Châtelet-Les Halles). Tues–Sun 8am–6pm. Specialist in products from the Landes region, *pâtés* in particular: Bayonne hams, goose and duck pâtés, conserves, etc.

Flo Prestige, 42 place du Marché-St-Honoré, 1ᵉʳ (Mᵒ Pyramides). Daily 8am–11pm. All sorts of super delicacies, plus wines, champagne and exquisite ready-made dishes.

Goldenberg's, 7 rue des Rosiers, 4e (Mº St-Paul). Daily 9am–2am. Superlative Jewish deli and restaurant.

Maison de la Truffe, 19 place de la Madeleine, 8e (Mº Madeleine). Mon–Sat 9am–9pm. Truffles, of course, and more from the Dordogne and Landes.

Aux Vrais Produits d'Auvergne, 46–48 rue Daubenton, 5e (Mº Censier-Daubenton). 8.30am–12.30pm & 4–7.30pm; closed Sun pm, Mon & July 15–Sept. An excellent chain, with numerous outlets across the city, selling genuine Auvergne fare.

CHEESE

Androuët, 41 rue d'Amsteray, 8e (Mº Liège). Mon–Sat 10am–1.30pm & 2.30–7.30pm). One of the most famous food shops in Paris, specializing in cheese – dozens of types. A rather expensive restaurant above the shop, whose menu features . . . lots of cheese.

Barthélémy, 51 rue de Grenelle, 7e (Mº Rue-du-Bac). Tues–Fri 8.30am–1pm & 3.30–7.30pm, Sat 8.30am–1pm & 3–7.30pm; closed Aug. Purveyors of cheeses to the rich and powerful; orders can be faxed on ☎ 01.xx.xx.xx.xx.

Carmès et Fils, 24 rue de Lévis, 17e (Mº Villiers). Tues–Sat 8.30am–1pm & 4–7.30pm, Sun 8.30am–1pm; closed Aug. In the rue de Lévis market. A family of experts, who bring on many of the cheeses in their own cellars and can advise you exactly which one is ripe for the picking. Said to be the only place in Paris where you can buy (whole) Cheddar cheeses.

Maison du Fromage, 62 rue de Sèvres, 6e (Mº Sèvres-Babylone). Mon–Fri 9am–1pm & 3–7.30pm, Sat 9am–7.45pm. Specializes in goat, sheep and mountain cheeses.

CHOCOLATES AND PÂTISSERIES

Debauve et Gallais, 30 rue des Sts-Pères, 6e (Mº St-Germain-des-Près).

Mon–Sat 10am–7pm. A beautiful and ancient shop, specializing since time began in chocolate and elaborate sweets.

Ladurée, 16 rue Royale, 8e (Mº Madeleine). Mon–Sat 8.30am–7pm. Delectable and pricey *pâtisseries*.

A la Mère de Famille, 35 rue du Faubourg-Montmartre, 9e (Mº Le Peletier). Tues–Sat 8.30am–1.30pm & 3–7pm. A nineteenth-century *confiserie* selling *marrons glacés*, prunes from Agen, dried fruit, sweets, chocolates and even some wines.

Le Moule à Gâteaux, at several addresses including 111 rue Mouffetard, 5e (Mº Censier-Daubenton); 17 rue Daguerre, 14e (Mº Denfert-Rochereau); 25 rue de Lévis, 17e (Mº Villiers); 53 rue des Abbesses, 18e (Mº Abbesses). All open Tues–Sat 8am–8pm, Sun 8am–2pm. A chain of *pâtisseries*.

Pâtisserie Stohrer, 51 rue Montorgueil, 2e (Mº Sentier). Tues–Sat 8am–8pm. Bread, *pâtisseries*, chocolate and *charcuterie*. Discover what standard-fare *pain aux raisins* should really taste like.

HERBS, SPICES AND DRIED FOODS

Aux Cinq Continents, 75 rue de la Roquette, 11e (Mº Bastille). Tues–Fri 9.30am–1.30pm & 3.30–10pm, Sun 9.30am–1.30pm, Mon 3.30–10pm. Boxes, trays, sacks of rice, pulses, herbs, spices, tarama, vine leaves, alcohol, etc, from the world over.

Izraël, 30 rue François-Miron, 4e (Mº St-Paul). Tues–Sat 9.30am–1pm & 2.30–7pm. Another cosmopolitan emporium of goodies from all round the globe.

HEALTH FOOD

Naturalia, 52 rue St-Antoine, 4e; ☎01.48.87.87.50 (Mº St-Paul/Bastille). Mon–Sat 10am–7.30pm. Feel like you need a vitamin boost? Or after too many rich meals you fancy some rice cakes and seaweed? This is where to come – the equivalent of *Holland & Barrett*. Seven other branches.

Shops and Markets

off rue Bastille

Hotel de ville → St Paul metro (nr Bastille)

Shops and Markets

up from Place ~~Concorde~~ Concorde

between Bourse de C and Chatelet

from back of St-Eustache → NW.

HONEY

Les Abeilles, 21 rue Butte-aux-Cailles, 13e (Mº Corvisart/Place d'Italie). Tues–Sat 11am–8pm. Honey from all over France and further afield, sold by an experieced bee keeper. Pots from 23F to 43F.

KITCHEN EQUIPMENT

Au Bain Marie, 10 rue Boissy-d'Anglas, 8e (Mº Concorde). Mon–Sat 10am–7pm. An Aladdin's cave of things for the kitchen: pots, pans, books, antiques, napkins.

E Dehillerin, 18–20 rue Coquillière, 1er (Mº Châtelet-Les Halles). Mon–Sat 8am–6pm. Laid out like a traditional ironmonger's: no fancy displays, prices buried in catalogues, but good-quality stock at reasonable prices.

MORA, 13 rue Montmartre, 1er (Mº Châtelet-Les Halles). Mon–Fri 8.30am–5.45pm, Sat 8.30am–1pm. An exhaustive collection of tools of the trade for the top professionals.

SALMON, SEAFOOD AND CAVIAR

In addition to the establishments below, more caviar, along with truffles, *foie gras*, etc, is to be found at the lower end of rue Montmartre by the Forum des Halles in the 1er.

Caviar Kaspia, 17 place de la Madeleine, 8e (Mº Madeleine). 9am–12.30am. Blinis, smoked salmon and Beluga caviar.

Comptoir du Saumon, 60 rue François-Miron, 4e (Mº St-Paul). Mon–Sat 10am–10pm. Salmon especially, but eels, trout and all things fishy as well. Plus a delightful little restaurant in which to taste the fare.

Petrossian, 18 bd de Latour-Maubourg, 7e (Mº Latour-Maubourg). 10am–7pm. More gilt-edge fish eggs, but other Russian and French delicacies too.

SNAILS

La Maison de l'Escargot, 79 rue Fondary, 15e (Mº Dupleix). Tues–Sat 8.30am–8pm, Sun 9am–1pm. The most delicious snails and stuffings in town. Here they sauce and re-shell them while you wait. There is a restaurant for *dégustation* opposite at no. 70 (55–65F, with a glass of wine).

VEGETARIAN

Diététique D J Fayer, 45 rue St-Paul, 4e (Mº St-Paul). Tues–Sat 9am–1.30pm, 2.45–8.45pm. One of the city's oldest specialists, selling dietary, macrobiotic and vegetarian products.

WINE

Le Baron Rouge, 1 rue Théophile-Roussel, 12e (Mº Ledru-Rollin). Tues–Sat 10am–2pm & 5–9.30pm, Sun 10am–2pm. A good selection of dependable lower-range French wines. Very drinkable *Merlot* at 16F a litre, if you bring your own containers.

Aux Caves Royales, 137 bd de l'Hôpital, 13e (Mº Campo-Formio). 9.30am–1pm, 3.30–7.45pm; closed Mon in Aug. & Sun pm. Another good selection of wines, from 17F a litre.

Les Caves St-Antoine, 95 rue St-Antoine, 4e (Mº St-Paul). Mon–Sat 9am–1pm, 3–8pm, Sun 9am–1pm. Another small, amicable outfit.

Maison de la Vigne et du Vin de France, 21 rue François-1er, 8e (Mº Franklin-D-Roosevelt). Mon–Fri 9.30am–12.30pm & 1.30–6.30pm. The headquarters of the French wine industry, with wine tasting, a shop, and information about all the wine regions. English spoken.

Michel Renaud, 12 place de la Nation, 12e (Mº Nation). 9am–1pm & 2–8.30pm; closed Sun pm and Mon am. Superb value and a huge selection of French and Spanish wines (drinkable plonk for around £1 a bottle), champagnes and Armagnac.

Nicolas, 31 place de la Madeleine, 8e (Mº Madeleine). Mon–Sat 9am–8pm. A reliable merchant, with dozens of shops across the city. A good general selection.

Le Repaire de Bacchus, 112 rue Mouffetard, 5e (Mº Censier-Daubenton), and several other addresses. Tues–Sat 9.30am–1pm & 3.30–8pm. A good chain to look out for, with many lesser-known and cheaper wines.

Music

Records, **cassettes** and **CDs** are not particularly cheap in Paris, but you may come across selections that are novel enough to tempt you. Brazilian, Caribbean, Antillais, African and Arab albums that would be **specialist rarities** in London, as well as every kind of jazz, abound in Paris. Rue Keller and rue des Taillandeurs, in the 11e (Mº Bastille), have a wide range of offbeat record shops selling current trends. Second-hand bargains can be scratchy treats – anything from the Red Army choir singing the *Marseillaise* to African drummers on skins made from spider ovaries. The **flea markets** (St-Ouen especially), and the *bouquinistes* along the Seine are good places to look for old records. In the **classical** department, the choice of interpretations is very generous and multinational. For all **new and mainstream** records, *FNAC Musique* usually has the best prices.

Also listed below are a couple of **bookshops** selling sheet music, scores and music literature, and some that sell instruments. Victor-Massé, Douai, Houdon, bd Clichy and other streets in the Pigalle area are full of instrument and sound system shops (guitarists will enjoy a look in at 16 rue V-Massé, 9e – afternoons only – where François Guidon builds jazz guitars for the greats and the gifted amateurs). For instruments and scores, head for *Paul Beuscher*, at the Bastille, which has amazing sales in spring.

Afric' Music, 3 rue des Plantes, 14e; ☎01.45.42.43.52 (Mº Mouton-Duvernet). Mon–Sat 10am–7pm. A small shop with an original selection of African, Caribbean and reggae discs.

Blue Moon, 7 rue Pierre-Sarrazin, 6e; ☎01.46.34.63.89 (Mº Odéon). Mon–Sat 11am–7pm. Exclusive imports from Jamaica and Africa: ska and reggae.

BPM Records, 1 rue Keller, 11e; ☎01.40.21.02.88 (Mº Bastille). Tues–Sat 1–9pm. Specialists in house, including acid, hip-hop and rap.

Camara, 45 rue Marcadet, 18e; ☎01.42.51.33.18 (Mº Marcadet-Poissonnière). Mon–Sat noon–8pm. Paris' best selection of West African music on cassette and video.

Crocodisc, 40–42 rue des Écoles, 5e; ☎01.43.54.47.95 (Mº Maubert-Mutualité). Tues–Sat 11am–7pm. Folk, oriental, Afro-Antillais, funk, reggae, soul, country, new and second-hand. Some of the best prices in town.

Crocojazz, 64 rue de la Montagne-Ste-Geneviève, 5e; ☎01.46.34.78.38 (Mº Maubert-Mutualité). Tues–Sat 11am–1pm & 2–7pm. Jazz, blues and gospel: mainly new imports.

Disc' Inter, 2 rue des Rasselins, 20e; ☎01.43.73.63.48 (Mº Porte-de-Montreuil). Mon–Sat 10am–7pm. Wide-ranging stock of Afro-Caribbean music on CD, cassette, video and vinyl.

Dream Store, 4 place St-Michel, 6e, ☎01.43.26.49.75 (Mº St-Michel). Tues–Sat 9.30am–7pm. Good discounted prices on blues, jazz, rock, folk and classical.

FNAC Musique, 4 place de la Bastille, 12e (next to opera house); ☎01.49.54.30.00 (Mº Bastille). Mon–Sat 10am–8pm, Wed & Fri 10am–10pm. Extremely stylish shop in black, grey and chrome with computerized catalogues, every variety of music, books, and a concert booking agency. Branch at 24 bd des Italiens, 9e ☎01.48.01.02.03, Mº Richelieu-Drouot), with a greater emphasis on rock and popular music. The other FNAC shops (see above under *Bookshops*) also sell music and hi-fi. Try *FNAC-Étoile* at 26 av des Ternes, 17e (Mº Ternes), Mon–Sat 10am–7pm, which is particularly good for jazz.

Hamm, 135 rue de Rennes, 6e; ☎01.44.39.35.35 (Mº St-Placide). Mon

Shops and Markets

The Cité de la Musique, *in La Villette, has a range of shops devoted to all things musical.*

Shops and Markets

2–7pm, Tues–Sat 10am–7pm. The biggest general music shop in Paris, selling instruments new and old, sheet music, scores, manuals, librettos, etc.

Istanbul Express, 3 rue de Metz, 10e; (Mº Strasbourg-St-Denis). Mon–Sat 10am–7pm. *The* address for Turkish music.

Librairie Musicale de Paris, 68bis rue Réaumur, 3e; ☎01.42.72.30.72 (Mº Réaumur-Sébastopol). Mon–Sat 10am–12.45pm & 2–7pm. Huge selection of books, on music and of music, from Baroque oratorios to heavy metal.

Maison Sauviat, 124 bd de la Chapelle, 18e; ☎01.46.06.31.84 (Mº Barbès). Mon–Sat 10am–7.30pm. Wonderful shop that's been going strong since the 1920s. Now selling African and Arab music.

Parallèles, 47 rue St-Honoré, 1er; ☎01.42.33.62.70 (Mº Châtelet-Les Halles). The bookshop (see p.324) also sells records and cheap second-hand CDs.

Paris Musique, 10 bd St-Michel, 6e; ☎01.43.26.96.41 (Mº St-Michel). Mon–Sat 10am–8pm, Sun 2–8pm. Second-hand, bootlegs and new – jazz, classical and rock.

Paul Beuscher, 15–29 bd Beaumarchais, 4e; ☎01.44.54.36.00 (Mº Bastille). Mon–Fri 9.45am–12.30pm & 2–7pm, Sat 9.45am–7pm. A music department store that's been going strong for over 100 years. Instruments, scores, books, recording equipment, etc.

Rough Trade, 38 rue de Charonne, 11e; ☎01.40.21.61.62 (Mº Ledru-Rollin). Mon–Sat 11am–7pm. Indie labels and fanzines – an offshoot of London's Portobello Road store.

Virgin Megastore, 56–60 av des Champs-Élysées, 8e (Mº Franklin-D-Roosevelt); and Carrousel du Louvre, under the Louvre, 1er (Mº Palais-Royal/Musée-du-Louvre). Mon–Sat 10am–midnight, Sun 2pm–midnight. *Virgin* has trumped all Paris music shops. It's the biggest and the trendiest, but

lacks the wax rock heroes of the London store. Concert booking agency and expensive ilnternet connection.

Sport

Bicloune, 7 rue Froment, 11e; ☎01.48.05.47.75 (Mº Bréguet-Sabin). Tues–Fri 10.30am–1.30pm & 2–7pm, Sat 10am–1pm & 2–6.30pm. A bike shop with some bizarre models on show. Repairs carried out.

La Boutique Gardien du But, 89 ter rue de Charenton, 12e; ☎01.43.45.99.66 (Mº Gare-de-Lyon). Tues–Sat 10am–1pm & 2–7pm. "The Goalkeeper": a very friendly, young shop specializing in French soccer. Stock includes shirts of every French club.

Le Ciel est à Tout le Monde, 10 rue Gay-Lussac, 5e; ☎01.46.33.21.50 (Mº Luxembourg); 7 av Trudaine, 9e (Mº Anvers). Tues–Sat 10am–7pm; closed Mon in Aug. The best kite shop in Europe also sells frisbees, boomerangs and anything else that flies without a motor. Prices from 120F, up to 1500F for really serious models. Also, material for making your own.

La Haute Route, 33 bd Henri-IV, 4e; ☎01.42.72.38.43 (Mº Bastille). Mon 2–7pm, Tues–Sat 9.30am–1pm & 2–7pm. Mainly skiing and mountaineering equipment: to rent or to buy – new and second-hand.

La Maison du Vélo, 11 rue Fenelon, 10e; ☎01.42.81.24.72 (Mº Gare-du-Nord). Tues–Sat 10am–5pm. Classic models, mountain bikes, tourers and racers.

Marathon, 29 rue de Chazelles, 17e; ☎01.42.27.48.18 (Mº Monceau). Tues–Sat 10am–7pm. Specialists in running shoes. The shop is owned by an experienced marathon runner.

La Roue d'Or, 7 rue de la Fidelité, 10e; ☎01.42.46.41.84 (Mº Gare-de-l'Est). Tues–Sat 9am–6.30pm; closed Aug. Another cycling enthusiast.

Au Vieux Campeur, 48 rue des Écoles, 5e; ☎01.43.29.12.32 (Mº Maubert-

Mutualité). Mon 2–7pm, Tues–Fri 9.30am–8.30pm, Sat 9.30am–8pm. Maps, guides, climbing, hiking, camping, ski gear and mountain bikes – and a climbing wall for kids. With its various mushrooming departments, the shop now occupies half the *quartier*.

A Miscellany

Cipière, 26 bd Beaumarchais, 11ᵉ; ☎01.47.00.37.25 (Mº Bastille). Mon 10am–1pm & 2–7pm, Tues–Sat 9.30am–7pm. New and second-hand photographic equipment.

Ivan Estivalet, 9 rue Oberkampf, 11ᵉ; ☎01.40.21.09.44 (Mº Filles-du-Calvaire); 77 rue du Cherche-Midi, 6ᵉ (Mº Vaneau). A florist who creates bouquets in outlandish holders made of cane, hemp, bamboo and other plant material.

Au Facteur Cheval, 66 rue de Javel, 15ᵉ; ☎01.45.79.59.93 (Mº Charles-Michels). Tues–Sat 9.30am–1.30pm & 3–7pm. Small antiques shop with reasonably priced glass and chinaware, perfume bottles, knick-knacks and furniture.

Laguiole-Paris, 6 rue du Pas de la Mule, 3ᵉ; ☎01.48.87.46.88 (Mº Chemin-Vert). Mon–Sat 10am–1pm & 2–7pm. Tiny shops selling a large range of the celebrated knives from Laguiole in the Massif Central.

La Maison du Collectionneur, 137 av Émile-Zola, 15ᵉ (Mº Émile-Zola). Old books, hats, newspapers of the wartime liberation, and assorted junk.

La Maison de la Fausse Fourrure, 34 bd Beaumarchais, 11ᵉ; ☎01.43.55.24.21 (Mº Chemin-Vert). Mon–Sat 11am–7pm. Sumptuous lengths of fake fur draped and pinned over every surface imaginable. Some of the cheapest leopard-print around at 225F a metre.

Marché St-Pierre, 2 rue Charles-Nodier, 18ᵉ; ☎01.42.64.66.26 (Mº Anvers). Mon 2–7pm, Tues–Sat 10am–7pm. Four floors of fabrics. Very cheap and definitely worth a visit.

Paris American Art, 2 & 4 rue Bonaparte, 6ᵉ; ☎01.43.26.09.93 (Mº St-Germain-des-Près). Tues–Sat 10am–1pm & 2–6.30pm. Local art suppliers for the Beaux-Arts students residing around the corner.

Pentagram, 15 rue Racine, 6ᵉ (Mº Cluny). Hand-blown glass pens, pharaonic board games, stationery and PCs for kids.

Pylones, 57 rue St-Louis-en-l'Ile, 4ᵉ; ☎01.46.34.05.02 (Mº Sully-Morland), and many other branches. Daily 10.30am–7.30pm. Playful and silly things, including inflatable fruit bowls, ceramic bowls painted with cow-print, and sparkly resin jewellery.

Thé-Troc, 52 rue J.P.-Timbaud, 11ᵉ (Mº Parmentier). Mon–Sat 9am–8pm. Wide selection of teas, plus second-hand records, books, jewellery and assorted junk.

Travelingue, 20 rue Boulard, 14ᵉ (Mº Denfert-Rochereau). Lots of bizarre accessories: ties, earrings, kitchenware and socks.

Trousselier, 73 bd Haussmann, 8ᵉ; ☎01.42.66.16.16 (Mº St-Augustin). Mon–Sat 10.30am–7pm. Described in French *Vogue* as *the* artificial flower shop. Every conceivable species of flora fashioned from man-made fibre; gilt egg-timers, too! Decadent and pricey, but fun!

Markets

Several of the markets listed below are described in the text of Chapters 2 to 11. These, however, are the details – and the highlights. The map on the next page shows the location of them all.

Books, Stamps and Art

As well as the specialized book markets listed below, you should of course remember the wide array of books and all forms of printed material on sale from the **bouquinistes**, who hook their green padlocked boxes onto the riverside *quais* of the Left Bank (see p.113).

Paris' **stamp market** is at the junction of avs Marigny and Gabriel, on the north side of place Clemenceau in the 8ᵉ (Thurs, Sat, Sun & hols 10am–dusk).

MARKETS

FLEA MARKETS:

A Puces St-Ouen (Porte de Clignancourt)
B Belleville (Place des Fêtes)
C Carreau du Temple
D Porte de Montreuil
E Place d'Aligre
F Porte de Vanves

SPECIALIST MARKETS:

G Place des Ternes (Flowers)
H Stamp Market
I Place de la Madeleine (Flowers)
J Quai de la Mégisserie (Plants & Pets)
K Place Lépine (Flowers)
L Seine Quais (Books)
M Marché aux Livres (Books)

STREET MARKETS:

1 Rue de Lévis
2 Rue Cler
3 Convention
4 Edgar Quinet
5 Raspail
6 St-Germain
7 Buci
8 Carmes
9 Mouffetard
10 Monge
11 Port Royal
12 Montorgueil
13 Enfants-Rouges
14 Porte St-Martin
15 Sécretan
16 Belleville

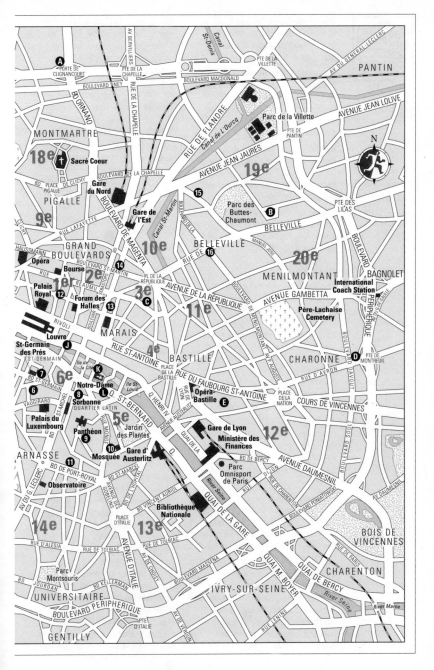

Shops and Markets

For a detailed description of the Puces de St-Ouen, *see p.166.*

Marché aux Cartes Postales Anciennes, Marché St-Germain, 3 ter rue Mabillon, 6e (Mº Mabillon). Wed & Thurs 9am–1pm & 4–6.30pm. Old postcards.

Marché de la Création Mouton-Duvernet, cnr rues Mouton-Duvernet, Boulard & Brézin, 14e (Mº Mouton-Duvernet). Sun 10.30am–5pm. Artists, many with studios nearby, display and sell their work here.

Marché du Livre Ancien et d'Occasion, Pavillon Baltard, Parc Georges-Brassens, rue Brancion, 15e (Mº Porte-de-Vanves). Sat & Sun 9am onwards. Second-hand and antiquarian books.

Marché aux Vieux Papiers de St-Mandé, av de Paris (Mº St-Mandé). Wed 10am–6pm. Old books, postcards and prints.

Flea Markets

Paris has three main flea markets (*marchés aux puces*) of ancient descent gathered about the old gates of the city. No longer the haunts of the flamboyant gypsies and petty crooks of literary tradition, they are nonetheless good entertainment, and if you go early enough you might just find something special. Some of the food markets have spawned second-hand clothes and junk stalls, notably the place d'Aligre, in the 12e, and the place des Fêtes, in the 20e.

Carreau du Temple, betw rue Perrée & rue du Petit-Thouars, 3e (Mº Temple). Tues–Fri until noon, Sat & Sun until 1pm. Specializes in plain and practical new clothes.

Porte de Montreuil, 20e (Mº Porte-de-Montreuil). Sat, Sun & Mon 6.30am–1pm. Best of the flea markets for second-hand clothes – cheapest on Mon when leftovers from the weekend are sold off.

Porte de Vanves, (av Georges-Lafenestre/av Marc-Sangnier) 14e (Mº Porte-de-Vanves). Sat & Sun 7am–6pm. The obvious choice for bric-a-brac searching, with professional dealers operating alongside amateurs. See account on p.000.

St-Ouen/Porte de Clignancourt, 18e (Mº Porte-de-Clignancourt). Sat, Sun & Mon 7.30am–7pm. The biggest and most touristy, with stalls selling clothes, shoes, records, books and junk of all sorts as well as expensive antiques. Trading usually starts well before the official opening hour – as early as 5am.

Flowers and Birds

Paris used to have innumerable **flower markets** around the streets, but today just the three listed below remain. Throughout the week, however, there's also the heavy concentration of plant and pet shops along the quai de la Mégisserie, between Pont-Neuf and Pont-au-Change.

Place Lépine, Île de la Cité, 1er. Daily 8am–7.30pm. On Sun flowers give way to birds and pets.

Place de la Madeleine, 8e. Tues–Sun 8am–7.30pm. Flowers and plants.

Place des Ternes, 8e. Tues–Sun 8am–7.30pm. Flowers and plants.

Food

The street **food markets** provide one of the capital's more exacting tests of willpower. At the top end of the scale, there are the Satanic arrays in rue de Lévis in the 17e and rue Cler in the 7e, both of which are more market street than street market, with their stalls mostly metamorphosed into permanent shops. The **real street markets** include a tempting scattering in the Left Bank – in rue de Buci (the most photographed) near St-Germain-des-Près, rue Mouffetard, place Maubert and place Monge. Bigger ones are at Montparnasse, in bd Edgar-Quinet, and opposite Val-de-Grâce in bd Port-Royal. The largest is in rue de la Convention, in the 15e.

For a different feel and more exotic foreign produce, take a look at the **Mediterranean/Oriental** displays in bd de Belleville and rue d'Aligre.

Markets usually start between 7am and 8am and tail off around midday. The covered markets have specific **opening** hours, which are given below along with details of locations and days of operation.

Belleville, bd de Belleville, 20e (Mᵒ Belleville/Ménilmontant). Tues & Fri.

Buci, rue de Buci & rue de Seine, 6e (Mᵒ Mabillon). Tues–Sun.

Carmes, place Maubert, 5e (Mᵒ Maubert-Mutualité). Tues, Thurs & Sat.

Convention, rue de la Convention, 15e (Mᵒ Convention). Tues, Thurs & Sun.

Dejean, place du Château-Rouge, 18e (Mᵒ Château-Rouge). Tues–Sun.

Edgar-Quinet, bd Edgar-Quinet, 14e (Mᵒ Edgar-Quinet). Wed & Sat.

Enfants-Rouges, 39 rue de Bretagne, 3e (Mᵒ Filles-du-Calvaire). Tues–Sat 8am–1pm & 4–7.30pm, Sun 8am–1pm.

Monge, place Monge, 5e (Mᵒ Monge). Wed, Fri & Sun.

Montorgueil, rue Montorgueil & rue Montmartre, 1er (Mᵒ Châtelet-Les Halles/Sentier). Daily.

Mouffetard, rue Mouffetard, 5e (Mᵒ Censier-Daubenton). Daily.

Place d'Aligre, 12e (Mᵒ Ledru-Rollin). Tues–Sat. Until noon.

Port-Royal, bd Port-Royal, near Val-de-Grâce, 5e (Mᵒ Port-Royale). Tues, Thurs & Sat.

Porte-St-Martin, rue du Château-d'Eau, 10e (Mᵒ Château-d'Eau). Tues–Sat 8am–1pm & 4–7.30pm, Sun 8am–1pm.

Rue Cler, 7e (Mᵒ École-Militaire). Tues–Sat.

Rue de Lévis, 17e (Mᵒ Villiers). Tues–Sun.

Rue du Poteau, 18e (Mᵒ Jules-Joffrin). Tues–Sat.

Raspail, bd Raspail, betw rue du Cherche-Midi & rue de Rennes, 6e (Mᵒ Rennes). Tues & Fri. Organic on Sun.

St-Germain, rue Mabillon, 6e (Mᵒ Mabillon). Tues–Sat 8am–1pm & 4–7.30pm, Sun 8am–1pm.

Secrétan, av Secrétan/rue Riquet, 19e (Mᵒ Bolivar). Tues–Sat 8am–1pm & 4–7.30pm, Sun 8am–1pm.

Tang Frères, 48 av d'Ivry, 13e (Mᵒ Porte-d'Ivry). Tues–Sun 9am–7.30pm. Not really a market, but a vast emporium of all things Oriental, where speaking French will not help you discover the nature and uses of what you see before you. In the same yard, there is also a Far Eastern flower shop.

Ternes, rue Lemercier, 17e (Mᵒ Ternes). Tues–Sat 8am–1pm & 4–7.30pm, Sun 8am–1pm.

Shops and
Markets

Chapter 18

Music and Nightlife

The strength of the Paris music scene is its diversity – a reputation gained mainly from its absorption of immigrant and exile populations. The city has no rivals in Europe for the variety of world music to be discovered: West and Central African, Caribbean and Latin American sounds are represented in force both by city-based groups and touring bands. You can spend any number of nights sampling mixtures of salsa, calypso, reggae and African sounds from Zaire, Congo, Senegal and Nigeria. Algerian raï has come out from the immigrant ghettoes, and the French language has been discovered to be a great vehicle for rap and hip-hop or the ragamuffin combination.

Jazz fans, too, are in for a treat. Paris has long been home to new styles and old-time musicians. The *Caveau de la Huchette* and *Le Petit Journal*, both in the Latin Quarter and both associated with traditional jazz, are two of the oldest clubs in the city. The *New Morning*, doyen of the modern clubs, hosts big names from all over the world. *Hot Brass*, in the 19e, is the hottest of the newcomers, and it's not hard to fill the late hours passing from one club to another in St-Germain or Les Halles – assuming your wallet can take it. Standards are high and the line-ups varied, and the ancient cellars housing many of the clubs make for great acoustics and atmosphere.

One variety of home-grown popular music is the tradition of **chansons**,

epitomized by Édith Piaf and developed to its greatest heights by Georges Brassens and the Belgian Jacques Brel. This music has been undergoing something of a revival since the return of the 1950s star Juliette Greco to the *Olympia* stage in 1991 brought rapt media attention. Another retrospective experience is **ballroom dancing** at the old music halls or surburban *guinguettes*.

Commercial French popular music is, on the whole, to be avoided. Although most singers – like Patrick Bruel, idol of depressed adolescents – lay claim to the *chansonniers* tradition, few have genuine roots in it, with the notable exception of Patricia Kaas. Vanessa Paradis went so far as to switch to English in order to pursue an international career. Two bands whose music is worth listening to for its fascinating mix of all kinds of styles are Mano Negra and Les Négresses Vertes.

Classical music, as you might expect in this Neoclassical city, is alive and well and takes up twice the space of "jazz-pop-folk-rock" in the listings magazines. The **Paris Opéra** with its two homes – the Opéra Garnier and Opéra Bastille – puts on a fine selection of opera and ballet. **Le Chatelet Théâtre Musical de Paris** also puts on interesting productions. For **concerts**, the choice is enormous. The two main orchestras are the Orchestre de Paris, based at the Salle Pleyel, and the Orchestre Nationale. Many concerts are put on in the city's churches – at very reasonable prices – but the need for advance reservations is a major inhibiting factor. If you're interested in the **contemporary** scene of Systems composition and the like, check out the state-sponsored experiments of Laurent Bayle at Beaubourg, L' Ensemble Intercontemporain at La Villette's Cité de la Musique, and Iannis Xenakis out at Issy-Les-Moulineaux.

In the listings in this chapter, **nightlife** recommendations – for **dance clubs and discos** – are to some extent incorporated in those for rock, world music and jazz, with which they merge. Separate sections, however, detail places that are mainly disco, and which cater for a gay or lesbian clientele.

The chapter's final section details all the **big venues**, where major concerts – from heavy metal to opera – are promoted.

Tickets and Information

The best place to get **tickets** for concerts, whether rock, jazz, *chansons* or classical, is *FNAC Forum des Halles*, 1–5 rue Pierre-Lescot, 1er, ☎01.40.41.40.00 (M° Chatelet-Les Halles), which takes more than fifty percent of sales. Or try the *FNAC*

Musique branches at 4 place de la Bastille, 12e (M° Bastille; Mon, Tues, Thurs & Sat 10am–8pm, Wed & Fri 10am–10pm), and 24 bd des Italiens, 9e (M° Richelieu-Drouot/Quatre-Septembre/Chaussée-d'Antin; Mon–Sat 10am–midnight; the *FNAC* bookshops (see p.323); the *Virgin Megastore*, 56–60 av des Champs-Élysées, 8e (M° Franklin-D-Roosevelt); or the Carrousel du Louvre, beneath the Louvre, 1er (M° Palais-Royal/Musée-du-Louvre; Mon–Thurs 10am–midnight, Fri & Sat 10am–1am, Sun 2pm–midnight).

Pariscope, Officiel des Spectacles and *Paris Free Voice* list a fair selection of concerts, clubs, etc, and you'll see posters around town (particularly in the Latin Quarter). *Les Inrockuptibles* is the serious magazine with in-depth analysis and interviews on the independent music scene. At *Parallèles*, 47 rue St-Honoré, 1er (M° Châtelet-les-Halles), you're likely to come across phone numbers for **raves**, if you're interested. For information about African music gigs, good places to go are the record shops *Blue Moon*, 7 rue Pierre-Sarrazin, 6e, ☎01.46.34.63.89 (M° Odéon; Mon–Sat 11am–7pm); and *Crocodisc*, 42 rue des Écoles, 5e (M° Maubert-Mutualité; Tues–Sat 11am–7pm).

Music and Nightlife

Music on TV and Radio

The private **TV** channel *Canal Plus* broadcasts big European concerts (Michael Jackson, Dire Straits, etc) and was responsible for initiating presenter Antoine de Caunes' *Rapido* to bring new popular sounds to a wider audience. *M6* has some late-night music programmes as well as numerous video clips during the day, while *Arte*, the fifth channel (after 7pm), shows contemporary opera productions and documentaries on all types of music.

Of the **local radio stations**, *Radio Nova* (101.5 MHz) plays a good cross-section of what's new from rap to funk; *Radio Beur* (106.7 MHz) and *Radio France-Mahgreb* (99.5MHz) have raï; *FIP* (105.1 MHz) has plenty of jazz; *Africa Numero 1* (107.5MHz) has African music; *Radio Latina* (99.0MHz) is the Latin American music station; and *Oui* (102.3 MHz) is the all-day rock radio. The national station *Europe 1* (104.7 MHz) has some imaginative music programming, and *France - Musique* (91.7 and 92.1 MHz) carries classical, contemporary, jazz, opera and anything really big. Under strict new language laws, forty percent of pop music played by any radio station has to be French, and there is now a dire Parisian radio station playing nothing but French music, *Chante France* (90.9 MHz).

Music and Nightlife

World Music and Rock

The last few years have seen considerable diversification in the Paris clubs and rock venues, which now concentrate more on international sounds, leaving the big Western rock bands to play the major arenas. Almost every club features **Latin and African** dance music, and big names from these worlds – in particular **zouk** musicians from the French Caribbean, for whom Paris is a second home – are almost always in town. The divisions between world sounds are mixing more and more, too. Even "ethnically French" Parisians have produced their own rewarding hybrids, best exemplified in the Pogue-like chaos of Les Négresses Vertes, who have successfully survived the death in 1993 of their lead singer, Helno. One brilliant vocalist to look out for at the moment is Angélique Kidjo, from Benin.

The only rock'n'roll megastar of France turned 50 in 1993. His birthday, celebrated with solo gigs at the Parc des Princes, was fêted by the (then) prime minister, Balladur, the culture minister, Jacques Toubon, and mayor of Paris, Jacques Chirac. But fortunately **Johnny Halliday** does not represent contemporary French rock. Until their recent demise, the best "alternative" rock band has been the Franco-Spanish **Mano Negra**, whose music, heavily influenced by their Latin American tours, combines rap, reggae, rock and salsa sounds. Other quality rock musicians include Louis Bertignac and Paul Personne. However, half of all albums bought in France are still recorded by British and American bands.

There are numerous **heavy metal** bands with English names like "Megadeath". Then there's **trashpop**, an amalgam of funk, punk and splashes of bebop, heavy metal and psychedelia. An emerging new trend is French "country" music, known as **Astérix rock**, a bawdy, raucous, energetic sound with accordions as the main instruments; two current bands making this are Les French Lovers and Les Garçons Bouchers.

Algerian raï continues to flourish, with singers like Cheb Khaled enjoying megastar status. But the rage is increasingly for professionally produced techno raves and the "marginale" culture of the *banlieue*, the dispossessed immigrant suburbs, depicted so powerfully in the movie *La Haine*, and finding musical expression in rap and hip-hop. Names to look out for are NTM, IAM and MC Solaar, who moves beyond traditional rap to something a good deal more melodic and musical, with superb words that you need to be pretty fluent to appreciate.

Music venues

Most of the venues listed below are clubs. A few of them will have live music all week, but the majority host bands on just a couple of nights, usually Friday and Saturday, when admission prices are also hiked up. *La Locomotive* and *Le Saint* are your best bets for a not-too-expensive good night out.

MAINLY ROCK

Chapelle des Lombards, 19 rue de Lappe, 11e; ☎01.43.57.24.24 (Mº Bastille). See p.344, under "Bals musettes and guinguettes".

La Cigale, 120 bd de Rochechouart, 18e; ☎01.42.23.15.15 (Mº Pigalle). Music from 8.30pm. *Rita Mitsouko*, punk, indie, etc; an eclectic programming policy in an old-fashioned converted theatre, long a fixture on the Pigalle scene.

Le Divan du Monde, 75 rue des Martyrs, 18e; ☎01.42.55.48.50 (Mº Notre-Dame-de-Lorette). Daily 7pm–5am. A new and youthful venue in a café whose regulars included Toulouse-Lautrec. An eclectic and exciting programming policy.

Élysée Montmartre, 72 bd de Rochechouart, 18e; ☎01.44.92.45.45 (Mº Anvers). An historic Montmartre nightspot, now dedicated to rock. Inexpensive and fun, it pulls in a young and excitable crowd.

Erotika, 2 rue Couston, 18e; ☎01.46.07.53.03 (Mº Blanche). Salsa, raï, acid jazz – rock on Thurs. 50F admission.

Fahrenheit, Espace Icare, 31 bd Gambetta, Issy-les-Moulineaux; ☎01.40.93.44.48 (Mº Corentin-Cariou). An energetic, sweaty, suburban venue for mainly (but not exclusively) heavy metal bands. Around 50F.

Le Gibus, 18 rue du Faubourg-du-Temple, 11e; ☎01.47.00.78.88 (Mº République). Tues–Sat 11pm–5am; Sat only in Aug. For twenty years English rock bands on their way up have played their first Paris gig at *Le Gibus*, the Clash and Police among them. Fourteen nights of dross will turn up perhaps one decent band, but it's always hot, loud, energetic, and crowded with young Parisians heavily committed to the rock scene. 70F admission; 80F with drink.

La Locomotive, 90 bd de Clichy, 18e; ☎01.42.57.37.37 (Mº Blanche). Concerts start at 1am. Closed Mon. Enormous high-tech nightclub refurbished in the 1980s. Three dance floors: one for techno; one for rock, heavy metal and concerts; and one for rap and funk. One of the most crowded, popular and democratic in the city, and you're sure of a good time. 60F weekdays; 100F weekends, including one drink.

New Riverside, 7 rue Grégoire-de-Tours, 6e; ☎01.43.54.46.33 (Mº Odéon). Daily 11pm–dawn. Good, friendly club playing rock and pop music in a sixteenth-century cellar. At weekends, breakfast included

in admission price; and free admission for women weekdays and before midnight Fri and Sat. Otherwise, Mon–Thurs 70F; Fri, Sat & Sun 100F.

Le Rex Club, 5 bd Poissonnière, 2e; ☎01.42.36.83.98 (Mº Montmartre). Tues–Sun 11pm–6am; sometimes closed Sun & Mon. Mainly live music – rock, funk, soul, raï, rap (generally Tues & Sat from 8pm; rave night, Thurs) – for which you pay 50–100F. Disco from 11pm, 60–90F.

Le Saint, 7 rue St-Séverin, 5e; ☎01.43.25.50.04 (Mº St-Michel). Tues–Sun 11am–dawn. Good value, varied music played in an ancient cellar; popular with students. 50F including one drink Tues–Thurs; 80F weekends.

MAINLY LATIN AND CARIBBEAN

L'Escale, 15 rue Monsieur-le-Prince, 6e; ☎01.43.25.55.22 (Mº Odéon). 11pm–4am. More Latin American musicians must have passed through here than any other club. The dancing sounds, salsa mostly, are in the basement (disco on Wed), while on the ground floor every variety of South American music is given an outlet. Drinks 80F.

Mambo Club, 20 rue Cujas, 5e; ☎01.43.54.89.21 (Mº St-Michel/Odéon). Wed–Sat 11pm–dawn, Sunday 4pm–dawn for "themed *soirées*". Afro-

Music and Nightlife

Karaoke

Rather a lot of French people have decided that karaoke is a wonderful way of showing off their talents (and practising their English). Unlike the average Brit, French karaoke-ists don't need to get completely plastered before they'll take the microphone, and they're depressingly good at it. There's now a weekly karaoke show on the TV, and French songs are coming on the market. If you keep your eye out, you're certain to see bars advertising the "sport", particularly around Les Halles.

A couple of popular venues are:

Le Grand Café de New York, Centre Beaugrenelle, 36 rue Linois, 15e (Mº Charles-Michels). Weekdays 10pm–2am, weekends 10pm–6am. Big and sophisticated as karaoke goes. Also a restaurant and bar. 100F for table; 45F first drink.

Nuits Elysées, 4 rue Arséne-Moussaye, 8e; ☎01.45.63.02.58 (Mº Étoile). Tues-Sun 11pm–6am. Can get hot 'n'steamy. Disco also.

Music and Nightlife

Details of afternoon sessions at the Balajo are given on p.302.

Cuban and Antillais music in a seedy dive with people of all ages and nationalities.

BALS MUSETTES AND GUINGUETTES

Balajo, 9 rue de Lappe, 11e; ☎01.47.00.07.87 (Mº Bastille). Mon, Fri & Sat 10pm–4.30am. The last and greatest survivor of the old-style dance halls of working-class and slightly louche Paris. The *Balajo* dates from the 1930s and has kept its extravagant contemporary décor, with a balcony for the orchestra above the vast dance floor. The clientele is all sorts now, and all ages, though recently the bouncers have started to show a preference for teenyboppers. The music encompasses everything from mazurka to tango, cha-cha, twist, and the slurpy *chansons* of between the wars. There are disco and modern hits as well, but that's on Mon nights when the kids from across town come and all the popular nostalgia disappears. Admission price is around 100F. Mon, free for women between 11.30pm and 1am.

Chapelle des Lombards, 19 rue de Lappe, 11e; ☎01.43.57.24.24 (Mº Bastille). Mon–Sat and the eve of public holidays 8pm–dawn; closed Sun. This erstwhile *bal musette* of the rue de Lappe still plays the occasional waltz and tango, but for the most part the music is salsa, reggae, steel drums, gwo-kâ, zouk, raï and the blues. The doormen are not too friendly and we've heard bad stories of serious hassle and harassment inside. 100F admission and first drink; 50F upwards for the next drinks.

Chez Gégène, 162bis quai de Polangis, Joinville-le-Pont; ☎01.48.83.29.43 (RER Joinville-le-Pont). Open mid-March to mid-Oct, Fri & Sat 9pm–2am, Sun 3–7pm. Just the other side of the Bois de Vincennes, this is a genuine *guinguette* (riverside eating, drinking and dancing venue) established in the 1900s. You don't have to dine to dance (around 70F extra for non-diners).

Le Petit Robinson, fifty metres along from *Chez Gégène* (above) and a bit more upmarket, is the place where very serious dancers go to show off their immaculate waltzes, foxtrots and tangos. Like its neighbour, it has a huge dance floor, with *rétro* Tues–Thurs nights and disco at the weekend. Admission and drink 80F evening; 75F afternoon.

Le Tango, 13 rue au-Maire, 3e; ☎01.42.72.17.78 (Mº Arts-et-Métiers). Fri, Sat & the eve of public hols only, 11pm–dawn. No vetting here. People wear whatever clothes they happen to be in and dance with abandon to please themselves, not the adjudicators of style. The music is jazzy Latin American: salsa, calypso and reggae. It is, however, a prime pick-up joint, and women are likely to be propositioned in no uncertain terms the moment they've agreed to a dance. Best to go with friends. Admission 60F Sat; 40F Fri. Drinks from 30F; obligatory cloakroom fee.

Nightclubs and Discos

Clubs listed below are essentially **discos**, though a few have the odd live group. They come and go at an exhausting rate, the business principle being to take over

---

Late-night bars with music

Several of the bars listed in Chapter 13 have occasional live music and small dance floors with a juke box.

a place, make a major investment in the décor, and close after two years, well in the black. As a customer, you contribute on a financial level – and in many places your ornamentation potential is equally important. Being sized up by a leather-clad American bouncer acting as the ultimate arbiter of style and prosperity can be a very demeaning experience. Men generally have a harder time than women. English-speakers are at an advantage, blacks are not. The one place that doesn't discriminate and should be at the top of any disco list is *Le Palace*.

L'Arc, 12 rue de Presbourg, 16e; ☎01.45.00.45.00 (Mº Charles-de-Gaulle-Étoile). Daily 11.30pm–dawn; 100F with first drink. Model types and *vedettes* are the norm in this upmarket fashionable spot. Restaurant too: Mon–Sat 9pm–1am; around 300F.

Les Bains, 7 rue du Bourg-l'Abbé, 3e; ☎01.48.87.01.80 (Mº Étienne-Marcel). Midnight–dawn every day (Sun, rock; Mon, "disturbance of the peace"; Wed, "disco inferno"). 150F admission, drinks expensive. This is as posey as they come – an old Turkish bathhouse where the Stones filmed part of their *Undercover of the Night* video, now redone in the anti-perspirant, passionless style pioneered for the *Café Costes*. The music is house, rap and funk, with occasional live (usually dross) bands. It's not a place where a 500F note has much life expectancy. The décor features a plunging pool by the dance floor in which the punters are wont to ruin their non-colour-fast designer creations. Whether you can watch this spectacle depends on the bouncers, who have fixed ideas. If you're turned away, be thankful and head down the road to *Le Tango* (see p.344).

Barde La Plage, 12 rue du Colonel-Oudot, 12e; ☎01.43.45.55.55 (Mº Porte-Dorée). Tues–Sat 11.30pm–dawn. Solarium, deckchairs, fine sand, parasols and cocktails.

La Casbah, 18–20 rue de la Forge-Royale, 11e; ☎01.43.71.71.89. (Mº Bastille). 9pm–5am. Admission around 100F; 150F for a table. Bar upstairs, dancing down. The outstanding feature of this rather fancy and exclusive place is the décor: beautiful and authentic stuff from Morocco – doors, furniture, plaster-work – matched by the *zouave* costumes of the waiters and waitresses. North African food served.

El Globo, 8 bd Strasbourg, 10e; ☎01.45.18.07.37 (Mº Strasbourg-St-Denis). Sat, Sun & public hols 10pm–dawn; entry 100F. Currently very popular with Beaux Quartiers rebels, 10e *arrondissement* punks and all sorts. Lots of room to dance to international hits past and present. Drinks 50F; 25F between 11pm and midnight. 1970s disco on Saturday night.

Flash Back, 37 rue Grégoire-de-Tours, 6e; ☎01.43.25.56.70 (Mº Mabillon). Tues–Sun 11am–dawn; 70F entry. Techno and commercial rock in a futuristic décor.

Keur Samba, 79 rue la Boétie, 8e; ☎01.43.59.03.10 (Mº Franklin-D-Roosevelt). Daily until breakfast. An expensive and fashionable Arab and African venue, where you need to be very well dressed. Afro-Antillais music. 120F for a drink.

Le Moloko, 26 rue Fontaine, 9e; ☎01.48.74.50.26 (Mº Blanche). Daily 9pm–6am; admission on Wed & Sat only 20F/40F. A new, fashionable and successful addition to the night scene, frequented by the young and gorgeous, the trendy and posey, all sorts. Jukebox instead of DJs, occasionally live music in the early evening. Drinks from 50F.

Niel's, 27 av des Ternes, 17e; ☎01.47.66.45.00 (Mº Ternes). Disco daily 12.30am–dawn; restaurant daily 9pm–midnight (around 350F). Like *L'Arc*, this place attracts the stars, but there's always the restaurant-booking technique to guarantee entry. Fri & Sat 100F with drink; weekdays 95F.

Le Palace, 8 rue du Faubourg-Montmartre, 9e; ☎01.47.70.75.02 (Mº Montmartre). 11pm–dawn. Entry 100F

Music and Nightlife

Music and Nightlife

For gay and lesbian contacts and information, see Basics, p.52.

Mon–Thurs; 120F weekend; drinks from 50F. Time was when everyone went to the *Palace*; it's still packed nightly with revellers, whether they've scraped together their week's savings or are just out to exercise the credit cards, and they all don their best party gear. Some nights it's thematic fancy dress, some nights the music is all African, other times the place is booked for TV dance shows. It's big, the bopping is good, and the clientele are an exuberant spectacle in themselves. Weekends are mainly techno and attract a gay crowd.

Le Shéhérazade, 3 rue de Liège, 9e; ☎01.42.85.53.78 (Mº Liège). Mon–Thurs 11pm–dawn, weekends midnight–dawn; 100F admission plus drink. Popular with the youthful, mixed, dancing crowd. House music, with occasional variant evenings. Exotic décor in a former Russian cabaret; vodka 80–90F a shot.

Zed Club, 2 rue des Anglais, 5e; ☎01.43.54.93.78 (Mº Maubert-Mutualité). Wed–Sat 10.30pm–3.30am; admission 50F Wed; 50F plus drink Thurs; 100F plus drink Fri & Sat. *The* rock 'n' roll club.

Lesbian and Gay Bars, Clubs and Discos

Lesbian clubs find it hard to be exclusively female, and you may find that none of the varied atmospheres is agreeable. The pleasures of **gay men** are far better catered for, though some Marais bars have been forced to close and others prosecuted for noise, contravention of drinking laws, and even for allowing plants to spread over the pavement. It seems that the residents of the Marais have become a good deal less tolerant.

While the selection of gay male-oriented establishments below only scratches the surface, for gay women our listings more or less cover all that's available. Lesbians, however, are welcome in some of the predominantly male clubs. For a complete rundown, consult *Paris Scene* (Gay Men's Press, £5.99), *Gai-Pied's Guide Gai* or the newspaper *Exit.*

WOMEN

La Champmeslé, 4 rue Chabanais, 2e; ☎01.42.96.85.20 (Mº Opéra). Daily 6pm–2am. Intimate, relaxed bar with yuppie clientèle. Cabaret on Thurs and weekends. Drinks 25–40F.

Chez Moune, 54 rue Pigalle, 18e; ☎01.45.26.64.64 (Mº Pigalle). 10pm–dawn. In the red-light heart of Paris, this mixed but predominantly women's cabaret and disco may shock or delight feminists. The evening includes a striptease (by women) without the standard audience for such shows (any man causing the slightest fuss is kicked out). Sunday afternoon teadances (4.30–8pm) are strictly women-only.

L'Entracte, 25 bd Poissonnière, 2e; ☎01.40.26.01.93 (Mº Montmartre). Sun–Fri from 11pm; Sat & Sun 50F entrance from midnight. Happy Hour 11pm–1.30am. Drinks 40F. Diverse music – from techno to Madonna.

Entre Nous, 17 rue Laferrière, 9e; ☎01.48.78.11.67 (Mº St-Georges). Sat only, 11pm–dawn. A small women-only club with an intimate atmosphere and catholic taste in music.

Le New Monocle, 60 bd Edgar-Quinet, 14e; ☎01.43.20.81.12 (Mº Montparnasse). Mon–Sat 11pm–dawn. This women's cabaret has been revitalized since the closing of its rival, *Le Baby Doll*. A small scattering of men is allowed in every evening.

Le Privilège-Kat, 3 cité Bergère, 9e; ☎01.42.46.50.98 (Mº Rue-Montmartre). Fri & Sat 11.30pm–6am. Entry 90F; drinks from 60F. A venue run by two stylish women. Women only Fri & Sat; all other days, men too.

El Scandalo, 21 rue Keller, 11e; ☎01.47.00.24.59 (Mº Voltaire/Bastille). Tues–Sun 8pm–2pm. Very friendly lesbian bar; men allowed in Tues & Sun after 7pm.

MIXED

Le Bar Central, 33 rue Vieille-du-Temple, 4e; ☎01.48.87.99.33 (Mº Hôtel-de-Ville).

Daily 2pm–2am. Small, crowded, friendly bar. Mostly men. Drinks 20–60F.

MEN

Banana Café, 13 rue de la Ferronerie, 1er; ☎01.42.33.35.31 (Mº Chatelet-Les Halles). Daily 4.30pm–dawn. Popular, expensive and very trendy.

Bar Bi, 23 rue Ste-Croix de la Bretonnerie, 4e; ☎01.42.78.26.20 (Mº Hôtel-de-Ville). Daily 5pm–2am. Another popular and crowded Marais bar, which the law has been particularly heavy with.

Club 18, 18 rue de Beaujolais, 1er; ☎01.42.97.52.13 (Mº Bourse). Tues–Sun 11pm–dawn; entry 60F Fri & Sat. Mainly young gay clientele in this friendly cellar bar with Sun cabaret.

La Luna, 28 rue Keller, 11e; ☎01.40.21.09.91 (Mº Bastille). Wed–Sun 11pm–6am. Weekend entry 50F; drinks from 45F. The latest high-tech rendezvous for the gay Bastille, complete with mirrors to dance in front of.

Open Bar, end of rue Vieille-du-Temple & rue des Archives, 4e (Mº Hôtel-de-Ville). The first gay bar/café to have pavement tables.

Le Palace Tea Dance. See under "Afternoon tangos", Chapter 15.

Le Piano Zinc, 49 rue des Blancs-Manteaux, 4e; ☎01.42.74.32.42 (Mº Rambuteau/Hôtel-de-Ville). Tues–Sun 6pm–2am. From 10pm, when the piano-playing starts, this bar becomes a happy riot of songs, music-hall acts, and dance, which may be hard to appreciate if you don't follow French very well. Drinks 36–47F.

Le Queen, 102 av des Champs-Élysées, 8e; ☎01.42.89.31.32 (Mº George-V). 11pm–dawn. Admission free weekdays; weekends 80F including drink. Women welcome except Thurs. Drag queens and model types mostly. Racy theme nights Mon, Wed & Sun.

Le Quetzal, 10 rue de la Verrerie, 4e; ☎01.48.87.99.07 (Mº Hôtel-de-Ville). Lots of beautiful bodies crammed into a popular space.

Jazz, Blues and Chansons

Jazz has long enjoyed an appreciative audience in France, most especially since the end of World War II, when the intellectual rigour and agonized musings of bebop struck an immediate chord of sympathy in the existentialist hearts of the *après-guerre*. Charlie Parker, Dizzy Gillespie, Bud Powell, Miles Davis – all were being listened to in the 1950s, when in Britain their names were known only to a tiny coterie of fans.

Gypsy guitarist Django Reinhardt and his partner, violinist Stéphane Grappelli, whose work represents the distinctive and undisputed French contribution to the jazz canon, had much to do with the music's popularity. But it was also greatly enhanced by the presence of many front-rank black American musicians, for whom Paris was a haven of freedom and culture after the racial prejudice and philistinism of the States. Among them were the soprano sax player Sidney Bechet, who set up in legendary partnership with French clarinettist Claude Luter, and Bud Powell, whose turbulent exile partly inspired the tenor man played by Dexter Gordon (himself a veteran of the *Montana* club) in the film *Round Midnight*.

Jazz is still alive and well in the city, with new venues opening all the time, where you can hear all styles from New Orleans to current experimental. Some **local names** to look out for are saxophonists François Jeanneau, Barney

Music and Nightlife

A note on prices

With virtually all of the jazz clubs listed below, expense is a real drawback to enjoyment – the *Théâtre Dunois*, *L'Eustache* and *Utopia* are the cheaper ones. Admission charges are generally high and, when they're not levied, there's usually a whacking charge for your first drink. Subsequent drinks, too, are absurdly priced – about twice what you'd pay in a similar club in London, and more than double that in New York.

Music and Nightlife

Willen, Didier Malherbe, André Jaume and Steve Lacey; violinist Didier Lockwood; British-born but long Paris-resident guitarist John McLaughlin; pianist Alain Jeanmarie; accordionist Richard Galliano; and bass player Jean-Jacques Avenel. All of them can be found playing small gigs, regardless of the size of their reputations.

MAINLY JAZZ

Le Baiser Salé, 58 rue des Lombards, 1er; ☎01.42.33.37.71 (Mº Châtelet). 8am–5am. 123F first drink includes charge for music. A bar downstairs and a small, crowded upstairs room with live music every night from 11pm – usually jazz, rhythm & blues, Latino-rock, reggae or Brazilian.

Le Bilboquet, 13 rue St-Benoît, 6e; ☎01.45.48.81.84 (Mº St-Germain). Mon–Sat 9pm–dawn; no admission, but pricey drinks, (120F). A rather smart, comfortable bar/restaurant with live jazz every night – local and international stars. Food served until 1am. The music starts at 10.45pm. This is the street where Dexter Gordon, Miles Davis, Bud Powell and others played and hung out in the 1950s.

Caveau de la Huchette, 5 rue de la Huchette, 5e; ☎01.43.26.65.05 (Mº St-Michel). Daily 9.30pm–2am or later. Sun–Thurs 60F (students 55F); Fri & Sat 70F; drinks from 20F. A wonderful slice of old Paris life in this horribly touristified area. Live jazz music, usually trad, to dance to on a floor surrounded by tiers of benches, and a bar decorated with caricatures of the barman drawn on any material to hand.

Au Duc des Lombards, 42 rue des Lombards, 1er; ☎01.42.33.22.88 (Mº Châtelet-Les Halles). Tues–Sat until 6am. Drinks from 58F or 78F. Small, unpretentious bar with performances every night from 11pm – jazz piano, blues, ballads, fusion. Sometimes big names.

L'Eustache, 37 rue Berger, 1er; ☎01.40.26.23.20 (Mº Châtelet-Les Halles). 11am–4am; Thurs, Fri & Sat live

jazz 10.30pm–2am and cheap beer in this young and friendly Les Halles café – in fact, the cheapest good jazz in the capital.

Hot Brass, parc de la Villette, 211 av Jean-Jaurés, 19e; ☎01.42.00.14.14 (Mº Porte-de-Pantin). Tues–Sat 8pm–2am; 120F/80F with first drink; music from 9.30pm. Successful and popular club, with some big names in international jazz. Also rap, soul and Latin music.

Instants Chavirés, 7 rue Richard-Lenoir, Montreuil; ☎01.42.87.25.91 (Mº Robespierre). Tues–Sat 8pm–1am; concerts at 9.30pm. Admission 35–80F, depending on the celebrity of the band; drinks from 15F. Avant-garde jazz joint – no comforts – on the eastern edge of the city, close to the Porte de Montreuil. A place where musicians go to hear each other play. Its reputation has already attracted subsidies from both state and local authorities.

Le Latitudes Jazz Club, 7–11 rue St-Benoît, 6e; ☎01.42.60.23.02 (Mº St-Germain-des-Près). Daily 6pm–2am; live jazz Wed–Sat 10.30pm–2am. 120F for the first drink, thereafter 15–65F depending on your choice. French and foreign stars play in the swish downstairs bar of the hotel.

Lionel Hampton Bar, Hôtel Méridien, 81 bd Gouvion-St-Cyr, 17e; ☎01.40.68.30.42 (Mº Porte-Maillot). Mon–Sat 10pm–2am. Drinks from 130F. First-rate jazz venue, with big-name musicians. Inaugurated by Himself, but otherwise the great man is only an irregular visitor.

New Morning, 7–9 rue des Petites-Écuries, 10e; ☎01.45.23.56.39 (Mº Château-d'Eau). 9pm–1.30am (concerts start around 10pm); admission around 110F. This is the place where the big international names in jazz come to play. Blues and Latin, too.

Passage du Nord-Ouest, 13 rue du Faubourg-Montmartre, 9e; ☎01.36.68.03.32 (Mº Rue-Montmartre). Music starts around 9pm, generally jazz, blues or salsa. 80–120F.

Old films, shorts, etc, 2–7pm. Bar around 45F.

Le Petit Journal, 71 bd St-Michel, 5e; ☎01.43.26.28.59 (Mº Luxembourg). Mon–Sat 10pm–2am; closed Aug. A small, smoky bar, long frequented by Left Bank student types, with good, mainly French, traditional and mainstream sounds. First drink 100–150F. Rather middle-aged and tourist-prone.

Le Petit Journal Montparnasse, 13 rue du Commandant-Mouchotte, 14e; ☎01.43.21.56.70 (Mº Montparnasse). Mon–Sat 9pm–2am. First drink 100F. Under the *Hôtel Montparnasse*, and sister establishment to the above, with bigger visiting names, both French and international.

Le Petit Opportun, 15 rue des Lavandières-Ste-Opportune, 1er; ☎01.42.36.01.36 (Mº Châtelet-Les Halles). Tues–Sat 9pm–3am. Music from 11pm. First drink 100F. It's worth arriving early to get a seat for the live music in the dungeon-like cellar where the acoustics play strange tricks and you can't always see the musicians. Fairly eclectic policy and a crowd of genuine connoisseurs.

Quai des Blues, 17 bd Vital-Bouhot, Île de la Jatte, Neuilly; ☎01.46.24.22.00 (Mº Pont-de-Levallois, then down the steps from the bridge). Not the easiest of places to get to. Thurs–Sat, music at 10.45pm & midnight; 80F. Mainly blues, R&B, gospel – American musicians.

Slow Club, 130 rue de Rivoli, 1er; ☎01.42.33.84.30 (Mº Châtelet/Pont-Neuf). Tues–Sat 10pm–4am. Admission 60F; Fri & Sat 75F. A jazz club where you can bop the night away to the sounds of Claude Luter's sextet and visiting New Orleans musicians.

Le Sunset, 60 rue des Lombards, 1er; ☎01.40.26.46.20 (Mº Châtelet-Les Halles). Mon–Sat 8pm–4am. Admission and first drink 80F. Restaurant upstairs, jazz club in the basement, featuring the best musicians – the likes of Alain Jeanmarie and Turk Mauro – and frequented by musicians in the wee small hours.

Théâtre Dunois, 108 rue du Chevaleret, 13e; ☎01.45.70.81.16 (Mº Chevaleret). Daily from 7pm; closed July & Aug. 70F admission; 50F students. Concerts Mon–Fri & Sun 8.30–11.30pm. A new location for the *Dunois*, more modern, no stage, and a bigger bar. The musical policy still gives consistent support to free and experimental jazz. One of the few places in Paris to hear improvised music, as opposed to free jazz..

Utopia, 1 rue de l'Ouest, 14e; ☎01.43.22.79.66 (Mº Pernety). Mon–Sat 10.30pm–dawn; closed Aug. No genius here, but good French blues singers interspersed with jazz and blues tapes, the people listening mostly young and studentish. Drinks from 50F. Generally very pleasant atmosphere.

La Villa, 29 rue Jacob, 6e; ☎01.43.26.60.00 (Mº St-Germain-des-Près). Mon–Sat 10pm–3am. Admission 120F with first drink. Popular joint with a good atmosphere and usually well-established musicians.

MAINLY CHANSONS

Casino de Paris, 19 rue de Clichy, 9e; ☎01.49.95.99.99 (Mº Trinité). Tickets from 100F to 200F. This decaying, once-plush casino in one of the seediest streets in Paris is a venue for all sorts of performances – *chansons*, poetry combined with flamenco guitar, cabaret. Check the listings magazines under "*Variétés*".

Caveau des Oubliettes, 11 rue St-Julien-le-Pauvre, 5e; ☎01.43.54.94.97 (Mº St-Michel). Fri & Sat only 9pm–2am; admission 70F; drinks from 20F. French popular music of bygone times – Piaf and earlier – sung with exquisite nostalgia in the ancient prisons of Châtelet.

Classical and Contemporary Music

Paris is a stimulating environment for **classical music**, both established and contemporary. The former is well represented with a choice of ten to twenty

Music and Nightlife

Music and Nightlife

concerts every day of the week, with numerous performances taking place in the appropriate acoustic setting of churches, often for free or very cheap. **Contemporary and experimental computer-based** work flourishes too; leading exponents are Paul Mefano and Pierre Boulez, founder of Beaubourg's *IRCAM* centre and himself one of the first pupils of Olivier Messiaen, the grand old man of modern French music, who died in 1992.

The new **Cité de la Musique**, at La Villette in the 19e, is an important new venue, with regular concerts in the Conservatoire (the Academy) and in the fabulously designed "modular" Salle des Concerts. Ancient music, contemporary works, jazz, *chansons* and music from all over the world are featured.

The city hosts a good number of **music festivals**, which vary from year to year. For details, pick up the current year's festival schedule from the tourist office or the Hôtel de Ville.

Two **periodicals** for those with a serious interest in the music scene are *Le Mélomane*, published monthly by the *Maison de la Radio*; and the trimonthly *Résonance*, published by *IRCAM* at the Centre Beaubourg and specializing in contemporary music.

Regular Concert Venues

Tickets for classical concerts are best bought at the box offices, though for big names you may find overnight queues, and a large number of seats are always booked by subscribers. The price range is very reasonable. The listings magazines and daily newspapers will have details of concerts in these venues, in the churches and in the suburbs. Look out for posters as well.

The top **auditoriums** are:

Cité de la Musique, 221 av Jean-Jaurès, 19e; ☎01.44.84.44.84 (Mº Porte-de-Pantin).

Conservatoire National Supérieur de Musique et de Danse de Paris, 209 av Jean-Jaurès, 19e; ☎01.40.40.46.46 (Mº Porte-de-Pantin).

Salle Gaveau, 45 rue de la Boétie; ☎01.45.62.09.71 (Mº Miromesnil).

Salle Pleyel, 252 rue du Faubourg-St-Honoré, 8e; ☎01.45.61.06.30 (Mº Ternes). Home of the *Orchestre de Paris*, the Paris symphony orchestra.

Théâtre des Champs-Élysées, 15 av Montaigne, 8e; ☎01.49.52.50.50 (Mº Alma-Marceau).

Théâtre Musical de Paris, Théâtre du Châtelet, 1 place du Châtelet, 1er; ☎01.40.28.28.40 (Mº Châtelet).

Opera

Opera would seem to have had its rewards in President Mitterrand's millennial endowments. The **Opéra-Bastille**

Radio-France free concerts

Squeezed by the all-too-familiar business reasoning of the age, the state radio's music station, *France-Musique*, has adopted a more commercial programming policy, aimed at wider public taste and better audience ratings, to the dismay, inevitably, of purists. However, a major advantage has been a significant increase in the number of **admission-free concerts** at the *Maison de la Radio*, 166 av du Président-Kennedy, 16e; ☎01.42.30.15.16 (Mº Passy). All you have to do is turn up half an hour in advance at Studio 106, the main auditorium, renamed *Salle Olivier Messiaen* in memory of the composer, to secure a yellow *carton d'invitation*.

Another interesting opportunity for music lovers is the daily programme **Les démons de Midi**, which goes out live at 12.30pm from Studio 101. It consists of recitals of all kinds of music from medieval to modern, with discussions and interventions by young musicians who turn up to take part. Again, all you have to do to attend is turn up half an hour early, at noon, and collect your *carton*.

(see p.108) was his most extravagant legacy to the city. It opened, with all due pomp, in 1989. Its first production – a six-hour performance of Berlioz's *Les Troyens* – cast something of a shadow on the project's proclaimed commitment to popularizing the art. "We are audacious", was the defence of the president, Pierre Bergé, who got his job after a lot of acrimonious political wrangling which included the dismissal of Daniel Barenboim as musical director. This was shortly followed by the dismissal of Rudolph Nureyev from the same post. Both Jessye Norman and Dietrich Fischer-Dieskau have boycotted the place. Resignations and a severe loss of morale followed the company's accident at the Seville Expo 92, when a chorus singer was killed and many others injured. The relatively unknown South Korean, Myung Whun Chung, was a controversial but popular musical director until he was sacked by the new chief, Hughes Gall, who has decided to take smaller productions back to the lavishly refurbished old **Opéra Garnier**, place de l'Opéra, 9e; ☎01.47.42.53.71 (Mº Opéra; tickets 60–750F).

Opera in Paris creams off almost two-thirds of the whole annual state budget for music. Potentially the Bastille orchestra is one of the best, but people disagree about the acoustics. And there is a feeling that productions are too big and stagey (and not the best on offer). To judge the place for yourself: **tickets** (60–590F) can be booked Monday to Saturday 11am to 6pm on ☎01.44.73.13.00 or at the ticket offices (Mon–Sat 11am–6.30pm within two weeks of the performance). The cheapest seats are only available to personal callers; unfilled seats are sold at discount to students five minutes before the curtain goes up. For programme details, phone ☎01.43.43.96.96.

More large-scale opera productions are staged at the **Théâtre Musical de Paris**, part of the **Théâtre du Châtelet** (see opposite). Rather less grand opera is performed at the **Opéra-Comique** (Salle Favard, 5 rue Favart, 2e;

☎01.42.86.88.83; Mº Richelieu-Drouot). Occasional operas and concerts by solo singers are hosted by the **Théâtre des Champs Elysées** (see opposite). Both opera and recitals are also put on at the multipurpose performance halls (see final section, p.352).

Contemporary Music

One of the few disadvantages of the high esteem in which the French hold their intellectual and artistic life is that it encourages, at the extremes, a tendency to sterile *intellectualisme*, as the French themselves call it. In the eyes of many music lovers, and musicians, this has been nowhere more evident than in music, where the avant-garde is split into post-serialist and spectral music factions. Doyen of the former is composer Pierre Boulez; of the latter, it is Paul Mefano, director of the *2E2M* ensemble.

Boulez's experiments for many years received massive public funding in the form of a vast laboratory of acoustics and "digital signal processing" – a complex known as **IRCAM** – housed underneath the Beaubourg arts centre. Boulez's Ensemble Intercontemporain is now based in the Cité de la Musique, but IRCAM occasionally opens its doors to the public.

An overground extension to IRCAM on place Igor-Stravinsky, next door to Beaubourg, should now be completed, and the *mediathèque* is open for public consultation Mon, Wed, Thurs & Fri 1.30–5.30pm (closed second half July & first half Aug; 20F). Concerts are advertised in *Pariscope*, etc.

Other Paris-based practitioners of contemporary and experimental music include Laurent Bayle, Jean-Claude Eloy, Pascal Dusapin, Luc Ferrarie, and the English composer George Benjamin. Among the younger generation of less sectarian composers, some names to look out for are Nicos Papadimitriou, Thierry Pécourt, François Leclere, Marc Dalbavie, and Georges Aperghis, whose speciality is musical theatre.

Music and Nightlife

Music and Nightlife

The Big Performance Halls

Events at any of the performance spaces listed below will be well advertised on billboards and posters throughout the city. Tickets can be obtained at the halls themselves, though it's easier to get them through agents like *FNAC* or *Virgin Megastore* (see p.341).

Le Bataclan, 50 bd Voltaire, 11e; ☎01.47.00.39.12 (Mº Oberkampf). One of the best places for visiting and native rock bands.

Forum des Halles, *niveau* 3, Porte Rambuteau, 15 rue de l'Équerre-d'Argent, 1er; ☎01.42.03.11.11 (Mº Châtelet). Varied functions – theatre, performance art, rock, etc, often with foreign touring groups.

Maison des Cultures du Monde, 101 bd Raspail, 6e; ☎01.45.44.72.30 (Mº Rennes). All the arts from all over the world, for once not dominated by Europeans.

Olympia, 28 bd des Capucines, 9e; ☎01.47.42.25.49 (Mº Madeleine/Opéra). An old music hall hosting occasional well-known rock groups and large popular concert performers.

Palais des Congrès, place de la Porte-Maillot, 17e; ☎01.40.68.22.22 (Mº Porte-Maillot). Opera, ballet, orchestral music, trade fairs, and the superstars of US and British rock.

Palais Omnisports de Bercy, 8 bd de Bercy, 12e; ☎01.43.46.12.21 (Mº Bercy). Opera, cycle racing, Bruce Springsteen, ice hockey, and Citroën launches – the newest multi-purpose stadium with seats to give vertigo to the most level-headed, but an excellent space when used in the round.

Palais des Sports, Porte de Versailles, 15e; ☎01.48.28.40.48 (Mº Porte-de-Versailles). Another vast-scale auditorium, ideal if you want to see your favourite rock star in miniature a kilometre away.

Zenith, Parc de la Villette, 211 av Jean-Jaurès, 20e; ☎01.42.08.60.00/ 01.42.40.60.00 (Mº Porte-de-Pantin). Seating for 6500 people in an inflatable stadium designed exclusively for rock and pop concerts. Head for the concrete column with a descending red aeroplane.

Film, Theatre and Dance

Movie-goers have a choice of around 300 films showing in Paris in any one week, which puts moving visuals on an equal footing with the still visuals of the art museums and galleries. And they cover every place and period, with new works (with the exception of British movies) arriving here long before they reach London and New York. If your French is good enough to cope with subtitles, go and see a Senegalese, Taiwanese, Brazilian or Finnish film that might never be seen in Britain or the US at all, except perhaps on television at 4am a year or two later.

Theatre, on the other hand, is less accessible to non-natives, especially the *café-théâtres* touted by "knowing" guide-writers. However, there is stimulation in the cult of the director; Paris is home to Peter Brook, Ariane Mnouchkine and other exiles, as well as French talent. Also, transcending language barriers, there are exciting developments in dance, much of it incorporating mime, which, alas, no longer seems to have a separate status.

Tipping

It is common practice in Parisian theatres and occasionally in independent cinemas for the ushers to expect a small tip from each customer (5F or so) and to ask for the money if it is not immediately forthcoming.

As for **sex shows** and **soft porn cabarets**, with names that conjure up the classic connotations of the sinful city – *Les Folies Bergères* or the *Moulin Rouge* – they thrive and will no doubt continue for as long as Frenchmen's culture excuses anything on the grounds of stereotyped female beauty. See p.168 for a fuller account.

Listings

Listings for all films and stage productions are detailed in *Pariscope*, etc, with brief résumés or reviews. Venues with wheelchair access will say "*accessible aux handicapés*".

Film

In recent years several of the tiny little *salles* in obscure corners of the city, where you could be the sole audience for an afternoon showing of *Hiroshima Mon Amour* or *The Maltese Falcon*, have closed. The big cinema chains, UGC and Gaumont, have opened new multi-screen cinemas equipped with escalators and popcorn carton holders by each seat. But there are more special film festivals these days, and Paris remains one of the few cities in the world in which it's possible to get not only serious entertainment but a serious film education from the programmes of regular – never mind the specialist – cinemas.

In a typical week it might be possible – not counting new and recent releases of American and other films – to catch retrospective seasons of films by Fassbinder, Antonioni, Orson Welles, Almodovar, David Lynch, Peter Greenaway, Polanski, and Serge Gainsbourg, a festival of contemporary Irish cinema, Vietnamese films, and any number of historically significant movies such as Fritz Lang's *Metropolis*, Oshima's *Empire of the Senses*, Kubrick's A *Clockwork Orange*, Orson Welles' *Citizen Kane*, Sergio Leone's *Once Upon a Time in the West*, Visconti's *Death in Venice*,

Film, Theatre and Dance

French cinema

The French have treated cinema as an art form, deserving of state subsidy, ever since its origination with the Lumière brothers in 1895. Investment in film production is nearly twice the level in the UK, and the number of films made annually is three times as great. The medium has (as yet) never had to bow down to TV, the seat of judgement stays in Cannes, and Paris remains the cinema capital of Europe.

The **Cinémathèque Française**, based at the Palais de Chaillot but at some point in the future to be moved to the new Palais du Cinéma in the west wing of the Palais de Tokyo, possesses the largest collection of silent and early talkie movies in the world. All the pre-1960 stock, whose celluloid nitrate is dissolving, is being transferred onto acetate. Some of these, including turn-of-the-century one-minute shorts featuring new inventions such as the hosepipe, can be seen during the Festival CinéMemoire.

While the old is treasured and preserved, the new in French cinema for a while revolved around the Nureyev of moviedom, **Gérard Depardieu**. Jean-Paul Rappeneau's 1990 screening of the late nineteenth-century play *Cyrano de Bergerac*, starring Depardieu and with rhyming couplets throughout, was the most expensive French film ever made and exceeded all box-office expectations in America and Britain. Depardieu went on to act in English in the American film *Green Card*, then played Columbus in the American-French co-production *1492: Conquest of Paradise* before returning to French cinema as as the collier Maheu in the movie version of Zola's *Germinal*.

Contemporary politics and cinematographic innovation made a dramatic comeback to French cinema with the 1996 winner of the French Césars award for best film, *La Haine* by Mathieu Kassovitz. A brilliant and strikingly original portrayal of exclusion and racism in the Paris *banlieue*, *La Haine* is worlds away from the early 1980s style of movies that used Paris as a backdrop, such as *Diva* and *Subway*. But *La Haine* would seem to be a one-off, with glossy star-vehicle "heritage" movies like *Beaumarchais l'Insolent* (a French equivalent of *The Madness of King George*) and *Le Hussard sur le Toit*, which broke budget records and flopped, lapping up funds. There is still no current force in French movie-making to touch on the prolific New Wave period of the Sixties, pioneered by **Jean-Luc Godard** and others. Luc Besson, Leos Carax, Agnès Varda, Bernard Tavernier and Patrice Chereau (also well known as a theatre director) are some of the stalwarts; and the mature talent of Jean-Paul Belmondo and Claude Lelouch was impressive in *Les Misérables*; and many foreign directors – notably Kurosawa, Wajda and Kieslowski – work or have worked in France, benefiting from public subsidies.

The row over cultural subsidies in the mid-1990s GATT negotiations revealed just how threatened France feels by American movie imports. The top box-office hits in Paris tend to be transatlantic imports, and a quick scan down the listings for any week shows a dominance of foreign films. Nonetheless, the city remains the perfect place to see movies, from the latest blockbuster to the least-known works of the earliest directors.

Louis Malle's *Zazie dans le Métro*, Carné's *Hôtel du Nord*, Rossellini's *Rome Open City* and Bresson's *Pickpocket*.

Almost all of the huge selection of **foreign films** will be shown at some cinemas in the original language – *version originale* or *v.o.* in the listings – as opposed to *version française* or *v.f.*, which means it's dubbed into French. *Version anglaise* or *v.a.* means it's the English version of an international co-production.

Among cinemas that run **seasons** of the work of a particular director or actor/actress, such as those outlined above, are the *Action* chain, the *Escurial*, the *Entrepôt* and *Le Studio 28*. In addition, some of the **foreign institutes** in the city have occasional screenings, so if your favourite director is a Hungarian, a Swede or a Korean, for example, check what's on at those countries' cultural centres. These will be listed along with other cinema-clubs and museum screenings under "*Séances exceptionnelles*" or "*Ciné-clubs*", and are usually cheaper than ordinary cinemas.

Times and Prices

Movie-going is not exclusively an evening occupation: the *séances* (programmes) start between 1 and 3pm at many places, sometimes even at 11am, and usually continue through to the early hours.

Cinema **tickets** rarely need buying in advance, and are cheap by European standards. The average price is around 40–45F; and most cinemas have lower rates on Monday or Wednesday, as well as reductions for students from Monday to Thursday. Some matinée *séances* also have discounts. UGC and Gaumont sell multi-tickets which work out at around 30F a seat, and some independents offer a *carte de fidélité*, giving you a free sixth entry.

For three days at the end of June during the **Fête du Cinéma**, any film ticket at a whole host of Paris cinemas gives you a "passport" to see as many other films as you like for 10F a go. In February there's a week of **18 hrs 18F** in which 6pm screenings cost 18F.

All Paris' cinemas are non-smoking, and in some cases the ushers are unwaged and so positively *have* to be tipped (see box on p.353).

Cinemas

L'Arlequin, 76 rue des Rennes, 6ᵉ (Mᵒ St-Sulpice). Owned by Jacques Tati in the

Film,
Theatre and
Dance

Film Festivals

Every year Paris plays host to an **International Festival of Women's Films**, which takes place at the end of March or beginning of April. It's organized by the *Maison des Arts* in Créteil, a southeastern suburb at the end of the Balard–Créteil métro line. 1996 was the eighteenth year of this festival, which has been very influential in promoting and encouraging works by women, particularly in France. Chinese, Indian, Russian, American, Japanese and European films compete for the eight awards, six of which are voted for by the audiences. Programme details are available from mid-March onwards, from the *Maison des Arts*, place Salvador-Allende, 94000 Créteil; ☎01.43.99.22.11 (Mᵒ Créteil-Préfecture) or on the Internet at http://www.coproductions.com/AFIFF/.

At the same time of year and also in the suburbs, in Bobigny to the northeast of the city, the *Magic Cinéma* (rue du Chemin-Vert, 9300 Bobigny; ☎01.48.30.32.87/01.41.60.00.71) runs a **Festival au Théâtre Cinéma**, which concentrates on the links between literature and the cinema.

CinéMemoire at the end of November and beginning of December, is a festival of restored old films in the city, shown with all the original trappings of organ or orchestral accompaniment (various venues; details from 29, rue du Colisée, 8e; ☎01.45.63.07.83).

Film,
Theatre and
Dance

1950s, then by the Soviet Union as the *cosmos* cinema until 1990, *L'Arlequin* has now been renovated and is once again the Latin Quarter's best cinephile's palace. There are special screenings of classics every Sunday at 11pm followed by debates in the café opposite.

L'Entrepôt, 7–9 rue Francis-de-Pressensé, 14e (M° Pernety). One of the best alternative Paris movie houses, which has been keeping ciné-addicts happy for years with its three screens dedicated to the obscure, the subversive and the brilliant, including among those categories many Arab and African films. It also shows videos, satellite and cable TV, and has a bookshop (Mon–Sat 2–8pm) and a restaurant (daily noon–midnight).

L'Escurial Panorama, 11 bd de Port-Royal, 13e (M° Gobelins). Combining plush seats, big screen, and more art than commerce in its programming policy, this cinema is likely to be showing something like *Eraserhead* on the small screen and the latest offering from a big-name director – French, Japanese or American – on the panoramic screen (never dubbed).

Grand Action & Action Écoles, 5 & 23 rue des Écoles, 5e (M° Cardinal-Lemoine/Maubert-Mutualité); **Action Christine Odéon**, 4 rue Christine, 6e (M° Odéon/St-Michel). The Action chain specializes in new prints of ancient classics and screens collections of contemporary films from different countries.

Le Grand Rex, 1 bd Poissonnière, 2e (M° Bonne-Nouvelle). Just as outrageous as the *Pagode* (see opposite) but in the kitsch line, with a Metropolis-style tower blazing its neon name, 2750 seats and a ceiling of stars and a Spanish city skyline. It's the good old Thirties public movie-seeing experience, though unfortunately all foreign films are dubbed.

Gaumont Grand Écran Italie, 30 place d'Italie, 13e (M° Place-d'Italie). Three screens – the *grand écran*, 24m wide, is the largest in Europe. Big-draw movies inevitably, with all foreign titles dubbed.

Le Latina, 20 rue du Temple, 4e (M° Hôtel-de-Ville). Specializes in Latin

American, Portuguese and Spanish films, as well as food and art in its gallery and restaurant.

Lucernaire Forum, 53 rue Notre-Dame-des-Champs, 6e (Notre-Dame-des-Champs/Vavin). An art complex with three screening rooms, two theatres, an art gallery, bar and restaurant, showing old arty movies and undubbed current films from all round the world.

Max Linder Panorama, 24 bd Poissonnière, 9e (M° Bonne-Nouvelle). Opposite *Le Grand Rex*, this always shows films in the original, and has almost as big a screen, state-of-the-art sound, and Art Deco décor.

La Pagode, 57bis rue de Babylone, 7e (M° François-Xavier). The most beautiful of all the capital's cinemas, originally transplanted from Japan at the turn of the century to be a rich Parisienne's party place. The wall panels of the *Grande Salle* are embroidered in silk; golden dragons and elephants hold up the candelabra; and a battle between Japanese and Chinese warriors rages on the ceiling. If you don't fancy the films being shown, you can still come here for tea and cakes (see p.258).

Le Studio des Ursulines, 10 rue des Ursulines, 5e (M° Censier-Daubenton). This was where *The Blue Angel* had its world première. Avant-garde movies are still premièred here, often followed by debates with the directors and actors.

Le Studio 28, 10 rue de Tholozé, 18e (M° Blanche/Abbesses). In its early days, after one of the first showings of Buñuel's *L'Age d'Or*, this was done over by extreme right-wing Catholics who destroyed the screen and the paintings by Dali and Ernst in the foyer. The cinema still hosts avant-garde premières, followed occasionally by discussions with the director, as well as regular festivals.

Cinémathèques

For the seriously committed film-freak, the best movie venues in Paris are the three **cinémathèques**, in the *Salle Garance* on the top floor of Beaubourg,

4e (Mº Rambuteau; closed Tues); the *Cinémathèque Française* in the Musée du Cinéma, Palais de Chaillot, corner of avs Président-Wilson and Albert-de-Mun, 16e (Mº Trocadéro); and at the *Salle République*, 18 rue du Faubourg-du-Temple, 11e (Mº République), with screenings every day. These give you a choice of over fifty different films a week, many of which would never be shown commercially, and tickets are only 28F (17F for students). Plans are afoot to transfer the *cinémathèque* and the Musée du Cinéma at the Palais de Chaillot to the new Palais du Cinéma in the west wing of the Palais de Tokyo (13 av Président Wilson, 16e; Mº Iéna). As well as watching movies, you'll be able to consult a vast amount of documentation, from film scripts and storyboards to photographs of shoots, film posters and reviews in the Bibliothèque de l'Image/Filmothèque (BIFI).

The *Vidéothèque de Paris*, in the Forum des Halles (see p.91), is another excellent-value venue for the bizarre or obscure on celluloid or video. Their repertoires are always based around a particular theme with some connection with Paris.

The Largest Screen

There is one cinematic experience that has to be recommended, however trite and vainglorious the film – and that's the 180-degree projection system called Omnimax, which works with a special camera and a 70mm horizontally progressing – rolling loop – film.

There are fewer than a dozen **Omnimax** cinemas in existence, of which two are to be found in Paris. One is **La Géode**, the mirrored globe bounced off the **Cité des Sciences** at La Villette, and the other, its offspring, is the new **Dôme-Imax** on the *Colline de l'Automobile* beside the Grande Arche at La Défense.

Unfortunately, Omnimax owners are not the sort to produce brilliant films. What you get is a *Readers' Digest* view of outer space, great cities of the world, monumental landscapes or whatever, on a screen wider than your range of vision

into which you feel you might fall at any moment. Low-flying shots, or shots taken from the front of moving trains, bobsleighs, cars and so on are sensational.

There are several screenings a day at both places, but you usually need to book in advance (**La Géode**: Tues–Sun 10am–9pm; tickets 57F/44F or 92F/79F for combined ticket with Cité des Sciences, programme details on ☎01.36.68.29.30, and best way to avoid the queues is to go at 9.30am for the first showing; Mº Porte-de-la-Villette/Corentin-Cariou; **Le Dôme-Imax**; daily 1–8.15pm; tickets 55F/40F; information ☎01.46.92.45.45; Mº/RER line A, Grande-Arche-de-la-Défense). The films are the same for months at a time (listed in *Pariscope*, etc). Don't worry if you don't understand French – in this instance it's a positive advantage.

Also in the Parc de la Villette is the **Cinaxe**, which shows high-resolution action film with seats that move in synchronization with the image (part of the Cité des Sciences; Tues–Sun 11am–6pm; 33F/29F or 29F supplement to Cité des Sciences ticket; not recommended if you're pregnant or have a weak heart; no admission for under-4s).

Finally, from mid-July to mid-Aug, epics, musicals, westerns and old-time Hollywood classics are shown in the **open air** on the Prairie du Triangle in the Parc de la Villette (☎01.40.03.75.00; free).

Television

At the other end of the scale of screen size, **French TV** has six channels – three public, *F2*, *Arte* and *F3*; one subscription, *Canal Plus* (with some unencrypted programmes); and two commercial open broadcasts, *TF1* and *M6*.

In addition there are the **cable** networks, including *France Infos* French news, *CNN*, the *BBC World Service*, *Euronews* with news in the original version from around Europe, *MTV* and *Planète* specializing in documentaries.

Arte, which took over the defunct La Cinq channel in September 1992, is a joint Franco-German cultural venture. Its

Film, Theatre and Dance

For more details of La Villette, *see p.178.*

Film, Theatre and Dance

highbrow programmes, daily documentaries, *Horizon* from the BBC, art criticism, serious French and German movies and complete operas are transmitted simultaneously in French and German.

Canal Plus is the main **movie channel** (and funder of the French film industry), with repeats of foreign films usually shown at least once in the original language. *F3* screens a fair selection of serious movies, with its *Cinéma de Minuit* slot late on Sunday nights good for foreign, undubbed films.

The main French **news broadcasts** are at 8.30pm on *Arte* and at 8pm on *F2* and *TF1*. At 7am on *Canal Plus* (unencrypted) you can watch the American *CBS* evening news.

Theatre

Certain directors in France do extraordinary things with the medium of **theatre**. Classic texts are shuffled into theatrical moments, where spectacular and dazzling sensation takes precedence over speech. Their shows are overwhelming: huge casts, vast sets (sometimes real buildings never before used for theatre), exotic lighting effects, original music scores. A unique experience, even if you haven't understood a word.

Ariane Mnouchkine, whose *Théâtre du Soleil* is based at the *Cartoucherie* in Vincennes, is the director par excellence of this form. Her production of *Les Atrides* (*The House of Atreus* in her own translation from Euripides and Aeschylus) stunned and delighted audiences in France, Britain and the United States. It lasted ten hours – relatively short for the *Théâtre du Soleil*, some of whose performances have gone on for several days. In 1996 she again dazzled French and foreign critics with her interpretation of Molière's *Tartuffe*, set in a contemporary North African city with Tartuffe as a young mullah.

Peter Brook, the English director based at the *Bouffes du Nord* theatre, is another great magician of the all-embracing several-day show. Another big name, though often involved in films rather than the theatre, is **Patrice Chereau**. Any show by these three

should not be missed, and there are likely to be other weird and wonderful productions by younger directors such as Jérôme Savary following their example.

At the same time, bourgeois farces, postwar classics, Shakespeare, Racine and the like, are staged with the same range of talent or lack of it that you'd find in London or New York. What you'll rarely find are the home-grown, socially concerned and realist dramas of the sort that have in the past kept theatre alive in Britain. An Edward Bond or David Edgar play crops up in translation often enough, although, frequently, such adaptations are not very successful because of the enormous differences between the British and French ways of thinking. The French equivalent, however, hardly exists.

The great generation of French or Francophone dramatists, which included Anouilh, Genet, Camus, Sartre, Adamov, Ionesco and Cocteau, came to an end with the death of **Samuel Beckett** in 1990 and Ionesco in 1994. Their plays, however, are still frequently performed. The Huchette has been playing Ionesco's *La Cantatrice Chauve* every night since October 1952, and Genet's *Les Paravents*, which set off riots on its opening night, can now be included alongside Corneille and Shakespeare in the programme of the **Comédie Française**, the national theatre for the classics.

Perhaps partly as a corollary of this pre-eminence of directors, the general standard of acting is not as high as in Britain. A production is more likely to be sustained by one or two big-name actors, supported by a cast of nonentities. Growing commercial pressures don't help either.

But one of the encouraging things about France and its public authorities is that they take their culture, including the theatre, seriously. Numerous theatres and theatre companies in Paris are subsidized, either wholly or in part, by the government or the Ville de Paris. And the suburbs are not left out, thanks to the ubiquitous **Maisons de Culture**, which were the brainchildren of André Malraux, man of letters, de Gaulle's wartime aide, and, eventually, in the 1960s, his Minister of Culture. Ironically, however, although they were designed to bring culture to the masses, their productions are often among the most "difficult" and intellectually inaccessible.

Another plus is the openness to **foreign influence** and foreign work. There is little xenophobia in Paris theatre; Argentinian Jorge Lavelli and Catalan Lluis Pasqual direct at the Théâtre National de la Colline and at the Odéon, and foreign artists are as welcome as they've always been. In any month there might be an Italian, Mexican, German or Brazilian production playing in the original language, or offerings by radical groups from Turkey, Iraq or China, who have no possibilities of a home venue.

The best time of all for theatre lovers to come to Paris is for the **Festival d'Automne** from October to December (see p.78), an international festival of all the performing arts, which attracts stage directors of the calibre of the American Bob Wilson, who directed the Opéra Bastille's highly successful *Magic Flute*, and Polish director Tadeusz Kantor.

Noteworthy Venues

Bouffes du Nord, 37bis bd de la Chapelle, 10e; ☎01.46.07.34.50 (Mº La Chapelle). Peter Brook has made this his permanent base in Paris, where he produces such events as the nine-hour show of the Indian epic, *Mahabharata*.

Cartoucherie, rte du Champ-de-Manoeuvre, 12e (Mº Château-de-Vincennes). As well as the *Théâtre du Soleil* (see p.358; ☎01.43.74.24.08), the *Cartoucherie* is home to the French-Spanish troupe, *Théâtre de l'Épée de Bois* (☎01.43.08.39.74), the *Théâtre de la Tempête* (☎01.43.28.36.36), the *Théâtre du Chaudron* (☎01.43.28.97.04) and the *Théâtre de l'Aquarium* (☎01.43.74.99.61).

Théâtre de Gennevilliers, Centre Dramatique National, 41 av des Grésillons, Gennevilliers; ☎01.41.32.26.26 (Mº Gabriel-Péri). Several stimulating productions by Bernard Sobel have brought acclaim – and audiences – to this suburban venue in recent years.

Comédie Française (national theatre), 2 rue de Richelieu, 1er; ☎01.40.15.00.15 (Mº Palais-Royal). The national theatre for the classics. However, the trend now seems to be to cut down on traditional productions, with the exception of Molière and Feydeau, in favour of more contemporary work and modernized versions of the classics.

Film, Theatre and Dance

Buying Theatre Tickets

The easiest place to get tickets to see a stage performance in Paris, with the possible exception of one of the *FNAC* shops and *Virgin Megastore* (see pp.323 and 341), is at the ticket kiosks on place de la Madeleine, 8e, opposite no. 15 and on the parvis of the Gare du Montparnasse, 14e (Tues–Sat 12.30–8pm, Sun 12.30–4pm). They sell same-day tickets at half price and 16F commission, but queues can be very long.

Booking well in advance is essential for new productions and all shows by the superstar directors. These are sometimes a lot more expensive – quite reasonably so when they are the much-favoured epics, lasting seven hours or even carrying on over several days.

Prices for the theatre vary between 30F (up in the gods) and 170F for state theatres, 60F and 260F for privately owned ones, and around 115F for the suburban venues. Previews at half price are advertised in *Pariscope*, etc, and there are weekday discounts for students. Most theatres are closed on Monday and Sunday. For three days at the end of April or beginning of May the Mairie de Paris sponsors a free second ticket for every theatre ticket bought (info on ☎01.42.78.44.72).

Film,
Theatre and
Dance

Maison des Arts de Créteil, place Salvador-Allende, Créteil; ☎01.43.99.22.11 (Mᵒ Créteil-Préfecture). As well as its movie programmes (see box on p.235), this also serves as a lively suburban theatre with a festival near the beginning of May, *Festival Exit*, of multi-cultural performance.

Maison de la Culture de Bobigny, 1 bd Lénine, Bobigny; ☎01.41.60.72.72 (Mᵒ Pablo-Picasso). The resident company, MC93, succeeds with highly challenging productions, for example a dramatization of *De Rerum Natura (The Nature of Things)* a scientific treatise by the first-century BC Roman poet Lucretius, using the auditorium as stage, considerable amounts of Latin, a boxing match, mime and giant swings.

Odéon Théâtre de l'Europe (national theatre), 1 place Paul-Claudel, 6e; ☎01.44.41.36.36 (Mᵒ Odéon). Contemporary plays, as well as *version originale* productions by well-known foreign companies. During May 1968, this theatre was occupied by students and became an open parliament with the backing of its directors, Jean-Louis Barrault (of Baptiste fame in *Les Enfants du Paradis* and who died in 1994) and Madeleine Renaud, one of the great French stage actresses. Promptly sacked by de Gaulle's Minister for Culture, they formed a new company and moved to the disused Gare d'Orsay. Their final years in the Théâtre du Rond-Point gave Paris its best performances of Beckett.

Théâtre des Amandiers, 7 av Pablo-Picasso, Nanterre, 92; ☎01.46.14.70.00 (*RER* Nanterre-Université and theatre bus). Renowned as the suburban base for Jean-Paul Vincent's exciting productions.

Théâtre des Artistic-Athévains, 45bis rue Richard-Lenoir, 11e; ☎01.43.56.38.32 (Mᵒ Voltaire). Small company heavily involved in community and educational theatre.

Théâtre de la Bastille, 79 rue de la Roquette, 11e; ☎01.43.57.42.14 (Mᵒ Bastille). One of the best places for new work and fringe productions.

Théâtre de la Colline (national theatre), 15 rue Malte-Brun, 20e; ☎01.43.66.43.60 (Mᵒ Gambetta). Most of the work put on by Jorge Lavelli is twentieth-century and innovative, and nearly always worth seeing.

Théâtre de la Commune, 2 rue Edouard-Poisson, Aubervilliers; ☎01.48.34.67.67 (Mᵒ Aubervilliers). Suburban theatre with an excellent reputation based on the work of director Brigitte Jacques.

Théâtre de l'Est Parisien, 159 av Gambetta, 20e; ☎01.43.64.80.80 (Mᵒ Gambetta). Well respected for its innovative work.

Théâtre de la Main-d'Or, 15 passage de la Main-d'Or, 11e; ☎01.48.05.67.89 (Mᵒ Bastille). An interesting experimental space, with occasional classics and English productions including a festival of English theatre in the spring.

Théâtre National de Chaillot (national theatre), Palais de Chaillot, place du Trocadéro, 16e; ☎01.47.27.81.15 (Mᵒ Trocadéro). The great Antoine Vitez may be no more, but the mega-spectacles go on under the directorship of Jérôme Savary. Roger Planchon from Lyon has his Parisian showings here.

Théâtre de Nesle, 8 rue de Nesle, 6e; ☎01.46.34.61.04 (Mᵒ Odéon). New French work, as well as English and American.

Théâtre Silvia-Montfort, Parc Georges-Brassens, 106 rue Briançon, 15e; ☎01.45.31.10.96 (Mᵒ Porte-de-Vanves). A pyramidal theatre, playing "classics" such as Anouilh, but also dedicated to staging original works.

Café-Théâtre

Literally a revue, monologue or mini-play performed in a place where you can drink, and sometimes eat, **café-théâtre** is probably less accessible than a Racine tragedy at the *Comédie Française*. The humour or puerile dirty jokes, wordplay, and allusions to current fads, phobias and politicians can leave even a fluent French speaker in the dark.

If you want to give it a try, the main **venues** are concentrated around the Marais. Tickets average around 80F and it's best to book in advance – the spaces are small – though you have a good chance of getting in on the night during the week.

Blancs-Manteaux, 15 rue des Blancs-Manteaux, 4e; ☎01.48.87.15.84 (Mº Hôtel-de-Ville/Rambuteau). Somewhat cramped venue, beneath a restaurant.

Café de la Gare, 41 rue du Temple, 4e; ☎01.42.78.52.51 (Mº Hôtel-de-Ville/Rambuteau). This may not be operating its turn-of-the-wheel admission price system any more, but it has retained a reputation for novelty.

Point Virgule, 7 rue Ste-Croix-de-la-Bretonnerie, 4e; ☎01.42.78.67.03 (Mº Hôtel-de-Ville/St-Paul). Occasionally interesting, but more often predictable and self-regarding.

Dance and Mime

In the 1970s all the dancers left Paris for New York, and only **mime** remained as the great performing art of the French, thanks to the *Lecoq School of Mime and Improvisation*, and the famous practitioner **Marcel Marceau**. Since Marceau's demise, no new pure mime artists of his stature have appeared. Lecoq foreign graduates return to their own countries, while the French incorporate their skills into dance, comedy routines and improvisation. While this cross-fertilization has given rise to new standards in performing art, it is still a pity that mime by itself is rarely seen (except on the streets, and on Beaubourg's piazza in particular).

The best-known and loved French clown, **Coluche**, died in a motorcycle accident in 1986. Most of his acts were incomprehensible to foreigners, save jests such as starting a campaign for the presidency, for which he posed nude with a feather up his bum. A troupe of mimes and clowns who debunk the serious in literature rather than politics are *La Clown Kompanie*, famous for their Shakespearean tragedies turned into farce. Joëlle Bouvier and Régis Obadia trained both at dance school and at Lecoq's; their company, *L'Esquisse*, combines both disciplines, takes inspiration from paintings, and portrays a dark, hallucinatory world.

The renaissance of French **dance** in the 1980s was not, on the whole, Paris-based. Subsidies have gone to regional companies expressly to decentralize the arts. But all the best contemporary practitioners come to the capital regularly. Names to look out for are Régine Chopinot's troupe from La Rochelle, Jean-Claude Gallotta's from Grenoble, Roland Petit's from Marseille, Dominique Bagouet's from Montpellier, and Joëlle Bouvier and Régis Obadia's from Angers. Creative choreographers based in or around Paris include Maguy Marin, Karine Saporta, François Verret, Jean-François Duroure and the Californian Carolyn Carlson.

Humour, everyday actions and obsessions, social problems, and the darker shades of life find expression in the myriad current dance forms. A multi-dimensional performing art is created by combinations of movement, mime, ballet, music from the medieval to contemporary jazz-rock, speech, noise, and theatrical effects. The Gallotta-choreographed film *Rei-Dom* opened up a whole new range of possibilities. Many of the traits of the modern epic theatre are shared with dance, including crossing international frontiers.

Many of the theatres listed above under drama include both mime and dance in their programmes: the Théâtre de la Bastille shows works by young dancers and choreographers; Maguy Marin's company is based at the Créteil Maison des Arts and François Verret's at the Maison de la Culture in Bobigny, where a prestigious competition for young choreographers is held in March; and the Théâtre des Amandiers in Nanterre hosts major contemporary works.

Film, Theatre and Dance

Film, Theatre and Dance

Plenty of space and critical attention are also given to **tap**, **tango**, **folk** and **jazz dancing**, and visiting traditional dance troupes from all over the world. There are also a dozen or so black African companies in Paris, who, predictably, find it hard to to compete with Europeans and the fashionable Japanese *butoh* for venues, as well as several Indian dance troupes, the *Ballet Classique Khmer*, and many more from exiled cultures.

As for **ballet**, the principal stage is at the newly renovated Opéra Garnier, home to the *Ballet de l'Opéra National de Paris* whose current star choreographer is Jérôme Robbins. After a troubled period under the directorship of the late, great Rudolf Nureyev, many of the best French classical dancers have returned to the company, with the exception, however, of the ravishing superstar Sylvie Guillem who is determined to plough her own independent furrow. Paris has also lost Maurice Béjart – wooed back to his home town of Marseille – who used to run the *Ballet du XXe Siècle*. But ballet fans can still be sure of masterly performances, at the Opéra Garnier, the Opéra Bastille, the Théâtre des Champs-Elysées and the Théâtre Musical de Paris.

The highlight of the year for dance is the *Concours International de Danse de Paris* in October and November, which involves contemporary, classical and different national traditions (☎01.45.22.28.74). The *Danses d'Avril* festival at the *Ferme du Boisson* (see below) is a showcase for contemporary dance. Other festivals combining theatre, dance, mime, classical music and its descendants include the *Festival Exit* in Creteil (see p.306), the *Paris Quartier d'Été* from mid-July to mid-August (☎01.44.83.64.40) and the *Festival d'Automne* from mid-September to mid-December (☎01.42.96.12.27), where Trisha Brown always makes an appearance.

Venues

Centre Beaubourg, rue Beaubourg, 4ᵉ; ☎01.44.78.13.15 (Mº Rambuteau/RER Châtelet-Les Halles). The *Grande Salle* in the basement is used for dance performances by visiting companies.

Centre Mandapa, 6 rue Wurtz, 13ᵉ; ☎01.45.89.01.60 (Mº Glacière). The one theatre dedicated to traditional dances from around the world.

Ferme du Boisson, 77 allée de la Ferme, Noisiel; ☎01.64.62.77.77 (*RER* Noisiel). A suburban venue reknowned for avant-garde perfomances and its *Danses d'Avril* festival in April.

L'Espace Kiron, 10 rue la Vacquerie, 11ᵉ; ☎01.44.64.11.50 (Mº Voltaire). Venue for experimental dance and performance art.

Opéra de Bastille, place de la Bastille, 12ᵉ; ☎01.40.01.17.89 (Mº Bastille). Stages some productions by the *Ballet de l'Opéra National de Paris.*

Opéra de Paris-Garnier, place de l'Opéra, 9ᵉ; ☎01.40.01.17.89 (Mº Opéra). Main home of the *Ballet de l'Opéra National de Paris* and the place to see ballet classics.

Regard du Cygne, 210 rue de Belleville, 20ᵉ; ☎01.43.58.55.93 (Mº Place-des-Fêtes). Innovative and exciting new work by companies such as Fabrice Dugied's troupe are performed here.

Théâtre de la Bastille, 76 rue de la Roquette, 11ᵉ; ☎01.43.57.42.14 (Mº Bastille). As well as more traditional theatre (see p.360), there are also dance and mime performances including productions by the *Théâtre Contemporain de la Danse.*

Théâtre des Champs-Élysées, 15 av Montaigne, 8ᵉ; ☎01.49.52.50.50 (Mº Alma-Marceau). Forever aiming to outdo the Opéra with even grander and more expensive ballet productions.

Théâtre Musical de Paris, place du Châtelet, 4ᵉ; ☎01.40.28.28.40 (Mº Châtelet). It was here, in 1910, that Diaghilev put on the first season of

Russian ballet, assisted by Cocteau, Rodin, Proust and others. Though mainly used for classical concerts and opera it hosts topnotch visiting ballet companies.

Théâtre de la Ville, 2 place du Châtelet, 4e; ☎01.42.74.22.77 (Mº Châtelet). The height of success for dance productions is to end up here. Karine Saporta's work is regularly featured as is Maguy Marin and Pina Bausch, together with modern theatre classics, comedy and concerts.

Film,
Theatre and
Dance

Beyond the City

Chapter 20

Day Trips from Paris

T he region that surrounds Paris – known as the Île de France – and the borders of the neighbouring provinces are studded with large-scale **châteaux.** In this chapter, we detail a select few of them. Many were royal or noble retreats for hunting and other leisured pursuits; some, such as **Versailles**, were for more serious state show. However, if you have limited time and even the slightest curiosity about church buildings, your first priority should be to make instead for the **cathedral of Chartres** – which is all it is cracked up to be, and more. Also, much closer in, on the edge of the city itself, **St-Denis** has a cathedral second only to Notre-Dame among Paris churches. A visit to it could be combined with an unusual approach to the city: a walk back (the best direction to follow) along the banks of the **St-Denis canal.**

Note that Disneyland Paris has a chapter to itself, starting on p.392.

Whether the various outlying **museums** deserve your attention will depend on your degree of interest in the subjects they represent. Several, however, have authoritative collections: **china** at Sèvres, **French prehistory** at St-Germain-en-Laye, the **history of flying machines** at Le Bourget, and the **Île de France** at Sceaux.

But the most satisfying experience is undoubtedly **Monet's garden** at Giverny, the inspiration for all his water-lily canvases in the Marmottan and Musée d'Orsay.

We've also included a brief foray into the architecture and planning of the suburbs since the 1950s, culminating in the bizarre constructions in the sprawling satellite town of **Marne-la-Vallée.**

The Cathedrals

An excursion to **Chartres** can seem a long way to go from Paris just to see one building; but then you'd have to go a very long way indeed to find any edifice to beat it. The cathedral of **St-Denis**, right on the edge of Paris, predates Chartres and represents the first breakthroughs in Gothic art. It is also the burial place of almost all the French kings.

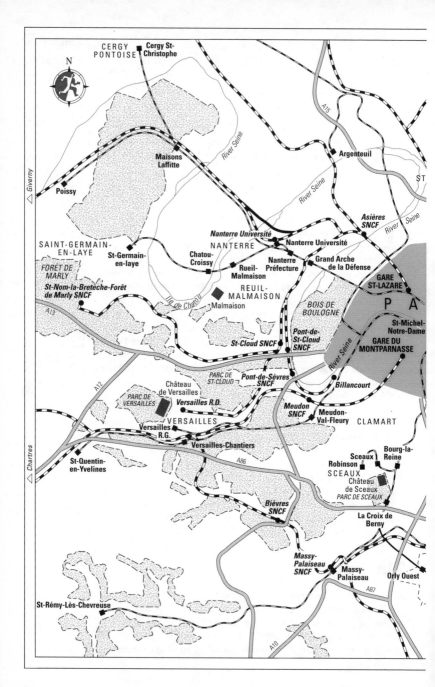

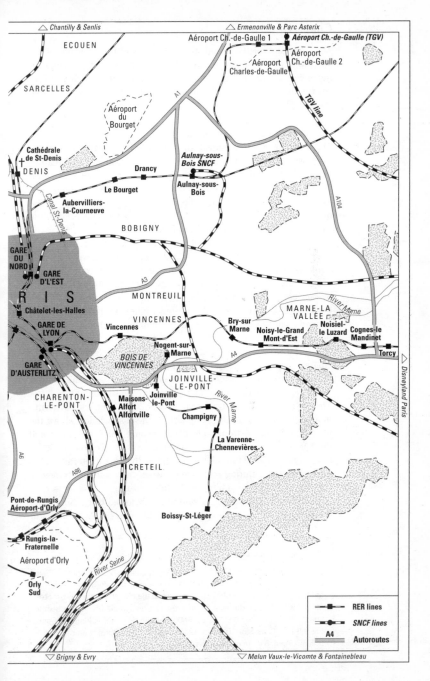

Chartres

The small and relatively undistinguished city of **Chartres** lies 80km southwest of Paris; an hour-long journey by train which brings an immediate reward in the moment as you approach, when you first see the great cathedral standing as if alone on the slight rise above the River Eure.

The Cathédrale Notre-Dame

The mysticism of medieval thought on life, death and deity, expressed in material form by the glass and masonry of the **cathedral** at Chartres (open for services only Sat after 5.45pm & Sun until 1pm), should best be experienced on a cloud-free winter's day. The low sun transmits the stained-glass colours to the interior stone, the quiet scattering of people leaves the acoustics unconfused, and the exterior is unmasked for miles around.

The best-preserved medieval cathedral in Europe is, for today's visitors, only flawed by changes in Roman Catholic worship. The immense distance from the door to the altar which, through mists of incense and drawn-out harmonies, emphasized the distance that only priests could mediate between worshippers and worshipped, has been abandoned. The central altar undermines (from a secular point of view) the theatrical dogma of the building and puts cloth and boards where the coloured lights should play.

A less recent change, that of allowing the congregation to use chairs, covers up the labyrinth on the floor of the nave – an original thirteenth-century arrangement and a great rarity, since the authorities at other cathedrals had them pulled up as distracting frivolities. The **Chartres labyrinth** traces a path over 200m long, enclosed within a diameter of 13m, the same size as the rose window above the main doors. The centre used to have a bronze relief of Theseus and the Minotaur and the pattern of the maze was copied from classical texts – the medieval Catholic idea of the path of life to eternity echoing Greek myth. During pilgrimages, when the chairs are removed, you may be lucky enough to see the full pattern.

But any medieval pilgrims who were projected to contemporary Chartres would think the battle of Armaggedon had been lost. For

---

Getting to Chartres

Hourly trains run to Chartres from Paris-Montparnasse (120F return), with a journey time of just under an hour. From the station, av J-de-Beauce leads up to place Châtelet. Diagonally opposite, past all the parked coaches, is rue Ste-Même, which meets rue Jean-Moulin. Turn left and you'll find the cathedral and the tourist office (☎02.37.21.50.00; summer Mon–Fri 9.30am–6.45pm, Sat 9.30am–6pm, Sun 10.30am–12.30pm & 2.30–6.30pm; winter Mon–Fri 9.30am–6pm, Sat 10am–5pm, Sun 10.30am–1pm).

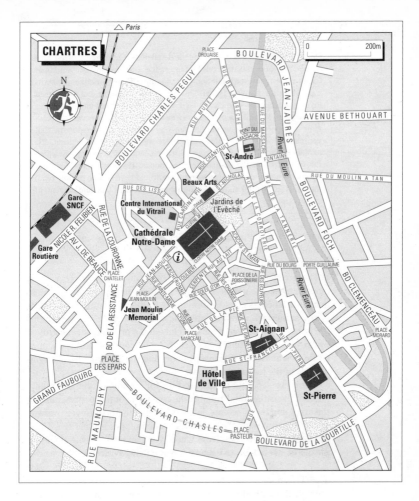

them, the cathedral would seem like an abandoned shrine with its promise of the New Jerusalem shattered. In **the Middle Ages** all the sculptures above the doors were painted and gilded while inside the walls were whitewashed. The colours in the clean stained-glass windows would have been so bright they would have glittered from the outside along with the gold of the crowns and halos of the statuary. Inside, the reflected patterns from the windows on the white walls would have jewelled the entire building.

It is difficult now to appreciate just how important **colour** used to be, when the minerals or plant and animal extracts to make the different shades cost time, effort and considerable amounts of money to procure. Perhaps, in a later age, the statues will again be painted.

Chartres

Demands for whitewash are occasionally made and ignored. Cleaning the windows does go on, but each one takes years and costs run into millions.

There remain, however, more than enough wonders to enthral modern eyes: the geometry of the building, unique in being almost unaltered since its consecration in the thirteenth century; the details of the stonework, most notably the western façade which includes the Portail Royal saved from the cathedral's predecessor, destroyed by fire in 1195 the Renaissance choir screen, and the hosts of sculpted figures above each transept door; and the shining circular symmetries of the transept windows.

There are separate admission fees for various of the less public parts of the cathedral. Probably the best value of these, preferable to the crypt and the treasures, is the climb up the **north tower** (crowds permitting; times vary, check in the cathedral; price 20F/12F). There are gardens at the back from where you can contemplate the complexity of stress factors balanced by the flying buttresses.

The Town

Though the cathedral is the main attraction, a wander round the **town** of Chartres also has its rewards. The **tourist office** on place de la Cathédrale can supply free maps and help with accommodation.

Occasionally stunning exhibitions of stained glass are displayed in a medieval wine and grain store, now the **Centre International du Vitrail**, at 5 rue du Cardinal Pie on the north side of the cathedral (Mon–Fri 9.30am–12.30pm & 1.30–6pm, Sat & Sun 10am–12.30pm & 1.30–7.15pm; 15F). The **Beaux Arts museum** in the former episcopal palace just north of the cathedral has some beautiful tapestries, a room full of Vlaminck, and Zurbaran's *Sainte Lucie*, as well as good temporary exhibitions (April–Sept daily 10am–6pm except Sun pm & Tues; Oct–March same days 10am–noon & 2–5pm; 20F/10F). Behind it, rue Chantault leads past old town houses to the

River Eure and Pont des Massacres. You can follow this reedy river lined with ancient wash-houses upstream via **rue des Massacres** on the right bank. On the left bank you'll see the Romanesque **church of St-André**, now used for art exhibitions, concerts, and so on.

Crossing the river at the end of rue de la Tannerie into rue du Bourg brings you back to the **medieval town**. At the top of rue du Bourg there's a turreted staircase attached to a house, and at the eastern end of place de la Poissonnerie, a carved salmon decorates an entrance. The **food market** takes place on place Billard and rue des Changes, and there's a **flower market** on place du Cy (Tues, Thurs & Sat).

Cloître-Notre-Dame, along the south side of the cathedral, has mainly expensive eating places, an exception being the popular *Café Serpente*, at no. 2. The best meals are at *La Truie qui File*, place de la Poissonnerie (☎02.37.21.53.90; closed Sun even, Mon & Aug); *Le Buisson Ardent*, 10 rue du Lait (☎02.37.34.04.666; closed Sun even). There are also innumerable *faste foude* joints. The liveliest place to drink on market days is *Le Brazza*, on place Billard.

At the edge of the old town, on the junction of bd de la Résistance and rue Jean-Moulin (to the right as you're coming up from the station), stands a memorial to **Jean Moulin**, Prefect of Chartres until he was sacked by the Vichy government in 1942. When the Germans occupied the town in 1940, Moulin refused under torture to sign a document to the effect that black soldiers in the French army were responsible for Nazi atrocities. He later became de Gaulle's number-one man on the ground, coordinating the Resistance. He died at the hands of Klaus Barbie in 1943.

St-Denis

St-Denis, just 10km north of the centre of Paris and accessible by métro, nonetheless remains a very distinct community, focused its magnificent cathedral, the **basilica of St-Denis**. Numbering 30,000 in 1870, 100,000 strong today, its people have seen their town grow into the most heavily industrialized community in France, bastion of the Red suburbs and stronghold of the Communist Party, with nearly all the principal streets bearing some notable left-wing name. Today, recession and the advance of the Pacific Rim have taken a heavy toll, though the decision to stage the 1998 Football World Cup finals in St-Denis may reverse its fortune somewhat – in honour of the occasion, a vast hi-tech stadium is being built just south of town. For all information about the event, call Mme Kouloumbri at eh St-Denis Office de Tourisme ☎01.42.43.33.35.

Although the centre of St-Denis still retains traces of its small town origins, the area immediately abutting the cathedral has been transformed in the last ten years into a fortress-like housing and shopping complex. The thrice-weekly **market**, however (Tues, Fri & Sun), still takes place in the square by the Hôtel de Ville and in the covered *halles* nearby. It is a multi-ethnic affair these days, and the quantity

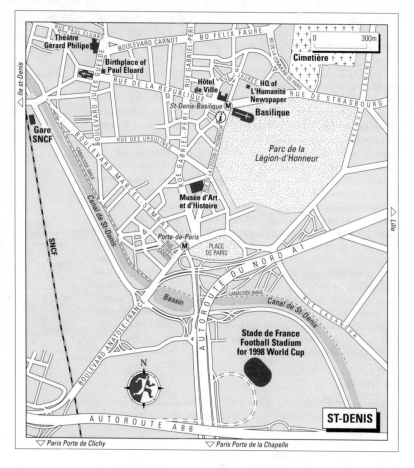

Map labels:

RUE PAUL ELUARD

Théâtre Gérard Philipe

BOULEVARD CARNOT

BD FELIX FAURE

Cimetière

0   300m

Birthplace of Paul Éluard

Île st-Denis

RUE DE LA RÉPUBLIQUE

BOULEVARD JULES GUESDE

RUE GABRIEL-PÉRI

Hôtel de Ville

RUE JAURÈS

HQ of L'Humanité Newspaper

BD DE LA COMMUNE DE PARIS

RUE DE STRASBOURG

AVENUE LÉNINE

St-Denis-Basilique (M)

Basilique

Gare SNCF

RUE DES URSULINES

BOULEVARD MARCEL SEMBAT

RUE GABRIEL-PÉRI

RUE DE LA LÉGION D'HONNEUR

Parc de la Légion-d'Honneur

CANALSIDE WALK

SNCF

Canal de St-Denis

Musée d'Art et d'Histoire

Lille

Porte-de-Paris (M)

RUE DOBROPOL SANDRE

PLACE DE PARIS

AUTOROUTE DU NORD A1

Bassin

CANALSIDE WALK

Canal de St-Denis

RUE CASANOVA

BOULEVARD ANATOLE FRANCE

AUTOROUTE A86

Stade de France Football Stadium for 1998 World Cup

N

ST-DENIS

▽ Paris Porte de Clichy   ▽ Paris Porte de la Chapelle

of offal on the butchers' stalls – ears, feet, tails and bladders – shows this is not rich folks' territory.

The Cathedral

Begun by Abbot Suger, friend and adviser to kings, in the first half of the twelfth century, **St-Denis cathedral** (April–Sept Mon–Sat 10am–6pm, Sun noon–6pm; Oct–March Mon–Sat 10am–5.30pm, Sun noon–5.30pm; closed Jan 1, May 1, Nov 1, Nov 11 & Dec 25) is generally regarded as the birthplace of the Gothic style in European architecture. Though its west front was the first ever to have a rose window, it is in the choir that you see the clear emergence of the new style: the slimness and lightness that comes with the use of the pointed arch, the ribbed vault and the long shafts of half-column rising from pillar to roof. It is a remarkably well-lit church too, thanks to the clerestory being almost wholly glass – another first for St-Denis – and the transept windows being so big that they occupy their entire end walls.

St-Denis

Once the place where the kings of France were crowned, since 1000 AD the cathedral has been the burial place of all but three. Their very fine **tombs and effigies** are deployed about the transepts and ambulatory (28F/18F). Among the most interesting are the enormous Renaissance memorial to François 1er on the right just beyond the entrance, in the form of a triumphal arch with the royal family perched on top and battle scenes depicted below, and the tombs of Louis XII, Henri II and Catherine de Médicis on the left side of the church. Also on the left, close to the altar steps, Philippe the Bold's is one of the earliest lookalike portrait statues, while to the right of the ambulatory steps you can see the stocky little general, Bertrand du Guesclin, who gave the English a run-around after the death of the Black Prince; and on the level above him, invariably graced by bouquets of flowers from the royalist contingent, the undistinguished statues of Louis XVI and Marie-Antoinette. Around the corner on the far side of the ambulatory is Clovis himself, king of the Franks way back in 500AD, a canny little German who wiped out Roman Gaul and turned it into France, with Paris for a capital.

The **tourist office** is located directly opposite.

The Musée d'Art et d'Histoire

Not many minutes' walk away on rue Gabriel-Péri is the **Musée d'Art et d'Histoire de la Ville de St-Denis** (Mon & Wed–Sat 10am–5.30pm, Sun 2–6.30pm; 15F/10F). The quickest route is along rue de la Légion-d'Honneur, then take the third right.

The museum is housed in a former Carmelite convent, rescued from the clutches of the developers and carefully restored. The exhibits on display are not of spectacular interest, though the presentation is excellent. The **local archeology** collection is good, and there are some interesting paintings of nineteenth- and twentieth-century industrial landscapes, including the St-Denis canal. The one unique collection is of documents relating to **the Commune**: posters, cartoons, broadsheets, paintings, plus an audiovisual presentation. There is also an exhibition of manuscripts and rare editions of the Communist poet, Paul Éluard, native son of St-Denis.

Canal St-Denis

To get to the canal – at the St-Denis end – follow rue de la République from the Hôtel de Ville to its end by a church. (To the right, at 46 bd Jules-Guesde, is the birthplace of the poet Paul Éluard.) Go down the left side of the church until you reach the canal bridge. Turn left, and you can walk all the way back to Paris along the towpath, taking something between ninety minutes and two hours. You come out at Porte de la Villette. There are stretches where it looks as if you're probably not supposed to be there. Just pay no attention and keep going.

Not far from the start of the walk, past some peeling villas with lilac and cherry blossom in their unkempt gardens, you come to a cobbled ramp on the left by a now-defunct restaurant, *La Péniche* (The Barge). Rue Raspail leads thence to a dusty square where the town council named a side street for IRA hunger-striker Bobby Sands. The whole neighbourhood is calm, poor and forgotten.

Continuing along the canal, you pass patches of greenery, sand and gravel docks, waste ground where larks rise above rusting bedsteads and doorless fridges, lock-keepers' cottages with roses and vegetable gardens, decaying tenements and improvised shacks, derelict factories and huge sheds where trundling gantries load bundles of steel rods onto Belgian barges. Barge traffic is regular and the life appears attractive, for these barges are proper family homes, with a dog at the prow, lace curtains at the window, potted plants, a bike propped against the cabin side, a couple of kids. But the keynote is decay and nothing looks set to last.

The Châteaux

The mansions and palaces around the capital are all very impressive on first sighting, but they can be hard work, if not downright tedious, to tour around – and none more so than **Versailles**.

That said, **Vaux-le-Vicomte**'s classical magnificence and **Fontainebleau**'s Italianate decoration are easy to appreciate; **Chantilly** has a gorgeous Book of Hours and a bizarre horse connection; and **Malmaison** is interesting for its former occupants. The main satisfaction, however, is in breathing country air in the **gardens, parks and forests** that surround the châteaux, and being able to get back to Paris comfortably in a day. If you get a bout of château mania, there are many more places in addition to those detailed in this section. Some, whose principal function these days is to house museums, are described later in this chapter, while the tourist office in Paris can provide full lists of others.

Versailles

The **Palace of Versailles** is one of the three most visited monuments in France. It was inspired by the young Louis XIV's envy of his finance minister's château at Vaux-le-Vicomte (see p.379), which he was determined to outdo. He recruited the design team of Vaux-le-Vicomte architect Le Vau, painter Le Brun and gardener Le Nôtre, and ordered something a hundred times the size. Versailles is a monster from every aspect – a mutated building gene allowed to run like a pounding fist for lengths no feet or eyes were made for, its décor a grotesque homage to the self-propaganda of the Sun King.

Getting to Versailles

Much the simplest way to get to Versailles from Paris is to take the *RER ligne* C5 to Versailles-Rive Gauche (40min). Once there, turn right out of the station and almost immediately left; the château itself, as big as a small town, is in front of you (10min walk).

The **tourist office** is at 7 rue des Réservoirs (☎01.39.50.36.22; daily May–Oct 9am–7pm, Nov–April 9am–12.30pm & 2–6.15pm), with an information desk (free maps of the park) in the *Manèges* shopping centre opposite the station. In summer there are additional information booths in the place d'Armes in front of the château.

In the park, a mere four square kilometres in area, the fountains only gush on selected days. The rest of the time the statues on the empty pools look like gargoyles dismantled from cathedral walls. It's hard to know why so many tourists come out here in preference to all except the most obvious sights of Paris. Yet they do, and the château is always a crush of bodies.

That this is not just a modern judgement could have no better witness than the English poet Alexander Pope. Satirizing the vainglorious and tasteless buildings of his rich contemporaries, he wrote in his *Epistle to the Earl of Burlington* of 1731:

Something there is more needful than Expence,
And something previous ev'n to Taste – 'tis Sense:
. . . Without it, proud Versailles, thy glory falls . . .

The Château

May–Sept Tues–Sun 9am–6.30pm; Oct–April Tues–Fri 9am–5.30pm, Sat & Sun 10am–5.30pm; closed Mon & hols. Last admission 30min before closing. Grands Appartements & Chambre du Roi 70F, 52F 18–25s; Grands Appartements only 45F, 35F 18–25s, 35F after 3.30pm & all day Sun.

Visitors to the château have a choice of itineraries, and whether to be guided or not. Apart from the state apartments of the king and queen and the Galerie des Glaces (the Hall of Mirrors, where the Treaty of Versailles was signed to end World War I), which you can visit on your own, most of the palace can only be viewed in guided groups, whose times are much more restricted. Long queues are common.

Don't set out to see all the palace in one day – it's not possible. Quite apart from the size, tours of some of the apartments run concurrently.

If you want to be sure of a place on a **guided tour**, it is wise to phone ahead (*Bureau d'Action Culturelle* for information ☎01.30.84.76.18, reservations ☎01.30.84.74.00). A word of warning, however, about guided tours: first, there are often several going on around you simultaneously in a distracting Babel of languages; second, the guides' spiel consists largely of anecdotes about court life with a heavy emphasis on numbers of mistresses and details of the cost, weight and so on of various items of furniture. There are more stimulating thematic tours lasting several hours and with a supplement of as much as 50F; information from the *Bureau d'Action Culturelle*; reservations must be made in person on the same day.

The construction of the château began in 1664 and lasted virtually until Louis XIV's death in 1715. It was never meant to be a home; kings were not homely people. Second only to God, and the head of an immensely powerful state, Louis XIV was an institution rather than a private individual. His risings and sittings, comings and goings, were minutely regulated and rigidly encased in ceremony, attendance at which was an honour much sought after by courtiers. Versailles was the headquarters of every arm of the state. More than twenty thousand people – nobles, administrative staff, merchants, soldiers and servants – lived in the palace in a state of unhygienic squalor according to contemporary accounts.

Following Louis XIV's death, the château was abandoned for a few years before being reoccupied by Louis XV in 1722. It remained the residence of the royal family until the Revolution of 1789, when the furniture was sold and the pictures dispatched to the Louvre. Thereafter it fell into ruin and was nearly demolished by Louis-Philippe. In 1871, during the Paris Commune, it became the seat of the nationalist government, and the French parliament continued to meet in Louis XV's opera building until 1879. Restoration only began in earnest between the two world wars.

The Park and Grand and the Petit Trianons

If you just feel like taking a look and a walk, the **park** (daily 7am–dusk, fountains play May–Sept Sun 11.15–11.45am & 3.30–5pm) is free except on Sundays (21F) and the scenery better the further you go from the palace. There are even informal groups of trees near the lesser outcrops of royal mania: the Italianate **Grand Trianon**, designed by Hardouin-Mansart in 1687 as a "country retreat" for Louis XIV, and the more modest Greek **Petit Trianon**, built by Gabriel in the 1760s (summer Tues–Sun 10am–6.30pm, winter Tues–Sun 10am–12.30pm & 2–5.30pm; Grand Trianon 25F/15F, Petit Trianon 15F/10F, combined ticket 30F/20F).

More charming and rustic than either of these is **Le Hameau de Marie-Antoinette**, a play-village and farm built in 1783 for Louis XVI's queen to indulge the fashionable Rousseau-inspired fantasy of returning to the natural life.

Distances in the park are considerable. If you can't manage them on foot, a *petit train* shuttles between the terrace in front of the château and the Trianons (30F/17F for kids aged 3–12). There are **bikes** for hire next door to the *Hôtel Palais Trianon* (see below), and **boats** for hire on the Grand Canal, within the park.

The Town

Versailles has a wonderfully posh place to take **tea**: the *Hôtel Palais Trianon*, where the final negotiations for the Treaty of

Versailles took place in 1919. Near the park entrance at the end of bd de la Reine, it offers trayfuls of *pâtisseries* to the limits of your desire for about 100F. The style of the hotel is very much that of the town in general. The dominant population is aristocratic, with those holding pre-revolutionary titles disdainful of those dating merely from Napoléon. On Bastille Day both lots show their colours, with black ribbons and ties in mourning for the guillotined monarchy.

Oddly enough, though, Versailles' **markets** offer excellent bargains, both for food (Sun, Tues & Fri 8am–1pm) and for second-hand stuff (Tues, Wed, Fri & Sat noon–7pm). The markets take place in the centre of town in the Marché Notre-Dame.

Vaux-le-Vicomte

April–Oct daily 10am–6pm, Nov–March closed much of the time – essential to phone ☎01.64.14.41.90. Château, gardens and Musée des Équipages 48F/38F; garden and museum 27F/22F.

Of all the great mansions within reach of a day's outing from Paris, the classical **château of Vaux-le-Vicomte** is the most architecturally harmonious, the most aesthetically pleasing and the most human in scale. It stands isolated in the countryside amid fields and woods, and its gardens make a lovely place to picnic.

The château was built between 1656 and 1661 for **Nicolas Fouquet**, Louis XIV's finance minister, to the designs of three of the finest French artists of the day. Fouquet, however, had little chance to enjoy his magnificent residence. On August 17, 1661, he invited the king and his courtiers to a sumptuous housewarming party. Three weeks later he was arrested – by d'Artagnan of Musketeer fame – charged with embezzlement, and clapped into jail for the rest of his life. Thereupon, the design team of Le Vau, Le Brun and Le Nôtre were carted off to build the king's own gross and gaudy piece of one-upmanship, the palace of Versailles.

Stripped of much of its furnishings by the king, the château remained in the possession of Fouquet's widow until 1705, when it was sold to the Maréchal de Villars, an adversary of the Duke of Marlborough in the War of Spanish Succession. In 1764 it was sold,

---

Getting to Vaux-le-Vicomte

By road, Vaux-le-Vicomte is 7km east of Melun, which is itself 46km southeast of Paris by the A4 autoroute (exit Melun-Sénart) or a little further by the A6 (exit Melun). **By rail** there are regular services from Gare de Lyon as far as Melun (40min), but, short of walking, the only means of covering the last 7km is **by taxi** (approximately 100–120F). There is a taxi rank on the forecourt of the train station, with telephone numbers to call if there are no taxis waiting. A cheaper way would be to take a coach tour – check the Paris **tourist office** (see p.37).

---

again, to the Duc de Choiseul-Praslin, Louis XV's navy minister.
His family kept it until 1875, when, in a state of utter dereliction –
the gardens had vanished completely – it was taken over by Alfred
Sommier, a French industrialist, who made its restoration and
refurbishment his life's work. It was finally opened to the public in
1968.

The Château and Gardens

Seen from the entrance the **château** is a rather austere grey pile built
on a stone terrace surrounded by an artificial moat and flanked by
two matching brick courtyards. It is only when you go through to the
south side, where the gardens decline in measured formal patterns of
grass and water, clipped box and yew, fountains and statuary, that
you can look back and appreciate the very harmonious and very
French qualities of the building – the combination of steep, tall roof
and central dome with classical pediment and pilasters. It is a building which manages to have charm in spite of its size.

As to the interior, the predominant impression as you wander
through is inevitably of opulence and monumental cost. The main
artistic interest lies in the work of **Le Brun**. He was responsible for
the two fine **tapestries** in the entrance, made in the local workshops
set up by Fouquet specifically to adorn his house (and subsequently
removed by Louis XIV to become the famous Gobelins works in
Paris), as well as numerous **painted ceilings**, notably in Fouquet's
bedroom, the Salon des Muses, his *Sleep* in the Cabinet des Jeux,
and the so-called King's bedroom, whose décor is the first example
of the style that became known as Louis Quatorze. The two oval marble tables in the Salle d'Hercule are the only pieces of furniture never
to have left the château.

Other points of interest are the **kitchens**, which have not been
altered since construction, and – if you read French – a room displaying **letters** in the hand of Fouquet, Louis XIV and other notables.
One, dated November 1794 (ie in mid-Revolution), addresses the
incumbent Duc de Choiseul-Praslin as *tu*. "Citizen," it says, "you've
got a week to hand over one hundred thousand pounds . . ." and signs
off with, "Cheers and brotherhood". You can imagine the shock to
the aristocratic system.

The **Musée des Équipages** in the stables comprises a collection of
horsedrawn vehicles, including the method of transport used by
Charles X fleeing Paris and the Duc de Rohan retreating from
Moscow (a Russian model).

Every Saturday evening from May to mid-October, between
8.30pm and 11pm, the state rooms are illuminated with a thousand
candles, as they probably were on the occasion of Fouquet's fateful
party (75F/65F entrance). **The fountains and other waterworks**
can be seen in action on the second and last Saturdays of each month
between April and October, from 3pm until 6pm.

Fontainebleau

Daily except Tues 9.30am–12.30pm & 2–5pm; 31F/20F/under-18s free, Sun 20F. Grands Appartements June–Oct 9.30am–5/6pm, Nov–May 9.30am–noon & 2–5pm. The Musée Napoléon and Musée Chinois are frequently – and unpredictably – closed for lack of staff. The Petits Appartements can only be seen on guided tours (Mon & public hols only). It's a mess. Phone before undertakng the journey: ☎01.60.71.50.77.

The **château of Fontainebleau**, 70km south of Paris, owes its existence to its situation in the middle of a magnificent forest, which made it the perfect base for royal hunting expeditions. Its transformation into a luxurious palace only took place in the sixteenth century on the initiative of François 1er, who imported a colony of Italian artists to carry out the decoration: among them Rosso il Fiorentino and Niccolò dell'Abate. It continued to enjoy royal favour well into the nineteenth century; Napoléon spent huge amounts of money on it, as did Louis-Philippe. And, after World War II, when it was liberated from the Germans by General Patton, it served for a while as Allied military HQ in Europe. The town in the meantime has become the seat of *INSEAD*, a prestigious and elite multi-lingual business school.

The **buildings**, unpretentious and attractive despite their extent, have none of the architectural unity of a purpose-built residence like Vaux-le-Vicomte. Their distinction is the sumptuous interiors worked by the Italians, notably the celebrated **Galerie François-1er** – which had a seminal influence on the subsequent development of French aristocratic art and design – the Salle de Bal, the Salon Louis-XIII, and the Salle du Conseil with its eighteenth-century decoration.

The **gardens** are equally luscious. If you want to escape into the relative wilds, head for the surrounding **Forest of Fontainebleau**, which is full of walking and cycling trails, all marked on Michelin map 196 (*Environs de Paris*). Its rocks are a favourite training ground for Paris-based climbers.

Getting to Fontainebleau

Getting to Fontainebleau from Paris is straightforward. By road it is 16km from the A6 autoroute (exit Fontainebleau). By train, it is 50 minutes from the Gare de Lyon to Fontainebleau-Avon station, whence bus #A takes you to the château gates in a few minutes. For further information, contact the SI at 31 place Napoléon (Mon–Sat 9am–12.30pm & 1.30–7pm, Sun 9am–12.30pm & 1.30–5pm; ☎01.64.22.25.68).

Chantilly

The main association with **Chantilly**, a small town 40km north of Paris, is horses. Some 3000 thoroughbreds prance the forest rides of a morning, and two of the season's classiest flat races are held here. The stables in the château are given over to a **museum** dedicated to live horses.

The Château

Château daily except Tues 10am–6pm, 39F/34F; park daily, 17F/10F; ☎01.44.57.08.00.

The Chantilly estate used to belong to two of the most powerful clans in France: first to the Montmorencys, then through marriage to the Condés. The present château was put up in the late nineteenth century. It replaced a palace, destroyed in the Revolution, which had been built for the Grand Condé, who smashed Spanish military power for Louis XIV in 1643. It's an imposing rather than beautiful structure, too heavy for grace, but it stands well, surrounded by water and looking out in a haughty manner over a formal arrangement of pools and pathways designed by the busy Le Nôtre.

The entrance to the château is across a moat past two realistic bronzes of hunting hounds. The visitable parts are all museum (same hours as the château): mainly an enormous collection of paintings and drawings. They are not well displayed and you quickly get visual indigestion from the massed ranks of good, bad and indifferent, deployed as if of equal value. Some highlights, however, are a collection of portraits of sixteenth- and seventeenth-century French monarchs and princes in the Galerie de Logis; interesting Greek and Roman bits in the tower room called the Rotonde de la Minerve; a big series of sepia stained glass illustrating Apuleius' *Golden Ass* in the Galerie de Psyche, together with some very lively portrait drawings; and, in the so-called Sanctuario, some Raphaels, a Filippino Lippi, and forty miniatures from a fifteenth-century Book of Hours attributed to the French artist Jean Fouquet.

The museum's single greatest treasure is in the library, the Cabinet des Livres, entered only in the presence of the guide. It is **Les Très Riches Heures du Duc de Berry**, the most celebrated of all Books of Hours. The illuminated pages illustrating the months of the year with representative scenes from contemporary (early 1400s) rural life – like harvesting and ploughing, sheep-shearing and pruning – are richly coloured and drawn with a delicate naturalism, as well as being of sociological interest. Unfortunately, and understandably, only facsimiles are on display, but they give an excellent idea of the original. Sets of postcards, of middling fidelity, are on sale at the entrance. There are thousands of other fine books here as well.

Chantilly

Sleeping Beauty's castle at Disneyland Paris *is based on an illustration in* Les Très Riches Heures; *see p.70.*

The Horse Museum

Daily except Tues April & July–Oct 10.30am–5.30pm, daily May & June 10.30am–5.30pm, Nov–March Mon–Fri 2–5pm Sat & Sun 10.30am–5pm; 50F/40F; ☎*01.44.57.13.13.*

Five minutes' walk along the château drive at Chantilly, the colossal stable block has been transformed into a museum of the horse, the **Musée Vivant du Cheval**. The building was erected at the beginning of the eighteenth century by the incumbent Condé prince, who believed he would be reincarnated as a horse and wished to provide fitting accommodation for 240 of his future relatives.

In the main hall horses of different breeds from around the world are stalled, with a ring for **demonstrations** (April–Oct 11.30am, 3.30pm & 5.15pm; Nov–March weekends & public hols 11.30am, 3.30pm & 5.15pm, weekdays 3.30pm only), followed by a series of life-size models illustrating the various activities horses are used for. In the rooms off the hall are collections of paintings, horseshoes, veterinary equipment, bridles and saddles, a mock-up of a blacksmith's, children's horse toys (including a chain-driven number, with handles in its ears, which belonged to Napoléon III), and a fanciful Sicilian cart painted with scenes of Crusader battles.

Malmaison

Daily except Tues May–Oct 10am–1pm & 1.30–6pm, Nov–March 10am–1pm & 1.30–5pm; combined ticket with Bois-Préau museum 28F/18F; guided tours only; ☎*01.1.29.05.55.*

The relatively small and surprisingly enjoyable **château of Malmaison** is set in the beautiful grounds of the Bois-Préau, about 15km west of central Paris. This was the home of the Empress Josephine. During the 1800–1804 Consulate, Napoléon would drive out at weekends, though by all accounts his presence was hardly guaranteed to make the party go with a bang. Twenty minutes was all the time allowed for meals, and when called upon to sing in party games, the great man always gave a rendition of *Malbrouck s'en Va-t'en Guerre* (*Malbrouck Goes to War*), out of tune. A slightly odd

Malmaison

choice, too, when you remember that it was Malbrouck, the Duke of Marlborough, who had given the French armies a couple of drubbings 100 years earlier. According to his secretary, Malmaison was "the only place next to the battlefield where he was truly himself". After their divorce, Josephine stayed on here, occasionally receiving visits from the emperor, until her death in 1814.

Visits today include private and official apartments, with some of their original furnishings, as well as Josephine's clothes, china, glass and personal possessions. During the Nazi occupation, the imperial chair in the library was rudely violated by the fat buttocks of Reichsmarschall Goering, dreaming perhaps of promotion or the conquest of Egypt. There are other Napoleonic bits in the **Bois-Préau museum** nearby.

On a high bump of ground behind the château, and not easy to get to without a car, is the 1830s fort of **Mont Valérien**. It was once a place of pilgrimage, but the Germans killed 4500 hostages and Resistance people there during the war. It is again a national shrine, though the memorial itself is not much to look at.

Other Museums

Of the assortment of museums in the general vicinity of Paris, the one with the widest appeal must be the **Musée de l'Île-de-France** at Sceaux, with its delightfully eclectic collection of mementos of the region. But for specialist interest, the **ceramics** at Sèvres, **prehistory** at St-Germain-en-Laye, and **aviation** at Le Bourget are all excellent. Some of the museums also provide a good excuse for wanderings in the countryside.

Musée de l'Air et de l'Espace

Aéroport du Bourget, Le Bourget (15km northeast of Paris). Daily except Mon 10am–5/6pm; 25F/20F. Take RER line B from Gare du Nord to Gare du Bourget, then bus #152 to Le Bourget/Musée de l'Air. Alternatively, take bus #350 from Gare du Nord, Gare de l'Est, and Porte de la Chapelle, or #152 from Porte de la Villette.

The French were always adventurous, pioneering aviators, and the name of **Le Bourget** is intimately connected with their earliest exploits. Lindbergh landed here after his epic first flight across the

At **Drancy**, near the Aéroport du Bourget, the Germans and the French Vichy regime had a transit camp for Jews en route to Auschwitz – this was where the poet Max Jacob, among others, died. A cattle wagon and a stone stele in the courtyard of a council estate commemorate the nearly 100,000 Jews who passed through here, of whom only 1518 returned.

Atlantic. From World War I until the development of Orly in the 1950s, it was Paris' principal airport.

Today Le Bourget is used only for internal flights (and for international arms fairs), while some of the older buildings have been turned into the museum of flying machines. It consists of five adjacent hangars, the first devoted to **space**, with rockets, satellites, space capsules, etc. Some are mock-ups, some the real thing. Among the latter are a Lunar Roving Vehicle, the Soyuz craft in which a French astronaut flew, and France's own first successful space rocket. Everything is accompanied by extremely good explanatory panels – though in French only.

The remainder of the exhibition is arranged in chronological order, starting with **Hangar A** (the furthest away from the entrance), which covers the period 1919–39. Several record-breakers here, including the *Bréguet XIX*, which made the first ever crossing of the South Atlantic in 1927. Also here is the corrugated iron job that featured so long on US postage stamps: a *Junkers F13*, which the Germans were forbidden to produce after World War I and which was taken over instead by the US mail.

Hangar B shows a big collection of World War II planes, including a *V-1* flying bomb and the Nazis' last jet fighter, the largely wooden *Heinkel 162A*. Incredibly, the plans were completed on September 24, 1944, and it flew on December 6. There are photographic displays and some revealing statistics on war damage in France. The destruction included two-thirds of rail wagons, four-fifths of barges, 115 large train stations, 9000 bridges, 80 wharves, and 1 house in 22 (plus 1 in 6 partially destroyed).

Hangars C and D cover the years 1945 to the present day, during which the French aviation industry, having lost eighty percent of its capacity in 1945, has recovered to a pre-eminent position in the world. Its high-tech achievement is represented here by the supersophisticated best-selling *Mirage* fighters, the first *Concorde* prototype and the *Ariane* space launcher (the two latter parked on the tarmac outside). No warheads on site, as far as we know . . . **Hangar E** has light and sporty aircraft.

Musée des Antiquités Nationales

Château de St-Germain-en-Laye, opposite St-Germain-en-Laye RER station (terminus of line A1); Wed–Sun 9am–5.15pm; 23F/16F/under-18s free.

The unattractively renovated château of St-Germain-en-Laye, 10km west of Malmaison and a total of 25km out of Paris, was one of the

Musée des Antiquités Nationales

main residences of the French court before the construction of Versailles. It now houses the extraordinary **national archeology museum**, which will prove of immense interest to anyone who has been to the prehistoric caves of the Dordogne.

The presentation and lighting make the visit a real pleasure. The extensive Stone Age section includes a mock-up of the **Lascaux caves** and a profile of Abbé Breuil, the priest who made prehistoric art respectable, as well as a beautiful collection of decorative objects, tools and so forth. All ages of prehistory are covered, right on down into historical times with Celts, Romans and Franks: abundant evidence that the French have been a talented arty lot for a very long time. The end piece is a room of **comparative archeology**, with objects from cultures across the globe.

From right outside the château, a **terrace** – Le Nôtre arranging the landscape again – stretches for more than 2km above the Seine with a view over the whole of Paris. All behind it is the **forest of St-Germain**, a sizable expanse of woodland, but crisscrossed by too many roads to be convincing as wilderness.

Musée de l'Île-de-France

Château de Sceaux. Take RER line B4 to Parc de Sceaux (15min from Denfert-Rochereau): turn left on av de la Duchesse-du-Maine, right into av Rose-de-Launay and right again on av Le-Nôtre and you'll find the château gates on your left (5–10min walk). Mon & Wed–Sun 10am–6pm, Oct–March closes 5pm; 23F/15F; disabled access.

The **château of Sceaux**, 20km south of Paris, is a nineteenth-century replacement of the original – demolished post-Revolution – which matched the now-restored Le Nôtre grounds of terraces, water and woods in classical geometry. It houses the newly renovated **Musée de l'Île de France**, which evokes the Paris countryside of the *ancien régime* with its aristocratic and royal domains; of the nineteenth century, with its riverside scenes and eating and dancing places, the *guinguettes*, that inspired so many artists; and documents the twentieth century's new towns and transport systems. There are models, pictures and diverse objects: a backpack hot chocolate dispenser with a choice of two brews, 1940s métro seats, early bicycles and a series of plates and figurines inspired by the arrival of the first giraffe in France in the 1830s. The changes since the days of the treehouse music and dance venue in Robinson are graphically illustrated, and though some of the rooms hold little excitement, most people, kids included, should find enough to make the visit worthwhile.

Temporary exhibitions and a summer **festival of classical chamber music** (mid-July to third week in Sept) are held in the Orangerie, which, along with the Pavillon de l'Aurore (in the northeast corner of the park), survives from the original residence (details of the concerts on ☎01.46.60.07.79). In the summer you can get snacks and drinks in the park.

Musée National de la Céramique

Place de la République, Sèvres. Daily except Tues 10am–5pm; 20F/13F/under-18s free. Take the métro to the Pont-de-Sèvres terminus, cross the bridge and spaghetti junction – the museum is the massive building facing the river bank on your right.

A ceramics museum may possibly seem a bit too rarefied an attraction to justify a trip out of Paris, but if you do have the taste, there is much to be savoured at Sèvres' **Musée National de la Céramique**. As well as French pottery and china, there's also Islamic, Chinese, Italian, German, Dutch and English produce, though the displays inevitably centre around a comprehensive collection of Sèvres ware, as the stuff is made right here.

Right by the museum is the **Parc de St-Cloud**, good for fresh air and visual order, with a geometrical sequence of pools and fountains. You could, if you wanted, take a train from St-Lazare to St-Cloud and head south through the park to the museum.

Giverny

Giverny, Normandy. Gardens all year Tues–Sun 10am–6pm; house April–Oct Tues–Sun 10am–noon & 2–6pm. Combined admission 36F/25F students, 15F under-12s; entrance to the gardens alone 25F/20F. Painters are allowed into the garden on Mon but by appointment only;: ☎01.32.51.28.21.

Monet's gardens in Giverny are in a class by themselves. They are a long way out from Paris (80km), in the direction of Rouen, and there's no direct transport. If you're planning a future holiday in Normandy, or if you're visiting in winter, leave them for another time. But, if not, consider making the effort – the rewards are greater than all the châteaux put together.

Monet lived in Giverny from 1883 till his death in 1926, and the gardens he laid out leading down from his house towards the river were considered by most of his friends to be his greatest masterpiece. Each month is reflected in a dominant colour, as are each of the rooms, hung as he left them with his collection of Japanese prints. May and June, when the rhododendrons flower round the lily pond and the wisteria winds over the Japanese bridge, are the best of all times to visit. But any month, from spring to autumn, is overwhelming in the beauty of this arrangement of living shades and shapes. Although you have to contend with crowds photographing

---

Getting to Giverny

Without a car, the easiest approach to Giverny is by **train** to Vernon from Paris-St-Lazare (35min–1hr; hourly). **Buses** meet each train for the 6km ride to the gardens or you can rent a **bike** or **walk**, in which case cross the river and turn right on the D5; take care as you enter Giverny to take the left fork, otherwise you'll make a long detour to reach the garden entrance.

Giverny

images of the waterlilies far removed from Monet's renderings, there's no place like it.

New Towns and Grands Ensembles

Investigating life in the **suburbs** is hardly a prime holiday occupation but if you are interested in housing and urban development, or the arrogance of architects and nose-length perspectives of planners, then the "Greater Paris" **new towns** of the 1970s and 1980s, and the 1950s and 1960s vast housing estates known as **Grands Ensembles**, could be instructive.

Wealthy Parisians who have moved out from the Beaux Quartiers have always had their flats or houses (with tennis courts and swimming pools) southwest of the city, in the garden suburbs that now stretch out beyond Versailles. Those forced to move by rising rents, or who have never afforded a Paris flat, live, if they're lucky, in the soulless *Villes Nouvelles*, and if not, in the *Grands Ensembles* that were the quick-fix solution to the housing crisis brought on by the postwar population growth and city-slum clearance programmes.

The *Villes Nouvelles* became the mode in the late 1960s when the accumulating problems of high-rise low-income society first started to filter through to architects and planners. Unlike their English equivalents, the Parisian new towns were grafted onto existing towns but conceived as satellites to the capital rather than places in their own right. Streets of tiny detached *pavillons* with old-time residents cower beneath buildings from another world. There's the unsettling reversal that the people are there because of the town, not vice versa. Added to which the town seems to be there only because of the rail and *RER* lines.

Sarcelles, 12km to the north, is the most notorious of the *Grands Ensembles*. It gave a new word to the French language, "*sarcellitis*", the social disease of delinquency and despair spread by the horizons of interminable, identical, high-rise hutches.

The film *La Haine* was shot in La Noe, an estate built in the 1960s for immigrant car workers in the Chanteloup near Sénart (southeast of Paris on the way to Melun). The success of the film brought tourists, sociologists and political commentators by the busful, but no investment or jobs for La Noe's 7000 residents. Resources instead have flowed into developments such as Roissypôle, a "business city" around Charles-de-Gaulle airport.

La Grande Borne, Evry and Cergy-Pontoise

A few years after Sarcelles' creation, at the end of the 1960s, the architect Émile Aillaud tried a very different approach in the *Grand Ensemble* called **La Grande Borne**. Twenty-five kilometres south of Paris and directly overlooking the Autoroute du Sud, which cuts it off from the town centre and nearest rail connection of Grigny, it was hardly a promising site. But, for once, a scale was used that didn't belittle the inhabitants and the buildings were shaped by curves instead of corners. The façades are coloured by tiny glass and ceramic tiles, there are inbuilt artworks – landscapes, animals, including two giant sculpted pigeons, and portraits of Rimbaud and Kafka – and the whole ensemble is pedestrian-only. Unfortunately the planners failed to integrate any small businesses or community spaces, so La Grande Borne remains a dormitory complex.

To get there by public transport is a bit exhausting: train from the Gare de Lyon, direction Corbeil-Essones, to Grigny-Centre, then bus or walk; but by road it's a quick flit down the A6 from Porte d'Orléans: turn off to the right on the D13 and both the first and second right will take you into the estate.

Having come out this way, you could also take a look at **Evry**, one of the five new towns in the Paris region (Evry *SNCF*, two stops on from Grigny). Follow the signs from Evry station to the *centre commercial* and keep going through it till you surface on a walkway that bridges bd de l'Europe. This leads you into Evry 1 housing estate, a multi-matt-coloured ensemble resembling a group of ransacked wardrobes and chests-of-drawers. The architects call it pyramidal and blather on about how the buildings and the landscape articulate each other. But it's quite fun as a monument, even if the "articulating" motifs on the façade overlooking the park are more like fossils than plants.

Cergy-Pontoise, 30km northwest of Paris (*RER* line A3, Cergy-St-Christophe), has giant clocks decorating its station. Take the left-hand exit and keep going straight up through pedestrianized squares until you see a high white column. Circled by awful mock-classical colonnades and mirrored façades, this is the start of an "Axe Majeur" pointing towards La Défense. The 3km vista has yet to have its full complement of architectural fantasies and may not have for a long time given the recession. There are very few cafés and brasseries in Cergy, and those there are seem full of arcade machines and bored men.

Marne-la-Vallée

The new town with the most to shock or amuse, or even please, is undoubtedly **Marne-la-Vallée**, where Terry Gilliam's totalitarian fantasy *Brasil* was filmed. It starts 10km east of Paris and hops for 20km from one new outburst to the next, with odd bits of wood and water in between, until it reaches its apogee, **Disneyland Paris** (see Chapter 21). All the *RER* stops from Bry-sur-Marne to Marne-la-Vallée/Chessy are in Marne-la-Vallée; journeys north or south from the rail line are not so easy.

To sample the architectural styles of Marne-la-Vallée you need only go as far as **Noisy-Le-Grand-Mont-d'Est**. You surface on the

Arcades, a stony substitute for a town square. And there you have the poetic panorama of a controlled community environment: bright-blue tubing and light-blue tiling on split-level walkways and spaceless concrete fencing; powder-blue boxes growing plants on buildings beside grey-blue roofs of multi-angled leanings; walls of blue, walls of white, deep blue frames and tinted glass reflecting the water of a chopped-up lake; islands linked by bridges with more blue railings . . .

The two acclaimed architectural pieces in this monolith have only one thing in their favour – neither displays a hint of blue. They are both low-cost housing units, gigantic and unmitigatedly horrible. The **Arènes de Picasso** is in the group of buildings to the right of the *RER* line as you look at the lakes from the *Arcades*, about 500m away. It's soon visible as you approach: two enormous circles like loudspeakers facing each other across a space that would do nicely for a Roman stadium. Prepare to feel as if the lions are waiting. At the other end of Noisy-Mont d'Est, facing the capital, is the extraordinary semicircle, arch and half-square of **Le Théâtre et Palacio d'Abraxas**, creation of Ricardo Boffil. Ghosts of ancient Greek designs haunt the façades, but proportion there is none, whether classical or any other.

Auvers-Sur-Oise

In spite of the difficulty of getting there, at least by public transport, **Auvers**, on the banks of the River Oise, about 35km northeast of Paris, makes an attractive rural excursion. It is the place where **Van Gogh** spent the last two months of his life, in a frenzy of painting activity, producing more canvases than the days of his stay. It was here, too, that he died, by his own hand.

The church at Auvers, the portrait of Dr Gachet, black crows flapping across a wheatfield – many of Van Gogh's best-known works belong to this period. He kept them stacked under the bed in the pitiful room he rented in the attic of the *Auberge Ravoux*, where he also died, in the arms of his brother, Theo, after an incompetent attempt to shoot himself.

On high days and holidays, you will not be alone in Auvers. Yet, in spite of its international shrine status, it retains its village and rural

---

Getting to Auvers

To reach Auvers **by road**, take the autoroute A15 from La Défense to Pontoise, the exit for Saint-Ouen-L'Aumône, then the SD4 to Auvers-sur-Oise. Otherwise there are **trains** from Gare du Nord, changing at Persan-Beaumont, or Gare St-Lazare, changing at Pontoise.

For something **to eat**, there's the reasonably priced *salon de thé, Les Roses Écossaises*, in a street that turns up to the church (salads for 45F), or the *Hostellerie du Nord* for something more substantial (menu at 120F). In the *Auberge Ravoux* itself you will pay upwards of 140F.

---

character, pretty well untroubled by souvenirs and teashops. The *Auberge Ravoux* is still there, repaired and renovated, on the main street. Van Gogh's room can be visited (Sept 15–April 15 Tues–Sun 10am–6pm, April 16–Sept 14 daily 10am–7pm; 30F, families 60F). It is surprisingly moving. There is a short video about his time in Auvers.

The **tourist office** opposite the gate (Manoir des Colombières, rue de la Sansonne; ☎01.30.36.10.06; Mon–Fri 9.30am–12.15pm & 1.30–5.45pm, Sat 9.30am–12.30pm & 1.45–6pm, Sun 10am–12.30pm & 1.30–6.30pm) dispenses further information. Daubigny, a nineteenth-century forerunner of the Impressionists, built a house in the village in the 1860s, his presence serving to attract other painters. His studio at 61 rue Daubigny is open to visitors (☎01.34.48.03.63; Easter–Nov daily except Mon 2–6.30pm; 20F). You can also make a rather special and fascinating tour of the world that the Impressionists lived in, with an infra-red helmet on your head, at the Château d'Auvers, at the entrance to the village (☎01.34.48.48.48; Tues–Sun Nov–April 10am–6pm, May–Oct 10am–8pm; 50F/40F/35F).

Most evocative of all is a walk through the old part of the village, past the church and the red lane into the famous wheatfield and up the hill to the cemetery where, against the far left wall in a humble ivy-covered grave, the Van Gogh brothers lie side by side.

Chapter 21

Disneyland Paris

C hildren will love Disneyland Paris, 25km east of the capital – there are no two ways about it. What their minders will think of it is another matter. For a start, there has to be the question of whether it's worth the money. Quite why American parents might bring their charges here is hard to fathom: even British parents might well decide that it would be easier, and cheaper, to buy a family package to Florida, where sunshine is assured, where Disney World has better rides (though Disneyland Paris is adding new attractions by the month), and where the conflict between enchanted kingdom and enchanting city does not arise.

In fact, foul north European weather does have its advantages. On an off-season wet and windy weekday (Mon & Thurs are the best), you can probably get round every ride you want.

With the opening of *Space Mountain*, Disneyland Paris does now provide a variety of good fear and thrill rides, though the majority of attractions remain very safe and staid. It takes its inspiration from film sets, not funfairs or big tops, which is why it's so wonderful for children. These sets are "real" – you can go into them and round them and the characters talk to you. All the structures are incredibly detailed, and their shades and textures have been worked out with the precision of a brain surgeon. But if you're not a child, solid three-dimensional buildings masquerading as flimsy film sets and con-

---

Getting to Disneyland Paris

From Paris, take *RER* line A (Châtelet-Les Halles, Gare-de-Lyon, Nation) to Marne-la-Vallée/Chessy, the Disneyland Paris stop. The journey takes about 40min, and costs 80F return.

If you're coming straight from the airport, there is one **shuttle bus every 45 min.** from Charles de Gaulle, and Orly (80F, no reductions for children). Marne-la-Vallée/Chessy also has its own *TGV* train station, linked to Roissy Charles-de-Gaulle station, and to Lille and Lyon. *Eurostar* now run trains direct from Britain to Disneyland.

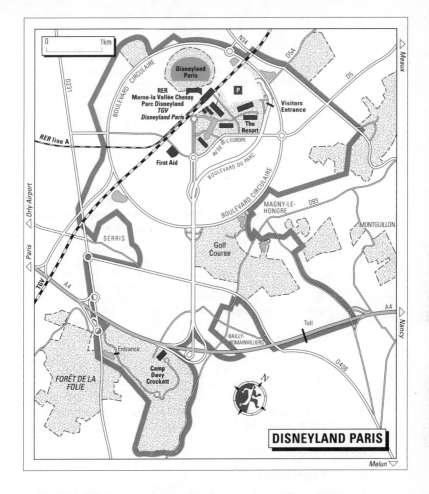

DISNEYLAND PARIS

stantly being filmed by swarming hordes of camcorder operators can well fail to fulfil any kind of escapist fantasy.

Besides the **Disneyland Paris Park**, the complex includes **Festival Disney** – the evening entertainments complex – and the Disney **hotels**. These, unlike the park, are radically different from their US or Japanese counterparts, having been designed especially for Europeans, who, according to Disney executives, invented fairy-tales and castles, but have run out of good ideas since.

Michael Eisner, Chair and Chief Executive of *Disney USA*, stated that "Euro Disney introduces a new level of design and innovation to Europe". Paris can take such bombast; it has existed for about 27 times the 71 years that Mr Eisner's company has been in business, and at the end of two millennia of sustained design achievement it remains the most innovative and stylish capital city in Europe. Disney's publicizing of Paris as a sideline tourist attraction is perhaps the most objectionable feature of the whole enterprise.

The Park

The introduction to Disneyland Paris is the same as in Florida, LA and Tokyo. **Main Street USA** is a mythical vision of a 1900s American town, West Coast with a dash of East Coast, but more the mishmash memories of a thousand and one American movies – without the mud.

Main Street leads to **Central Plaza**, the hub of the standard radial layout. Clockwise from Main Street are **Frontierland**, **Adventureland**, **Fantasyland** and **Discoveryland**. The **castle**, directly opposite Main Street across Central Plaza, belongs to Fantasyland. A steam train **Railroad** runs round the park with stations at each "land" and at the entrance.

Information and Access

You enter the park under Main Street Station. **City Hall** is to the left, where you can get **information** about the day's programming of events and about the hotels and evening's entertainments. For people in **wheelchairs** there's the *Guest Special Services Guide* that details accessibility of the rides. All the loos, phones, shops and restaurants have wheelchair access. Wheelchairs and pushchairs can be rented (30F plus 20F deposit) in the building opposite City Hall (you are allowed to bring in your own).

The **lost property office** is in City Hall. **Lost children** can be found in the Baby Care Centre by the Plaza Gardens Restaurant in the block between Main Street and Discoveryland. **Luggage** can be left in lockers in "Guest Storage" under Main Street Station (10F).

Food and Drink

The former Disney policy of no alcohol has been abandoned. Adults can now sip wine or beer at any of the park's restaurants, at a considerable price, of course. Coke, fruit juices, tea, coffee, chocolate, mineral water, fizzy drinks and alcohol-free cocktails are also readily available, and coffee away from Main Street is reasonably priced, if a bit weak compared to the French café norm. The **food** in Disneyland Paris, however, tastes as if it's been first cooked, then sterilized, then put on your plate. This is certainly not the place to blow precious meal money, so avoid the restaurants on Main Street and go for hamburgerish snacks at the various themed eateries around the park.

Officially, you're not allowed to bring any refreshments into the park, but, if you don't want to spend anything more than the entrance fee, eat a good Parisian breakfast and smuggle in some

---

Admission Fees for the Park

	Low season Oct–March excl Christmas Hols	High season April–Sept & 3rd week Dec–1st week Jan
1 day	150/120F	195/150F
2 days	290/230F	375/290F
3 days	405/325F	530/405F

Reduced tarif: children aged 3–11; under 3s free.

Passes, known as passports, can be purchased in advance at the Paris Tourist Office and at all Disney shops. Multi-day passes don't have to be used on consecutive days. Your wrist is stamped with invisible ink when you leave the park, allowing you to return.

Opening hours: highly variable. Generally low season Mon–Fri 10am–6pm, Sat & Sun till 8pm; high season daily 9am–11pm – but check exact opening hours before you go.

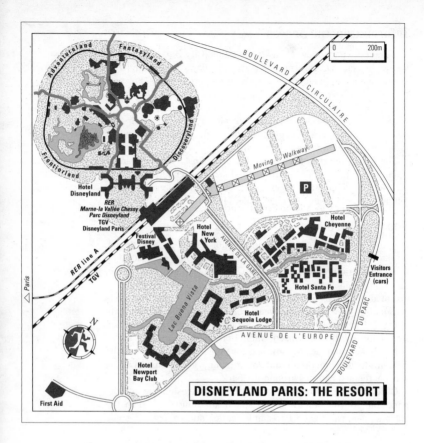

DISNEYLAND PARIS: THE RESORT

discreet snacks. Whether Goofy will turn nasty if he sees you eating a brand name not on the list of Disney sponsors is anyone's guess.

Smoking is allowed in the park, but not in the queues for the rides. You won't see a cigarette butt anywhere; all litter gets swept up instantaneously.

Main Street USA

On the corner of **Main Street**, *Town Square Photography* rents out still and video cameras, and sells film, lenses, cameras and tripods amid a collection of museum pieces. *Kodak* is one of Disney's main sponsors, and kiosks throughout the park sell film and offer two-hour print developing.

If you succumb at this stage to the idea of takeaway snapshots and the Disneyland Paris home movie, you'll be in serious financial trouble by the end of the day. As a practice run, see if you can get down Main Street without buying one of the following: a balloon, a hat with your name embroidered on it, an ice-cream, bag of sweets, silhouette portraits of your kids, the *Wall Street Journal* of 1902, a Disney version of a children's classic in hardback, an evening dress and suit and tie, a Donald Duck costume, a haircut, a model rocket, a genuine vintage car, a tea service and set of crystal glasses, some muffins, a Coke, a few cakes, a limited edition Disney lithograph, and a complete set of Disney characters in ceramics, metal, plastic, rubber or wool.

Leaving Main Street is quickest on foot (crowds permitting), although omnibuses, trams, horse-drawn streetcars, fire trucks and police vans are always on hand, plus the Disney *pièce de résistance*, the Railroad, for which **Main Street Station** has the longest queues.

The Railroad

The "attraction" on the circular Railroad is the **Grand Canyon Diorama** between Main Street and Frontierland. You enter a tunnel, and there below you, in all its tiny glory, is a miniature plastic Grand Canyon. While you ruminate on the fact that it is the *size* of the real Grand Canyon that is the source of its fascination, you can look out the window and appreciate how enormous Disneyland Paris is. Once you've been in the park a few hours, however, you may begin to find yourself unable to imagine any fantasy, discovery, adventure or "frontier experience" other than those created by the scenes laid out before you.

The Parades

La Parade Disney happens every day at 3pm. This is not a bad time to go on the most popular rides, but if you have kids they will no doubt force you to press against the barriers for the ultimate Disney event. The best place is on the queuing ramp for *It's a Small World*, right by the gates through which the floats appear. You can even see them over the fence "backstage", but Disney cast members are too well trained to be frowning and smoking a fag before their entrance. From here, the parade progresses, very slowly, to Town Square.

The parade floats represent all the top box-office Disney movies – *Dumbo, Snow White, Cinderella, Pinocchio, The Jungle Book, Peter Pan, Roger Rabbit, Beauty and the Beast, Aladdin* and *Toy Story*. Everyone waves and smiles, characters on foot shake hands with the kids who've managed to get to the front, and *Sleeping Beauty*'s medieval valets trundle bins and brushes to mop up behind the knights on horseback – a small concession to reality.

The night-time parades that feature in Florida are not a regular event here. They do have **Electrical Parades**, with characters' costumes strung with light bulbs, but not every night. **Firework displays** happen about twice a week during the summer (and have had to be toned down because of complaints by people living in villages 15km away). Check with the *Programme des Spectacles* available at City Hall for dates and times.

The Rides

The listings below are a selection of the best and worst rides, or "attractions", as they like to be called. As the guide you get on entry covers the park in a clockwise direction, this does the opposite in the hope that you might be competing with slightly fewer of your fellow *RER* travellers on the first few rides.

For the youngest kids, **Fantasyland** is likely to hold the most thrills. **Adventureland** has the most outlandish sets and two of the best rides – *Pirates of the Caribbean* and *Indiana Jones and the Temple of Doom.* Boat trips in canoes, keelboats and a paddle-steamer are to be had in **Frontierland,** where *Big Thunder Mountain* provides a decent roller-coaster ride. The one and only real heart-stopper, *Space Mountain,* is in **Discoveryland** along with Michael Jackson playing Captain Eo.

Discoveryland

Space Mountain
The star attraction and not for the faint-hearted. You're catapulted upwards, suspended weightless and then spun through an interstellar world at speeds of up to 40km, with a 360 degree sidewinder loop and corkscrew loop. The inspiration for the décor is Jules Verne's *From the Earth to the Moon.*

Le Visionarium
A slow build-up to a 360 degree film (shot with nine cameras and screened with nine projectors), presented by a robotic timekeeper host and his nervous android assistant. The story involves their travelling through time and picking up Jules Verne at the 1900 *Exposition Universelle* in Paris just as he and H G Wells are discussing time travel. They show Jules Verne all the wonders of contemporary life (*TGV*s and Mirages mainly), with bit parts for the likes of Gérard Depardieu as an airport baggage handler.

Queues

Disney's claim of average 15min queues are hard to believe. One-hour waits for the big rides are common – don't be fooled by the length of the visible queues; they often continue for a further 100m or more inside. After 5pm, first thing in the morning (though Disney hotel guests can enter the park up to an hour earlier than the general public) and during the (3pm) afternoon parade are the best times.

The only drawback to the complete surround film is that, not having nine eyes, you have to keep deciding which way to look. An English translation is available on headphones.

Les Mystères du Nautilus

More Jules Verne fetish, with a visit in a miniature *Nautilus* submarine – Captain Nemo's vessel in *20,000 Leagues Under the Sea* – through an oversize *Nautilus*. Apart from the giant squid attack on the big *Nautilus*' porthole window, what's supposed to impress you is the faithfulness of the décor to the original Disney set: the organ is even an exact replica.

Orbitron

The "rockets" on this hideous structure go round and round extremely slowly and go up (at your control) even more laggardly to a daring 30 degrees above the horizontal. Only suitable for small kids and for those who hate more violent rides (whatever the special boarding restrictions say).

Star Tours

Simulated ride in a spacecraft (with 60 other people all in neat rows) piloted by friendly incompetent C3PO of *Star Wars* fame. The projection of what you're supposed to be careering through is from the film, which is the only thing that makes this superior to space tour simulations elsewhere. When you come off the ride there's an arcade of video games, which only those adept at this kind of entertainment can work out how to use.

Cinémagique

A Michael Jackson movie with impressive animations, deafening sound, and 3-D specs to turn it from film into stage. Not for those with sensitive eyes or ears, nor for those whose sensitivities don't extend to adoring Mr Jackson.

Autopia

Miniature futuristic cars to drive on rails with no possibility of any dodgems stratagems.

Fantasyland

Le Château de la Belle au Bois Dormant

Sleeping Beauty was originally *La Belle au Bois*, heroine of a seventeenth-century French tale. Disney is very smug about having based the design of the castle on an illustration in the medieval manuscript *Les Très Riches Heures du Duc de Berry* (see p.383). In the picture, the château is a veritable fortress, grey and forbidding. In the foreground grumpy peasants till the fields. The château here copies the shapes of some of the turrets and the blue of the roof tiles, but that's about it. In fact, it has about the same connection as the originals of *Alice in Wonderland*, *The Jungle Book* and *La Belle au Bois* to the Disney versions.

You might wonder why after a hundred years' enforced slumber, finally rescued by the Prince's kiss, Sleeping Beauty should decide to turn her place of torment into a shopping arcade – but she has. The one thing you can't buy are the tapestries of Disney scenes that adorn the walls; these are genuine one-offs, painstakingly manufactured by the d'Aubusson workshops. Down below, in the dungeon, you'll find one of the better bits of fantasy apparatus: a huge dragon with red eyes that wakes on cue to snap its jaws and flick its tail.

Peter Pan's Flight
Disney must have cursed the appearance of *Hook* in the same year that Disneyland Paris opened. Anyone who has seen Spielberg's movie will have problems returning to the Disney version. But the very young will probably appreciate the jerky ride above Big Ben and the lights of London to Never-Never Land.

Le Pays des Contes de Fées
An unenthralling ride through fairytale scenes: *Alice in Wonderland*, *Pinocchio*, etc. Fine for little kids.

Le Carrousel de Lancelot
No complaints about this stately merry-go-round, whose every horse has its own individual medieval equerry in glittering paint.

Blanche-Neige et les Sept Nains
Unlike *Peter Pan*, *Snow White and the Seven Dwarfs* no longer exist as anything but their Disney manifestations. So this ride, through lots of menacing moving trees, swinging doors and cackling witches, is less grating than some of the others.

Mad Hatter's Tea Cups
These look wonderful – great big whirling teacups sliding past each other on a chequered floor – even if the connection with *Alice* is a little strained. Again, not a whizzy ride, but fun for younger ones.

Dumbo the Flying Elephant
Dumbo and his clones provide yet another safe, slow and low aerial ride.

Alice's Curious Labyrinth
The best things about this maze are the slow-motion fountains spurting jets of water over your head. There are passages that only those

under 1m can pass through, and enough false turns and exits to make it an irritatingly good labyrinth. As for the Disneyized White Rabbit, Tweedledum and Tweedledee and the Cheshire Cat, think of them as fellow tourists.

It's a Small World

This is a quintessential Disney experience: there's one in every Disneyland, and Walt considered it to be the finest expression of his corporation's philosophy. For a jaded adult, it is certainly one of the most entertaining of all the "attractions". It is quite definitively, and spectacularly, revolting. Your boat rides through a polystyrene and glitter world where animated dolls in national/ethnic/tribal costumes dance beside their most famous landmarks or landscapes, singing the song *It's a Small World*. The lyrics and the context make it clear that what unites the human race is the possibility that every child could have its imagination totally fed by Disney products. What a relief that the global telecommunications network trumpeted by *France Telecom*, who sponsor this "attraction", does not in fact reach every corner of the globe.

Adventureland

Le Passage enchanté d'Aladdin
A magic carpet ride – of course, with the film's soundtrack and all the highlights of the film, which rather lose their charm in three dimensions.

Pirates of the Caribbean
Disney are dead proud of this ride, which doesn't exist in the other Disneylands. The animated automata are the best yet, to the extent

that it's hard to be convinced that they're not actors (perhaps they are). The ride consists of an underground ride on water and down waterfalls, past scenes of evil piracy. Baddies in jail try coaxing a dog who has the keys in its mouth, sitting just out of reach. Battles are staged across the water, skeletons slide into the water, parrots squawk, chains rattle and a treasure trove is revealed. Note that queues for this one are horrendous, and once you're inside there's still a very long way to go.

Indiana Jones and the Temple of Doom (Le Temple du Péril)

This is a fast and quite violent roller-coaster with the first 360 degree loop on a Disney ride. Impressive stone vipers wait for you above the flame torches after you've lined up through tents filled with fossils and the ruined temple. Visually one of the best, though the ride itself doesn't last long.

La Cabane des Robinson

The 27-metre mock Banyan tree at the top of Adventure Isle is one of Disneyland Paris' most obsessively detailed creations, complete with hundreds of thousands of false leaves and blossoms. Not much point, though, unless you're a dedicated Swiss Family Robinson fan.

Adventureland Bazaar

This is a clever bit of shopping mall, disguised as a *souk*, with traditional Arab latticed walls, desert pastel colours, and all sorts of genuine Hollywood details. In the alleyway to the right of the archway (with Adventureland behind you) there's an inset in the wall where a laughing genie appears out of Aladdin's lamp every few minutes.

Frontierland

Big Thunder Mountain

A proper heart-in-the-mouth funfair thrill, this is a roller-coaster round the "mining mountain", under the lake to the other island and back again, with wicked twists and turns, splashes and collapsing roofs. The modelling on the upward sections is very effective; there are no Disney characters, and the dogs and goats do very good impressions of ordinary dogs and goats. Also, all the mining bits and pieces are genuine articles, bought up by Disney from museums and old mines in California and Nevada.

Phantom Manor

This starts off very promisingly: a *Psycho*-style house on the outside and Hammer Horror Edwardian mansion within. Holographic ghosts appear before cobweb-covered mirrors and ancestral portraits. But horror is not part of Disney's world; the dead bride story suddenly switches to a Wild West graveyard dance, and any lurking heebie-jeebies are well and truly scuttled. The other problem with Disney doing a Ghost Train ride is that the last thing they want to do is to scare you. So nothing jumps out and screams at you, no deathly hand skims your hair.

Rustler Roundup Shootin' Gallery
The only "attraction" for which there's a fee (10F), because, without some check, people stay for hours and hours when they might otherwise be consuming.

River Rogue Keelboats and Indian Canoes
Northern European weather is a problem here. If it's raining and there's more than a ripple on the lake's surface, the boats don't go out.

Festival Disney and the Hotels

When the park gates close, you're not supposed to hop it back to Paris. Oh no. It's Disney **festival** time. *Buffalo Bill's Wild West Show, Billy Bob's Country Western Saloon, Hurricanes, Annette's Diner, Rock 'n' Roll America* and the *Champions Sports Bar* await you with live music on summer nights: bluegrass bands, rock 'n' roll and the Top 40 hits.

When you're nearing exhaustion from so much enchantment, you can return to your themed **hotel** and have a sauna, a jacuzzi or a whirlpool dip, eat and drink some more, purchase more "giftware", play video games and be in bed in time to feel fresh and fit to meet Mickey and Minnie again over breakfast. Then out for a round of golf, a workout, some pony or bike riding or serious team sports. You can skate (in winter), sail (in summer), jog on a special "health circuit", shop some more, mainline more video games, and return to the park for another go at the queues.

In reality, partaking of this end of the resort on top of the park is well beyond most people's budgets. The cheapest hotel room off season is 300F (for 2 adults, 2 children), the Davey Crockett Campsite is 300F for a campsite or a cabin (again low season), and entertainments such as *Buffalo Bill's Wild West Show* (real guns, horses, bulls and bison) is 325F (200F for 3–11-year-olds) for the dinner and show. Accommodation is based on a family of four sharing a room or campsite.

Special packages are available (for details, phone ☎ 03.60.30.60.30 in France, ☎ 0990 030303 in the UK, ☎ 407/IN-DISNEY in the US).

Even if you don't stay, you may be intrigued enough to take a look at the state of **contemporary American architecture,** as patronized by the Disney Corporation. Producing some way-out buildings with big signatures was an important ploy in persuading the French cultural establishment to accept Disneyland Paris. Two hundred internationally renowned architects were invited to compete. Only one, James Stirling, turned down the offer, and only one non-American won a contract. The star of the show is **Frank D Gehry**, currently the most fashionable architect in the US, and renowned for "deconstructing" buildings (making them look as if a bomb's gone off in them).

A tour of **Festival Disney** and the **six hotels** would be quite an effort on foot. The hotels spread as if they've been given growth hormones, and the whole site is twice that of the park. Fortunately, however, you can get around by hopping in and out of the free bright yellow shuttle buses.

Festival Disney

This is the shops, shows, bars and restaurants complex between the station and the lake. It's Frank Gehry's work, and the bomb here has carried off the circus top tent, in case you were wondering what all the wires and zigzag towers were. There's a huge great red thing, a shiny white rocket cone thing, some greenhouses, and lots of slanting roofs and fairy lights.

Disneyland Hotel

Situated over the entrance to the park with wings to either side, the *Disneyland Hotel* is in the Main Street *à la Hollywood* style, and is the most upmarket. Rooms vary from 1650F off season to 1995F in peak season.

Hotel New York

The architect of the *Hotel New York*, Michael Graves, says things like "The idea of two dimensions versus three is something that Disney, in a sense, teaches in a very solemn way." A peculiar statement for anyone, even an architect and one who has spectacularly failed to translate the skyline of New York onto the outline of this hotel. It is a very ugly building, mixing Mickey-ear-shapes with post-modernist triangles, stripes and upright tombs in ochres and greys. Within, the furnishings are pseudo Art Deco with lots of apples – in case you'd failed to recognize New York from outside. The rooms are 1025F all year round.

Newport Bay Club

This "New England seaside resort circa 1900" spreads like a game of dominoes, with no apparent reason why the wings have turned one way rather than another. Blue and white striped canopies over the balconies fail to give it that cosy guesthouse feel, while the cupola roof resembles a cross between a Kaiser Wilhelm and a Nazi helmet. Robert Stern is the architect. Rooms start at 625F; 895F peak season.

Sequoia Lodge

Prison blocks, minus fence and watchtowers, masquerading as the National Parks of the western United States, by the only non-

American architect, Antoine Grumbach. Rooms from 525F to over 895F.

Hotel Cheyenne
Along with *Sante Fe*, *Cheyenne* deals with the scale problem by breaking into small units: the film-set buildings of a Western frontier town, complete with wagons, cowboys, a hanging tree and scarecrows. The architect is again Robert Stern. Rooms from 400F to 695F.

Hotel Santa Fe
Accommodation in the *Hotel Santa Fe* takes the form of smooth, mercifully unadorned, imitation sun-baked mud buildings in various shapes and sizes. Between them are tasteful car wrecks, a cactus in a glass case, irrigation systems, strange geological formations, ancient desert ruins and other products of the distinctly un-Disney imagination of New Mexican architect Antoine Predock. He cites Wim Wenders' film *Paris, Texas*, the Roman archeological site in Marne-la-Vallée and UFOs as part of his reference material. But the dominant icon, visible from the autoroute, is a scowling cheroot-chewing Clint Eastwood. This gigantic mural creates the drive-in movie entrance to *Santa Fe*. This is the cheapest hotel, at 300F (low season) to 595F.

Davy Crockett Range and camping
The log cabin experience at the Davy Crockett Range costs from 300F to 795F for a cabin (4–6 people). Camping on the ranch is 300F for the site (for 4 people). The range is a 15-minute drive from the park, with no transport laid on.

The Contexts

Paris in History

Two thousand years of compressed history – featuring riots and revolutions, shantytowns, palaces, new street plans, sanitation and the Parisian people.

Beginnings

It was **Rome** that put Paris on the map, as it did the rest of western Europe. When Julius Caesar's armies arrived in 52 BC, they found a Celtic settlement confined to an island in the Seine – the Île de la Cité. It must already have been fairly populous, as it had sent a contingent of eight thousand men to stiffen the Gallic chieftain Vercingétorix's doomed resistance to the invaders.

Under the name of Lutetia, it remained **a Roman colony** for the next three hundred years, prosperous commercially because of its commanding position on the Seine trade route, but insignificant politically. The Romans established their administrative centre on the Île de la Cité, and their town on the Left Bank on the slopes of the Montagne Ste-Geneviève. Though no monuments of their presence remain today, except the baths by the *Hôtel de Cluny* and the amphitheatre in rue Monge, their **street plan**, still visible in the north–south axis of rue St-Martin and rue St-Jacques, determined the future growth of the city.

When Roman rule disintegrated under the impact of **Germanic invasions** around 275 AD,

Paris held out until it fell to **Clovis the Frank** in 486. In 511 Clovis' son commissioned the cathedral of St-Étienne, whose foundations can be seen in the *crypte archéologique* under the square in front of Notre-Dame. Clovis' own conversion to Christianity hastened the **Christianization** of the whole country, and under his successors Paris saw the foundation of several rich and influential monasteries, especially on the Left Bank.

With the election of **Hugues Capet**, Comte de Paris, as king in 987, the fate of the city was inextricably identified with that of the **monarchy**. The presence of the kings, however, prevented the development of the middle-class, republican institutions that the rich merchants of Flanders and Italy were able to obtain for their cities. The result was recurrent political tension, which led to open **rebellion**, for instance, in 1356, when Étienne Marcel, a wealthy cloth merchant, demanded greater autonomy for the city. Further rebellions, fuelled by the hopeless poverty of the lower classes, led to the king and court abandoning the capital in 1418, not to return for more than a hundred years.

The Right Bank, Latin Quarter and Louvre

As the city's livelihood depended from the first on its river-borne trade, commercial activity naturally centred round the place where the goods were landed. This was the **place de Grève** on the **Right Bank**, where the Hôtel de Ville now stands. Marshy ground originally, it was gradually drained to accommodate the business quarter. Whence the continuing association of the Right Bank with commerce and banking today.

The **Left Bank**'s intellectual associations are similarly ancient, dating from the growth of schools and student accommodation round the two great **monasteries** of Ste-Geneviève and St-Germain-des-Prés. The first, dedicated to the city's patron saint who had saved it from destruction by Attila's raiders, occupied the site of the present Lycée Henri-IV on top of the hill behind the Panthéon. In 1215 a papal licence allowed the formation of what gradually became the renowned **University of Paris**, eventually to be known as **the Sorbonne**, after Robert de Sorbon, founder of a college for poor scholars. It was the fact that Latin was the language of the schools both inside and outside the classroom that gave the district its name of Latin Quarter.

To protect this burgeoning city, Philippe Auguste (king from 1180 to 1223) built the Louvre fortress (whose excavated remains are now on display beneath the Louvre museum) and a wall, which swung south to enclose the Montagne Ste-Geneviève and north and east to encompass the Marais. The administration of the city remained in the hands of the king until 1260, when St Louis ceded a measure of responsibility to the leaders of the Paris watermen's guild, whose power was based on their monopoly control of all river traffic and taxes thereon. The city's government, when it has been allowed one, has been conducted ever since from the place de Grève/place de l'Hôtel-de-Ville.

Civil Wars and Foreign Occupation

From the mid-thirteenth to mid-fourteenth centuries Paris shared the same unhappy fate as the rest of France, embroiled in the long and destructive **Hundred Years War** with the English. Étienne Marcel let the enemy into the city in 1357, the Burgundians did the same in 1422, when the Duke of Bedford set up his government of northern France here. Joan of Arc made an unsuccessful attempt to drive them out in 1429 and was wounded in the process at the Porte St-Honoré. The following year the English king, Henry VI, had the cheek to have himself crowned king of France in Notre-Dame.

It was only when the English were expelled – from Paris in 1437 and from France in 1453 – that the economy had the chance to recover from so many decades of devastation. It received a further boost when **François 1er** decided to re-establish the royal court in Paris in 1528. Work began on reconstructing the Louvre and building the Tuileries palace for Cathérine de Médicis, and on transforming Fontainebleau and other country residences into sumptuous Renaissance palaces.

But before these projects reached completion,

war again intervened, this time **civil war** between Catholics and Protestants, in the course of which Paris witnessed one of the worst atrocities ever committed against French Protestants. Some three thousand of them were gathered in Paris for the wedding of Henri III's daughter, Marguerite, to Henri, the Protestant king of Navarre. On August 25, 1572, St Bartholomew's Day, they were massacred at the instigation of the Catholic Guise family. When, through this marriage, Henri of Navarre became heir to the French throne in 1584, the Guises drove his father-in-law, Henri III, out of Paris. Forced into alliance, the two Henris laid siege to the city. Five years later, Henri III having been assassinated in the meantime, Henri of Navarre entered the city as king **Henri IV**. "Paris is worth a Mass", he is reputed to have said to justify renouncing his Protestantism in order to soothe Catholic susceptibilities.

The Paris he inherited was not a very salubrious place. It was overcrowded. No domestic building had been permitted beyond the limits of Philippe-Auguste's twelfth-century walls because of the guilds' resentment of the unfair advantage enjoyed by craftsmen living outside the jurisdiction of the city's tax regulations. The population had doubled to around 400,000, causing an acute housing shortage and a terrible strain on the rudimentary water supply and drainage system. It is said that the first workmen who went to clean out the city's cesspools in 1633 fell dead from the fumes. It took seven months to clean out 6420 cartloads of filth that had been accumulating for two centuries. The overflow ran into the Seine, whence Parisians drew their drinking water.

Planning and Expansion

The first systematic attempts at **planning** were introduced by Henri IV at the beginning of the seventeenth century: regulating street lines and uniformity of façade, and laying out the first geometric squares. The **place des Vosges** dates from this period, as does the **Pont Neuf**, the first of the Paris bridges not to be cluttered with medieval houses. Henri thus inaugurated a tradition of grandiose public building, which was to continue to the Revolution and beyond, that perfectly symbolized the bureaucratic, centralized power of the newly self-confident state concentrated in the person of its absolute monarch.

The process reached its apogee under **Louis XIV**, with the construction of the **boulevards** from the Madeleine to the Bastille, the places Vendôme and Victoire, the Porte St-Martin and St-Denis gateways, the Invalides, Observatoire and the Cour Carrée of the Louvre – not to mention the vast palace at **Versailles**, whither he repaired with the court in 1671. The aristocratic *hôtels* or mansions of the Marais were also erected during this period, to be superseded early in the eighteenth century by the Faubourg St-Germain as the fashionable quarter of the rich and powerful.

The underside of all this bricks and mortar self-aggrandizement was the general neglect of the living conditions of the ordinary citizenry of Paris. The centre of the city remained a densely packed and insanitary warren of medieval lanes and tenements. And it was only in the years immediately preceding the 1789 Revolution that any attempt was made to clean it up. The buildings crowding the bridges were dismantled as late as 1786. Pavements were introduced for the first time and attempts were made to improve the drainage. A further source of pestilential infection was removed with the emptying of the overcrowded cemeteries into the catacombs. One gravedigger alone claimed to have buried more than ninety thousand people in thirty years, stacked "like slices of bacon" in the charnel house of the Innocents, which had been receiving the dead of 22 parishes for 800 years.

In 1786 Paris also received its penultimate ring of fortifications, the so-called wall of the Fermiers Généraux, with 57 *barrières* or toll gates (one of which survives in the middle of place Stalingrad), where a tax was levied on all goods entering the city.

The 1789 Revolution

The immediate cause of the Revolution of 1789 was a campaign by the privileged classes of the clergy and nobility to protect their status, especially exemption from taxation, against erosion by the royal government. The revolutionary movement, however, was quickly taken over by the middle classes, relatively well off but politically underprivileged. In the initial phases this meant essentially the provincial bourgeoisie. It was they who comprised the majority of the representatives of the **Third Estate**, the "order" that encompassed the whole of French society after the clergy, who formed the First Estate, and the

nobility who formed the Second. It was they who took the initiative in setting up the **National Assembly** on June 17, 1789. The majority of them would probably have been content with constitutional reforms that checked monarchical power on the English model. But their power depended largely on their ability to wield the threat of a Parisian popular explosion.

Although the effects of the Revolution were felt all over France and indeed Europe, it was in Paris that the most profound changes took place. Being as it were on the spot, the people of Paris discovered themselves in the Revolution. They formed the revolutionary shock troops, the driving force at the crucial stages of the Revolution. They marched on Versailles and forced the king to return to Paris with them. They stormed and destroyed the Bastille on July 14, 1789. They occupied the Hôtel de Ville, set up an insurrectionary Commune and captured the Tuileries palace on August 10, 1792. They invaded the Convention in May 1793 and secured the arrest of the more conservative Girondin faction of deputies.

Where the bourgeois deputies of the Convention were concerned principally with political reform, the **sans-culottes** – literally, the people without breeches – expressed their demands in economic terms: price controls, regulation of the city's food supplies, and so on. In so doing they foreshadowed the rise of the working-class and socialist movements of the nineteenth century. They also established by their practice of taking to the streets and occupying the Hôtel de Ville a tradition of revolutionary action that continued through to the 1871 Commune.

Napoléon – and the Barricades

Apart from some spectacular bloodletting, and yet another occupation of the city by foreign powers in 1814, Napoléon's chief legacy to France was a very centralized, authoritarian and efficient **bureaucracy** that put Paris in firm control of the rest of the country. In Paris itself, he left his share of pompous architecture – in the **Arcs de Triomphe** and **Carrousel**, rue de Rivoli and rue de la Paix, the Madeleine and façade of the Palais-Bourbon, plus a further extension for the Louvre and a revived tradition of court flummery and extravagant living among the well-to-do. For the rest of the nineteenth century after his demise, France was left to fight out the contradictions and unfinished business left behind by the Revolution of 1789. And the arena in which these conflicts were resolved was, literally, the streets of the capital.

On the one hand, there was a tussle between the class that had risen to wealth and power as a direct result of the destruction of the monarchy and the old order, and the survivors of the old order, who sought to make a comeback in the 1820s under the restored monarchy of **Louis XVIII** and **Charles X**. This conflict was finally resolved in favour of the new bourgeoisie. When Charles X refused to accept the result of the 1830 National Assembly elections, Adolphe Thiers – who was to become the veteran conservative politician of the nineteenth century – led the opposition in revolt. Barricades were erected in Paris and there followed three days of bitter street fighting, known as **les trois glorieuses**, in which 1800 people were killed (they are commemorated by the column on place de la Bastille). The outcome was the election of **Louis-Philippe** as constitutional monarch, and the introduction of a few liberalizing reforms, most either cosmetic or serving merely to consolidate the power of the wealthiest stratum of the population. Radical republican and working-class interests remained completely unrepresented.

The other, and more important, major political conflict was the extended struggle between this enfranchised and privileged bourgeoisie and the heirs of the 1789 *sans-culottes*, whose political consciousness had been awakened by the Revolution but whose demands remained unsatisfied. These were the people who died on the barricades of July to hoist the bourgeoisie firmly into the saddle.

As their demands continued to go unheeded, so their radicalism increased, exacerbated by deteriorating living and working conditions in the large towns, especially Paris, as the Industrial Revolution got underway. There were, for example, twenty thousand deaths from cholera in Paris in 1832, and 65 percent of the population in 1848 were too poor to be liable for tax. Eruptions of discontent invariably occurred in the capital, with insurrections in 1832 and 1834. In the absence of organized parties, opposition centred on newspapers and clandestine or informal political clubs in the tradition of 1789. The most notable – and the only one dedicated to the violent overthrow of the regime – was Auguste Blanqui's *Société Républicaine*.

In the 1840s the publication of the first Socialist works like Louis Blanc's *Organization of Labour* and Proudhon's *What is Property?* gave an additional spur to the impatience of the opposition. When the lid blew off the pot in **1848** and the **Second Republic** was proclaimed in Paris, it looked for a time as if working-class demands might be at least partly met. The provisional government included Louis Blanc and a Parisian manual worker. But in the face of demands for the control of industry, the setting up of co-operatives and so on, backed by agitation in the streets and the proposed inclusion of men like Blanqui and Barbès in the government, the more conservative Republicans lost their nerve. The nation returned a spanking reactionary majority in the April elections.

Revolution began to appear the only possible defence for the radical left. On June 23, 1848, **working-class Paris** – Poissonnière, Temple, St-Antoine, the Marais, Quartier Latin, Montmartre – rose in **revolt**. Men, women and children fought side by side against fifty thousand troops. In three days of fighting, nine hundred soldiers were killed. No-one knows how many of the *insurgés* – the insurgents – died. Fifteen thousand people were arrested and four thousand sentenced to prison terms.

Despite the shock and devastation of civil war in the streets of the capital, the ruling classes failed to heed the warning in the events of June 1848. Far from redressing the injustices which had provoked them, they proceeded to exacerbate them – by, for example, reducing the representation of what Adolphe Thiers called "the vile multitude". The Republic was brought to an end in a coup d'état by **Louis Napoléon**, who within twelve months had himself crowned Emperor Napoléon III.

Rewards of Colonialism

There followed a period of **foreign acquisitions** on every continent and of **laissez-faire capitalism** at home, both of which greatly increased the economic wealth of France, then lagging far behind Britain in the industrialization stakes. Foreign trade trebled, a huge expansion of the rail network was carried out, investment banks were set up, and so forth. The rewards, however, were very unevenly distributed, and the regime relied unashamedly on repressive measures – press censorship, police harassment and the forcible suppression of strikes – to hold the underdogs in check.

The response was entirely predictable. Opposition became steadily more organized and determined. In 1864, under the influence of Karl Marx in London, a French branch of the International was established in Paris and the youthful trade union movement gathered its forces in a federation. In 1869 the far from socialist Gambetta, briefly deputy for Belleville, declared, "Our generation's mission is to complete the French Revolution."

During these nearly twenty years of the Second Empire, while conditions were ripening for the most terrible of all Parisian revolutions, the 1871 Commune, the city itself suffered the greatest ever shock to its system. **Baron Haussmann**, appointed Prefect of the Seine department with responsibility for Paris by Napoléon III, undertook the total transformation of the city. In love with the straight line and grand vista, he drove 135km of broad new streets through the cramped quarters of the medieval city, linking the interior and exterior boulevards, and creating north–south, east–west cross-routes. His taste dictated the uniform grey stone façades, mansard roofs and six to seven storeys that are still the architectural hallmark of the Paris street today. In fact, such was the logic of his planning that construction of his projected streets continued long after his death, boulevard Haussmann itself being completed only in 1927.

While it is difficult to imagine how Paris could have survived without some Haussmann-like intervention, the scale of demolitions entailed by such massive redevelopment brought the direst social consequences. The city boundaries were extended to the 1840 fortifications where the *boulevard périphérique* now runs. The prosperous classes moved into the new western *arrondissements*, leaving the decaying older properties to the poor. These were divided and subdivided into ever smaller units as landlords sought to maximize their rents. Sanitation was nonexistent. Water standpipes were available only in the street. Migrant workers from the provinces, sucked into the city to supply the vast labour requirements, crammed into the old villages of Belleville and Ménilmontant. Many, too poor to buy furniture, lived in barely furnished digs or *demi-lits*, where the same bed was shared by several tenants on a shift basis. Cholera and TB were rife. Attempts to impose

sanitary regulations were resisted by landlords as covert socialism. Many considered even connection to Haussmann's water mains an unnecessary luxury. Until 1870 refuse was thrown into the streets at night to be collected the following morning. When in 1884 the Prefect of the day required landlords to provide proper containers, they retorted by calling the containers by his name, *poubelle* – and the name has stuck as the French word for "dustbin".

Far from being concerned with Parisians' welfare, Haussmann's scheme was at least in part designed to keep the workers under control. Barracks were located at strategic points like the place du Château-d'Eau, now République, controlling the turbulent eastern districts, and the broad boulevards were intended to facilitate troop movements and artillery fire. A section of the Canal St-Martin north of the Bastille was covered over for the same reason.

The Siege of Paris and the Commune

In September 1870, Napoléon III surrendered to Bismarck at the border town of Sedan, less than two months after France had declared war on the well-prepared and superior forces of the **Prussian** state. The humiliation was enough for a Republican government to be instantly proclaimed in Paris. The Prussians advanced and by September 19 were laying **siege** to the capital. Gambetta was flown out by hot-air balloon to rally the provincial troops but the country was defeated and liaison with Paris almost impossible. Further balloon messengers ended up in Norway or the Atlantic; the few attempts at military sorties from Paris turned into yet more blundering failures. Meanwhile, the city's restaurants were forced to change menus to fried dog, roast rat or peculiar delicacies from the zoos. For those without savings, death from disease or starvation became an ever more common fate. At the same time, the peculiar conditions of a city besieged gave a greater freedom to collective discussion and dissent.

The government's half-hearted defence of the city – more afraid of revolution within than of the Prussians – angered Parisians, who clamoured for the creation of a 1789-style Commune. The Prussians meanwhile were demanding a proper government to negotiate with. In January 1871, those in power agreed to hold elections for a new national assembly with the authority to surrender officially to the Prussians. A large monarchist majority, with Thiers at its head, was returned, again demonstrating the isolation from the countryside of the Parisian leftists, among whom many prominent old-timers, veterans of 1848 and the empire's jails like Blanqui and Delescluze, were still active.

On March 1, Prussian troops marched down the Champs-Élysées and garrisoned the city for three days while the populace remained behind closed doors in silent protest. On March 18, amid growing resentment from all classes of Parisians, Thiers' attempt to take possession of the National Guard's artillery in Montmartre (see p.162) set the barrel alight. The Commune was proclaimed from the Hôtel de Ville and Paris was promptly subjected to a second siege by Thiers' government, which had fled to Versailles, followed by all the remaining Parisian bourgeoisie.

The **Commune** lasted 72 days – a festival of the oppressed, Lenin called it. Socialist in inspiration, it had no time to implement lasting reforms. Wholly occupied with defence against Thiers' army, it succumbed finally on May 28, 1871, after a week of street-by-street warfare, in which three thousand Parisians died on the barricades and another twenty to twenty-five thousand men, women and children were killed in random revenge shootings by government troops. Thiers could declare with satisfaction – or so he thought – "Socialism is finished for a long time."

Among the non-human casualties were several of the city's landmark buildings, including the Tuileries palace, Hôtel de Ville, Cours des Comptes (where the Musée d'Orsay now stands) and a large chunk of the rue Royale.

The Belle Époque

Physical recovery was remarkably quick. Within six or seven years few signs of the fighting remained. Visitors remarked admiringly on the teeming streets, the expensive shops and energetic nightlife. Charles Garnier's Opéra was opened in 1875. Aptly described as the "triumph of moulded pastry", it was a suitable image of the frivolity and materialism of the so-called naughty Eighties and Nineties. In 1889 the **Eiffel Tower** stole the show at the great Exposition. For the 1900 repeat, the **Métropolitain** (métro) – or *Nécropolitain*, as it was dubbed by one wit – was unveiled.

The lasting social consequence of the Commune was the confirmation of the them-and-us divide between bourgeoisie and working class. Any stance other than a revolutionary one after the Commune appeared not only feeble, but also a betrayal of the dead. None of the contradictions had been resolved. The years up to World War I were marked by the increasing organization of the Left in response to the unstable but thoroughly conservative governments of the Third Republic. The trade union movement unified in 1895 to form the **Confédération Générale du Travail** (*CGT*), and in 1905 Jean Jaurès and Jules Guesde founded the **Parti Socialiste** (also known as the *SFIO*). On the extreme right, fascism began to make its ugly appearance with Maurras' proto-Brownshirt organization, the *Camelots du Roi*, which inaugurated another French tradition, of violence and thuggery on the far Right.

Yet despite – or maybe in some way *because of* – these tensions and contradictions, Paris provided the supremely inspiring environment for a concentration of **artists and writers** – the so-called **Bohemians**, both French and foreign – such as Western culture has rarely seen. Impressionism, Fauvism and Cubism were all born in Paris in this period, while French poets like Apollinaire, Laforgue, Max Jacob, Blaise Cendrars and André Breton were preparing the way for Surrealism, concrete poetry and symbolism. Film, too, saw its first developments. After World War I, Paris remained the world's art centre, with an injection of foreign blood and a shift of venue from Montmartre to Montparnasse.

In the postwar struggle for recovery the interests of the urban working class were again passed over, with the exception of Clemenceau's eight-hour day legislation in 1919. An attempted general strike in 1920 came to nothing, and workers' strength was again weakened by the irredeemable split in the Socialist Party at the 1920 Congress of Tours. The pro-Lenin majority formed the **French Communist Party**, while the minority faction, under the leadership of Léon Blum, retained the old *SFIO* title.

As **Depression** deepened in the 1930s and Nazi power across the Rhine became more menacing, fascist thuggery and anti-parliamentary activity increased in France, culminating in a pitched battle outside the Chamber of Deputies in February 1934. (Léon Blum was only saved from being lynched by a funeral cortege through the intervention of some building workers who happened to notice what was going on in the street below.) The effect of this fascist activism was to unite the Left, including the Communists, led by the Stalinist Maurice Thorez, in the **Popular Front**. When they won the 1936 elections with a handsome majority in the Chamber, there followed a wave of strikes and factory sit-ins – a spontaneous expression of working-class determination to get their just deserts after a century and a half of frustration. Frightened by the apparently revolutionary situation, the major employers signed the Matignon Agreement with Blum, which provided for wage increases, nationalization of the armaments industry and partial nationalization of the Bank of France, a forty-hour week, paid annual leave and collective bargaining on wages. These reforms were pushed through parliament, but when Blum tried to introduce exchange controls to check the flight of capital the Senate threw the proposal out and he resigned. The Left returned to Opposition, where it remained, with the exception of coalition governments, until 1981. Most of the Popular Front's reforms were promptly undone.

The German Occupation

During the occupation of Paris in World War II, the Germans found some sections of Parisian society, as well as the minions of the Vichy government, only too happy to hobnob with them. For four years the city suffered fascist rule with curfews, German garrisons and a Gestapo HQ. Parisian Jews were forced to wear the star of David and in 1942 were rounded up – by other Frenchmen – and shipped off to Auschwitz (see p.385).

The **Resistance** was very active in the city, gathering people of all political persuasions into its ranks, but with communists and socialists, especially of East European Jewish origin, well to the fore. The job of torturing them when they fell into Nazi hands – often as a result of betrayals – was left to their fellow citizens in the fascist militia. Those who were condemned to death – rather than the concentration camps – were shot against the wall below the old fort of Mont Valérien above St-Cloud.

As Allied forces drew near to the city in 1944, the FFI (armed Resistance units), determined to play their part in driving the Germans out, called their troops onto the streets – some said, in a Leftist attempt to seize political power. To their credit, the Paris police also joined in, holding their Île de la Cité HQ for three days against German attacks. Liberation finally came on August 25, 1944.

Postwar Paris – One More Try at Revolution

Postwar Paris has remained no stranger to **political battles** in its streets. Violent demonstrations accompanied the Communist withdrawal from the coalition government in 1947. In the Fifties the Left took to the streets again in protest against the colonial wars in Indochina and Algeria. And, in 1961, in one of the most shameful episodes in modern French history, some two hundred Algerians were killed by the police during a civil rights demonstration.

This **"secret massacre"**, which remained covered by a veil of total official silence until the 1990s, took place during the Algerian war. It began with a peaceful demonstration against a curfew on North Africans imposed by de Gaulle's government in an attempt to inhibit FLN resistance activity in the French capital. Whether the police were acting on higher orders or merely on the authority of their own commanders is not clear. What is clear from hundreds of eyewitness accounts, including some from horrified policemen, is that the police went berserk. They opened fire, clubbed people and threw them in the Seine to drown. Several dozen Algerians were killed in the courtyard of the police HQ on the Île de la Cité. For weeks afterwards, corpses were recovered from the Seine, but the French media remained silent, in part through censorship, in part perhaps unable to comprehend that such events had happened in their own capital. Maurice Papon, the police chief at the time, was subsequently decorated by de Gaulle. He is now finally under investigation for war crimes.

The state attempted censorship again during the events of **May 1968**, though with rather less success. Through this extraordinary month, a radical, libertarian, Leftist movement spread from the Paris universities to include, eventually, the occupation of hundreds of factories across the country and a general strike by nine million workers. The old-fashioned and reactionary university structures that had triggered the revolt were reflected in the hierarchical and rigid organizations of many other institutions in French life. The position of women and of youth, of culture and modes of behaviour, were suddenly highlighted in the general dissatisfaction with a society in which big business ran the state.

There was no revolutionary situation on the 1917 model. The vicious battles with the para-military CRS police on the streets of Paris shook large sectors of the population – France's silent majority – to the core, as the government cyni-cally exploiting the scenes for TV knew full well. There was no shared economic or political aim in the ranks of the opposition. With the exception of Michel Rocard's small *Parti Socialiste Uni*, the tra-ditional parties were taken completely by sur-prise and uncertain how to react. The French Communist Party, stuck with its Stalinist traditions, was far from favourably disposed to the adven-turism of the students and their numerous Maoist, Trotskyist and anarchist factions or *grou-puscules*. Right-wing and "nationalist" demon-strations orchestrated by de Gaulle left public opinion craving stability and peace; and a great many workers were satisfied with a new system for wage agreements. It was not, therefore, sur-prising that the elections called in June returned the Right to power.

The occupied buildings emptied and the bar-ricades in the Latin Quarter came down. For those who thought they were experiencing The Revolution, the defeat was catastrophic. But French institutions and French society did change, shaken and loosened by the events of May 1968. And most importantly it opened up the debate of a new road to socialism, one in which no old models would give all the answers.

Modern Developments of the City

Until World War II, Paris remained pretty much as Haussmann had left it. Housing conditions showed little sign of improvement. There was even an outbreak of bubonic plague in Clignancourt in 1921. In 1925 a third of the hous-es still had no sewage connection. Of the seven-teen worst blocks of slums designated for clear-ance, most were still intact in the 1950s, and

even today they have some close rivals in parts of Belleville and elsewhere.

Migration to the suburbs continued, with the creation of **shantytowns** to supplement the hopelessly inadequate housing stock. Post-World War II, these became the exclusive territory of **Algerian** and other **North African immigrants**. In 1966 there were 89 of them, housing 40,000 immigrant workers and their families.

Only in the last thirty years have the authori-ties begun to grapple with the housing problem, though not by expanding possibilities within Paris, but by siphoning huge numbers of people into a ring of **satellite towns** encircling the greater Paris region.

In Paris proper this same period has seen the final breaking of the mould of Haussmann's influ-ence. Intervening architectural fashions, like Art Nouveau, Le Corbusier's International style and the Neoclassicism of the 1930s, had little more than localized cosmetic effects. It was devotion to the needs of the motorist – a cause unhesi-tatingly espoused by Pompidou – and the devel-opment of the high-rise tower that finally did the trick, starting with the **Tour Maine-Montparnasse** and **La Défense**, the redevelopment of the 13e and, in the 1970s, projects like **Beaubourg**, the **Front de Seine** and **Les Halles**. In recent years, new colossal public buildings in myriad conflict-ing styles have been inaugurated at an ever-more astounding rate. At the same time, the fab-ric of the city – the streets, the métro and the graffitied walls – have been ignored.

When the Les Halles flower and veg market was dismantled, it was not just the nineteenth-century architecture that was mourned. As a sign posted during the redevelopment of Les Halles lamented, "The centre of Paris will be beautiful. Luxury will be king. But we will not be here." The city's social mix has changed more in 25 years than in the previous 100. Gentrification of the remaining working-class districts has accelerated, and the population has become essentially mid-dle-class and white-collar.

The Political Present

François Mitterrand's presidency came to an end in April 1995. He had been the French head of state for fourteen years, presiding over two Socialist and two Gaullist governments. When he won the elections in 1981, he embodied all the hopes of a generation of socialists who had never seen their party in power. The last years of his presidency saw him becoming ill and aged, his reputation tarnished and his party's popularity reduced to an all-time low. His death in January 1996, following the massive popular strikes against welfare cuts in December 1995, signalled the end of an era.

The recession started to take hold during Mitterrand's presidency, official unemployment figures passed three million, and scandals touched the president, politicians of all parties and businesspeople. Socialist Lionel Jospin did surprisingly well in the presidential elections, but it was a foregone conclusion that Jacques Chirac, former Mayor of Paris, would win.

The Mitterrand Era, 1981–95

The **Socialists'** first government after 23 years in opposition included four Communist ministers: an alliance reflected in the government commitments to expanded state control of industry, high taxation for the rich, support for liberation struggles around the world, and a public spending programme to raise the living standards of the least well-off. By 1984, however, the government had done a complete volte-face with Laurent Fabius presiding over a cabinet of centrist to conservative "socialist" ministers, clinging desperately to power.

The commitments had come to little. Attempts to bring private education under state control were defeated by mass protests in the streets; ministers were implicated in cover-ups and corruption; unemployment continued to rise. Any idea of peaceful and pro-ecological intent was dashed, as far as international opinion was concerned, by the French Secret Service's murder of a Greenpeace photographer on the *Rainbow Warrior* in New Zealand.

There were sporadic achievements – in labour laws and women's rights, notably – but no cohe-sive and consistent socialist line. The Socialists' 1986 election slogan was "Help – the Right is coming back", a bizarrely self-fulfilling tactic. **Jacques Chirac** became prime minister (and continued as Mayor of Paris).

Throughout 1987 the chances of Mitterrand's winning the presidential election in 1988 seemed very slim. But Chirac's economic policies of privatization and monetary control failed to deliver the goods. Millions of first-time investors in "popular capitalism" lost all their money on Black Monday. Terrorists planted bombs in Paris and took French hostages in Lebanon. Unemployment steadily rose and Chirac made the fatal mistake of flirting with the extreme right. Several leading politicians of the centre-right, among them Simone Weil, a concentration-camp survivor, denounced Chirac's concessions to Le Pen, and a new alignment of the centre started to emerge. **Mitterrand**, the grand old man of politics, with decades of experience, played off all the groupings of the Right in an all-but-flawless campaign, and won another mandate.

His party, however, failed to win an absolute majority in the parliamentary elections soon afterwards. The austerity measures of Mitterrand's new prime minister, **Michel Rocard**, upset traditional Socialist supporters in the public-service sector, with nurses, civil servants, teachers and the like quick to take industrial action. Though Chirac's programmes were halted, they were not reversed.

The 1980s ended with the most absurd blowout of public funds ever – the **Bicentennial celebrations of the French Revolution**. They symbolized a culture industry spinning mindlessly around the vacuum at the centre of the French vision for the future. And they highlighted the contrast between the unemployed and homeless begging on the streets and the limitless cash available for prestige projects.

In 1991, Mitterrand sacked Michel Rocard and appointed **Édith Cresson** as prime minister. Initially the French were happy to have their first woman prime minister, who promised to wage economic war against the Germans and the Japanese. The Left, including the Communists, were pleased with Cresson's socialist credentials. But she soon began to turn a few heads with her comments about special charters for illegal immigrants; her dismissal of the stock exchange as a waste of time; her description of the Japanese as yellow ants and British males as homosexual; and by attacks on her own ministers. Cresson became the most unpopular prime minister in the history of the Fifth Republic.

Cresson's worst move was to propose a tax on everyone's insurance contributions to pay for compensation to haemophiliacs infected with HIV. The knowing use of infected blood in transfusions in 1985 became one of the biggest scandals of the Socialist regime.

Pierre Bérégovoy succeeded Cresson in 1992. Universally known as *Béré*, and mocked for his bumbling persona, he survived strikes by farmers, dockers, car workers and nurses, the scandals touching the Socialists, and the Maastricht referendum. But then a private loan was revealed from one Roger-Patrice Pelat, a friend of Mitterrand's accused of insider dealing. Mitterrand distanced himself from his prime minister, who then shot himself two months after losing the elections, leaving no note of explanation.

The new prime minister, **Edouard Balladur**, a fresh and fatherly face from the Right, started off with great popularity. But a series of U-turns after demonstrations by *Air France* workers, teachers, farmers, fishermen and school pupils, and the state's rescue of the *Crédit Lyonnais* bank after spectacular losses, wiped away his successes over GATT and keeping the franc strong and inflation down.

His home affairs minister, **Charles Pasqua** (who served in the same post under Chirac), was a highly unpopular right-winger with a strong anti-immigration and anti-immigrant line. In 1992, Pasqua joined forces with another senior Gaullist bully boy, Philippe Séguin, and the extreme *UDF* right-winger Philippe de Villiers, to oppose the Maastricht treaty. Opposition to the treaty also came from the *PCF*, the breakaway socialist Jean-Pierre Chevènement and the *Front National*. Clearly, the long-established certainty of the absolute divide between Right and Left loyalties was no longer tenable. The actual voters divided along the lines of the poorer rural areas voting "No" and the rich urbanites voting "Yes". In Paris the "Yes" vote was overwhelming. Disillusionment with the established parties was

confirmed in the 1994 Euro elections. The *RPR/UDF* lost votes to the anti-Europeans and for the *Parti Socialiste* it was a total disaster. Rocard had to resign as the party secretary – his attempts to "modernize" the party had failed.

Meanwhile Mitterrand tottered on to the end of his presidential term, looking less and less like the nation's favourite uncle. Two months after Bérégovoy's suicide, Réné Bousquet, who was head of police in the Vichy government and supervised the rounding up of Jews in 1942, was murdered. He was a friend of Mitterrand's and thought to have known shady secrets about the president. The following year a secret service agent and close adviser and friend, Jacques Attali, had to resign from the European Bank for Reconstruction and Development for suspected filching of the bank's money.

On the twentieth anniversary of President Pompidou's death in April 1994, there was a wave of nostalgia for a time when "things were right and proper". A month later, a leading French businessman was arrested for corruption, soon followed by other corruption scandals touching businesspeople and politicians, including ministers. Cracks had opened up in the French establishment and the recession was biting.

In 1995, with **Mitterrand dying from cancer** but refusing to step down before the end of his term, revelations surfaced about his war record as an official in the Vichy regime before he joined the Resistance. A biography of Mitterrand, *Le Grand Secret*, detailing a whole host of scandals, was banned in France but published on the Internet.

The Socialist Party was desperate for **Jacques Delors**, chair of the European Commission, to stand as their presidential candidate. When he finally refused, it looked as if the party was doomed. But **Lionel Jospin**, the uncharismatic former education minister, performed remarkably well, topping the poll in the first round – in which right-wing votes were split between Balladur, Chirac, the extreme-right Le Pen and the anti-European Philippe de Villiers. Le Pen scored 15.5 percent and called on his followers to abstain in the second round run-off between Jospin and Chirac. Chirac stole the Left's clothes by placing **unemployment and social exclusion** at the top of the political agenda, and heaped promises of better times on every section of the electorate. He won, by a small margin, and was inaugurated as the new president of France in May 1995.

Mitterrand died eight months later in January 1996. Despite everything, he was genuinely mourned as a man of culture and vision, a supreme political operator, and for his unwavering commitment to the European Union.

Chirac's Presidency

Mitterrand had predicted that Jacques Chirac as president would become the laughing stock of the world. But it was international condemnation rather than derision that greeted the first significant act of his presidency, the decision to resume **nuclear testing** on the Pacific island of Muroroa. A typically Gaullist move, it provoked boycotts of French produce and a revival of the French peace and environmental movements.

Municipal elections in June 1995 gave the *Front National* control of three towns, including the major port of Toulon. The Socialists, who did not do too badly, accused the Right of refusing tactical alliances to defeat Le Pen. The increasing popularity of racist measures was noted by the political establishment in Paris, but it was happy to ignore the shock of Le Pen's best ever electoral success.

With a very comfortable right-wing majority in both houses of parliament, Chirac followed his demonstration of French machismo on the world stage with constitutional changes to **presidential powers**, giving him the right to call referenda on any subject with or without parliamentary approval.

Chirac's new prime minister, replacing Balladur who had treacherously stood against Chirac in the presidentials, was **Alain Juppé**, a clever, clinical technocrat to whom the French could not warm easily. It was down to him to square the circle of Chirac's election pledges of job creation, maintaining the value of pensions and welfare benefits and reducing the number of homeless, with tax cuts, a continuing strong franc and a reduction in the budget deficit to stay on course for monetary union.

Juppé was in trouble right from the start due to allegations of **corruption** concerning his luxury flat in Paris (see below). A summer of **bomb attacks** by Islamic fundamentalists diminished public confidence in the government as guardians of law and order. By October Juppé had broken all records for prime ministerial unpopularity. Having sacked his finance minister, Alain Madelin, for proposing tax cuts and radical reductions in public spending, Juppé raised VAT along with other taxes and provoked a round of strikes with an austerity budget freezing public sector pay.

But that was nothing compared to the **strikes of November and December 1995**, sparked off by Juppé's announcement of dramatic changes in social security provision and a restructuring of the state-owned railways involving job losses and branch line closures. Suddenly, and en masse, the French decided they had had enough of arrogant, elitist politicians, their false election promises and the austerity measures demanded by a free-market approach to European union. Students, teachers and nurses, workers in the transport, energy, post and telecommunications industries, bank clerks and civil servants – all took to the streets with the strong support of private sector employees struggling to get to work. Even the police showed sympathy to the strikers.

With five million people out over a period of 24 days, it was the strongest show of protest in France since May 1968. The mood this time, however, was not joyful liberation but anxiety about unemployment and social welfare, and disillusionment with politicians of both Right and Left, seen as lackeys of the global financial markets. There were no positive demands; indeed no united voice at all from the protestors who ranged from working-class *Front National* supporters to middle-class Gaullists to Communist trade unionists. But it was the clearest indication in Europe to date that there are limits to people's acceptance of neoliberalism, and that dressing up the free pay of market forces as "modernization" or "realism" does not wash.

Amazingly Juppé survived this "winter of discontent", abandoning some proposals, such as upping the public sector retirement age, but only delaying others. A new tax to pay off the social security deficit has been imposed; cuts in the health service are going ahead along with a market restructuring along British lines; shortening the working week has been ruled out.

Unemployment stood at 12.3 percent in April 1995, a tiny reduction since the all-time high in March 1994. The figure for the young is 27.7 percent. Jobs are being lost in banks and in the defence industries; the plight of the "*exclus*" has not been ameliorated, and demonstrations continue. In Lyon during the G7 summit in the summer of 1996, 50,000 people marched under banners calling for a Europe of social solidarity, inclusion and justice.

Parties and Politicians

ON THE LEFT

PS (Parti Socialiste). The Socialist Party to which **François Mitterrand** belonged but whose difficulties he chose to ignore during the "cohabitation" years of right-wing governments in his second presidential term. The party had its all-time electoral low in 1993 followed by a very poor showing in the Euro elections of 1994. Corruption in Socialist-controlled town halls was revealed and party secretary **Henri Emmanuelli** charged with fraud. Though it has not exactly cleaned up its act, the party's fortunes have been restored by a few bye-election successes and the creditable performance in the presidential elections of **Lionel Jospin**, now party leader. Other key figures include **Michel Rocard**, prime minister 1988–91, who tried to push the party towards the centre ground; **Laurent Fabius**, prime minister 1984-86 and now leader of the parliamentary group; and **Martine Aubry**, daughter of Jacques Delors, who is seen as a possible future first woman president. The left wing of the party favours a coalition with the Greens, the Communists and the *Mouvement des Radicaux de Gauche (MRG)*.

PCF (Parti Communiste Français). Robert Hue succeeded the veteran Stalinist leader **Georges Marchais** as party leader. Hue has proposed a new broad coalition with progressive Greens, Socialists, community groups, churches, etc, which forms a big break from the old line, but has probably come too late to get very far. The *PCF* remains influential with the country's trade unions and also in local government.

Mouvement des Citoyens (MDC). Small radical socialist grouping led by **Jean-Pierre Chevènement**, who resigned as defence minister in protest at the Gulf War.

Lutte Ouvrière Trotskyist party whose presidential candidate, **Arlette Laguillier**, has stood in every contest since 1974 (with an identical workers' revolutionary programme). In 1995 she was credited with being the only honest candidate and won five percent of the vote in the first round – her highest ever score.

ON THE RIGHT

UDF (Union pour la Démocratie Française). Confederation of centre-right parties in alliance with the *RPR* (see below) created by aloof, aristocratic **Valéry Giscard d'Estaing**, French president 1974–81. It failed to put up a presidential candidate in 1995 after Giscard decided not to stand and members split their support between Balladur and Chirac. It was then embroiled in a leadership battle after Giscard stepped down in 1996. **François Léotard**, culture minister under Chirac and defence minister under Balladur (despite charges of corruption), is now the leader. **Raymond Barre**,

Political Issues in Paris

In the twenty years that Paris has had its own Mairie (Town Hall), it has always been in the hands of the Right. Indeed, from 1977 to 1995 there was only one mayor, Jacques Chirac. Over the same period, the mairies of the *arrondissements* have also been controlled by Gaullists or *UDF* members, and Paris deputés have rarely been from the Left. It was only in the suburbs that voters chose Socialist or Communist representatives.

But in the local elections of 1995, the Left tripled its number of councillors and won the 3e, 10e, 11e, 18e, 19e and 20e *arrondissements*, with several ecologists, communists and members of the *Mouvement des Citoyens* elected. Though still the largest party, the Gaullists lost their absolute majority in the Mairie de Paris, where the real power resides. The *arrondissement* Mairies have tiny budgets, their main function being to distribute grants to local organizations. In theory they do have a veto over planning consents, in practice, however, the city mairie gets its way.

The Fabric of the city

Presidents of France traditionally make their mark on the capital, though none has left such a notable legacy as François Mitterrand. His "*grands projets*" included the Parc de la Villette (inherited from Giscard), the Louvre Pyramid, the Grande Arche de la Défense, the Institut du Monde Arabe, the Opéra Bastille and the Bibliothèque Nationale de France.

mayor of Lyon and prime minister under Giscard, is an old stalwart who may yet return to high office.

PR (Parti Républicain). Part of the *UDF*, though some members want to form their own independent group. Key figures are Léotard (see above), who supported Balladur in the presidentials, and his rival for the *UDF* leadership, **Alain Madelin**, the finance minister sacked by Juppé, who headed the pro-Chirac camp.

RPR (Rassemblement Pour la République). Gaullist, conservative party headed by **Jacques Chirac**, mayor of Paris 1977–95, prime minister 1974–76 and 1986–88 and now president. **Edouard Balladur**, prime minister 1993–95 and known by his opponents in the media as "Ballamou" (Balla-wimp), stood against Chirac in the presidentials. **Philippe Séguin**, Speaker of the French Parliament, is a strong anti-European, and main rival to **Alain Juppé**, who he may yet replace as prime minister. Also in the running as a possible successor to Juppé is **Charles Pasqua**, home affairs minister under Chirac and Balladur, renowned for his hard line on immigration and law and order. Unlike the two prime ministers he has served, Pasqua is another anti-European.

Mouvement Pour La France. Anti-European party created by former Gaullist **Philippe de Villiers**, a Catholic aristocrat **against abortion, divorce, immigration, state education,** etc, and by UK industrialist **Jimmy Goldsmith**. De Villiers won twelve percent of the vote in the 1994 Euro elections but did not fare as well in the presidentials.

FN (Front National). Extreme-right party led by arch-racist **Jean-Marie Le Pen** and his unspeakable deputy **Bruno Mégret**. The *FN* has eleven *MEP*s, several hundred local councillors, controls three town halls and scored over fifteen percent in the first round of the presidential elections. Its current strategy is to oppose the *RPR* and *UDF* at all costs, even if it allows a socialist or communist to be elected.

GREEN PARTIES

GE (Génération Écologie). One of the two Green parties, led by **Brice Lalonde**, who served in the Socialist government of 1988–91 but switched allegiance in 1993 to the Gaullists and failed to win a local council seat in 1994. He supported Chirac for president in 1995.

Les Verts. The other Greens, more "pure" than *GE*, led by **Dominique Voynet**. All eight Green European seats were lost in 1994, and Voynet scored very badly in the 1995 presidentials. Unofficial coalitions at local level take place with left-wing socialists, anti-racists, reforming communists, etc. Many Greens, including 1988 presidential candidate **André Waechter**, now stand independently from *Les Verts* and *GE* (known together as *L'Écologistes*).

Parisians may be proud of their ever-evolving and architecturally innovative city, but they have begun to question the massive drain on public funds represented by these projects, particularly as the numbers of poor and homeless in the city have rocketed.

Eighties-style private sector development projects, like the "Seine Rive Gauche", have run into trouble, with office space no longer at a premium and private buyers unattracted by lifeless new complexes. But neighbourhood action has had its successes. The Enfants-Rouge covered market, which the former right-wing mayor of the 3e *arrondissement* wanted to pull down and replace with a concrete mall, was saved by determined local campaigning. The gardens of square Villemin, in the 8e, have been preserved for pub-

lic use, and groups of "*amis du quartier*" have sprung up in several areas to combat unwelcome development.

For the first time since World War II, the population of the city has started to drop. Single people are occupying flats that would previously have housed families, as people with children move out in search of more generous living space and a cleaner environment. Those who can work from home are beginning to doubt whether the charms of the city outweigh its congestion, crime and, most of all, the air pollution that is said to kill several hundred Parisians a year. Many businesses are beginning to relocate away from the city, along the TGV lines, to lower tax zones, faster communications and environments more attractive to the thirtysomething generation.

The City of Light is not going to empty overnight. But Parisians may be forced, not before time, to rethink their relationship with the motor car; and the tourist industry that fills the city centre with poison-belching coaches will have to consider whether Paris as a collection of monuments and museums is, in the end, as attractive as Paris as a city in which people can live and bring up their kids.

Racism

The fate of immigrants and their French descendants has never been so precarious. Fury and frustration at discrimination, assault, abuse and economic deprivation has erupted into battles on the street. Several young blacks have died at the hands of the police, while the right-wing media have revelled in images of violent Arab youths.

Parisians of Algerian origin have long been used to frequent identity checks and harassment by the police. However, since the 1995 bombing campaign in Paris, thought to be the work of Algerian fundamentalists, in which seven people died and over a hundred were injured, their experiences at the hands of the law have deteriorated dramatically; the assumption that Arabs must be fundamentalist sympathizers has added another layer to the burden of racist treatment.

In 1992, tent cities were erected by homeless Africans in the 13e arrondissement and in the Bois de Vincennes to protest against discrimination in housing allocation. There was some public sympathy, but the issue was used as a political football between Mitterrand as President and Chirac as Mayor of Paris, and a clear distinction promoted between the "deserving" and the "undesirable undeserving".

In March 1996, three hundred Malian immigrants, many of them failed asylum seekers, sought refuge in the church of St-Ambroise, in the 11e arrondissement. On the eve of the International Day Against Racism, they were forcibly evicted by truncheon-wielding riot police with the complicity of the local bishop and the curé of the church who had even provided the police with the keys. There was considerable outrage, though aimed more against the Church than the "Pasqua Law" of 1993, which took away the automatic entitlement to French citizenship of those born in France and made it far harder for legal immigrants' families to enter France, for asylum seekers and for long-term students.

In its annual report, the National Commission on Human Rights underlined a dramatic increase in racist assaults in 1995 and said that France had gone backwards ten years, with xenophobic opinions becoming accepted platitudes. Following the success of the Front National in the local elections of 1995, the government announced plans to deport 20,000 illegal immigrants a year on charter planes. In 1996, the government began work on amending "Pasqua's Law" with even more draconian measures.

The "Excluded"

Unemployment in Paris, standing at around thirteen percent, is significantly higher than the national average. The problem is even worse in many of the suburbs, some of which have a youth unemployment rate of over fifty percent. The numbers of homeless (SDF – Sans Domicile Fixe) in Paris has continued to grow – reaching an estimated 250,000 – along with the numbers of people with no option but to beg on the streets and in the métro.

Despite the visibility of poverty in the city, Parisians like to imagine that all the associated problems of drugs, violence and delinquency belong to la banlieue (the suburbs). Whenever trouble occurs on the capital's streets, it is banlieusards who are blamed.

In July 1996, Prime Minister Juppé announced yet another package of measures to create jobs in the most deprived suburban estates. But the experience of residents is that new businesses lured in by tax incentives end up employing outsiders. Nor have they found much comfort in the extra police contingents, armed with plastic bullets. The widely shared view, stongly expressed in the winter strikes of 1995, is that the problems of the dissaffected younger generation go right to the heart of the general malaise of French society, something that needs a much more profound solution than the creation of enterprise zones.

There are small-scale initiatives that give some hope; like the projects in Argenteuil and Gennevilliers where young people, equipped with a battered old van, buy fresh food directly from the producers in the countryside to sell on the estates. The producers get a better price, the food is sold more cheaply than in supermarkets, and the young people earn a living. But such "self-help" ideas receive no media coverage and fall well outside the conventional framework of the political parties.

The 1995 Winter Strikes

Other cities in France saw larger demonstrations than Paris, but that was largely because public transport stoppages in the capital made it virtually inaccessible. Roads into the city were blocked with traffic jams 100km long. People walked, cycled, roller-skated and hitched to work, and, despite the cold and the traffic-snarled streets, the majority of Parisians gave the strikers their full support.

The first Paris demonstrations, in November, were by students demanding more money for understaffed and overcrowded universities. As is always the case, a minority indulged in looting and car-burning, but even café and shop owners whose windows had been smashed remained sympathetic to the strike. There were typical scenes of French revolt: railway sleepers being burnt by the Arc de Triomphe; tear-gas canisters, petrol bombs and stones flying between students and riot police; jazz bands, balloons and food stalls in place de la République. On one day 120 women's groups demonstrated for equal pay and tougher action against anti-abortion campaigners. A call by the government for a counter-demonstration brought out a miserable straggle.

Rubbish continued to be collected, the dead to be buried and bread to be baked. Parisians found themselves talking animatedly to strangers on the streets; the final mood was elation that the city's tradition of public protest was still alive.

Town Hall Scandals

In 1994 it was revealed that Chirac, then mayor of Paris, was renting – at half the going rate – an apartment in the 7e belonging to an obscure civic trust controlled by the Mairie. Since then revelations of town hall officers and politicians being awarded desirable municipal residences have multiplied.

Soon after Jean Tiberi became mayor in 1995, it was discovered that his two children were living in council flats for next to nothing while raking in market rents from apartments they owned.

(The waiting list for Paris council flats is around 60,000.) In addition, city funds were used for an extravagant refit of Tiberi's son's property.

Prime Minister Juppé, formerly deputy mayor of Paris in charge of finances, was living in a St-Germain mansion owned by the Mairie, again paying below market rents. In 1993 he reduced the rent on his son's flat and found prestigious homes owned by the Mairie for other family members.

In addition, there have been allegations of bribery by construction companies seeking contracts from the city's housing department, headed at the time by Tiberi, and of misappropriation of municipal funds earmarked for public housing. The money, it was said, was finding its way into *RPR* party funds.

The magistrate examining the case raided Tiberi's home in June 1996, but corruption proceedings against the mayor have since been shelved and the magistrate in question taken off the case. This has led to another row about the impartiality of the Minister for Justice, fellow Gaullist Jacques Toubon, who went on to sack the head of the anti-corruption agency whose investigations into the homes-for-the-boys scandal were paving the way for a prosecution against Juppé.

Juppé has been cleared of any wrongdoing; he has had to move out of his mansion, but has kept his job. The two senior prosecutors appointed in July 1996 to examine whether fraud proceedings should go ahead against Tiberi and others are Gaullist sympathizers – a cover-up is expected.

In the past, politicians feathering their own nests never roused much public anger. But times have changed. People are disgusted at seeing the "elites" profiting from subsidized housing while hundreds of thousands are homeless. Even the normally obsequious right-wing press has been asking questions about the judiciary's independence, something Chirac promised to uphold in his election manifesto. The scandal typifies the increasing gap between the governors and the governed, which was one of the key themes of the 1995 strikes.

Books

An extraordinary number of books have been written about Paris and all things Parisian. Most of the following are published in the UK and US.

History

Alfred Cobban, *A History of Modern France* (3 vols: 1715–99, 1799–1871 and 1871–1962. Complete and very readable account of the main political, social and economic strands in French – and inevitably Parisian – history.

Colin Jones, *The Cambridge Illustrated History of France*. A political and social history of France from prehistoric times to the mid-1990s, concentrating on issues of regionalism, gender, race and class. Good illustrations and a friendly, non-academic writing style.

Norman Hampson, *A Social History of the French Revolution*. An analysis that concentrates on the personalities involved. Its particular interest lies in the attention it gives to the *sans-culottes*, the ordinary poor of Paris.

Christopher Hibbert, *The French Revolution*. Good, concise popular history of the period and events.

Lissagaray, *Paris Commune*. A highly personal and partisan account of the politics and fighting by a participant. Although Lissagaray himself is reticent about it, history has it that the last solitary Communard on the last barricade – in the rue Ramponneau in Belleville – was in fact himself.

Karl Marx, *Surveys from Exile; On the Paris Commune*. *Surveys* includes Marx's speeches and articles at the time of the 1848 Revolution and after, including an analysis, riddled with jokes, of Napoléon III's rise to power. *Paris Commune* – more rousing prose – has a history of the Commune by Engels.

Paul Webster, *Pétain's Crime: The Full Story of French Collaboration in the Holocaust*. The fascinating and alarming story of the Vichy regime's more than willing collaboration with the German authorities' campaign to implement the "final solution" in occupied France, and the bravery of those, especially the Communist resistance, who attempted to prevent it. A mass of hitherto unpublished evidence.

Theodore Zeldin, *France, 1845–1945* (5 paperback vols). Series of thematic volumes on diverse French matters – all good reads.

Society and Politics

John Ardagh, *France Today*. Comprehensive journalistic overview, covering food, film, education and holidays as well as politics and education. Good on detail about the urban suburbs (and the shift there from the centre) of Paris.

Roland Barthes, *Mythologies; Selected Writings; A Barthes Reader*. The first, though dated, is the classic: a brilliant description of how the ideas, prejudices and contradictions of French thought and behaviour manifest themselves, in food, wine, cars, travel guides and other cultural offerings. Barthes' piece on the Eiffel Tower doesn't appear, but it's included in the *Selected Writings*, published in the US as *A Barthes Reader* (ed Susan Sontag).

Simone de Beauvoir, *The Second Sex*. One of the prime texts of western feminism, written in 1949, covering women's inferior status in history, literature, mythology, psychoanalysis, philosophy and everyday life.

Denis Belloc *Slow Death in Paris*. A harrowing account of a heroin addict in Paris. Not recommended holiday reading, but if you want to know about the seemy underbelly of the city, this is the book.

James Campbell *Paris Interzone*. The feuds, passions and destructive lifestyles of Left Bank writers

1946–60 are evoked here. The cast includes Richard Wright, James Baldwin, Samuel Beckett, Boris Vian, Alexander Trocchi, Eugene Ionesco, Sartre, de Beauvoir, Nabokov and Allan Ginsberg.

Gisèle Halim, *Milk for the Orange Tree*. Born in Tunisia, daughter of an Orthodox Jewish family; ran away to Paris to become a lawyer; defender of women's rights, Algerian *FLN* fighters and all unpopular causes. A gutsy autobiographical story.

Peter Lennon, *Foreign Correspndents: Paris in the Sixties*. Irish journalist Peter Lennon went to Paris in the early 1960s unable to speak a word of French. He became a close friend of Samuel Beckett and was a witness to the May 1968 events.

François Maspero, *Roissy Express*, photographs Anaïk Frantz. A "travel book" along the *RER* B line from Roissy to St-Rémy-lès-Chevreuse (excluding the Paris stops). Brilliant insights into the life of the Paris suburbs, and fascinating digressions into French history and politics. As the blurb on the back says, this is "proof that a month on the *RER* can teach one more about *la France profonde* than a year in Provence".

William Wiser *The Great Good Place*. An account of American expatriate women in Paris, from the Impressionist painter Mary Cassatt, through to writer Edith Wharton, publisher Caresse Crosby, the sad socialite novelist's wife Zelda Fitzgerald and finally the singer Josephine Baker.

Theodore Zeldin *The French*. A coffee-table book without the pictures, based on the author's conversations with a wide range of people, about money, sex, phobias, parents and everything else.

Art, Architecture and Photography

Brassaï, *Le Paris Secret des Années 30*. Extraordinary photos of the capital's nightlife in the 1930s – brothels, music halls, street cleaners, transvestites and the underworld – each one a work of art and a familiar world (now long since gone) to Brassaï and his mate, Henry Miller, who accompanied him on his nocturnal expeditions.

Norma Evenson, *Paris: A Century of Change, 1878–1978*. A large illustrated volume which makes the development of urban planning and the fabric of Paris an enthralling subject, mainly because the author's concern is always with people, not panoramas.

John James, *Chartres*. The story of Chartres cathedral, with insights into the medieval context, the character and attitudes of the masons, the symbolism, and the advanced mathematics of the building's geometry.

Edward Lucie-Smith, *Concise History of French Painting*. If you're after an art reference book, then this will do as well as any, though there are of course dozens of other books available on particular French artists and art movements.

William Mahder (ed), *Paris Arts: The '80s Renaissance*. Illustrated, magazine-style survey of French arts. The design and photos are reason enough in themselves to look it up. Fortunately, the French edition, *Paris Creation: Une Renaissance*, remains available; the English one is out of print.

Willy Ronis, *Belleville Ménilmontant*. Misty black-and-white photographs of people and streets in the two "villages" of eastern Paris in the 1940s and 1950s.

Vivian Russell, *Monet's Garden*. An exceptional book illustrated with sumptious colour photographs by the author, old photographs of the artist and reproductions of his paintings. Superb opening chapter on Monet as "poet of nature", plus a detailed description of the garden's evolution, seasonal cycle and current maintenance, which will delight serious gardeners.

Paris in Literature

British/American

Charles Dickens, *A Tale of Two Cities*. Paris and London during the 1789 Revolution and before. The plot's pure Hollywood, but the streets and at least some of the social backdrop are for real.

Robert Ferguson, *Henry Miller*. Very readable biography of the old rogue and his rumbustious doings, including his long stint in Paris and affair with Anaïs Nin.

Brion Gysin, *The Last Museum*. The setting is the *Hôtel Bardo*, the Beat hotel: the co-residents are Kerouac, Ginsberg and Burroughs. Published posthumously, this is 1960s Paris in its most manic mode.

Ernest Hemingway, *A Moveable Feast*. Hemingway's American-in-Paris account of life in the 1930s with Ezra Pound, F. Scott Fitzgerald, Gertrude Stein, etc. Dull, pedestrian stuff, despite its classic and best-seller status.

Jack Kerouac, *Satori in Paris . . . and in Brittany*, too. Uniquely inconsequential Kerouac experiences.

Herbert Lottman, *Colette: A Life*. An interesting if somewhat dry account of this enigmatic Parisian writer's life.

Henry Miller, *Tropic of Cancer; Quiet Days in Clichy*. Again 1930s Paris, though from a more focused angle – sex, essentially. Erratic, wild, self-obsessed writing, but with definite flights of genius.

Anaïs Nin, *The Journals 1931–1974* (7 vols). A detailed literary narrative of French and US artists and fiction-makers from the first half of this century – not least, Nin herself – in Paris and elsewhere. The more famous *Erotica* was also written in Paris, for a local connoisseur of pornography.

George Orwell, *Down and Out in Paris and London*. Documentary account of breadline living in the 1930s – Orwell at his best.

Paul Rambali, *French Blues*. Movies, sex, down-and-outs, politics, fast food, bikers – a cynical, streetwise look at modern urban France.

French (in Translation)

Baudelaire's Paris, translated by Laurence Kitchen. Gloom and doom by Baudelaire, Gérard de Nerval, Verlaine and Jiménez – in bilingual edition.

André Breton, *Nadja*. A surrealist evocation of Paris. Fun.

Blaise Cendrars, *To the End of the World*. An outrageous bawdy tale of a randy septuagenarian Parisian actress, having an affair with a deserter from the Foreign Legion.

Didier Daeninckx, *Murder in Memoriam*. A thriller involving two murders: one of a Frenchman during the massacre of the Algerians in Paris in 1961, the other of his son twenty years later. The investigation by an honest detective lays bare dirty tricks, corruption, racism and the cover-up of the massacre.

Alexandre Dumas, *The Count of Monte Cristo*. One hell of a good yarn, with Paris and Marseilles locations.

Gustave Flaubert, *Sentimental Education*. A lively, detailed 1869 reconstruction of the life, manners, characters and politics of Parisians in the 1840s, including the 1848 Revolution.

Victor Hugo, *Les Misérables*. A racy, eminently readable novel by the French equivalent of Dickens, about the Parisian poor and low-life in the first half of the nineteenth century. Book Four contains an account of the barricade fighting during the 1832 insurrection.

François Maspero, *Le Sourire du Chat* (translated as *Cat's Grin*). Semi-autobiographical novel of the young teenager Luc in Paris during World War II, with his adored elder brother in the Resistance, his parents taken to concentration camps as Paris is liberated, and everyone else busily collaborating. An intensely moving and revealing account of the war period.

Georges Perec *Life: A User's Manual*. An extraordinary literary jigsaw puzzle of life, past and present, human, animal and mineral, extracted from the residents of an imaginary apartment block in the 17e *arrondissement* of Paris.

Édith Piaf, *My Life*. Piaf's dramatic story told pretty much in her words.

Marcel Proust, *Remembrance of Things Past*. Written in and of Paris: absurdly long but bizarrely addictive.

Jean-Paul Sartre, *Roads to Freedom Trilogy*. Metaphysics and gloom, despite the title.

Georges Simenon, *Maigret at the Crossroads*, or any other of the Maigret novels. Literary crime thrillers; the Montmartre and seedy criminal locations are unbeatable.

Michel Tournier, *The Golden Droplet*. A magical tale of a Saharan boy coming to Paris, where strange adventures, against the backdrop of immigrant life in the slums, overtake him because he never drops his desert oasis view of the world.

Émile Zola, *Nana*. The rise and fall of a courtesan in the decadent times of the Second Empire. Not bad on sex, but confused on sexual politics. A great story nevertheless, which brings mid-nineteenth-century Paris alive, direct, to present-day senses. Paris is also the setting for Zola's *L'Assommoir*, *L'Argent* and *Thérèse Raquin*.

Language

French can be a deceptively familiar language because of the number of words and structures it shares with English. Despite this it's far from easy, though the bare essentials are not difficult to master and can make all the difference. Even just saying "Bonjour Madame/Monsieur" and then gesticulating will usually get you a smile and helpful service. People working in tourist offices, hotels and so on almost always speak English and tend to use it when you're struggling to speak French – be grateful, not insulted.

French Pronunciation

One easy rule to remember is that **consonants** at the end of words are usually silent. *Pas plus tard* (not later) is thus pronounced "pa-plu-tarr". But when the following word begins with a vowel, you run the two together: *pas aprés* (not after) becomes "pazapray".

Vowels are the hardest sounds to get right. Roughly:

a	as in h**a**t	*i*	as in mach**i**ne
e	as in g**e**t	*o*	as in h**o**t
é	between g**e**t and g**a**te	*o/au*	as in **o**ver
è	between g**e**t and g**u**t	*ou*	as in f**oo**d
eu	like the **u** in h**u**rt	*u*	as in pursed-lip version of **u**se

More awkward are the **combinations** in/im, en/em, on/om, un/um at the ends of words, or followed by consonants other than n or m. Again, roughly:

in/im	like the **an** in **an**xious	*on/om*	like the **on** in D**on**caster
an/am, en/em	like the **on** in D**on**caster when said with a nasal accent		said by someone with a heavy cold
		un/um	like the **u** in **u**nderstand

Consonants are much as in English, except that: ch is always sh, h is silent, th is the same as t, ll is like the y in "yes", w is v, and r is growled (or rolled).

Learning Materials

Rough Guide French Phrasebook (Rough Guides). Mini dictionary-style phrasebook with both English–French and French–English sections, along with cultural tips for tricky situations and a menu reader.

Mini French Dictionary (Harrap/Prentice Hall). French–English and English–French, plus a brief grammar and pronunciation guide.

Breakthrough French (Pan; book and two cassettes). Excellent teach-yourself course.

French and English Slang Dictionary (Harrap); **Dictionary of Modern Colloquial**

French (Routledge). Both volumes are a bit large to carry, but they are the key to all you ever wanted to understand.

Verbaid (Verbaid, Hawk House, Heath Lane, Farnham, Surrey GF9 0PR). CD-size laminated paper "verb wheel" giving tense endings for regular verbs.

A Vous La France; Franc Extra; Franc Parler (BBC Publications; each has a book and two cassettes). BBC radio courses, running from beginners' to fairly advanced language.

Basic Words and Phrases

French nouns are divided into masculine and feminine. This causes difficulties with adjectives, whose endings have to change to suit the gender of the nouns they qualify. If you know some grammar, you will know what to do. If not, stick to the masculine form, which is the simplest – it's what we have done in this glossary.

today	*aujourd'hui*	that one	*celà*
yesterday	*hier*	open	*ouvert*
tomorrow	*demain*	closed	*fermé*
in the morning	*le matin*	big	*grand*
in the afternoon	*l'après-midi*	small	*petit*
in the evening	*le soir*	more	*plus*
now	*maintenant*	less	*moins*
later	*plus tard*	a little	*un peu*
at one o'clock	*à une heure*	a lot	*beaucoup*
at three o'clock	*à trois heures*	cheap	*bon marché*
at ten-thirty	*à dix heures et demie*	expensive	*cher*
		good	*bon*
at midday	*à midi*	bad	*mauvais*
man	*un homme*	hot	*chaud*
woman	*une femme*	cold	*froid*
here	*ici*	with	*avec*
there	*là*	without	*sans*
this one	*ceci*		

Accommodation

a room for one/two people	*une chambre pour une/deux personnes*	do laundry	*faire la lessive*
a double bed	*un lit double*	sheets	*draps*
a room with a shower	*une chambre avec douche*	blankets	*couvertures*
		quiet	*calme*
a room with a bath	*une chambre avec salle de bain*	noisy	*bruyant*
		hot water	*eau chaude*
For one/two/three nights	*Pour une/deux/trois nuit(s)*	cold water	*eau froide*
		Is breakfast included?	*Est-ce que le petit déjeuner est compris?*
Can I see it?	*Je peux la voir?*		
a room in the courtyard	*une chambre sur la cour*	I would like breakfast	*Je voudrais prendre le petit déjeuner*
a room over the street	*une chambre sur la rue*	I don't want breakfast	*Je ne veux pas le petit déjeuner*
first floor	*premier étage*	Can we camp here?	*On peut camper ici?*
second floor	*deuxième étage*	campsite	*un camping/terrain de camping*
with a view	*avec vue*		
key	*clef*	tent	*une tente*
to iron	*repasser*	tent space	*un emplacement*
		youth hostel	*auberge de jeunesse*

Days and Dates

January	*janvier*	May	*mai*	September	*septembre*
February	*février*	June	*juin*	October	*octobre*
March	*mars*	July	*juillet*	November	*novembre*
April	*avril*	August	*août*	December	*décembre*

Sunday	*dimanche*	August 1	*le premier août*
Monday	*lundi*	March 2	*le deux mars*
Tuesday	*mardi*	July 14	*le quatorze juillet*
Wednesday	*mercredi*	November 23, 1997	*le vingt-trois*
Thursday	*jeudi*		*novembre, dix-*
Friday	*vendredi*		*neuf-cent-quatre-*
Saturday	*samedi*		*vingt--dix-sept*

Numbers

1	un	11	onze	21	vingt-et-un	95	quatre-vingt-
2	deux	12	douze	22	vingt-deux		quinze
3	trois	13	treize	30	trente	100	cent
4	quatre	14	quatorze	40	quarante	101	cent-et-un
5	cinq	15	quinze	50	cinquante	200	deux cents
6	six	16	seize	60	soixante	300	trois cents
7	sept	17	dix-sept	70	soixante-dix	1000	mille
8	huit	18	dix-huit	75	soixante-quinze	2000	deux milles
9	neuf	19	dix-neuf	80	quatre-vingts	5000	cinq milles
10	dix	20	vingt	90	quatre-vingt-dix	1,000,000	un million

Talking to people

When addressing people you should always use *Monsieur* for a man, *Madame* for a woman, *Mademoiselle* for a girl. Plain *bonjour* by itself is not enough. This isn't as formal as it seems, and it has its uses when you've forgotten someone's name or want to attract someone's attention.

Excuse me	*Pardon*	please	*s'il vous plaît*
Do you speak English?	*Vous parlez anglais?*	thank you	*merci*
		hello	*bonjour*
How do you say in French?	*Comment ça se dit en français?*	goodbye	*au revoir*
What's your name?	*Comment vous appelez-vous?*	good morning/ afternoon	*bonjour*
		good evening	*bonsoir*
My name is...	*Je m'appelle...*	good night	*bonne nuit*
I'm English/ Irish/	*Je suis anglais(e)/ irlandais(e)/*	How are you?	*Comment allez-vous?/Ça va?*
Scottish/	*écossais(e)/*		
Welsh/	*gallois(e)/*	Fine, thanks	*Très bien, merci*
American/	*américan(e)/*	I don't know	*Je ne sais pas*
Australian/	*australien(ne)*	Let's go	*Allons-y*
Canadian/	*canadien(ne)*	See you tomorrow	*A demain*
a New Zealander	*néo-zélandais(e)*	See you soon	*A bientôt*
yes	*oui*	Sorry	*Pardon, Madame/je*
no	*non*		*m'excuse*
I understand	*Je comprends*	Leave me alone (aggressive)	*Fichez-moi la paix!*
I don't understand	*Je ne comprends pas*		
Can you speak slower?	*S'il vous plaît, parlez moins vite*	Please help me	*Aidez-moi, s'il vous plaît*
OK/agreed	*d'accord*		

Questions and Requests

The simplest way of asking a question is to start with *s'il vous plaît* (please), then name the thing you want in an interrrogative tone of voice. For example:

Where is there a bakery?	*S'il vous plaît, la boulangerie?*
Which way is it to the Eiffel Tower?	*S'il vous plaît, la route pour la Tour Eiffel?*

Similarly with requests:

We'd like a room for two.	*S'il vous plaît, une chambre pour deux.*
Can I have a kilo of oranges?	*S'il vous plaît, un kilo d'oranges.*

Question words:

where?	*où?*	when?	*quand?*
how?	*comment?*	why?	*pourquoi?*
how many/how much?	*combien?*	at what time?	*à quelle heure?*
		what is/which is?	*quel est?*

Getting around

bus	*autobus, bus, car*	hitchhiking	*autostop*
bus station	*gare routière*	on foot	*à pied*
bus stop	*arrêt*	Where are you going?	*Vous allez où?*
car	*voiture*	I'm going to . . .	*Je vais à . . .*
train/taxi/ferry	*train/taxi/ferry*	I want to get off at . . .	*Je voudrais descendre à . . .*
boat	*bâteau*		
plane	*avion*	the road to . . .	*la route pour . . .*
railway station	*gare*	near	*près/pas loin*
platform	*quai*	far	*loin*
What time does it leave?	*Il part à quelle heure?*	left	*à gauche*
		right	*à droite*
What time does it arrive?	*Il arrive à quelle heure?*	straight on	*tout droit*
		on the other side of	*à l'autre côté de*
a ticket to . . .	*un billet pour . . .*	on the corner of	*à l'angle de*
single ticket	*aller simple*	next to	*à côté de*
return ticket	*aller retour*	behind	*derrière*
validate your ticket	*compostez votre billet*	in front of	*devant*
valid for	*valable pour*	before	*avant*
ticket office	*vente de billets*	after	*aprés*
how many kilometres?	*combien de kilomètres?*	under	*sous*
		to cross	*traverser*
how many hours?	*combien d'heures?*	bridge	*pont*

Cars

garage	*garage*	air line	*ligne à air*
service	*service*	put air in the tyres	*gonfler les pneus*
to park the car	*garer la voiture*	battery	*batterie*
car park	*un parking*	the battery is dead	*la batterie est morte*
no parking	*défense de stationner/ stationnement interdit*	plugs	*bougies*
		to break down	*tomber en panne*
		petrol can	*bidon*
		insurance	*assurance*
petrol station	*poste d'essence*	green card	*carte verte*
petrol	*essence*	traffic lights	*feux*
fill it up	*faire le plein*	red light	*feu rouge*
oil	*huile*	green light	*feu vert*

French and Architectural Terms: a Glossary

These are either terms you'll come across in this book, or come up against on signs, maps, etc, while travelling around. For food items see p.236 onwards.

ABBAYE abbey

AMBULATORY covered passage around the outer edge of a choir of a church

APSE semicircular termination at the east end of a church

ARRONDISSEMENT district of the city

ASSEMBLÉE NATIONALE the French parliament

AUBERGE DE JEUNESSE (AJ) youth hostel

BAROQUE High Renaissance period of art and architecture, distinguished by extreme ornateness

BEAUX ARTS fine arts museum (and school)

CAR bus

CAROLINGIAN dynasty (and art, sculpture, etc) founded by Charlemagne, late eighth to early tenth centuries

CFDT Socialist trade union

CGT Communist trade union

CHASSE, CHASSE GARDÉE hunting grounds

CHÂTEAU mansion, country house, castle

CHÂTEAU FORT castle

CHEMIN path

CHEVET end wall of a church

CIJ (Centre d'Informations Jeunesse) youth information centre

CLASSICAL architectural style incorporating Greek and Roman elements – pillars, domes, colonnades, etc – at its height in France in the seventeenth century and revived in the nineteenth century as **NEOCLASSICAL**

CLERESTORY upper storey of a church, incorporating the windows

CODENE French *CND*

CONSIGNE luggage consignment

COURS combination of main square and main street

COUVENT convent, monastery

DÉFENSE DE . . . It is forbidden to . . .

DÉGUSTATION tasting (wine or food)

DÉPARTEMENT county – more or less

ÉGLISE church

EN PANNE out of order

ENTRÉE entrance

FERMETURE closing period

FLAMBOYANT florid form of Gothic

FN (*Front National*) fascist party led by Jean-Marie Le Pen

FO Catholic trade union

FRESCO wall painting – durable through application to wet plaster

GALLO-ROMAIN period of Roman occupation of Gaul (first to fourth centuries AD)

GARE station; **ROUTIÈRE** – bus station; **SNCF** – train station

GOBELINS famous tapestry manufacturers, based in Paris; its most renowned period was in the reign of Louis XIV (seventeenth century)

GRANDE RANDONÉE (GR) long-distance footpath

HALLES covered market

HLM public housing development

HÔTEL a hotel, but also an aristocratic townhouse or mansion

HÔTEL DE VILLE town hall

JOURS FÉRIÉS public holidays

MAIRIE town hall

MARCHÉ market

MEROVINGIAN dynasty (and art, etc), ruling France and parts of Germany from the sixth to mid-eighth centuries

NARTHEX entrance hall of church

NAVE main body of a church

PCF Communist Party of France

PLACE square

PORTE gateway

PS Socialist party

PTT post office

QUARTIER district of a town

RENAISSANCE art/architectural style developed in fifteenth-century Italy and imported to France in the early sixteenth century by François 1er

RETABLE altarpiece

REZ-DE-CHAUSSÉE (RC) ground floor

RN (*Route Nationale*) main road

ROMANESQUE early medieval architecture distinguished by squat, rounded forms and naive sculpture

RPR Gaullist party led by Jacques Chirac

SI (*Syndicat d'Initiative*) tourist information office; also known as *OT, OTSI* and *Maison du Tourisme*

SNCF (*Société Nationale des Chemins de Fer*) French railways

SORTIE exit

STUCCO plaster used to embellish ceilings, etc

TABAC bar or shop selling stamps, cigarettes, etc

TOUR tower

TRANSEPT cross arms of a church

TYMPANUM sculpted panel above a church door

UDF centre-right party headed by Giscard d'Estaing

VAUBAN seventeenth-century military architect – his fortresses still stand all over France

VILLA a mews or a series of small residential streets, built as a unity

VOUSSOIR sculpted rings in an arch over church door

ZONE BLEUE restricted parking zone

ZONE PIÉTONNE pedestrian zone

Index

N

O

Odéon, Théâtre de l' 122
Opéra-Bastille 108
Opéra Garnier (formerly, de Paris) 85
Orangerie 77, 286
Orsay, Musée d' 131, 280
Orwell, George 139

P

Packages 7, 10, 16
Palais de Chaillot 124
Palais de Justice 69
Palais des Omnisports de Bercy 195
Palais Royal 79
Palais Soubise 101
Palais de Tokyo 125
Panthéon 114
Paradis, rue de 171
Parks
 Bois de Boulogne 204
 Bois de Vincennes 196
 Champs-de-Mars 312
 Jardin d'Acclimatation 204, 311
 Jardin Albert Kahn 202
 Jardin des Halles 312
 Jardin du Luxembourg 122, 313
 Jardin des Plantes 116
 Jardin du Ranelagh 313
 Jardin de Reuilly 195
 Jardin de Ste-Périne 201
 Jardin des Serres d'Auteuil 202
 Jardin du Trocadéro 313
 Jardin des Tuileries 77
 Parc André-Citroën 142
 Parc de Bagatelle 204
 Parc de Belleville 184
 Parc des Buttes-Chaumont 182, 312
 Parc Floral 198, 312
 Parc Georges Brassens 143, 313
 Parc Monceau 205, 313
 Parc Montsouris 147, 313
 Parc de St-Cloud 387
 Parc de la Villette 178, 311
Passage Choiseul 87
Passage du Grand-Cerf 88
Passage Jouffroy 88
Passage des Panoramas 88
Passage des Princes 88
Passage Verdeau 88
Passy 203
Pei, I.M. 78
Père-Lachaise cemetery 187
Pernety, quartier 144
Petit Palais 76, 289
Pharmacists 23
Philippe-Auguste 78, 101, 115, 410
Piaf, Édith 184, 297
Picasso 102, 287
Pigalle 167
Place des Abbesses 158

Place d'Aligre 194
Place de Catalogne 145
Place Clichy 168
Place du Colonel-Fabien 178
Place de la Concorde 77
Place de la Contrescarpe 116
Place Denfert-Rochereau 138
Place de l'Étoile 74
Place des Fêtes 183
Place Furstemberg 121
Place du 18-Juin-1940 133
Place d'Italie 151
Place du Marché-Ste-Catherine 103
Place des Petit-Pères 89
Place Pigalle 168
Place de la République 173
Place St-Georges 169
Place St-Germain-des-Prés 121
Place St-Michel 109
Place St-Sulpice 122
Place de Stalingrad 177
Place du Tertre 159
Place Vendôme 89
Place des Victoires 89
Place des Vosges 100
Plaisance, quartier 144
Police 55
Politics 397
Pompidou Centre 94, 284
Pont d'Arcole 70
Pont des Arts 117
Pont Neuf 67
Port de Sully 113
Porte de Clignancourt 166
Porte de Versailles 143
Porte St-Denis 171
Porte St-Martin 171
Post offices 42
Postwar Paris 415
Printemps, Magasins du 86
Public transport 30
Puces de St-Ouen 166

Q

Quartier du Citroën-Cévennes 142
Quartier Juif 103
Quartier Latin 109
Quartier du Temple 100
Quincampoix, rue 99

R

Racism 54
Radio 44
Rafle du Vel d'Hiv 139
RER 30, 32
Restaurants, see "Eating and drinking"
Revolution 411
Richelieu Chapel (Sorbonne) 114

direct orders from

		UK£	US$	CAN$
Amsterdam	1-85828-218-7	UK£8.99	US$14.95	CAN$19.99
Andalucia	1-85828-219-5	9.99	16.95	22.99
Australia	1-85828-220-9	13.99	21.95	29.99
Bali	1-85828-134-2	8.99	14.95	19.99
Barcelona	1-85828-221-7	8.99	14.95	19.99
Berlin	1-85828-129-6	8.99	14.95	19.99
Belgium & Luxembourg	1-85828-222-5	10.99	17.95	23.99
Brazil	1-85828-223-3	13.99	21.95	29.99
Britain	1-85828-208-X	12.99	19.95	25.99
Brittany & Normandy	1-85828-224-1	9.99	16.95	22.99
Bulgaria	1-85828-183-0	9.99	16.95	22.99
California	1-85828-181-4	10.99	16.95	22.99
Canada	1-85828-130-X	10.99	14.95	19.99
China	1-85828-225-X	15.99	24.95	32.99
Corfu	1-85828-226-8	8.99	14.95	19.99
Corsica	1-85828-227-6	9.99	16.95	22.99
Costa Rica	1-85828-136-9	9.99	15.95	21.99
Crete	1-85828-132-6	8.99	14.95	18.99
Cyprus	1-85828-182-2	9.99	16.95	22.99
Czech & Slovak Republics	1-85828-121-0	9.99	16.95	22.99
Egypt	1-85828-188-1	10.99	17.95	23.99
Europe	1-85828-289-6	14.99	19.95	25.99
England	1-85828-160-1	10.99	17.95	23.99
First Time Europe	1-85828-270-5	7.99	9.95	12.99
Florida	1-85828-184-4	10.99	16.95	22.99
France	1-85828-228-4	12.99	19.95	25.99
Germany	1-85828-128-8	11.99	17.95	23.99
Goa	1-85828-275-6	8.99	14.95	19.99
Greece	1-85828-300-0	12.99	19.95	25.99
Greek Islands	1-85828-163-6	8.99	14.95	19.99
Guatemala	1-85828-189-X	10.99	16.95	22.99
Hawaii: Big Island	1-85828-158-X	8.99	12.95	16.99
Hawaii	1-85828-206-3	10.99	16.95	22.99
Holland	1-85828-229-2	10.99	17.95	23.99
Hong Kong	1-85828-187-3	8.99	14.95	19.99
Hungary	1-85828-123-7	8.99	14.95	19.99
India	1-85828-200-4	14.99	23.95	31.99
Ireland	1-85828-179-2	10.99	17.95	23.99
Italy	1-85828-167-9	12.99	19.95	25.99
Jamaica	1-85828-230-6	9.99	16.95	22.99
Kenya	1-85828-192-X	11.99	18.95	24.99
London	1-85828-231-4	9.99	15.95	21.99
Mallorca & Menorca	1-85828-165-2	8.99	14.95	19.99
Malaysia, Singapore & Brunei	1-85828-232-2	11.99	18.95	24.99
Mexico	1-85828-044-3	10.99	16.95	22.99
Morocco	1-85828-040-0	9.99	16.95	21.99
Moscow	1-85828-118-0	8.99	14.95	19.99
Nepal	1-85828-190-3	10.99	17.95	23.99
New York	1-85828-296-9	9.99	15.95	21.99
Norway	1-85828-234-9	10.99	17.95	23.99
Pacific Northwest	1-85828-092-3	9.99	14.95	19.99
Paris	1-85828-235-7	8.99	14.95	19.99

around the world

Poland	1-85828-168-7	10.99	17.95	23.99
Portugal	1-85828-180-6	9.99	16.95	22.99
Prague	1-85828-122-9	8.99	14.95	19.99
Provence	1-85828-127-X	9.99	16.95	22.99
Pyrenees	1-85828-093-1	8.99	15.95	19.99
Rhodes & the Dodecanese	1-85828-120-2	8.99	14.95	19.99
Romania	1-85828-097-4	9.99	15.95	21.99
San Francisco	1-85828-185-7	8.99	14.95	19.99
Scandinavia	1-85828-236-5	12.99	20.95	27.99
Scotland	1-85828-166-0	9.99	16.95	22.99
Sicily	1-85828-178-4	9.99	16.95	22.99
Singapore	1-85828-237-3	8.99	14.95	19.99
South Africa	1-85828-238-1	12.99	19.95	25.99
Soutwest USA	1-85828-239-X	10.99	16.95	22.99
Spain	1-85828-240-3	11.99	18.95	24.99
St Petersburg	1-85828-133-4	8.99	14.95	19.99
Sweden	1-85828-241-1	10.99	17.95	23.99
Thailand	1-85828-140-7	10.99	17.95	24.99
Tunisia	1-85828-139-3	10.99	17.95	24.99
Turkey	1-85828-242-X	12.99	19.95	25.99
Tuscany & Umbria	1-85828-243-8	10.99	17.95	23.99
USA	1-85828-161-X	14.99	19.95	25.99
Venice	1-85828-170-9	8.99	14.95	19.99
Vietnam	1-85828-191-1	9.99	15.95	21.99
Wales	1-85828-245-4	10.99	17.95	23.99
Washington DC	1-85828-246-2	8.99	14.95	19.99
West Africa	1-85828-101-6	15.99	24.95	34.99
More Women Travel	1-85828-098-2	10.99	16.95	22.99
Zimbabwe & Botswana	1-85828-186-5	11.99	18.95	24.99
Phrasebooks				
Czech	1-85828-148-2	3.50	5.00	7.00
French	1-85828-144-X	3.50	5.00	7.00
German	1-85828-146-6	3.50	5.00	7.00
Greek	1-85828-145-8	3.50	5.00	7.00
Italian	1-85828-143-1	3.50	5.00	7.00
Mexican	1-85828-176-8	3.50	5.00	7.00
Portuguese	1-85828-175-X	3.50	5.00	7.00
Polish	1-85828-174-1	3.50	5.00	7.00
Spanish	1-85828-147-4	3.50	5.00	7.00
Thai	1-85828-177-6	3.50	5.00	7.00
Turkish	1-85828-173-3	3.50	5.00	7.00
Vietnamese	1-85828-172-5	3.50	5.00	7.00
Reference				
Classical Music	1-85828-113-X	12.99	19.95	25.99
European Football	1-85828-256-X	14.99	23.95	31.99
Internet	1-85828-288-8	5.00	8.00	10.00
Jazz	1-85828-137-7	16.99	24.95	34.99
Opera	1-85828-138-5	16.99	24.95	34.99
Reggae	1-85828-247-0	12.99	19.95	25.99
Rock	1-85828-201-2	17.99	26.95	35.00
World Music	1-85828-017-6	16.99	22.95	29.99

In the USA, or for international orders, charge your order by Master Card or Visa (US$15.00 minimum order): call 1-800-253-6476; or send orders, with complete name, address and zip code, and list price, plus $2.00 shipping and handling per order to: Consumer Sales, Penguin USA, PO Box 999 – Dept #17109, Bergenfield, NJ 07621. No COD. Prepay foreign orders by international money order, a cheque drawn on a US bank, or US currency. No postage stamps are accepted. All orders are subject to stock availability at the time they are processed. Refunds will be made for books not available at that time. Please allow a minimum of four weeks for delivery.

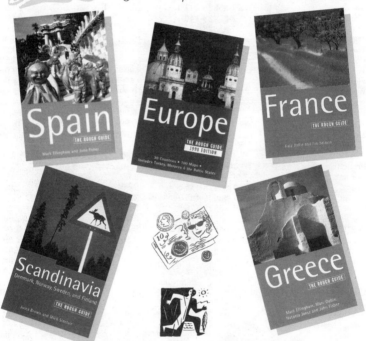

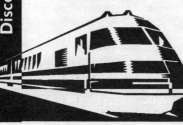

Asteria 1 →9, 11, 14, 15
(want: 10, 12, 13, 16)